JLA PRESENTS

AZTEK

THE ULTIMATE MAN

JLA PRESENTS

AZTEK

THE ULTIMATE MAN

Written by
GRANT MORRISON & MARK MILLAR

Pencilled by
N. STEVEN HARRIS

Inked by
KEITH CHAMPAGNE

Colored by
MIKE DANZA

Lettered by
CHRIS ELIOPOULOS & CLEM ROBINS

Original Series Covers by
**N. STEVEN HARRIS/KEITH CHAMPAGNE, DAVE JOHNSON,
MIKE WIERINGO, ED BENES, NORM BREYFOGLE,
STEVE LIGHTLE**

AZTEK created by
GRANT MORRISON, MARK MILLAR
and **N. STEVEN HARRIS**

Cover art by N. Steven Harris and Keith Champagne.
Publication design by Brainchild Studios/NYC.

JLA PRESENTS: AZTEK THE ULTIMATE MAN

Published by DC Comics. Cover and compilation Copyright © 2008 DC Comics. All Rights Reserved.

DC Comics, 1700 Broadway, New York, NY 10019
A Warner Bros. Entertainment Company
Printed in Canada. First Printing.

ISBN: 978-1-4012-1688-7

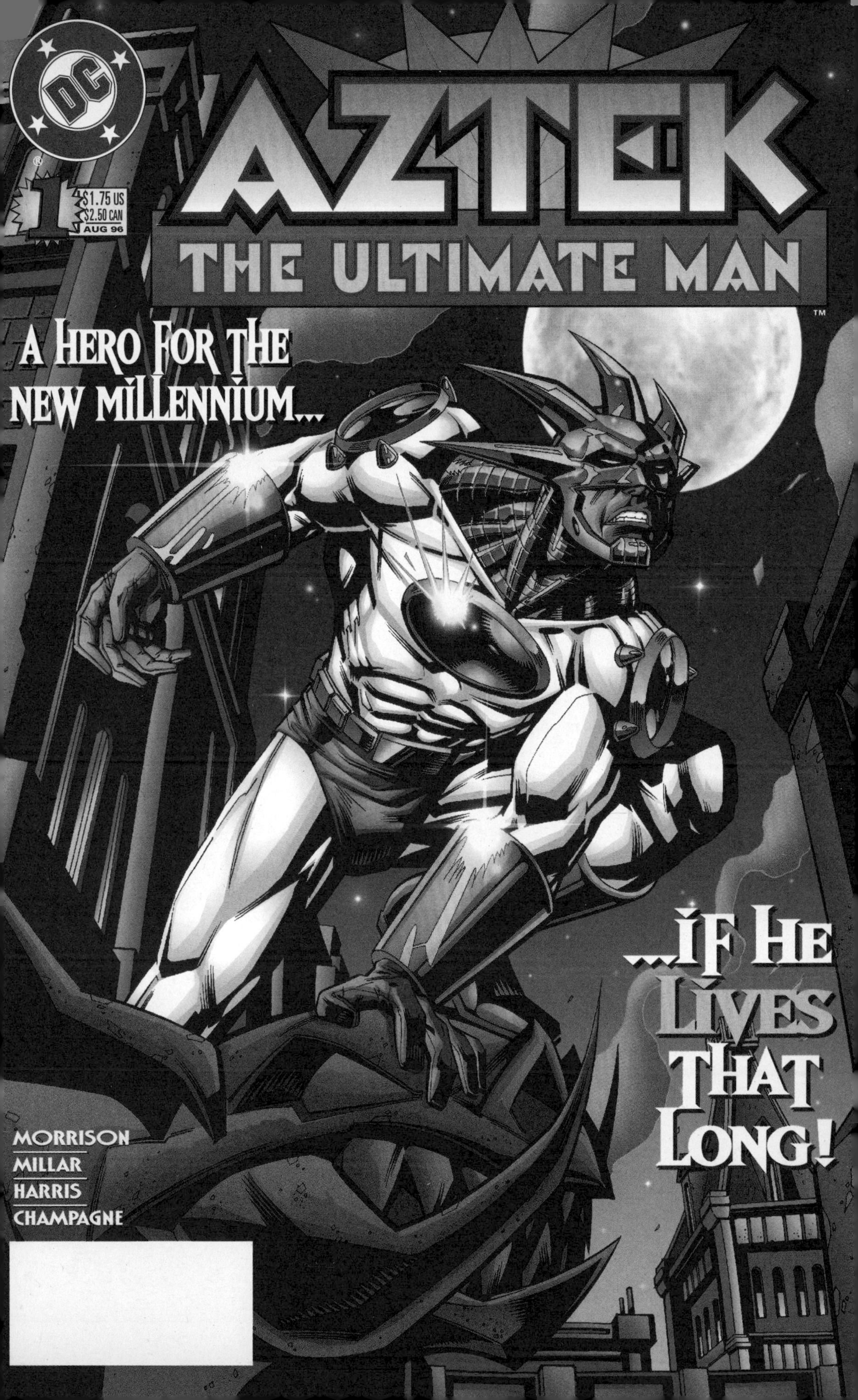

DC
1
$1.75 US
$2.50 CAN
AUG 96
AZTEK
THE ULTIMATE MAN
A HERO FOR THE NEW MILLENNIUM...
...IF HE LIVES THAT LONG!
MORRISON
MILLAR
HARRIS
CHAMPAGNE

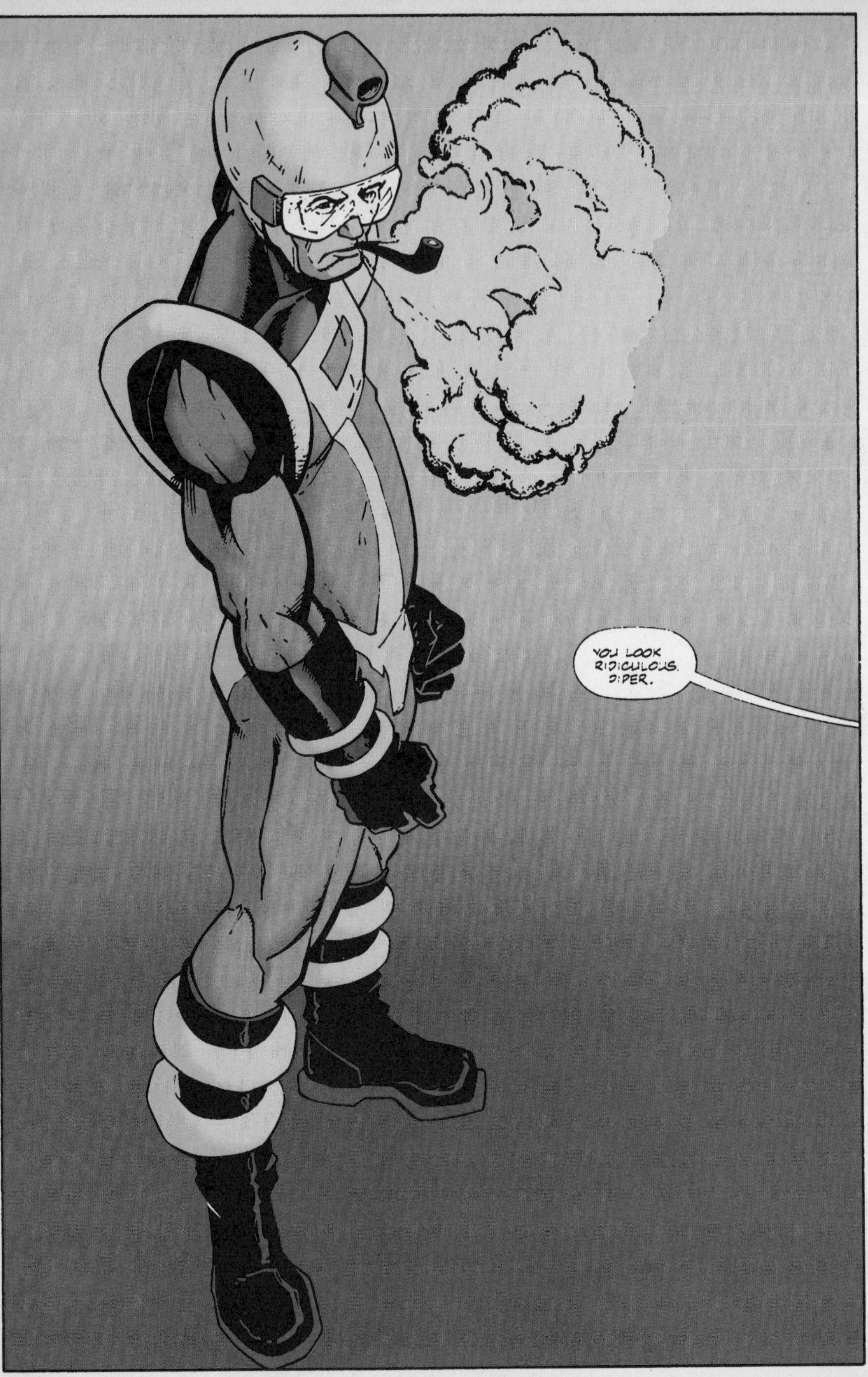
YOU LOOK RIDICULOUS. DIPER.

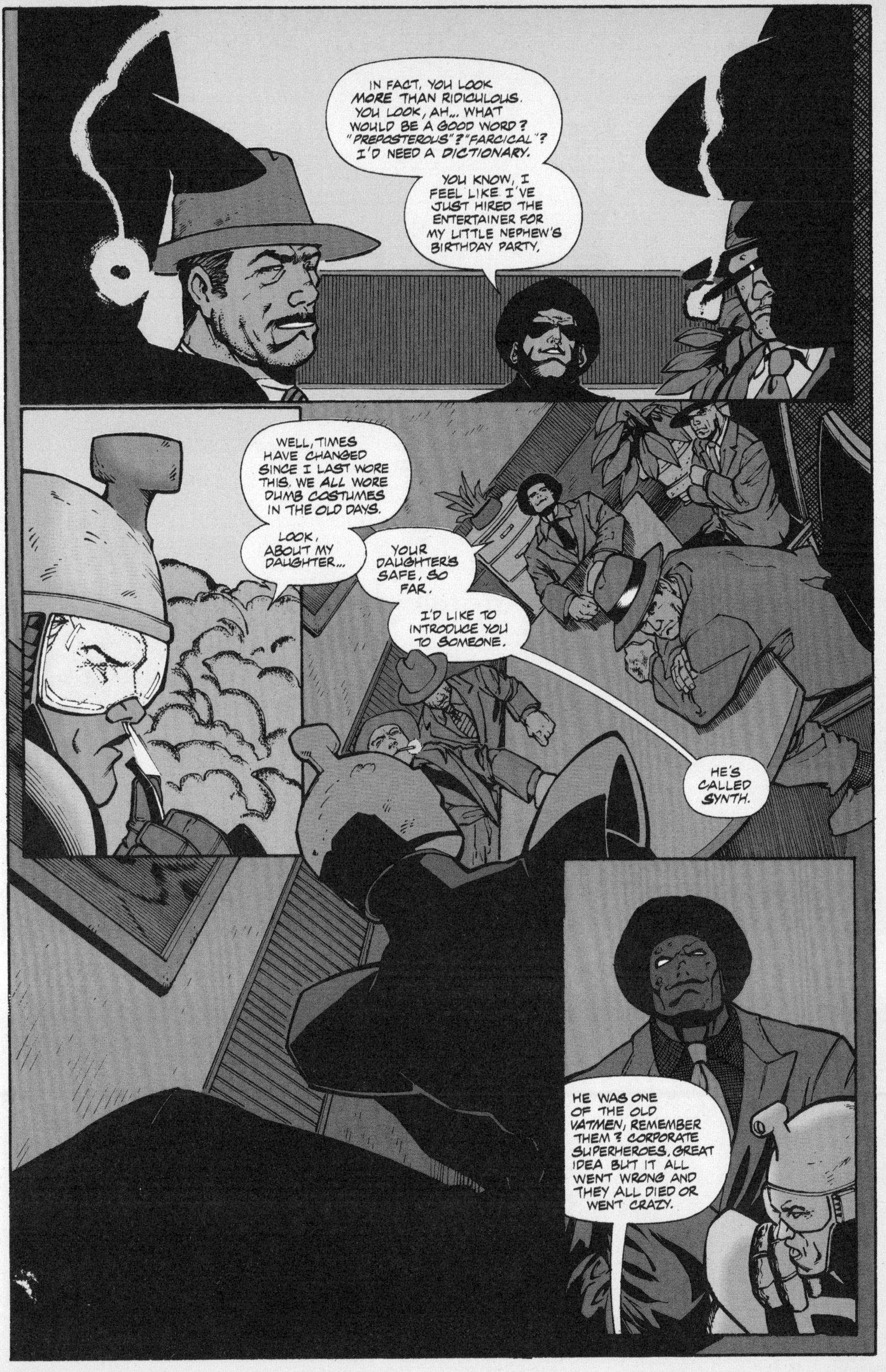
IN FACT, YOU LOOK MORE THAN RIDICULOUS. YOU LOOK, AH... WHAT WOULD BE A GOOD WORD? "PREPOSTEROUS"? "FARCICAL"? I'D NEED A DICTIONARY.
YOU KNOW, I FEEL LIKE I'VE JUST HIRED THE ENTERTAINER FOR MY LITTLE NEPHEW'S BIRTHDAY PARTY.
WELL, TIMES HAVE CHANGED SINCE I LAST WORE THIS. WE ALL WORE DUMB COSTUMES IN THE OLD DAYS.
LOOK, ABOUT MY DAUGHTER...
YOUR DAUGHTER'S SAFE, SO FAR.
I'D LIKE TO INTRODUCE YOU TO SOMEONE.
HE'S CALLED SYNTH.
HE WAS ONE OF THE OLD VATMEN, REMEMBER THEM? CORPORATE SUPERHEROES. GREAT IDEA BUT IT ALL WENT WRONG AND THEY ALL DIED OR WENT CRAZY.

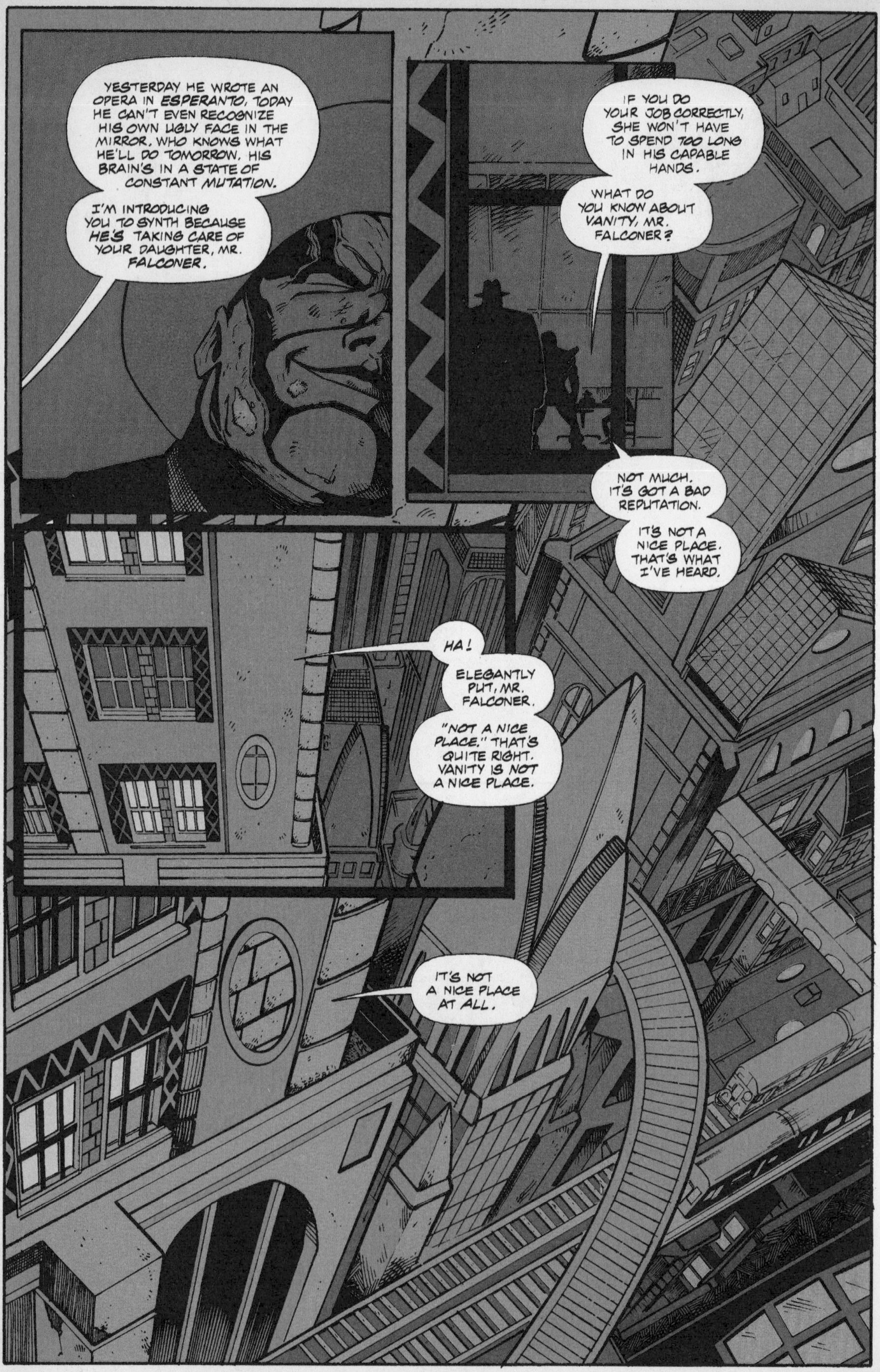
YESTERDAY HE WROTE AN OPERA IN ESPERANTO, TODAY HE CAN'T EVEN RECOGNIZE HIS OWN UGLY FACE IN THE MIRROR. WHO KNOWS WHAT HE'LL DO TOMORROW. HIS BRAIN'S IN A STATE OF CONSTANT MUTATION.
I'M INTRODUCING YOU TO SYNTH BECAUSE HE'S TAKING CARE OF YOUR DAUGHTER, MR. FALCONER.
IF YOU DO YOUR JOB CORRECTLY, SHE WON'T HAVE TO SPEND TOO LONG IN HIS CAPABLE HANDS.
WHAT DO YOU KNOW ABOUT VANITY, MR. FALCONER?
NOT MUCH. IT'S GOT A BAD REPUTATION.
IT'S NOT A NICE PLACE. THAT'S WHAT I'VE HEARD.
HA!
ELEGANTLY PUT, MR. FALCONER.
"NOT A NICE PLACE." THAT'S QUITE RIGHT. VANITY IS NOT A NICE PLACE.
IT'S NOT A NICE PLACE AT ALL.

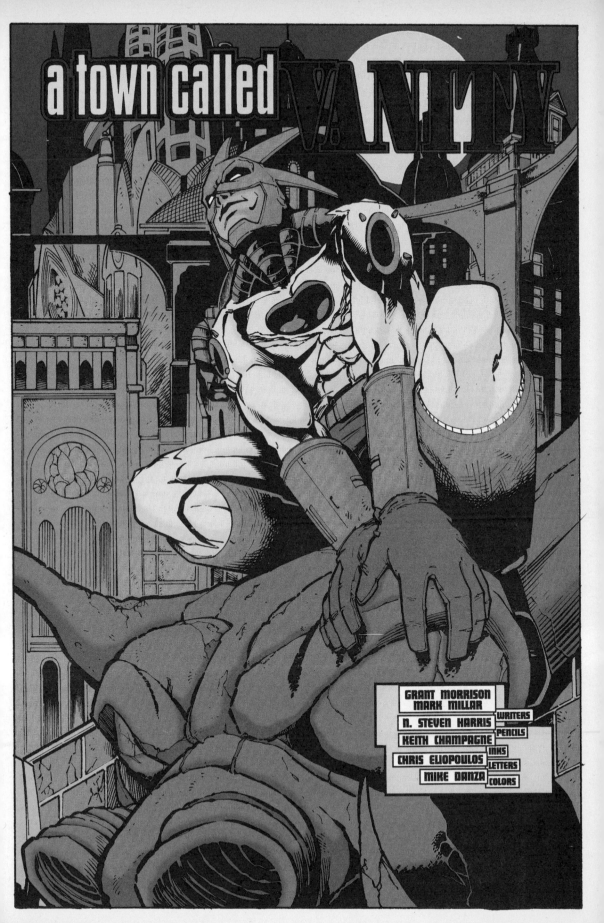

a town called VANITY

GRANT MORRISON
MARK MILLAR — WRITERS

N. STEVEN HARRIS — PENCILS

KEITH CHAMPAGNE — INKS

CHRIS ELIOPOULOS — LETTERS

MIKE DANZA — COLORS

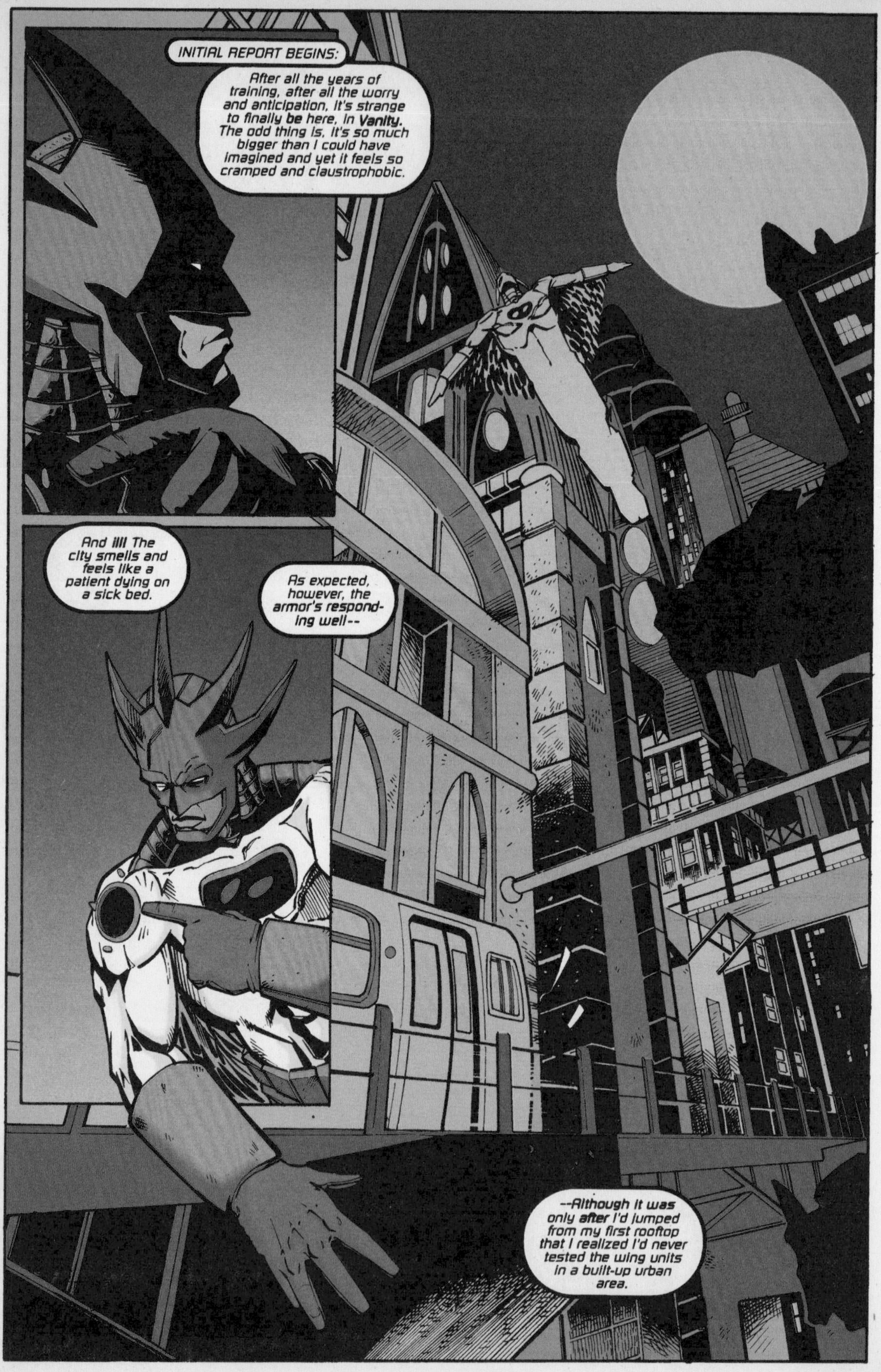
INITIAL REPORT BEGINS:
After all the years of training, after all the worry and anticipation, it's strange to finally be here, in Vanity. The odd thing is, it's so much bigger than I could have imagined and yet it feels so cramped and claustrophobic.
And ill! The city smells and feels like a patient dying on a sick bed.
As expected, however, the armor's respond-ing well--
--Although it was only after I'd jumped from my first rooftop that I realized I'd never tested the wing units in a built-up urban area.

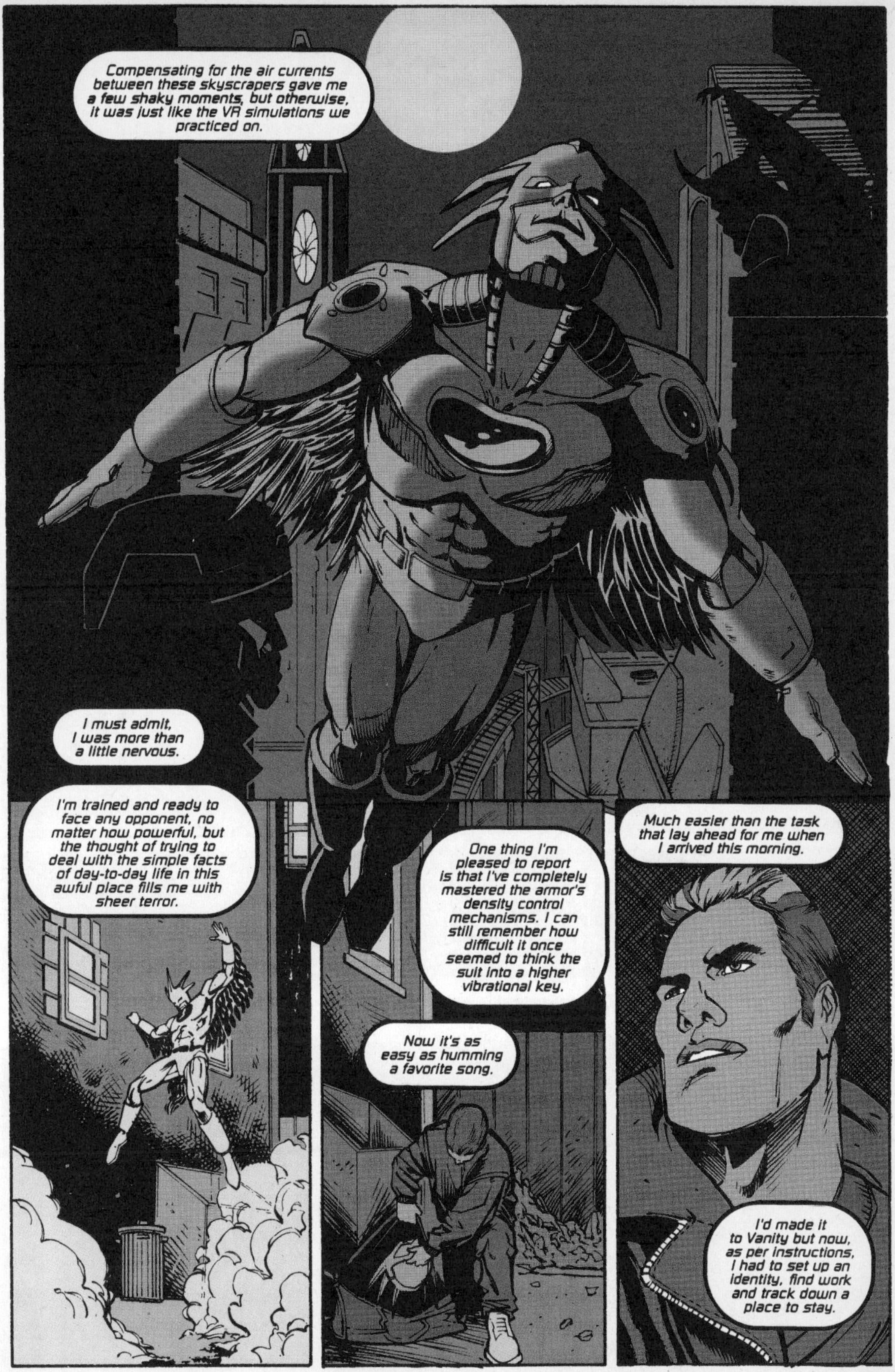
Compensating for the air currents between these skyscrapers gave me a few shaky moments, but otherwise, it was just like the VR simulations we practiced on.
I must admit, I was more than a little nervous.
I'm trained and ready to face any opponent, no matter how powerful, but the thought of trying to deal with the simple facts of day-to-day life in this awful place fills me with sheer terror.
One thing I'm pleased to report is that I've completely mastered the armor's density control mechanisms. I can still remember how difficult it once seemed to think the suit into a higher vibrational key.
Now it's as easy as humming a favorite song.
Much easier than the task that lay ahead for me when I arrived this morning.
I'd made it to Vanity but now, as per instructions, I had to set up an identity, find work and track down a place to stay.

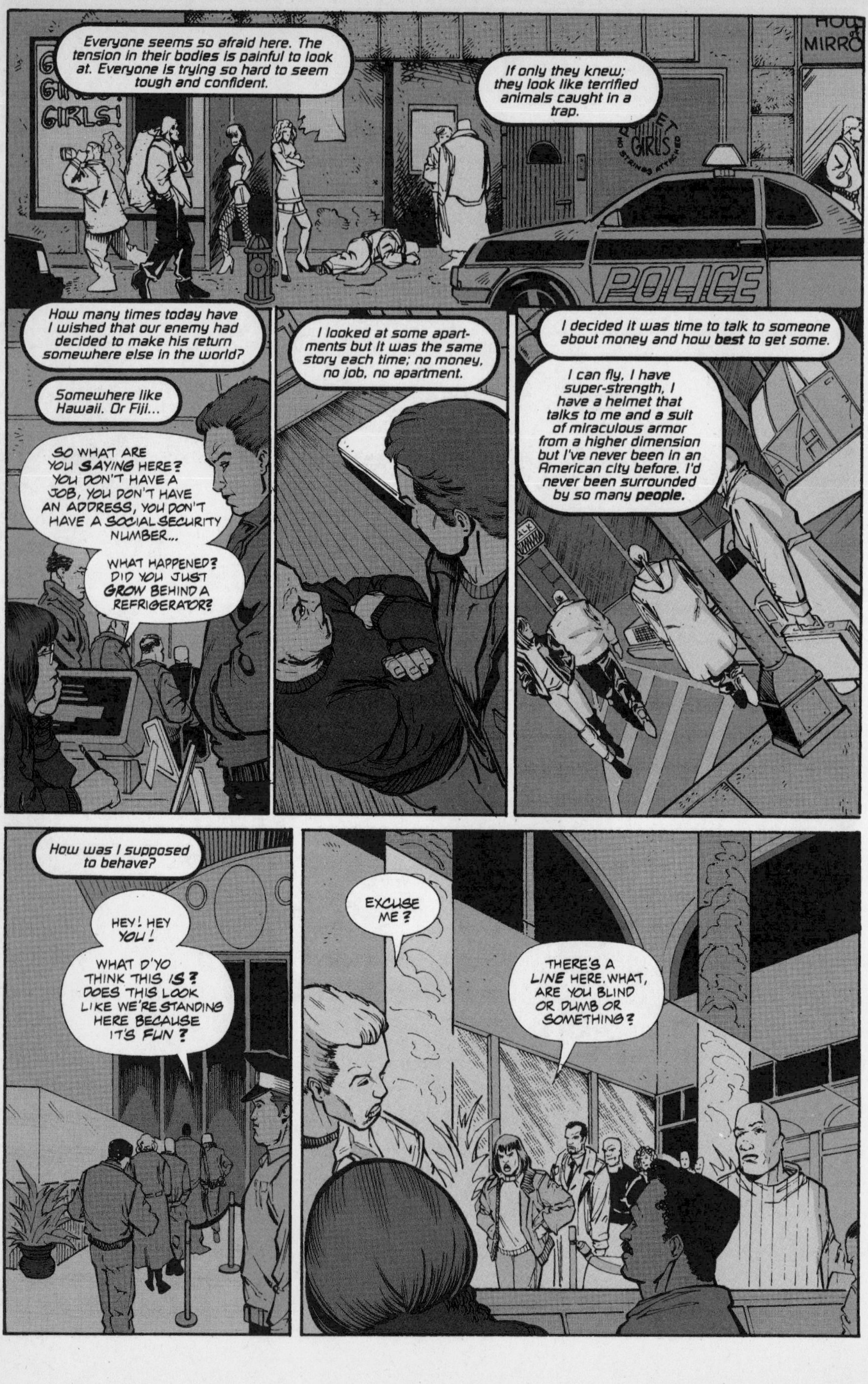

GIRLS!
Everyone seems so afraid here. The tension in their bodies is painful to look at. Everyone is trying so hard to seem tough and confident.
If only they knew; they look like terrified animals caught in a trap.
POLICE
How many times today have I wished that our enemy had decided to make his return somewhere else in the world?
Somewhere like Hawaii. Or Fiji...
SO WHAT ARE YOU SAYING HERE? YOU DON'T HAVE A JOB, YOU DON'T HAVE AN ADDRESS, YOU DON'T HAVE A SOCIAL SECURITY NUMBER...
WHAT HAPPENED? DID YOU JUST GROW BEHIND A REFRIGERATOR?
I looked at some apartments but it was the same story each time; no money, no job, no apartment.
I decided it was time to talk to someone about money and how best to get some.
I can fly, I have super-strength, I have a helmet that talks to me and a suit of miraculous armor from a higher dimension but I've never been in an American city before. I'd never been surrounded by so many people.
How was I supposed to behave?
HEY! HEY YOU!
WHAT D'YO THINK THIS IS? DOES THIS LOOK LIKE WE'RE STANDING HERE BECAUSE IT'S FUN?
EXCUSE ME?
THERE'S A LINE HERE. WHAT, ARE YOU BLIND OR DUMB OR SOMETHING?

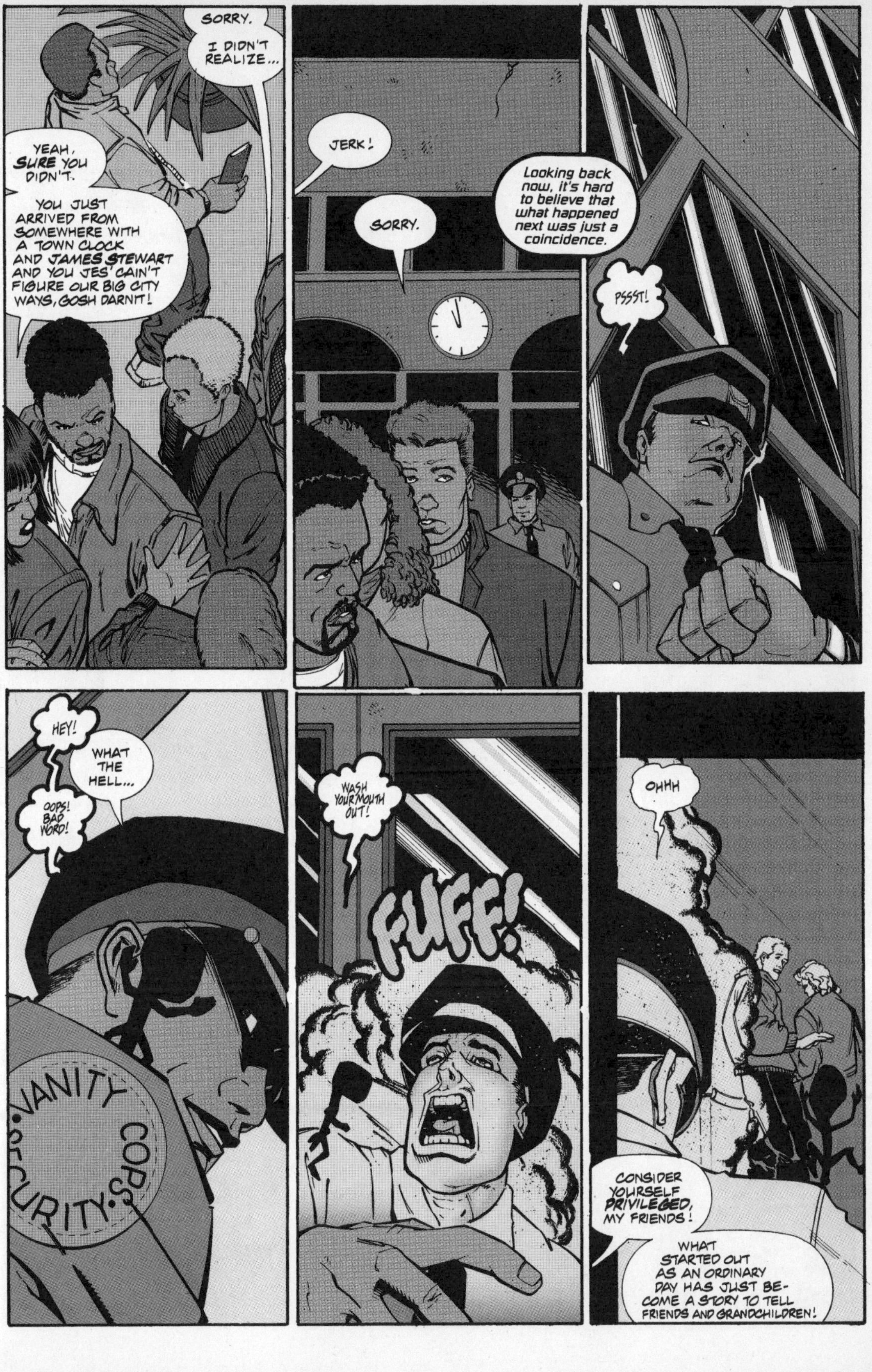

SORRY.
I DIDN'T REALIZE...
YEAH, SURE YOU DIDN'T.
YOU JUST ARRIVED FROM SOMEWHERE WITH A TOWN CLOCK AND JAMES STEWART AND YOU JES' CAIN'T FIGURE OUR BIG CITY WAYS, GOSH DARNIT!
JERK!
SORRY.
Looking back now, it's hard to believe that what happened next was just a coincidence.
PSSST!
HEY!
WHAT THE HELL...
OOPS! BAD WORD!
VANITY CORPS SECURITY
WASH YOUR MOUTH OUT!
FUFF!
OHHH
CONSIDER YOURSELF PRIVILEGED, MY FRIENDS!
WHAT STARTED OUT AS AN ORDINARY DAY HAS JUST BECOME A STORY TO TELL FRIENDS AND GRANDCHILDREN!

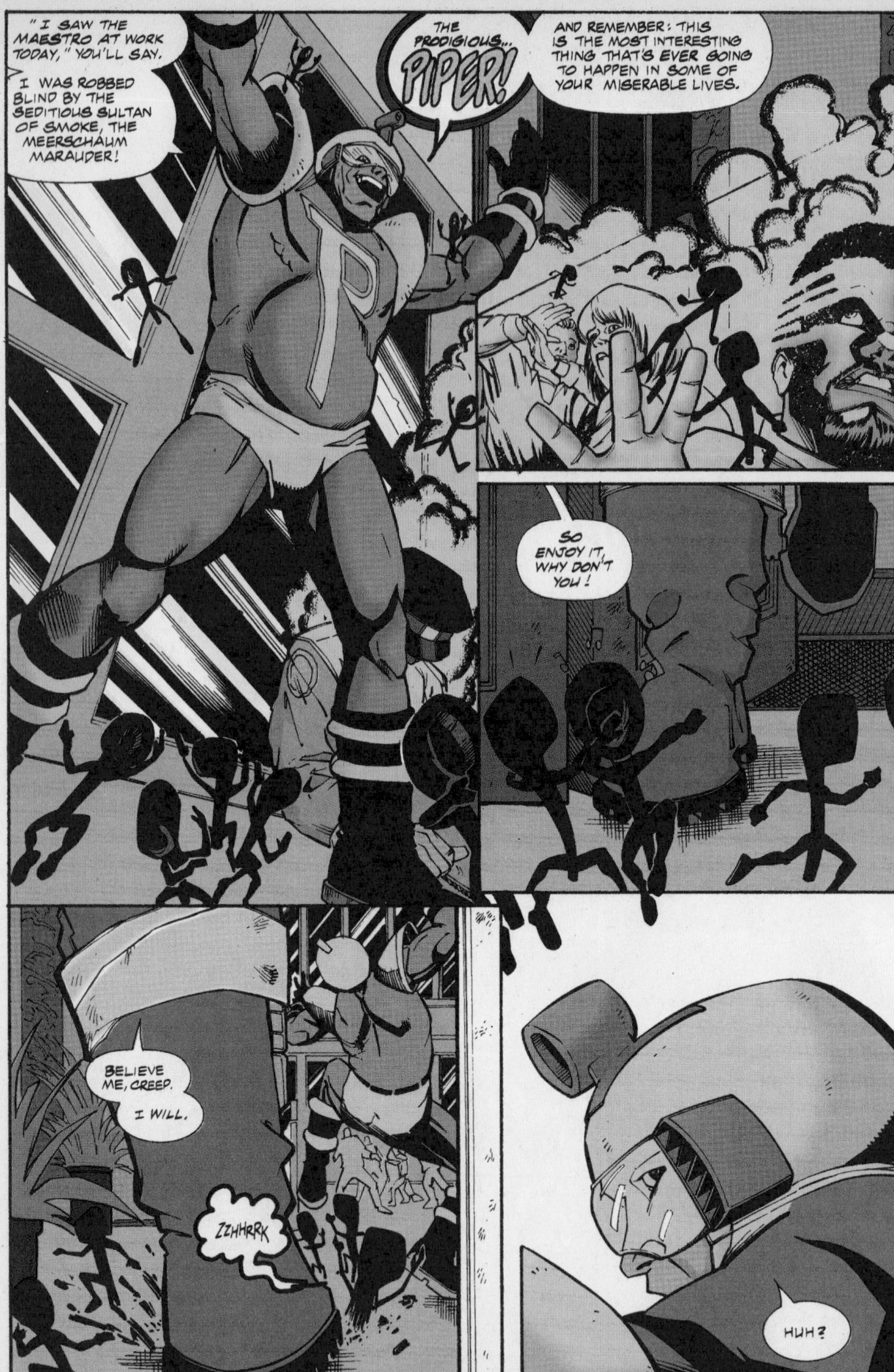
"I SAW THE MAESTRO AT WORK TODAY," YOU'LL SAY.
I WAS ROBBED BLIND BY THE SEDITIOUS SULTAN OF SMOKE, THE MEERSCHAUM MARAUDER!
THE PRODIGIOUS... PIPER!
AND REMEMBER: THIS IS THE MOST INTERESTING THING THAT'S EVER GOING TO HAPPEN IN SOME OF YOUR MISERABLE LIVES.
SO ENJOY IT, WHY DON'T YOU!
BELIEVE ME, CREEP.
I WILL.
ZZHHRRK
HUH?

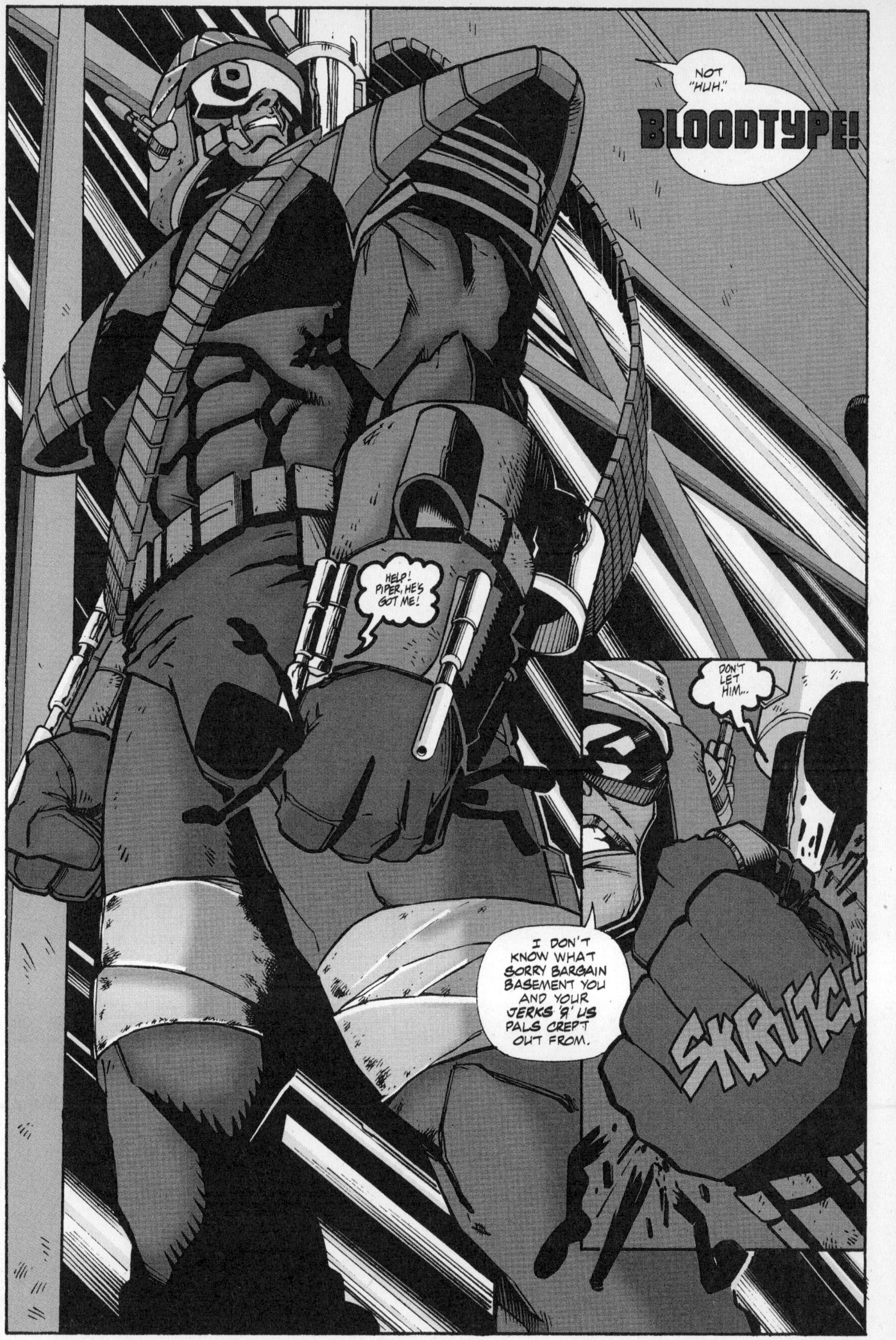
NOT "HUH."
BLOODTYPE!
HELP! PIPER, HE'S GOT ME!
DON'T LET HIM...
I DON'T KNOW WHAT SORRY BARGAIN BASEMENT YOU AND YOUR JERKS 'R' US PALS CREPT OUT FROM.
SKRUTCH

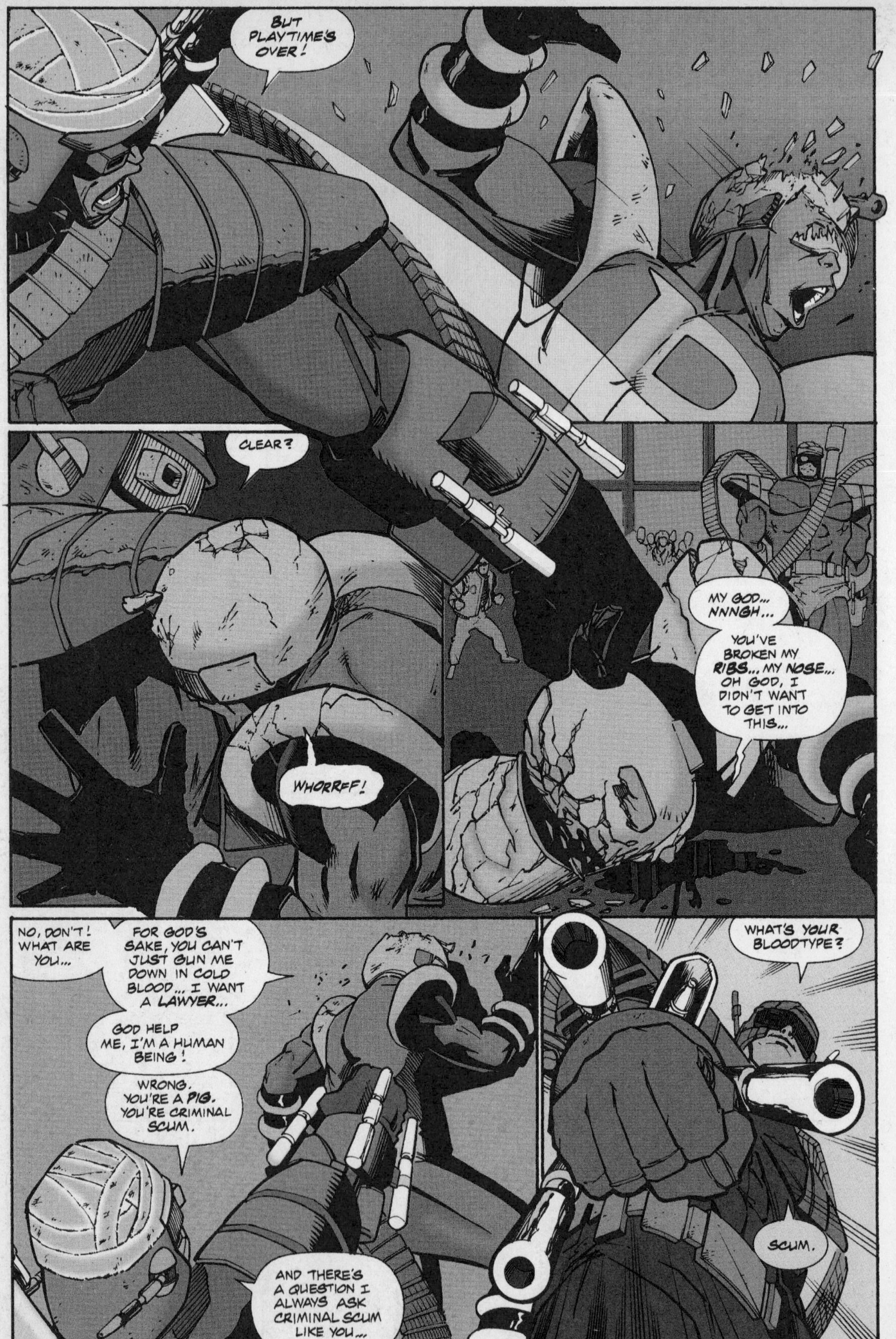

BUT PLAYTIME'S OVER!
CLEAR?
WHORRFF!
MY GOD... NNNGH...
YOU'VE BROKEN MY RIBS... MY NOSE... OH GOD, I DIDN'T WANT TO GET INTO THIS...
NO, DON'T! WHAT ARE YOU...
FOR GOD'S SAKE, YOU CAN'T JUST GUN ME DOWN IN COLD BLOOD... I WANT A LAWYER...
GOD HELP ME, I'M A HUMAN BEING!
WRONG. YOU'RE A PIG. YOU'RE CRIMINAL SCUM.
AND THERE'S A QUESTION I ALWAYS ASK CRIMINAL SCUM LIKE YOU...
WHAT'S YOUR BLOODTYPE?
SCUM.

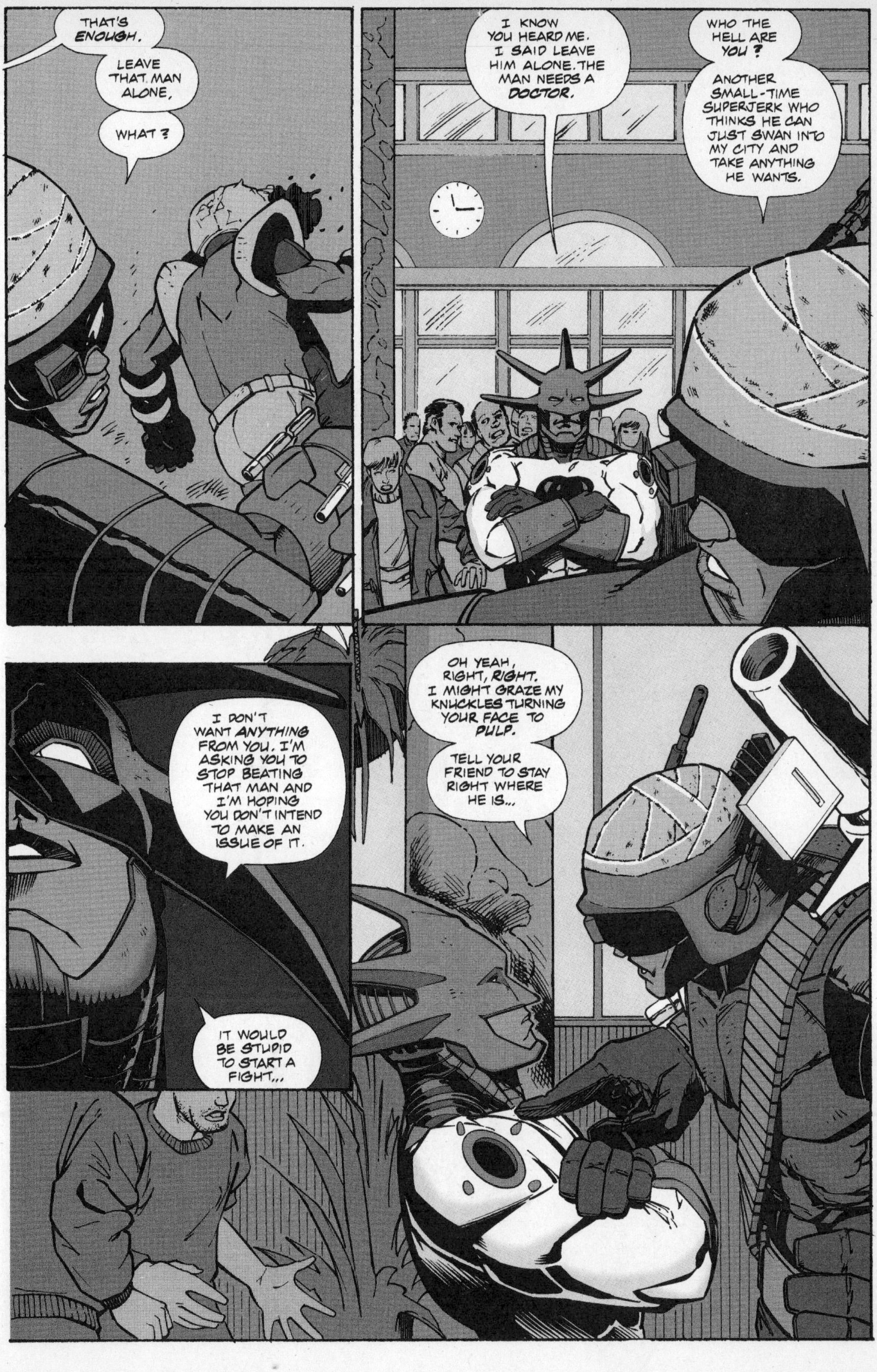
THAT'S ENOUGH.
LEAVE THAT MAN ALONE.
WHAT?
I KNOW YOU HEARD ME. I SAID LEAVE HIM ALONE. THE MAN NEEDS A DOCTOR.
WHO THE HELL ARE YOU?
ANOTHER SMALL-TIME SUPERJERK WHO THINKS HE CAN JUST SWAN INTO MY CITY AND TAKE ANYTHING HE WANTS.
I DON'T WANT ANYTHING FROM YOU. I'M ASKING YOU TO STOP BEATING THAT MAN AND I'M HOPING YOU DON'T INTEND TO MAKE AN ISSUE OF IT.
IT WOULD BE STUPID TO START A FIGHT...
OH YEAH, RIGHT, RIGHT. I MIGHT GRAZE MY KNUCKLES TURNING YOUR FACE TO PULP.
TELL YOUR FRIEND TO STAY RIGHT WHERE HE IS...

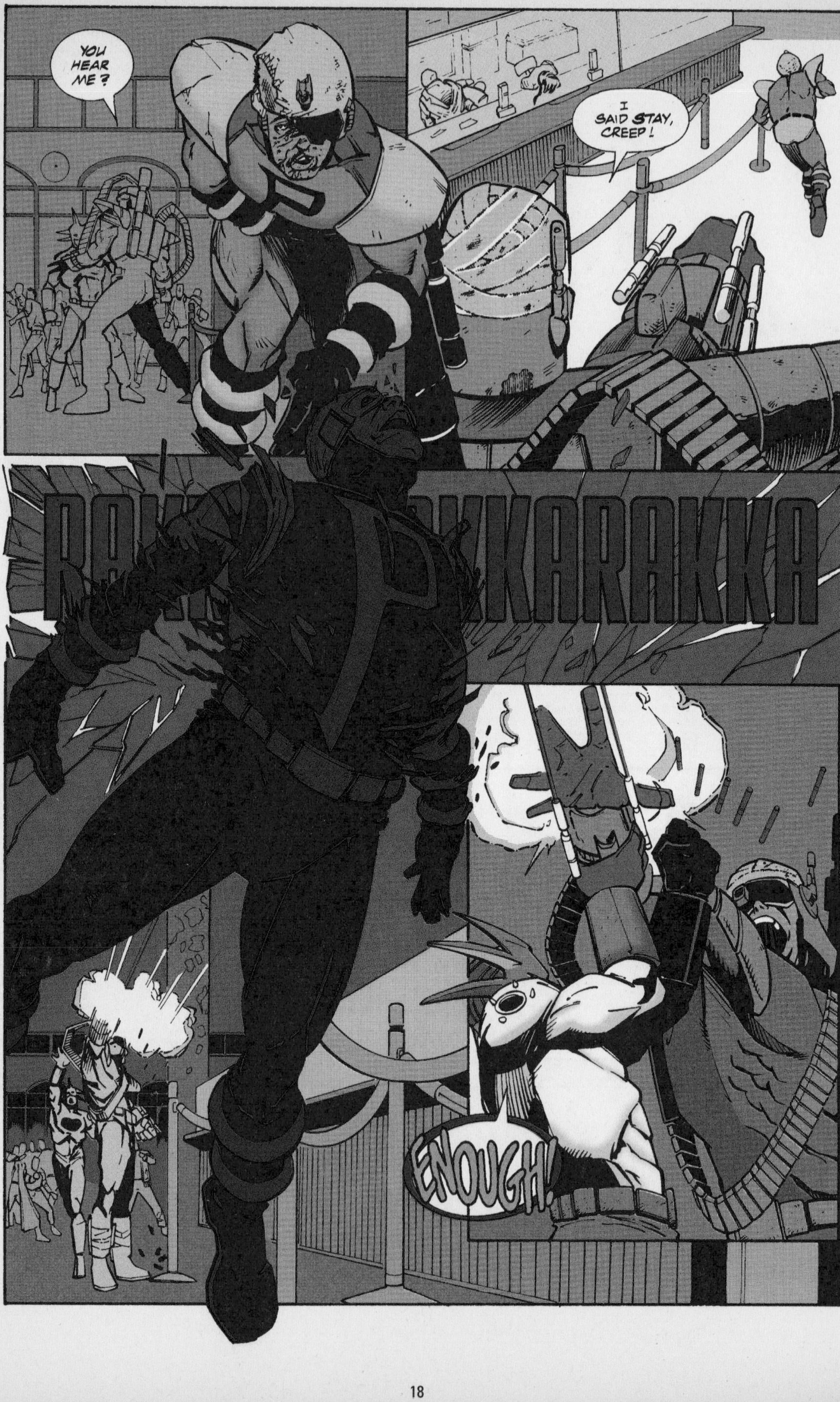
YOU HEAR ME?
I SAID STAY, CREEP!
ENOUGH!

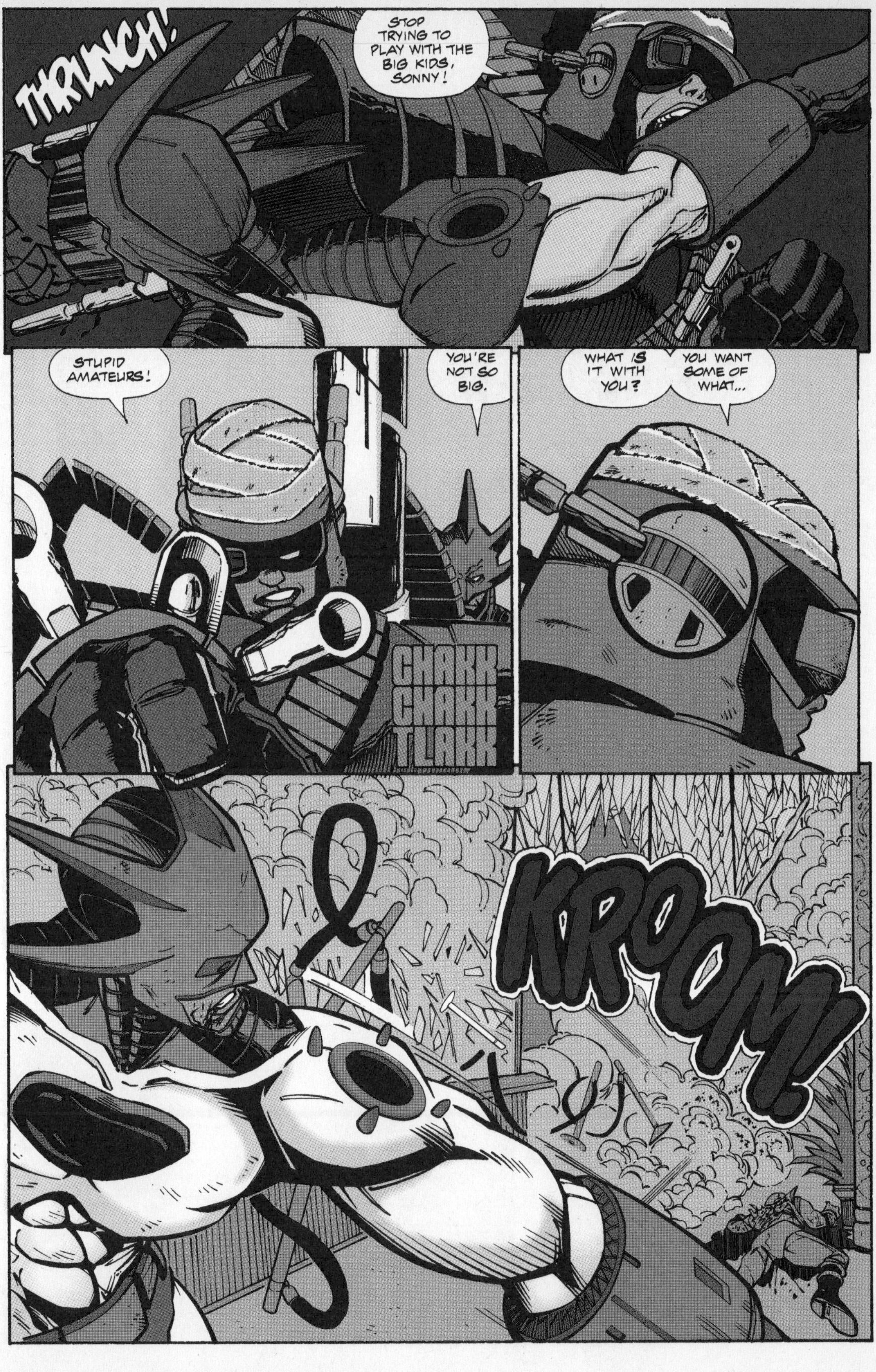
THRUNCH!
STOP TRYING TO PLAY WITH THE BIG KIDS, SONNY!
STUPID AMATEURS!
YOU'RE NOT SO BIG.
CHAKK CHAKK TLAKK
WHAT IS IT WITH YOU?
YOU WANT SOME OF WHAT...
KROOM!

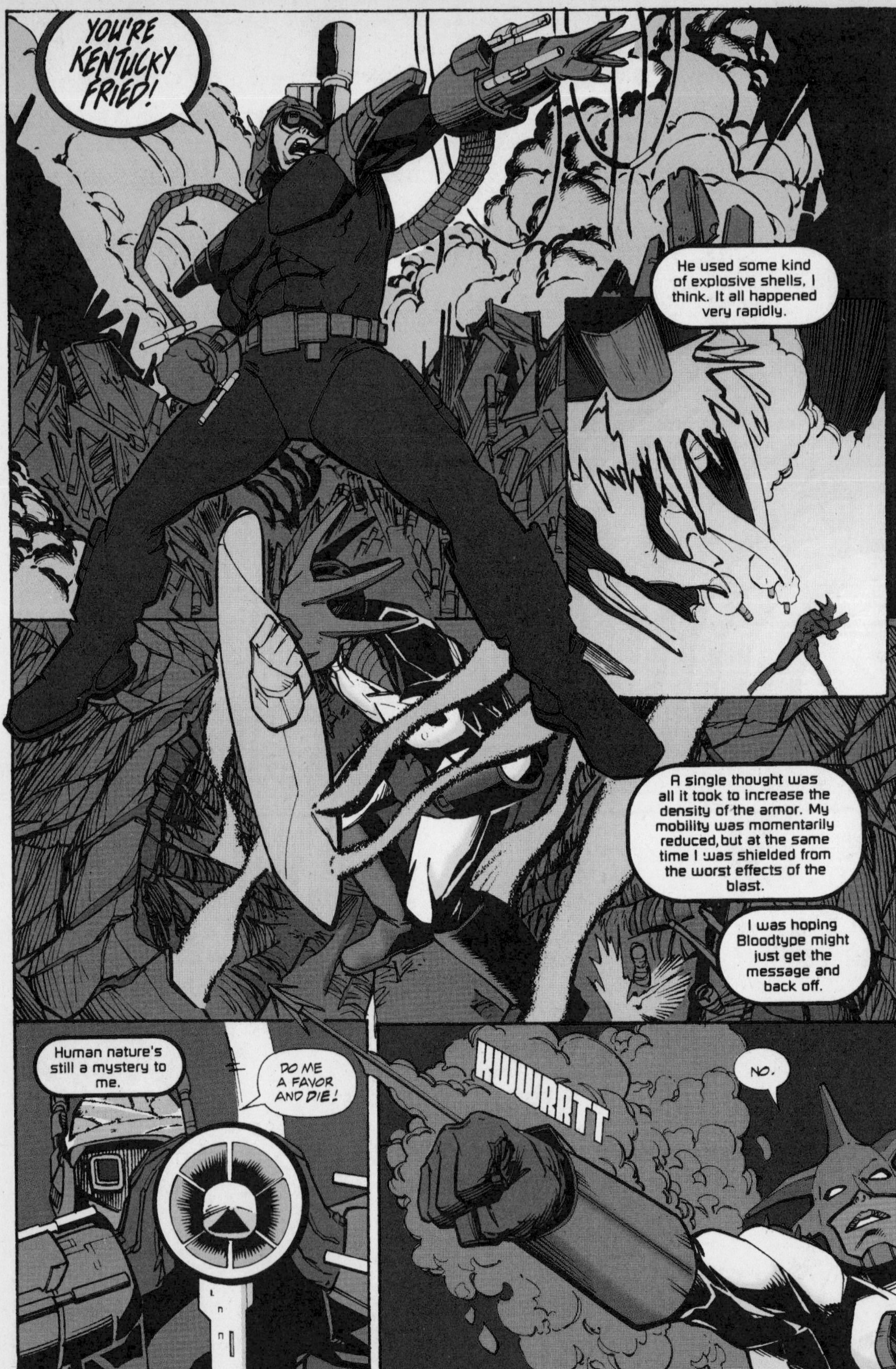
YOU'RE KENTUCKY FRIED!
He used some kind of explosive shells, I think. It all happened very rapidly.
A single thought was all it took to increase the density of the armor. My mobility was momentarily reduced, but at the same time I was shielded from the worst effects of the blast.
I was hoping Bloodtype might just get the message and back off.
Human nature's still a mystery to me.
DO ME A FAVOR AND DIE!
KWWRRTT
NO.

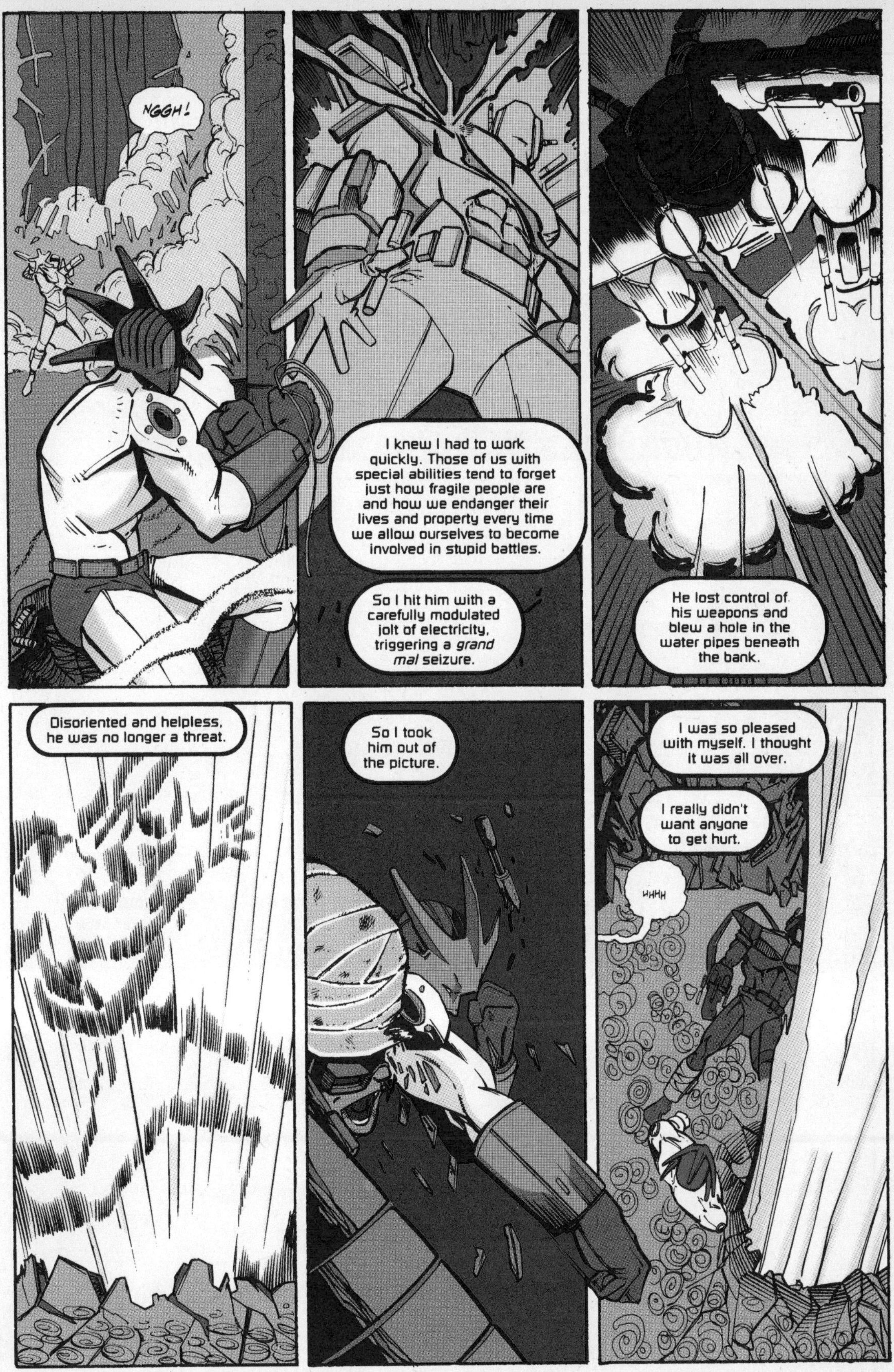
NGGH!
I knew I had to work quickly. Those of us with special abilities tend to forget just how fragile people are and how we endanger their lives and property every time we allow ourselves to become involved in stupid battles.
So I hit him with a carefully modulated jolt of electricity, triggering a *grand mal* seizure.
He lost control of his weapons and blew a hole in the water pipes beneath the bank.
Disoriented and helpless, he was no longer a threat.
So I took him out of the picture.
I was so pleased with myself. I thought it was all over.
I really didn't want anyone to get hurt.

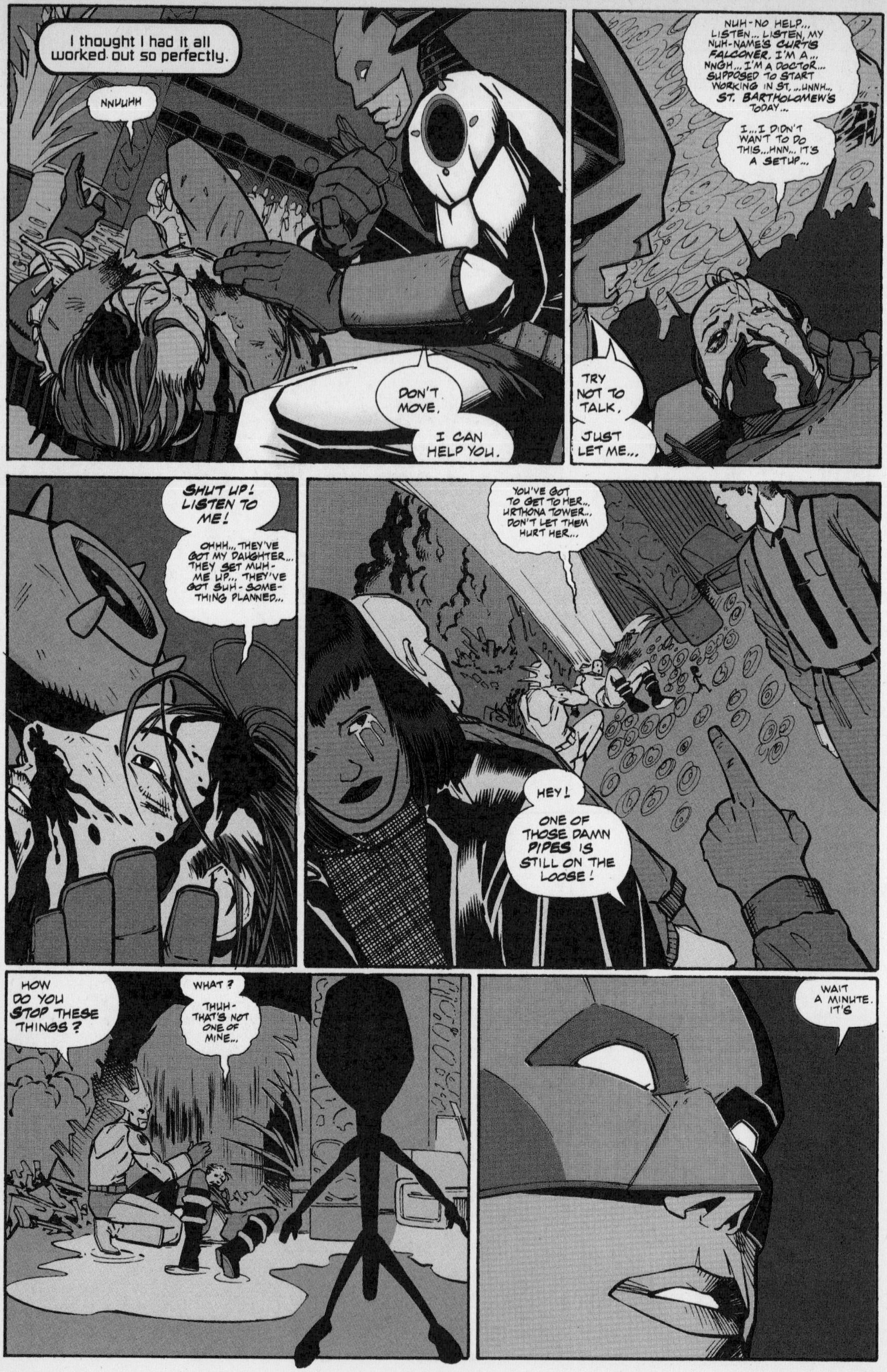
I thought I had it all worked out so perfectly.
NNUUHH
DON'T MOVE.
I CAN HELP YOU.
NUH-NO HELP... LISTEN... LISTEN, MY NUH-NAME'S CURTIS FALCONER. I'M A... NNGH... I'M A DOCTOR... SUPPOSED TO START WORKING IN ST. ...UNNH... ST. BARTHOLOMEW'S TODAY...
I...I DIDN'T WANT TO DO THIS...HNN... IT'S A SETUP...
TRY NOT TO TALK.
JUST LET ME...
SHUT UP! LISTEN TO ME!
OHHH... THEY'VE GOT MY DAUGHTER... THEY SET MUH-ME UP... THEY'VE GOT SUH- SOMETHING PLANNED...
YOU'VE GOT TO GET TO HER... URTHONA TOWER... DON'T LET THEM HURT HER...
HEY!
ONE OF THOSE DAMN PIPES IS STILL ON THE LOOSE!
HOW DO YOU STOP THESE THINGS?
WHAT?
THUH- THAT'S NOT ONE OF MINE...
WAIT A MINUTE. IT'S

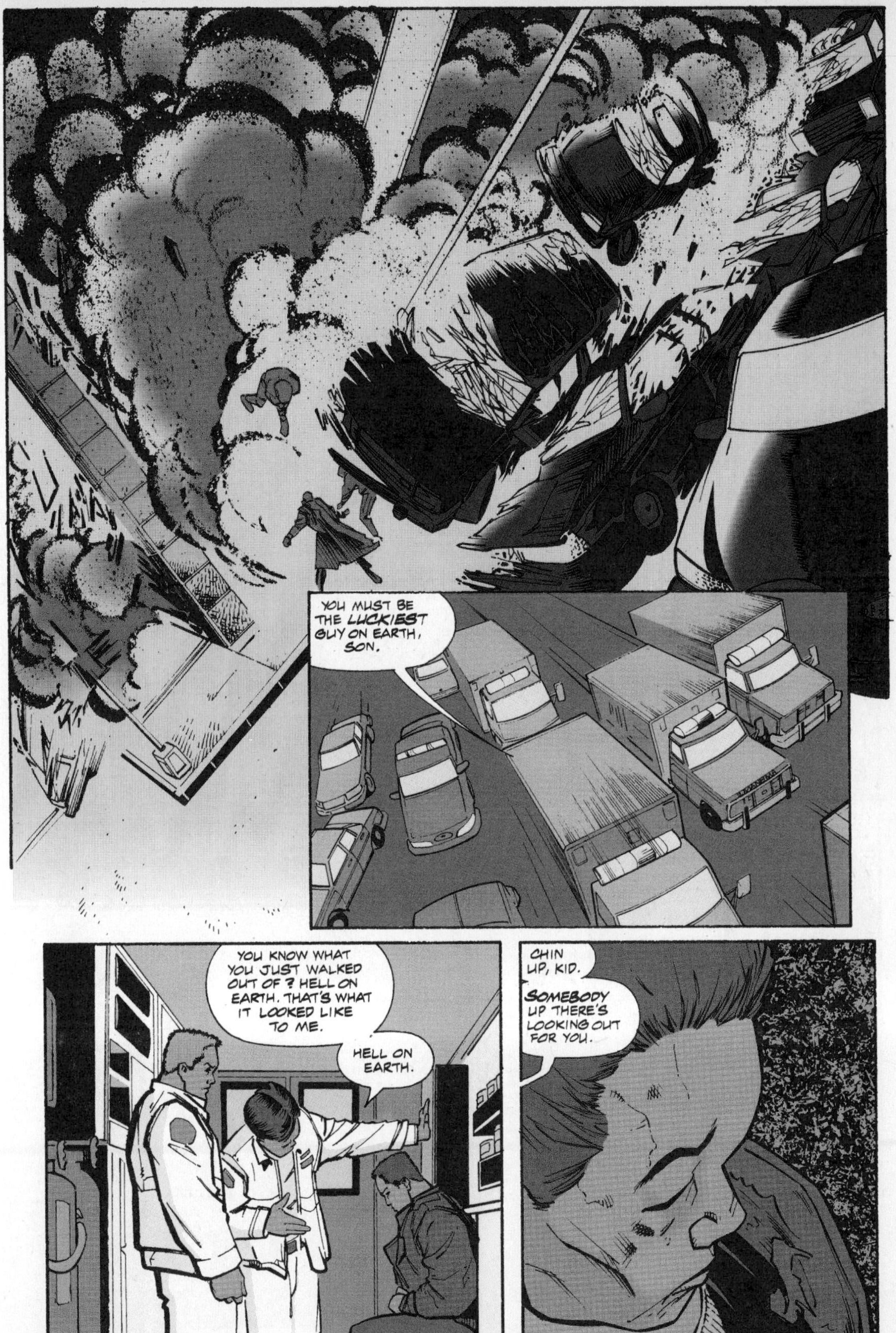
YOU MUST BE THE LUCKIEST GUY ON EARTH, SON.
YOU KNOW WHAT YOU JUST WALKED OUT OF ? HELL ON EARTH. THAT'S WHAT IT LOOKED LIKE TO ME.
HELL ON EARTH.
CHIN UP, KID.
SOMEBODY UP THERE'S LOOKING OUT FOR YOU.

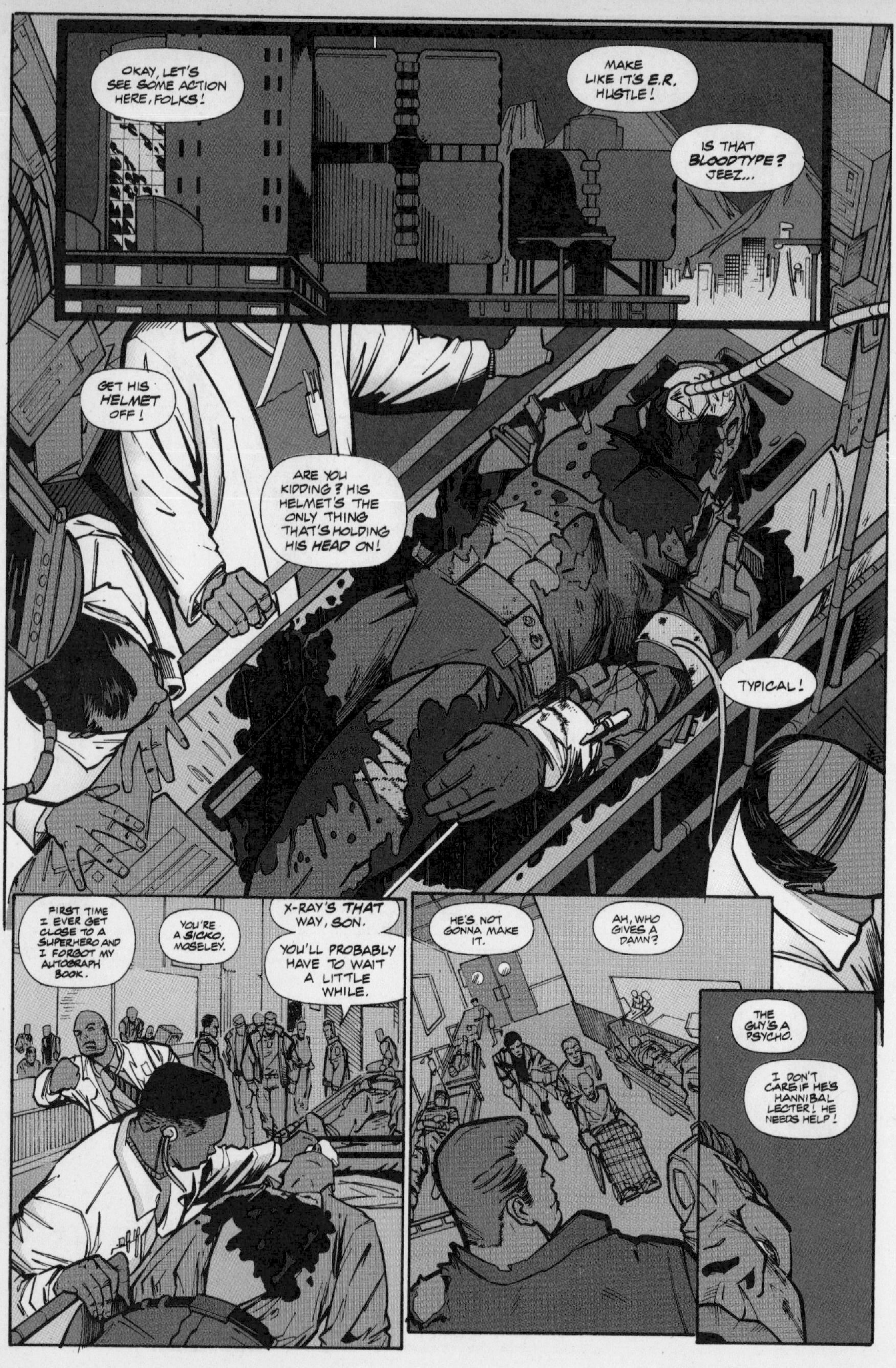
OKAY, LET'S SEE SOME ACTION HERE, FOLKS!
MAKE LIKE IT'S E.R. HUSTLE!
IS THAT BLOODTYPE? JEEZ...
GET HIS HELMET OFF!
ARE YOU KIDDING? HIS HELMET'S THE ONLY THING THAT'S HOLDING HIS HEAD ON!
TYPICAL!
FIRST TIME I EVER GET CLOSE TO A SUPERHERO AND I FORGOT MY AUTOGRAPH BOOK.
YOU'RE A SICKO, MOSELEY.
X-RAY'S THAT WAY, SON.
YOU'LL PROBABLY HAVE TO WAIT A LITTLE WHILE.
HE'S NOT GONNA MAKE IT.
AH, WHO GIVES A DAMN?
THE GUY'S A PSYCHO.
I DON'T CARE IF HE'S HANNIBAL LECTER! HE NEEDS HELP!

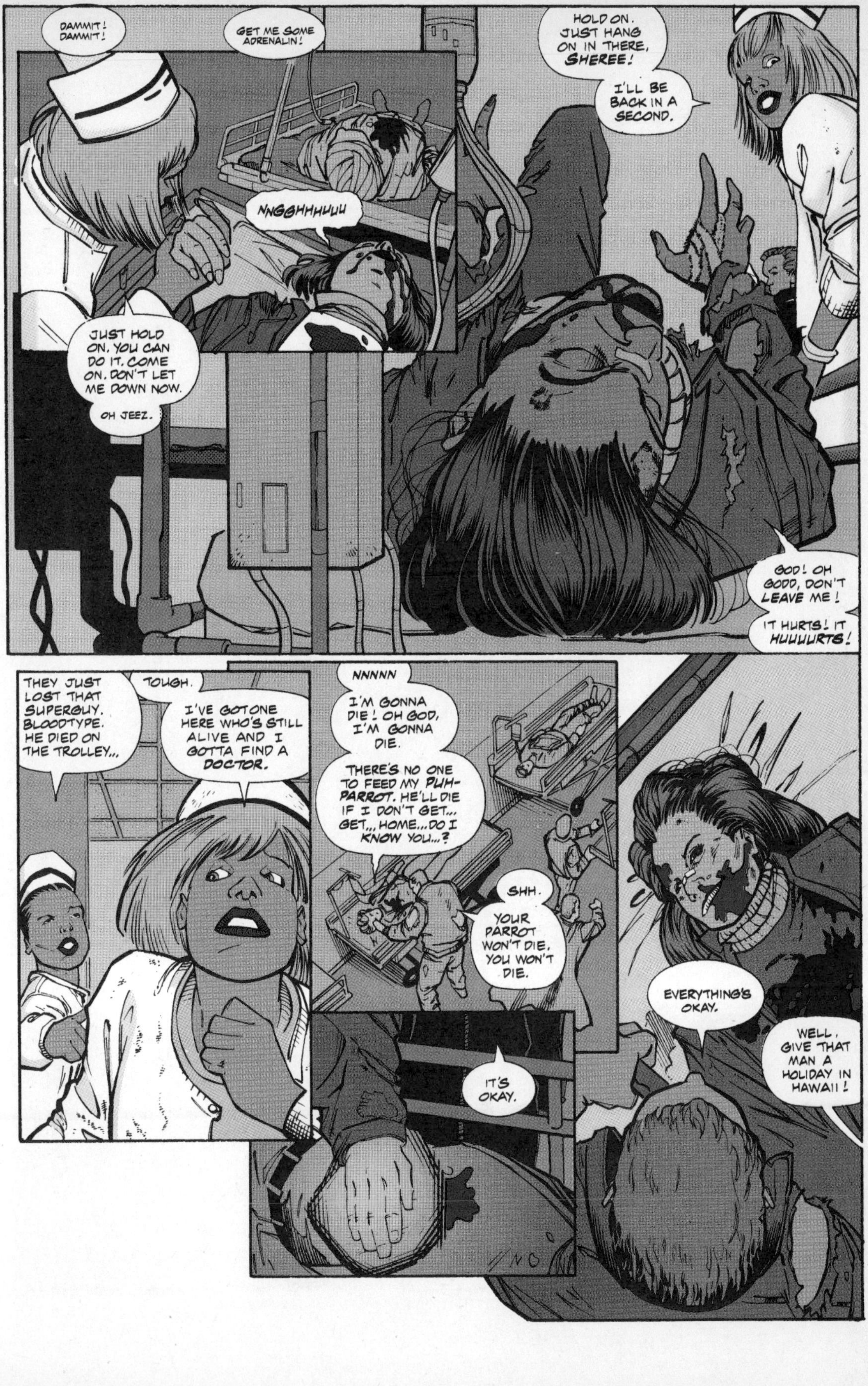
DAMMIT! DAMMIT!
GET ME SOME ADRENALIN!
HOLD ON. JUST HANG ON IN THERE, SHEREE!
I'LL BE BACK IN A SECOND.
NNGGHHHUUU
JUST HOLD ON. YOU CAN DO IT. COME ON. DON'T LET ME DOWN NOW.
OH JEEZ.
GOD! OH GODD, DON'T LEAVE ME!
IT HURTS! IT HUUUURTS!
THEY JUST LOST THAT SUPERGUY. BLOODTYPE. HE DIED ON THE TROLLEY...
TOUGH.
I'VE GOT ONE HERE WHO'S STILL ALIVE AND I GOTTA FIND A DOCTOR.
NNNNN
I'M GONNA DIE! OH GOD, I'M GONNA DIE.
THERE'S NO ONE TO FEED MY PUH-PARROT. HE'LL DIE IF I DON'T GET... GET... HOME... DO I KNOW YOU...?
SHH.
YOUR PARROT WON'T DIE. YOU WON'T DIE.
EVERYTHING'S OKAY.
IT'S OKAY.
WELL, GIVE THAT MAN A HOLIDAY IN HAWAII!

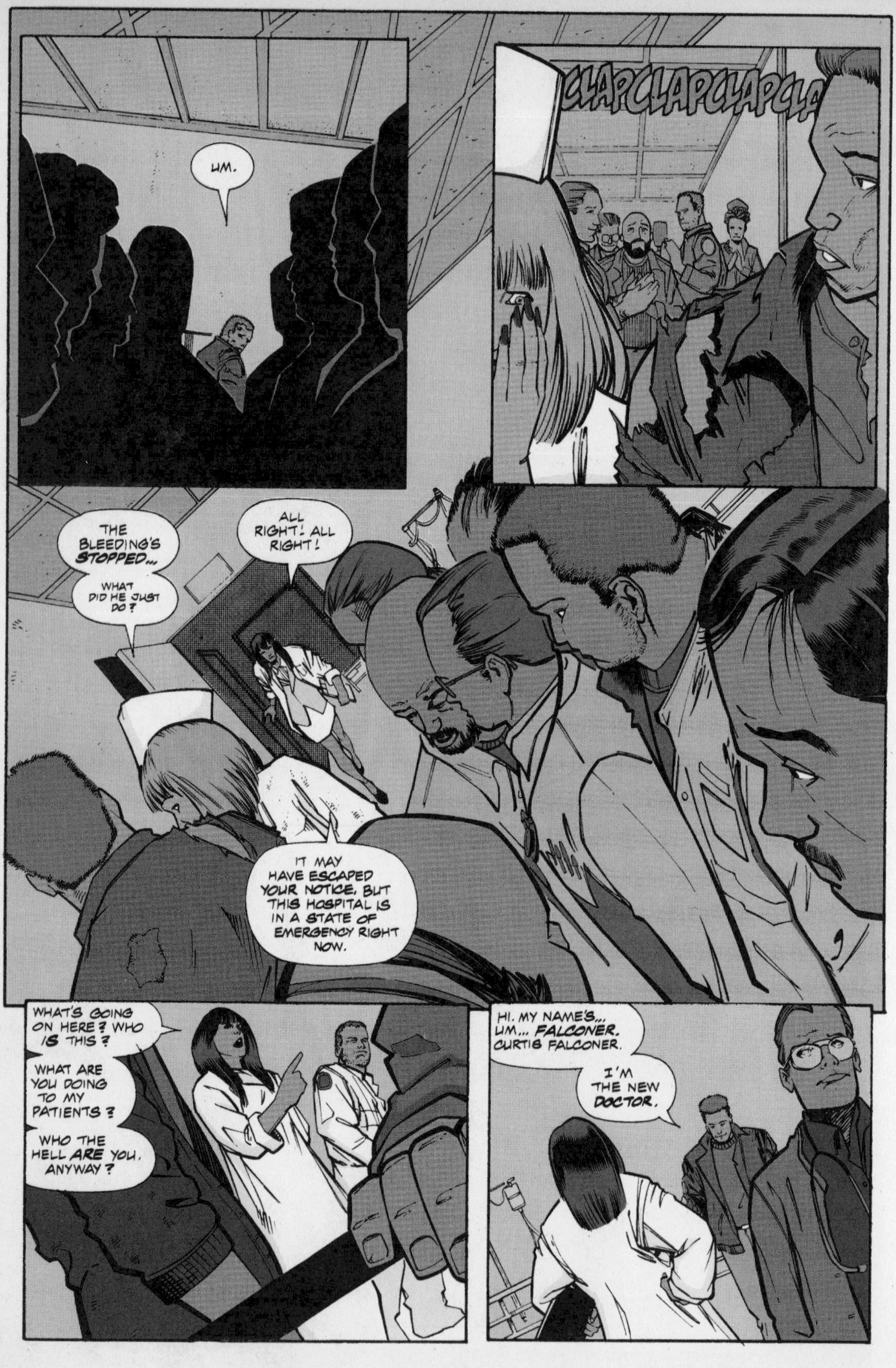
UM.
CLAPCLAPCLAPCLA
THE BLEEDING'S STOPPED...
WHAT DID HE JUST DO?
ALL RIGHT! ALL RIGHT!
IT MAY HAVE ESCAPED YOUR NOTICE, BUT THIS HOSPITAL IS IN A STATE OF EMERGENCY RIGHT NOW.
WHAT'S GOING ON HERE? WHO IS THIS?
WHAT ARE YOU DOING TO MY PATIENTS?
WHO THE HELL ARE YOU, ANYWAY?
HI. MY NAME'S... UM... FALCONER. CURTIS FALCONER.
I'M THE NEW DOCTOR.

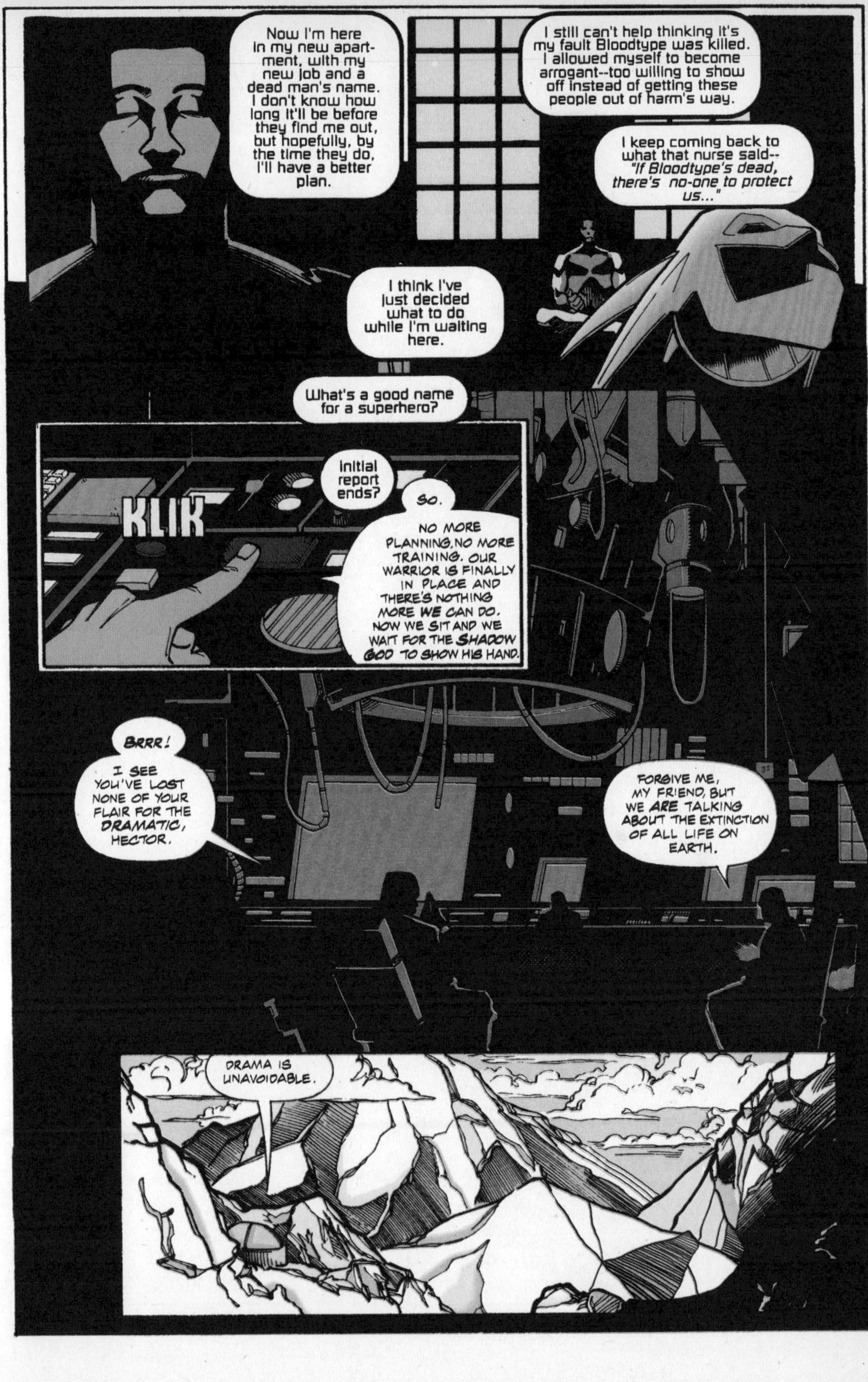
Now I'm here in my new apartment, with my new job and a dead man's name. I don't know how long it'll be before they find me out, but hopefully, by the time they do, I'll have a better plan.
I still can't help thinking it's my fault Bloodtype was killed. I allowed myself to become arrogant--too willing to show off instead of getting these people out of harm's way.
I keep coming back to what that nurse said-- "If Bloodtype's dead, there's no-one to protect us..."
I think I've just decided what to do while I'm waiting here.
What's a good name for a superhero?
KLIK
Initial report ends?
SO.
NO MORE PLANNING, NO MORE TRAINING. OUR WARRIOR IS FINALLY IN PLACE AND THERE'S NOTHING MORE WE CAN DO. NOW WE SIT AND WE WAIT FOR THE SHADOW GOD TO SHOW HIS HAND.
BRRR!
I SEE YOU'VE LOST NONE OF YOUR FLAIR FOR THE DRAMATIC, HECTOR.
FORGIVE ME, MY FRIEND, BUT WE ARE TALKING ABOUT THE EXTINCTION OF ALL LIFE ON EARTH.
DRAMA IS UNAVOIDABLE.

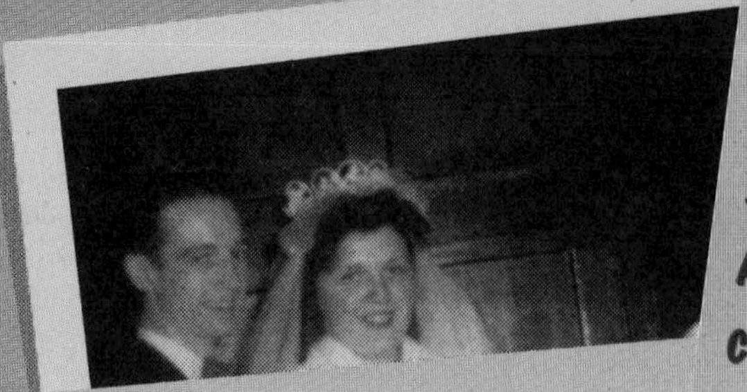

Letter forwarded by Vanity police department by roommate of missing college student, Mindy Falconer. Authenticity yet to be confirmed.

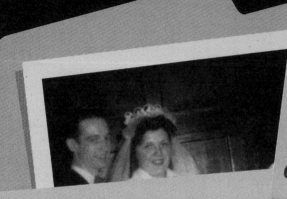

DR. CURT FALCONER, MD
APARTMENT 13C
66 LUCAS BOULEVARD
CHAPMAN, VANITY

June 13th 1996

Dear Mindy,

My little baby girl. You have every reason to despise me now. I am such a weak and foolish man. It's only right I should pay for my mistakes but so unfair that you should suffer. I pray to God that your kidnappers release you when I've done what they asked me to do. Should anything happen to you, then I would kill myself. You're all I have in the world and even you don't like me. Please be alive, baby girl. Please be alive.

I want this letter to say all the things I never could, but writing has never come naturally to me. I've always had a good brain in my head and yet I find it so hard to think of anything *nice* to say. Your mother told me I have never truly loved and so I am impossible to love. Please don't let this be true. I loved you since the moment I delivered you into this terrible world and cleaned the blood from your face with a hospital sponge. I never stopped caring no matter how much you hurt me, no matter what you said or did. You're my daughter and I'll always be there for you whatever the cost to myself. If I die tomorrow, then my sacrifice will be worth it, knowing I have saved your life.

My hands keep shaking. Typing is becoming so difficult, and my bowels aren't working properly. As you'll probably hear on the news, Vanity's gang-bosses have told me to rob the First National Bank, but I don't know if I have what it takes anymore. It's been ten years since I put on my Piper costume, and all my old friends from the Lawless Legion in New York are either dead or in jail. It's such a different world out there these days. I look at the super-heroes on television with their long hair and scowls and their violent new powers, and even *they* scare me now. The only risk I used to worry about was the disgrace of being caught and the premature end to my medical career, but now I wake in the middle of the night fearing heroes with guns and blades and the most awful grammar. I don't know if I belong in this world anymore. I wish we'd never come to Vanity.

Dressing up and stealing things was my way of dealing with the stress of working eighty hours a week in Accident and Emergency. Of course, your mother knew my little secret but we never spoke about it. We used to have dinner in silence every night just like any other family. The subject never once arose, not even when you found my costume upstairs in the bedroom cupboard and I told you they were just my new pajamas. Maybe if we'd all been a little more honest with each other, things would have worked out better between your mother and me. Between you and me. Coming here to Vanity is my biggest mistake in a life full of regrets. This hateful city is famous for turning good men bad, but perhaps the opposite is true in my case. I gave up my secret life and buried myself in my work. Now all I have to do is one last job and you'll be safe again. The

Letter forwarded by Vanity police department:

gangsters will leave us alone and you can move back home and everything will be different. I'll have my new job at a new hospital and we'll go to the movies and go out for dinner and talk to each other all the time. I promise.

My driver license expired today. So did my book club membership and vehicle insurance policy. A little voice in the back of my head keeps telling me to go to the police instead of pulling this final job, but I can't afford to be superstitious — not when the life of my dear daughter is at stake. I've checked my robot pipes over and over again. They're all working perfectly but I'll check them one more time before I go to bed. I found my old photo album earlier, the one filled with clippings of my greatest victories over The Elongated Man and The Atom. Reading about the good old days cheered me up and made me feel a little more confident about tomorrow. I found a photograph inside you might like to see: an old black and white picture someone must have taken on the day your mother and I were married. Possibly the only one in the world she never took a pair of scissors to. Put it somewhere nice. Think of us like we look in the picture.

All this worrying has made my ulcer flare up again. I've been taking my medicine but it isn't working. I haven't been able to eat anything for days. I saw Bloodtype interviewed on television tonight with the corpse of a tortured super-villain slung over his shoulder and I wished he was dead. God forgive me but that man scares me so much. I think of the heroes we used to have in this country — decent men and woman who *believed* in something. They were inspirational figures who showed us what we could aspire to. Not what depths we could reach. I wish we had someone like that watching over us again. We deserve better than this.

It's getting late. I can't think of anything else to say. I love you, Mindy. No matter what you hear them say about me on the news if I don't make it back, just remember that I've *always* loved you.

Dad

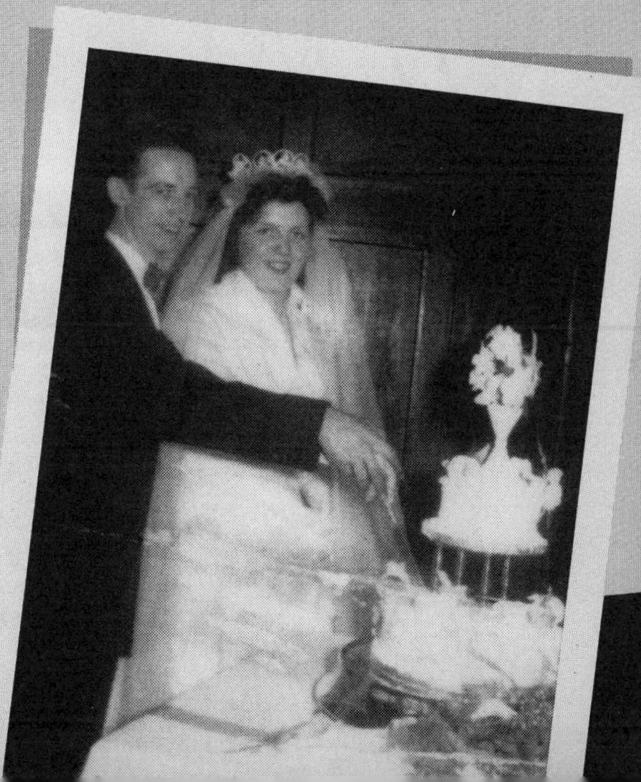

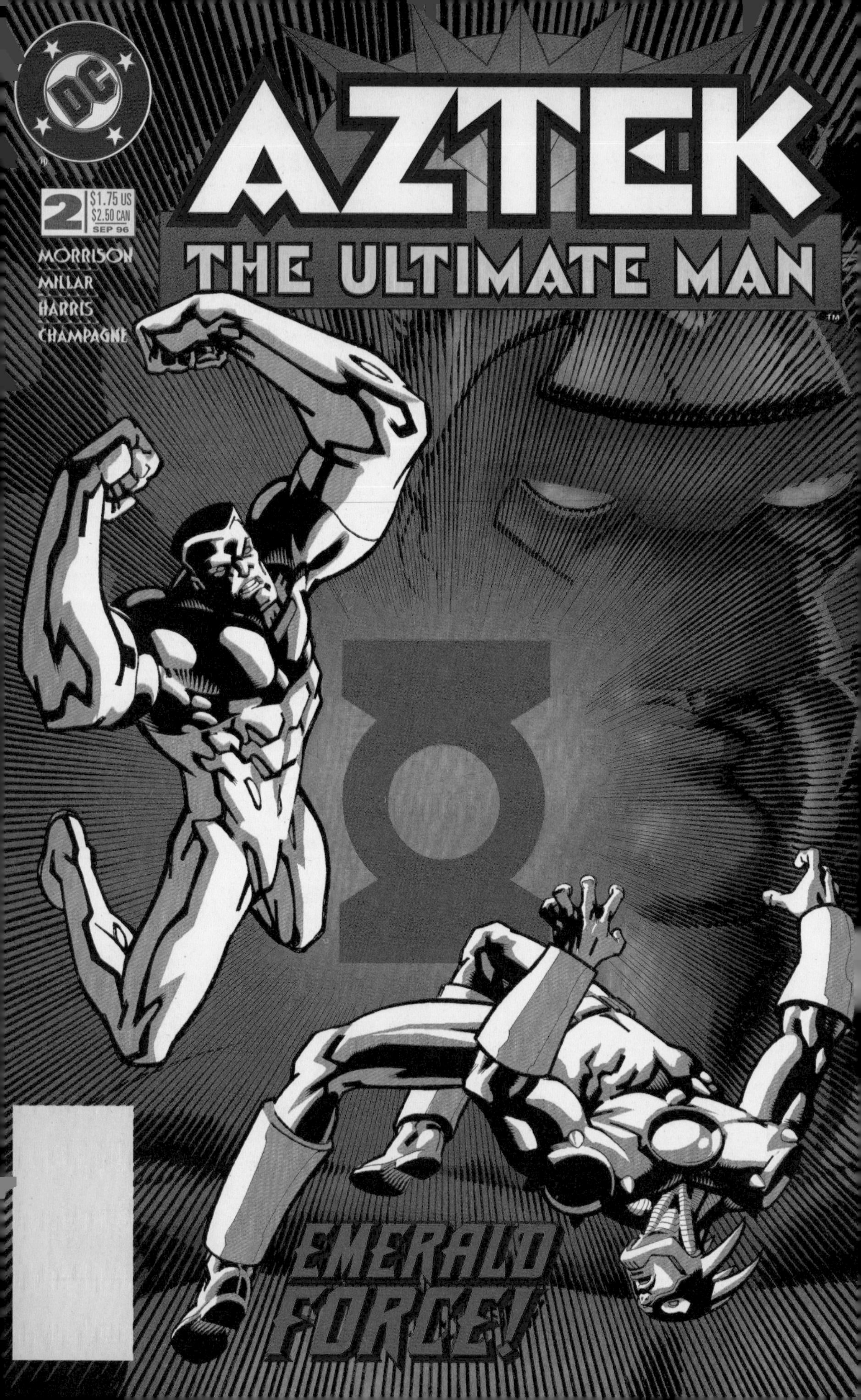
AZTEK
THE ULTIMATE MAN
2
$1.75 US
$2.50 CAN
SEP 96
MORRISON
MILLAR
HARRIS
CHAMPAGNE
EMERALD FORCE!

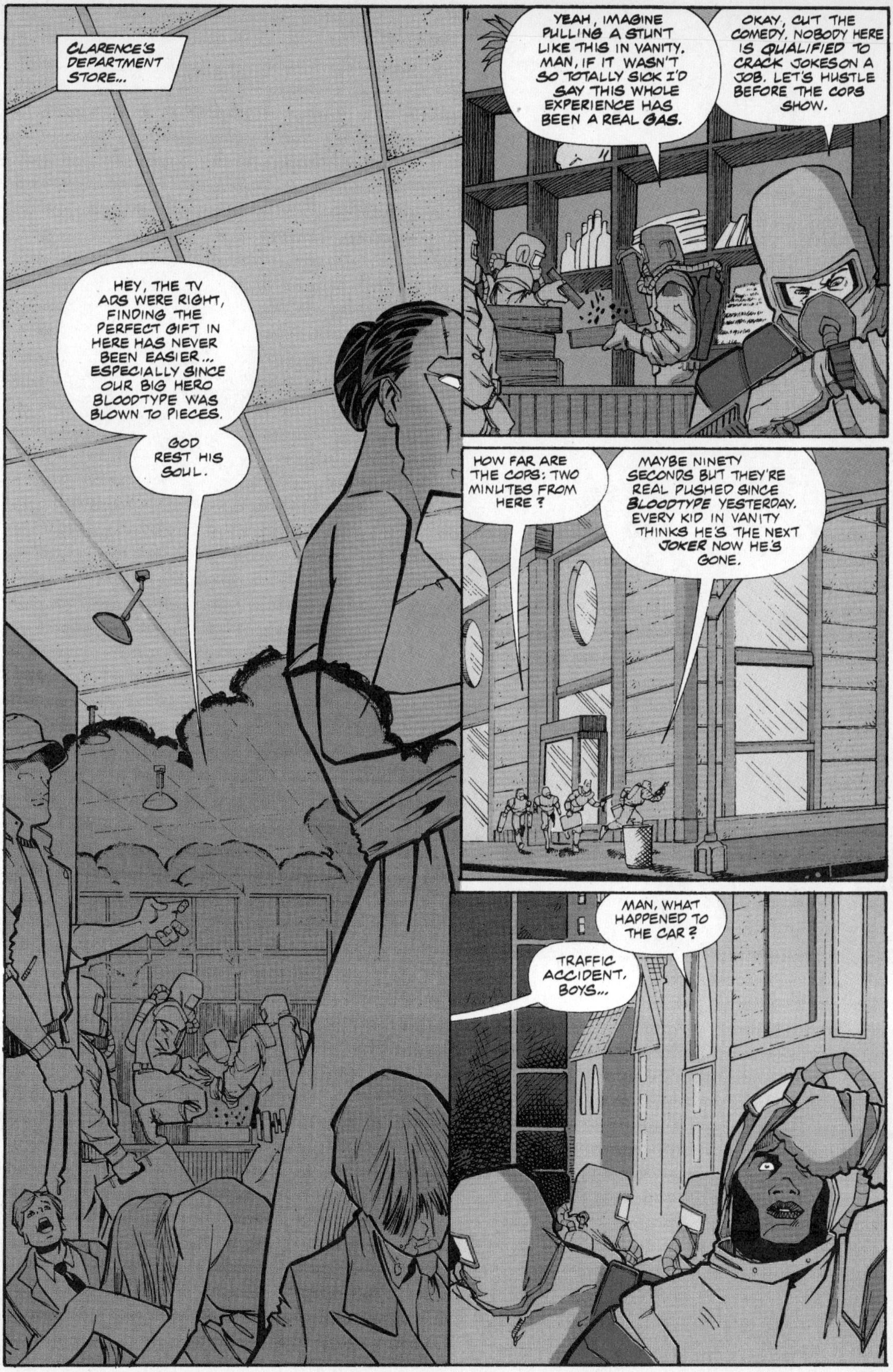
CLARENCE'S DEPARTMENT STORE...
HEY, THE TV ADS WERE RIGHT, FINDING THE PERFECT GIFT IN HERE HAS NEVER BEEN EASIER... ESPECIALLY SINCE OUR BIG HERO BLOODTYPE WAS BLOWN TO PIECES.
GOD REST HIS SOUL.
YEAH, IMAGINE PULLING A STUNT LIKE THIS IN VANITY. MAN, IF IT WASN'T SO TOTALLY SICK I'D SAY THIS WHOLE EXPERIENCE HAS BEEN A REAL GAS.
OKAY, CUT THE COMEDY. NOBODY HERE IS QUALIFIED TO CRACK JOKES ON A JOB. LET'S HUSTLE BEFORE THE COPS SHOW.
HOW FAR ARE THE COPS: TWO MINUTES FROM HERE?
MAYBE NINETY SECONDS BUT THEY'RE REAL PUSHED SINCE BLOODTYPE YESTERDAY. EVERY KID IN VANITY THINKS HE'S THE NEXT JOKER NOW HE'S GONE.
MAN, WHAT HAPPENED TO THE CAR?
TRAFFIC ACCIDENT, BOYS...

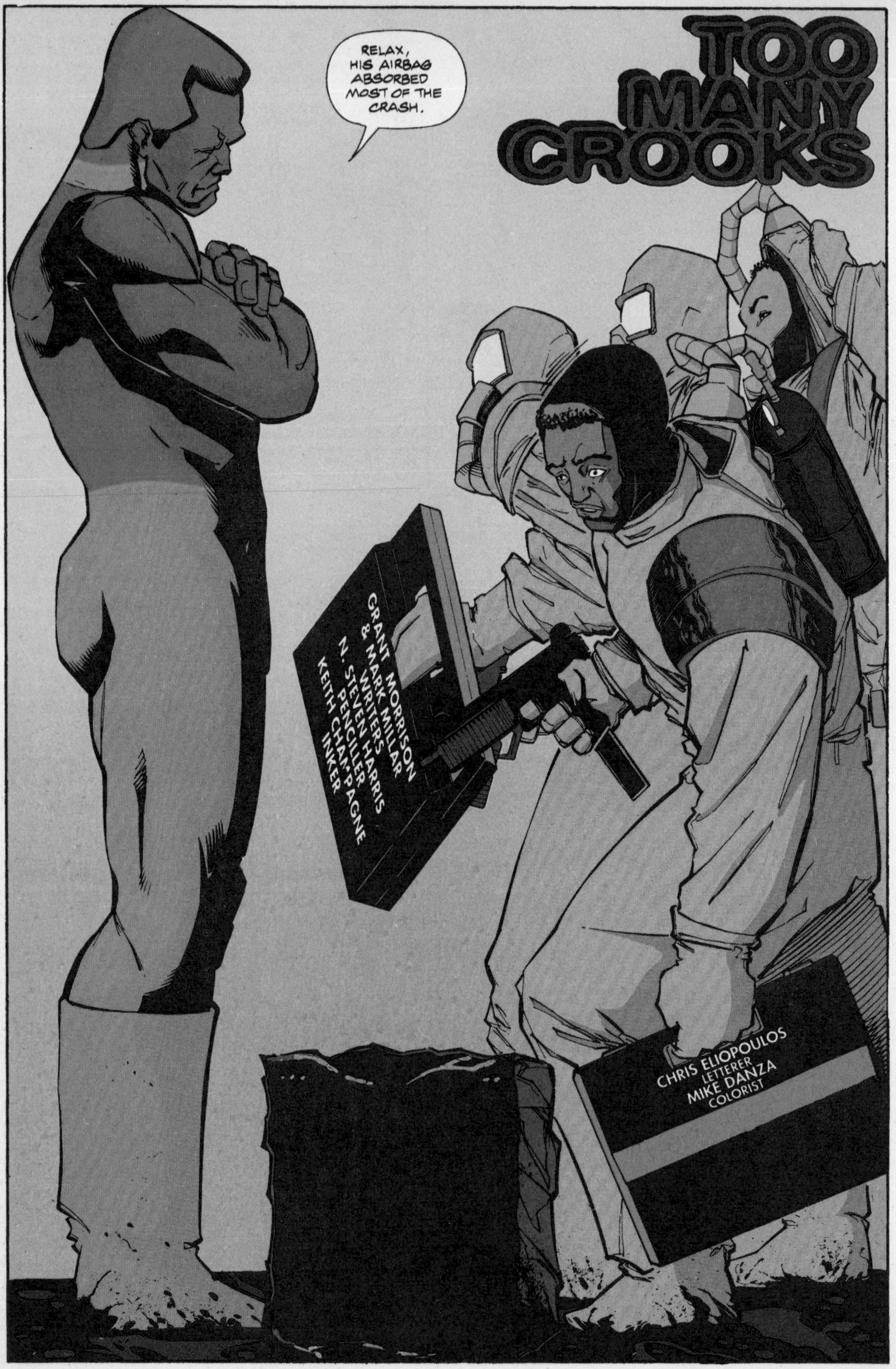

RELAX, HIS AIRBAG ABSORBED MOST OF THE CRASH.
TOO MANY CROOKS
GRANT MORRISON & MARK MILLAR WRITERS
N. STEVEN HARRIS PENCILLER
KEITH CHAMPAGNE INKER
CHRIS ELIOPOULOS LETTERER
MIKE DANZA COLORIST

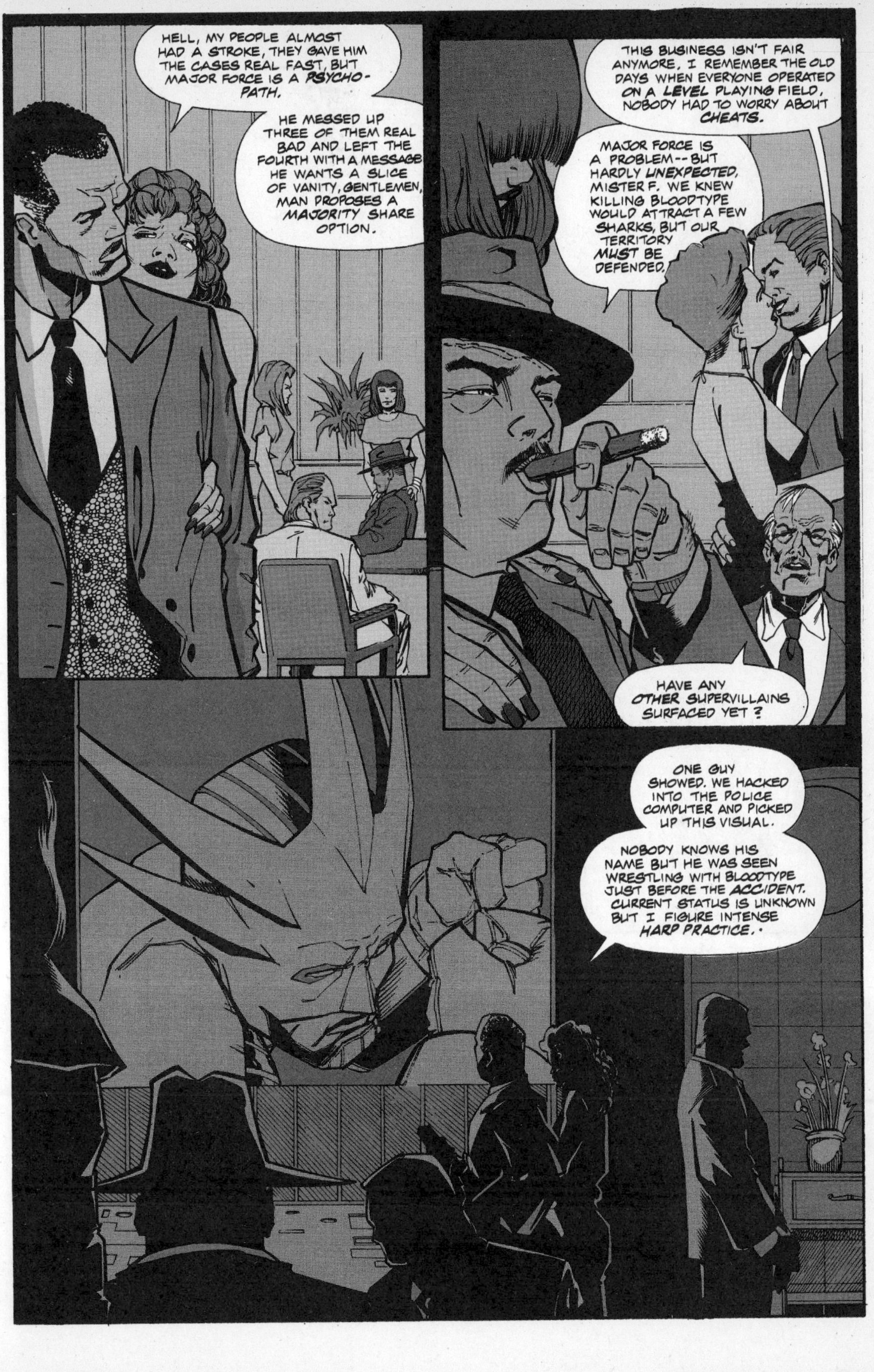

HELL, MY PEOPLE ALMOST HAD A STROKE, THEY GAVE HIM THE CASES REAL FAST, BUT MAJOR FORCE IS A PSYCHO-PATH.
HE MESSED UP THREE OF THEM REAL BAD AND LEFT THE FOURTH WITH A MESSAGE. HE WANTS A SLICE OF VANITY, GENTLEMEN, MAN PROPOSES A MAJORITY SHARE OPTION.
THIS BUSINESS ISN'T FAIR ANYMORE. I REMEMBER THE OLD DAYS WHEN EVERYONE OPERATED ON A LEVEL PLAYING FIELD, NOBODY HAD TO WORRY ABOUT CHEATS.
MAJOR FORCE IS A PROBLEM--BUT HARDLY UNEXPECTED, MISTER F. WE KNEW KILLING BLOODTYPE WOULD ATTRACT A FEW SHARKS, BUT OUR TERRITORY MUST BE DEFENDED.
HAVE ANY OTHER SUPERVILLAINS SURFACED YET?
ONE GUY SHOWED. WE HACKED INTO THE POLICE COMPUTER AND PICKED UP THIS VISUAL.
NOBODY KNOWS HIS NAME BUT HE WAS SEEN WRESTLING WITH BLOODTYPE JUST BEFORE THE ACCIDENT. CURRENT STATUS IS UNKNOWN BUT I FIGURE INTENSE HARD PRACTICE.

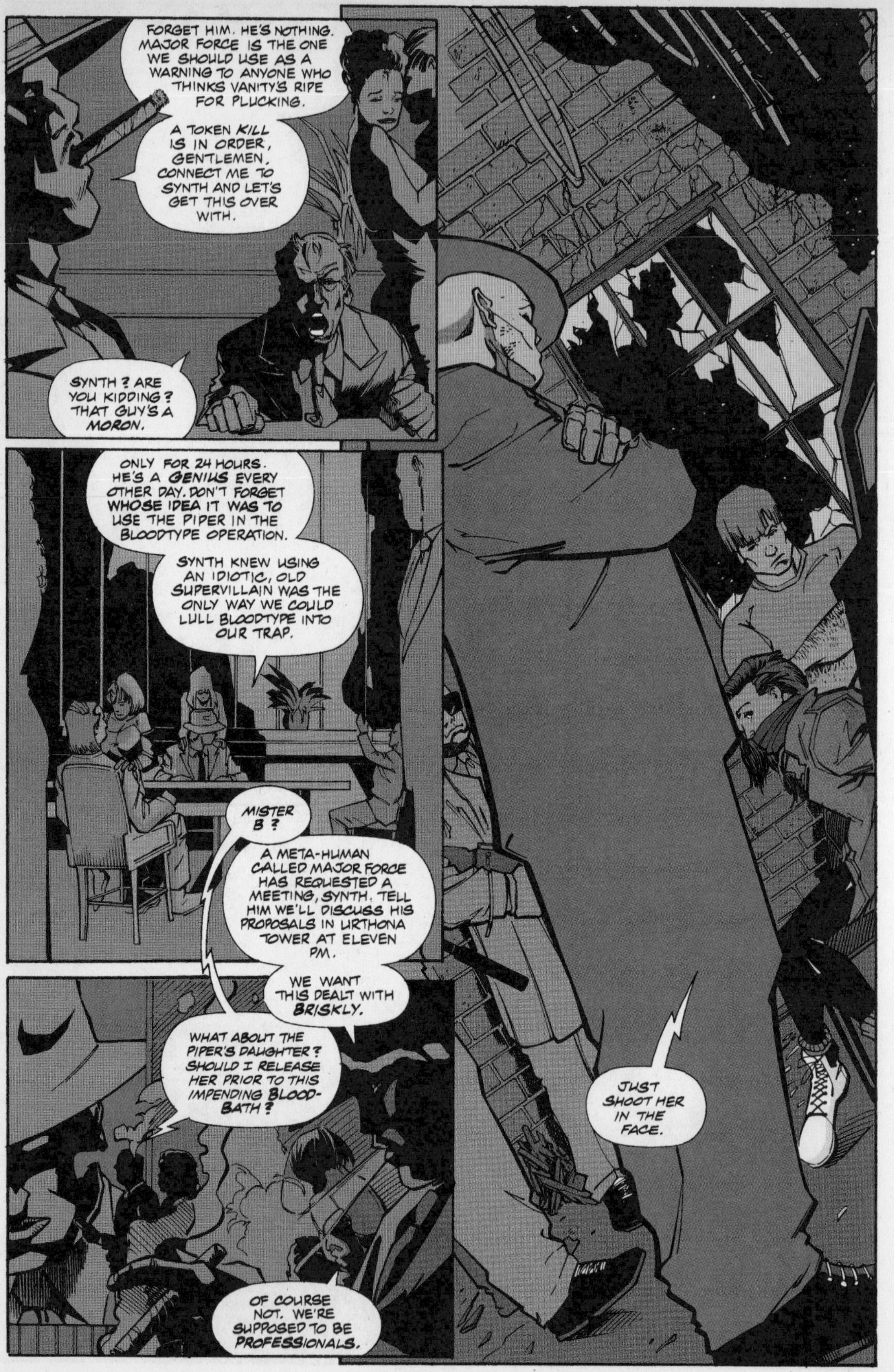
FORGET HIM. HE'S NOTHING. MAJOR FORCE IS THE ONE WE SHOULD USE AS A WARNING TO ANYONE WHO THINKS VANITY'S RIPE FOR PLUCKING.
A TOKEN KILL IS IN ORDER, GENTLEMEN. CONNECT ME TO SYNTH AND LET'S GET THIS OVER WITH.
SYNTH ? ARE YOU KIDDING ? THAT GUY'S A MORON.
ONLY FOR 24 HOURS. HE'S A GENIUS EVERY OTHER DAY. DON'T FORGET WHOSE IDEA IT WAS TO USE THE PIPER IN THE BLOODTYPE OPERATION.
SYNTH KNEW USING AN IDIOTIC, OLD SUPERVILLAIN WAS THE ONLY WAY WE COULD LULL BLOODTYPE INTO OUR TRAP.
MISTER B ?
A META-HUMAN CALLED MAJOR FORCE HAS REQUESTED A MEETING, SYNTH. TELL HIM WE'LL DISCUSS HIS PROPOSALS IN URTHONA TOWER AT ELEVEN PM.
WE WANT THIS DEALT WITH BRISKLY.
WHAT ABOUT THE PIPER'S DAUGHTER ? SHOULD I RELEASE HER PRIOR TO THIS IMPENDING BLOOD-BATH ?
JUST SHOOT HER IN THE FACE.
OF COURSE NOT. WE'RE SUPPOSED TO BE PROFESSIONALS.

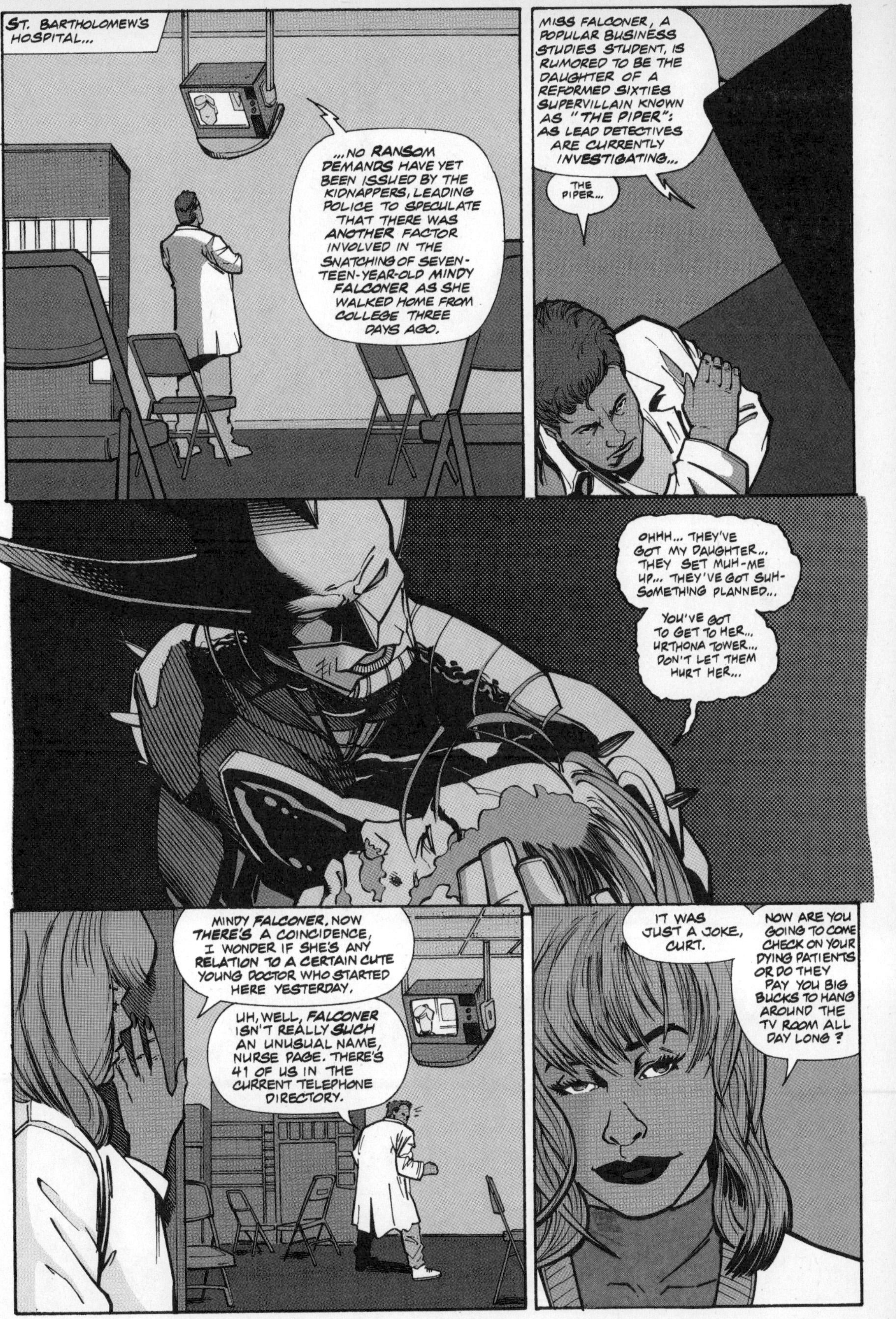
ST. BARTHOLOMEW'S HOSPITAL...
...NO RANSOM DEMANDS HAVE YET BEEN ISSUED BY THE KIDNAPPERS, LEADING POLICE TO SPECULATE THAT THERE WAS ANOTHER FACTOR INVOLVED IN THE SNATCHING OF SEVENTEEN-YEAR-OLD MINDY FALCONER AS SHE WALKED HOME FROM COLLEGE THREE DAYS AGO.
MISS FALCONER, A POPULAR BUSINESS STUDIES STUDENT, IS RUMORED TO BE THE DAUGHTER OF A REFORMED SIXTIES SUPERVILLAIN KNOWN AS "THE PIPER": AS LEAD DETECTIVES ARE CURRENTLY INVESTIGATING...
THE PIPER...
OHHH... THEY'VE GOT MY DAUGHTER... THEY SET MUH-ME UP... THEY'VE GOT SUH-SOMETHING PLANNED...
YOU'VE GOT TO GET TO HER... URTHONA TOWER... DON'T LET THEM HURT HER...
MINDY FALCONER. NOW THERE'S A COINCIDENCE. I WONDER IF SHE'S ANY RELATION TO A CERTAIN CUTE YOUNG DOCTOR WHO STARTED HERE YESTERDAY.
UH, WELL, FALCONER ISN'T REALLY SUCH AN UNUSUAL NAME, NURSE PAGE. THERE'S 41 OF US IN THE CURRENT TELEPHONE DIRECTORY.
IT WAS JUST A JOKE, CURT.
NOW ARE YOU GOING TO COME CHECK ON YOUR DYING PATIENTS OR DO THEY PAY YOU BIG BUCKS TO HANG AROUND THE TV ROOM ALL DAY LONG?

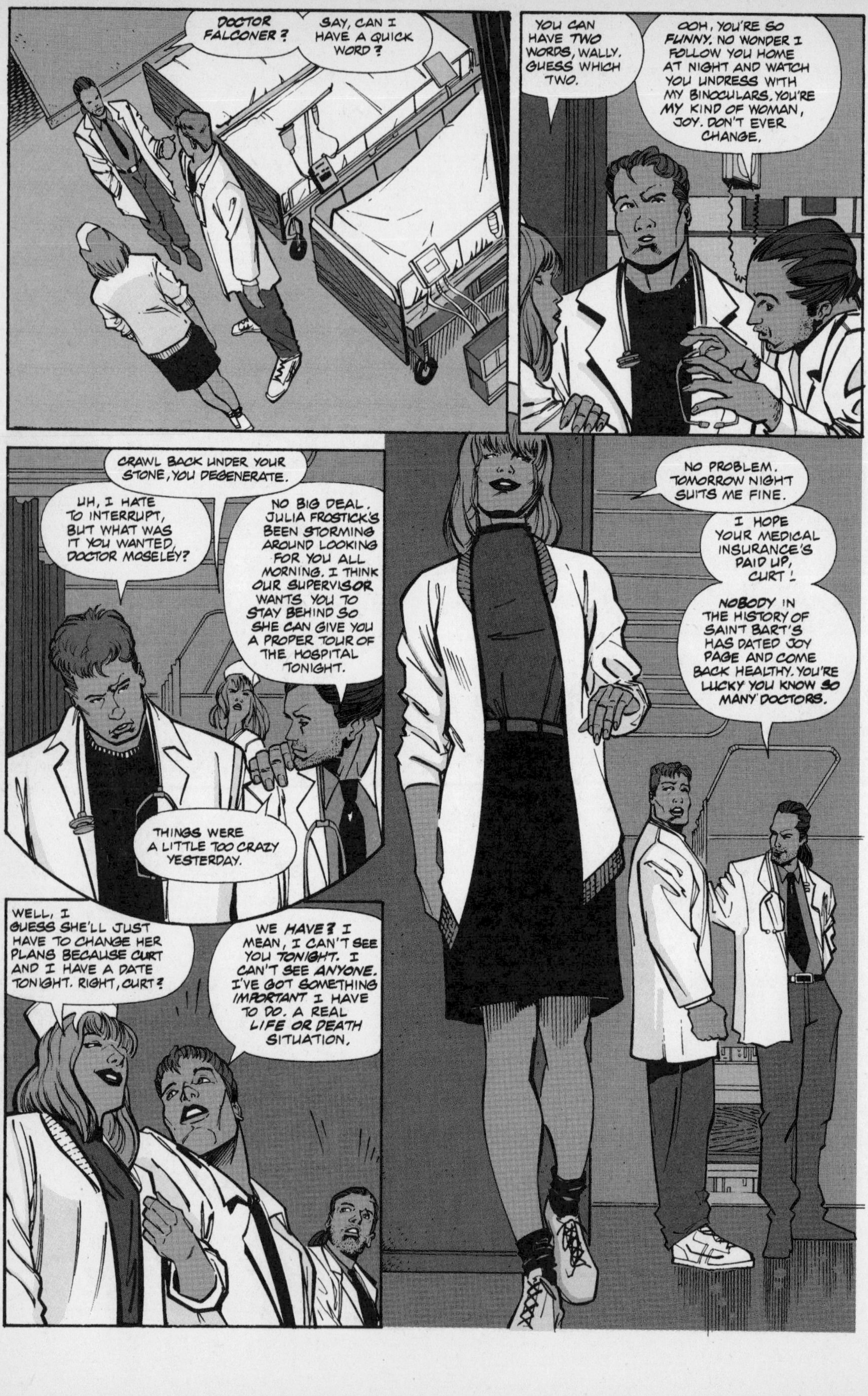
DOCTOR FALCONER?
SAY, CAN I HAVE A QUICK WORD?
YOU CAN HAVE TWO WORDS, WALLY. GUESS WHICH TWO.
OOH, YOU'RE SO FUNNY. NO WONDER I FOLLOW YOU HOME AT NIGHT AND WATCH YOU UNDRESS WITH MY BINOCULARS. YOU'RE MY KIND OF WOMAN, JOY. DON'T EVER CHANGE.
CRAWL BACK UNDER YOUR STONE, YOU DEGENERATE.
UH, I HATE TO INTERRUPT, BUT WHAT WAS IT YOU WANTED, DOCTOR MOSELEY?
NO BIG DEAL. JULIA FROSTICK'S BEEN STORMING AROUND LOOKING FOR YOU ALL MORNING. I THINK OUR SUPERVISOR WANTS YOU TO STAY BEHIND SO SHE CAN GIVE YOU A PROPER TOUR OF THE HOSPITAL TONIGHT.
THINGS WERE A LITTLE TOO CRAZY YESTERDAY.
WELL, I GUESS SHE'LL JUST HAVE TO CHANGE HER PLANS BECAUSE CURT AND I HAVE A DATE TONIGHT. RIGHT, CURT?
WE HAVE? I MEAN, I CAN'T SEE YOU TONIGHT. I CAN'T SEE ANYONE. I'VE GOT SOMETHING IMPORTANT I HAVE TO DO. A REAL LIFE OR DEATH SITUATION.
NO PROBLEM. TOMORROW NIGHT SUITS ME FINE.
I HOPE YOUR MEDICAL INSURANCE'S PAID UP, CURT!
NOBODY IN THE HISTORY OF SAINT BART'S HAS DATED JOY PAGE AND COME BACK HEALTHY. YOU'RE LUCKY YOU KNOW SO MANY DOCTORS.

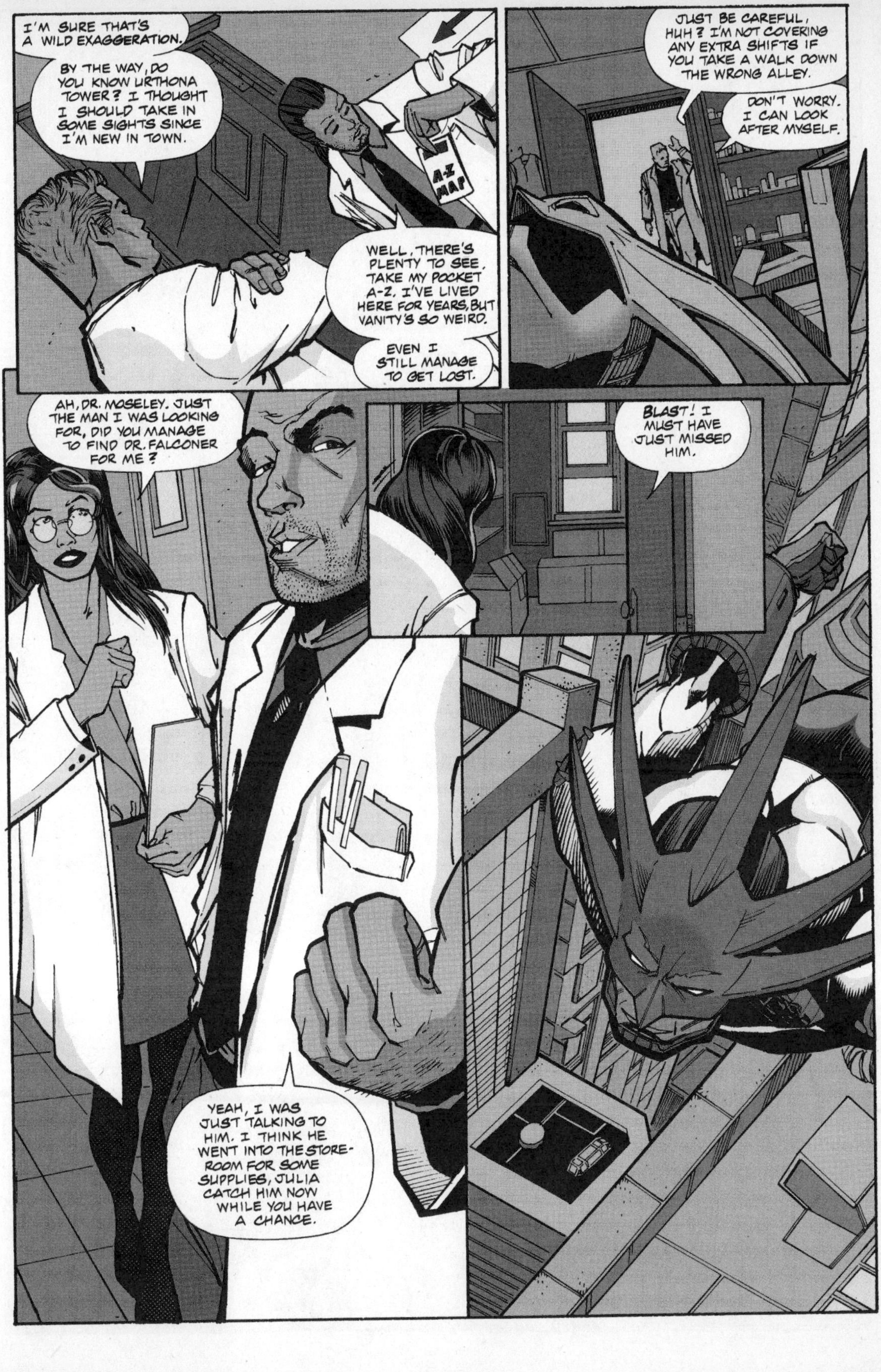
I'M SURE THAT'S A WILD EXAGGERATION.
BY THE WAY, DO YOU KNOW URTHONA TOWER? I THOUGHT I SHOULD TAKE IN SOME SIGHTS SINCE I'M NEW IN TOWN.
A-Z MAP
WELL, THERE'S PLENTY TO SEE. TAKE MY POCKET A-Z. I'VE LIVED HERE FOR YEARS, BUT VANITY'S SO WEIRD.
EVEN I STILL MANAGE TO GET LOST.
JUST BE CAREFUL, HUH? I'M NOT COVERING ANY EXTRA SHIFTS IF YOU TAKE A WALK DOWN THE WRONG ALLEY.
DON'T WORRY. I CAN LOOK AFTER MYSELF.
AH, DR. MOSELEY. JUST THE MAN I WAS LOOKING FOR. DID YOU MANAGE TO FIND DR. FALCONER FOR ME?
YEAH, I WAS JUST TALKING TO HIM. I THINK HE WENT INTO THE STORE-ROOM FOR SOME SUPPLIES, JULIA. CATCH HIM NOW WHILE YOU HAVE A CHANCE.
BLAST! I MUST HAVE JUST MISSED HIM.

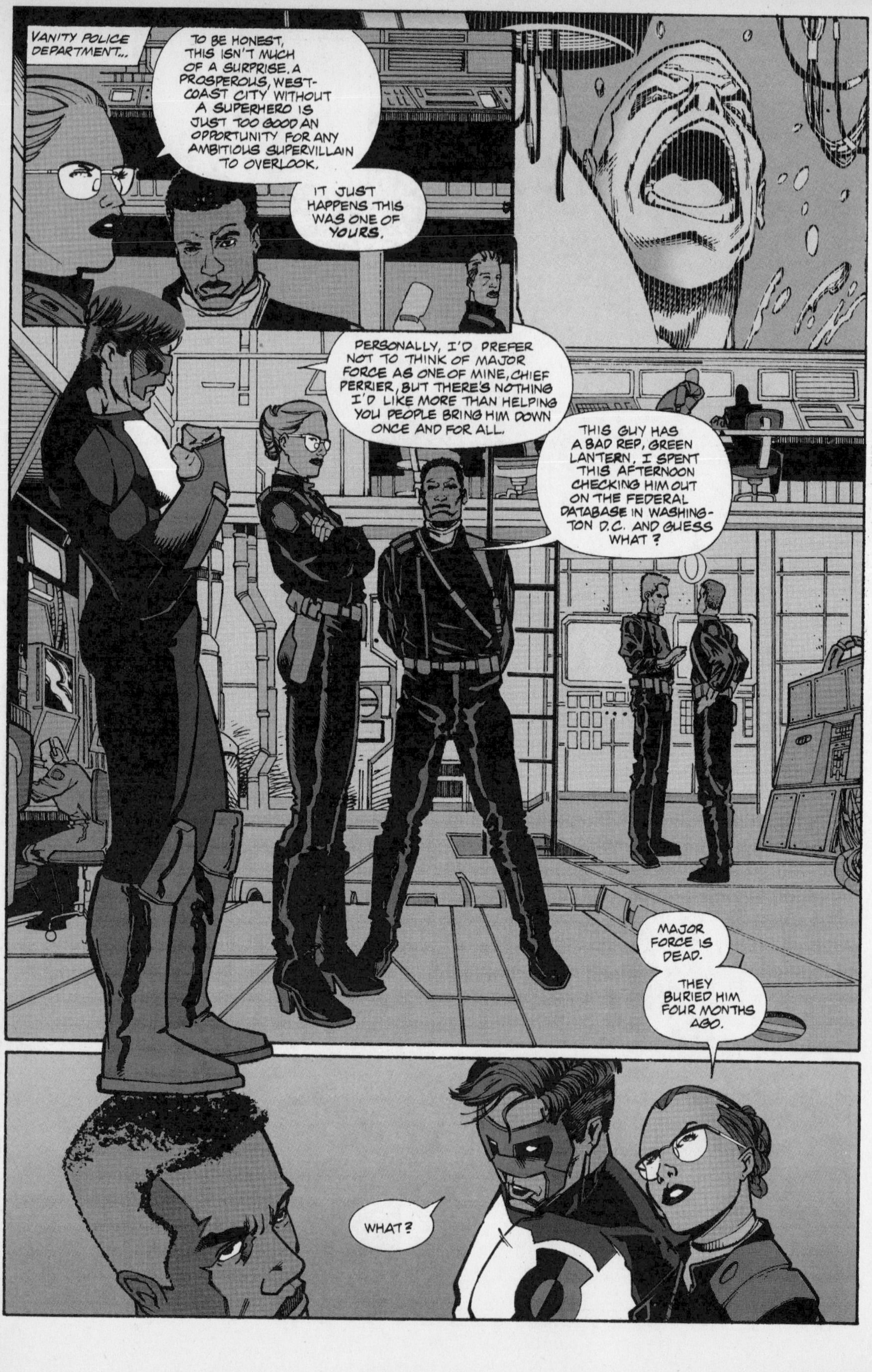
VANITY POLICE DEPARTMENT...
TO BE HONEST, THIS ISN'T MUCH OF A SURPRISE. A PROSPEROUS, WEST-COAST CITY WITHOUT A SUPERHERO IS JUST TOO GOOD AN OPPORTUNITY FOR ANY AMBITIOUS SUPERVILLAIN TO OVERLOOK.
IT JUST HAPPENS THIS WAS ONE OF YOURS.
PERSONALLY, I'D PREFER NOT TO THINK OF MAJOR FORCE AS ONE OF MINE, CHIEF PERRIER, BUT THERE'S NOTHING I'D LIKE MORE THAN HELPING YOU PEOPLE BRING HIM DOWN ONCE AND FOR ALL.
THIS GUY HAS A BAD REP, GREEN LANTERN. I SPENT THIS AFTERNOON CHECKING HIM OUT ON THE FEDERAL DATABASE IN WASHINGTON D.C. AND GUESS WHAT?
MAJOR FORCE IS DEAD.
THEY BURIED HIM FOUR MONTHS AGO.
WHAT?

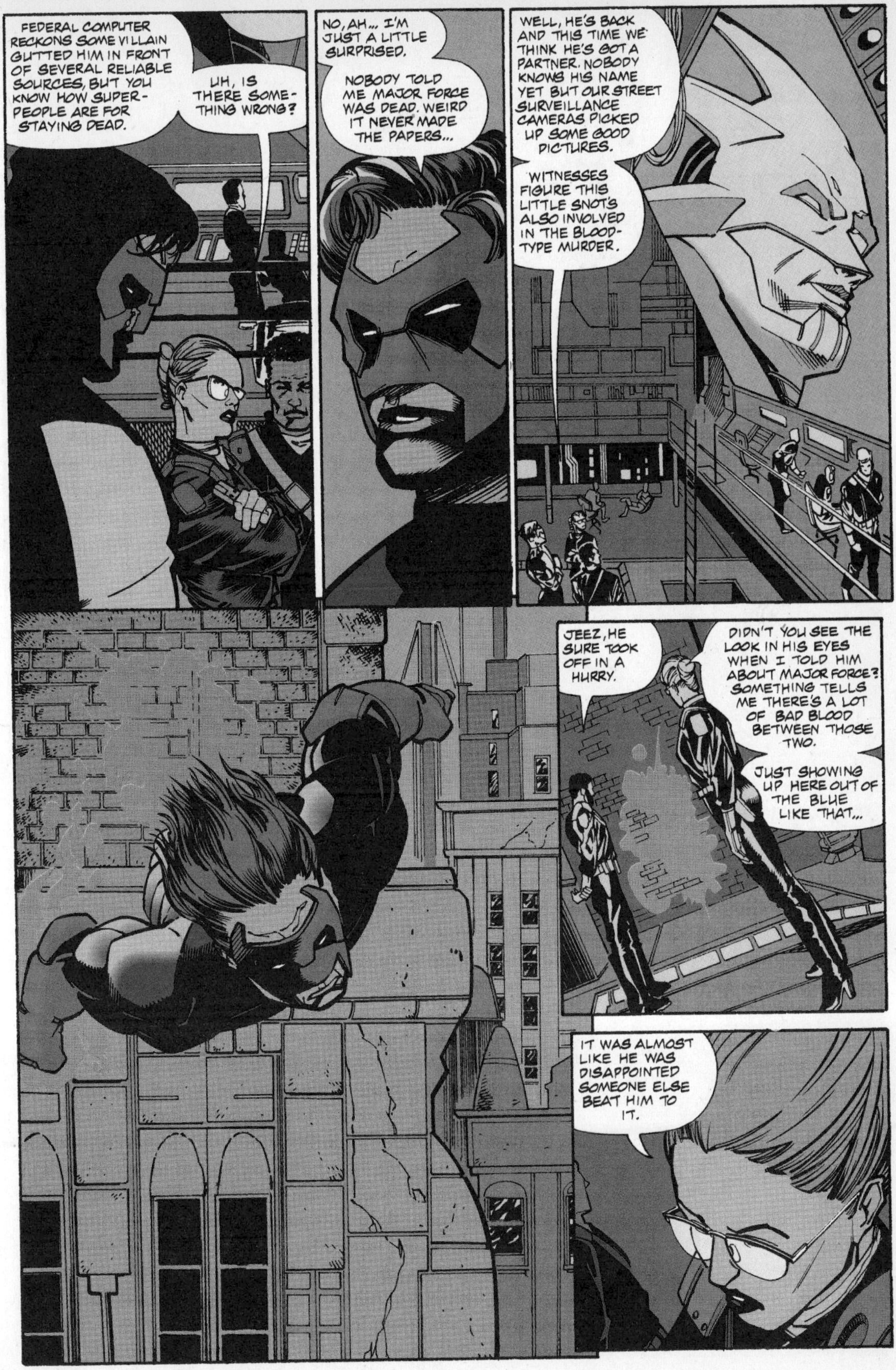
FEDERAL COMPUTER RECKONS SOME VILLAIN GUTTED HIM IN FRONT OF SEVERAL RELIABLE SOURCES, BUT YOU KNOW HOW SUPER-PEOPLE ARE FOR STAYING DEAD.
UH, IS THERE SOMETHING WRONG?
NO, AH... I'M JUST A LITTLE SURPRISED.
NOBODY TOLD ME MAJOR FORCE WAS DEAD. WEIRD IT NEVER MADE THE PAPERS...
WELL, HE'S BACK AND THIS TIME WE THINK HE'S GOT A PARTNER. NOBODY KNOWS HIS NAME YET BUT OUR STREET SURVEILLANCE CAMERAS PICKED UP SOME GOOD PICTURES.
WITNESSES FIGURE THIS LITTLE SNOT'S ALSO INVOLVED IN THE BLOOD-TYPE MURDER.
JEEZ, HE SURE TOOK OFF IN A HURRY.
DIDN'T YOU SEE THE LOOK IN HIS EYES WHEN I TOLD HIM ABOUT MAJOR FORCE? SOMETHING TELLS ME THERE'S A LOT OF BAD BLOOD BETWEEN THOSE TWO.
JUST SHOWING UP HERE OUT OF THE BLUE LIKE THAT...
IT WAS ALMOST LIKE HE WAS DISAPPOINTED SOMEONE ELSE BEAT HIM TO IT.

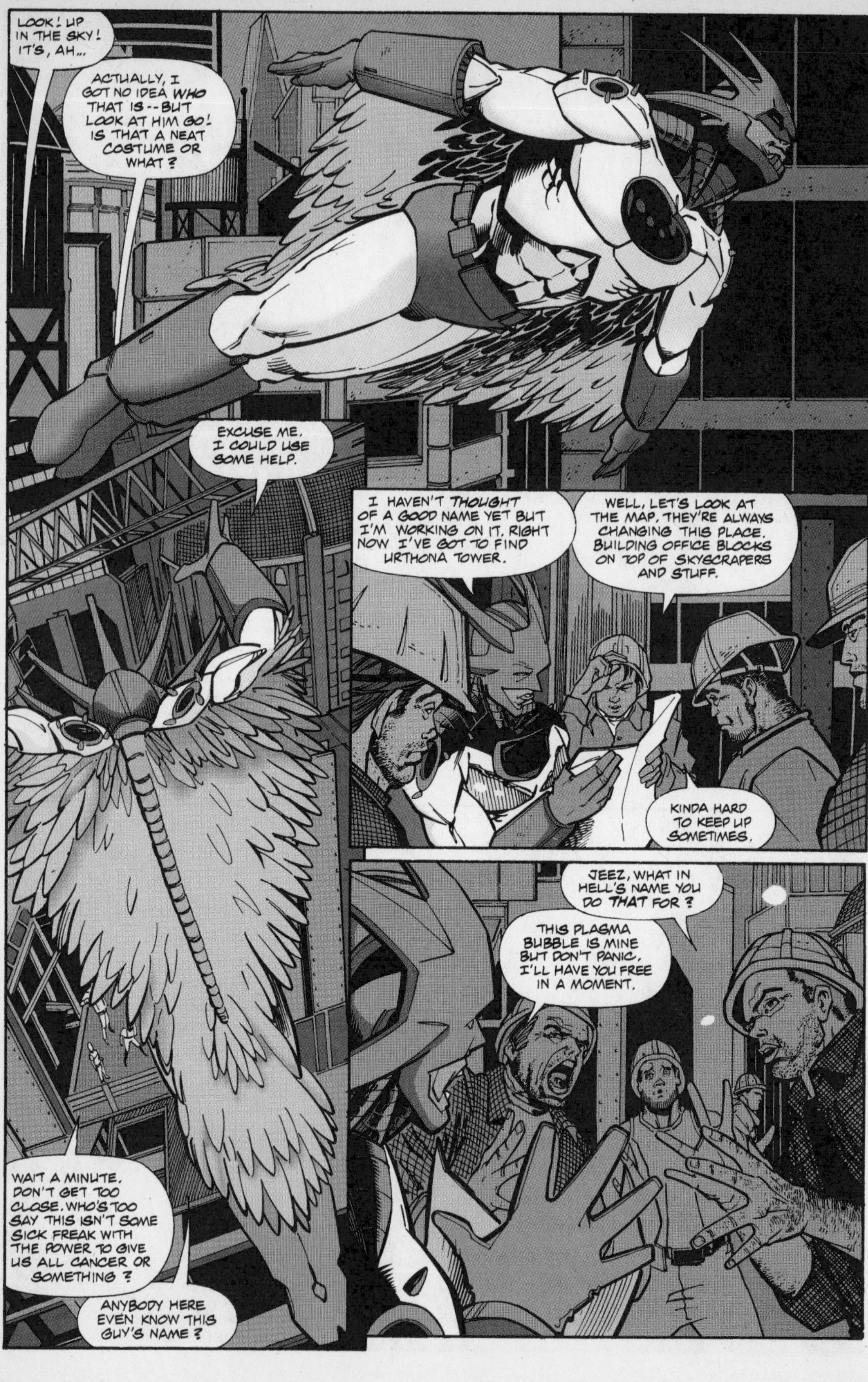
LOOK! UP IN THE SKY! IT'S, AH...
ACTUALLY, I GOT NO IDEA WHO THAT IS--BUT LOOK AT HIM GO! IS THAT A NEAT COSTUME OR WHAT?
EXCUSE ME. I COULD USE SOME HELP.
I HAVEN'T THOUGHT OF A GOOD NAME YET BUT I'M WORKING ON IT. RIGHT NOW I'VE GOT TO FIND URTHONA TOWER.
WELL, LET'S LOOK AT THE MAP. THEY'RE ALWAYS CHANGING THIS PLACE. BUILDING OFFICE BLOCKS ON TOP OF SKYSCRAPERS AND STUFF.
KINDA HARD TO KEEP UP SOMETIMES.
WAIT A MINUTE. DON'T GET TOO CLOSE. WHO'S TOO SAY THIS ISN'T SOME SICK FREAK WITH THE POWER TO GIVE US ALL CANCER OR SOMETHING?
ANYBODY HERE EVEN KNOW THIS GUY'S NAME?
JEEZ, WHAT IN HELL'S NAME YOU DO THAT FOR?
THIS PLASMA BUBBLE IS MINE BUT DON'T PANIC. I'LL HAVE YOU FREE IN A MOMENT.

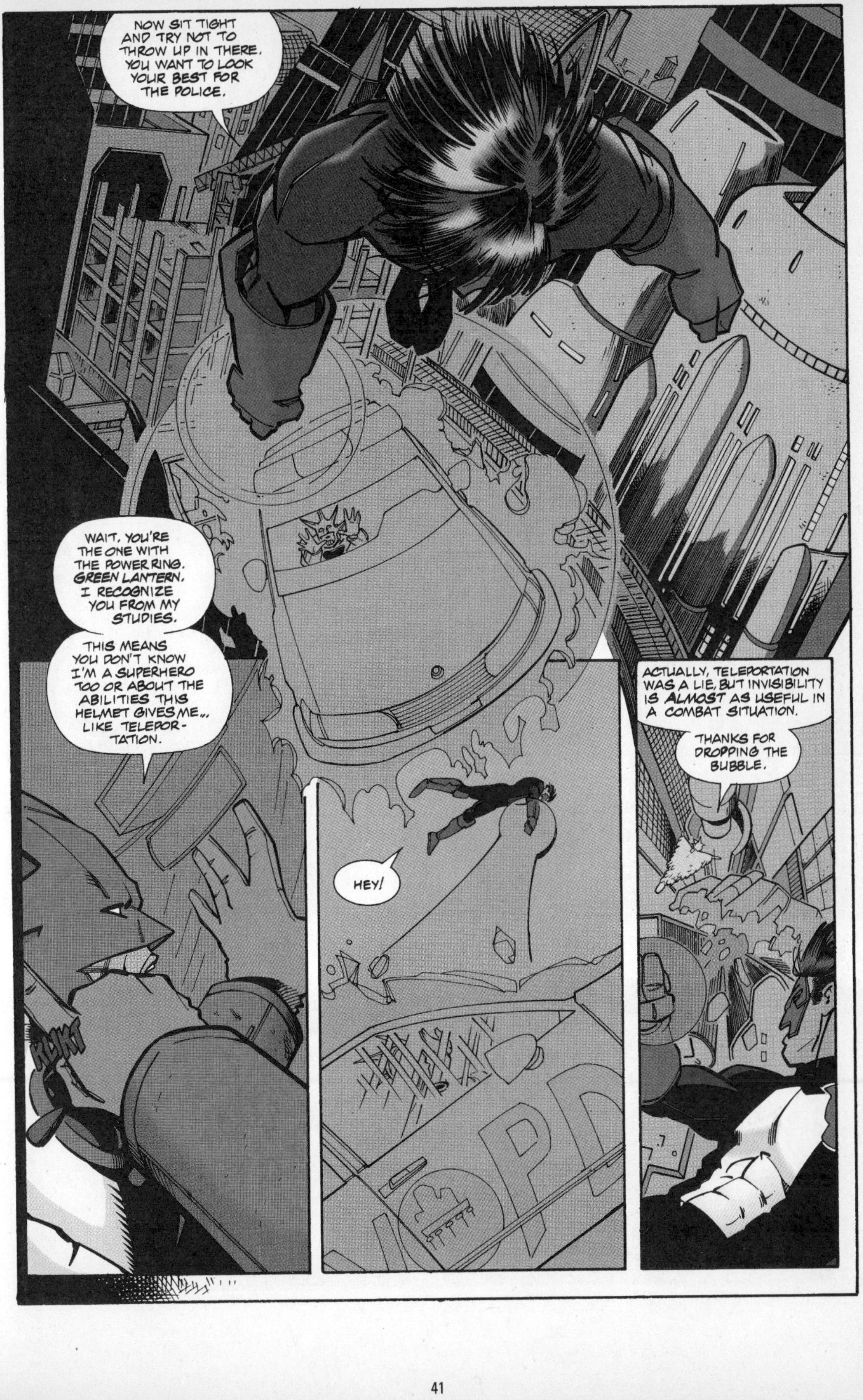
NOW SIT TIGHT AND TRY NOT TO THROW UP IN THERE. YOU WANT TO LOOK YOUR BEST FOR THE POLICE.
WAIT. YOU'RE THE ONE WITH THE POWER RING. GREEN LANTERN. I RECOGNIZE YOU FROM MY STUDIES.
THIS MEANS YOU DON'T KNOW I'M A SUPERHERO TOO OR ABOUT THE ABILITIES THIS HELMET GIVES ME... LIKE TELEPOR-TATION.
HEY!
ACTUALLY, TELEPORTATION WAS A LIE, BUT INVISIBILITY IS ALMOST AS USEFUL IN A COMBAT SITUATION.
THANKS FOR DROPPING THE BUBBLE.

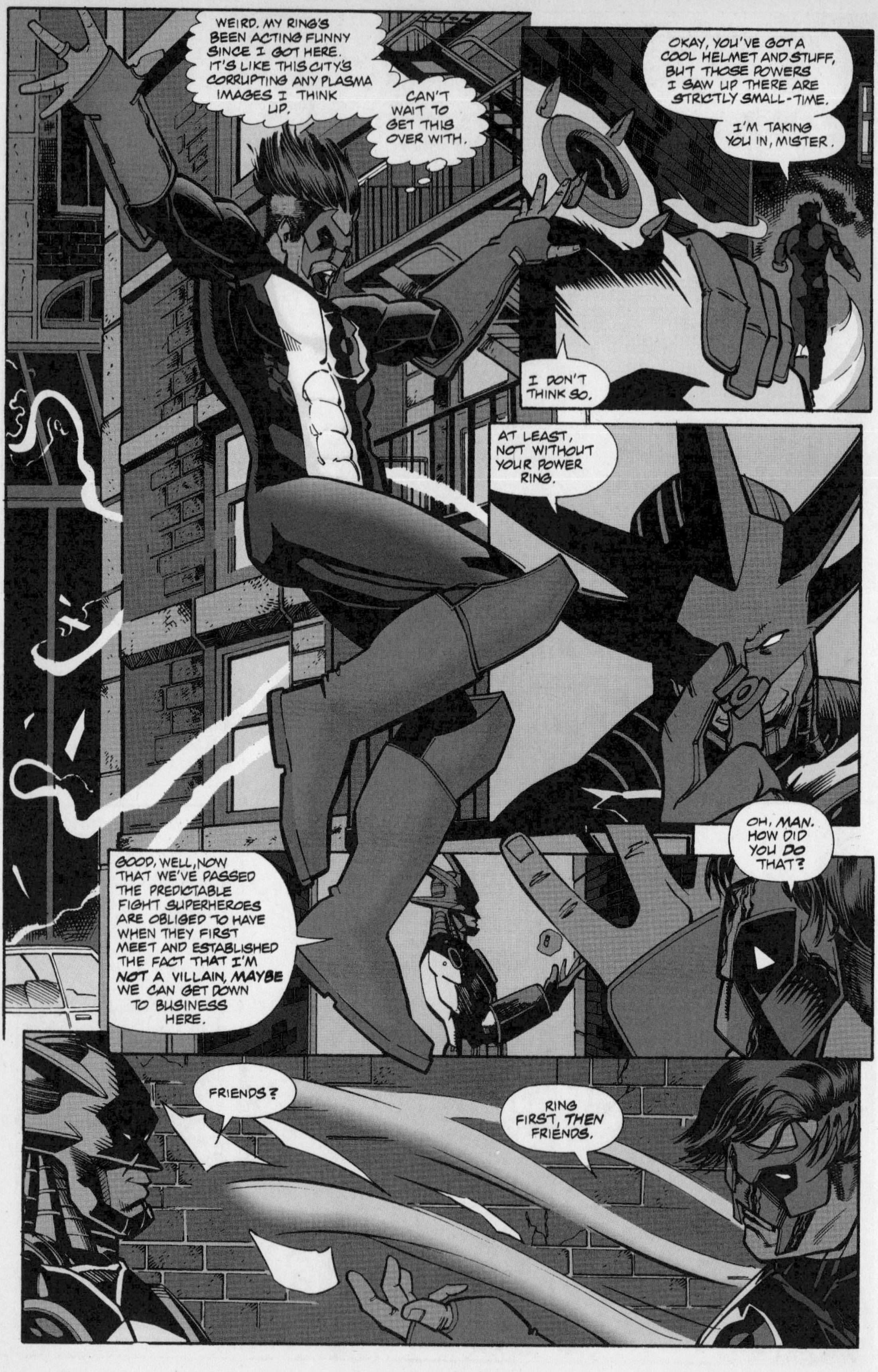
WEIRD. MY RING'S BEEN ACTING FUNNY SINCE I GOT HERE. IT'S LIKE THIS CITY'S CORRUPTING ANY PLASMA IMAGES I THINK UP.
CAN'T WAIT TO GET THIS OVER WITH.
OKAY, YOU'VE GOT A COOL HELMET AND STUFF, BUT THOSE POWERS I SAW UP THERE ARE STRICTLY SMALL-TIME.
I'M TAKING YOU IN, MISTER.
I DON'T THINK SO.
AT LEAST, NOT WITHOUT YOUR POWER RING.
OH, MAN. HOW DID YOU DO THAT?
GOOD, WELL, NOW THAT WE'VE PASSED THE PREDICTABLE FIGHT SUPERHEROES ARE OBLIGED TO HAVE WHEN THEY FIRST MEET AND ESTABLISHED THE FACT THAT I'M NOT A VILLAIN, MAYBE WE CAN GET DOWN TO BUSINESS HERE.
FRIENDS?
RING FIRST, THEN FRIENDS.

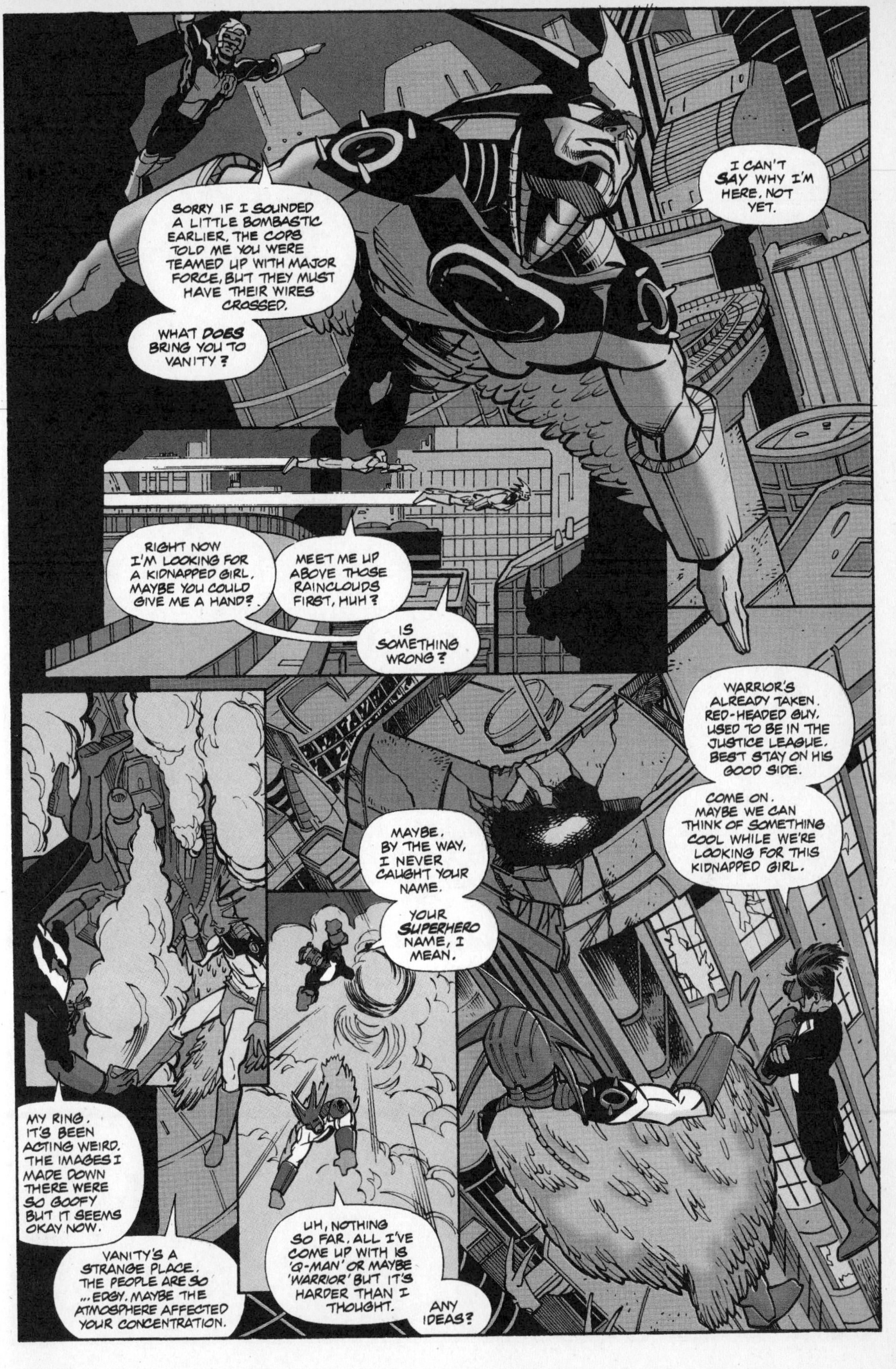
SORRY IF I SOUNDED A LITTLE BOMBASTIC EARLIER. THE COPS TOLD ME YOU WERE TEAMED UP WITH MAJOR FORCE, BUT THEY MUST HAVE THEIR WIRES CROSSED.
WHAT DOES BRING YOU TO VANITY?
I CAN'T SAY WHY I'M HERE. NOT YET.
RIGHT NOW I'M LOOKING FOR A KIDNAPPED GIRL. MAYBE YOU COULD GIVE ME A HAND?
MEET ME UP ABOVE THOSE RAINCLOUDS FIRST, HUH?
IS SOMETHING WRONG?
MY RING. IT'S BEEN ACTING WEIRD. THE IMAGES I MADE DOWN THERE WERE SO GOOFY BUT IT SEEMS OKAY NOW.
VANITY'S A STRANGE PLACE. THE PEOPLE ARE SO ...EDGY. MAYBE THE ATMOSPHERE AFFECTED YOUR CONCENTRATION.
MAYBE. BY THE WAY, I NEVER CAUGHT YOUR NAME.
YOUR SUPERHERO NAME, I MEAN.
UH, NOTHING SO FAR. ALL I'VE COME UP WITH IS 'Q-MAN' OR MAYBE 'WARRIOR' BUT IT'S HARDER THAN I THOUGHT.
ANY IDEAS?
WARRIOR'S ALREADY TAKEN. RED-HEADED GUY. USED TO BE IN THE JUSTICE LEAGUE. BEST STAY ON HIS GOOD SIDE.
COME ON. MAYBE WE CAN THINK OF SOMETHING COOL WHILE WE'RE LOOKING FOR THIS KIDNAPPED GIRL.

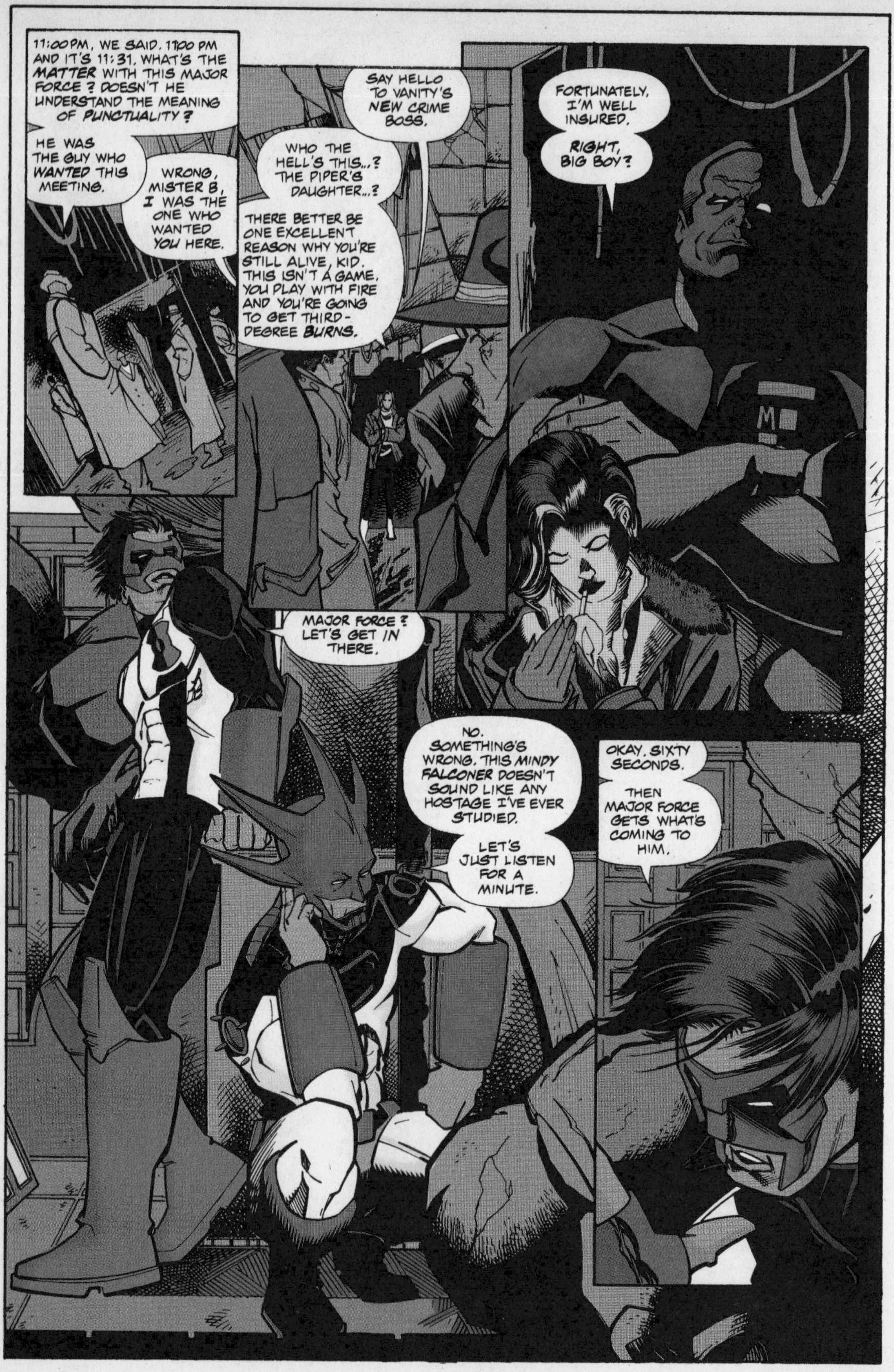
11:00 PM, WE SAID. 11:00 PM AND IT'S 11:31. WHAT'S THE MATTER WITH THIS MAJOR FORCE? DOESN'T HE UNDERSTAND THE MEANING OF PUNCTUALITY?
HE WAS THE GUY WHO WANTED THIS MEETING.
WRONG, MISTER B, I WAS THE ONE WHO WANTED YOU HERE.
SAY HELLO TO VANITY'S NEW CRIME BOSS.
WHO THE HELL'S THIS...? THE PIPER'S DAUGHTER...?
THERE BETTER BE ONE EXCELLENT REASON WHY YOU'RE STILL ALIVE, KID. THIS ISN'T A GAME. YOU PLAY WITH FIRE AND YOU'RE GOING TO GET THIRD-DEGREE BURNS.
FORTUNATELY, I'M WELL INSURED.
RIGHT, BIG BOY?
MAJOR FORCE? LET'S GET IN THERE.
NO. SOMETHING'S WRONG. THIS MINDY FALCONER DOESN'T SOUND LIKE ANY HOSTAGE I'VE EVER STUDIED.
LET'S JUST LISTEN FOR A MINUTE.
OKAY. SIXTY SECONDS.
THEN MAJOR FORCE GETS WHAT'S COMING TO HIM.

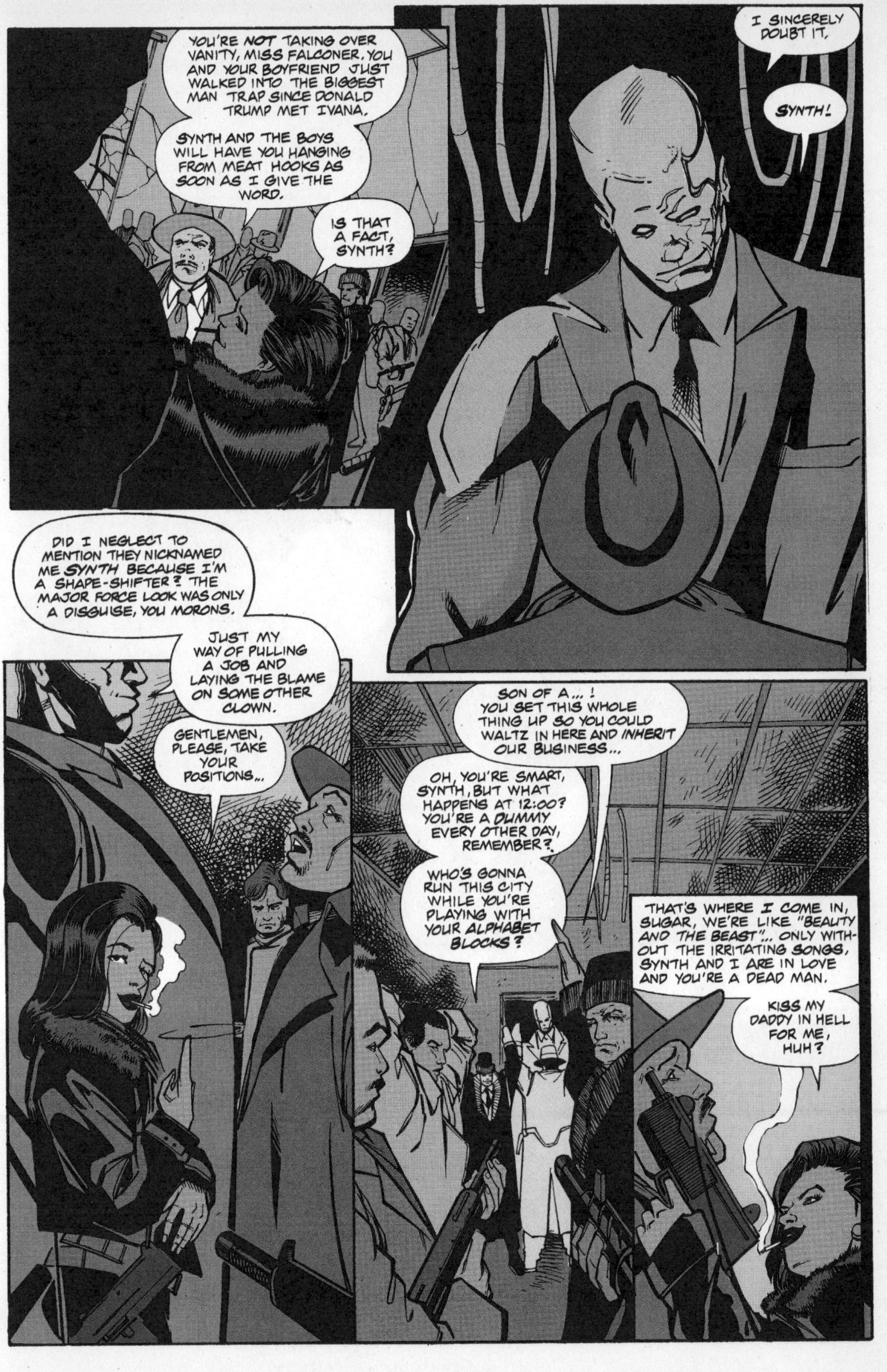
YOU'RE NOT TAKING OVER VANITY, MISS FALCONER. YOU AND YOUR BOYFRIEND JUST WALKED INTO THE BIGGEST MAN TRAP SINCE DONALD TRUMP MET IVANA.
SYNTH AND THE BOYS WILL HAVE YOU HANGING FROM MEAT HOOKS AS SOON AS I GIVE THE WORD.
IS THAT A FACT, SYNTH?
I SINCERELY DOUBT IT.
SYNTH!
DID I NEGLECT TO MENTION THEY NICKNAMED ME SYNTH BECAUSE I'M A SHAPE-SHIFTER? THE MAJOR FORCE LOOK WAS ONLY A DISGUISE, YOU MORONS.
JUST MY WAY OF PULLING A JOB AND LAYING THE BLAME ON SOME OTHER CLOWN.
GENTLEMEN, PLEASE, TAKE YOUR POSITIONS...
SON OF A... ! YOU SET THIS WHOLE THING UP SO YOU COULD WALTZ IN HERE AND INHERIT OUR BUSINESS...
OH, YOU'RE SMART, SYNTH, BUT WHAT HAPPENS AT 12:00? YOU'RE A DUMMY EVERY OTHER DAY, REMEMBER?
WHO'S GONNA RUN THIS CITY WHILE YOU'RE PLAYING WITH YOUR ALPHABET BLOCKS?
THAT'S WHERE I COME IN, SUGAR. WE'RE LIKE "BEAUTY AND THE BEAST"... ONLY WITHOUT THE IRRITATING SONGS. SYNTH AND I ARE IN LOVE AND YOU'RE A DEAD MAN.
KISS MY DADDY IN HELL FOR ME, HUH?

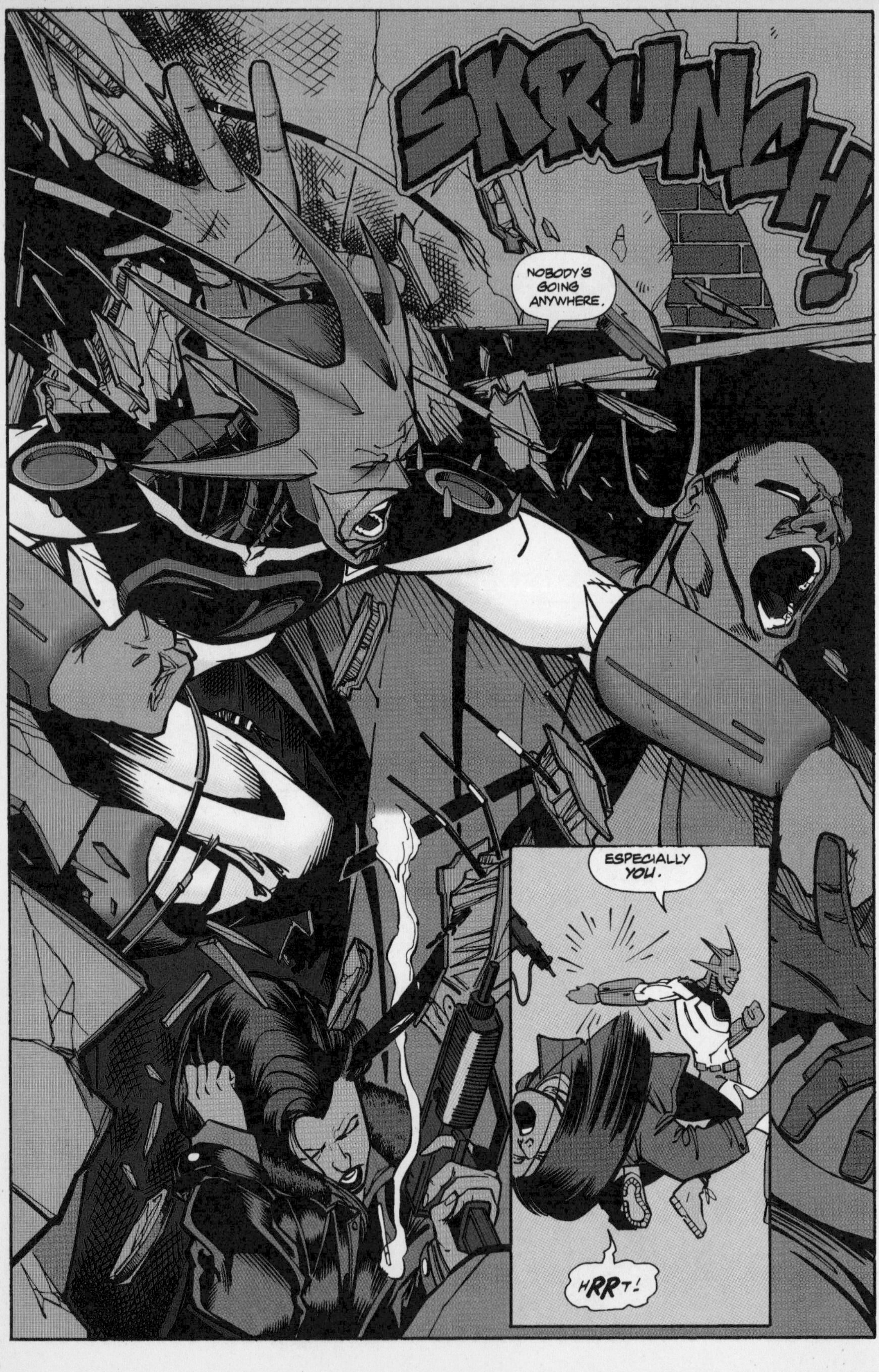
SKRUNCH!
NOBODY'S GOING ANYWHERE.
ESPECIALLY YOU.
HRRT!

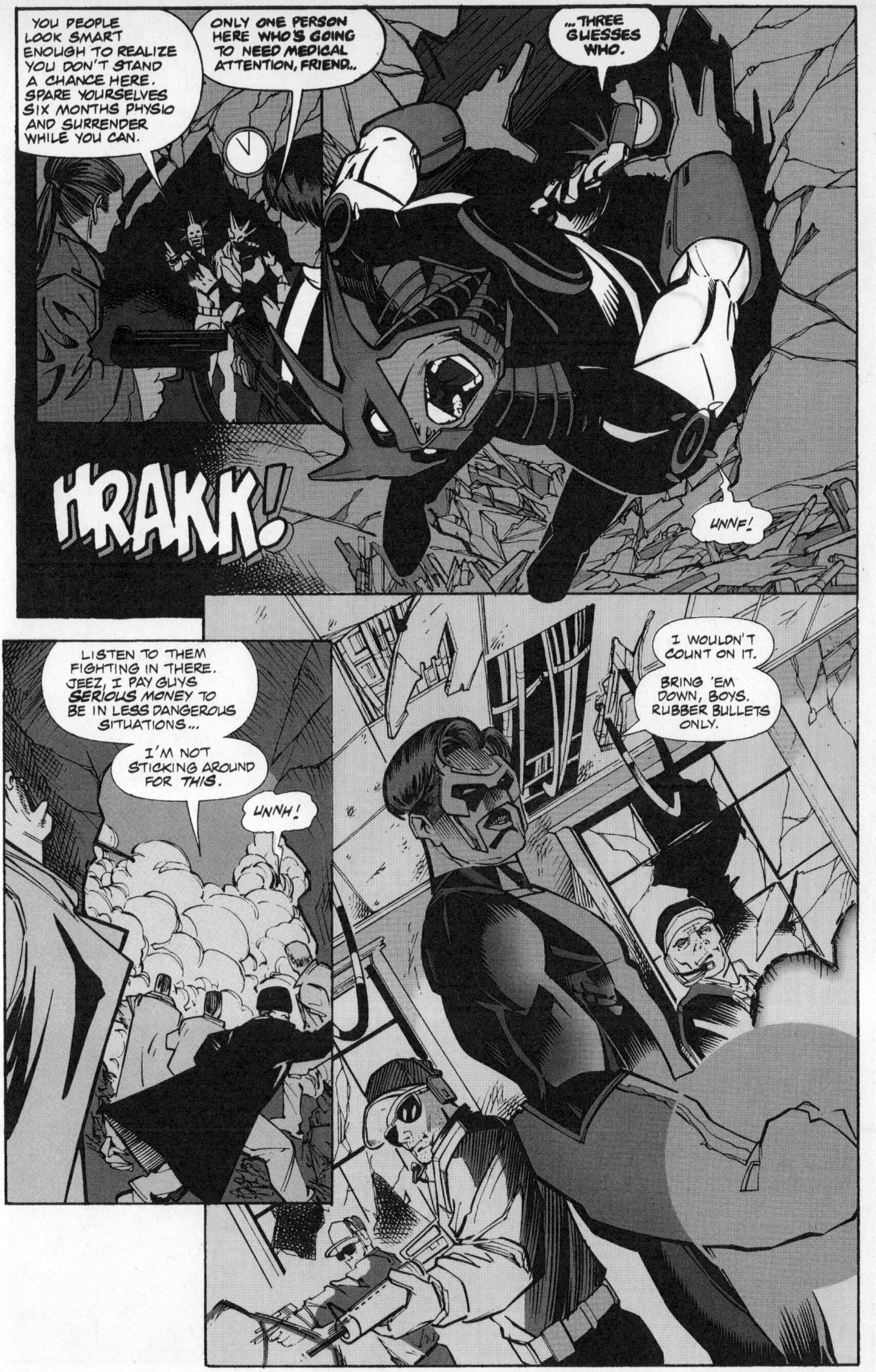
YOU PEOPLE LOOK SMART ENOUGH TO REALIZE YOU DON'T STAND A CHANCE HERE. SPARE YOURSELVES SIX MONTHS PHYSIO AND SURRENDER WHILE YOU CAN.
ONLY ONE PERSON HERE WHO'S GOING TO NEED MEDICAL ATTENTION, FRIEND...
...THREE GUESSES WHO.
HRAKK!
UNNF!
LISTEN TO THEM FIGHTING IN THERE. JEEZ, I PAY GUYS SERIOUS MONEY TO BE IN LESS DANGEROUS SITUATIONS...
I'M NOT STICKING AROUND FOR THIS.
UNNH!
I WOULDN'T COUNT ON IT.
BRING 'EM DOWN, BOYS. RUBBER BULLETS ONLY.

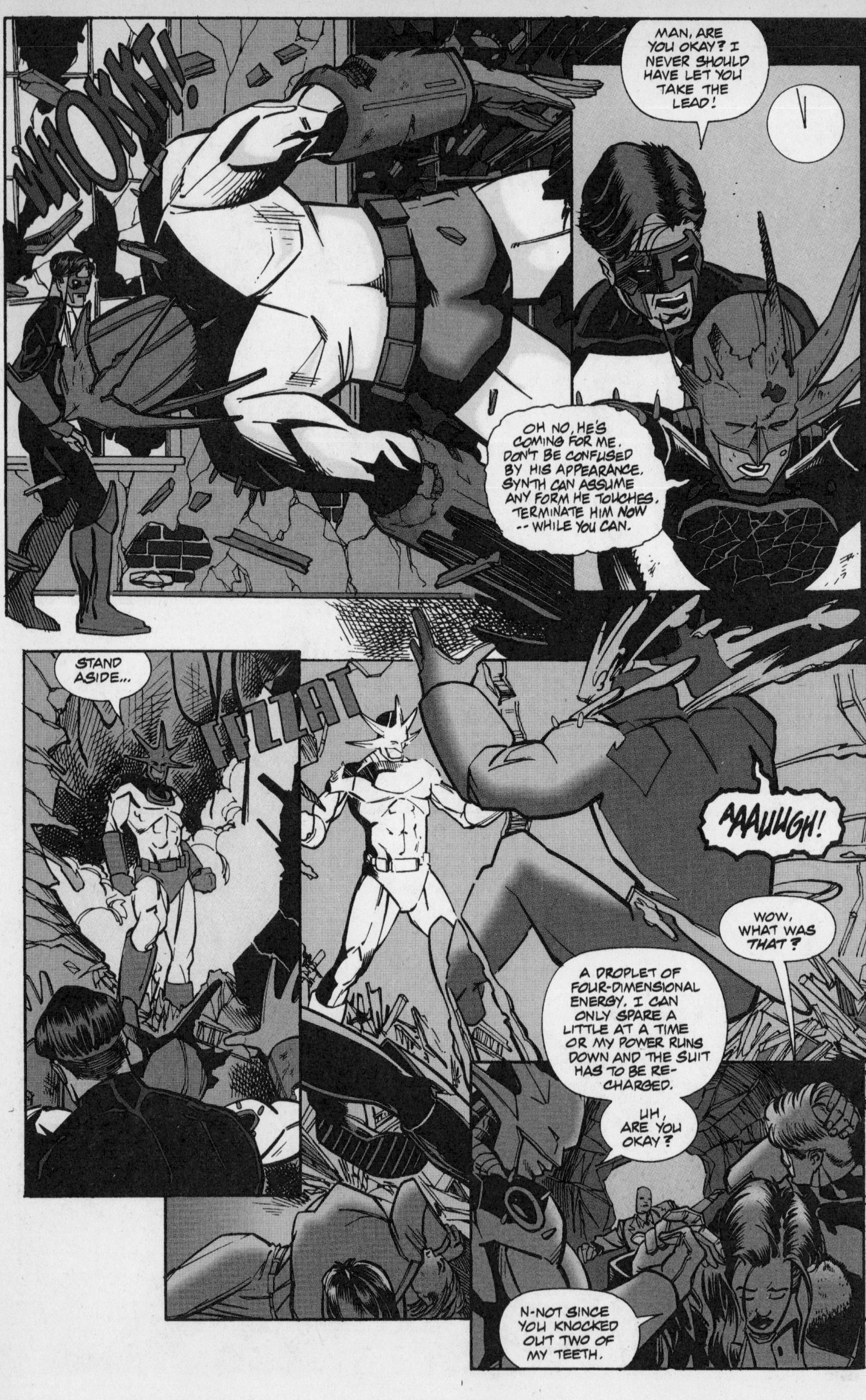
WHOKK!
MAN, ARE YOU OKAY? I NEVER SHOULD HAVE LET YOU TAKE THE LEAD!
OH NO, HE'S COMING FOR ME. DON'T BE CONFUSED BY HIS APPEARANCE. SYNTH CAN ASSUME ANY FORM HE TOUCHES. TERMINATE HIM NOW -- WHILE YOU CAN.
STAND ASIDE...
FZZAT
AAAUUGH!
WOW, WHAT WAS THAT?
A DROPLET OF FOUR-DIMENSIONAL ENERGY. I CAN ONLY SPARE A LITTLE AT A TIME OR MY POWER RUNS DOWN AND THE SUIT HAS TO BE RE-CHARGED.
UH, ARE YOU OKAY?
N-NOT SINCE YOU KNOCKED OUT TWO OF MY TEETH.

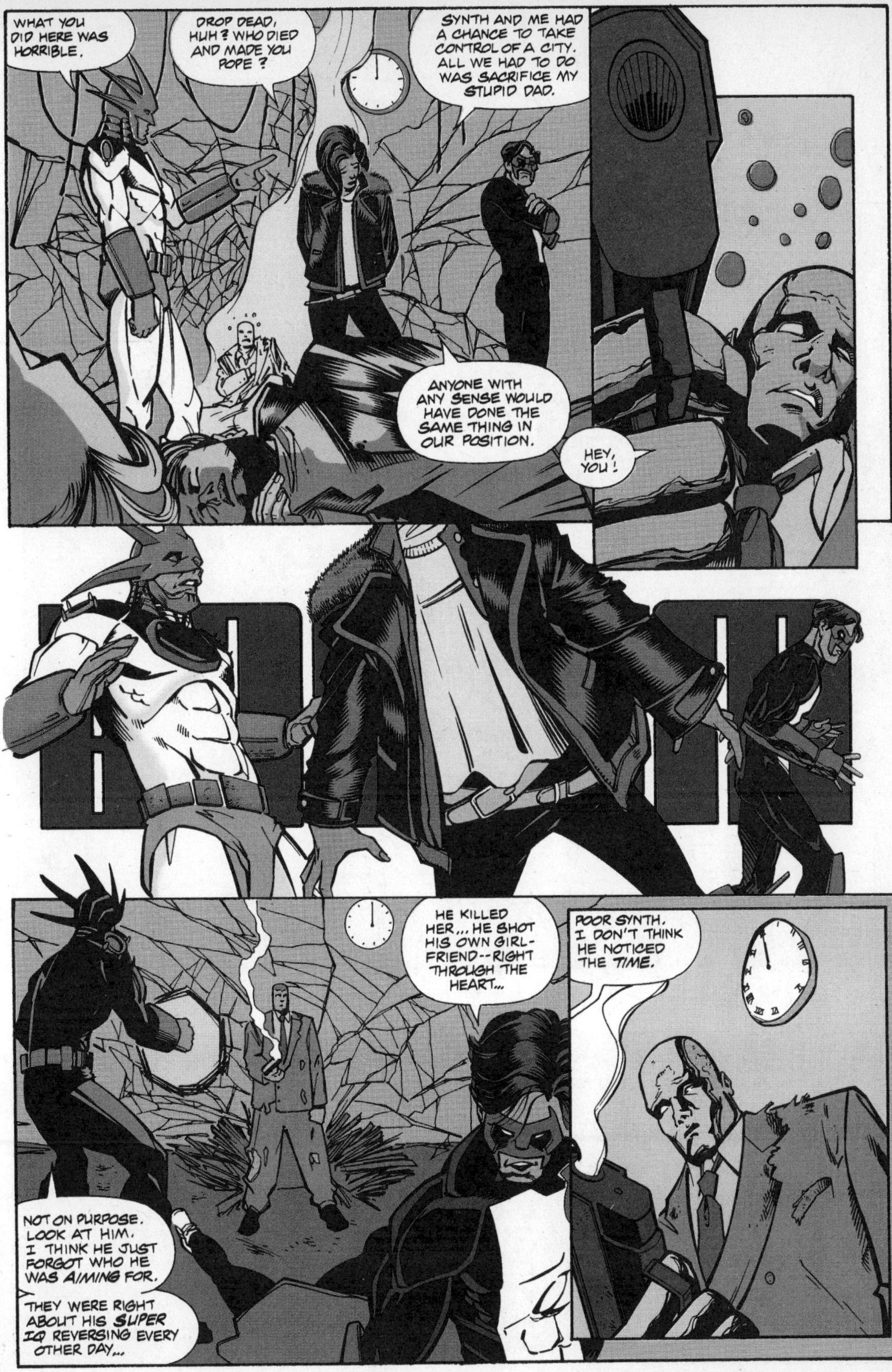
WHAT YOU DID HERE WAS HORRIBLE.
DROP DEAD, HUH? WHO DIED AND MADE YOU POPE?
SYNTH AND ME HAD A CHANCE TO TAKE CONTROL OF A CITY. ALL WE HAD TO DO WAS SACRIFICE MY STUPID DAD.
ANYONE WITH ANY SENSE WOULD HAVE DONE THE SAME THING IN OUR POSITION.
HEY, YOU!
HE KILLED HER... HE SHOT HIS OWN GIRL-FRIEND--RIGHT THROUGH THE HEART...
POOR SYNTH. I DON'T THINK HE NOTICED THE TIME.
NOT ON PURPOSE. LOOK AT HIM. I THINK HE JUST FORGOT WHO HE WAS AIMING FOR.
THEY WERE RIGHT ABOUT HIS SUPER IQ REVERSING EVERY OTHER DAY...

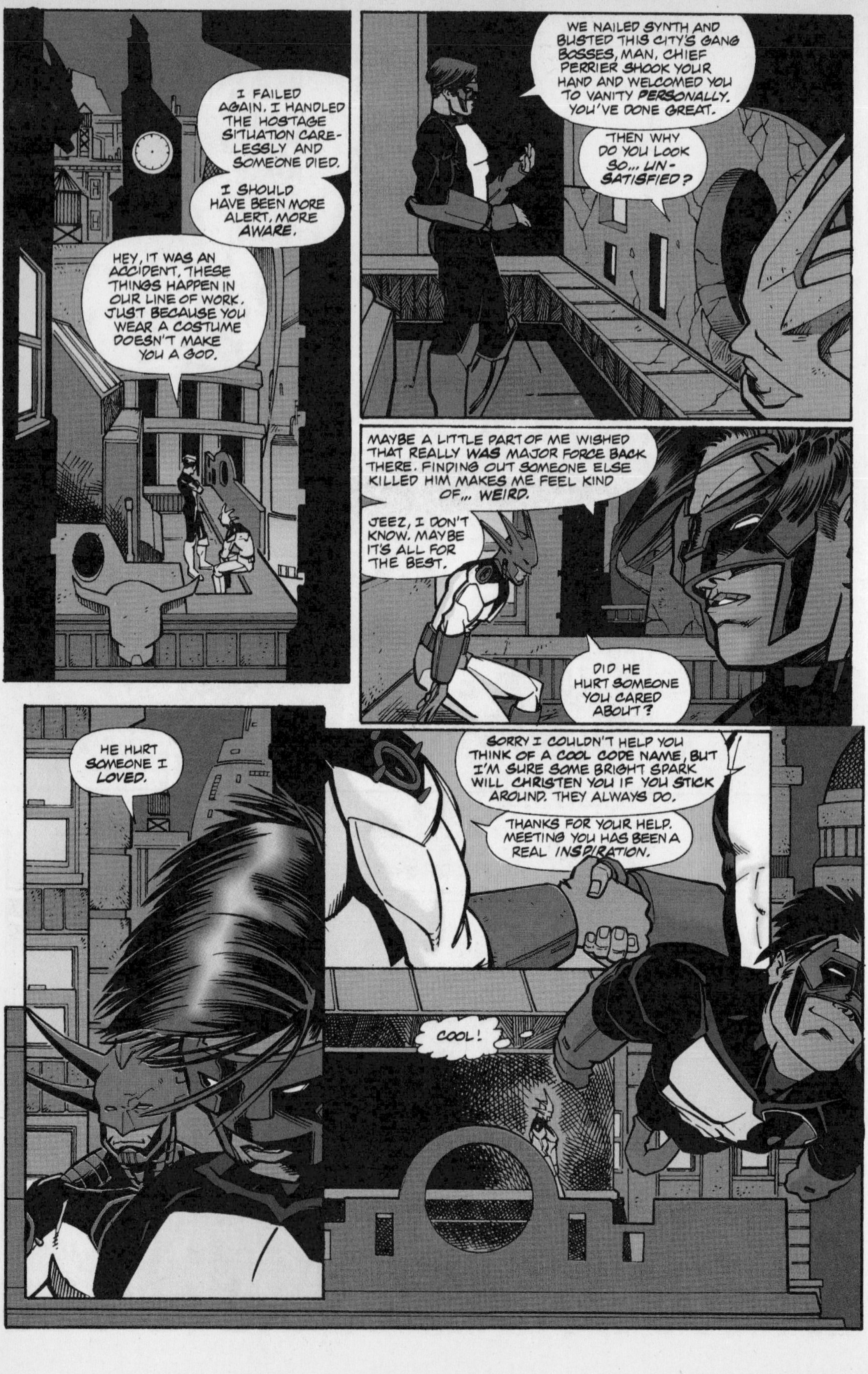
I FAILED AGAIN. I HANDLED THE HOSTAGE SITUATION CARE-LESSLY AND SOMEONE DIED.
I SHOULD HAVE BEEN MORE ALERT, MORE AWARE.
HEY, IT WAS AN ACCIDENT. THESE THINGS HAPPEN IN OUR LINE OF WORK. JUST BECAUSE YOU WEAR A COSTUME DOESN'T MAKE YOU A GOD.
WE NAILED SYNTH AND BUSTED THIS CITY'S GANG BOSSES, MAN. CHIEF PERRIER SHOOK YOUR HAND AND WELCOMED YOU TO VANITY PERSONALLY. YOU'VE DONE GREAT.
THEN WHY DO YOU LOOK SO... UN-SATISFIED?
MAYBE A LITTLE PART OF ME WISHED THAT REALLY WAS MAJOR FORCE BACK THERE. FINDING OUT SOMEONE ELSE KILLED HIM MAKES ME FEEL KIND OF... WEIRD.
JEEZ, I DON'T KNOW. MAYBE IT'S ALL FOR THE BEST.
DID HE HURT SOMEONE YOU CARED ABOUT?
HE HURT SOMEONE I LOVED.
SORRY I COULDN'T HELP YOU THINK OF A COOL CODE NAME, BUT I'M SURE SOME BRIGHT SPARK WILL CHRISTEN YOU IF YOU STICK AROUND. THEY ALWAYS DO.
THANKS FOR YOUR HELP. MEETING YOU HAS BEEN A REAL INSPIRATION.
COOL!

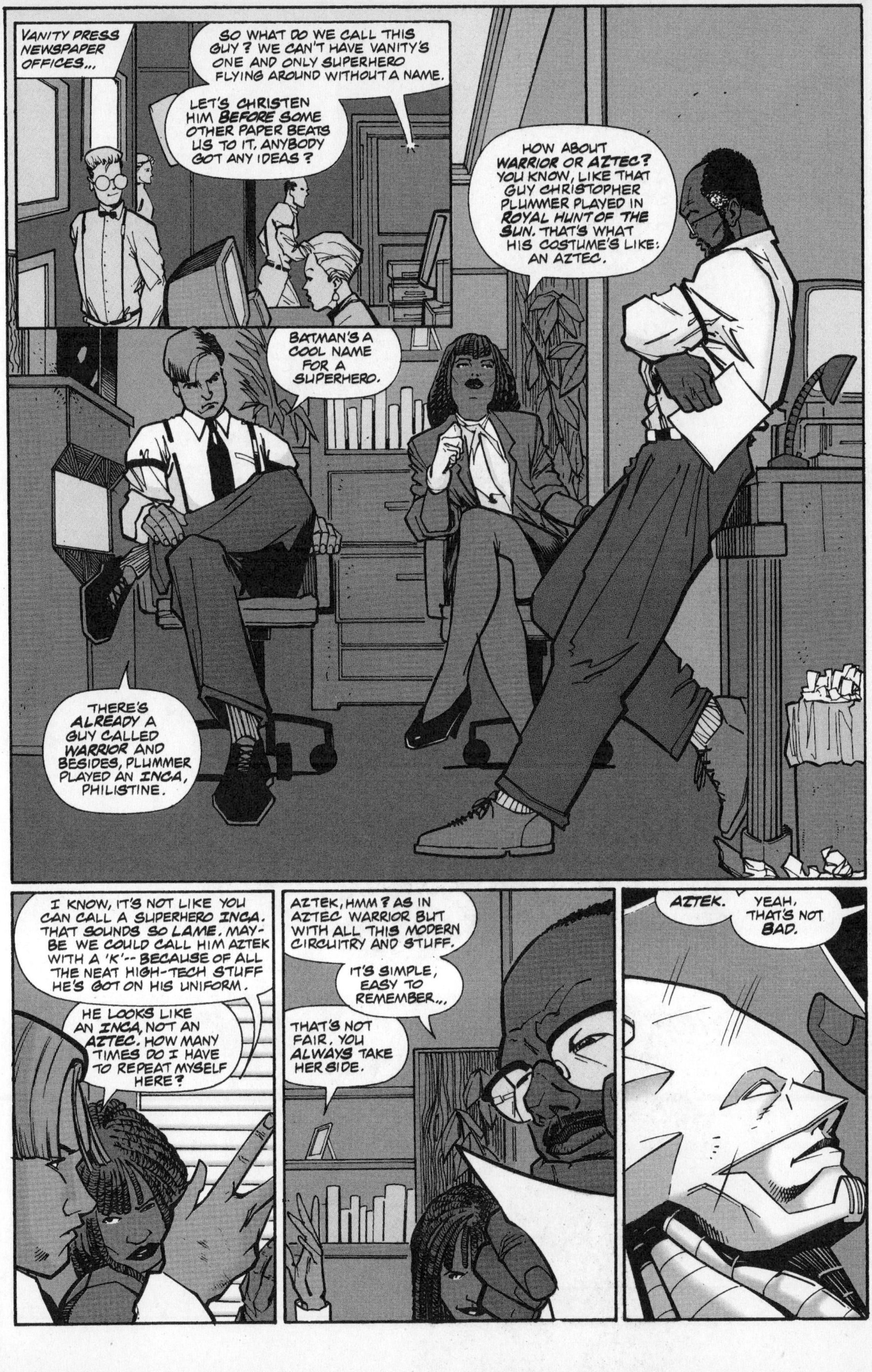
VANITY PRESS NEWSPAPER OFFICES...
SO WHAT DO WE CALL THIS GUY? WE CAN'T HAVE VANITY'S ONE AND ONLY SUPERHERO FLYING AROUND WITHOUT A NAME.
LET'S CHRISTEN HIM BEFORE SOME OTHER PAPER BEATS US TO IT. ANYBODY GOT ANY IDEAS?
HOW ABOUT WARRIOR OR AZTEC? YOU KNOW, LIKE THAT GUY CHRISTOPHER PLUMMER PLAYED IN ROYAL HUNT OF THE SUN. THAT'S WHAT HIS COSTUME'S LIKE: AN AZTEC.
BATMAN'S A COOL NAME FOR A SUPERHERO.
THERE'S ALREADY A GUY CALLED WARRIOR AND BESIDES, PLUMMER PLAYED AN INCA, PHILISTINE.
I KNOW, IT'S NOT LIKE YOU CAN CALL A SUPERHERO INCA. THAT SOUNDS SO LAME. MAY-BE WE COULD CALL HIM AZTEK WITH A 'K'-- BECAUSE OF ALL THE NEAT HIGH-TECH STUFF HE'S GOT ON HIS UNIFORM.
HE LOOKS LIKE AN INCA, NOT AN AZTEC. HOW MANY TIMES DO I HAVE TO REPEAT MYSELF HERE?
AZTEK, HMM? AS IN AZTEC WARRIOR BUT WITH ALL THIS MODERN CIRCUITRY AND STUFF.
IT'S SIMPLE, EASY TO REMEMBER...
THAT'S NOT FAIR. YOU ALWAYS TAKE HER SIDE.
AZTEK.
YEAH, THAT'S NOT BAD.

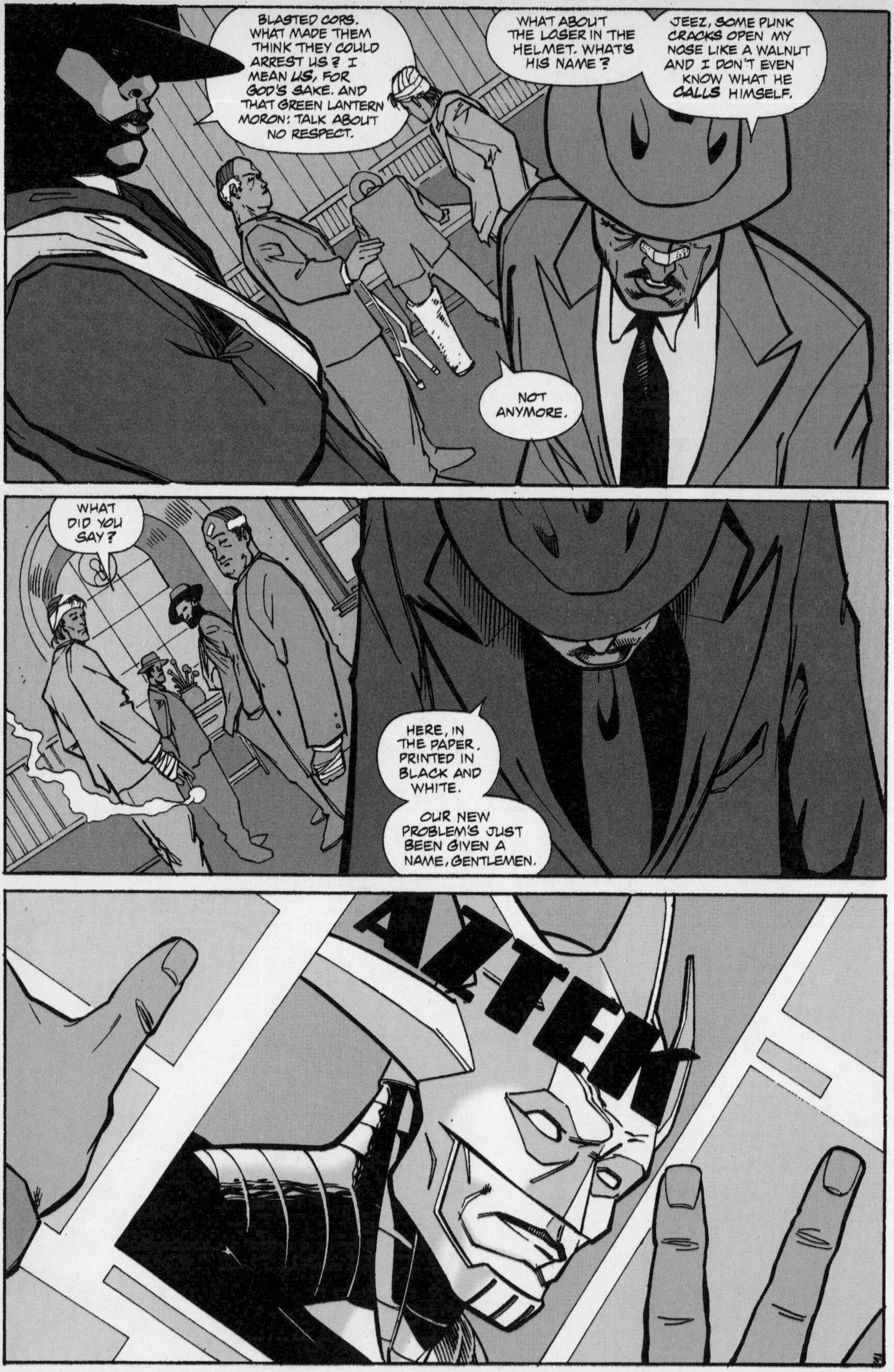
BLASTED COPS. WHAT MADE THEM THINK THEY COULD ARREST US? I MEAN US, FOR GOD'S SAKE. AND THAT GREEN LANTERN MORON: TALK ABOUT NO RESPECT.
WHAT ABOUT THE LOSER IN THE HELMET. WHAT'S HIS NAME?
JEEZ, SOME PUNK CRACKS OPEN MY NOSE LIKE A WALNUT AND I DON'T EVEN KNOW WHAT HE CALLS HIMSELF.
NOT ANYMORE.
WHAT DID YOU SAY?
HERE, IN THE PAPER, PRINTED IN BLACK AND WHITE.
OUR NEW PROBLEM'S JUST BEEN GIVEN A NAME, GENTLEMEN.
AZTEK

FEDERAL AUTHORITY REGISTERED META-HUMANS

WASHINGTON, DC

META-HUMAN License Application

FOR INTERDEPARTMENTAL USE ONLY *(Please print clearly)*

1 PERSONAL DATA

Name: AZTEK

Secret Identity: Police chief told me I didn't have to say

Date of Birth: December 24, 1975   **Place of Birth:** South America

Group Affiliation: Nobody you know

Height: 6 ft., 1 in.   **Weight:** 185 lbs.

Base of Operations: Vanity, U.S.A.

*If you are a non-terrestrial life-form, please ask for **FARM Registration form 2-867** and enclose details.*

2 POWERS AND WEAPONS *(Please describe in detail)*

Powers derived from ancient helmet include night-vision, infra-red and x-ray capability. Helmet also used to manifest costume which creates flight option and increased strength plus a variety of hidden weapons. Costume powered by chest battery.

IMPORTANT

Have you been bitten by anything radioactive? ☐ Yes ☑ No *(Check one)*

3 KNOWN ENEMIES

Please give details below of any super-villains of collective groups (Rogues Galleries) who would be inspired to attack your proposed place of residence if your were adopted as its official super-hero.

I've made a number of enemies since coming to Vanity, including Bloodtype (deceased) and Synth (currently serving a life sentence) but no one prior to my arrival.

4 PLEASE ANSWER THE FOLLOWING QUESTIONS

What is your motivation (e.g., vengeance)? I'm here on a mission. I've been trained for all my life. A menace is coming to Vanity, and I'm the only one who can deal with it.

Could your costume be described as sexually explicit? ☐ Yes ☑ No
I hope

Are you a former super-villain? ☐ Yes ☑ No *(If YES, please ask for FARM Registration form 2-675 and describe seriousness of crime.)*

Would you be prepared to take a human (or humanoid) life?
Only as a last resort. I've been taught to respect ALL life.

Do you seek a teenage sidekick? ☐ Yes ☑ No *(If YES, please ask for FARM Registration form 2-845 and state recognized public romances)*
No thanks.

Do you require legal advice regarding your name, costume and copyright situation in the event a third party seeks commercial gain from your reputation? I don't care about money. This isn't necessary.

Do any substances exist, natural or artificial, which cause you to change size, shape or intention?
Not that I'm aware of.

Will proposed city be a permanent residence? ☐ Yes ☑ No
Once my mission is complete I intend to return to my people. The rest of my life will be devoted to meditation and learning.

PLEASE SIGN AND DATE BELOW. *Any false information given in this form could lead to imprisonment, expulsion from a super-team or deportation from the planet Earth. Please allow 28 days for reply.*

SIGNED *aztek*

DATE June 19th, 1996

FOR OFFICE USE ONLY

Proposed super-hero is courteous, capable, and broadly supports the same laws we do. Vanity <u>needs</u> a protector since we lost Bloodtype, and Aztek's all we've got. <u>Please</u> <u>process</u> <u>quickly!</u>

COMMENTS

Helena Perrier

REQUESTED BY

June 20, 1996
DATE

Chief of Police, Vanity
POSITION

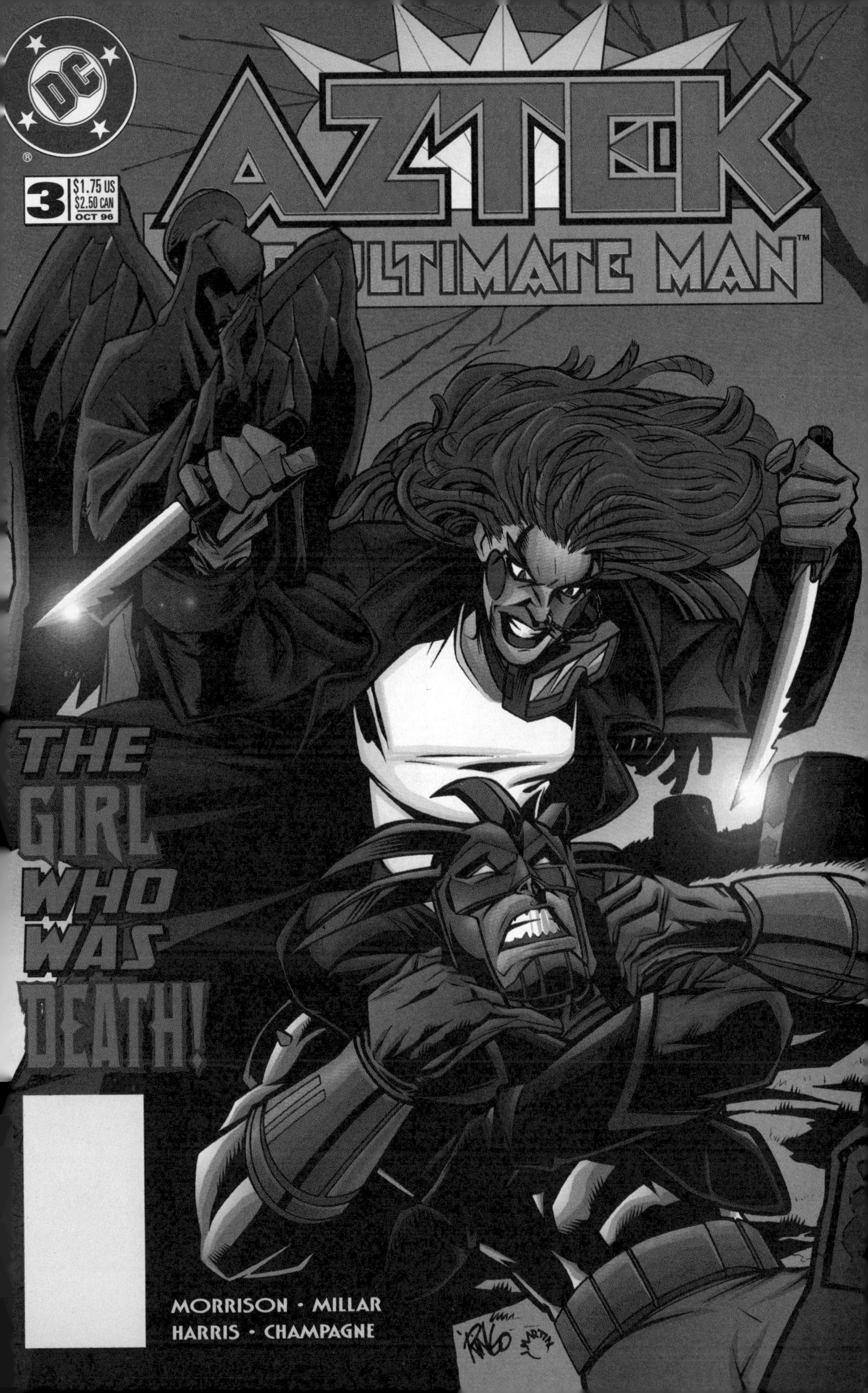
DC
3
$1.75 US
$2.50 CAN
OCT 96
AZTEK
THE ULTIMATE MAN™
THE GIRL WHO WAS DEATH!
MORRISON · MILLAR
HARRIS · CHAMPAGNE

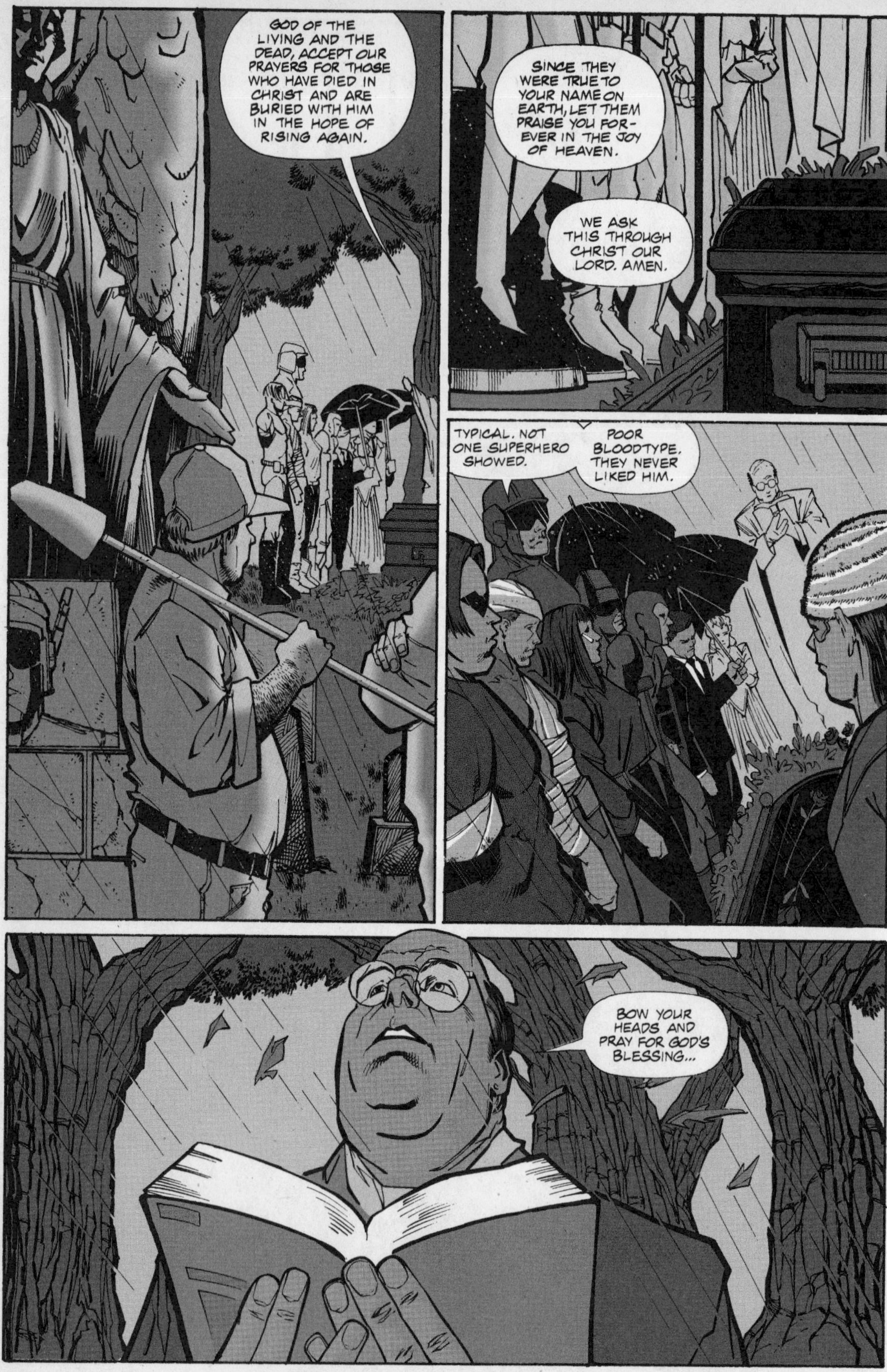
GOD OF THE LIVING AND THE DEAD, ACCEPT OUR PRAYERS FOR THOSE WHO HAVE DIED IN CHRIST AND ARE BURIED WITH HIM IN THE HOPE OF RISING AGAIN.
SINCE THEY WERE TRUE TO YOUR NAME ON EARTH, LET THEM PRAISE YOU FOR-EVER IN THE JOY OF HEAVEN.
WE ASK THIS THROUGH CHRIST OUR LORD. AMEN.
TYPICAL. NOT ONE SUPERHERO SHOWED.
POOR BLOODTYPE. THEY NEVER LIKED HIM.
BOW YOUR HEADS AND PRAY FOR GOD'S BLESSING...

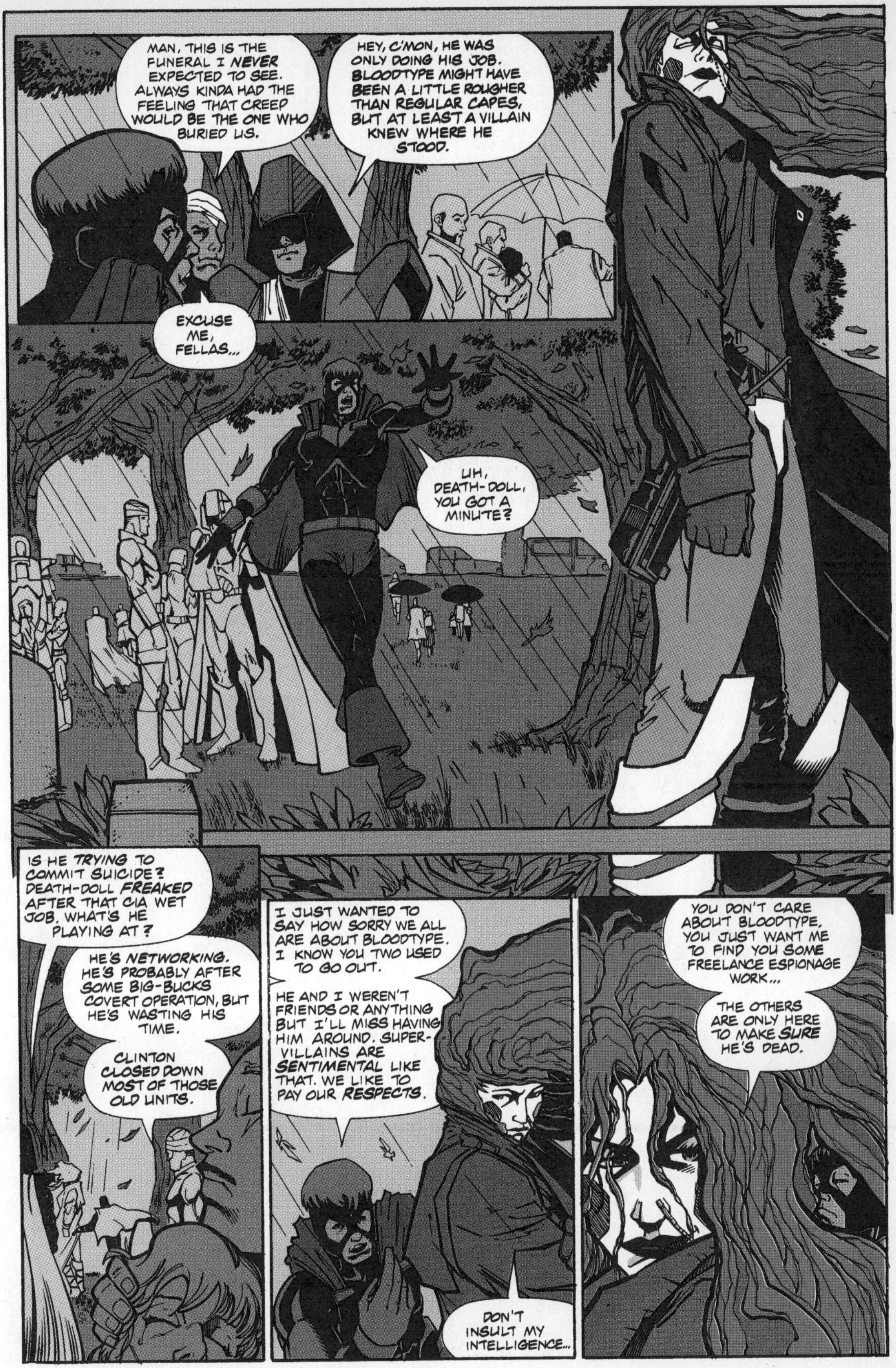
MAN, THIS IS THE FUNERAL I NEVER EXPECTED TO SEE. ALWAYS KINDA HAD THE FEELING THAT CREEP WOULD BE THE ONE WHO BURIED US.
HEY, C'MON, HE WAS ONLY DOING HIS JOB. BLOODTYPE MIGHT HAVE BEEN A LITTLE ROUGHER THAN REGULAR CAPES, BUT AT LEAST A VILLAIN KNEW WHERE HE STOOD.
EXCUSE ME, FELLAS...
UH, DEATH-DOLL, YOU GOT A MINUTE?
IS HE TRYING TO COMMIT SUICIDE? DEATH-DOLL FREAKED AFTER THAT CIA WET JOB. WHAT'S HE PLAYING AT?
HE'S NETWORKING. HE'S PROBABLY AFTER SOME BIG-BUCKS COVERT OPERATION, BUT HE'S WASTING HIS TIME.
CLINTON CLOSED DOWN MOST OF THOSE OLD UNITS.
I JUST WANTED TO SAY HOW SORRY WE ALL ARE ABOUT BLOODTYPE. I KNOW YOU TWO USED TO GO OUT.
HE AND I WEREN'T FRIENDS OR ANYTHING BUT I'LL MISS HAVING HIM AROUND. SUPER-VILLAINS ARE SENTIMENTAL LIKE THAT. WE LIKE TO PAY OUR RESPECTS.
DON'T INSULT MY INTELLIGENCE...
YOU DON'T CARE ABOUT BLOODTYPE. YOU JUST WANT ME TO FIND YOU SOME FREELANCE ESPIONAGE WORK...
THE OTHERS ARE ONLY HERE TO MAKE SURE HE'S DEAD.

UH, THE PRIEST GAVE A NICE SERMON, DIDN'T HE? THE STUFF ABOUT SUPERHEROES NEVER STAYING DOWN.

SOME OF THE PAPERS FIGURE BLOODTYPE COULD BE BACK IN SIX MONTHS' TIME, TOUGHER THAN EVER.

GIVE IT A REST. JUST TELL ME WHAT YOU KNOW ABOUT AZTEK. WAS HE IMPLICATED IN THE MURDER?

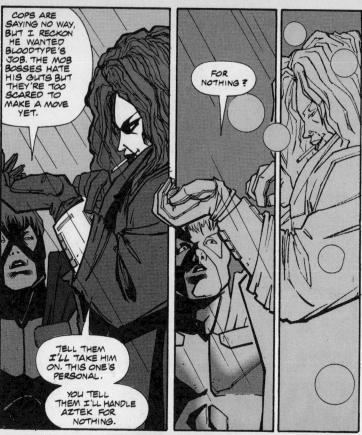

COPS ARE SAYING NO WAY, BUT I RECKON HE WANTED BLOODTYPE'S JOB. THE MOB BOSSES HATE HIS GUTS BUT THEY'RE TOO SCARED TO MAKE A MOVE YET.

TELL THEM I'LL TAKE HIM ON. THIS ONE'S PERSONAL.

YOU TELL THEM I'LL HANDLE AZTEK FOR NOTHING.

FOR NOTHING?

NOBODY IN VANITY DOES ANYTHING FOR NOTHING.

THANKS FOR EVERYTHING, PADRE.

YOU'LL FIND WHAT YOU ASKED FOR IN THE BACK SEAT.

PLEASURE DOING BUSINESS WITH YOU, YOUNG MAN.

ALWAYS A PLEASURE.

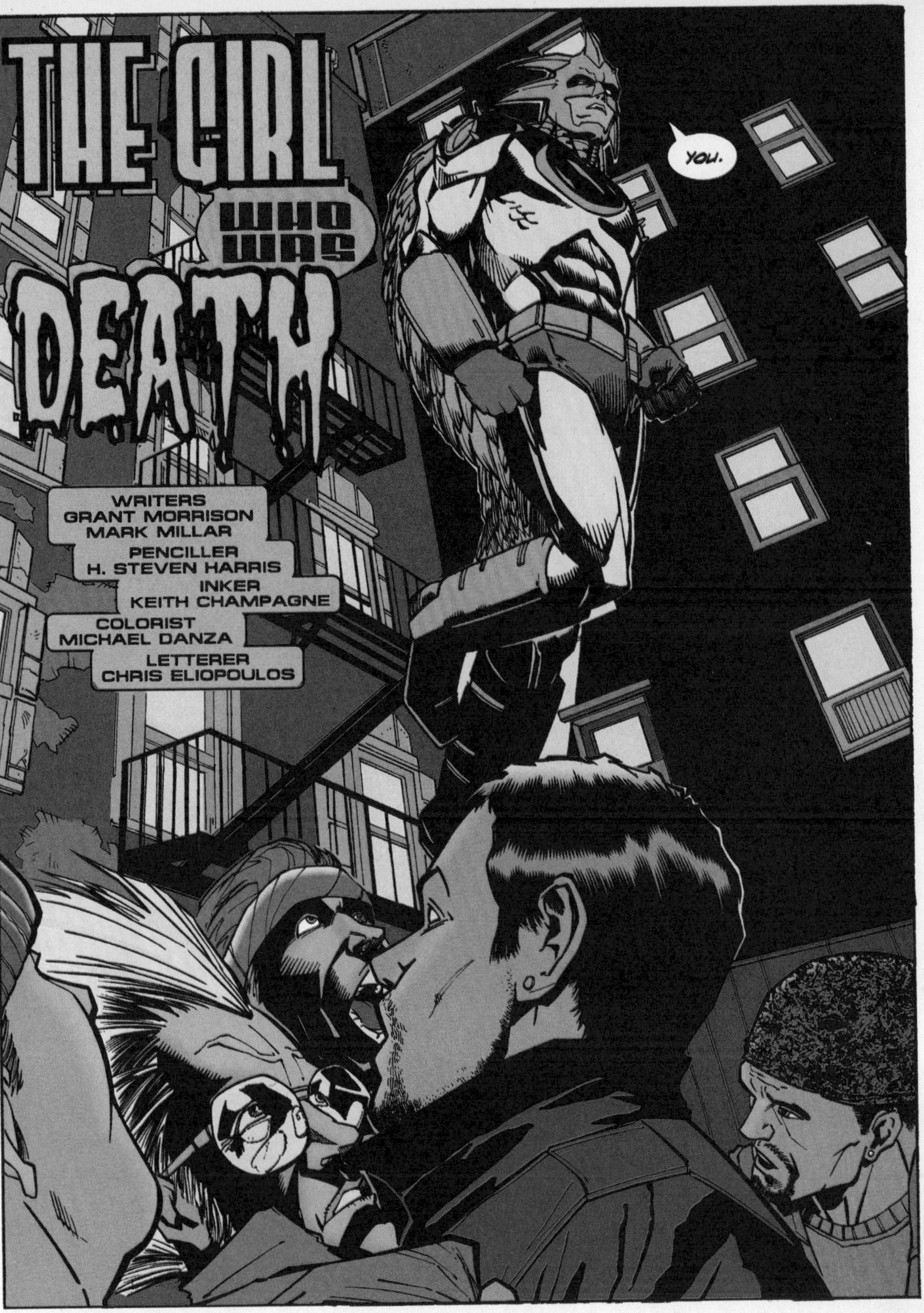
THE GIRL WHO WAS DEATH
YOU.
WRITERS
GRANT MORRISON
MARK MILLAR
PENCILLER
H. STEVEN HARRIS
INKER
KEITH CHAMPAGNE
COLORIST
MICHAEL DANZA
LETTERER
CHRIS ELIOPOULOS

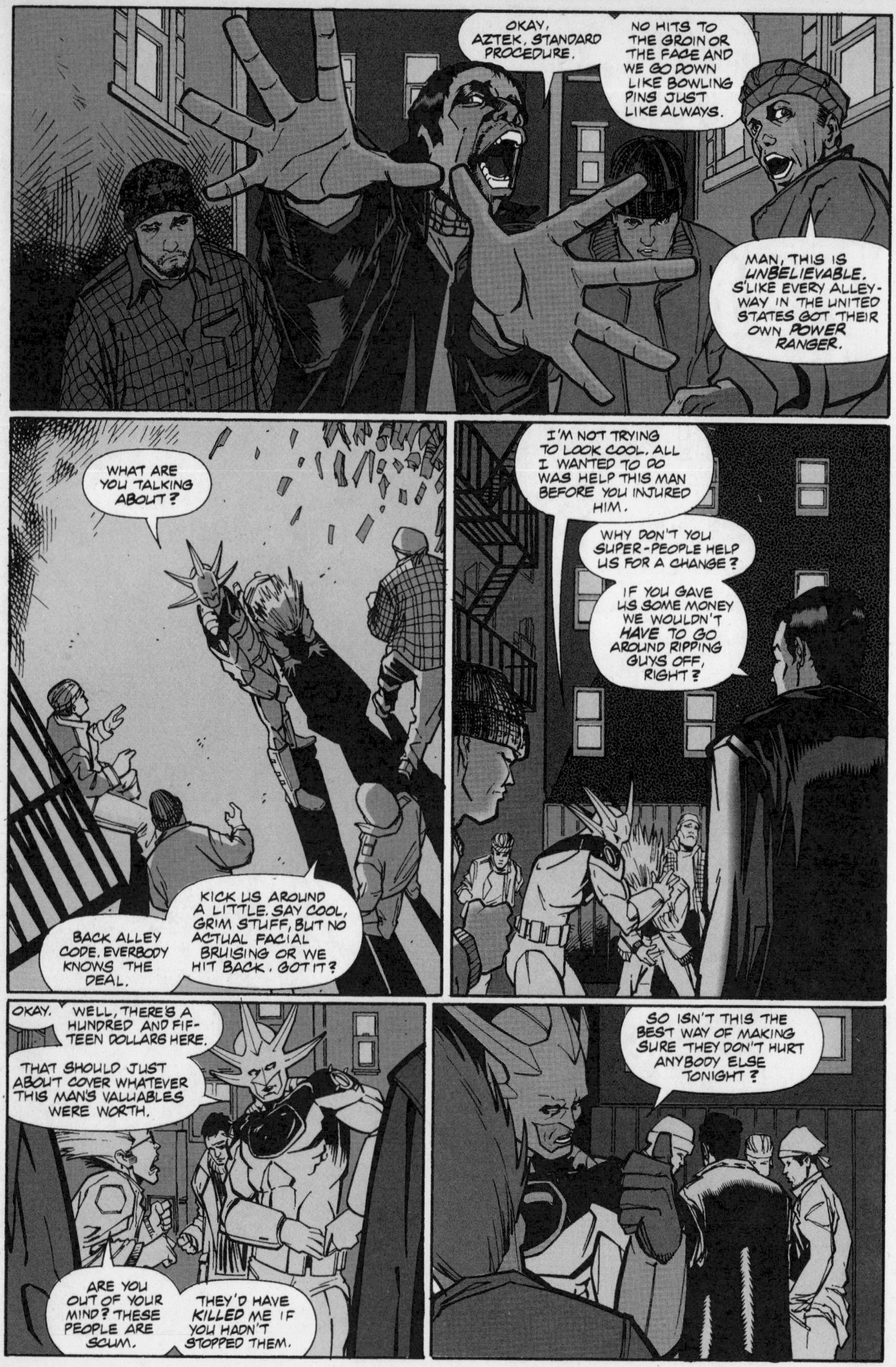
OKAY, AZTEK, STANDARD PROCEDURE.
NO HITS TO THE GROIN OR THE FACE AND WE GO DOWN LIKE BOWLING PINS JUST LIKE ALWAYS.
MAN, THIS IS UNBELIEVABLE. S'LIKE EVERY ALLEY-WAY IN THE UNITED STATES GOT THEIR OWN POWER RANGER.
WHAT ARE YOU TALKING ABOUT?
KICK US AROUND A LITTLE. SAY COOL, GRIM STUFF, BUT NO ACTUAL FACIAL BRUISING OR WE HIT BACK. GOT IT?
BACK ALLEY CODE. EVERBODY KNOWS THE DEAL.
I'M NOT TRYING TO LOOK COOL. ALL I WANTED TO DO WAS HELP THIS MAN BEFORE YOU INJURED HIM.
WHY DON'T YOU SUPER-PEOPLE HELP US FOR A CHANGE?
IF YOU GAVE US SOME MONEY WE WOULDN'T HAVE TO GO AROUND RIPPING GUYS OFF, RIGHT?
OKAY.
WELL, THERE'S A HUNDRED AND FIF-TEEN DOLLARS HERE.
THAT SHOULD JUST ABOUT COVER WHATEVER THIS MAN'S VALUABLES WERE WORTH.
ARE YOU OUT OF YOUR MIND? THESE PEOPLE ARE SCUM.
THEY'D HAVE KILLED ME IF YOU HADN'T STOPPED THEM.
SO ISN'T THIS THE BEST WAY OF MAKING SURE THEY DON'T HURT ANYBODY ELSE TONIGHT?

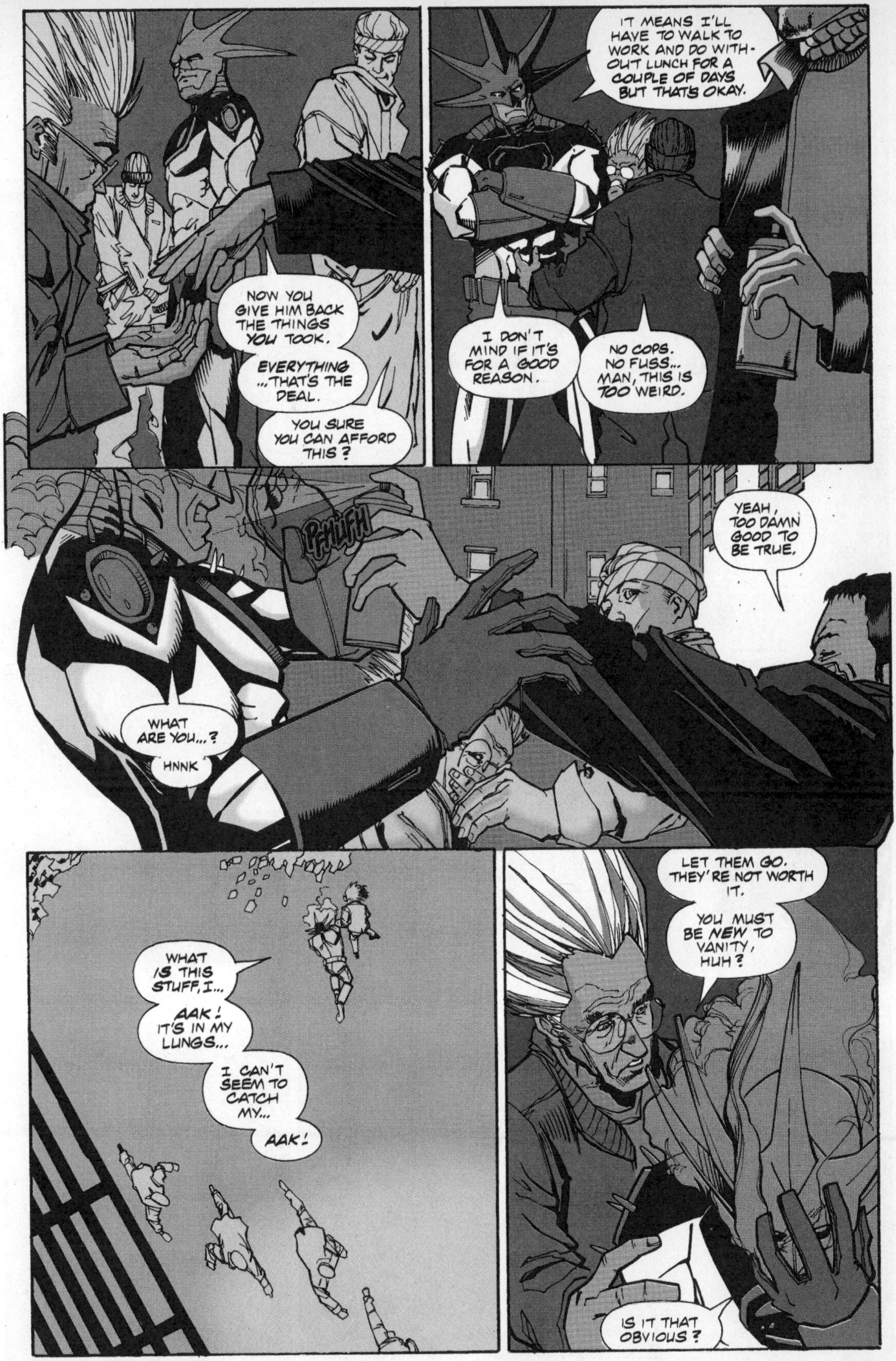
IT MEANS I'LL HAVE TO WALK TO WORK AND DO WITH-OUT LUNCH FOR A COUPLE OF DAYS BUT THAT'S OKAY.
NOW YOU GIVE HIM BACK THE THINGS YOU TOOK.
EVERYTHING ...THAT'S THE DEAL.
YOU SURE YOU CAN AFFORD THIS?
I DON'T MIND IF IT'S FOR A GOOD REASON.
NO COPS. NO FUSS... MAN, THIS IS TOO WEIRD.
PFHUFH
YEAH, TOO DAMN GOOD TO BE TRUE.
WHAT ARE YOU...?
HNNK
WHAT IS THIS STUFF, I...
AAK! IT'S IN MY LUNGS...
I CAN'T SEEM TO CATCH MY...
AAK!
LET THEM GO. THEY'RE NOT WORTH IT.
YOU MUST BE NEW TO VANITY, HUH?
IS IT THAT OBVIOUS?

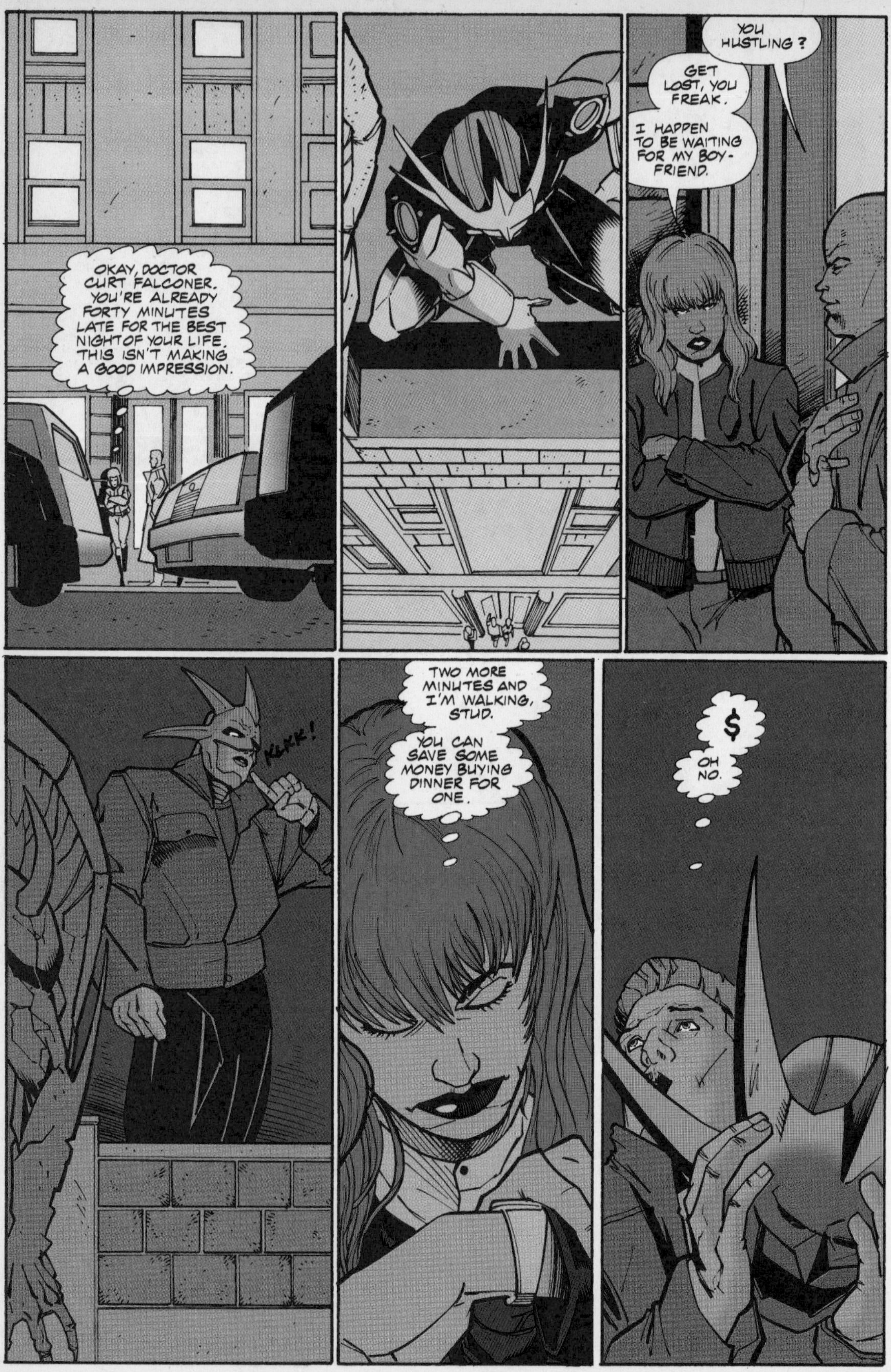
OKAY, DOCTOR CURT FALCONER. YOU'RE ALREADY FORTY MINUTES LATE FOR THE BEST NIGHT OF YOUR LIFE. THIS ISN'T MAKING A GOOD IMPRESSION.
YOU HUSTLING?
GET LOST, YOU FREAK.
I HAPPEN TO BE WAITING FOR MY BOY-FRIEND.
TWO MORE MINUTES AND I'M WALKING, STUD.
YOU CAN SAVE SOME MONEY BUYING DINNER FOR ONE.
$
OH NO.

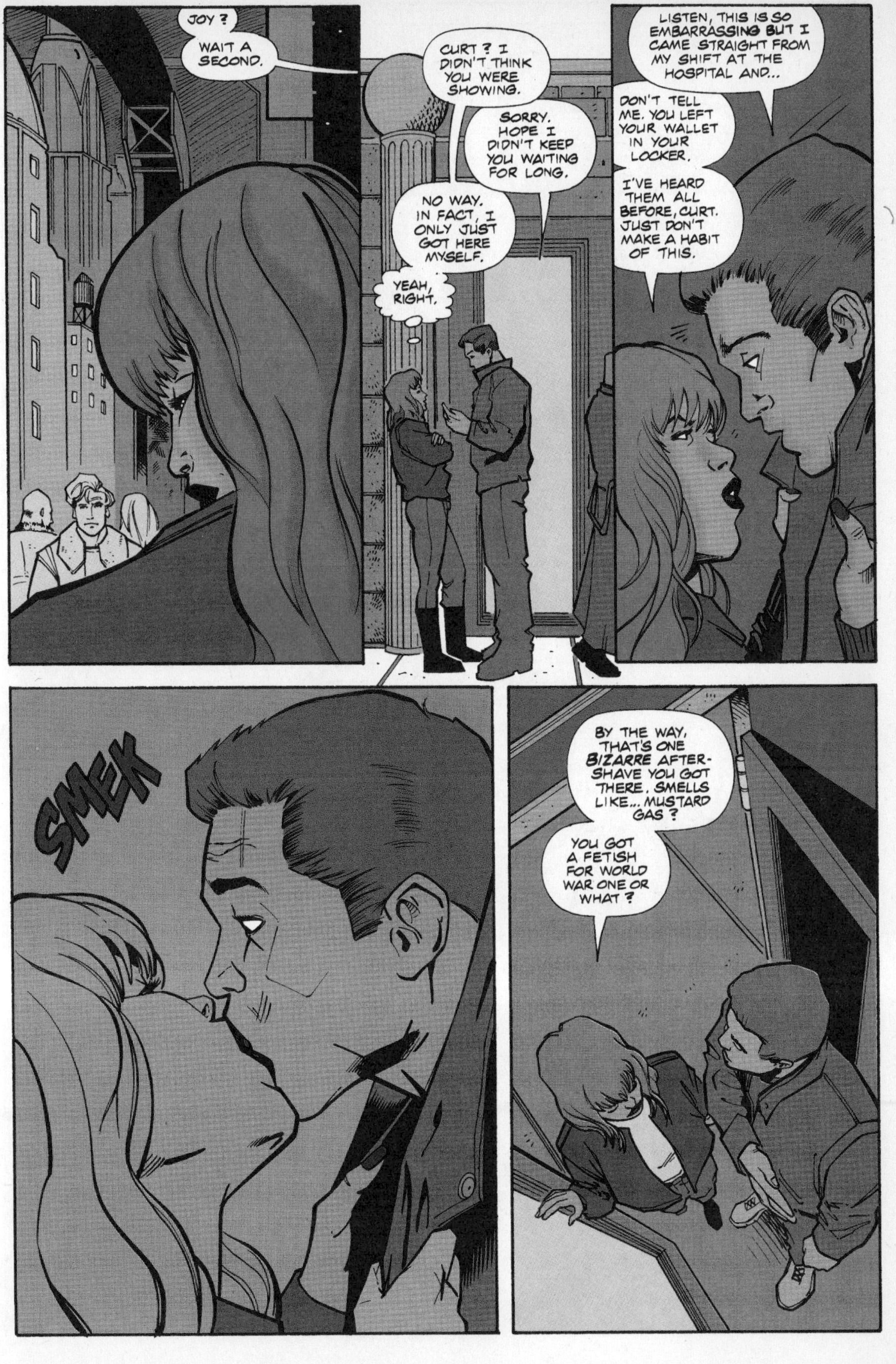
JOY ?
WAIT A SECOND.
CURT ? I DIDN'T THINK YOU WERE SHOWING.
SORRY. HOPE I DIDN'T KEEP YOU WAITING FOR LONG.
NO WAY. IN FACT, I ONLY JUST GOT HERE MYSELF.
YEAH, RIGHT.
LISTEN, THIS IS SO EMBARRASSING BUT I CAME STRAIGHT FROM MY SHIFT AT THE HOSPITAL AND...
DON'T TELL ME. YOU LEFT YOUR WALLET IN YOUR LOCKER.
I'VE HEARD THEM ALL BEFORE, CURT. JUST DON'T MAKE A HABIT OF THIS.
SMEK
BY THE WAY, THAT'S ONE BIZARRE AFTER-SHAVE YOU GOT THERE. SMELLS LIKE... MUSTARD GAS ?
YOU GOT A FETISH FOR WORLD WAR ONE OR WHAT ?

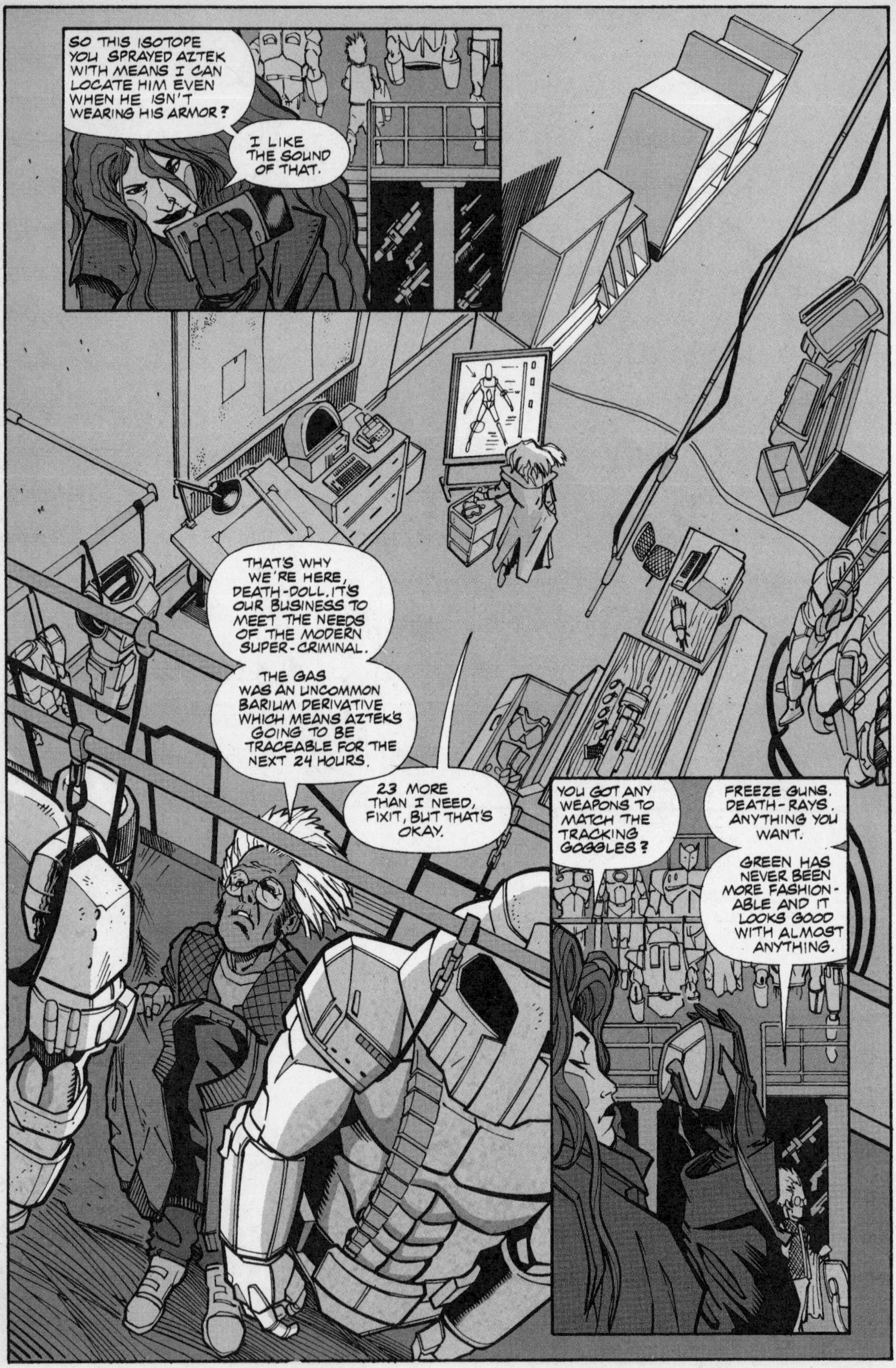
SO THIS ISOTOPE YOU SPRAYED AZTEK WITH MEANS I CAN LOCATE HIM EVEN WHEN HE ISN'T WEARING HIS ARMOR?
I LIKE THE SOUND OF THAT.
THAT'S WHY WE'RE HERE, DEATH-DOLL. IT'S OUR BUSINESS TO MEET THE NEEDS OF THE MODERN SUPER-CRIMINAL.
THE GAS WAS AN UNCOMMON BARIUM DERIVATIVE WHICH MEANS AZTEK'S GOING TO BE TRACEABLE FOR THE NEXT 24 HOURS.
23 MORE THAN I NEED, FIXIT, BUT THAT'S OKAY.
YOU GOT ANY WEAPONS TO MATCH THE TRACKING GOGGLES?
FREEZE GUNS. DEATH-RAYS. ANYTHING YOU WANT.
GREEN HAS NEVER BEEN MORE FASHION-ABLE AND IT LOOKS GOOD WITH ALMOST ANYTHING.

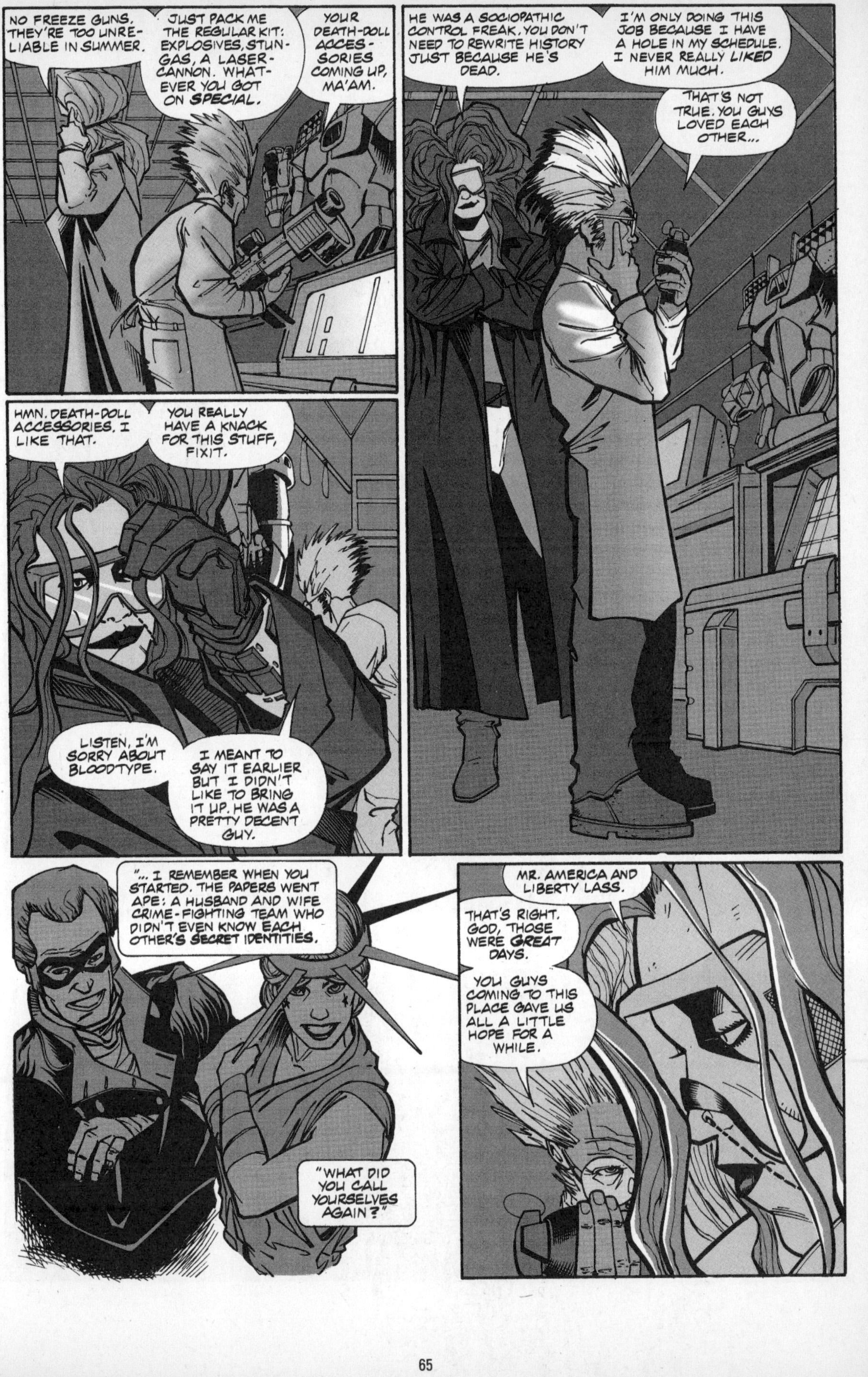

NO FREEZE GUNS. THEY'RE TOO UNRELIABLE IN SUMMER.
JUST PACK ME THE REGULAR KIT: EXPLOSIVES, STUN-GAS, A LASER-CANNON. WHATEVER YOU GOT ON SPECIAL.
YOUR DEATH-DOLL ACCESSORIES COMING UP, MA'AM.
HMN. DEATH-DOLL ACCESSORIES. I LIKE THAT.
YOU REALLY HAVE A KNACK FOR THIS STUFF, FIXIT.
LISTEN, I'M SORRY ABOUT BLOODTYPE.
I MEANT TO SAY IT EARLIER BUT I DIDN'T LIKE TO BRING IT UP. HE WAS A PRETTY DECENT GUY.
HE WAS A SOCIOPATHIC CONTROL FREAK. YOU DON'T NEED TO REWRITE HISTORY JUST BECAUSE HE'S DEAD.
I'M ONLY DOING THIS JOB BECAUSE I HAVE A HOLE IN MY SCHEDULE. I NEVER REALLY LIKED HIM MUCH.
THAT'S NOT TRUE. YOU GUYS LOVED EACH OTHER...
"... I REMEMBER WHEN YOU STARTED. THE PAPERS WENT APE: A HUSBAND AND WIFE CRIME-FIGHTING TEAM WHO DIDN'T EVEN KNOW EACH OTHER'S SECRET IDENTITIES.
"WHAT DID YOU CALL YOURSELVES AGAIN?"
MR. AMERICA AND LIBERTY LASS.
THAT'S RIGHT. GOD, THOSE WERE GREAT DAYS.
YOU GUYS COMING TO THIS PLACE GAVE US ALL A LITTLE HOPE FOR A WHILE.

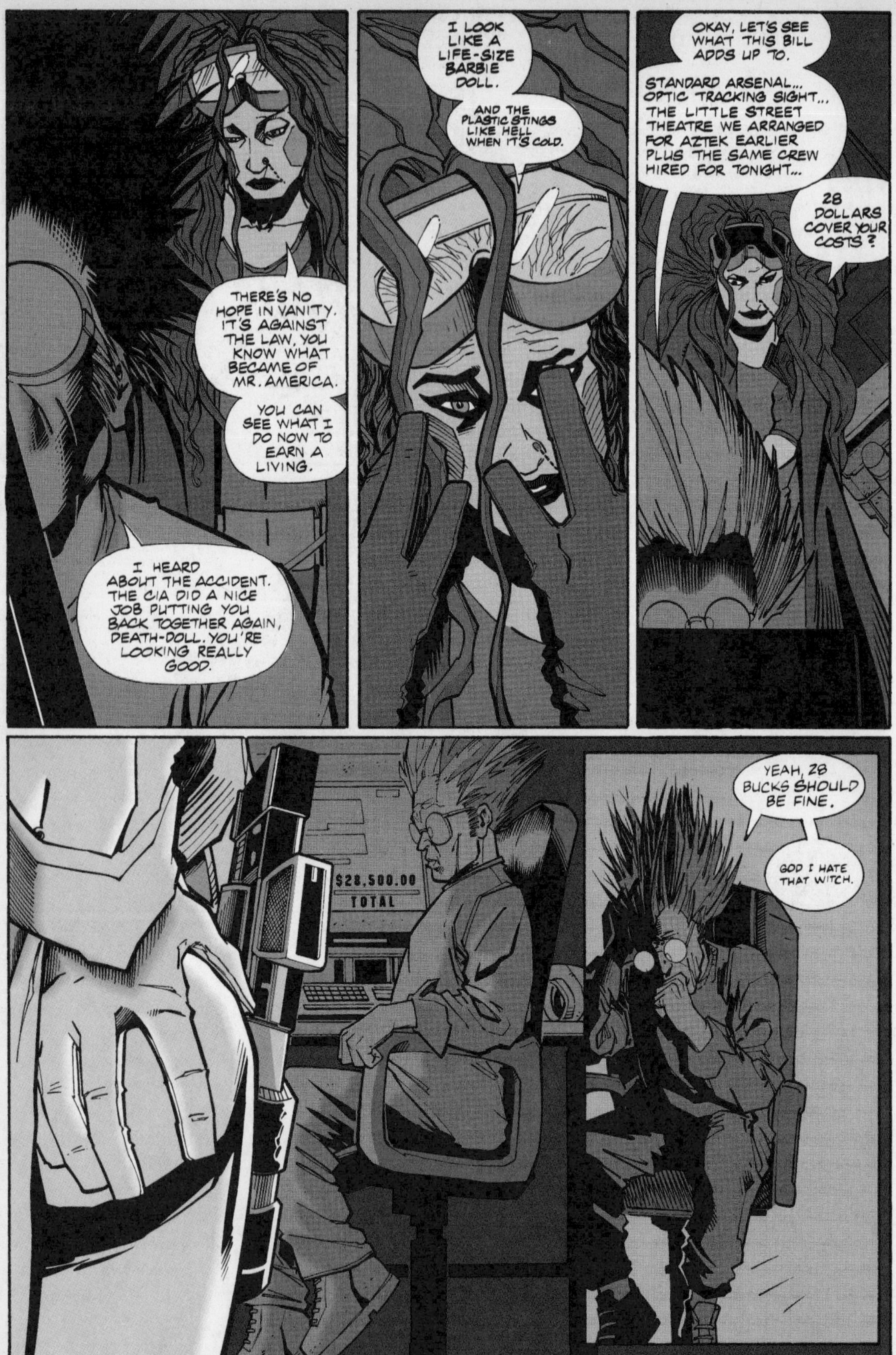
THERE'S NO HOPE IN VANITY. IT'S AGAINST THE LAW. YOU KNOW WHAT BECAME OF MR. AMERICA.
YOU CAN SEE WHAT I DO NOW TO EARN A LIVING.
I HEARD ABOUT THE ACCIDENT. THE CIA DID A NICE JOB PUTTING YOU BACK TOGETHER AGAIN, DEATH-DOLL. YOU'RE LOOKING REALLY GOOD.
I LOOK LIKE A LIFE-SIZE BARBIE DOLL.
AND THE PLASTIC STINGS LIKE HELL WHEN IT'S COLD.
OKAY, LET'S SEE WHAT THIS BILL ADDS UP TO.
STANDARD ARSENAL... OPTIC TRACKING SIGHT... THE LITTLE STREET THEATRE WE ARRANGED FOR AZTEK EARLIER PLUS THE SAME CREW HIRED FOR TONIGHT...
28 DOLLARS COVER YOUR COSTS?
$28,500.00
TOTAL
YEAH, 28 BUCKS SHOULD BE FINE.
GOD I HATE THAT WITCH.

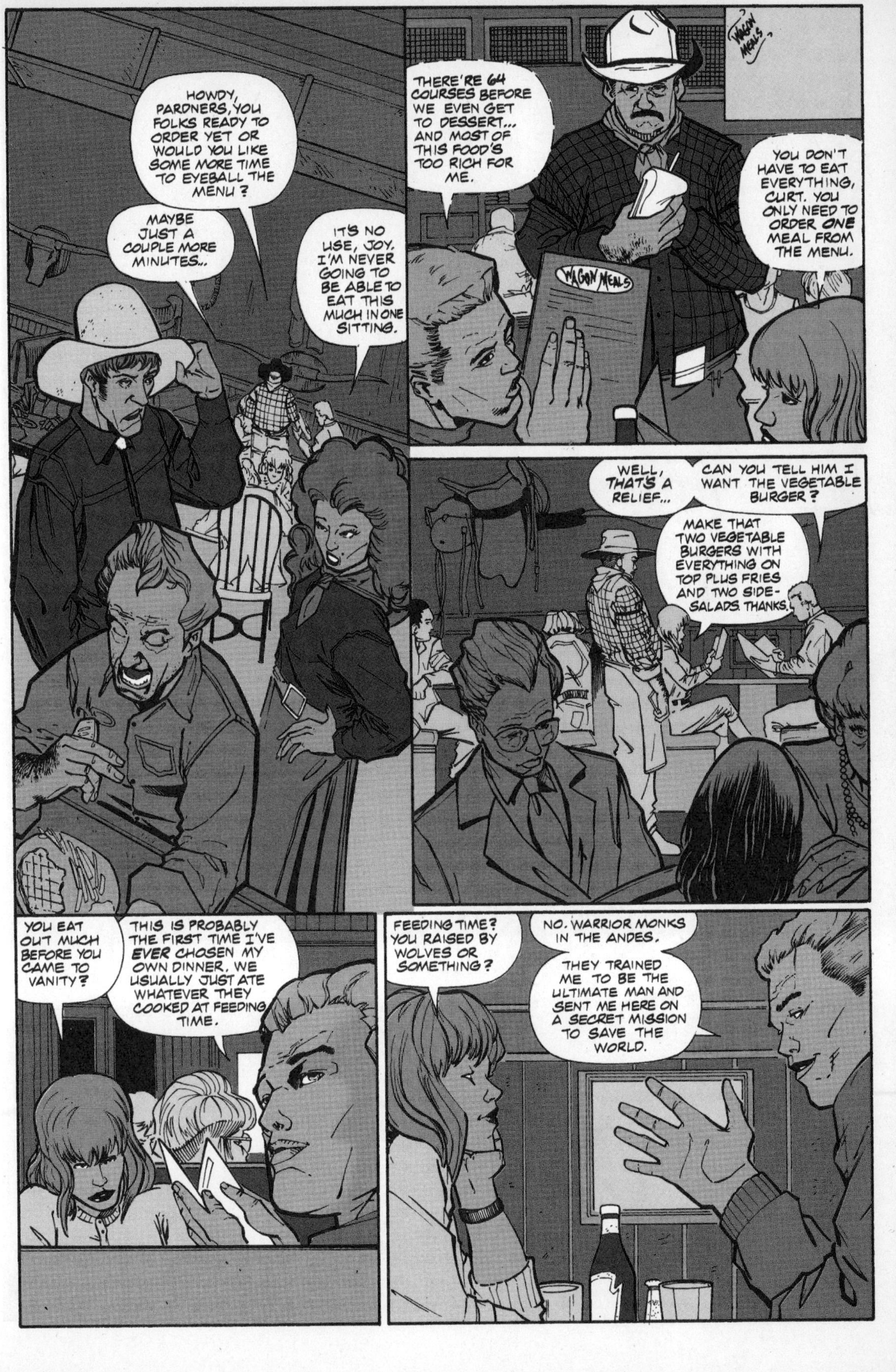
HOWDY, PARDNERS, YOU FOLKS READY TO ORDER YET OR WOULD YOU LIKE SOME MORE TIME TO EYEBALL THE MENU?
MAYBE JUST A COUPLE MORE MINUTES...
IT'S NO USE, JOY. I'M NEVER GOING TO BE ABLE TO EAT THIS MUCH IN ONE SITTING.
THERE'RE 64 COURSES BEFORE WE EVEN GET TO DESSERT... AND MOST OF THIS FOOD'S TOO RICH FOR ME.
YOU DON'T HAVE TO EAT EVERYTHING, CURT. YOU ONLY NEED TO ORDER ONE MEAL FROM THE MENU.
WAGON MEALS
WELL, THAT'S A RELIEF...
CAN YOU TELL HIM I WANT THE VEGETABLE BURGER?
MAKE THAT TWO VEGETABLE BURGERS WITH EVERYTHING ON TOP PLUS FRIES AND TWO SIDE-SALADS. THANKS.
YOU EAT OUT MUCH BEFORE YOU CAME TO VANITY?
THIS IS PROBABLY THE FIRST TIME I'VE EVER CHOSEN MY OWN DINNER. WE USUALLY JUST ATE WHATEVER THEY COOKED AT FEEDING TIME.
FEEDING TIME? YOU RAISED BY WOLVES OR SOMETHING?
NO. WARRIOR MONKS IN THE ANDES.
THEY TRAINED ME TO BE THE ULTIMATE MAN AND SENT ME HERE ON A SECRET MISSION TO SAVE THE WORLD.

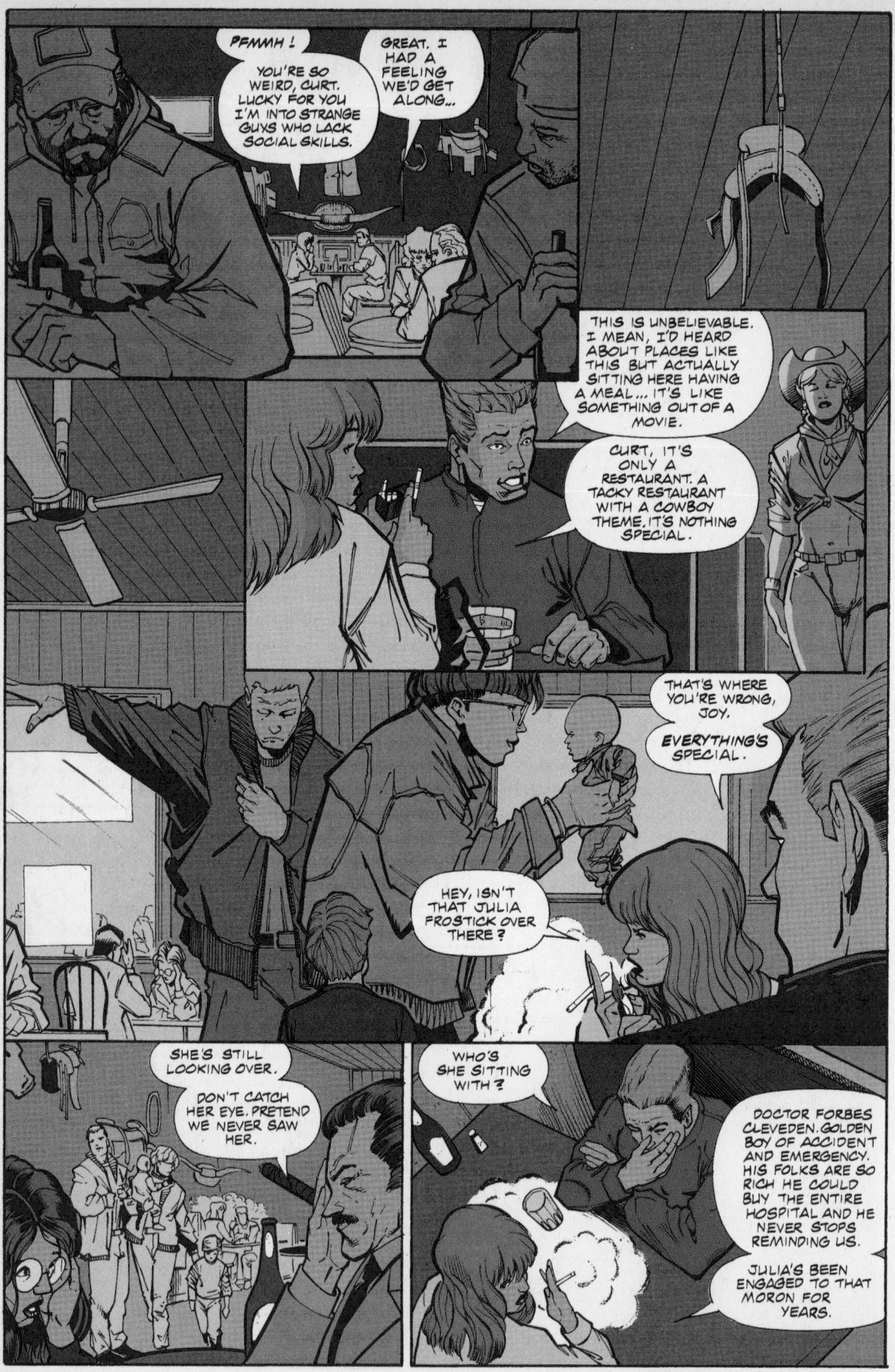
PFMMH! YOU'RE SO WEIRD, CURT. LUCKY FOR YOU I'M INTO STRANGE GUYS WHO LACK SOCIAL SKILLS.
GREAT. I HAD A FEELING WE'D GET ALONG...
THIS IS UNBELIEVABLE. I MEAN, I'D HEARD ABOUT PLACES LIKE THIS BUT ACTUALLY SITTING HERE HAVING A MEAL... IT'S LIKE SOMETHING OUT OF A MOVIE.
CURT, IT'S ONLY A RESTAURANT. A TACKY RESTAURANT WITH A COWBOY THEME. IT'S NOTHING SPECIAL.
THAT'S WHERE YOU'RE WRONG, JOY.
EVERYTHING'S SPECIAL.
HEY, ISN'T THAT JULIA FROSTICK OVER THERE?
SHE'S STILL LOOKING OVER.
DON'T CATCH HER EYE. PRETEND WE NEVER SAW HER.
WHO'S SHE SITTING WITH?
DOCTOR FORBES CLEVEDEN. GOLDEN BOY OF ACCIDENT AND EMERGENCY. HIS FOLKS ARE SO RICH HE COULD BUY THE ENTIRE HOSPITAL AND HE NEVER STOPS REMINDING US.
JULIA'S BEEN ENGAGED TO THAT MORON FOR YEARS.

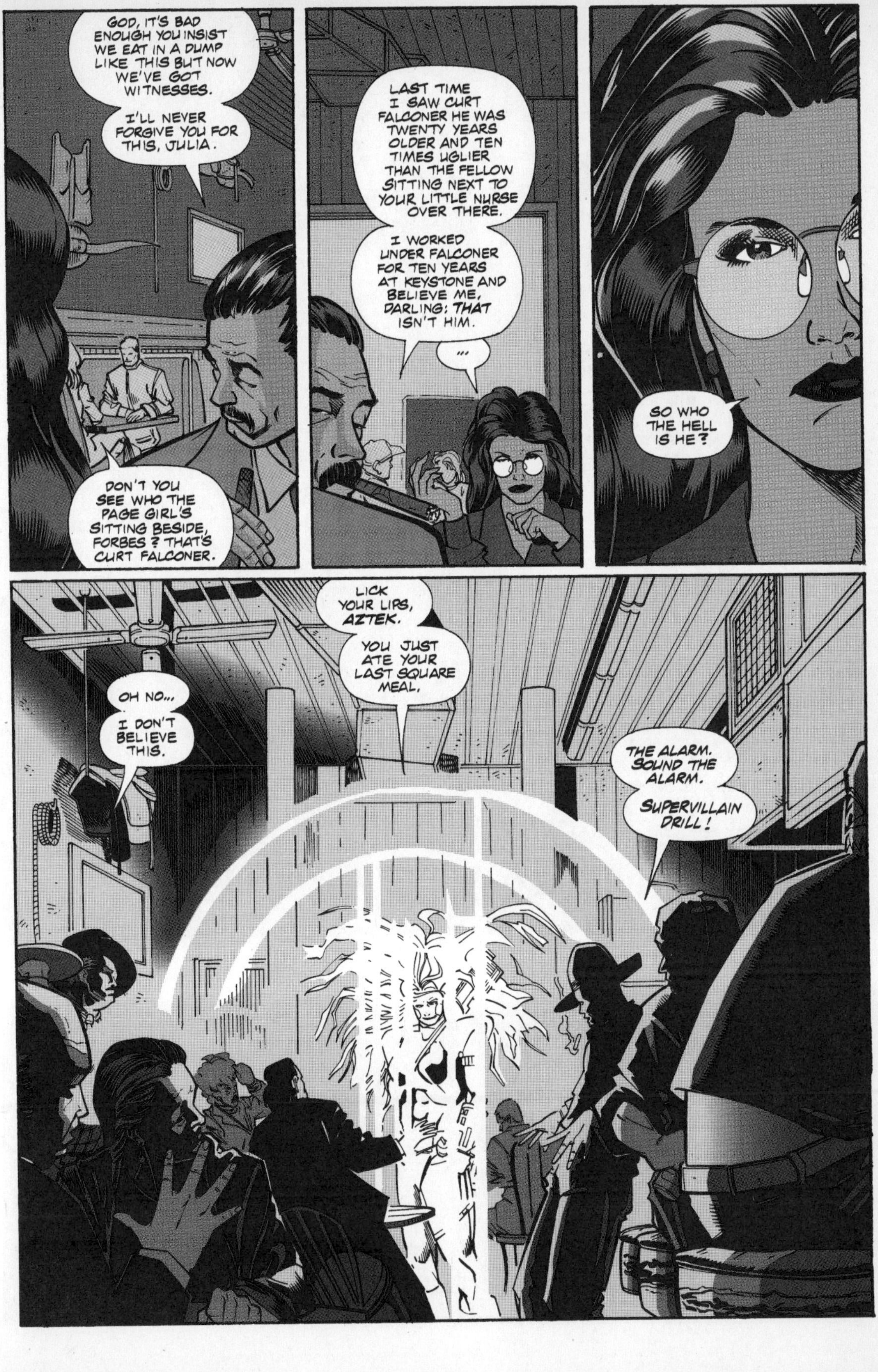
GOD, IT'S BAD ENOUGH YOU INSIST WE EAT IN A DUMP LIKE THIS BUT NOW WE'VE GOT WITNESSES.
I'LL NEVER FORGIVE YOU FOR THIS, JULIA.
DON'T YOU SEE WHO THE PAGE GIRL'S SITTING BESIDE, FORBES? THAT'S CURT FALCONER.
LAST TIME I SAW CURT FALCONER HE WAS TWENTY YEARS OLDER AND TEN TIMES UGLIER THAN THE FELLOW SITTING NEXT TO YOUR LITTLE NURSE OVER THERE.
I WORKED UNDER FALCONER FOR TEN YEARS AT KEYSTONE AND BELIEVE ME, DARLING: THAT ISN'T HIM.
...
SO WHO THE HELL IS HE?
LICK YOUR LIPS, AZTEK.
YOU JUST ATE YOUR LAST SQUARE MEAL.
OH NO... I DON'T BELIEVE THIS.
THE ALARM. SOUND THE ALARM.
SUPERVILLAIN DRILL!

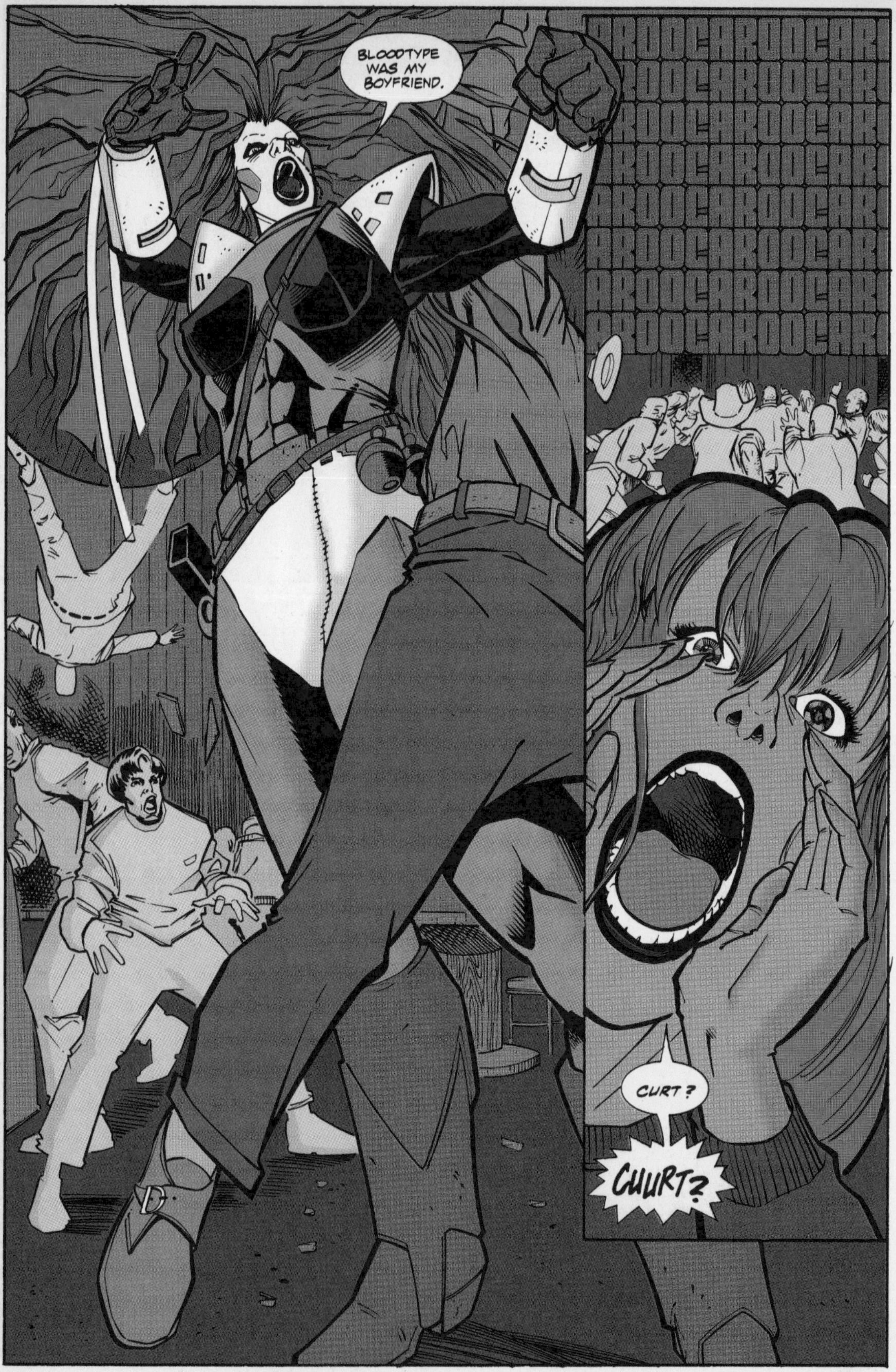
BLOODTYPE WAS MY BOYFRIEND.
AROOCAROOCAR
CURT?
CUURT?

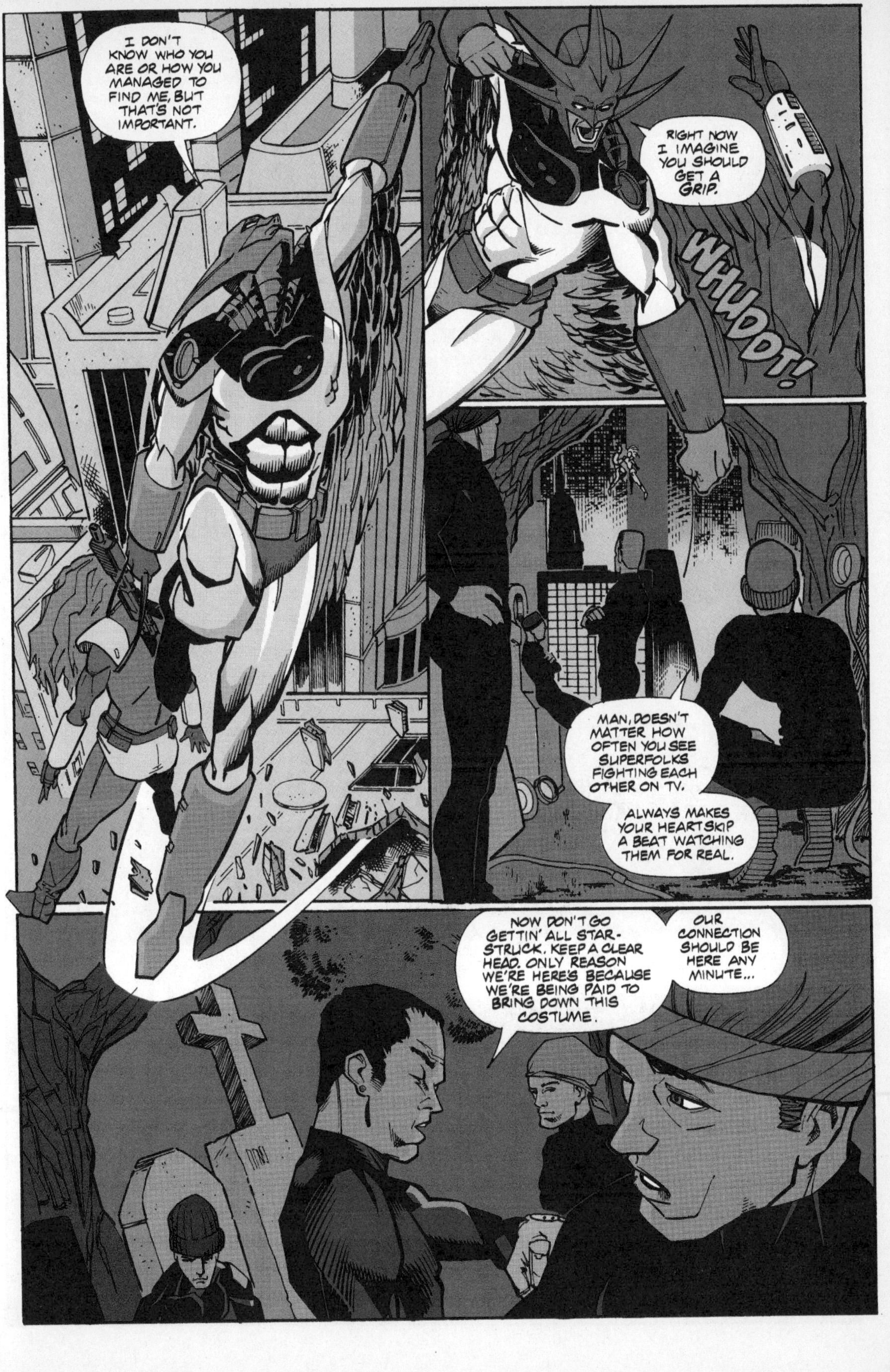
I DON'T KNOW WHO YOU ARE OR HOW YOU MANAGED TO FIND ME, BUT THAT'S NOT IMPORTANT.
RIGHT NOW I IMAGINE YOU SHOULD GET A GRIP.
WHUDDT!
MAN, DOESN'T MATTER HOW OFTEN YOU SEE SUPERFOLKS FIGHTING EACH OTHER ON TV.
ALWAYS MAKES YOUR HEART SKIP A BEAT WATCHING THEM FOR REAL.
NOW DON'T GO GETTIN' ALL STAR-STRUCK. KEEP A CLEAR HEAD. ONLY REASON WE'RE HERE'S BECAUSE WE'RE BEING PAID TO BRING DOWN THIS COSTUME.
OUR CONNECTION SHOULD BE HERE ANY MINUTE...

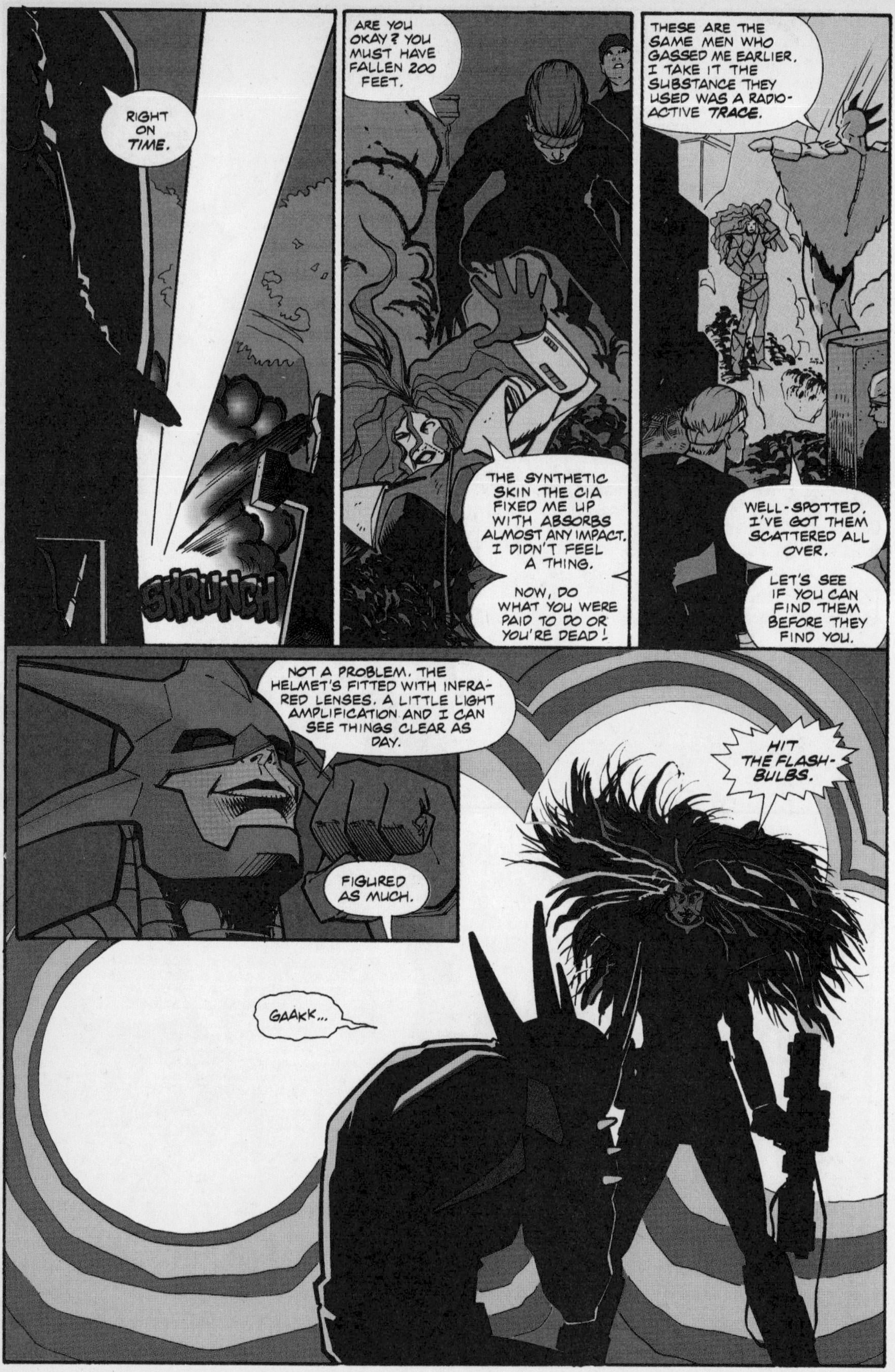
RIGHT ON TIME.
SKRUNCH
ARE YOU OKAY? YOU MUST HAVE FALLEN 200 FEET.
THE SYNTHETIC SKIN THE CIA FIXED ME UP WITH ABSORBS ALMOST ANY IMPACT. I DIDN'T FEEL A THING.
NOW, DO WHAT YOU WERE PAID TO DO OR YOU'RE DEAD!
THESE ARE THE SAME MEN WHO GASSED ME EARLIER. I TAKE IT THE SUBSTANCE THEY USED WAS A RADIO-ACTIVE TRACE.
WELL-SPOTTED. I'VE GOT THEM SCATTERED ALL OVER.
LET'S SEE IF YOU CAN FIND THEM BEFORE THEY FIND YOU.
NOT A PROBLEM. THE HELMET'S FITTED WITH INFRA-RED LENSES. A LITTLE LIGHT AMPLIFICATION AND I CAN SEE THINGS CLEAR AS DAY.
FIGURED AS MUCH.
HIT THE FLASH-BULBS.
GAAKK...

WHAT'S WRONG? TEMPORARY BLINDNESS?

JEEZ. THAT'S TOO BAD.

WOULDN'T WANT YOU TO MISS YOUR OWN FUNERAL.

HHRT!

C'MON. MOVE. WE'RE DONE HERE.

WE CAN'T LEAVE HIM LIKE THIS. AZTEK HELPED US OUT MORE THAN SHE EVER DID. HE GAVE US MONEY.

WE CAN'T JUST LET HER KILL THE GUY.

THIS WASN'T REALLY ABOUT REVENGE.

IT WAS ABOUT MAKING MY NAME AS A PLAYER AGAIN IN A WORLD ALREADY CRAWLING WITH SUPERVILLAINS.

NOW PEOPLE KNOW DEATH-DOLL'S BACK IN BUSINESS.

CHOOM!

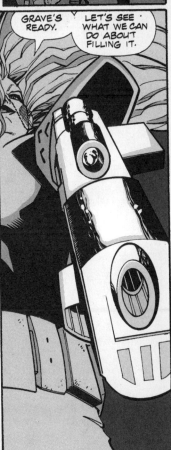

GRAVE'S READY.

LET'S SEE WHAT WE CAN DO ABOUT FILLING IT.

73

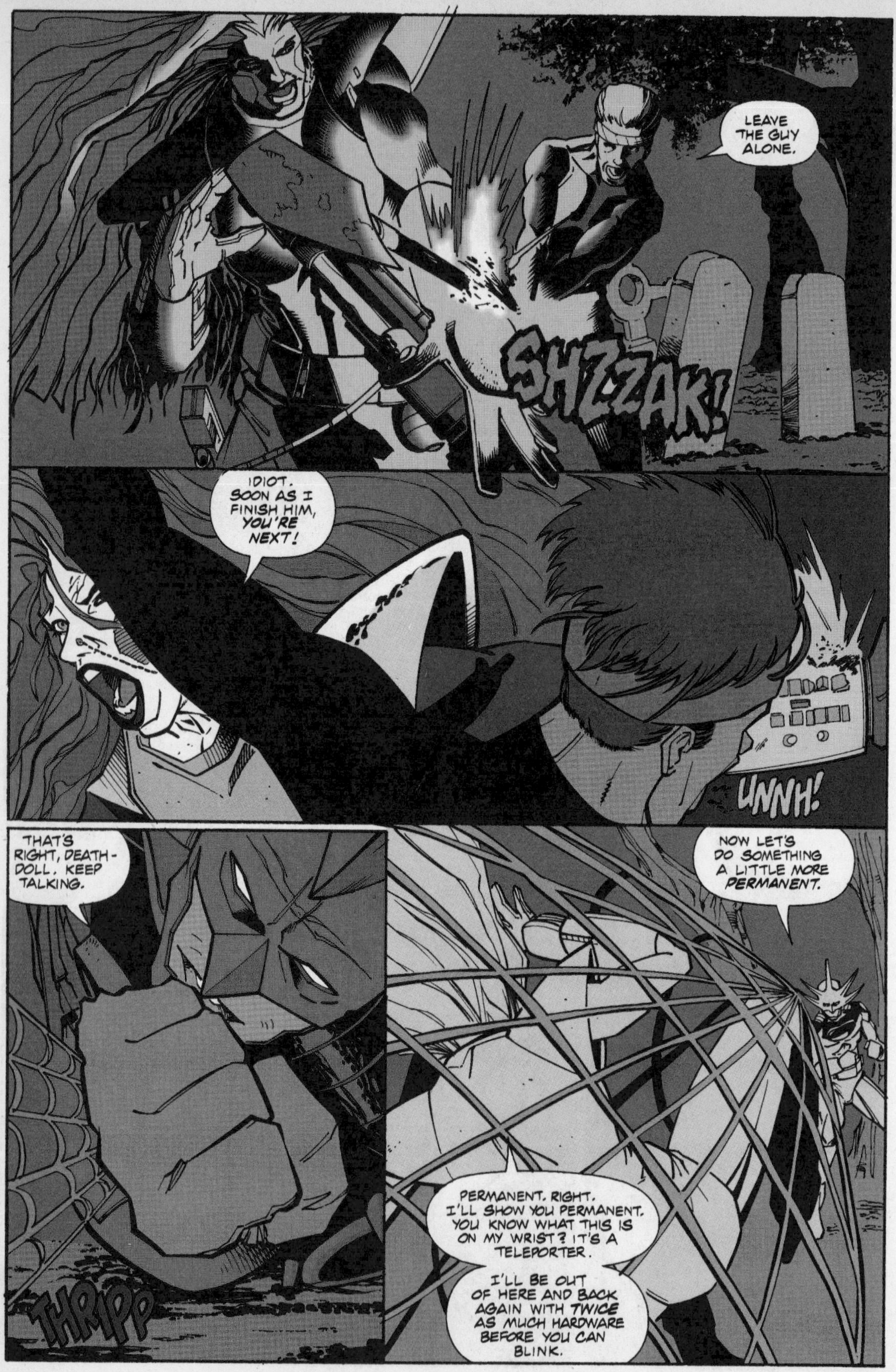
LEAVE THE GUY ALONE.
SHZZAK!
IDIOT. SOON AS I FINISH HIM, YOU'RE NEXT!
UNNH!
THAT'S RIGHT, DEATH-DOLL. KEEP TALKING.
THRIPP
NOW LET'S DO SOMETHING A LITTLE MORE PERMANENT.
PERMANENT. RIGHT. I'LL SHOW YOU PERMANENT. YOU KNOW WHAT THIS IS ON MY WRIST? IT'S A TELEPORTER.
I'LL BE OUT OF HERE AND BACK AGAIN WITH TWICE AS MUCH HARDWARE BEFORE YOU CAN BLINK.

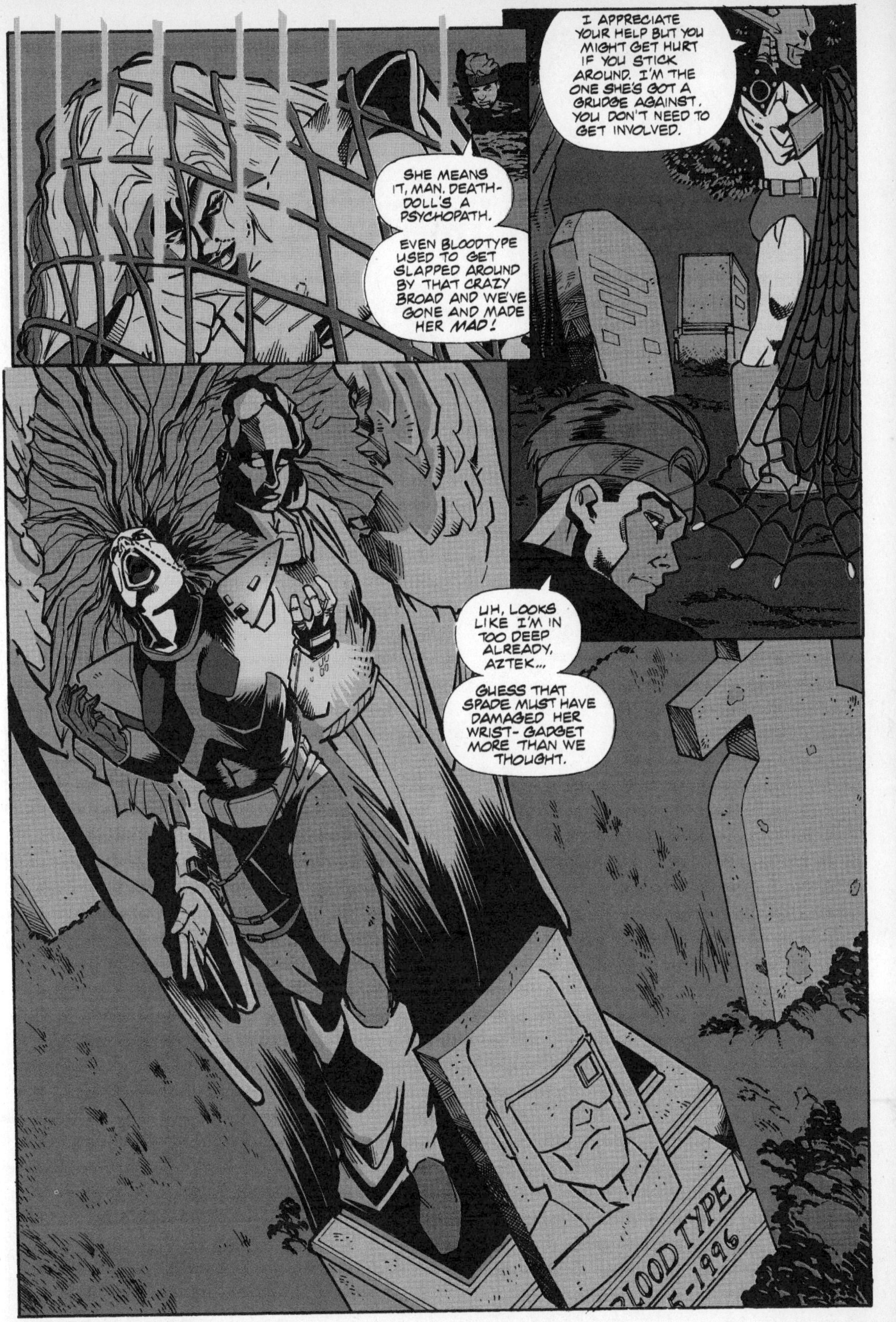
SHE MEANS IT, MAN. DEATH-DOLL'S A PSYCHOPATH.
EVEN BLOODTYPE USED TO GET SLAPPED AROUND BY THAT CRAZY BROAD AND WE'VE GONE AND MADE HER *MAD*!
I APPRECIATE YOUR HELP BUT YOU MIGHT GET HURT IF YOU STICK AROUND. I'M THE ONE SHE'S GOT A GRUDGE AGAINST. YOU DON'T NEED TO GET INVOLVED.
UH, LOOKS LIKE I'M IN TOO DEEP ALREADY, AZTEK...
GUESS THAT SPADE MUST HAVE DAMAGED HER WRIST-GADGET MORE THAN WE THOUGHT.
BLOOD TYPE
5-1996

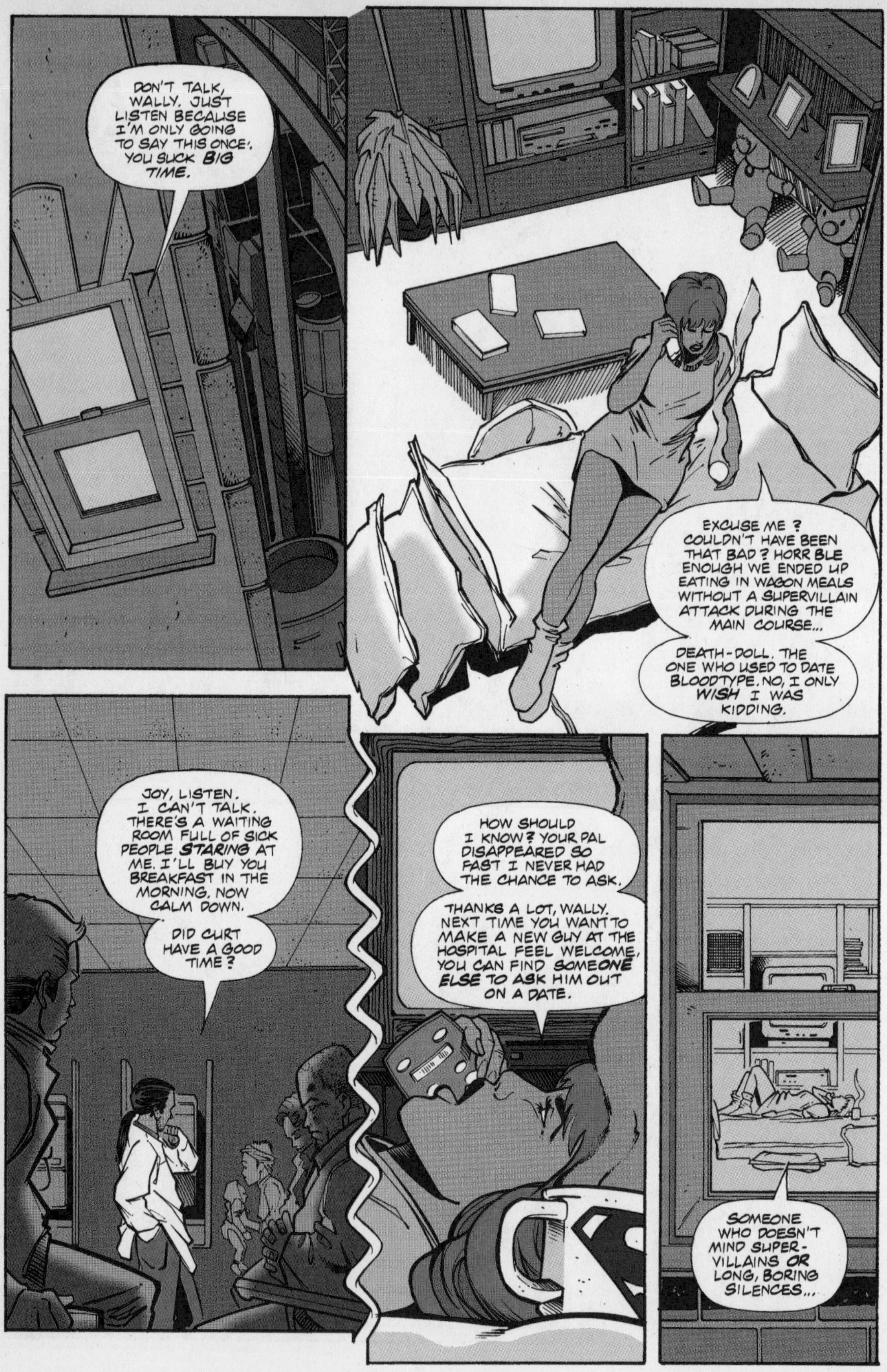
DON'T TALK, WALLY. JUST LISTEN BECAUSE I'M ONLY GOING TO SAY THIS ONCE: YOU SUCK BIG TIME.
EXCUSE ME ? COULDN'T HAVE BEEN THAT BAD ? HORR BLE ENOUGH WE ENDED UP EATING IN WAGON MEALS WITHOUT A SUPERVILLAIN ATTACK DURING THE MAIN COURSE...
DEATH-DOLL. THE ONE WHO USED TO DATE BLOODTYPE. NO, I ONLY WISH I WAS KIDDING.
JOY, LISTEN. I CAN'T TALK. THERE'S A WAITING ROOM FULL OF SICK PEOPLE STARING AT ME. I'LL BUY YOU BREAKFAST IN THE MORNING. NOW CALM DOWN.
DID CURT HAVE A GOOD TIME ?
HOW SHOULD I KNOW ? YOUR PAL DISAPPEARED SO FAST I NEVER HAD THE CHANCE TO ASK.
THANKS A LOT, WALLY. NEXT TIME YOU WANT TO MAKE A NEW GUY AT THE HOSPITAL FEEL WELCOME, YOU CAN FIND SOMEONE ELSE TO ASK HIM OUT ON A DATE.
SOMEONE WHO DOESN'T MIND SUPER-VILLAINS OR LONG, BORING SILENCES...

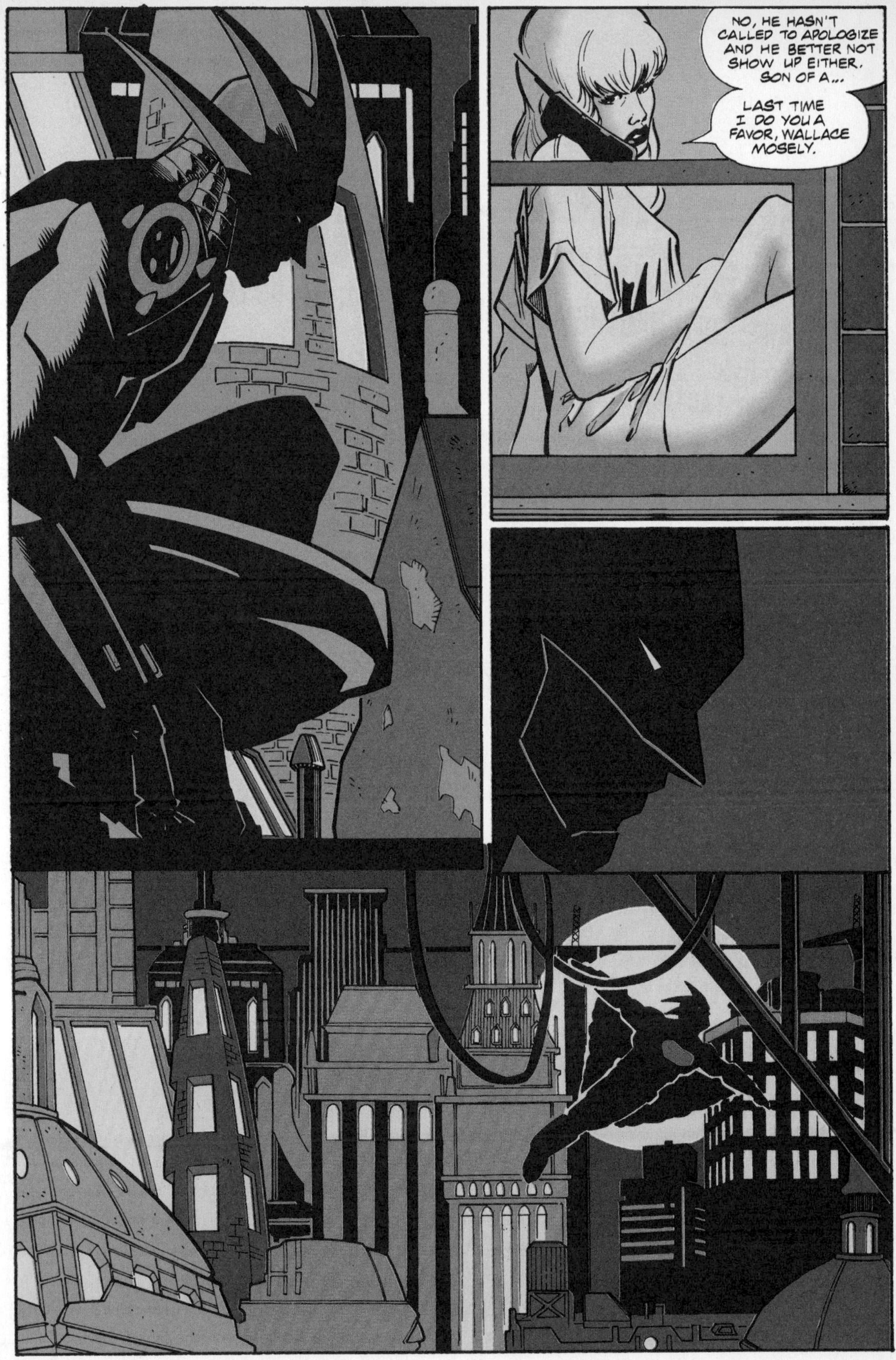
NO, HE HASN'T CALLED TO APOLOGIZE AND HE BETTER NOT SHOW UP EITHER. SON OF A...
LAST TIME I DO YOU A FAVOR, WALLACE MOSELY.

A Monument To His Own Hubris

CITIZEN VANE: THE UNAUTHORIZED BIOGRAPHY OF AN AMERICAN TYCOON

by Jonathan Ryle
435PP ■ WAYNE FACTION ■ $24.95

Reviewed by Adam Kennedy-Vane

Sometimes we need to read between the lines to understand the real meaning behind a story, but here we only have to open the inside cover and read the name of the publisher to discover the truth. This extraordinary, paranoid and poorly-researched biography, supposedly shedding light upon the secret life of my late father, has been published by the grandson of perhaps his greatest business rival: Gotham surgeon and successful stockbroker Anthony Thomas Wayne. Forensic investigative journalism is one thing, but this book amounts to little more than a petty and vindictive attack in a small-minded bid to settle a score more than half a century old. Anthony Wayne himself would never have allowed the publishing wing of his business empire to print such a cheap and down-market volume, and I regret to say Bruce Wayne may have inherited all his family's wealth but none of their manners. His endorsement of Mister Jonathan Ryle's sick character assassination brings the judgment of Gotham's notorious billionaire playboy into serious disrepute. As you might suspect, it was therefore with some trepidation that I endeavored to read any further.

The book begins with a bleak account of my father's funeral in nineteen thirty eight which neglects to mention the one million citizens of Vanity who lined the streets to solemnly watch the procession go by. No mention was made of the flowers which stretched ten miles from Hindley Plaza to Gein Street, the wreaths sent by Congressmen and daisy chains made by children as a mark of respect for a man who built one of this nation's greatest cities. No mention is made of the one-minute silence held all across the United States from log cabins in Arkansas to the White House itself to note the passing of a man who twice ran for President. Instead, Jonathan Ryle prefers to begin with the distasteful tabloid conspiracy theory that our family and friends buried an empty coffin on August twenty-sixth of that tragic year and my father's corpse is kept somewhere beneath this city in a state of suspended animation.

As the inheritor and publisher of Clarence Vane's media interests and the chief controller of his remaining stock, I would be expected to defend my own flesh and blood from such foul criticism; however, it's worth pointing out that I am the first to admit my father was not without his faults. He was a harsh and deeply religious man, a workaholic who seldom spoke or smiled. In fact, it would be safe to say there was no love in our vast household during my formative years, if there ever was at all. Clarence Vane was indeed a visionary, but this talent was also his greatest failing. He has often been compared to Charles Foster Kane and believed to be the inspiration for Welles's cinematic masterpiece released the year my father died. The only difference is that Clarence Vane's personal Xanadu was no mere castle but an entire city; a utopian marvel of shining buildings and magnificent bridges and fountain-filled

CONTINUED ON NEXT PAGE

VANITY PRESS BOOK REVIEW

CONTINUED FROM PREVIOUS PAGE

plazas. A project that consumed not only the billions of dollars he had earned from a life of hard, honest work but, in the end, also robbed him of his health. Ambition was his greatest vice, and he died from overindulgence.

In his opening chapter, Jonathan Ryle describes Vanity as "a monument to Vane's own hubris" but I suspect the term works equally well when applied to the author himself. His unauthorized biography, five years in the writing, is the headstone placed upon what was once a promising career as an investigative reporter. In fact, I should mention that Mister Ryle was once employed by this newspaper, which leads one to speculate that perhaps his primary motivation is not to uncover the truth as he tells us on the dust jacket but that he seeks revenge for his dismissal after being caught leafing through our family's most private papers.

His validity as a serious journalist is shattered by his most prominent charge that my late father is in some way responsible for Vanity's current spiraling suicide rate. He insists that Vanity was an early experiment in what crackpots have since termed "sick building syndrome" and speculates that Clarence Vane and his contemporaries designed the city for maximum discomfort. The truth of the matter is that the unusual layout and construction, particularly in the old heart of the city, was inspired by several innovative European art movements. The bizarre Mister Ryle suggests instead that a sinister "occult geometry" was its true inspiration and even implies that my father, a devout Methodist, was a devotee of The Dark. The suicide rate, he explains, is five times the national average, but he never tells us where he gets his questionable data. Vanity might indeed have a high number of young men and women taking their lives every year, but this is true of any major city; and capitalizing on the grief of others is a cheap method of publishing indeed.

Every century ends with panic as the world indulges in a state of periodic hysteria. It is almost as if the Earth itself worries about getting a little older. Reaching the end of the millennium is like a global amplification of how a man feels when he reaches middle age, and we often turn to the most extreme solutions when we feel insecure. People like Jonathan Ryle shamelessly exploit this millennium fever in an effort to make money by distorting the truth into an apocalyptic piece of horror fiction. He looks at the story of a brilliant man who poured almost all of his wealth into a magnificent folly and spots a business opportunity. My father was not a bad man. He was simply misguided and wanted to leave something behind that people would remember and respect him for. The idea that he set out to build something evil belongs on the colorful supermarket shelves beside blurred sightings of The Shaggy Man and rumors of the CIA's involvement in the death of Superman. There is no conspiracy to create a monster in the heart of Vanity. There never was and there never will be. Anyone with any evidence of my father's involvement in such a secret society is welcome to show me the details, but Jonathan Ryle fails to impress. His book is filled with speculation and innuendo. There are no hard facts, and without the facts there can be no truth.

Clarence Vane was a pioneer, a newspaperman who transformed the publishing world in the early part of this century and became the world's richest man for a time through a mixture of inspiration and perspiration. He was a unique and complex individual who deserves none of this cheap speculation almost sixty years after his death. Jonathan Ryle's biography concentrates perhaps a little too much on adolescent conspiracy theories and not enough on the contribution one man tried to make for a better future. Let my father rest in peace. ■

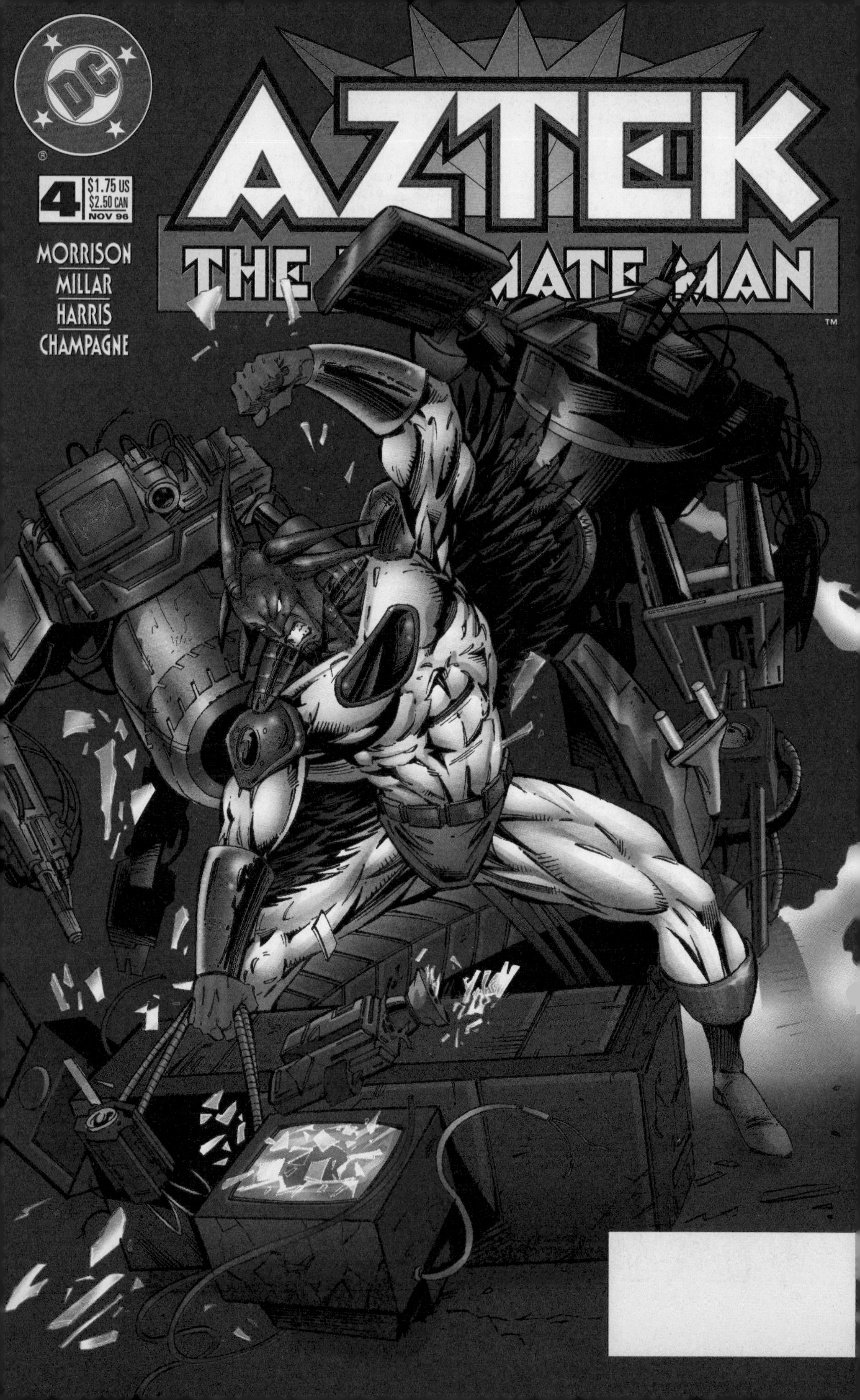
DC
AZTEK
THE ULTIMATE MAN
4
$1.75 US
$2.50 CAN
NOV 96
MORRISON
MILLAR
HARRIS
CHAMPAGNE
™

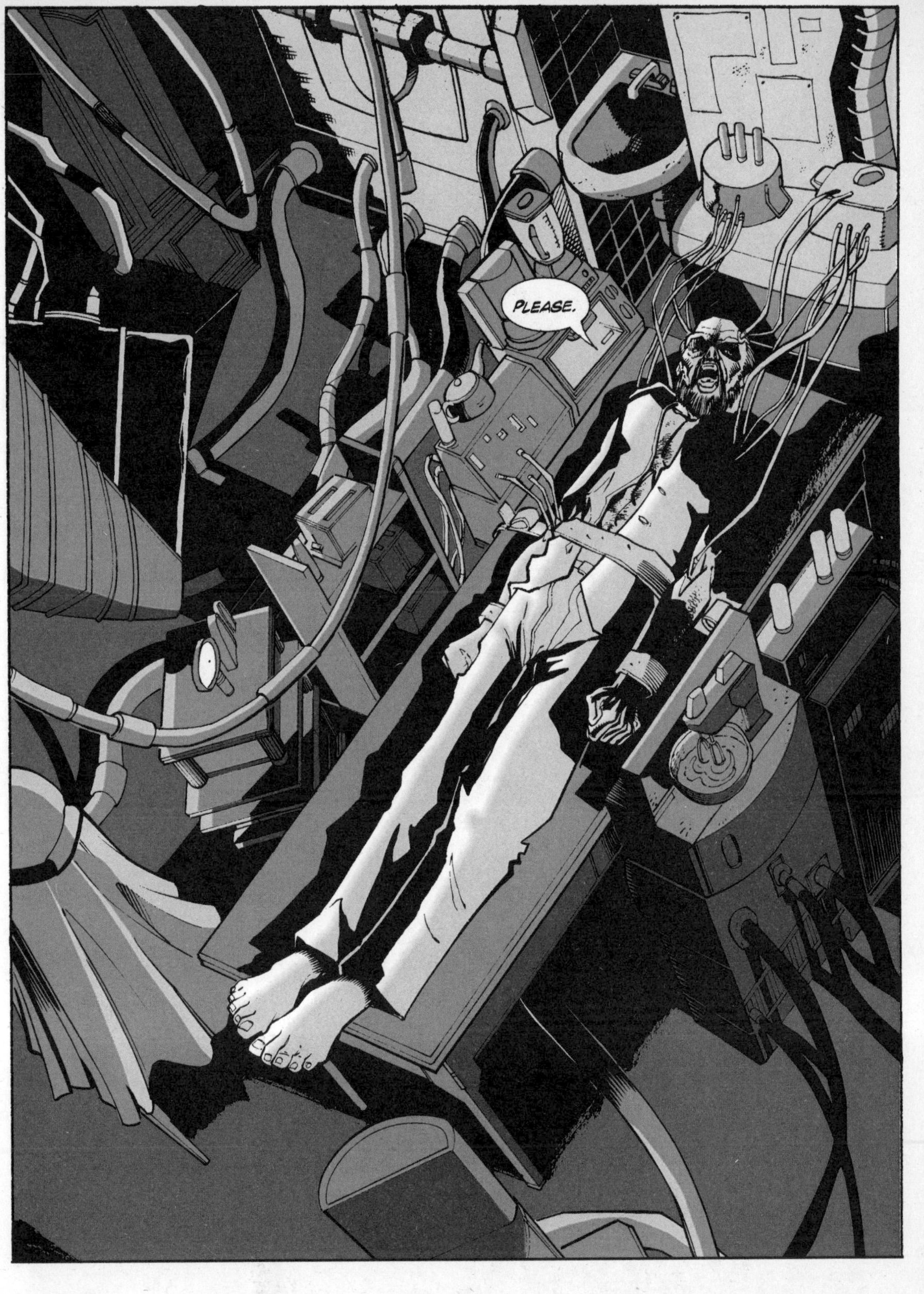
PLEASE.

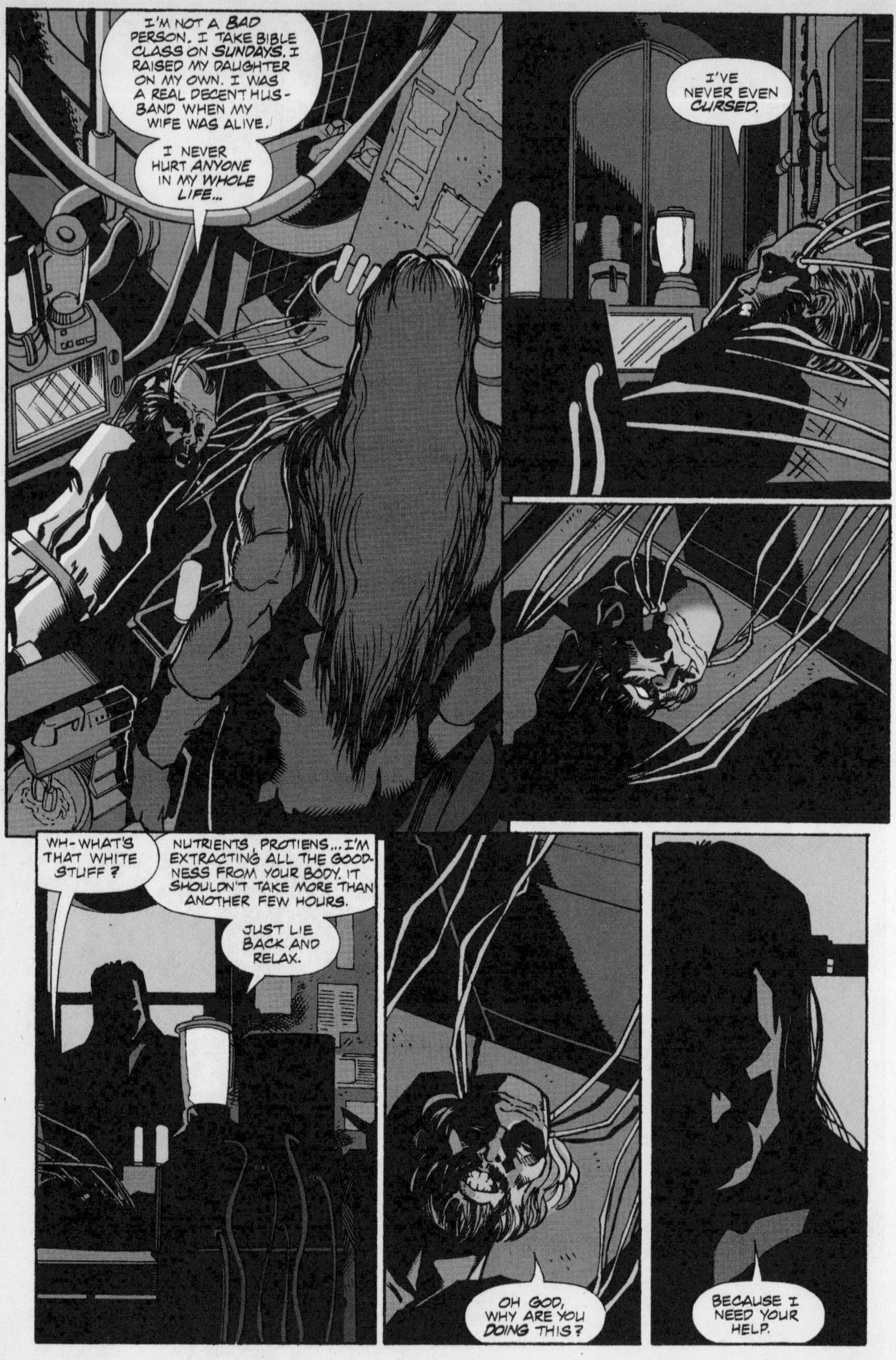

I'M NOT A BAD PERSON. I TAKE BIBLE CLASS ON SUNDAYS. I RAISED MY DAUGHTER ON MY OWN. I WAS A REAL DECENT HUS-BAND WHEN MY WIFE WAS ALIVE.
I NEVER HURT ANYONE IN MY WHOLE LIFE...
I'VE NEVER EVEN CURSED.
WH-WHAT'S THAT WHITE STUFF?
NUTRIENTS, PROTIENS... I'M EXTRACTING ALL THE GOOD-NESS FROM YOUR BODY. IT SHOULDN'T TAKE MORE THAN ANOTHER FEW HOURS.
JUST LIE BACK AND RELAX.
OH GOD, WHY ARE YOU DOING THIS?
BECAUSE I NEED YOUR HELP.

NFF

WHAT D'YOU MEAN...?

I CAME TO VANITY BECAUSE I WANT A JOB. THE POST'S ALREADY OCCUPIED AT THE MOMENT BUT YOU'RE GOING TO HELP *REMEDY* THE SITUATION.

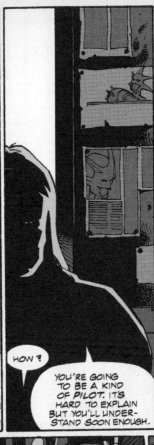

HOW?

YOU'RE GOING TO BE A KIND OF *PILOT.* IT'S HARD TO EXPLAIN BUT YOU'LL UNDERSTAND SOON ENOUGH.

I CHOSE YOU AND YOUR UNIT BECAUSE OF THE INHERENT DECENCY YOU SHARE. THE PURE SHOULD BE SPARED THE HORRORS WHICH ARE TO COME.

UNIT? WH-WHAT UNIT?

YOUR DAUGHTER, OF COURSE.

SHE WAS A GOOD DEAL SMALLER THAN YOU TO BEGIN WITH. PROBABLY CONSUMED LESS FATTY FOOD AND CANDY BARS. HER MODIFICATION TOOK HALF THE TIME.

AW NO PLEEASE...

SHE'S GOING TO BE YOUR CO-PILOT.

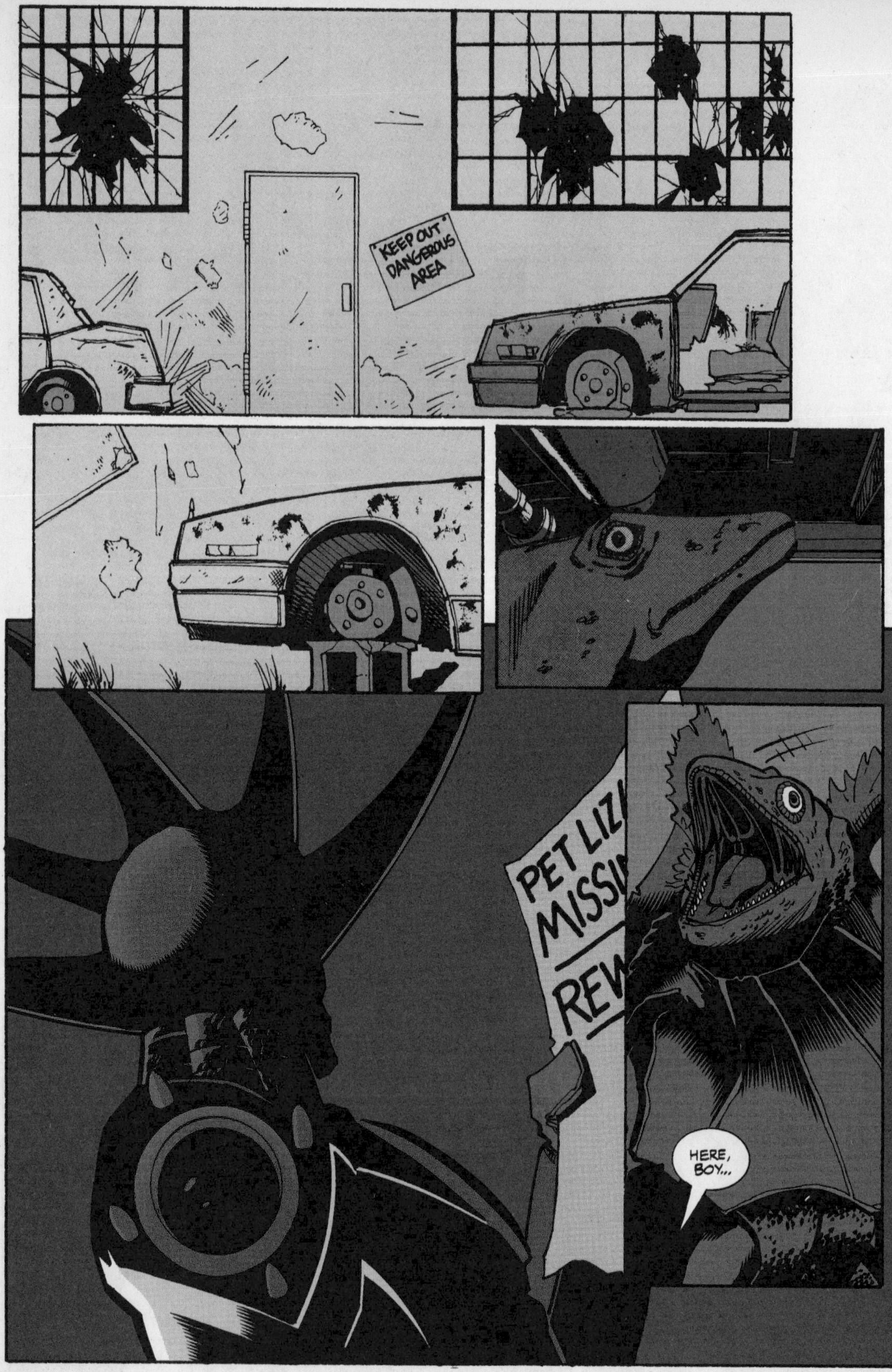
KEEP OUT DANGEROUS AREA
PET LIZ
MISSI
REW
HERE, BOY...

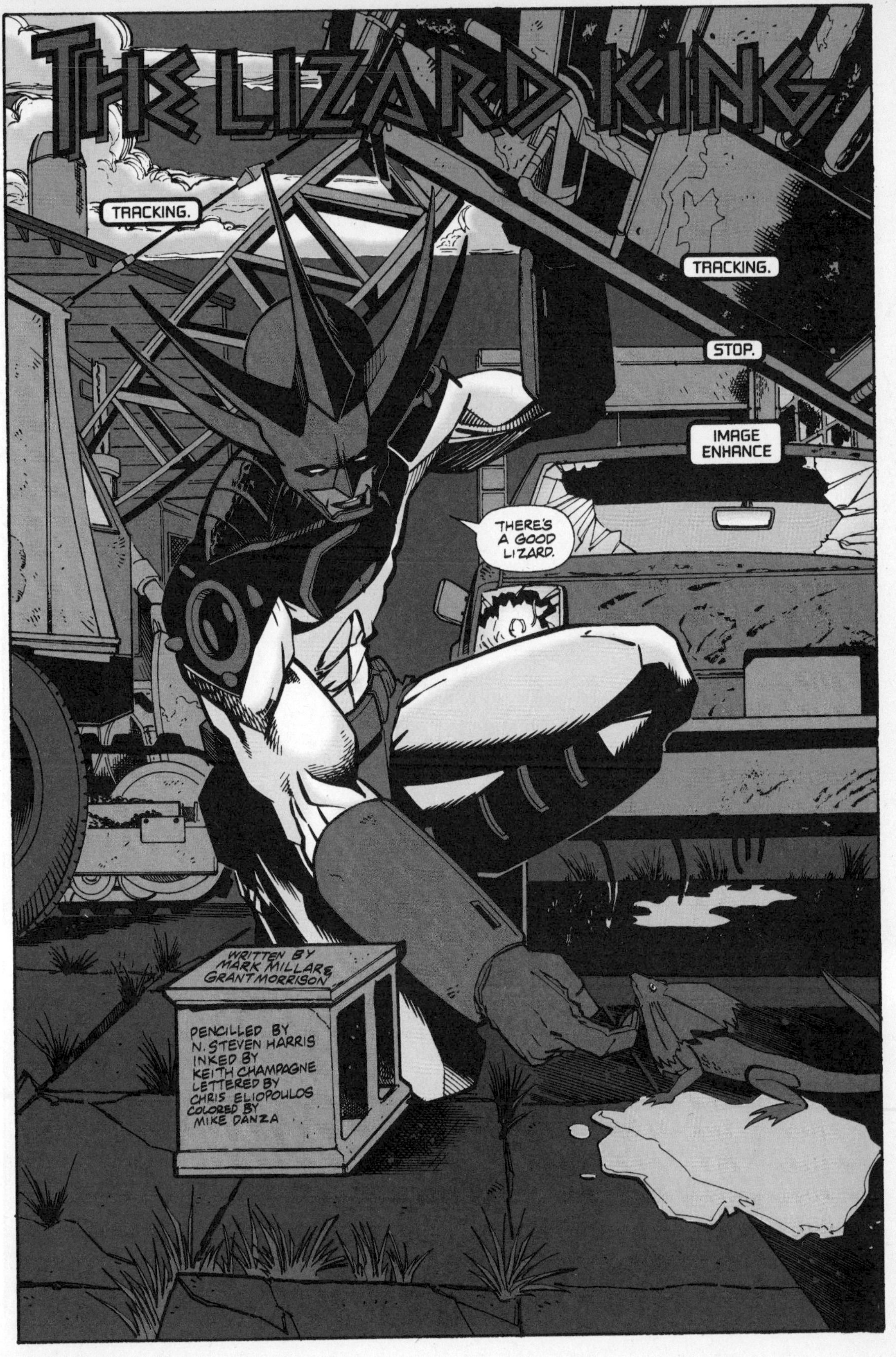
THE LIZARD KING
TRACKING.
TRACKING.
STOP.
IMAGE ENHANCE
THERE'S A GOOD LIZARD.
WRITTEN BY MARK MILLAR & GRANT MORRISON
PENCILLED BY N. STEVEN HARRIS
INKED BY KEITH CHAMPAGNE
LETTERED BY CHRIS ELIOPOULOS
COLORED BY MIKE DANZA

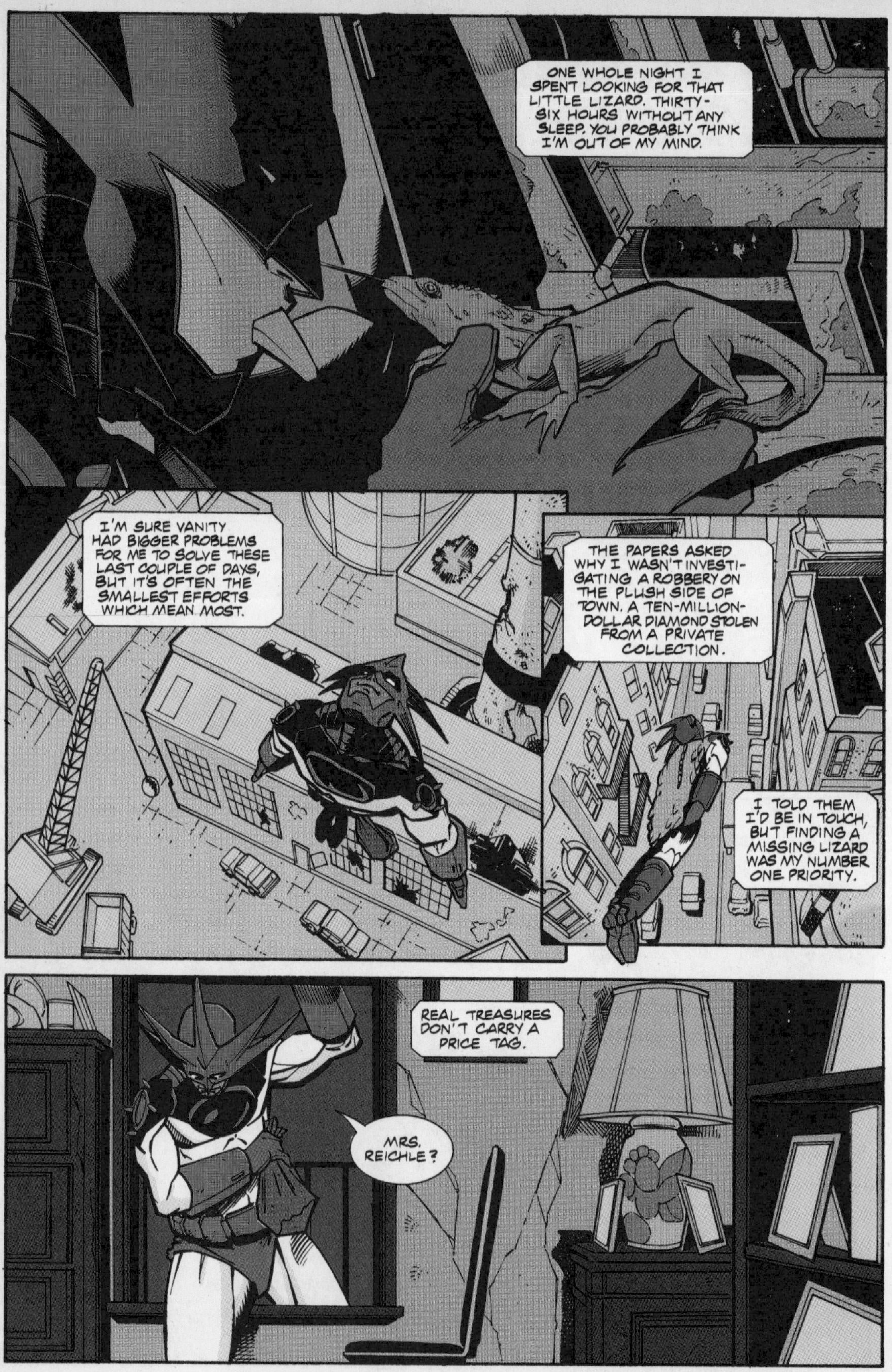
ONE WHOLE NIGHT I SPENT LOOKING FOR THAT LITTLE LIZARD. THIRTY-SIX HOURS WITHOUT ANY SLEEP. YOU PROBABLY THINK I'M OUT OF MY MIND.
I'M SURE VANITY HAD BIGGER PROBLEMS FOR ME TO SOLVE THESE LAST COUPLE OF DAYS, BUT IT'S OFTEN THE SMALLEST EFFORTS WHICH MEAN MOST.
THE PAPERS ASKED WHY I WASN'T INVESTIGATING A ROBBERY ON THE PLUSH SIDE OF TOWN. A TEN-MILLION-DOLLAR DIAMOND STOLEN FROM A PRIVATE COLLECTION.
I TOLD THEM I'D BE IN TOUCH, BUT FINDING A MISSING LIZARD WAS MY NUMBER ONE PRIORITY.
REAL TREASURES DON'T CARRY A PRICE TAG.
MRS. REICHLE?

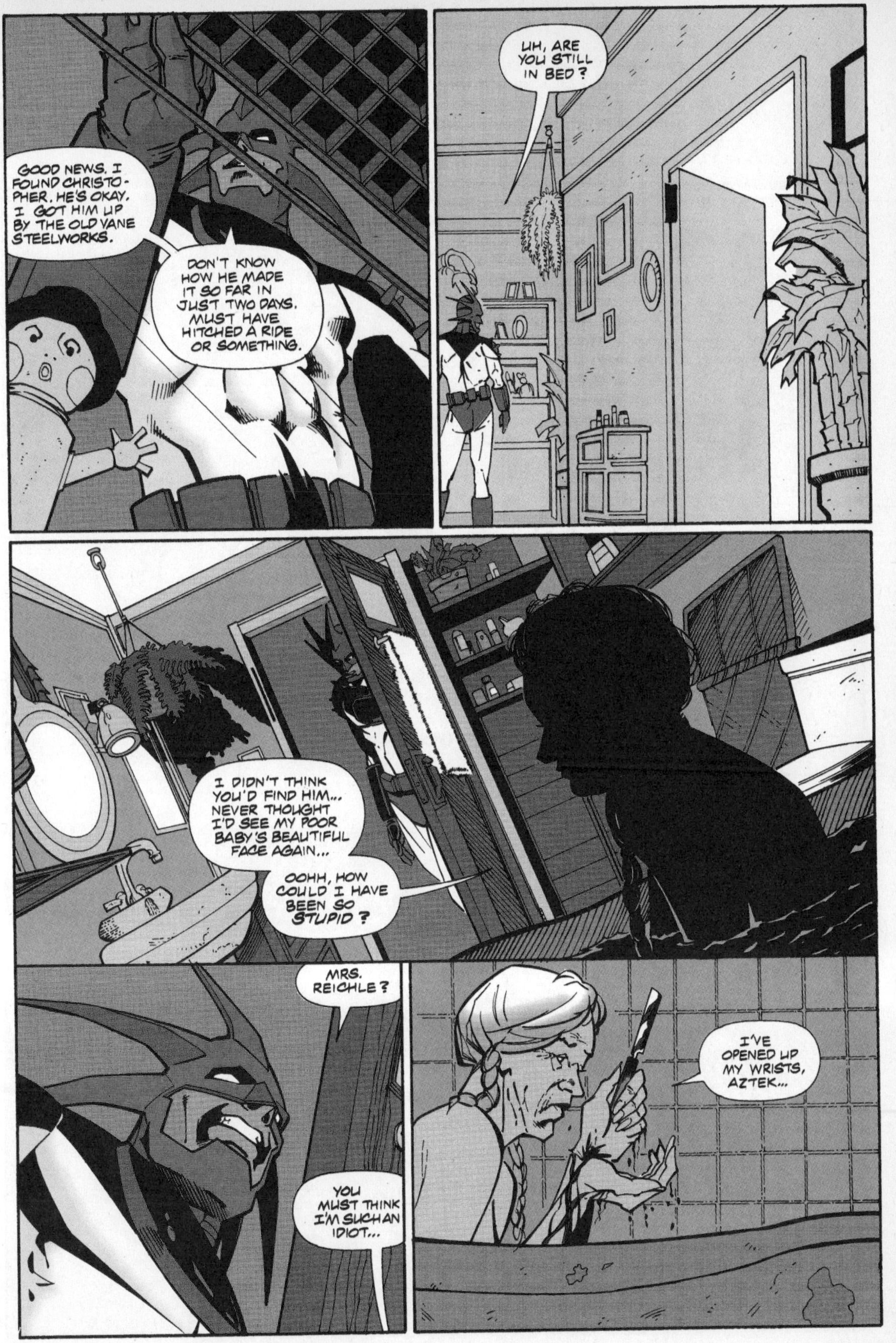
GOOD NEWS. I FOUND CHRISTO-PHER. HE'S OKAY. I GOT HIM UP BY THE OLD VANE STEELWORKS.
DON'T KNOW HOW HE MADE IT SO FAR IN JUST TWO DAYS. MUST HAVE HITCHED A RIDE OR SOMETHING.
UH, ARE YOU STILL IN BED?
I DIDN'T THINK YOU'D FIND HIM... NEVER THOUGHT I'D SEE MY POOR BABY'S BEAUTIFUL FACE AGAIN...
OOHH, HOW COULD I HAVE BEEN SO STUPID?
MRS. REICHLE?
YOU MUST THINK I'M SUCH AN IDIOT...
I'VE OPENED UP MY WRISTS, AZTEK...

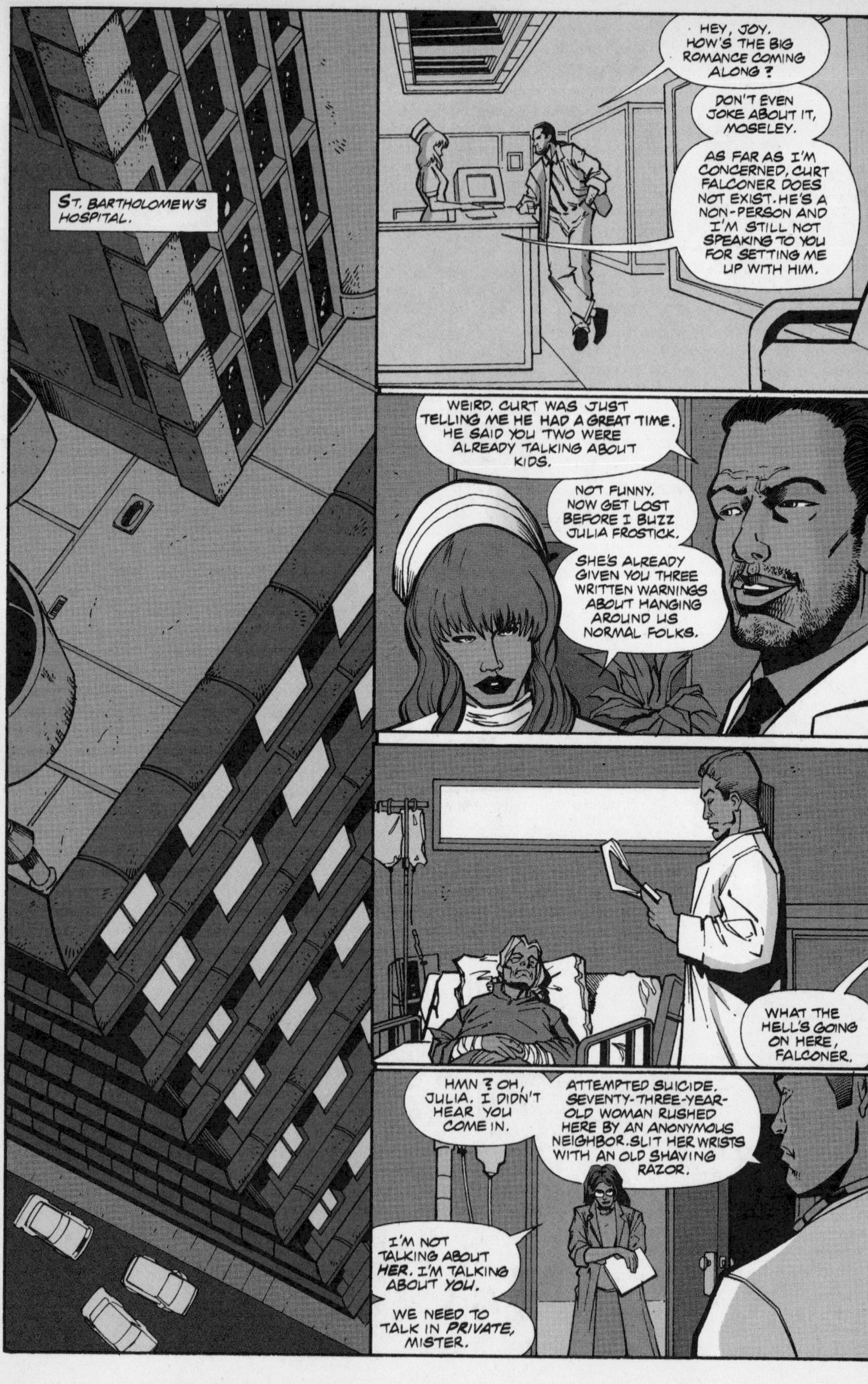
ST. BARTHOLOMEW'S HOSPITAL.
HEY, JOY. HOW'S THE BIG ROMANCE COMING ALONG?
DON'T EVEN JOKE ABOUT IT, MOSELEY.
AS FAR AS I'M CONCERNED, CURT FALCONER DOES NOT EXIST. HE'S A NON-PERSON AND I'M STILL NOT SPEAKING TO YOU FOR SETTING ME UP WITH HIM.
WEIRD. CURT WAS JUST TELLING ME HE HAD A GREAT TIME. HE SAID YOU TWO WERE ALREADY TALKING ABOUT KIDS.
NOT FUNNY. NOW GET LOST BEFORE I BUZZ JULIA FROSTICK.
SHE'S ALREADY GIVEN YOU THREE WRITTEN WARNINGS ABOUT HANGING AROUND US NORMAL FOLKS.
WHAT THE HELL'S GOING ON HERE, FALCONER.
HMN? OH, JULIA. I DIDN'T HEAR YOU COME IN.
ATTEMPTED SUICIDE. SEVENTY-THREE-YEAR-OLD WOMAN RUSHED HERE BY AN ANONYMOUS NEIGHBOR. SLIT HER WRISTS WITH AN OLD SHAVING RAZOR.
I'M NOT TALKING ABOUT HER. I'M TALKING ABOUT YOU.
WE NEED TO TALK IN PRIVATE, MISTER.

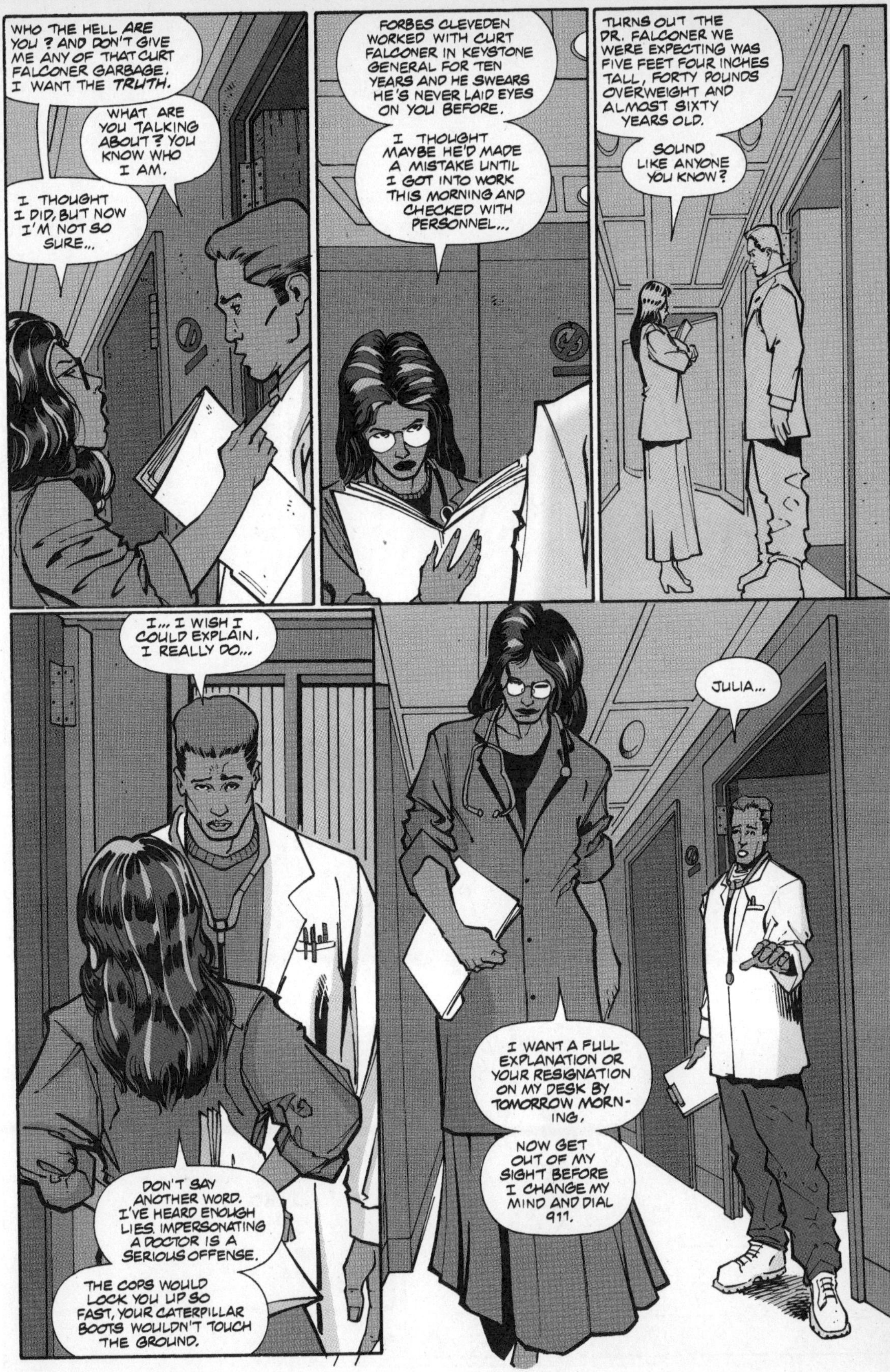
WHO THE HELL ARE YOU ? AND DON'T GIVE ME ANY OF THAT CURT FALCONER GARBAGE. I WANT THE TRUTH.
WHAT ARE YOU TALKING ABOUT? YOU KNOW WHO I AM.
I THOUGHT I DID, BUT NOW I'M NOT SO SURE...
FORBES CLEVEDEN WORKED WITH CURT FALCONER IN KEYSTONE GENERAL FOR TEN YEARS AND HE SWEARS HE'S NEVER LAID EYES ON YOU BEFORE.
I THOUGHT MAYBE HE'D MADE A MISTAKE UNTIL I GOT INTO WORK THIS MORNING AND CHECKED WITH PERSONNEL...
TURNS OUT THE DR. FALCONER WE WERE EXPECTING WAS FIVE FEET FOUR INCHES TALL, FORTY POUNDS OVERWEIGHT AND ALMOST SIXTY YEARS OLD.
SOUND LIKE ANYONE YOU KNOW?
I... I WISH I COULD EXPLAIN. I REALLY DO...
DON'T SAY ANOTHER WORD. I'VE HEARD ENOUGH LIES. IMPERSONATING A DOCTOR IS A SERIOUS OFFENSE.
THE COPS WOULD LOCK YOU UP SO FAST, YOUR CATERPILLAR BOOTS WOULDN'T TOUCH THE GROUND.
I WANT A FULL EXPLANATION OR YOUR RESIGNATION ON MY DESK BY TOMORROW MORN-ING.
NOW GET OUT OF MY SIGHT BEFORE I CHANGE MY MIND AND DIAL 911.
JULIA...

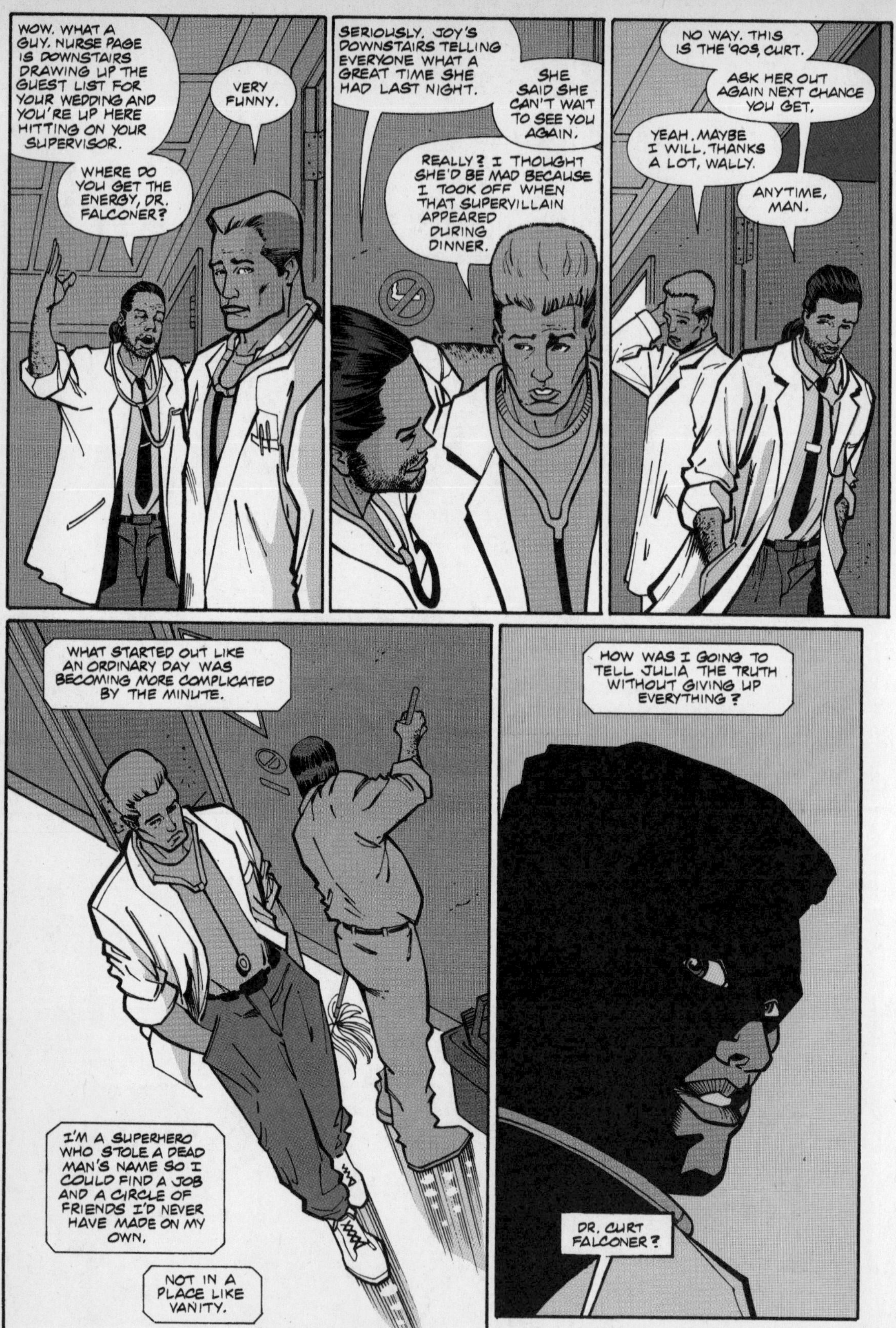
WOW. WHAT A GUY. NURSE PAGE IS DOWNSTAIRS DRAWING UP THE GUEST LIST FOR YOUR WEDDING AND YOU'RE UP HERE HITTING ON YOUR SUPERVISOR.
VERY FUNNY.
WHERE DO YOU GET THE ENERGY, DR. FALCONER?
SERIOUSLY. JOY'S DOWNSTAIRS TELLING EVERYONE WHAT A GREAT TIME SHE HAD LAST NIGHT.
SHE SAID SHE CAN'T WAIT TO SEE YOU AGAIN.
REALLY? I THOUGHT SHE'D BE MAD BECAUSE I TOOK OFF WHEN THAT SUPERVILLAIN APPEARED DURING DINNER.
NO WAY. THIS IS THE '90S, CURT.
ASK HER OUT AGAIN NEXT CHANCE YOU GET.
YEAH, MAYBE I WILL. THANKS A LOT, WALLY.
ANYTIME, MAN.
WHAT STARTED OUT LIKE AN ORDINARY DAY WAS BECOMING MORE COMPLICATED BY THE MINUTE.
I'M A SUPERHERO WHO STOLE A DEAD MAN'S NAME SO I COULD FIND A JOB AND A CIRCLE OF FRIENDS I'D NEVER HAVE MADE ON MY OWN.
NOT IN A PLACE LIKE VANITY.
HOW WAS I GOING TO TELL JULIA THE TRUTH WITHOUT GIVING UP EVERYTHING?
DR. CURT FALCONER?

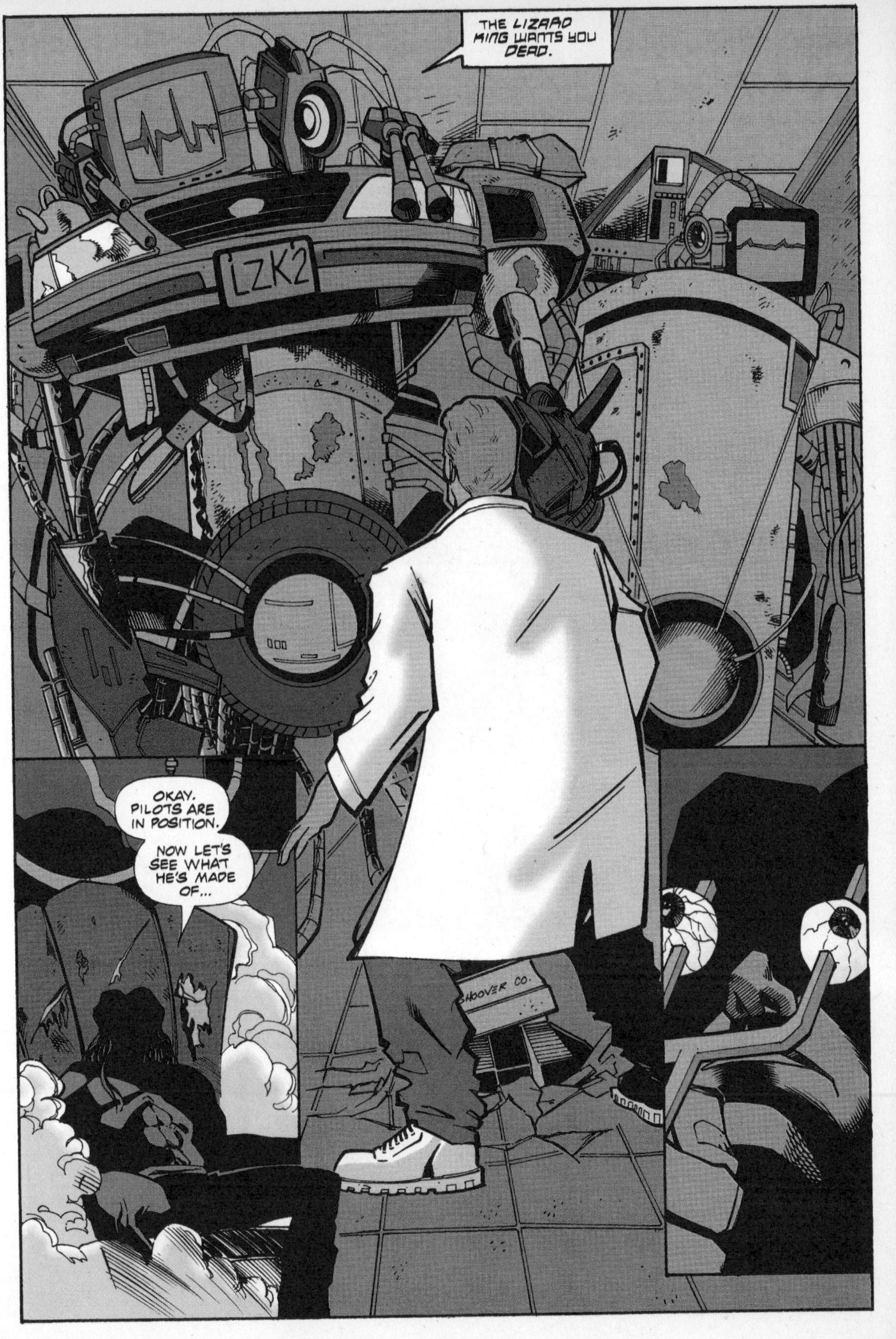
THE LIZARD KING WANTS YOU DEAD.
LZK2
OKAY. PILOTS ARE IN POSITION.
NOW LET'S SEE WHAT HE'S MADE OF...
SHOOVER CO.

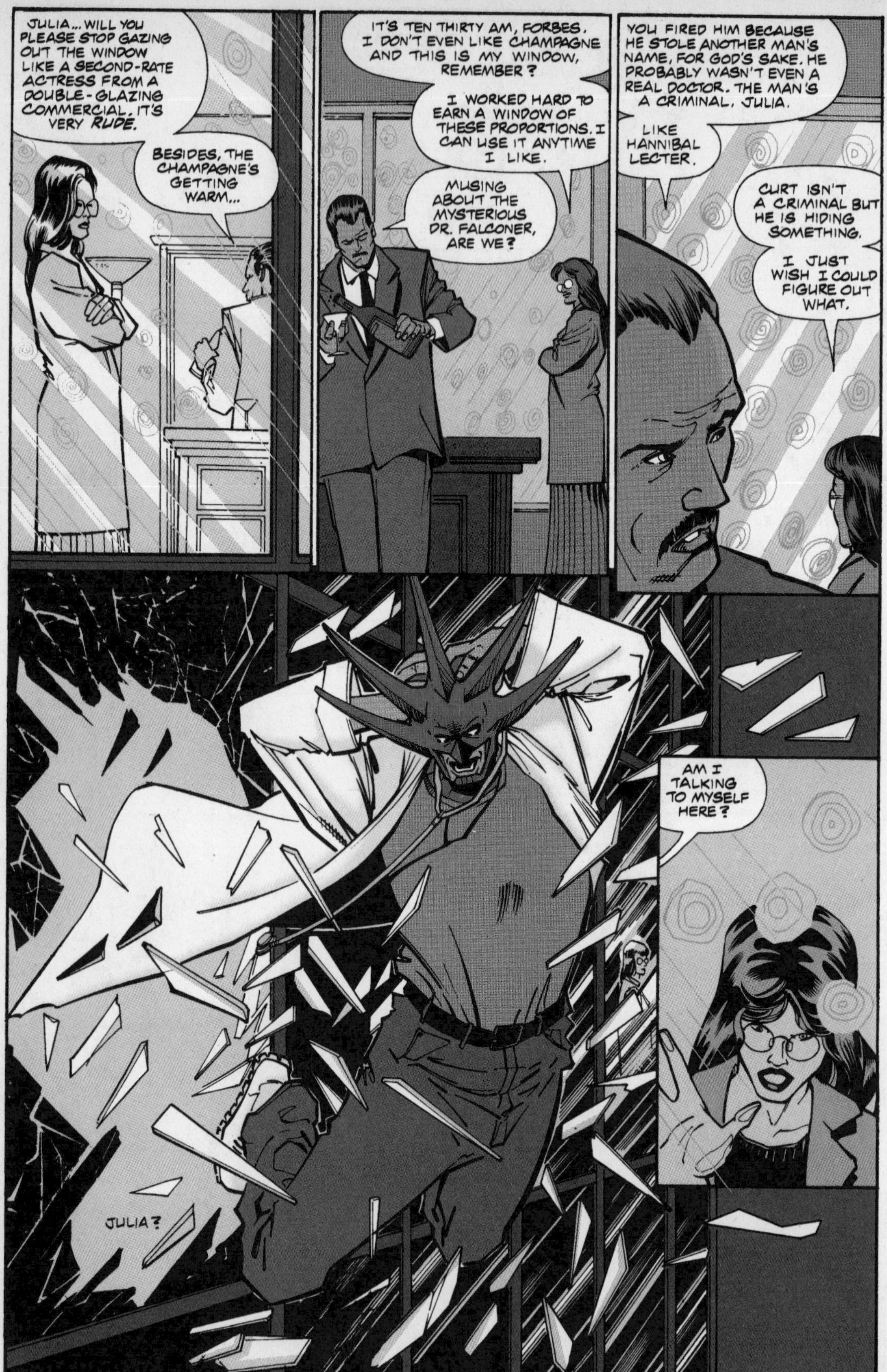
JULIA... WILL YOU PLEASE STOP GAZING OUT THE WINDOW LIKE A SECOND-RATE ACTRESS FROM A DOUBLE-GLAZING COMMERCIAL. IT'S VERY RUDE.
BESIDES, THE CHAMPAGNE'S GETTING WARM...
IT'S TEN THIRTY AM, FORBES. I DON'T EVEN LIKE CHAMPAGNE AND THIS IS MY WINDOW, REMEMBER?
I WORKED HARD TO EARN A WINDOW OF THESE PROPORTIONS. I CAN USE IT ANYTIME I LIKE.
MUSING ABOUT THE MYSTERIOUS DR. FALCONER, ARE WE?
YOU FIRED HIM BECAUSE HE STOLE ANOTHER MAN'S NAME, FOR GOD'S SAKE. HE PROBABLY WASN'T EVEN A REAL DOCTOR. THE MAN'S A CRIMINAL, JULIA.
LIKE HANNIBAL LECTER.
CURT ISN'T A CRIMINAL BUT HE IS HIDING SOMETHING.
I JUST WISH I COULD FIGURE OUT WHAT.
AM I TALKING TO MYSELF HERE?
JULIA?

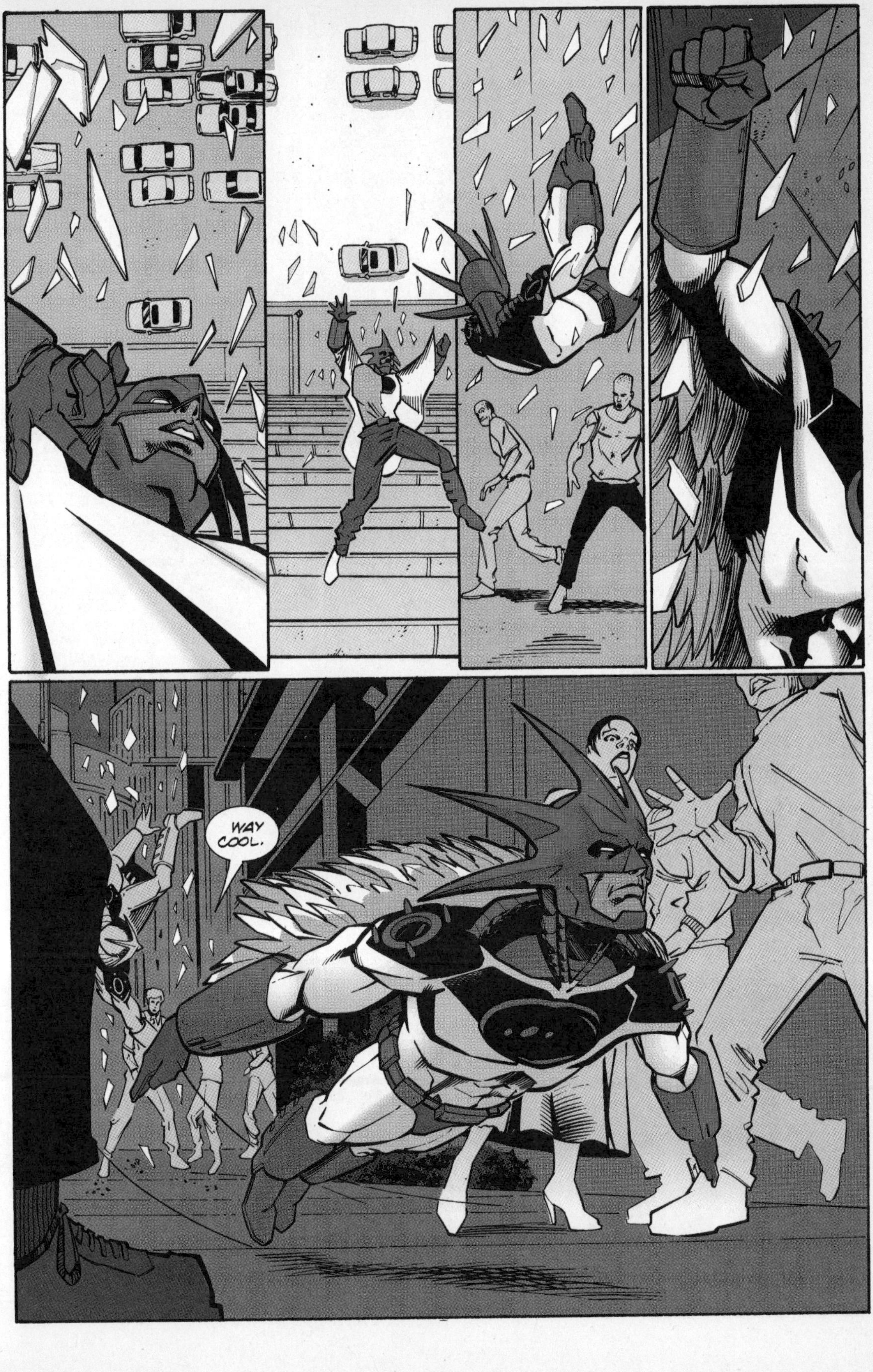
WAY COOL.

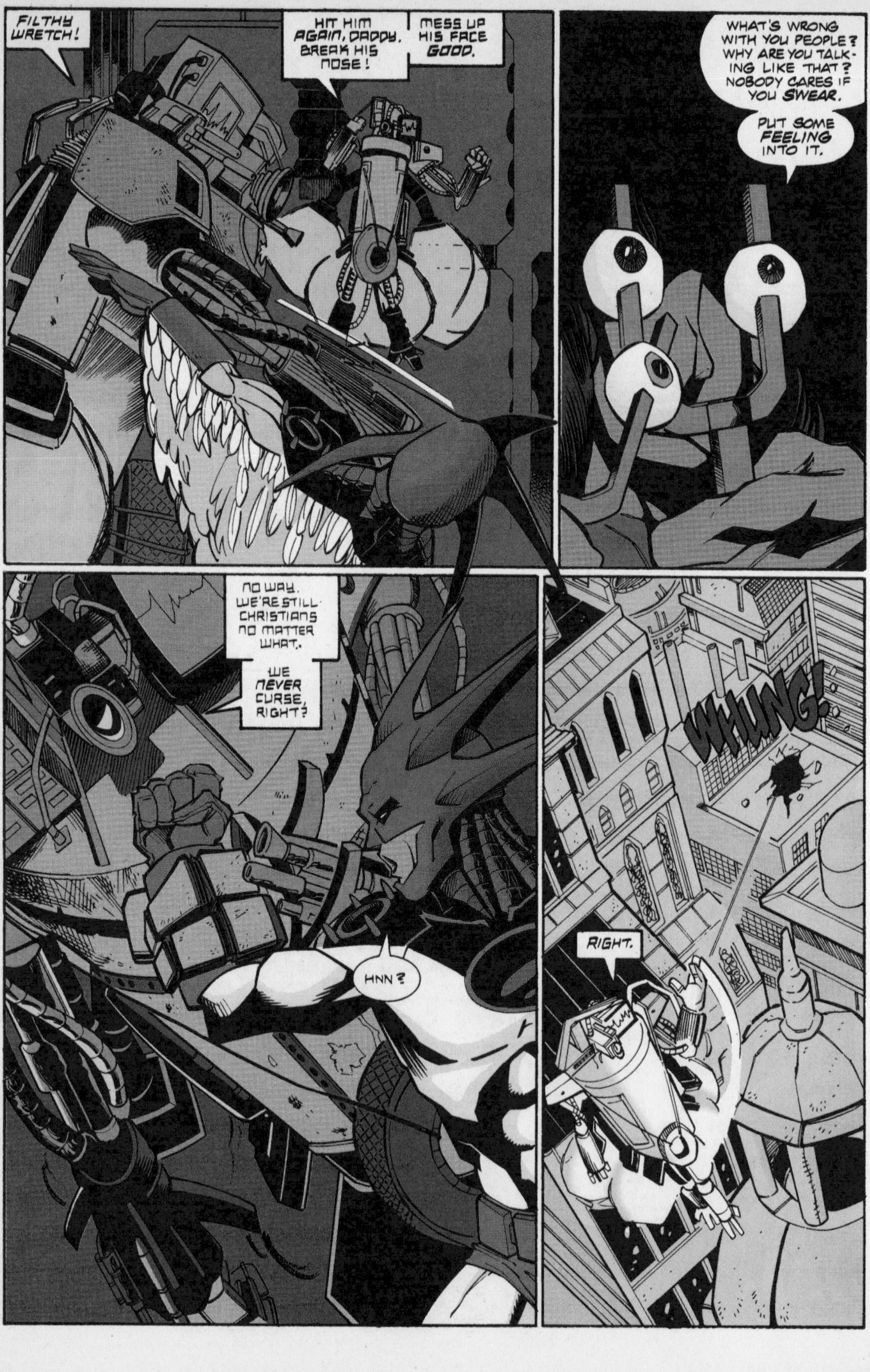
FILTHY WRETCH!
HIT HIM AGAIN, DADDY. BREAK HIS NOSE!
MESS UP HIS FACE GOOD.
WHAT'S WRONG WITH YOU PEOPLE? WHY ARE YOU TALKING LIKE THAT? NOBODY CARES IF YOU SWEAR.
PUT SOME FEELING INTO IT.
NO WAY. WE'RE STILL CHRISTIANS NO MATTER WHAT.
WE NEVER CURSE, RIGHT?
HNN?
RIGHT.
WHUNG!

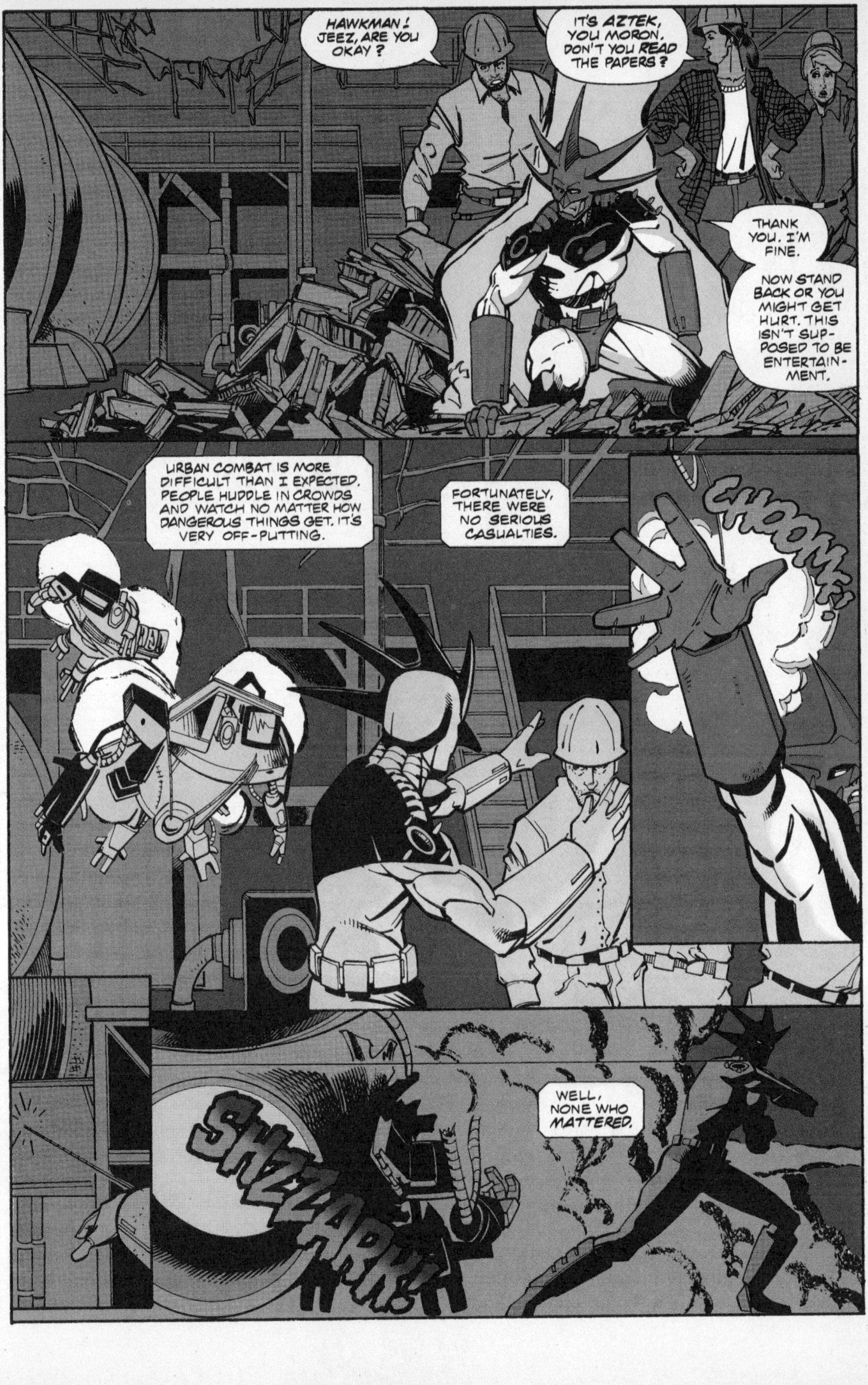
HAWKMAN! JEEZ, ARE YOU OKAY?
IT'S AZTEK, YOU MORON. DON'T YOU READ THE PAPERS?
THANK YOU. I'M FINE.
NOW STAND BACK OR YOU MIGHT GET HURT. THIS ISN'T SUP-POSED TO BE ENTERTAIN-MENT.
URBAN COMBAT IS MORE DIFFICULT THAN I EXPECTED. PEOPLE HUDDLE IN CROWDS AND WATCH NO MATTER HOW DANGEROUS THINGS GET. IT'S VERY OFF-PUTTING.
FORTUNATELY, THERE WERE NO SERIOUS CASUALTIES.
CHOOMK!
WELL, NONE WHO MATTERED.
SHZZARK!

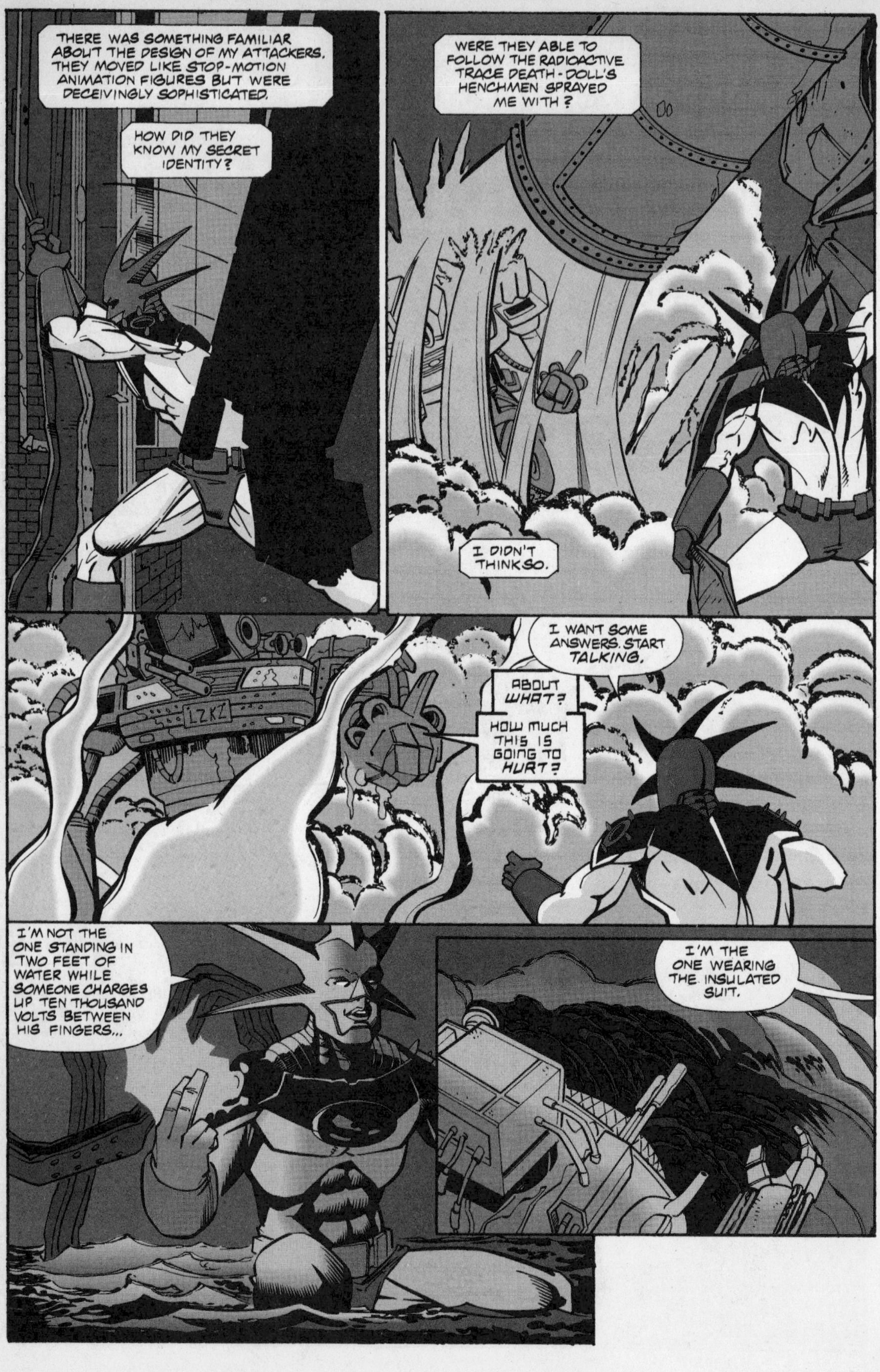

THERE WAS SOMETHING FAMILIAR ABOUT THE DESIGN OF MY ATTACKERS. THEY MOVED LIKE STOP-MOTION ANIMATION FIGURES BUT WERE DECEIVINGLY SOPHISTICATED.
HOW DID THEY KNOW MY SECRET IDENTITY?
WERE THEY ABLE TO FOLLOW THE RADIOACTIVE TRACE DEATH-DOLL'S HENCHMEN SPRAYED ME WITH?
I DIDN'T THINK SO.
I WANT SOME ANSWERS. START TALKING.
ABOUT WHAT?
HOW MUCH THIS IS GOING TO HURT?
I'M NOT THE ONE STANDING IN TWO FEET OF WATER WHILE SOMEONE CHARGES UP TEN THOUSAND VOLTS BETWEEN HIS FINGERS...
I'M THE ONE WEARING THE INSULATED SUIT.

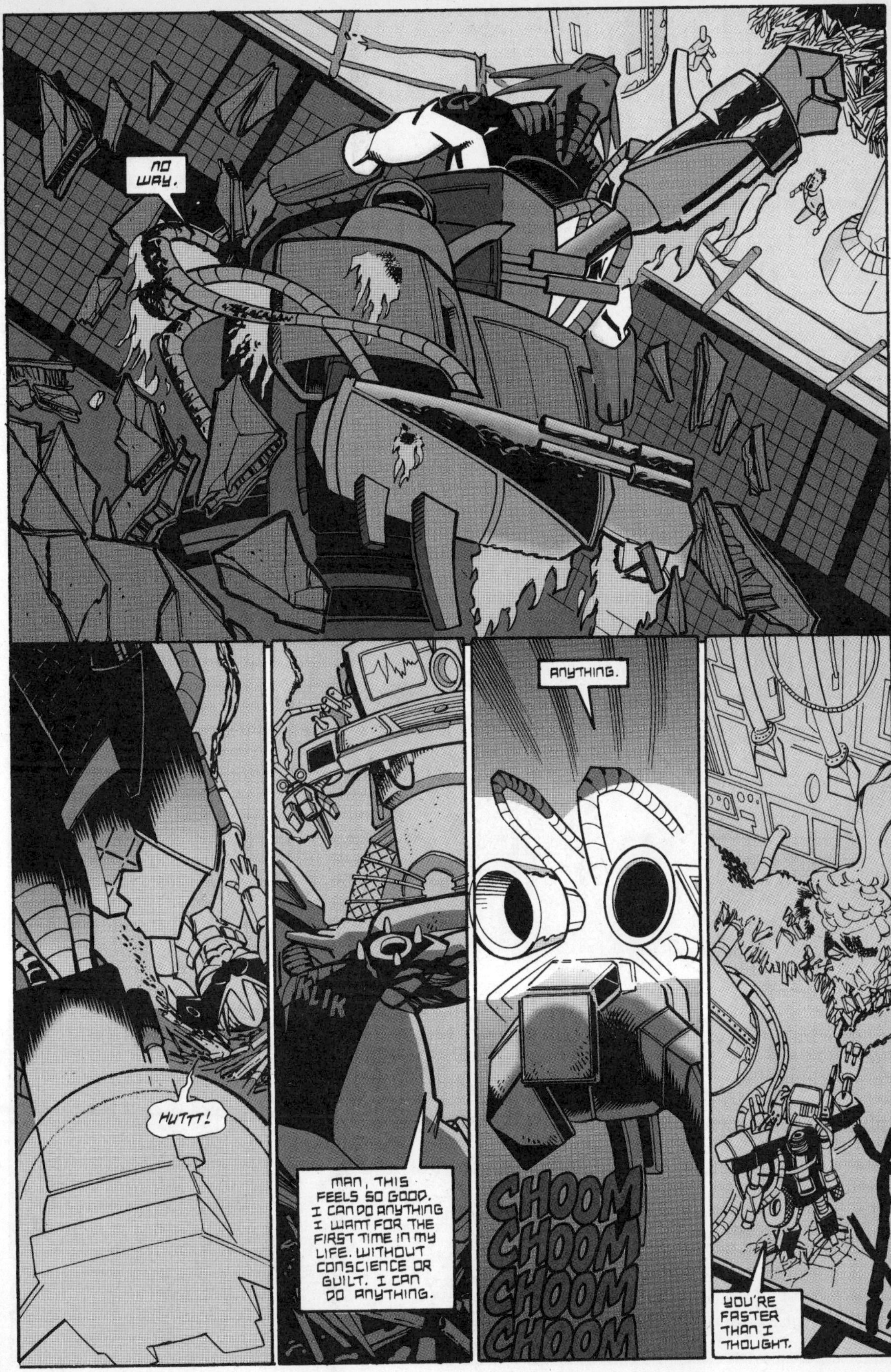
NO WAY.
HUTTT!
KLIK
MAN, THIS FEELS SO GOOD. I CAN DO ANYTHING I WANT FOR THE FIRST TIME IN MY LIFE. WITHOUT CONSCIENCE OR GUILT. I CAN DO ANYTHING.
ANYTHING.
CHOOM CHOOM CHOOM CHOOM
YOU'RE FASTER THAN I THOUGHT.

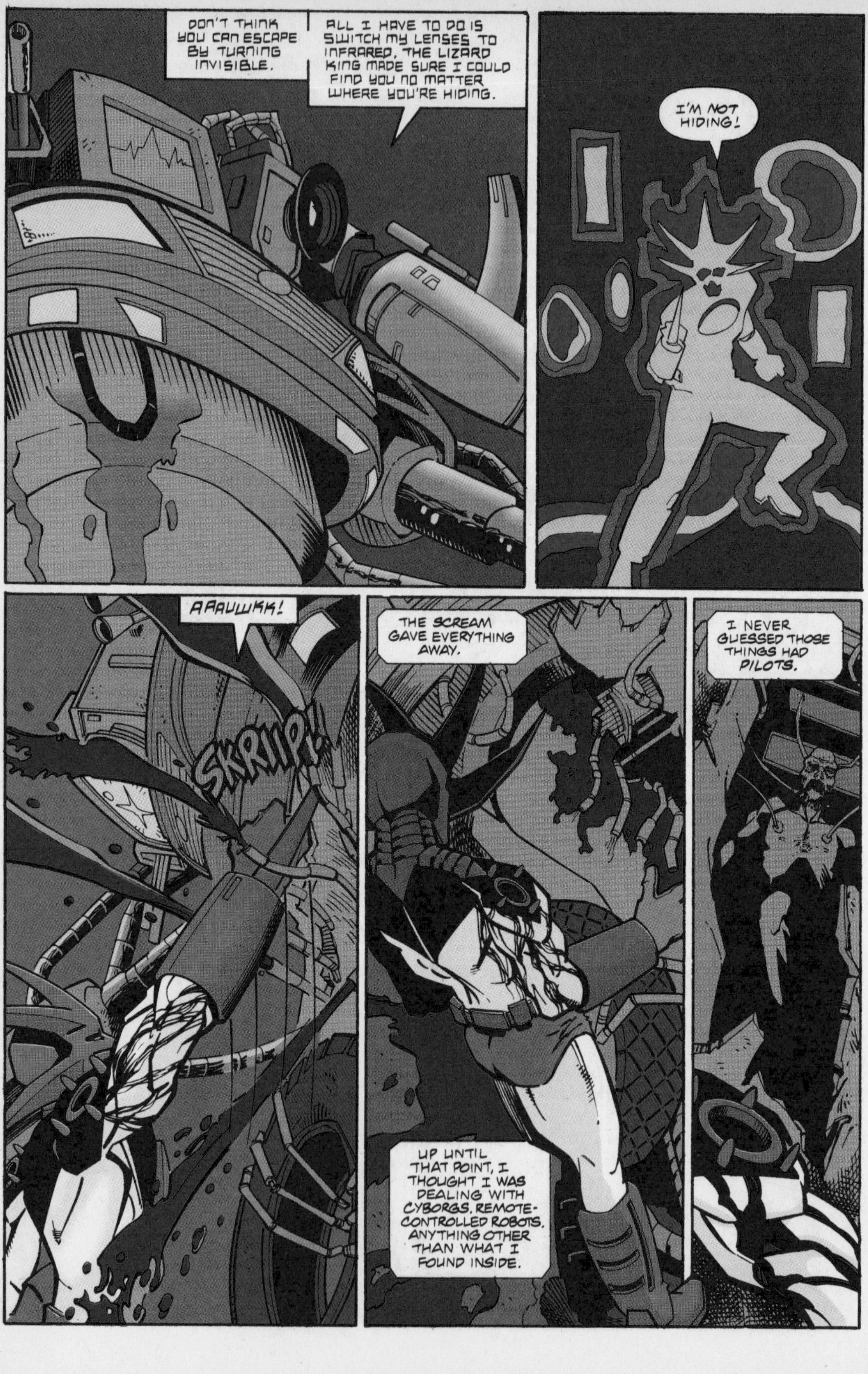
DON'T THINK YOU CAN ESCAPE BY TURNING INVISIBLE.
ALL I HAVE TO DO IS SWITCH MY LENSES TO INFRARED, THE LIZARD KING MADE SURE I COULD FIND YOU NO MATTER WHERE YOU'RE HIDING.
I'M NOT HIDING!
AARUWKK!
SKRIIP!
THE SCREAM GAVE EVERYTHING AWAY.
UP UNTIL THAT POINT, I THOUGHT I WAS DEALING WITH CYBORGS, REMOTE-CONTROLLED ROBOTS. ANYTHING OTHER THAN WHAT I FOUND INSIDE.
I NEVER GUESSED THOSE THINGS HAD PILOTS.

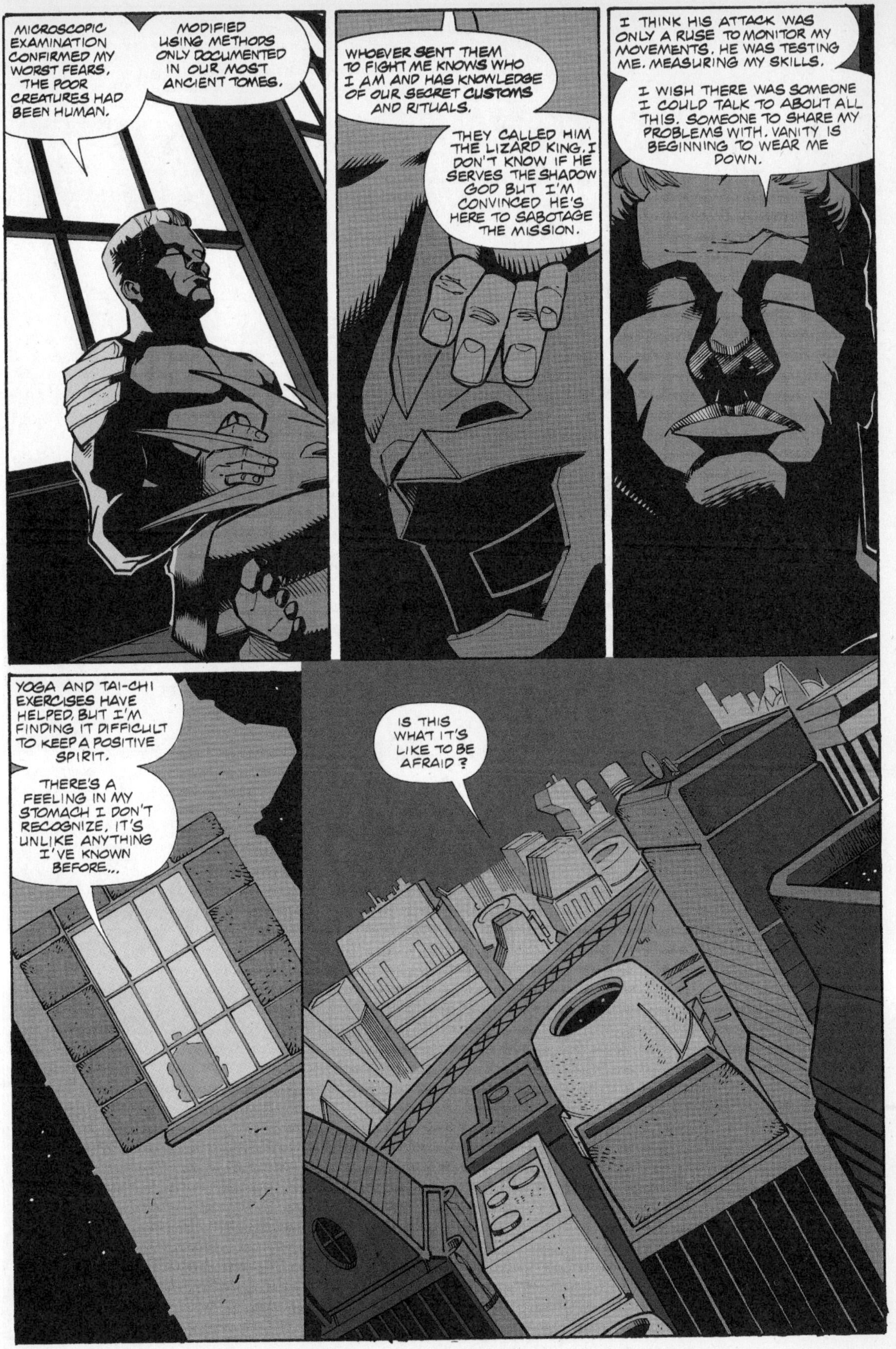
MICROSCOPIC EXAMINATION CONFIRMED MY WORST FEARS. THE POOR CREATURES HAD BEEN HUMAN.
MODIFIED USING METHODS ONLY DOCUMENTED IN OUR MOST ANCIENT TOMES.
WHOEVER SENT THEM TO FIGHT ME KNOWS WHO I AM AND HAS KNOWLEDGE OF OUR SECRET CUSTOMS AND RITUALS.
THEY CALLED HIM THE LIZARD KING. I DON'T KNOW IF HE SERVES THE SHADOW GOD BUT I'M CONVINCED HE'S HERE TO SABOTAGE THE MISSION.
I THINK HIS ATTACK WAS ONLY A RUSE TO MONITOR MY MOVEMENTS. HE WAS TESTING ME. MEASURING MY SKILLS.
I WISH THERE WAS SOMEONE I COULD TALK TO ABOUT ALL THIS. SOMEONE TO SHARE MY PROBLEMS WITH. VANITY IS BEGINNING TO WEAR ME DOWN.
YOGA AND TAI-CHI EXERCISES HAVE HELPED, BUT I'M FINDING IT DIFFICULT TO KEEP A POSITIVE SPIRIT.
THERE'S A FEELING IN MY STOMACH I DON'T RECOGNIZE. IT'S UNLIKE ANYTHING I'VE KNOWN BEFORE...
IS THIS WHAT IT'S LIKE TO BE AFRAID?

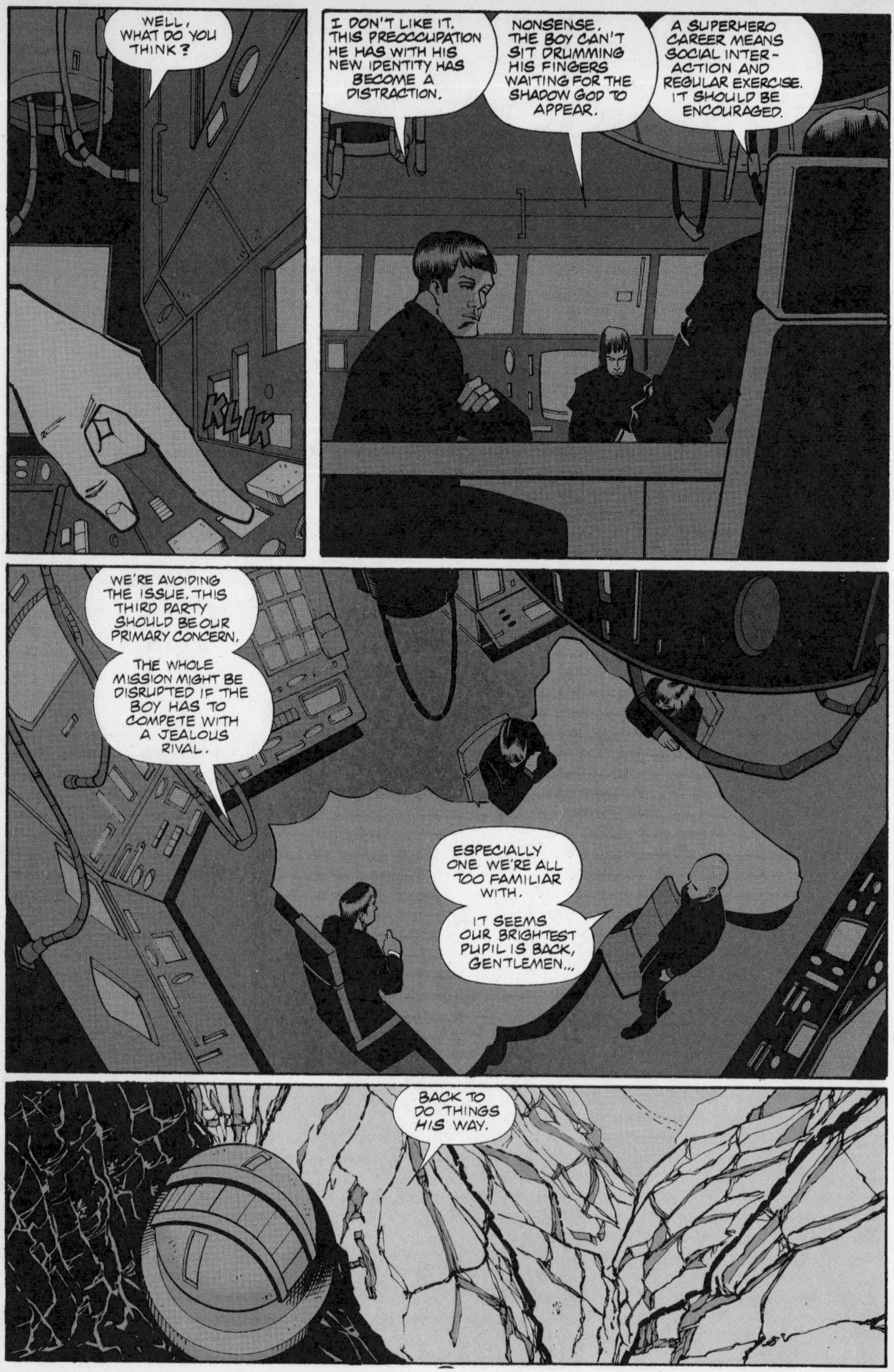
WELL, WHAT DO YOU THINK?
KLIK
I DON'T LIKE IT. THIS PREOCCUPATION HE HAS WITH HIS NEW IDENTITY HAS BECOME A DISTRACTION.
NONSENSE. THE BOY CAN'T SIT DRUMMING HIS FINGERS WAITING FOR THE SHADOW GOD TO APPEAR.
A SUPERHERO CAREER MEANS SOCIAL INTER-ACTION AND REGULAR EXERCISE. IT SHOULD BE ENCOURAGED.
WE'RE AVOIDING THE ISSUE. THIS THIRD PARTY SHOULD BE OUR PRIMARY CONCERN.
THE WHOLE MISSION MIGHT BE DISRUPTED IF THE BOY HAS TO COMPETE WITH A JEALOUS RIVAL.
ESPECIALLY ONE WE'RE ALL TOO FAMILIAR WITH.
IT SEEMS OUR BRIGHTEST PUPIL IS BACK, GENTLEMEN...
BACK TO DO THINGS HIS WAY.

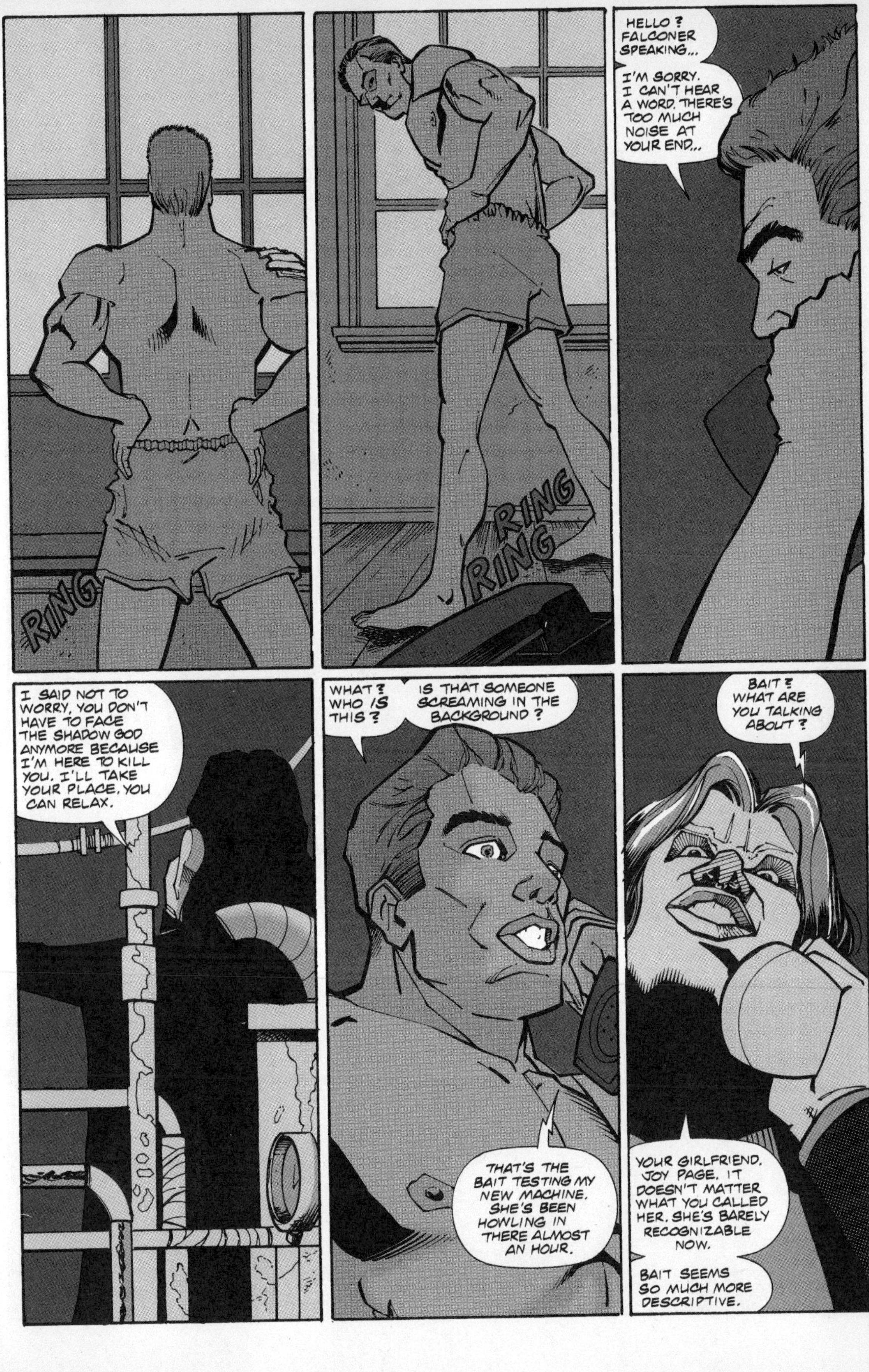
RING
RING RING
HELLO? FALCONER SPEAKING...
I'M SORRY. I CAN'T HEAR A WORD. THERE'S TOO MUCH NOISE AT YOUR END...
I SAID NOT TO WORRY. YOU DON'T HAVE TO FACE THE SHADOW GOD ANYMORE BECAUSE I'M HERE TO KILL YOU. I'LL TAKE YOUR PLACE. YOU CAN RELAX.
WHAT? WHO IS THIS?
IS THAT SOMEONE SCREAMING IN THE BACKGROUND?
THAT'S THE BAIT TESTING MY NEW MACHINE. SHE'S BEEN HOWLING IN THERE ALMOST AN HOUR.
BAIT? WHAT ARE YOU TALKING ABOUT?
YOUR GIRLFRIEND. JOY PAGE. IT DOESN'T MATTER WHAT YOU CALLED HER. SHE'S BARELY RECOGNIZABLE NOW.
BAIT SEEMS SO MUCH MORE DESCRIPTIVE.

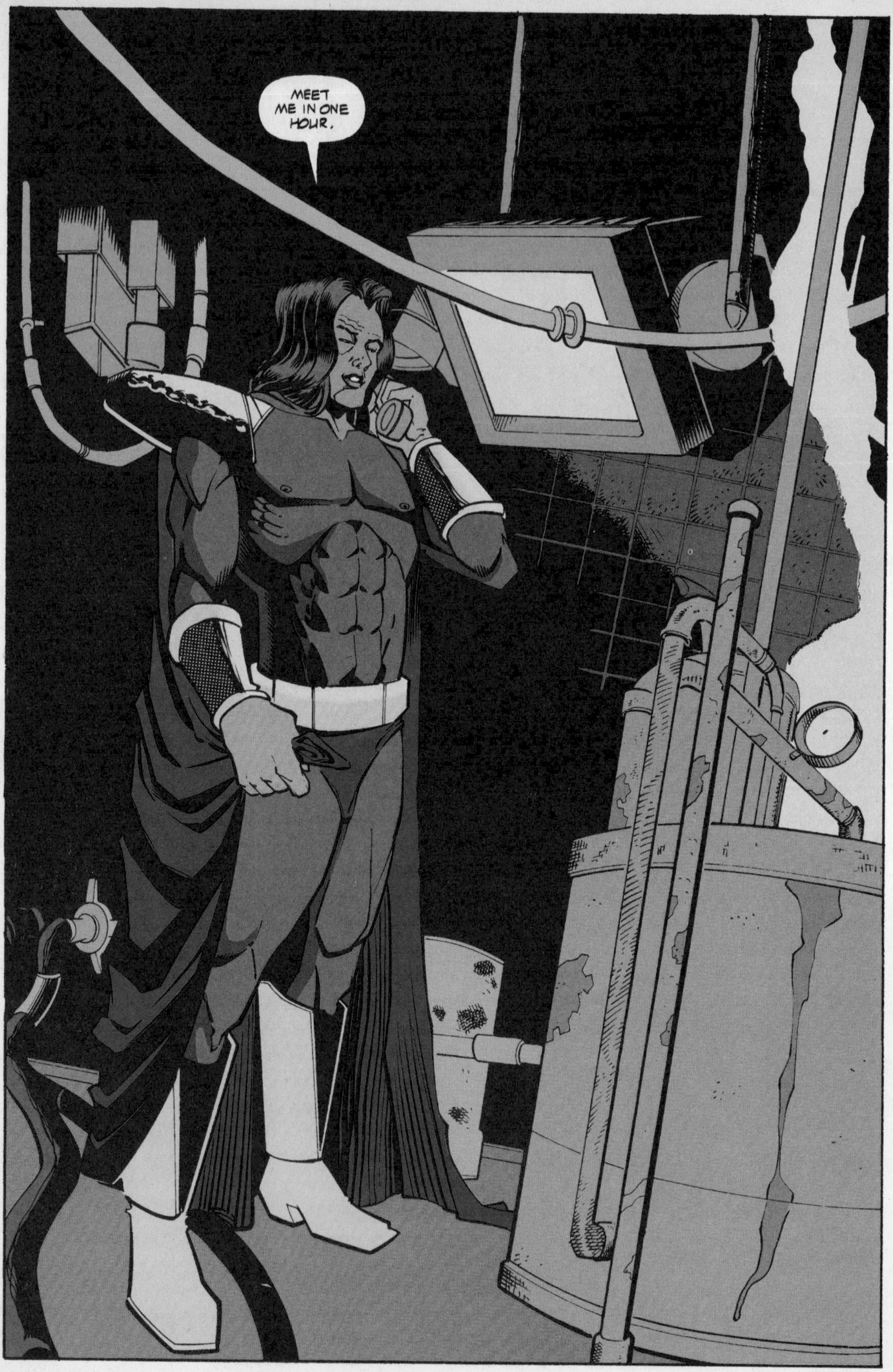
MEET ME IN ONE HOUR.

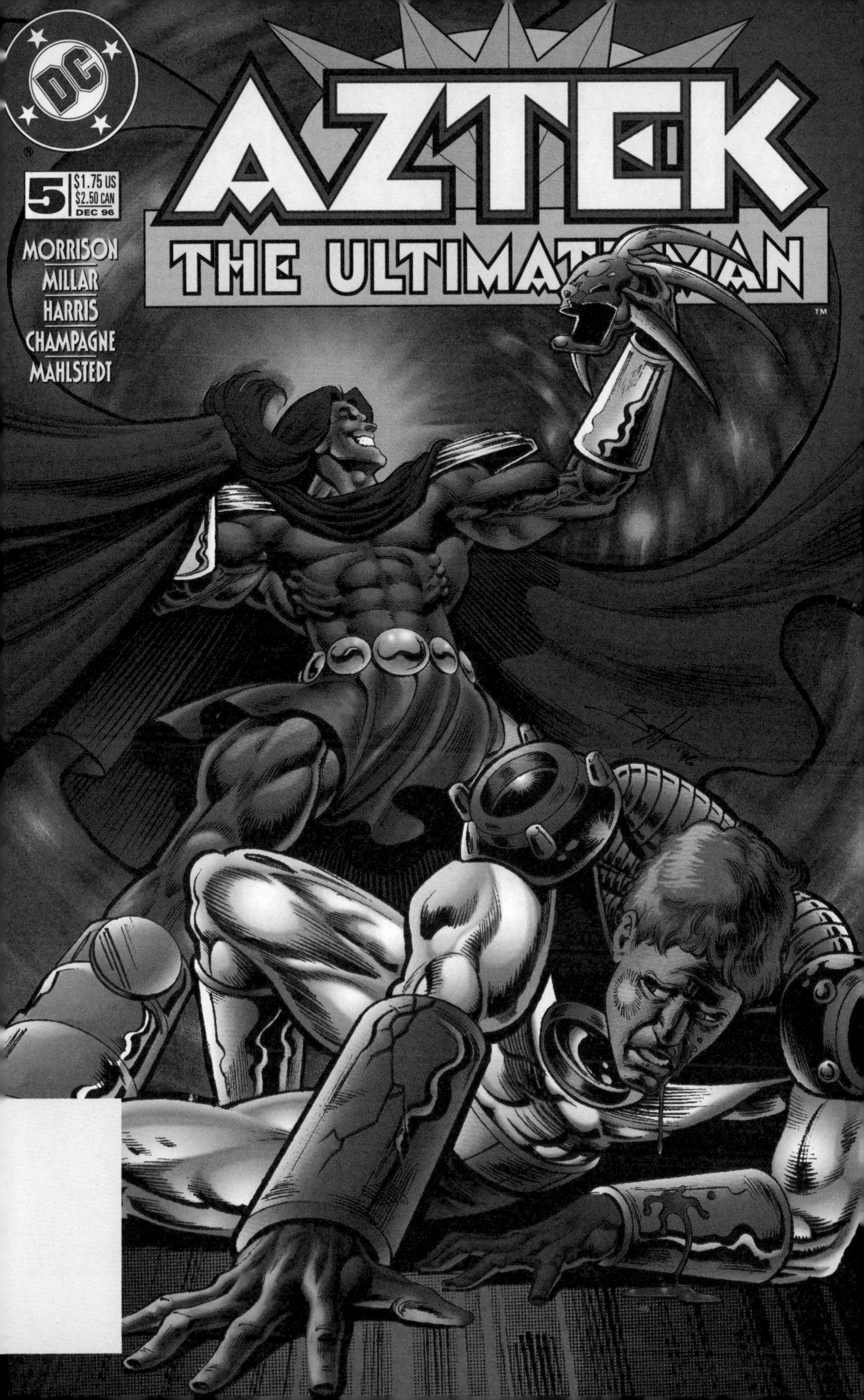
DC
AZTEK
THE ULTIMAT MAN
™
5
$1.75 US
$2.50 CAN
DEC 96
MORRISON
MILLAR
HARRIS
CHAMPAGNE
MAHLSTEDT

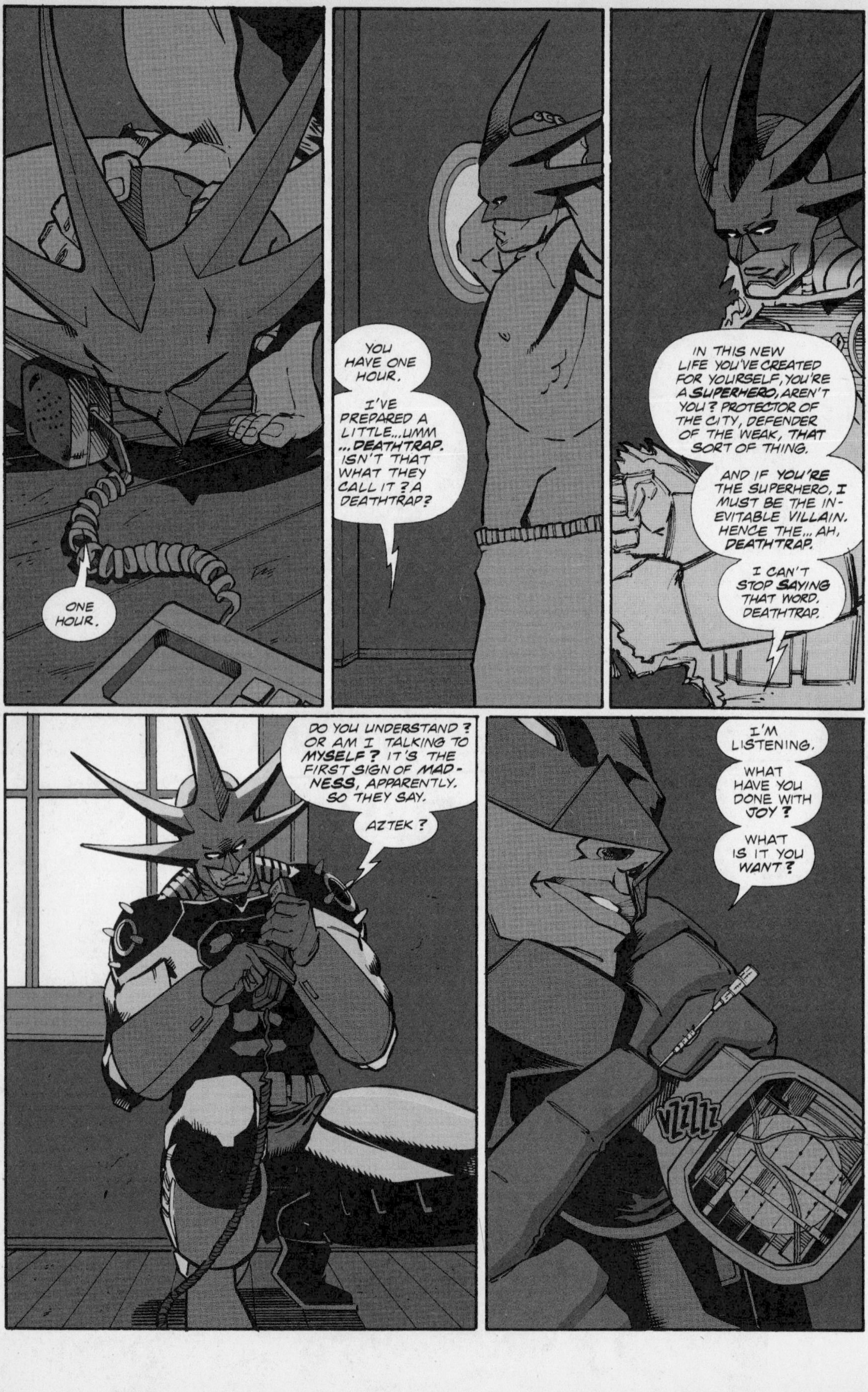
ONE HOUR.
YOU HAVE ONE HOUR.
I'VE PREPARED A LITTLE...UMM ...DEATHTRAP. ISN'T THAT WHAT THEY CALL IT? A DEATHTRAP?
IN THIS NEW LIFE YOU'VE CREATED FOR YOURSELF, YOU'RE A SUPERHERO, AREN'T YOU? PROTECTOR OF THE CITY, DEFENDER OF THE WEAK, THAT SORT OF THING.
AND IF YOU'RE THE SUPERHERO, I MUST BE THE IN-EVITABLE VILLAIN. HENCE THE... AH, DEATHTRAP.
I CAN'T STOP SAYING THAT WORD. DEATHTRAP.
DO YOU UNDERSTAND? OR AM I TALKING TO MYSELF? IT'S THE FIRST SIGN OF MAD-NESS, APPARENTLY. SO THEY SAY.
AZTEK?
I'M LISTENING.
WHAT HAVE YOU DONE WITH JOY?
WHAT IS IT YOU WANT?
VZZZZ

NURSE PAGE IS... ENTERTAINING ME.

AND WHAT I WANT, WHAT I WANT IS YOU. NO, NOT YOU, YOUR MASK. MY SCRAPPERS WERE SUPPOSED TO KILL YOU AND TAKE IT. I SHOULD HAVE KNOWN THEY'D BE INCAPABLE OF EVEN THAT SIMPLE TASK.

SKRRTTZ

THOSE THINGS... THERE WERE PEOPLE INSIDE... I'VE SEEN THE TECHNOLOGY BEFORE.

SCRAPPER PILOTS AREN'T PEOPLE. THEY'RE WHAT'S LEFT WHEN YOU TAKE ALL THE GOOD THINGS AWAY FROM A PERSON.

MY MACHINES EXTRACT THE GOODNESS, THE ESSENCE.

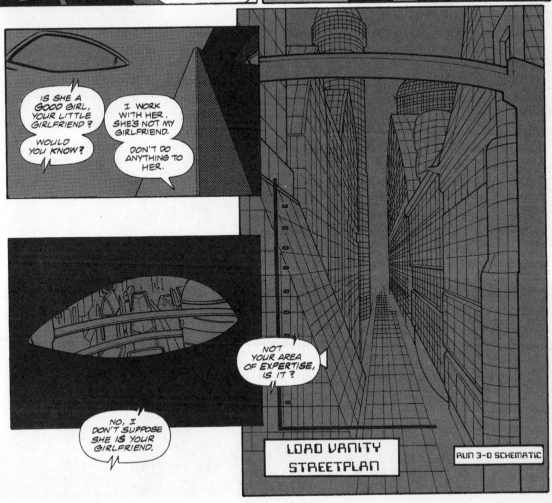

IS SHE A GOOD GIRL, YOUR LITTLE GIRLFRIEND?

WOULD YOU KNOW?

I WORK WITH HER. SHE'S NOT MY GIRLFRIEND.

DON'T DO ANYTHING TO HER.

NOT YOUR AREA OF EXPERTISE, IS IT?

NO, I DON'T SUPPOSE SHE IS YOUR GIRLFRIEND.

LORD VANITY STREETPLAN

RUN 3-D SCHEMATIC

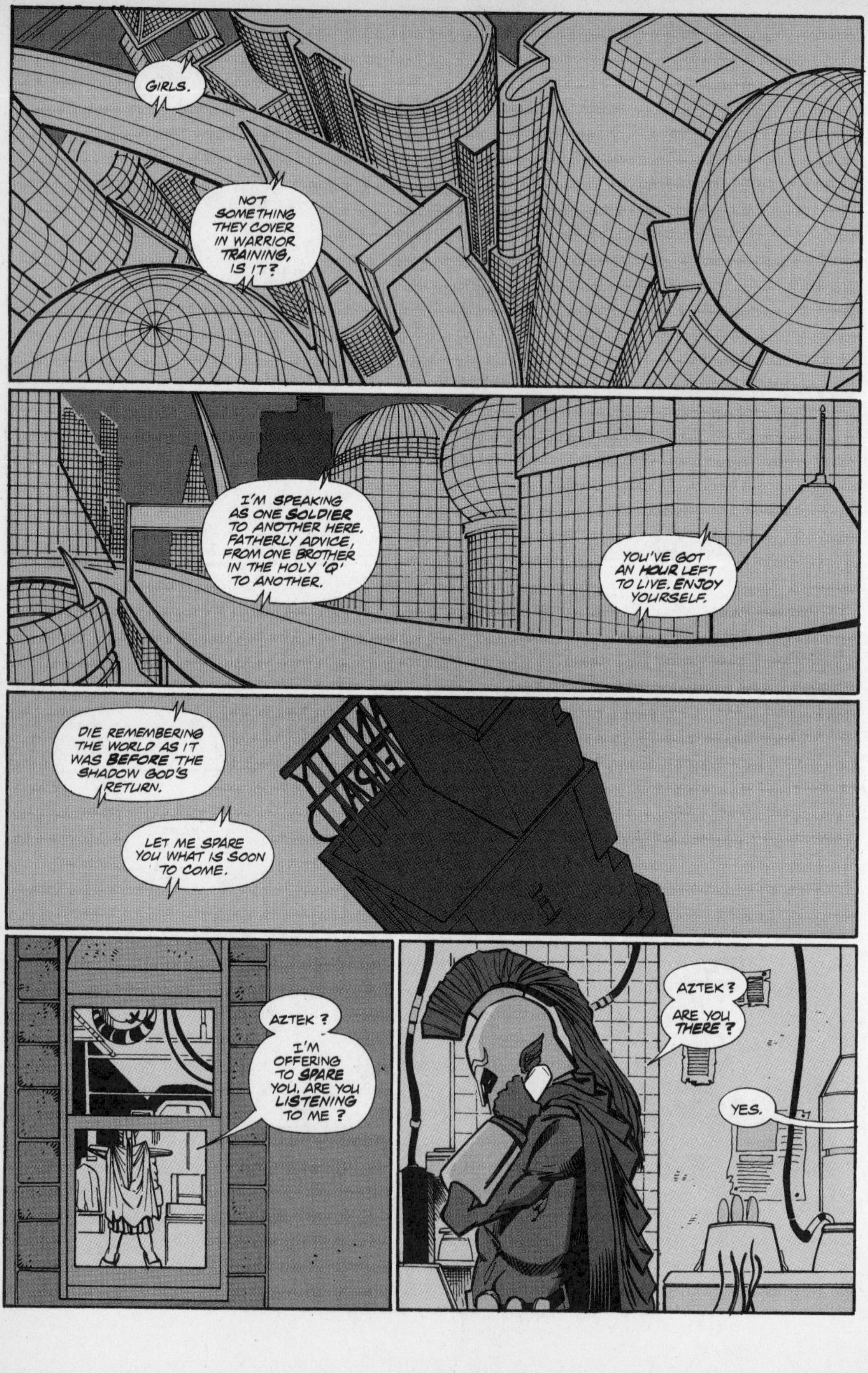
GIRLS.
NOT SOMETHING THEY COVER IN WARRIOR TRAINING, IS IT?
I'M SPEAKING AS ONE SOLDIER TO ANOTHER HERE. FATHERLY ADVICE, FROM ONE BROTHER IN THE HOLY 'Q' TO ANOTHER.
YOU'VE GOT AN HOUR LEFT TO LIVE. ENJOY YOURSELF.
DIE REMEMBERING THE WORLD AS IT WAS BEFORE THE SHADOW GOD'S RETURN.
LET ME SPARE YOU WHAT IS SOON TO COME.
AZTEK?
I'M OFFERING TO SPARE YOU. ARE YOU LISTENING TO ME?
AZTEK?
ARE YOU THERE?
YES.

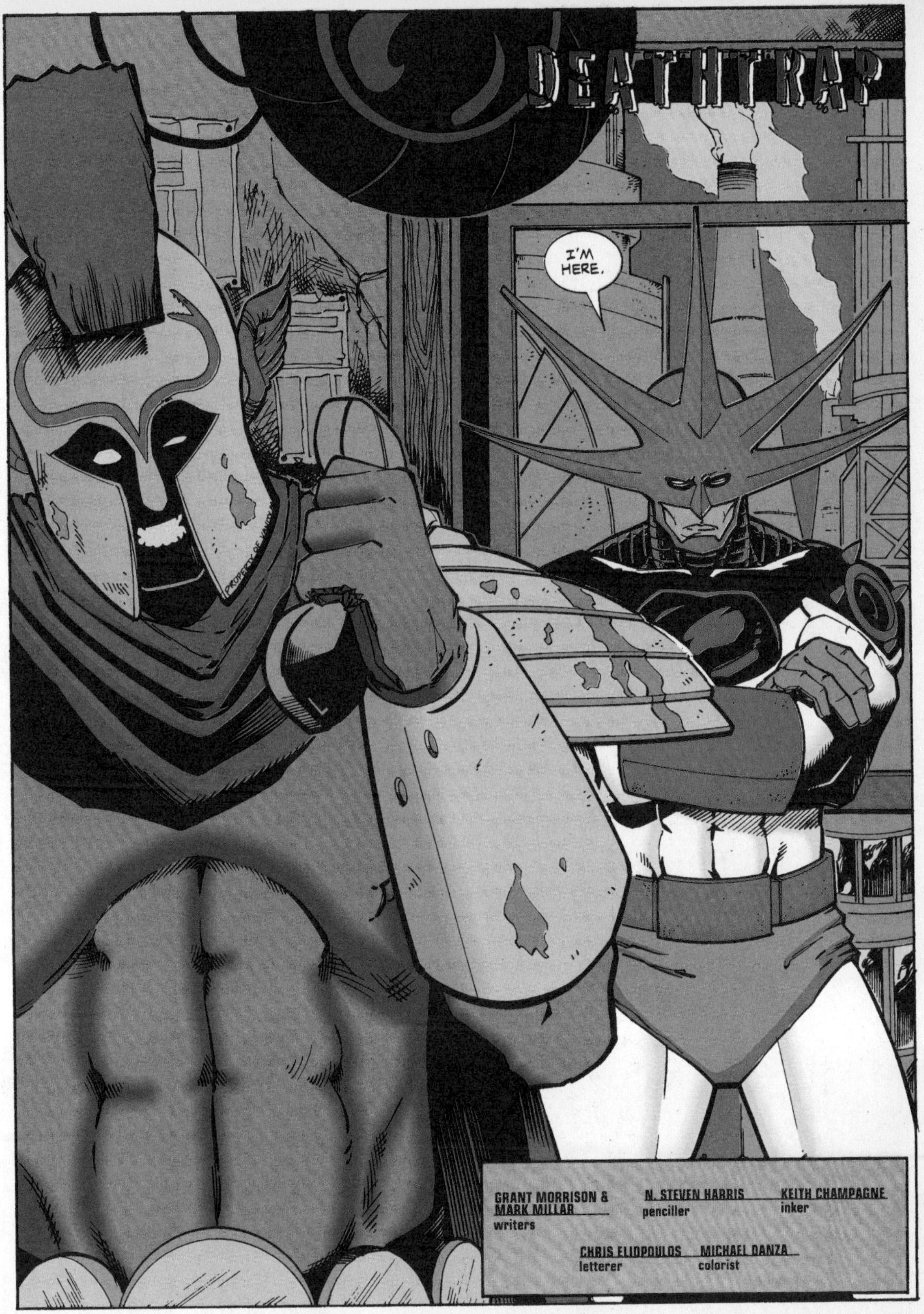
DEATHTRAP
I'M HERE.
PROPERTY OF VANITY
GRANT MORRISON & MARK MILLAR writers
N. STEVEN HARRIS penciller
KEITH CHAMPAGNE inker
CHRIS ELIOPOULOS letterer
MICHAEL DANZA colorist

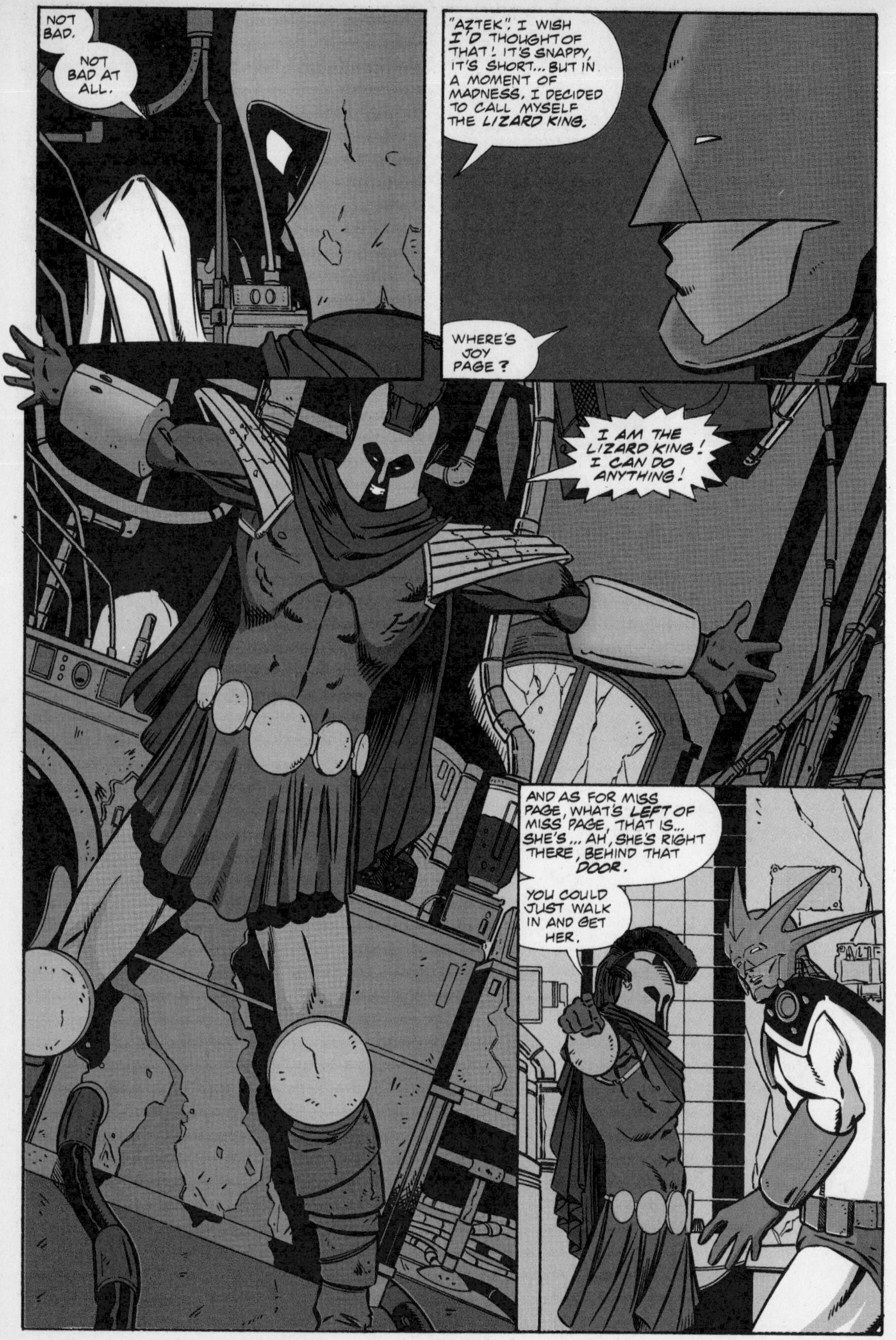
NOT BAD.
NOT BAD AT ALL.
"AZTEK". I WISH I'D THOUGHT OF THAT! IT'S SNAPPY, IT'S SHORT... BUT IN A MOMENT OF MADNESS, I DECIDED TO CALL MYSELF THE LIZARD KING.
WHERE'S JOY PAGE?
I AM THE LIZARD KING! I CAN DO ANYTHING!
AND AS FOR MISS PAGE, WHAT'S LEFT OF MISS PAGE, THAT IS... SHE'S... AH, SHE'S RIGHT THERE, BEHIND THAT DOOR.
YOU COULD JUST WALK IN AND GET HER.

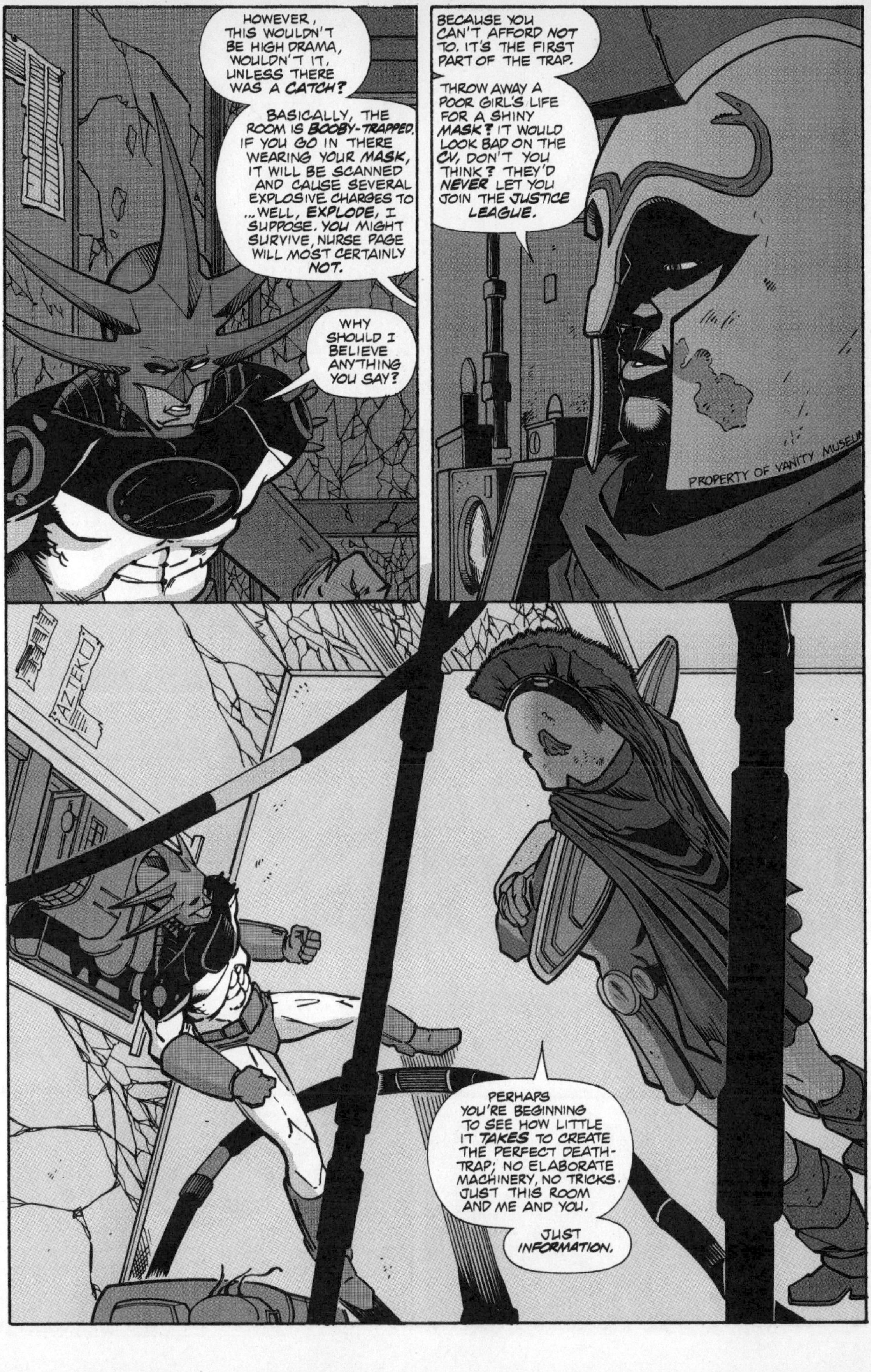
HOWEVER, THIS WOULDN'T BE HIGH DRAMA, WOULDN'T IT, UNLESS THERE WAS A CATCH?
BASICALLY, THE ROOM IS BOOBY-TRAPPED. IF YOU GO IN THERE WEARING YOUR MASK, IT WILL BE SCANNED AND CAUSE SEVERAL EXPLOSIVE CHARGES TO ...WELL, EXPLODE, I SUPPOSE. YOU MIGHT SURVIVE, NURSE PAGE WILL MOST CERTAINLY NOT.
WHY SHOULD I BELIEVE ANYTHING YOU SAY?
BECAUSE YOU CAN'T AFFORD NOT TO. IT'S THE FIRST PART OF THE TRAP.
THROW AWAY A POOR GIRL'S LIFE FOR A SHINY MASK? IT WOULD LOOK BAD ON THE CV, DON'T YOU THINK? THEY'D NEVER LET YOU JOIN THE JUSTICE LEAGUE.
PROPERTY OF VANITY MUSEUM
AZTEK
PERHAPS YOU'RE BEGINNING TO SEE HOW LITTLE IT TAKES TO CREATE THE PERFECT DEATH-TRAP; NO ELABORATE MACHINERY, NO TRICKS. JUST THIS ROOM AND ME AND YOU.
JUST INFORMATION.

I WILL KILL YOU. THAT MUCH IS CERTAIN. I JUST WANT YOU TO UNDERSTAND THAT I'M DOING IT TO SAVE YOU.

I'M DOING IT TO SAVE EVERYONE.

JUST LET HER GO. WHATEVER THIS IS ABOUT HAS NOTHING TO DO WITH JOY.

WILL YOU LET HER GO?

SOMETIMES INNOCENTS SUFFER.

ALL I WANT IS YOUR MASK. WITHOUT THE MASK I JUST DON'T HAVE THE RAW POWER TO FACE THE SHADOW GOD AND FRANKLY, I HAVE NO INTENTION OF FACING HIM WITHOUT THE RAW POWER.

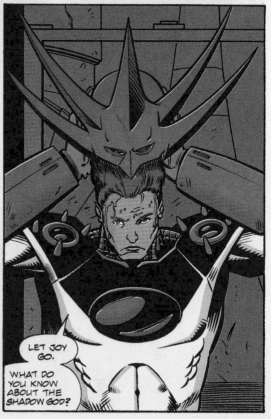

LET JOY GO.

WHAT DO YOU KNOW ABOUT THE SHADOW GOD?

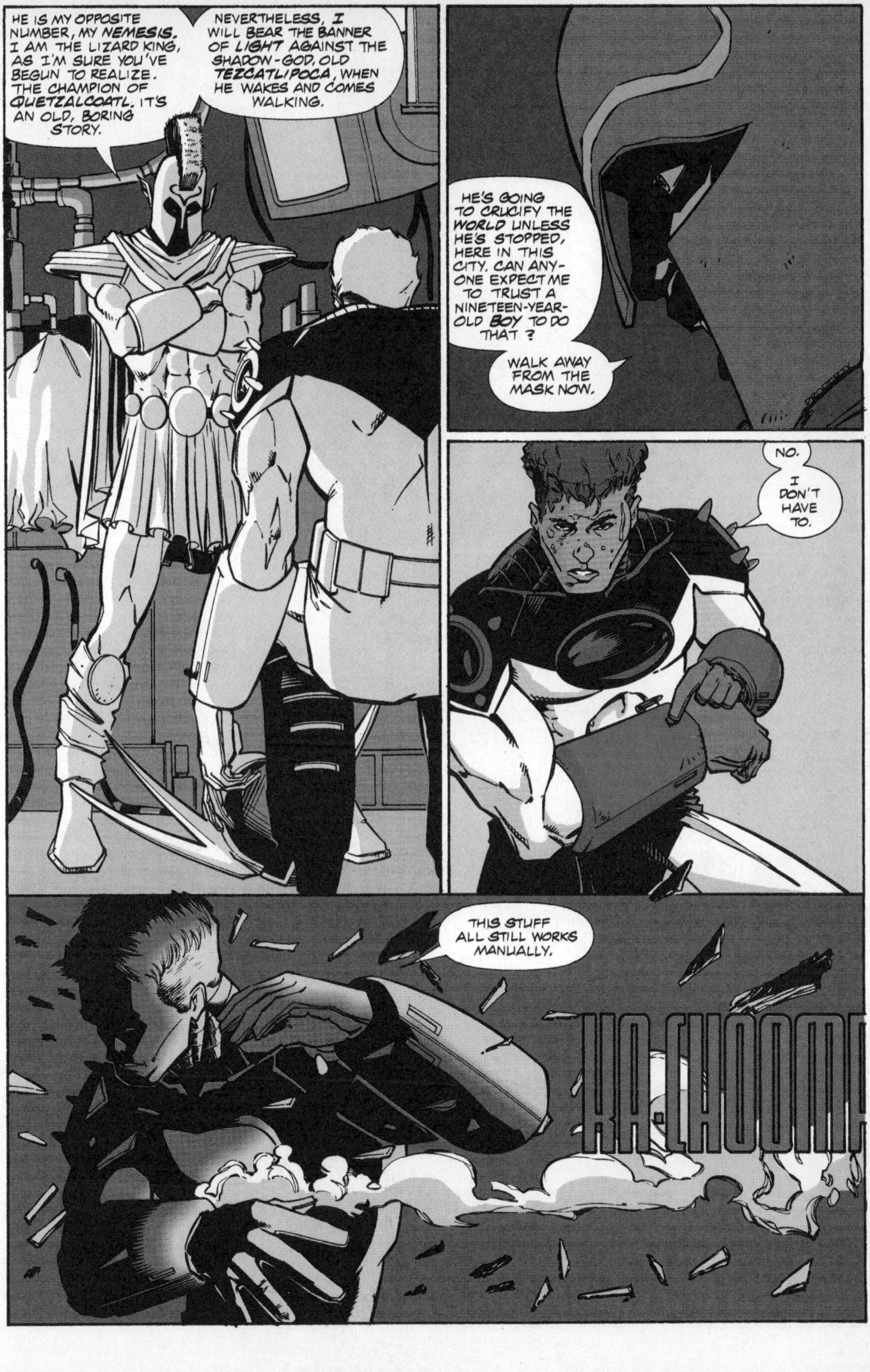
HE IS MY OPPOSITE NUMBER, MY NEMESIS. I AM THE LIZARD KING, AS I'M SURE YOU'VE BEGUN TO REALIZE. THE CHAMPION OF QUETZALCOATL. IT'S AN OLD, BORING STORY.
NEVERTHELESS, I WILL BEAR THE BANNER OF LIGHT AGAINST THE SHADOW-GOD, OLD TEZCATLIPOCA, WHEN HE WAKES AND COMES WALKING.
HE'S GOING TO CRUCIFY THE WORLD UNLESS HE'S STOPPED, HERE IN THIS CITY. CAN ANYONE EXPECT ME TO TRUST A NINETEEN-YEAR-OLD BOY TO DO THAT?
WALK AWAY FROM THE MASK NOW.
NO.
I DON'T HAVE TO.
THIS STUFF ALL STILL WORKS MANUALLY.
KA-CHOOM

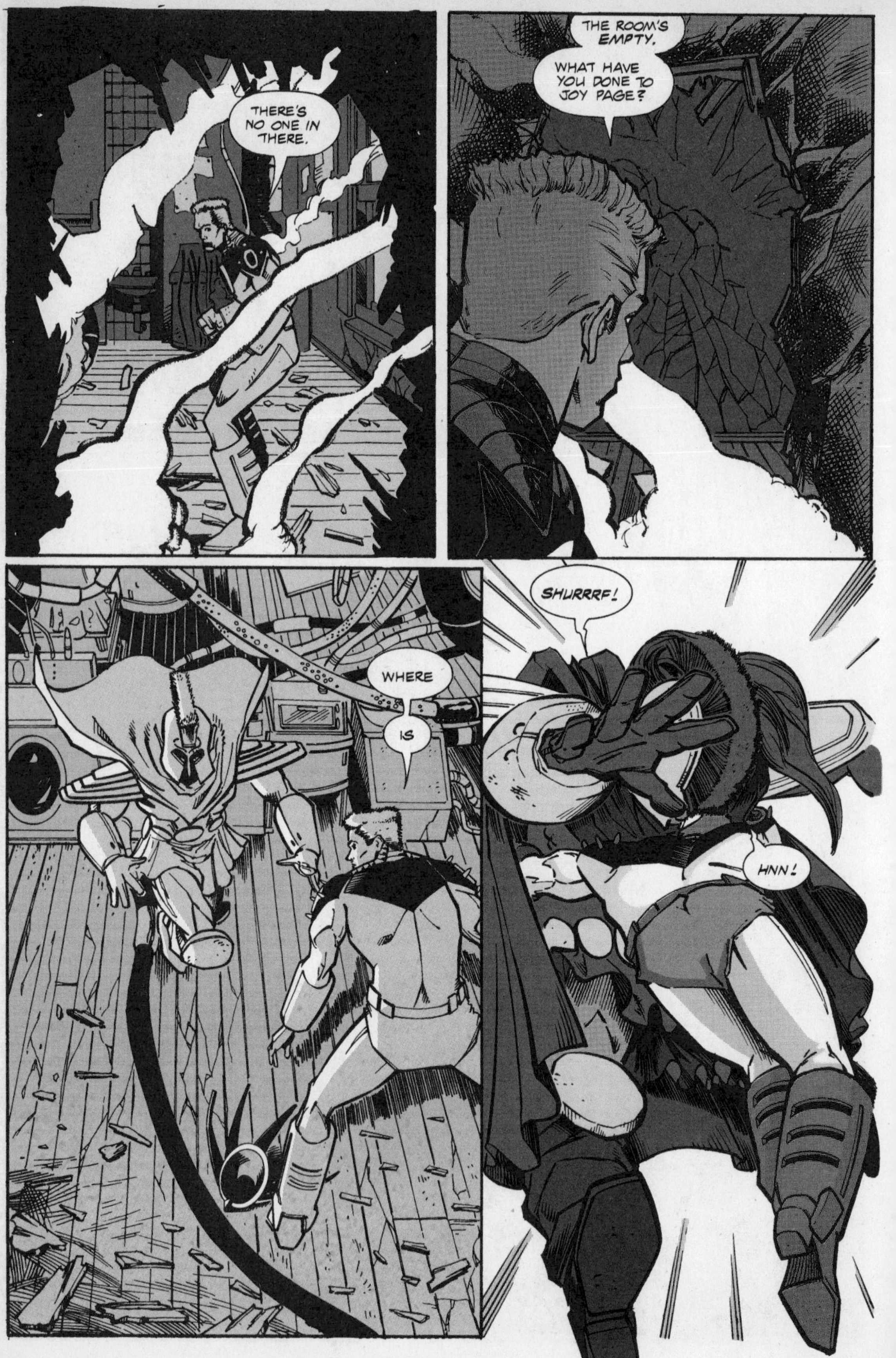
THERE'S NO ONE IN THERE.
THE ROOM'S EMPTY.
WHAT HAVE YOU DONE TO JOY PAGE?
WHERE
IS
SHURRRF!
HNN!

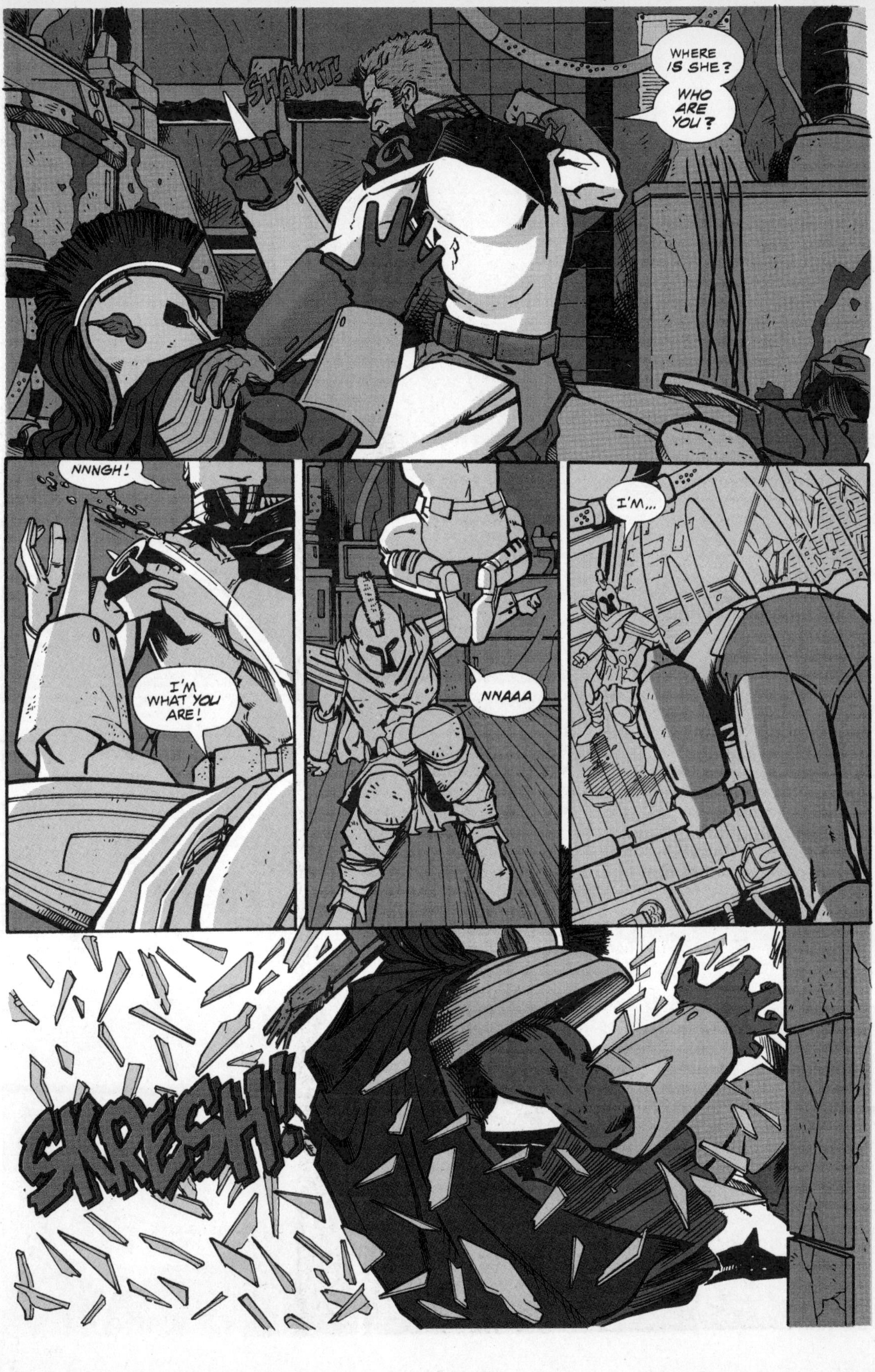
SHAKKT!
WHERE IS SHE?
WHO ARE YOU?
NNNGH!
I'M WHAT YOU ARE!
NNAAA
I'M...
SKRESH!!

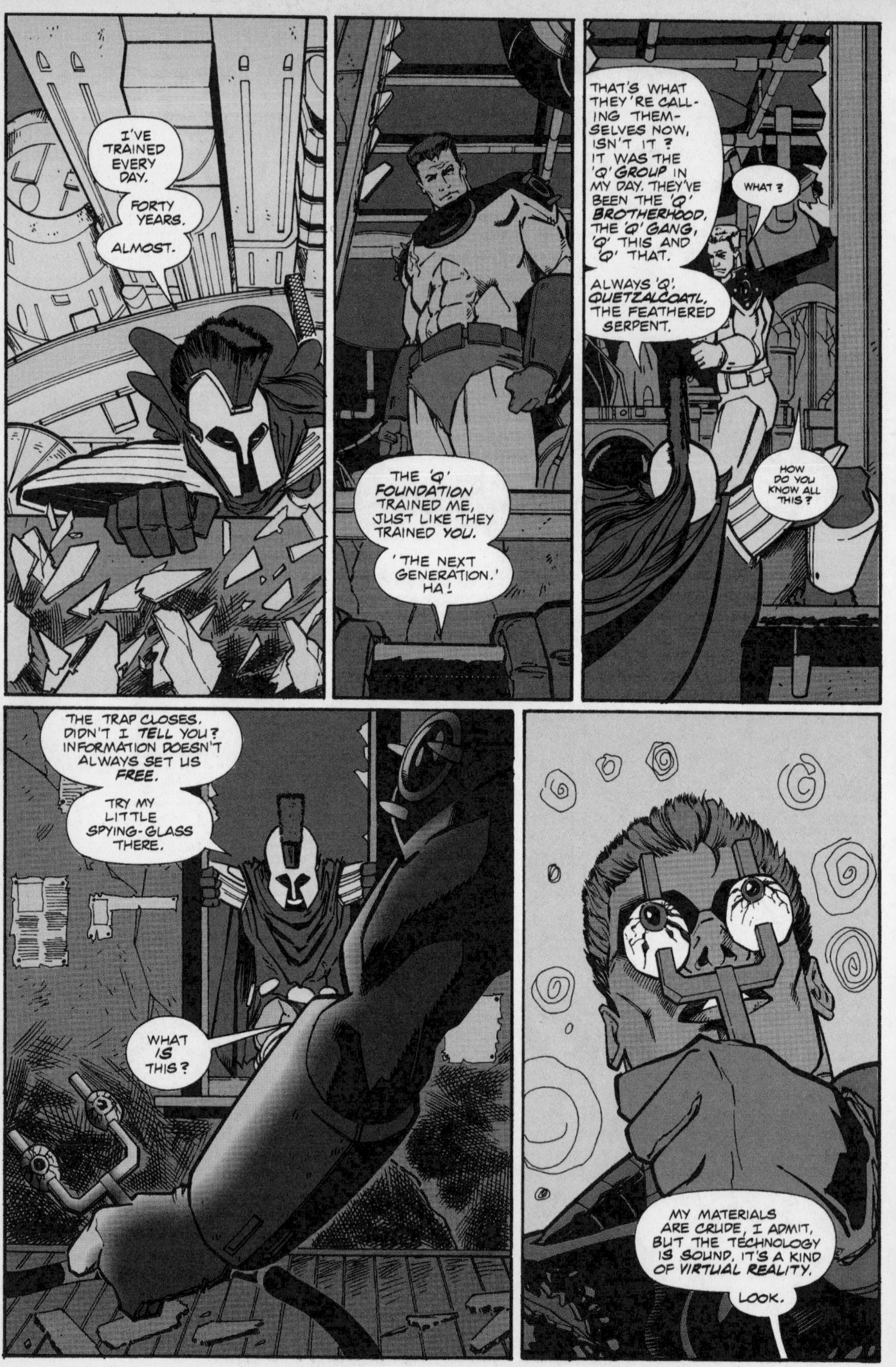
I'VE TRAINED EVERY DAY.
FORTY YEARS.
ALMOST.
THE 'Q' FOUNDATION TRAINED ME, JUST LIKE THEY TRAINED YOU.
'THE NEXT GENERATION.' HA!
THAT'S WHAT THEY'RE CALLING THEMSELVES NOW, ISN'T IT? IT WAS THE 'Q' GROUP IN MY DAY. THEY'VE BEEN THE 'Q' BROTHERHOOD, THE 'Q' GANG, 'Q' THIS AND 'Q' THAT.
WHAT?
ALWAYS 'Q'. QUETZALCOATL, THE FEATHERED SERPENT.
HOW DO YOU KNOW ALL THIS?
THE TRAP CLOSES. DIDN'T I TELL YOU? INFORMATION DOESN'T ALWAYS SET US FREE.
TRY MY LITTLE SPYING-GLASS THERE.
WHAT IS THIS?
MY MATERIALS ARE CRUDE, I ADMIT, BUT THE TECHNOLOGY IS SOUND. IT'S A KIND OF VIRTUAL REALITY.
LOOK.

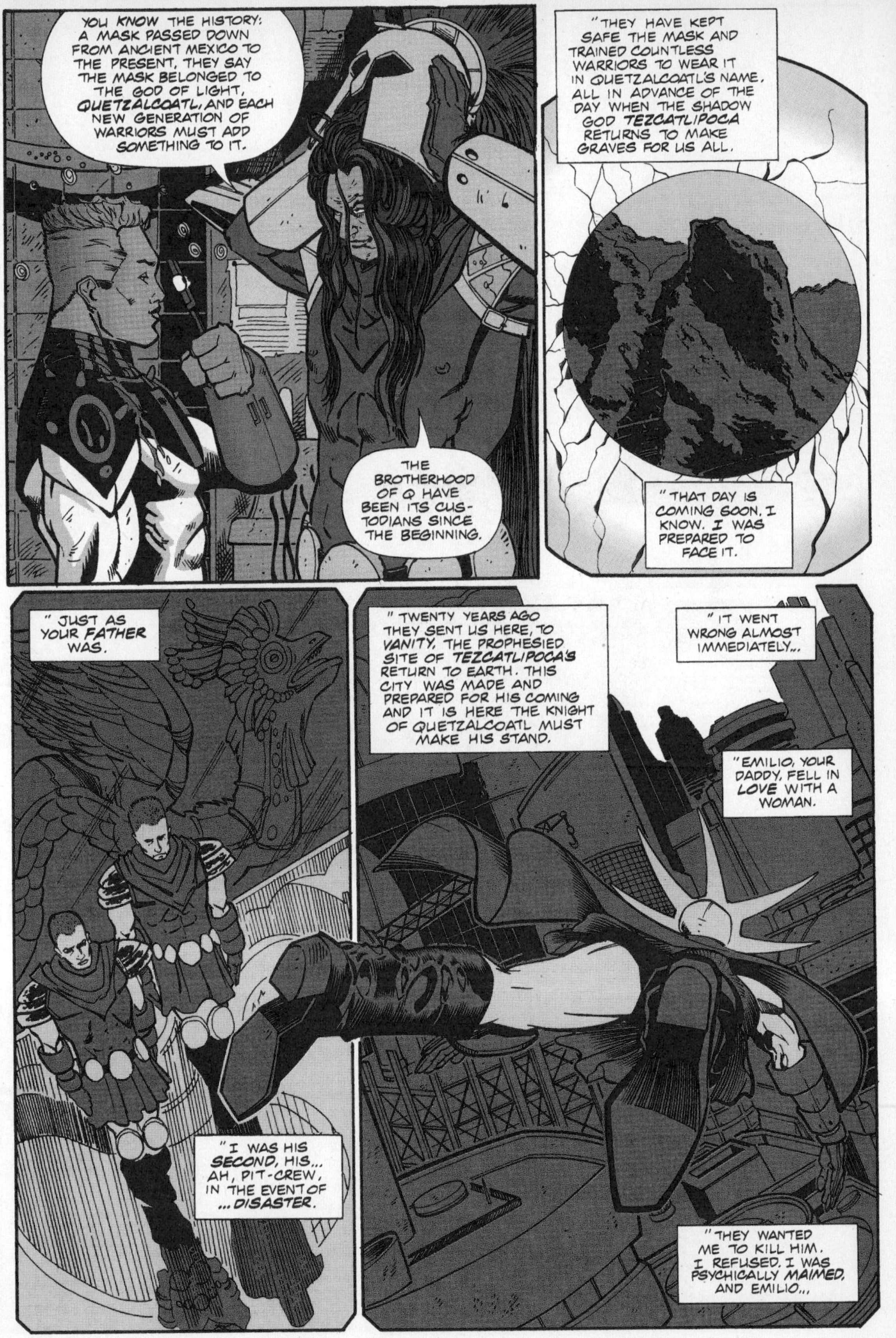
YOU KNOW THE HISTORY: A MASK PASSED DOWN FROM ANCIENT MEXICO TO THE PRESENT. THEY SAY THE MASK BELONGED TO THE GOD OF LIGHT, QUETZALCOATL, AND EACH NEW GENERATION OF WARRIORS MUST ADD SOMETHING TO IT.
THE BROTHERHOOD OF Q HAVE BEEN ITS CUSTODIANS SINCE THE BEGINNING.
"THEY HAVE KEPT SAFE THE MASK AND TRAINED COUNTLESS WARRIORS TO WEAR IT IN QUETZALCOATL'S NAME, ALL IN ADVANCE OF THE DAY WHEN THE SHADOW GOD TEZCATLIPOCA RETURNS TO MAKE GRAVES FOR US ALL.
"THAT DAY IS COMING SOON. I KNOW. I WAS PREPARED TO FACE IT.
"JUST AS YOUR FATHER WAS.
"I WAS HIS SECOND, HIS... AH, PIT-CREW, IN THE EVENT OF ...DISASTER.
"TWENTY YEARS AGO THEY SENT US HERE, TO VANITY, THE PROPHESIED SITE OF TEZCATLIPOCA'S RETURN TO EARTH. THIS CITY WAS MADE AND PREPARED FOR HIS COMING AND IT IS HERE THE KNIGHT OF QUETZALCOATL MUST MAKE HIS STAND.
"IT WENT WRONG ALMOST IMMEDIATELY...
"EMILIO, YOUR DADDY, FELL IN LOVE WITH A WOMAN.
"THEY WANTED ME TO KILL HIM. I REFUSED. I WAS PSYCHICALLY MAIMED, AND EMILIO...

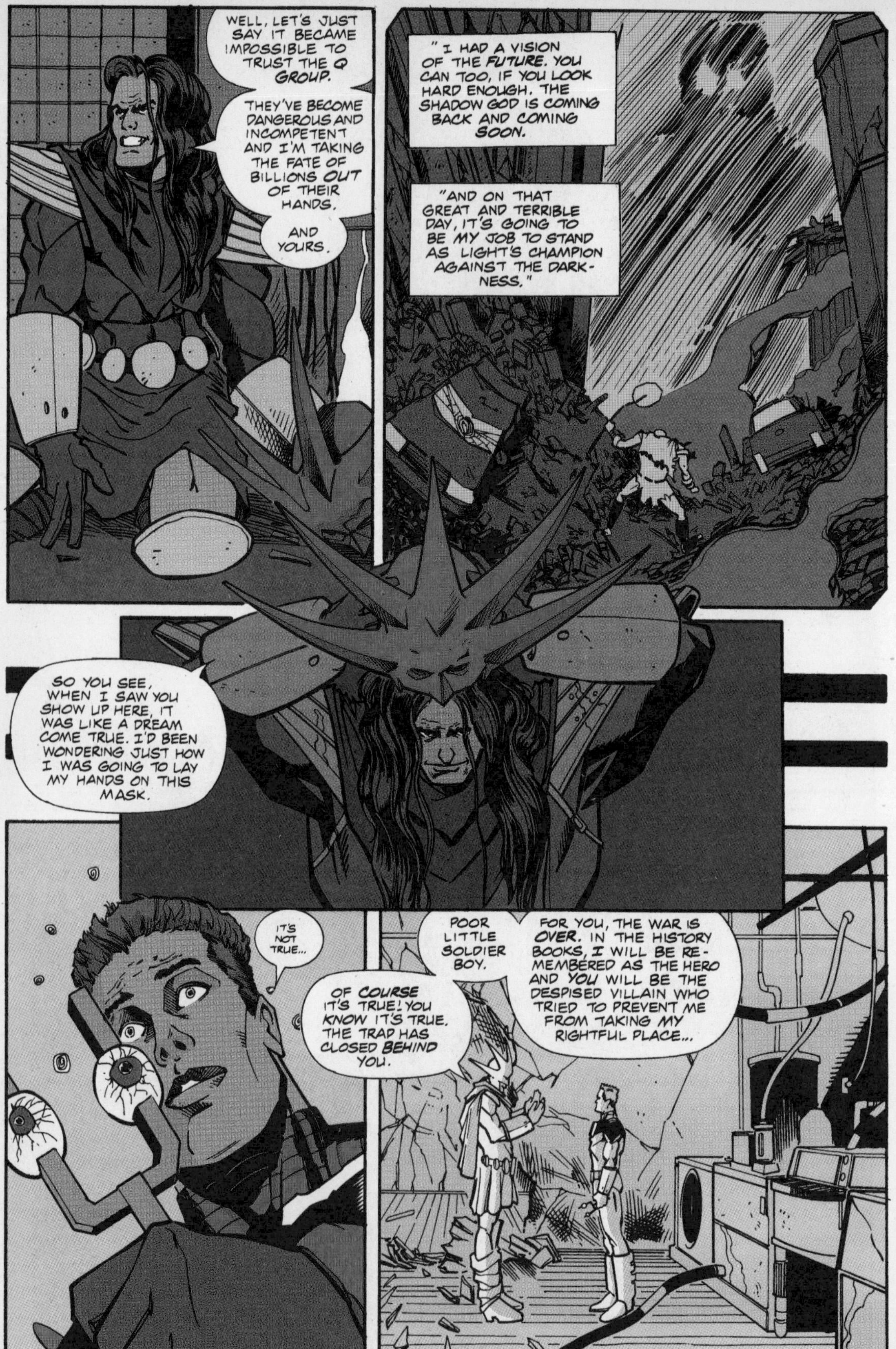
WELL, LET'S JUST SAY IT BECAME IMPOSSIBLE TO TRUST THE Q GROUP.
THEY'VE BECOME DANGEROUS AND INCOMPETENT AND I'M TAKING THE FATE OF BILLIONS OUT OF THEIR HANDS.
AND YOURS.
"I HAD A VISION OF THE FUTURE. YOU CAN TOO, IF YOU LOOK HARD ENOUGH. THE SHADOW GOD IS COMING BACK AND COMING SOON.
"AND ON THAT GREAT AND TERRIBLE DAY, IT'S GOING TO BE MY JOB TO STAND AS LIGHT'S CHAMPION AGAINST THE DARK-NESS."
SO YOU SEE, WHEN I SAW YOU SHOW UP HERE, IT WAS LIKE A DREAM COME TRUE. I'D BEEN WONDERING JUST HOW I WAS GOING TO LAY MY HANDS ON THIS MASK.
IT'S NOT TRUE...
OF COURSE IT'S TRUE! YOU KNOW IT'S TRUE. THE TRAP HAS CLOSED BEHIND YOU.
POOR LITTLE SOLDIER BOY.
FOR YOU, THE WAR IS OVER. IN THE HISTORY BOOKS, I WILL BE RE-MEMBERED AS THE HERO AND YOU WILL BE THE DESPISED VILLAIN WHO TRIED TO PREVENT ME FROM TAKING MY RIGHTFUL PLACE...

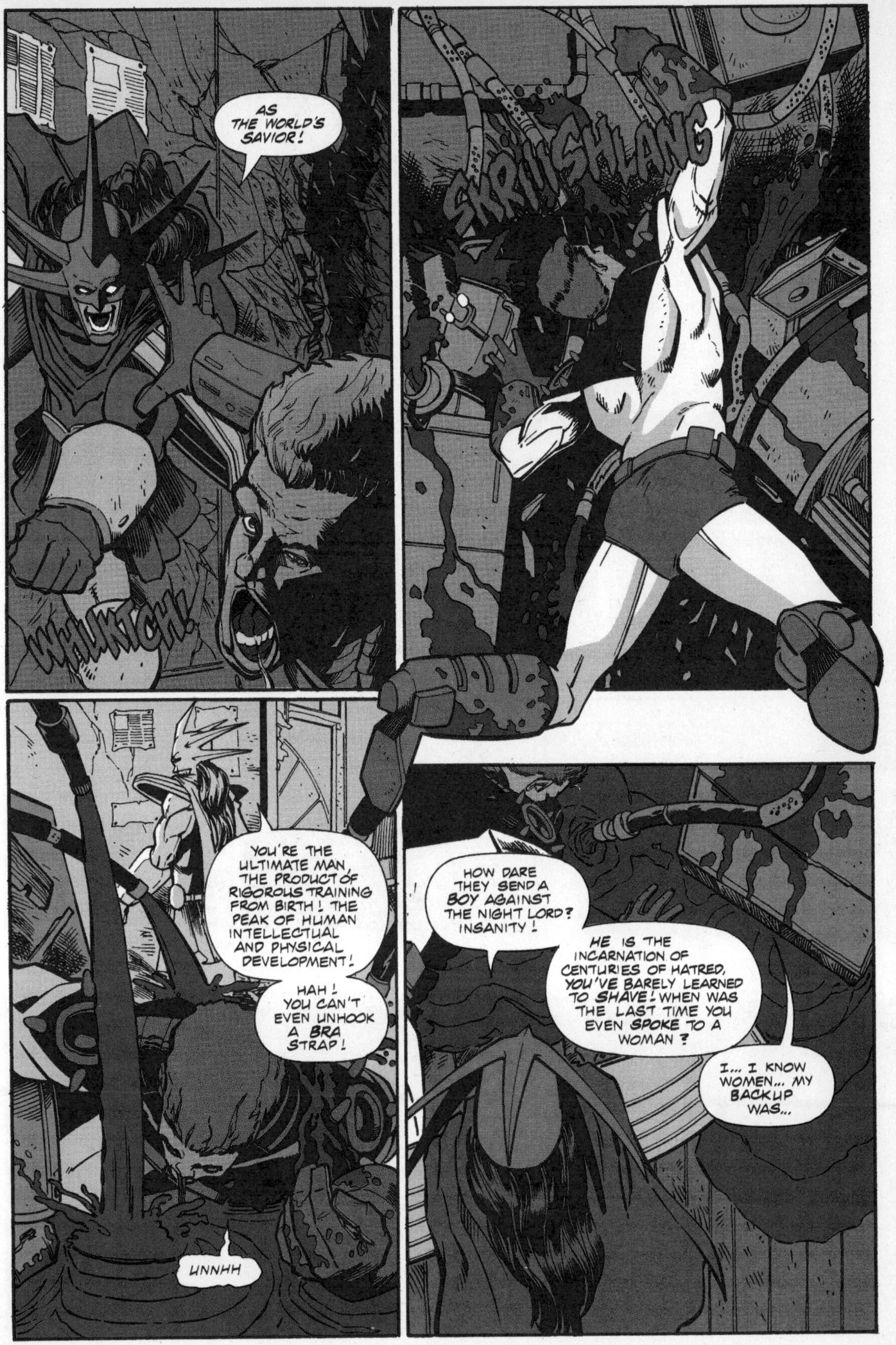
AS THE WORLD'S SAVIOR!
WHUKTCH!
SKRUSHLANG
YOU'RE THE ULTIMATE MAN, THE PRODUCT OF RIGOROUS TRAINING FROM BIRTH! THE PEAK OF HUMAN INTELLECTUAL AND PHYSICAL DEVELOPMENT!
HAH! YOU CAN'T EVEN UNHOOK A BRA STRAP!
UNNHH
HOW DARE THEY SEND A BOY AGAINST THE NIGHT LORD? INSANITY!
HE IS THE INCARNATION OF CENTURIES OF HATRED, YOU'VE BARELY LEARNED TO SHAVE! WHEN WAS THE LAST TIME YOU EVEN SPOKE TO A WOMAN?
I... I KNOW WOMEN... MY BACKUP WAS...

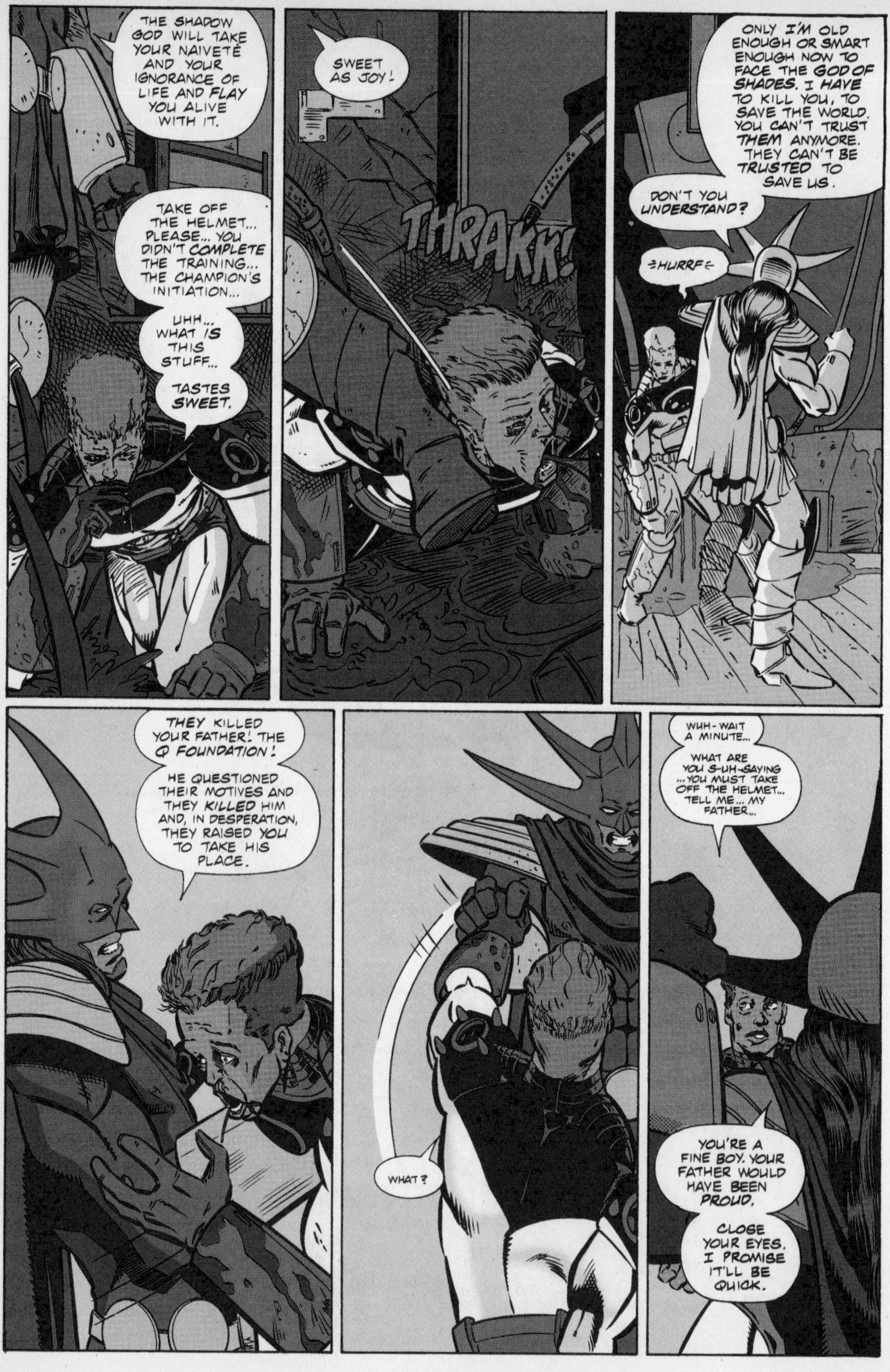
THE SHADOW GOD WILL TAKE YOUR NAIVETÉ AND YOUR IGNORANCE OF LIFE AND FLAY YOU ALIVE WITH IT.
TAKE OFF THE HELMET... PLEASE... YOU DIDN'T COMPLETE THE TRAINING... THE CHAMPION'S INITIATION...
UHH... WHAT IS THIS STUFF...
TASTES SWEET.
SWEET AS JOY!
THRAKK!
ONLY I'M OLD ENOUGH OR SMART ENOUGH NOW TO FACE THE GOD OF SHADES. I HAVE TO KILL YOU, TO SAVE THE WORLD. YOU CAN'T TRUST THEM ANYMORE. THEY CAN'T BE TRUSTED TO SAVE US.
DON'T YOU UNDERSTAND?
HURRF
THEY KILLED YOUR FATHER! THE Q FOUNDATION!
HE QUESTIONED THEIR MOTIVES AND THEY KILLED HIM AND, IN DESPERATION, THEY RAISED YOU TO TAKE HIS PLACE.
WHAT?
WUH-WAIT A MINUTE...
WHAT ARE YOU S-UH-SAYING ...YOU MUST TAKE OFF THE HELMET... TELL ME... MY FATHER...
YOU'RE A FINE BOY. YOUR FATHER WOULD HAVE BEEN PROUD.
CLOSE YOUR EYES. I PROMISE IT'LL BE QUICK.

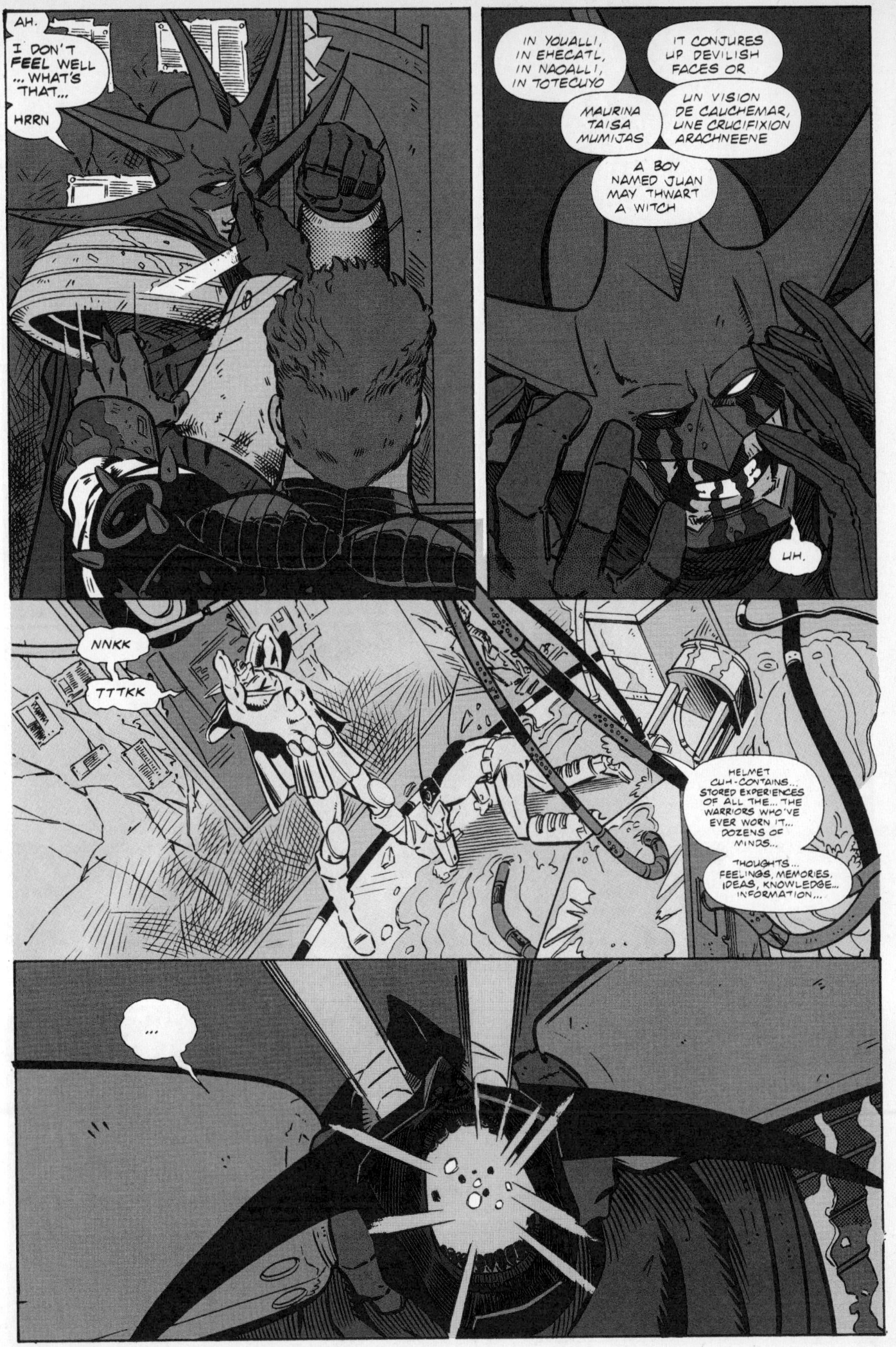

AH.
I DON'T FEEL WELL ...WHAT'S THAT...
HRRN
IN YOUALLI, IN EHECATL, IN NAOALLI, IN TOTECUYO
IT CONJURES UP DEVILISH FACES OR
MAURINA TAISA MUMIJAS
UN VISION DE CAUCHEMAR, UNE CRUCIFIXION ARACHNEENE
A BOY NAMED JUAN MAY THWART A WITCH
UH.
NNKK
TTTKK
HELMET CUH-CONTAINS... STORED EXPERIENCES OF ALL THE... THE WARRIORS WHO'VE EVER WORN IT... DOZENS OF MINDS...
THOUGHTS... FEELINGS, MEMORIES, IDEAS, KNOWLEDGE... INFORMATION...
...

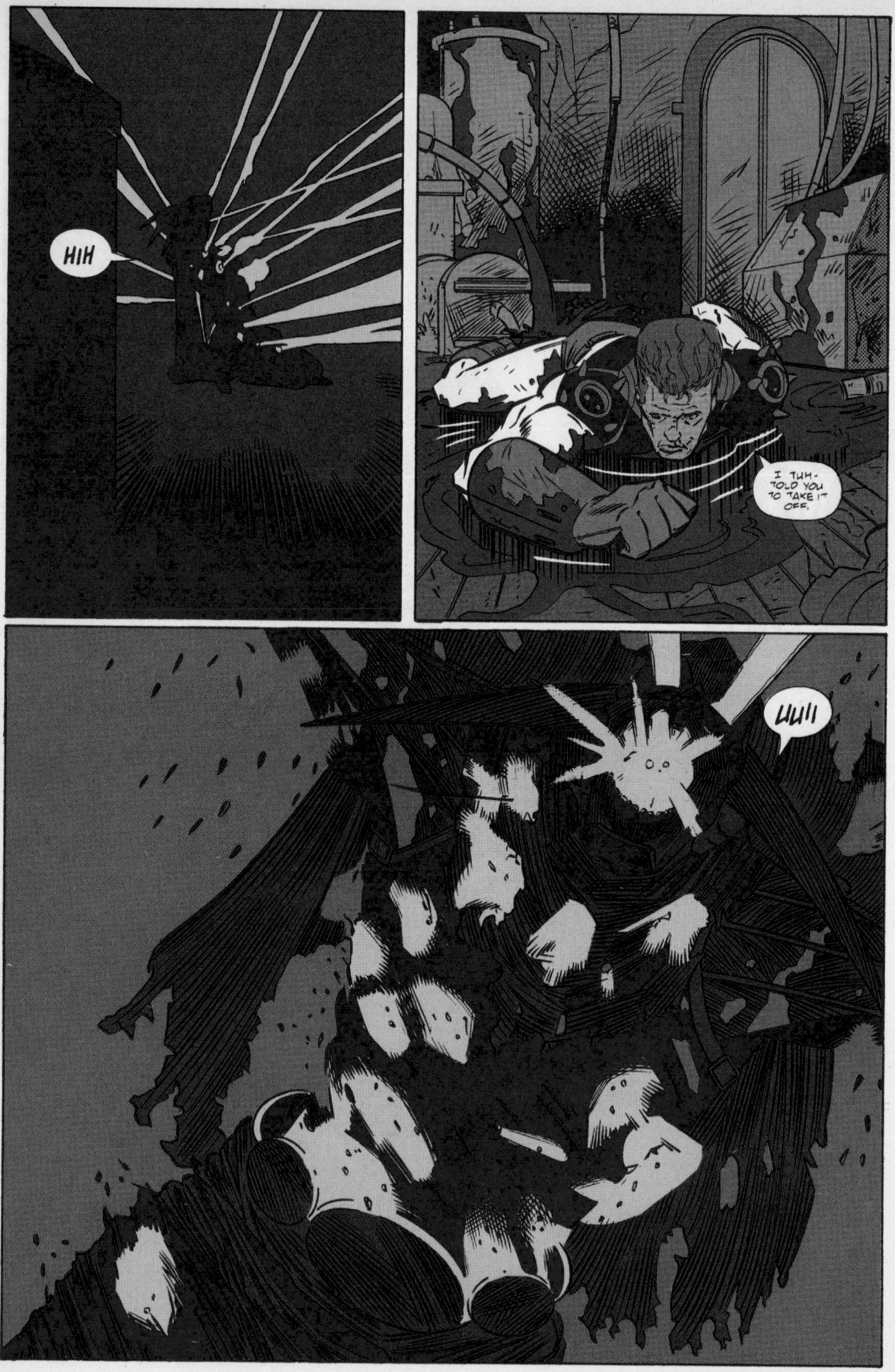
HIH
I THH-
TOLD YOU
TO TAKE IT
OFF.
UUll

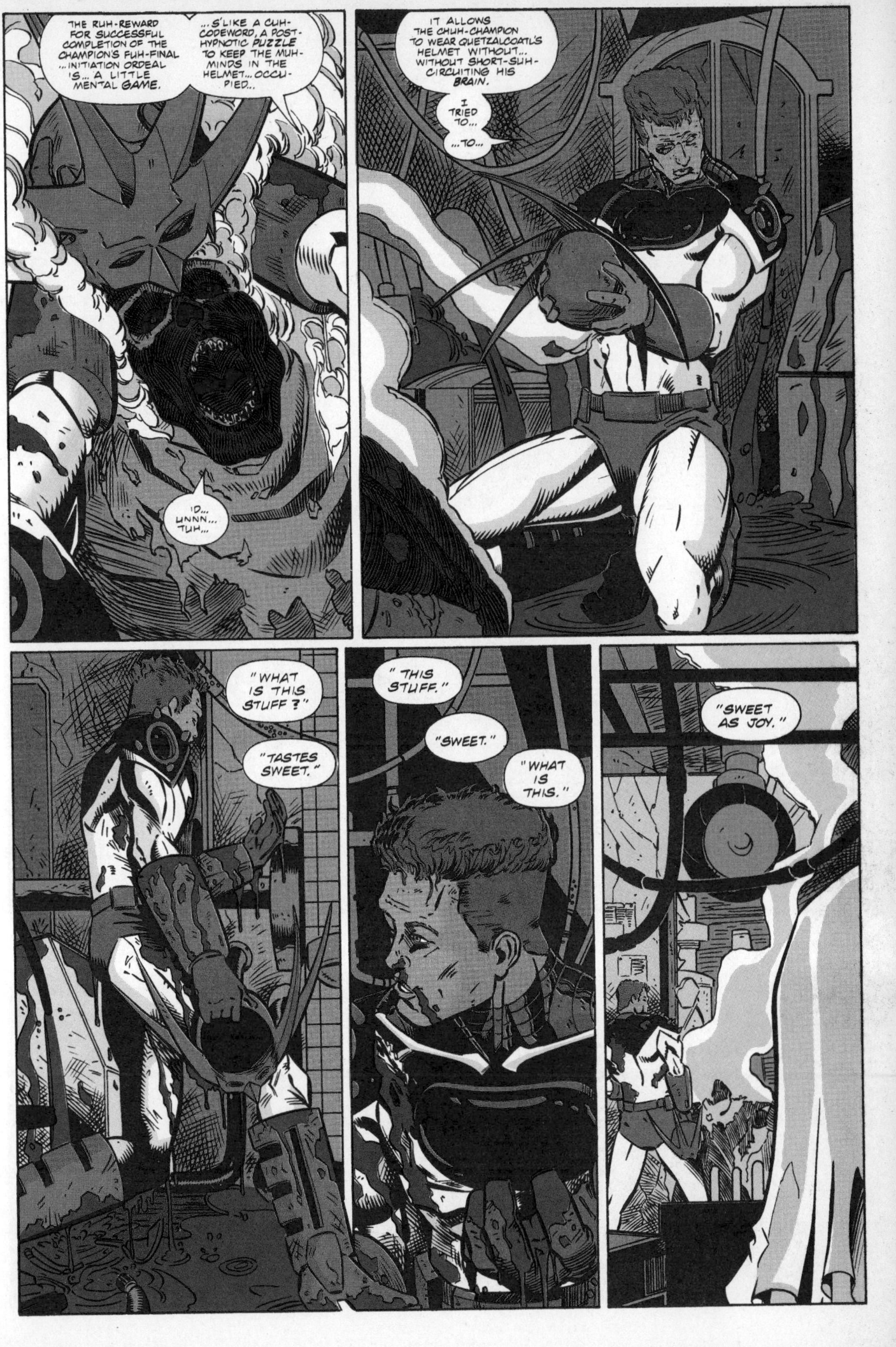
THE RUH-REWARD FOR SUCCESSFUL COMPLETION OF THE CHAMPION'S FUH-FINAL ...INITIATION ORDEAL 'S... A LITTLE MENTAL GAME.
...S'LIKE A CUH-CODEWORD, A POST-HYPNOTIC PUZZLE TO KEEP THE MUH-MINDS IN THE HELMET... OCCU-PIED...
ID... UNNN... TUH...
IT ALLOWS THE CHUH-CHAMPION TO WEAR QUETZALCOATL'S HELMET WITHOUT... WITHOUT SHORT-SUH-CIRCUITING HIS BRAIN.
I TRIED TO...
...TO...
"WHAT IS THIS STUFF?"
"TASTES SWEET."
"THIS STUFF."
"SWEET."
"WHAT IS THIS."
"SWEET AS JOY."

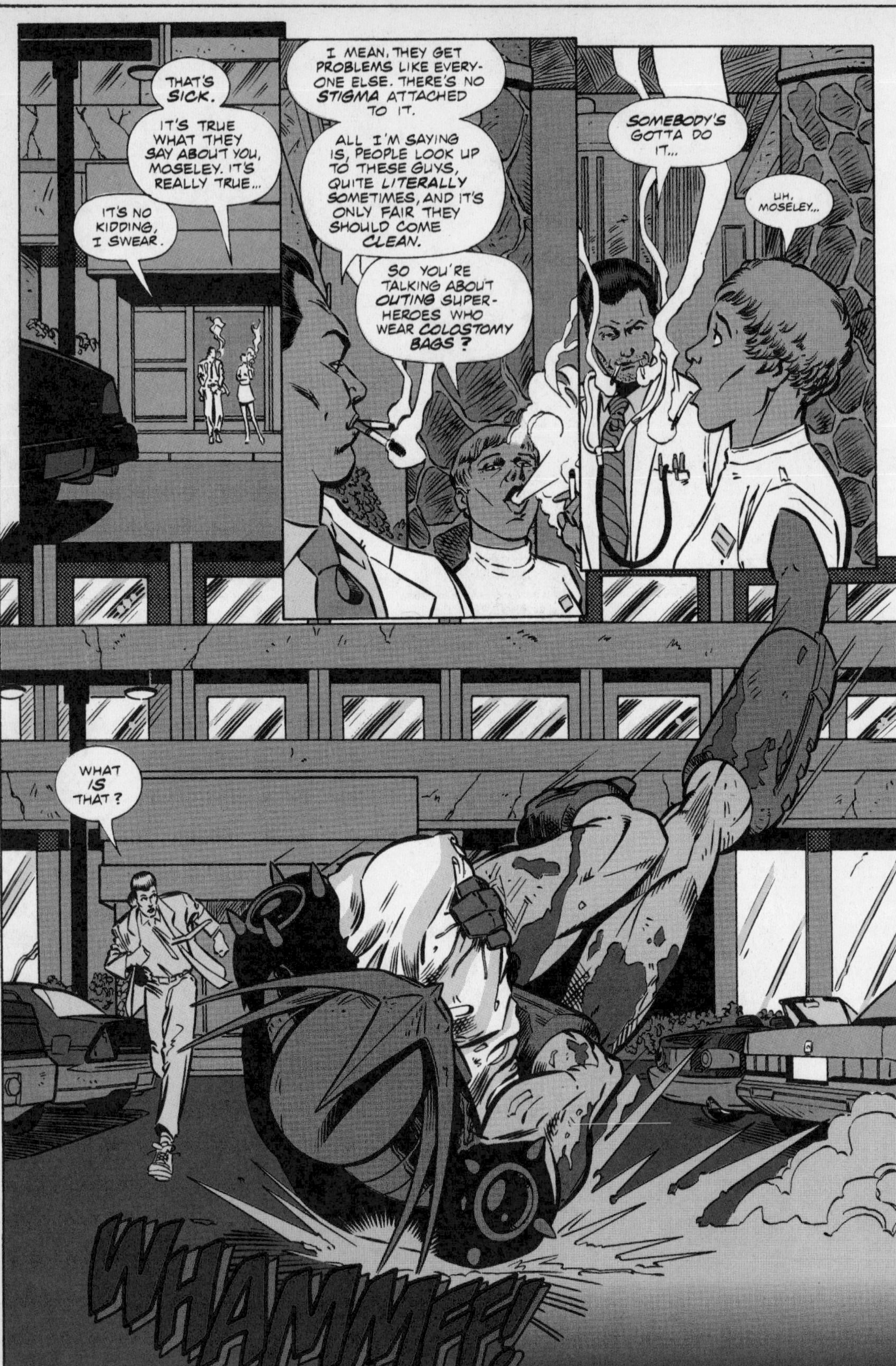

THAT'S SICK.
IT'S TRUE WHAT THEY SAY ABOUT YOU, MOSELEY. IT'S REALLY TRUE...
IT'S NO KIDDING, I SWEAR.
I MEAN, THEY GET PROBLEMS LIKE EVERY-ONE ELSE. THERE'S NO STIGMA ATTACHED TO IT.
ALL I'M SAYING IS, PEOPLE LOOK UP TO THESE GUYS, QUITE LITERALLY SOMETIMES, AND IT'S ONLY FAIR THEY SHOULD COME CLEAN.
SO YOU'RE TALKING ABOUT OUTING SUPER-HEROES WHO WEAR COLOSTOMY BAGS?
SOMEBODY'S GOTTA DO IT...
UH, MOSELEY...
WHAT IS THAT?
WHAMMFF!

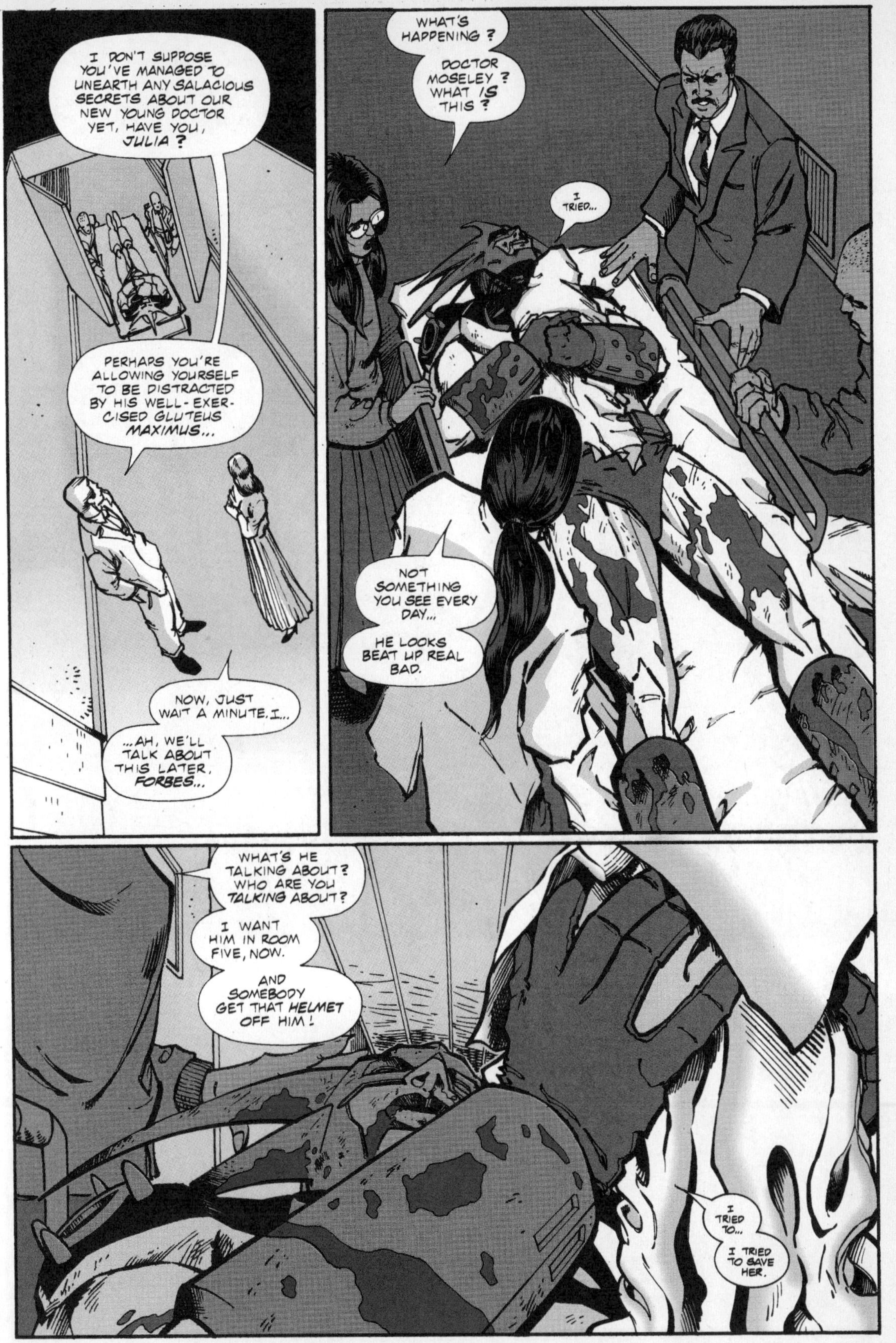
I DON'T SUPPOSE YOU'VE MANAGED TO UNEARTH ANY SALACIOUS SECRETS ABOUT OUR NEW YOUNG DOCTOR YET, HAVE YOU, JULIA?
PERHAPS YOU'RE ALLOWING YOURSELF TO BE DISTRACTED BY HIS WELL-EXERCISED GLUTEUS MAXIMUS...
NOW, JUST WAIT A MINUTE. I...
...AH, WE'LL TALK ABOUT THIS LATER, FORBES...
WHAT'S HAPPENING?
DOCTOR MOSELEY? WHAT IS THIS?
I TRIED...
NOT SOMETHING YOU SEE EVERY DAY...
HE LOOKS BEAT UP REAL BAD.
WHAT'S HE TALKING ABOUT? WHO ARE YOU TALKING ABOUT?
I WANT HIM IN ROOM FIVE, NOW.
AND SOMEBODY GET THAT HELMET OFF HIM!
I TRIED TO...
I TRIED TO SAVE HER.

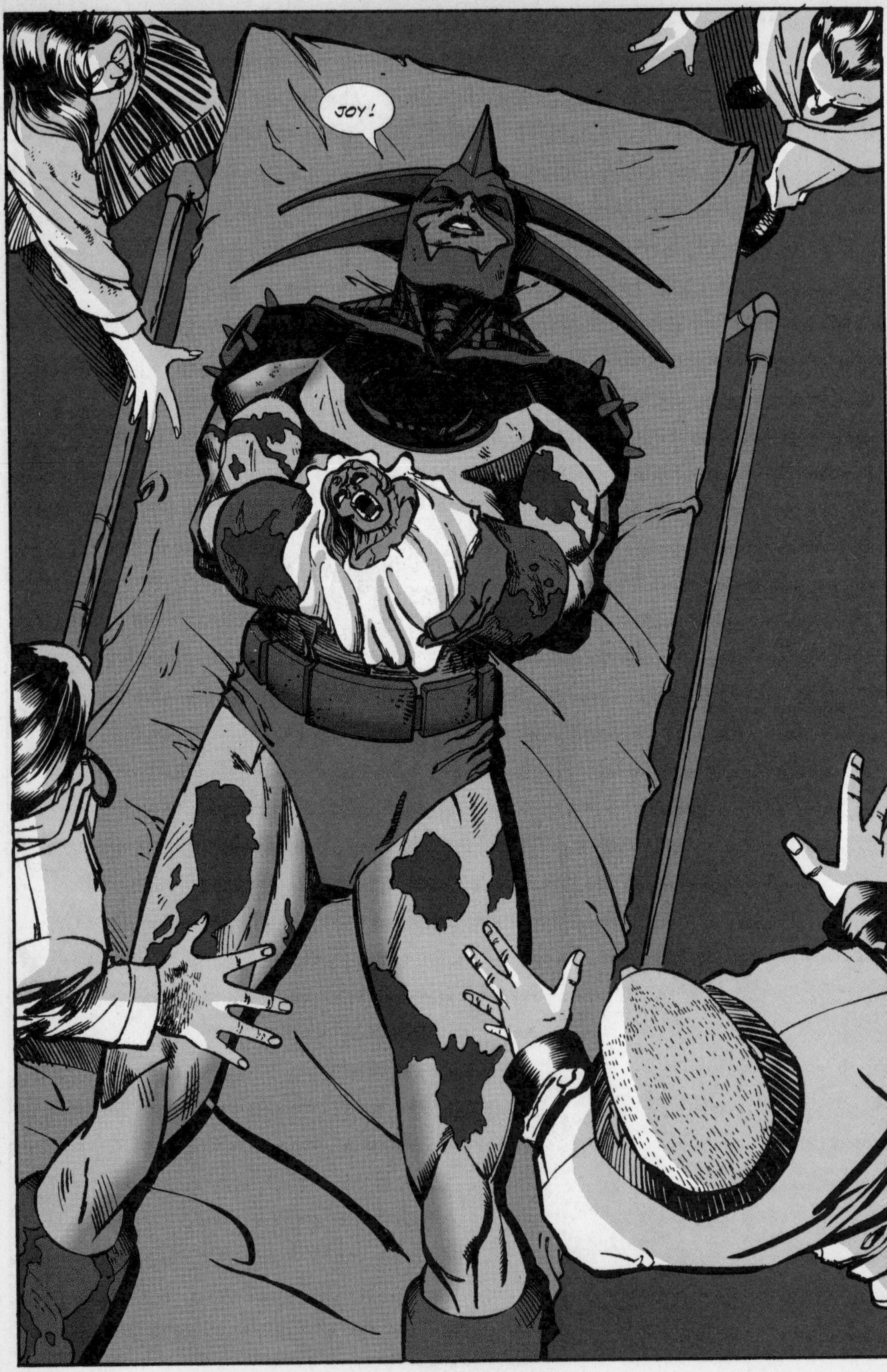
JOY!

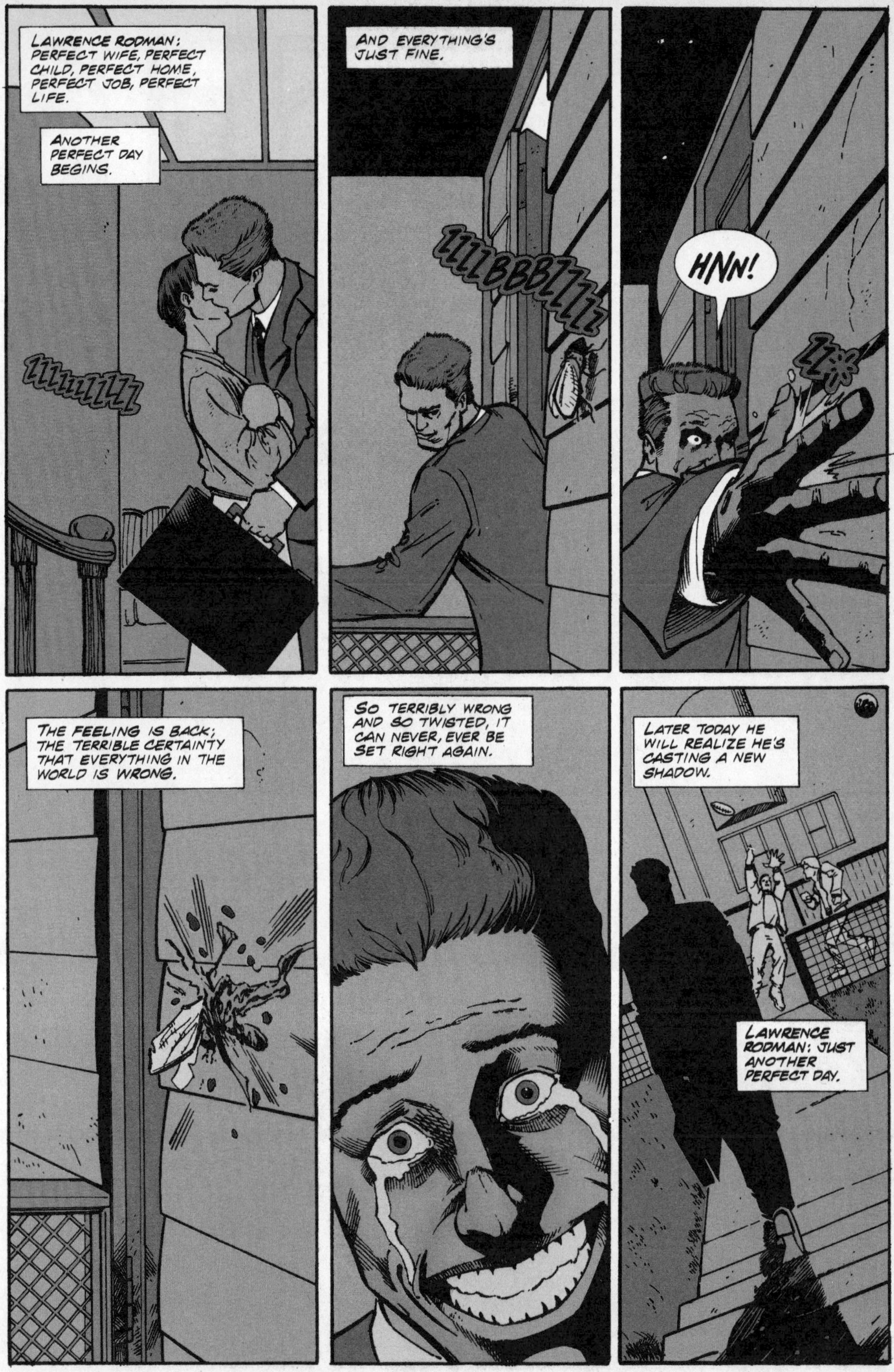
LAWRENCE RODMAN: PERFECT WIFE, PERFECT CHILD, PERFECT HOME, PERFECT JOB, PERFECT LIFE.
ANOTHER PERFECT DAY BEGINS.
ZZZzzzZZZZ
AND EVERYTHING'S JUST FINE.
ZZZZBBBZZZZZ
HNN!
ZZ
THE FEELING IS BACK; THE TERRIBLE CERTAINTY THAT EVERYTHING IN THE WORLD IS WRONG.
SO TERRIBLY WRONG AND SO TWISTED, IT CAN NEVER, EVER BE SET RIGHT AGAIN.
LATER TODAY HE WILL REALIZE HE'S CASTING A NEW SHADOW.
LAWRENCE RODMAN: JUST ANOTHER PERFECT DAY.

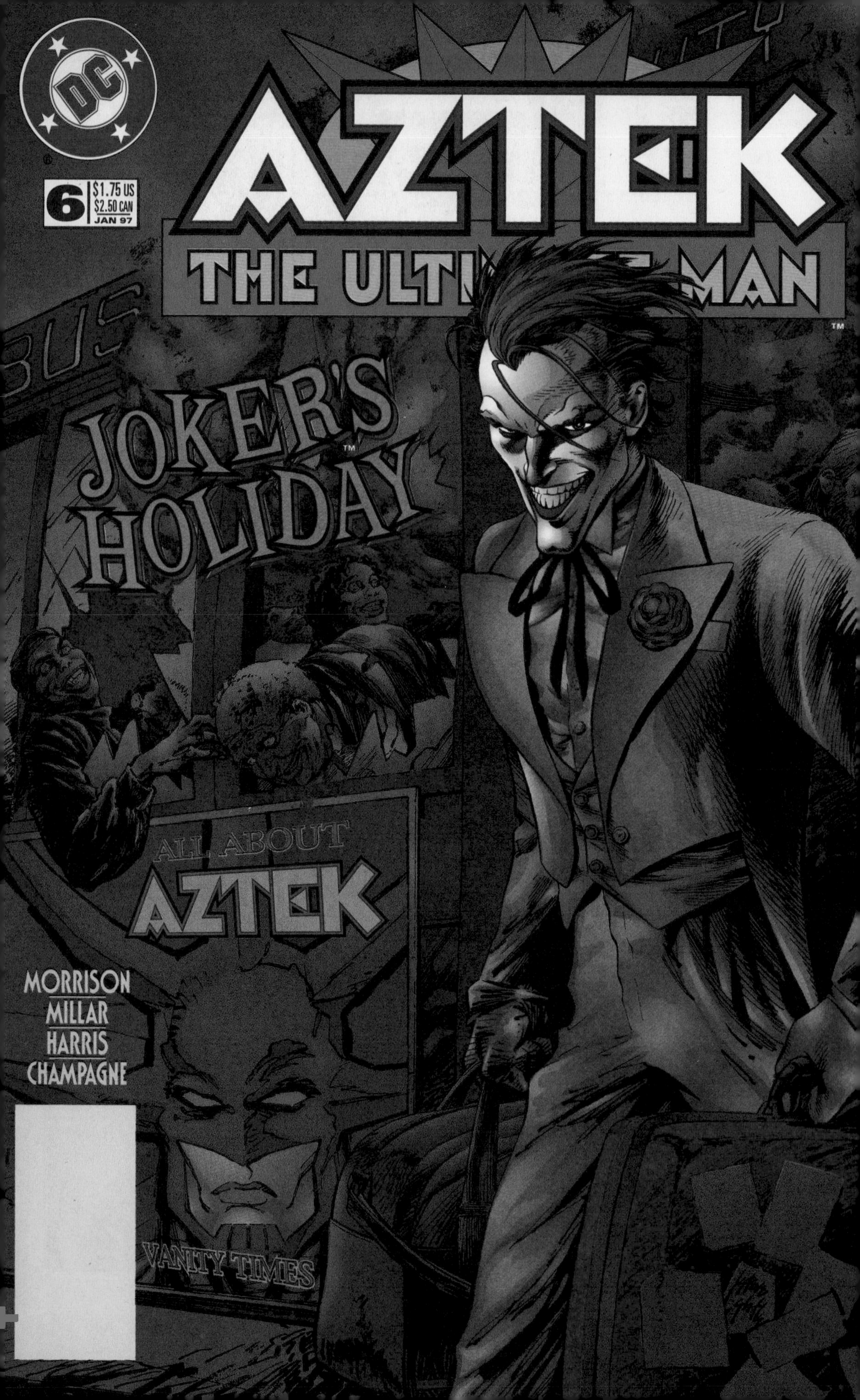
DC
AZTEK
THE ULTI
MAN
6
$1.75 US
$2.50 CAN
JAN 97
JOKER'S
HOLIDAY
ALL ABOUT
AZTEK
MORRISON
MILLAR
HARRIS
CHAMPAGNE
VANITY TIMES

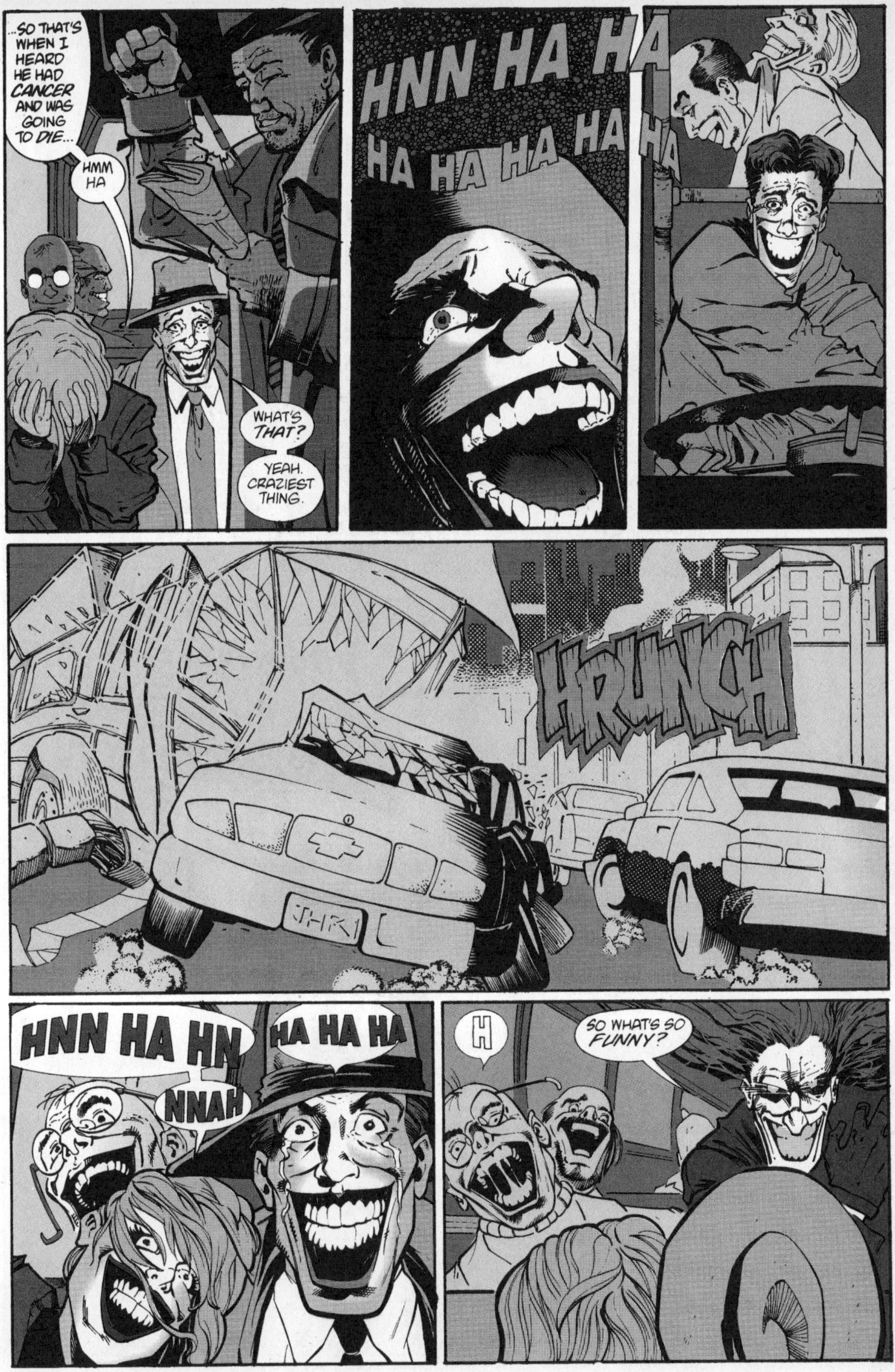
...SO THAT'S WHEN I HEARD HE HAD CANCER AND WAS GOING TO DIE...
HMM HA
WHAT'S THAT?
YEAH. CRAZIEST THING.
HNN HA HA
HA HA HA HA HA
HRUNCH
HNN HA HN
HA HA HA
NNAH
H
SO WHAT'S SO FUNNY?

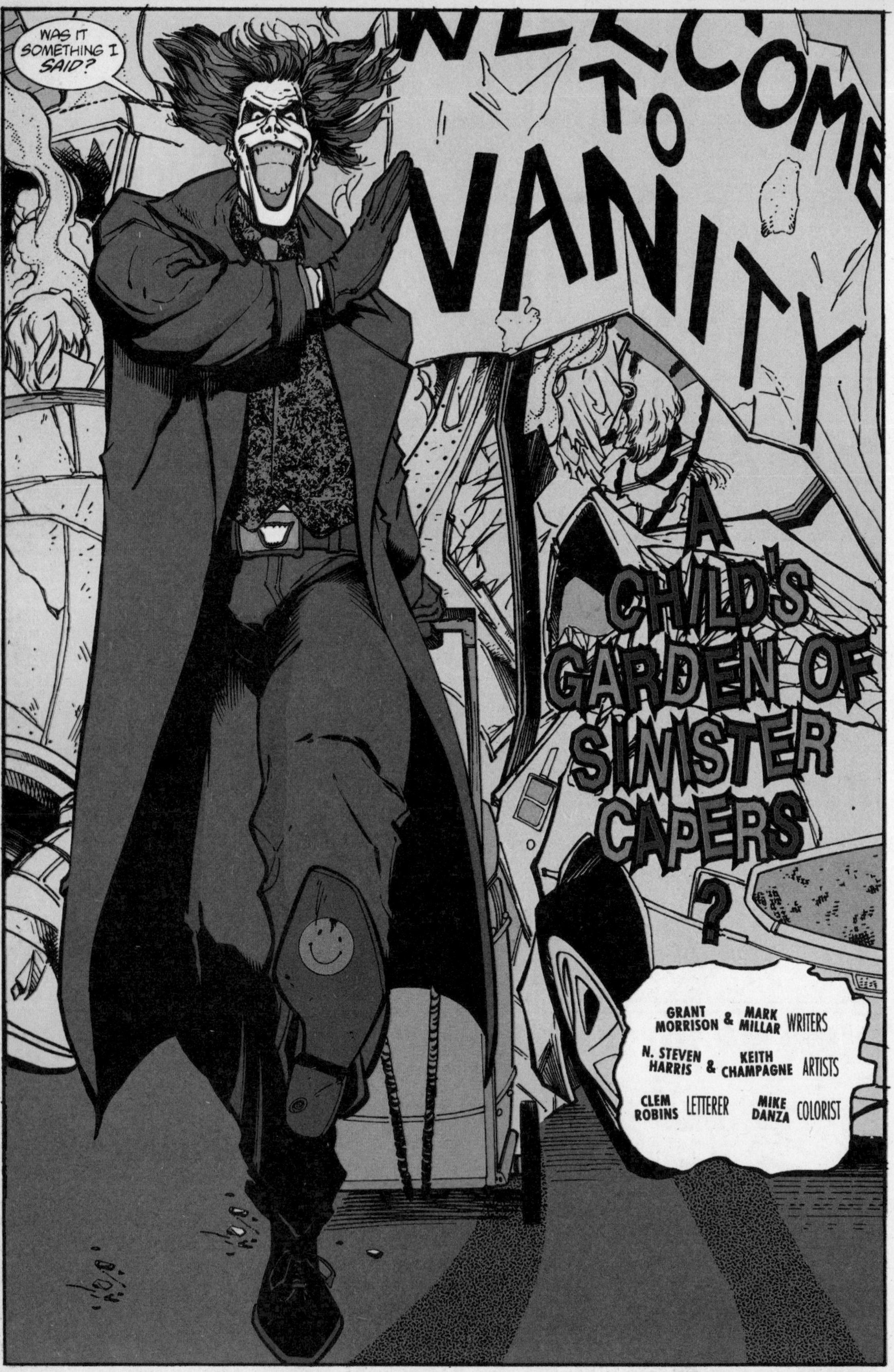
WAS IT SOMETHING I SAID?
WELCOME TO VANITY
A CHILD'S GARDEN OF SINISTER CAPERS?
GRANT MORRISON & MARK MILLAR WRITERS
N. STEVEN HARRIS & KEITH CHAMPAGNE ARTISTS
CLEM ROBINS LETTERER
MIKE DANZA COLORIST

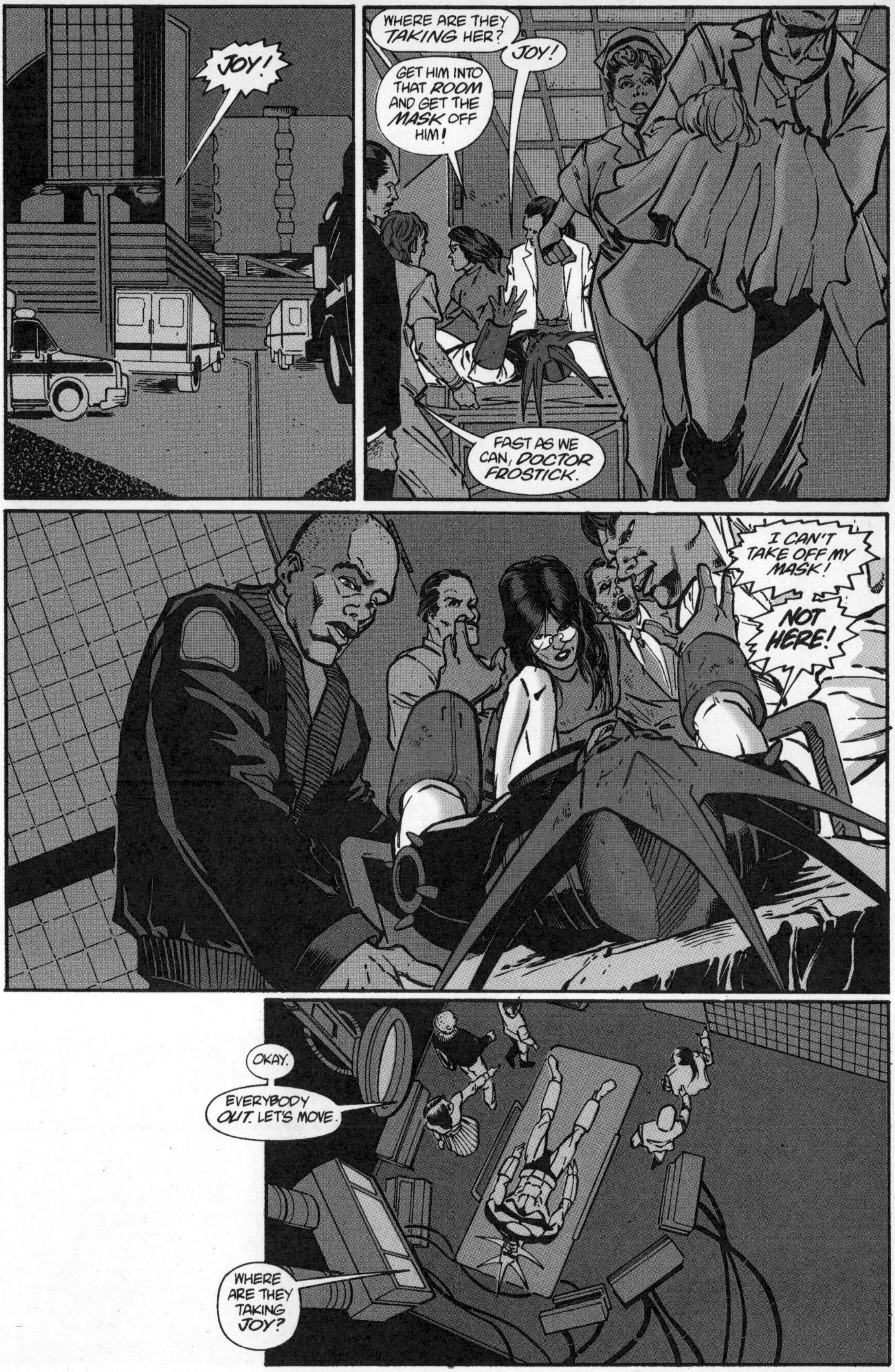
JOY!
WHERE ARE THEY TAKING HER?
JOY!
GET HIM INTO THAT ROOM AND GET THE MASK OFF HIM!
FAST AS WE CAN, DOCTOR FROSTICK.
I CAN'T TAKE OFF MY MASK!
NOT HERE!
OKAY.
EVERYBODY OUT. LET'S MOVE.
WHERE ARE THEY TAKING JOY?

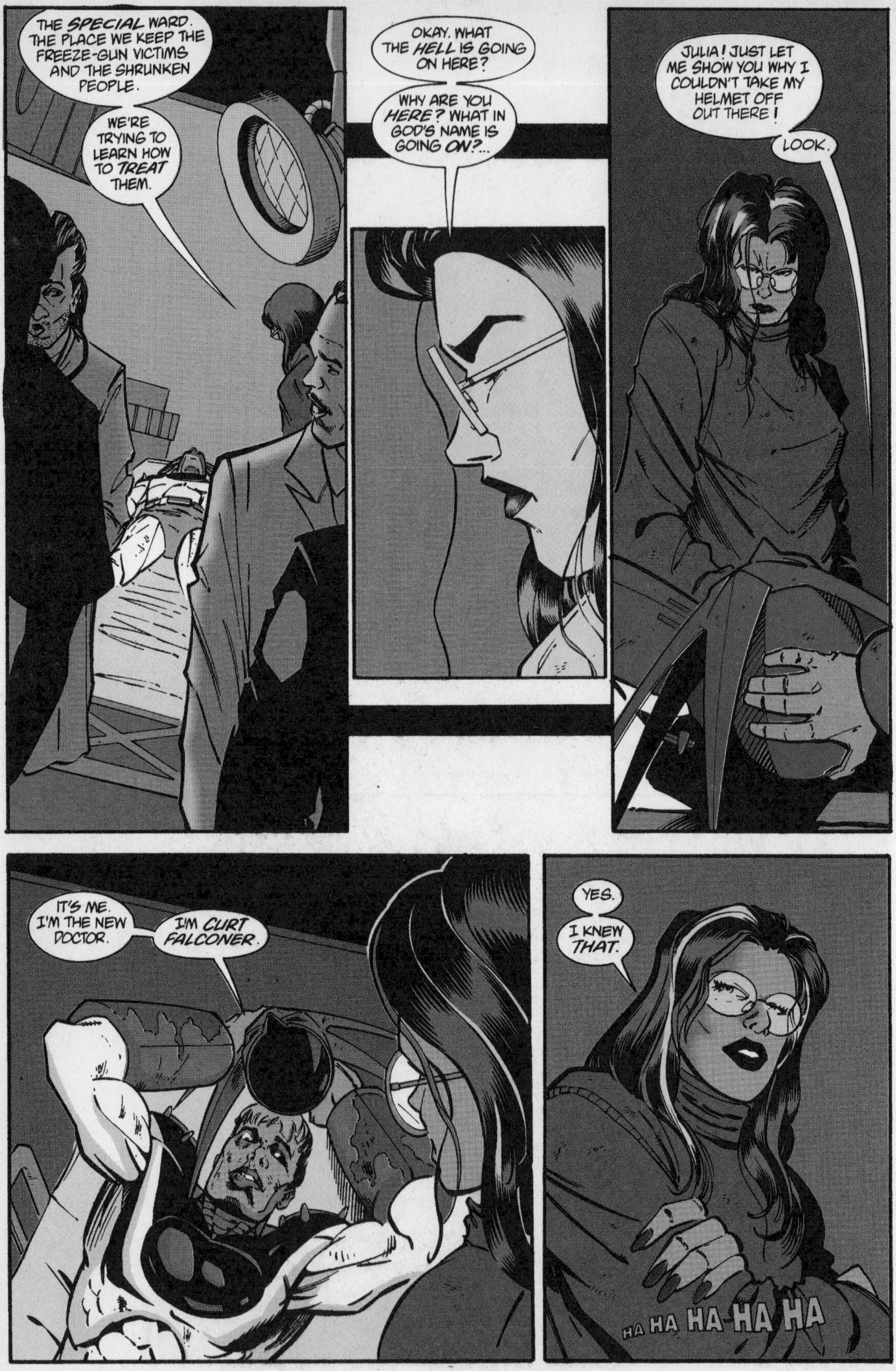
THE SPECIAL WARD. THE PLACE WE KEEP THE FREEZE-GUN VICTIMS AND THE SHRUNKEN PEOPLE.
WE'RE TRYING TO LEARN HOW TO TREAT THEM.
OKAY. WHAT THE HELL IS GOING ON HERE?
WHY ARE YOU HERE? WHAT IN GOD'S NAME IS GOING ON?...
JULIA! JUST LET ME SHOW YOU WHY I COULDN'T TAKE MY HELMET OFF OUT THERE!
LOOK.
IT'S ME. I'M THE NEW DOCTOR.
I'M CURT FALCONER.
YES.
I KNEW THAT.
HA HA HA HA HA HA

YOU KNEW?

THE REAL DOCTOR CURT FALCONER WAS *DEAD* THE LAST TIME WE LOOKED. AND YOU'RE NOT VERY GOOD AT *HIDING* WHAT YOU DO. YOU DON'T EVEN CHANGE YOUR *VOICE.*

WHAT I WANT TO KNOW *NOW* IS HOW YOU'RE GOING TO...

HA HA HA HA HA

HA HA HA HA

JULIA!

IT'S THE *JOKER!* HE'S HIT...*UMM...SIX* LOCATIONS IN THE CITY!

HA HA HA

WE'RE PULLING THEM IN FROM ALL OVER! WHAT ARE YOU *DOING?*

I HAVE TO HELP.

YOU'RE A *MESS!* YOU CAN HARDLY *STAND!*

YOU OWE ME AN *EXPLANATION!*

I KNOW.

I'M SORRY.

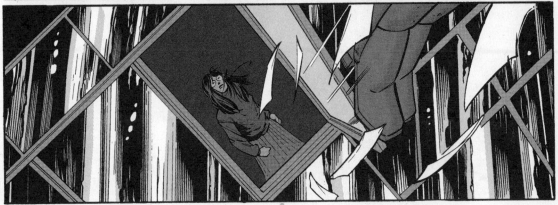

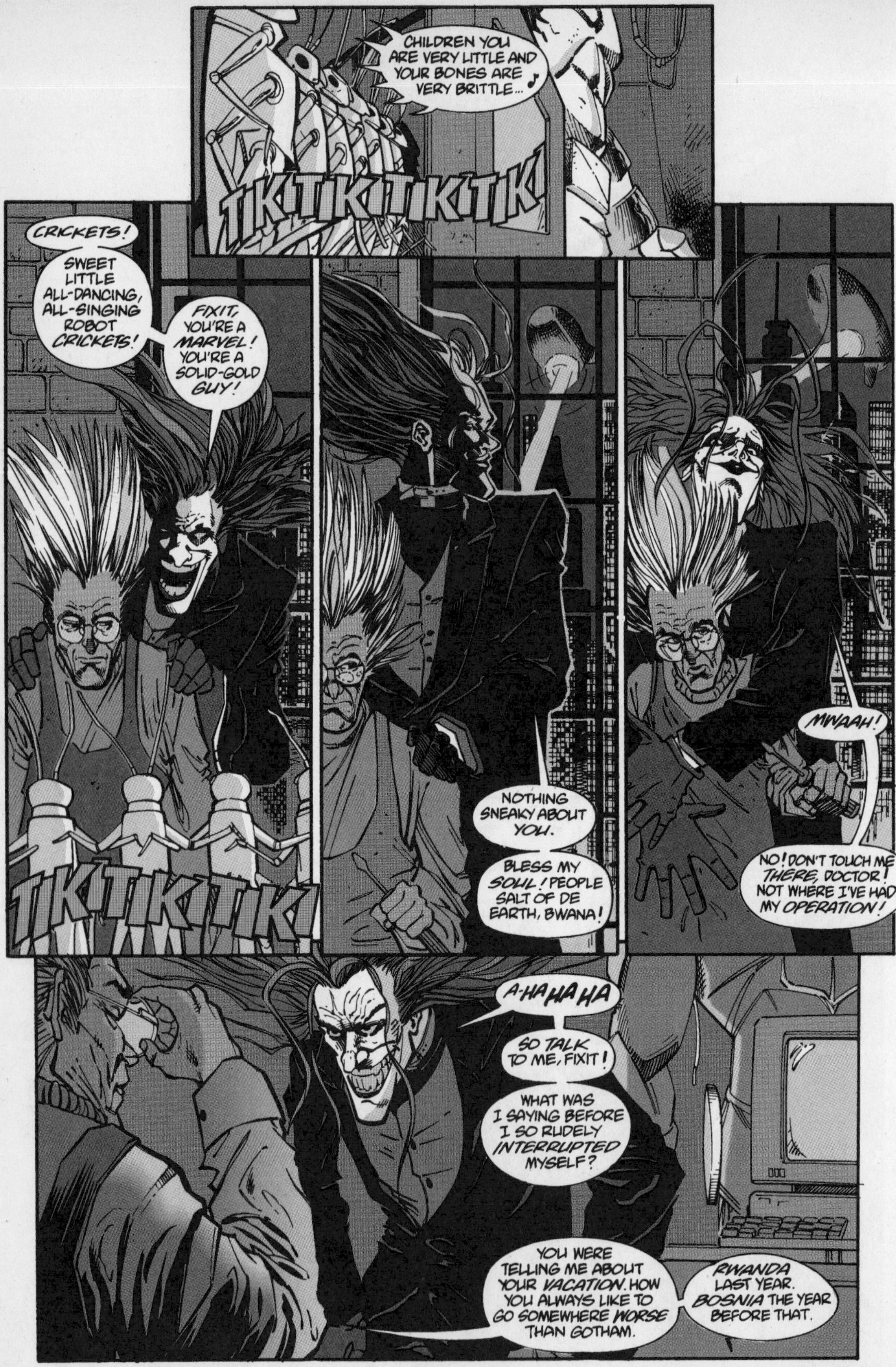
CHILDREN YOU ARE VERY LITTLE AND YOUR BONES ARE VERY BRITTLE...
TIKITIKITIKITIK!
CRICKETS!
SWEET LITTLE ALL-DANCING, ALL-SINGING ROBOT CRICKETS!
FIXIT, YOU'RE A MARVEL! YOU'RE A SOLID-GOLD GUY!
TIKITIKITIK!
NOTHING SNEAKY ABOUT YOU.
BLESS MY SOUL! PEOPLE SALT OF DE EARTH, BWANA!
MWAAH!
NO! DON'T TOUCH ME THERE, DOCTOR! NOT WHERE I'VE HAD MY OPERATION!
A-HA HA HA HA
SO TALK TO ME, FIXIT!
WHAT WAS I SAYING BEFORE I SO RUDELY INTERRUPTED MYSELF?
YOU WERE TELLING ME ABOUT YOUR VACATION. HOW YOU ALWAYS LIKE TO GO SOMEWHERE WORSE THAN GOTHAM.
RWANDA LAST YEAR. BOSNIA THE YEAR BEFORE THAT.

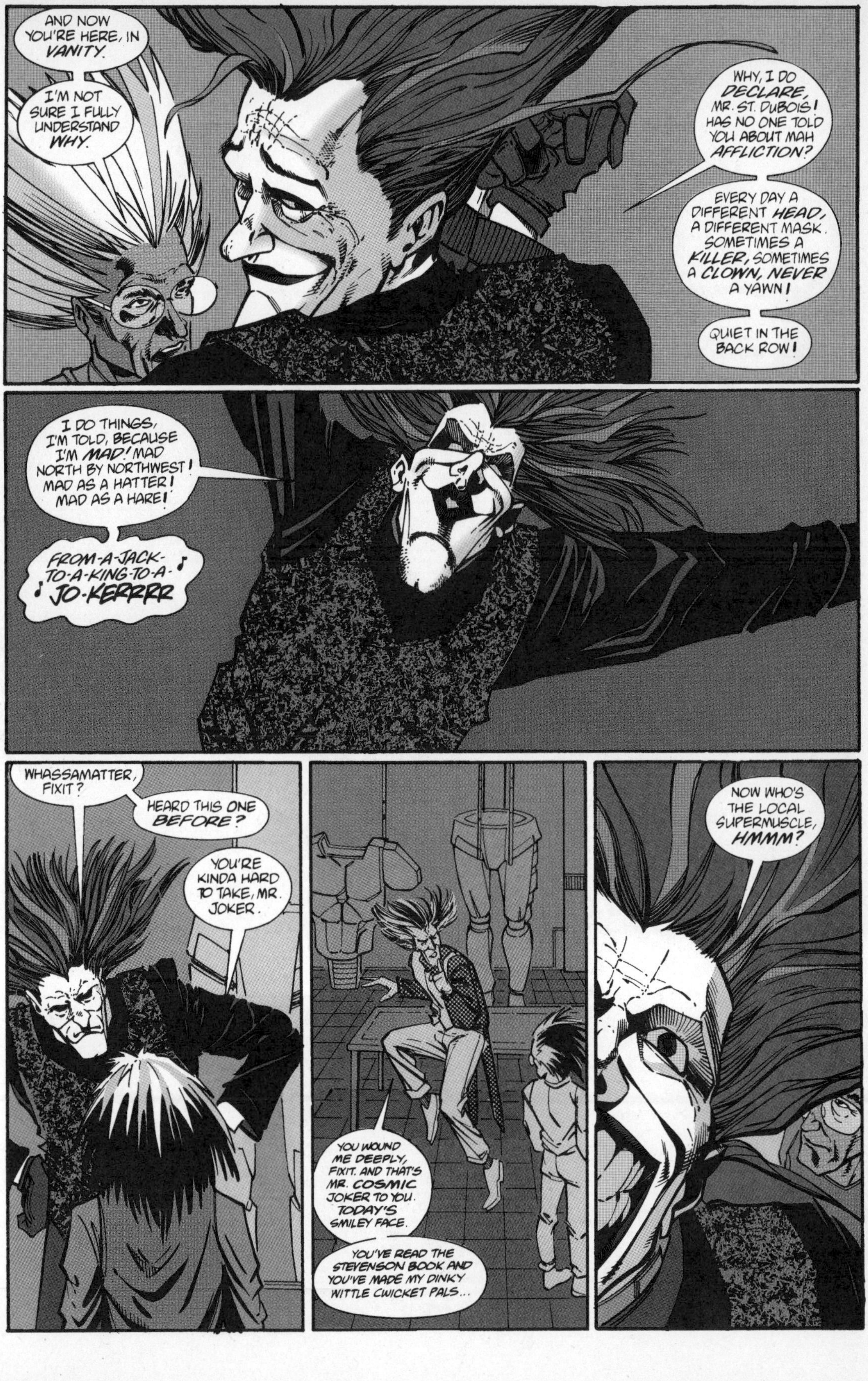
AND NOW YOU'RE HERE, IN VANITY.
I'M NOT SURE I FULLY UNDERSTAND WHY.
WHY, I DO DECLARE, MR. ST. DUBOIS! HAS NO ONE TOLD YOU ABOUT MAH AFFLICTION?
EVERY DAY A DIFFERENT HEAD, A DIFFERENT MASK. SOMETIMES A KILLER, SOMETIMES A CLOWN, NEVER A YAWN!
QUIET IN THE BACK ROW!
I DO THINGS, I'M TOLD, BECAUSE I'M MAD! MAD NORTH BY NORTHWEST! MAD AS A HATTER! MAD AS A HARE!
FROM-A-JACK-TO-A-KING-TO-A-JO-KERRRR
WHASSAMATTER, FIXIT?
HEARD THIS ONE BEFORE?
YOU'RE KINDA HARD TO TAKE, MR. JOKER.
YOU WOUND ME DEEPLY, FIXIT. AND THAT'S MR. COSMIC JOKER TO YOU. TODAY'S SMILEY FACE.
YOU'VE READ THE STEVENSON BOOK AND YOU'VE MADE MY DINKY WITTLE CWICKET PALS...
NOW WHO'S THE LOCAL SUPERMUSCLE, HMMM?

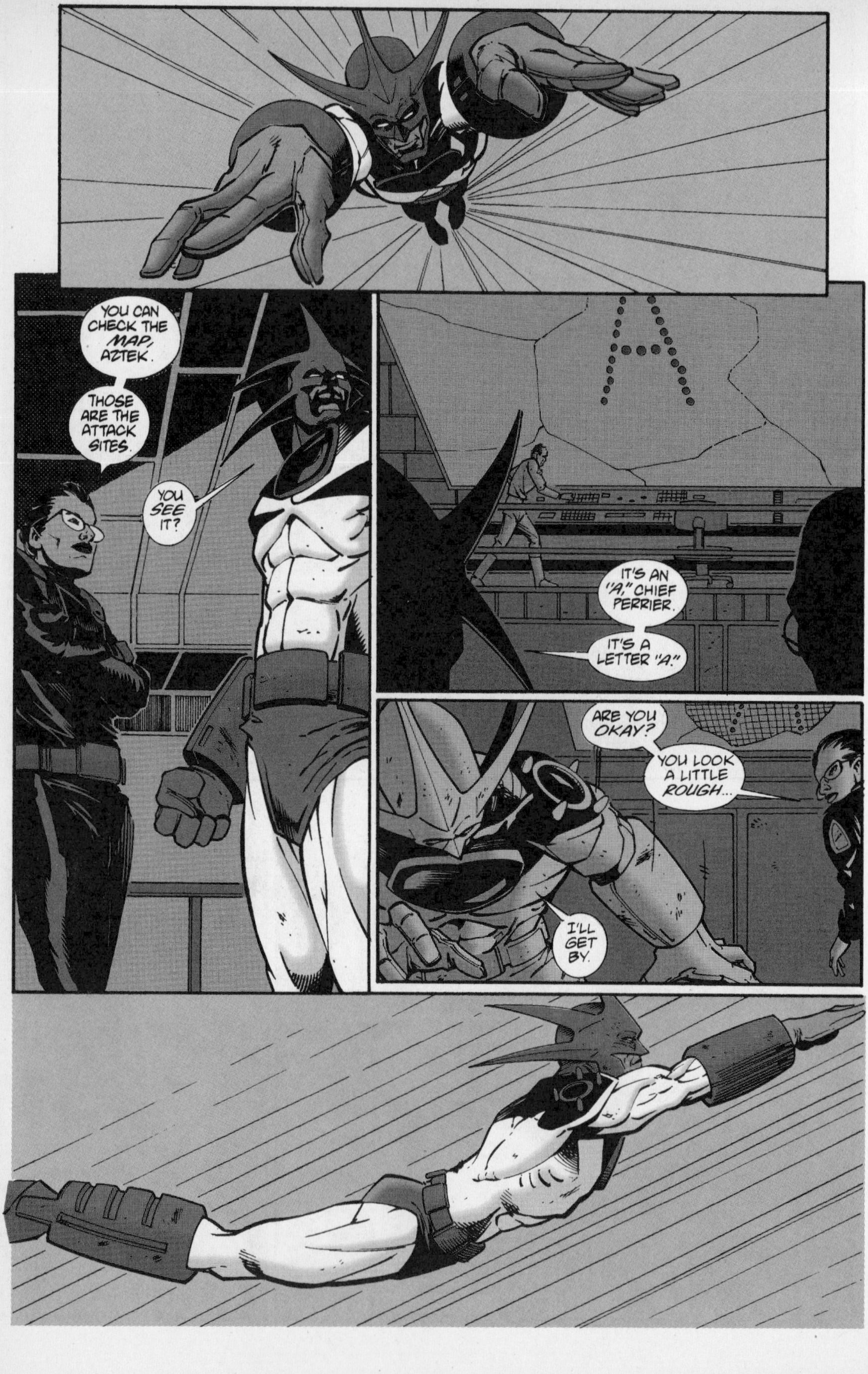
YOU CAN CHECK THE MAP, AZTEK.
THOSE ARE THE ATTACK SITES.
YOU SEE IT?
IT'S AN "A," CHIEF PERRIER.
IT'S A LETTER "A."
ARE YOU OKAY?
YOU LOOK A LITTLE ROUGH...
I'LL GET BY.

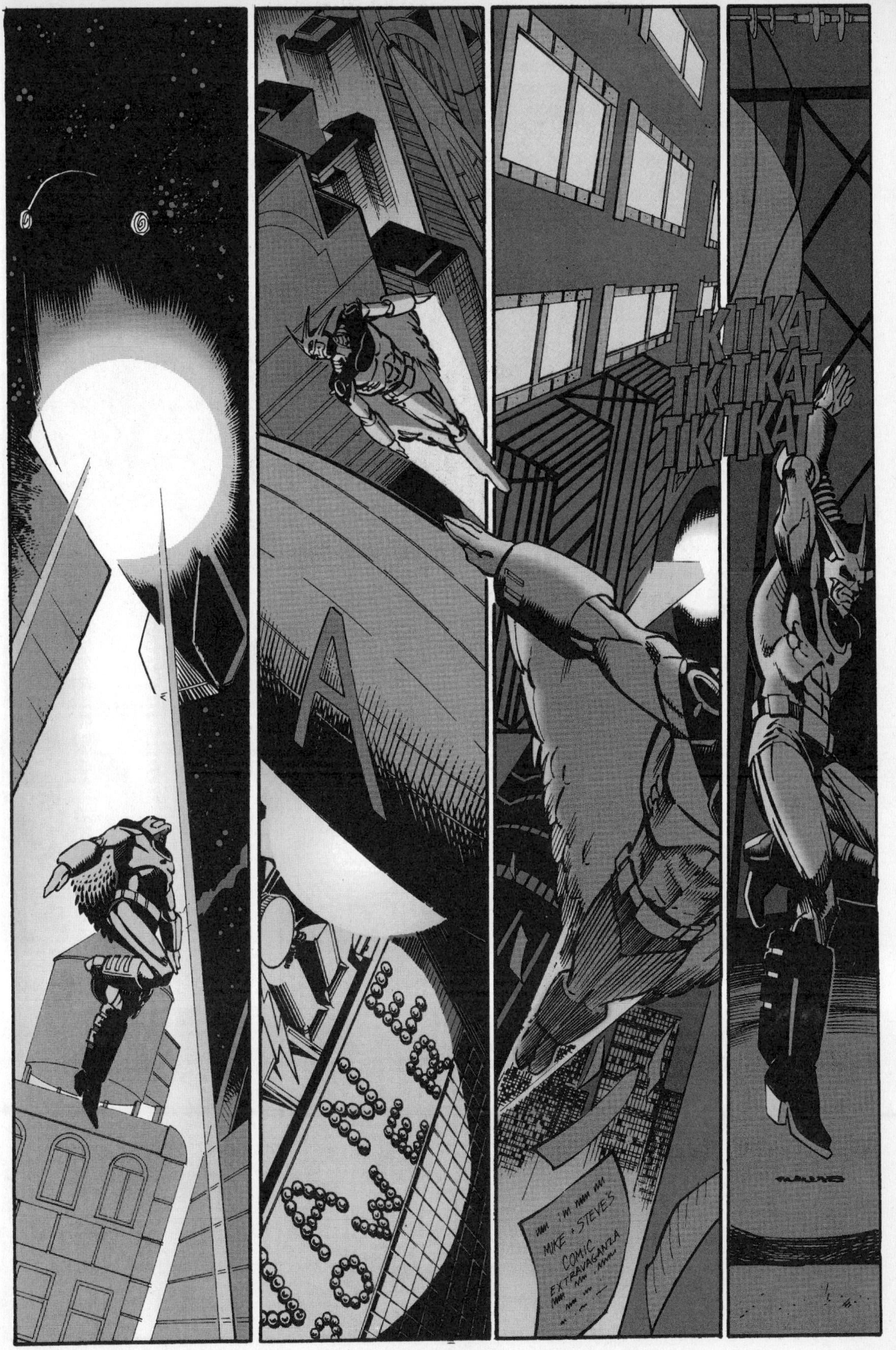
TIKITIKAT
TIKITIKAT
TIKITIKAT
MIKE & STEVE'S
COMIC
EXTRAVAGANZA

ANY PROGRESS?

WE HAVE PEOPLE *DYING* HERE!

HA HA HA HA

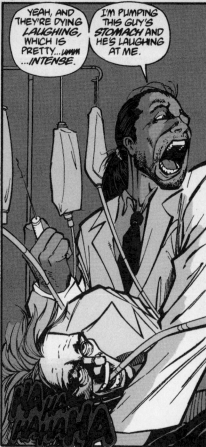

YEAH, AND THEY'RE DYING *LAUGHING,* WHICH IS PRETTY...UMM ...INTENSE.

I'M PUMPING THIS GUY'S *STOMACH* AND HE'S LAUGHING AT ME.

HAHA HAHAHA

THAT'S A MAN WITH A HELL OF A SENSE OF *HUMOR,* MOSELEY.

MAN, THIS IS SO *SICK.* WHERE'S WONDERKID *FALCONER* WHEN WE REALLY NEED HIM?

DOCTOR CLEVEDEN!

HA HAHA HAHA HA

HAHA AHAHA

ARE YOU GOING TO SIT THERE DRINKING CHAMPAGNE *ALL* DAY OR DO YOU WANT TO HELP US HERE?

FIGURE OUT AN *ANTITOXIN,* FORBES!

HAHA HAHA

YOUR WISH IS MY COMMAND, JULIA.

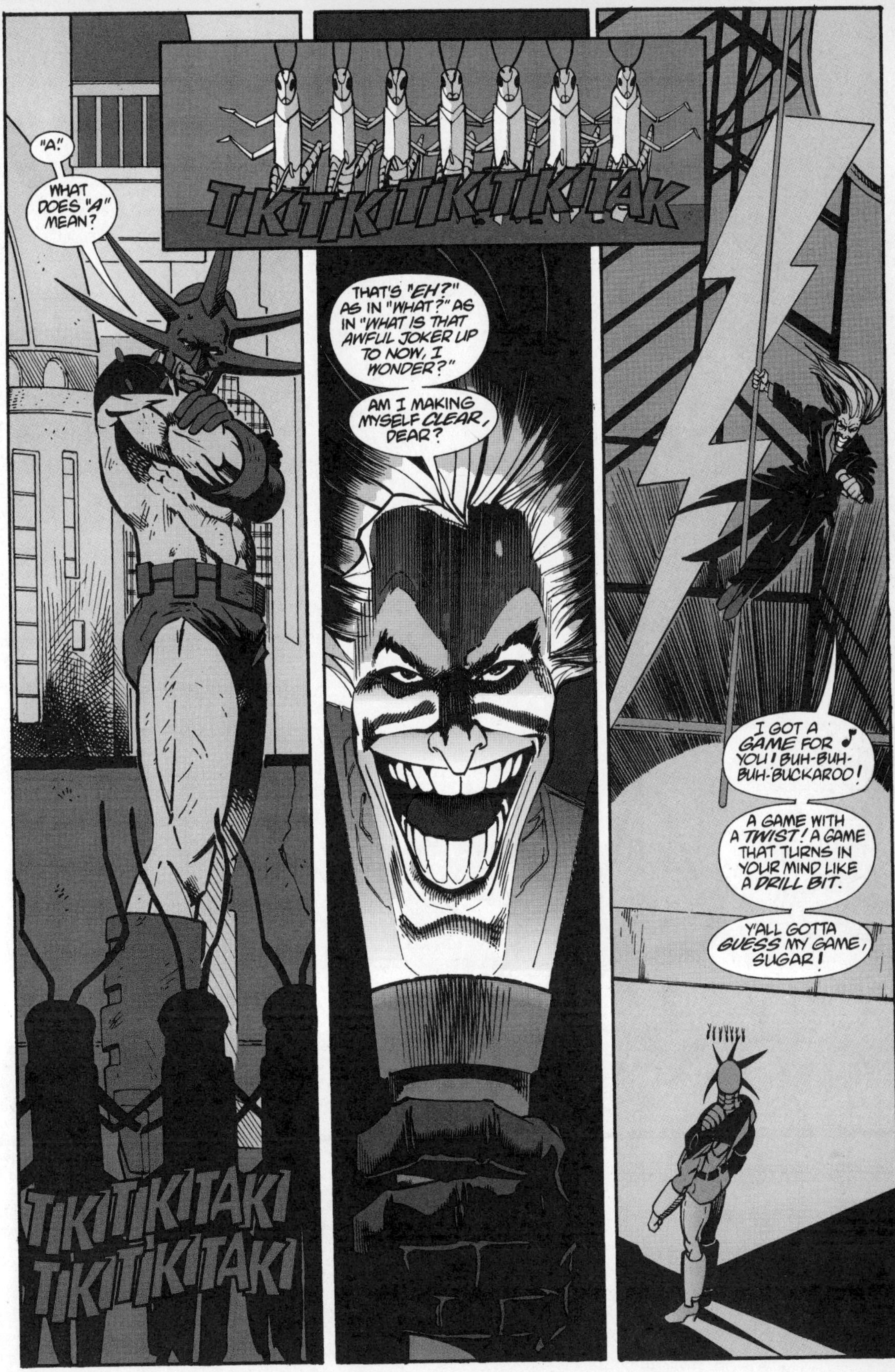
"A."
WHAT DOES "A" MEAN?
TIKITIKITIKITIKITAK
TIKITIKITAKI TIKITIKITAKI
THAT'S "EH?" AS IN "WHAT?" AS IN "WHAT IS THAT AWFUL JOKER UP TO NOW, I WONDER?"
AM I MAKING MYSELF CLEAR, DEAR?
I GOT A GAME FOR YOU! BUH-BUH-BUH-BUCKAROO!
A GAME WITH A TWIST! A GAME THAT TURNS IN YOUR MIND LIKE A DRILL BIT.
Y'ALL GOTTA GUESS MY GAME, SUGAR!

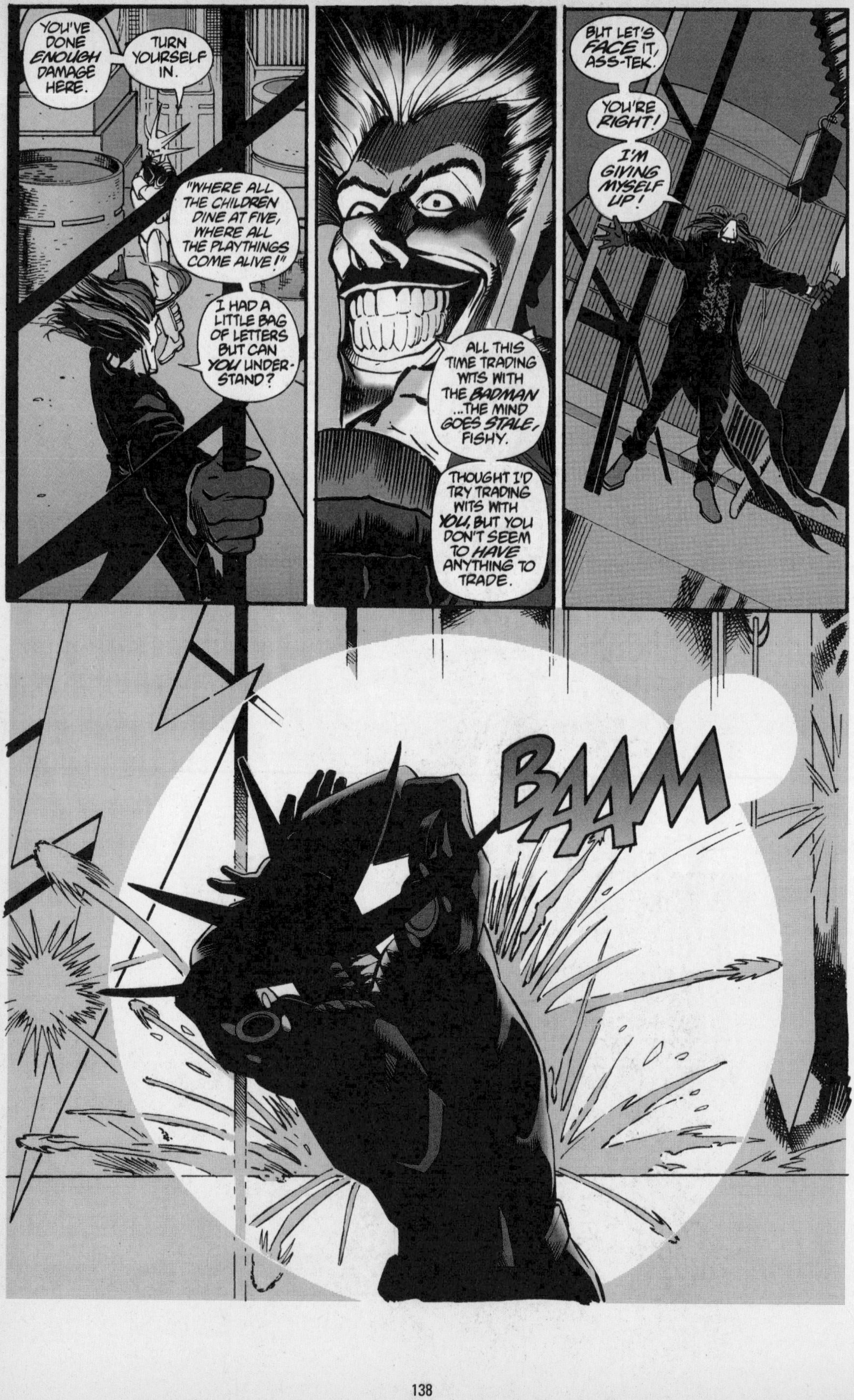
YOU'VE DONE ENOUGH DAMAGE HERE.
TURN YOURSELF IN.
"WHERE ALL THE CHILDREN DINE AT FIVE, WHERE ALL THE PLAYTHINGS COME ALIVE!"
I HAD A LITTLE BAG OF LETTERS BUT CAN YOU UNDERSTAND?
ALL THIS TIME TRADING WITS WITH THE BADMAN ...THE MIND GOES STALE, FISHY.
THOUGHT I'D TRY TRADING WITS WITH YOU, BUT YOU DON'T SEEM TO HAVE ANYTHING TO TRADE.
BUT LET'S FACE IT, ASS-TEK.
YOU'RE RIGHT!
I'M GIVING MYSELF UP!
BAAM

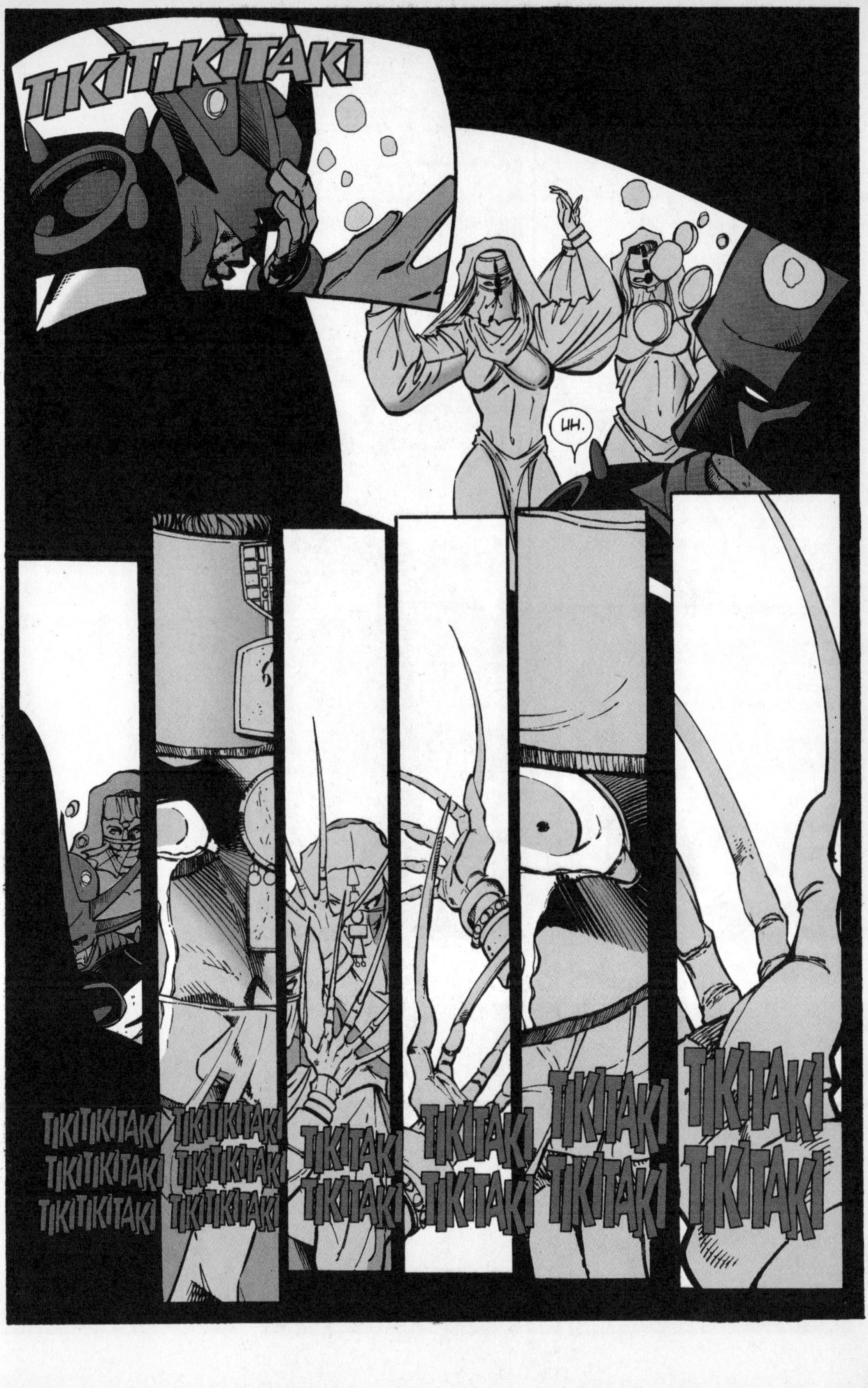
TIKITIKITAKI
UH.
TIKITIKITAKI
TIKITIKITAKI
TIKITIKITAKI
TIKITIKITAKI
TIKITIKITAKI
TIKITIKITAKI
TIKITAKI
TIKITAKI
TIKITAKI
TIKITAKI
TIKITAKI
TIKITAKI
TIKITAKI
TIKITAKI

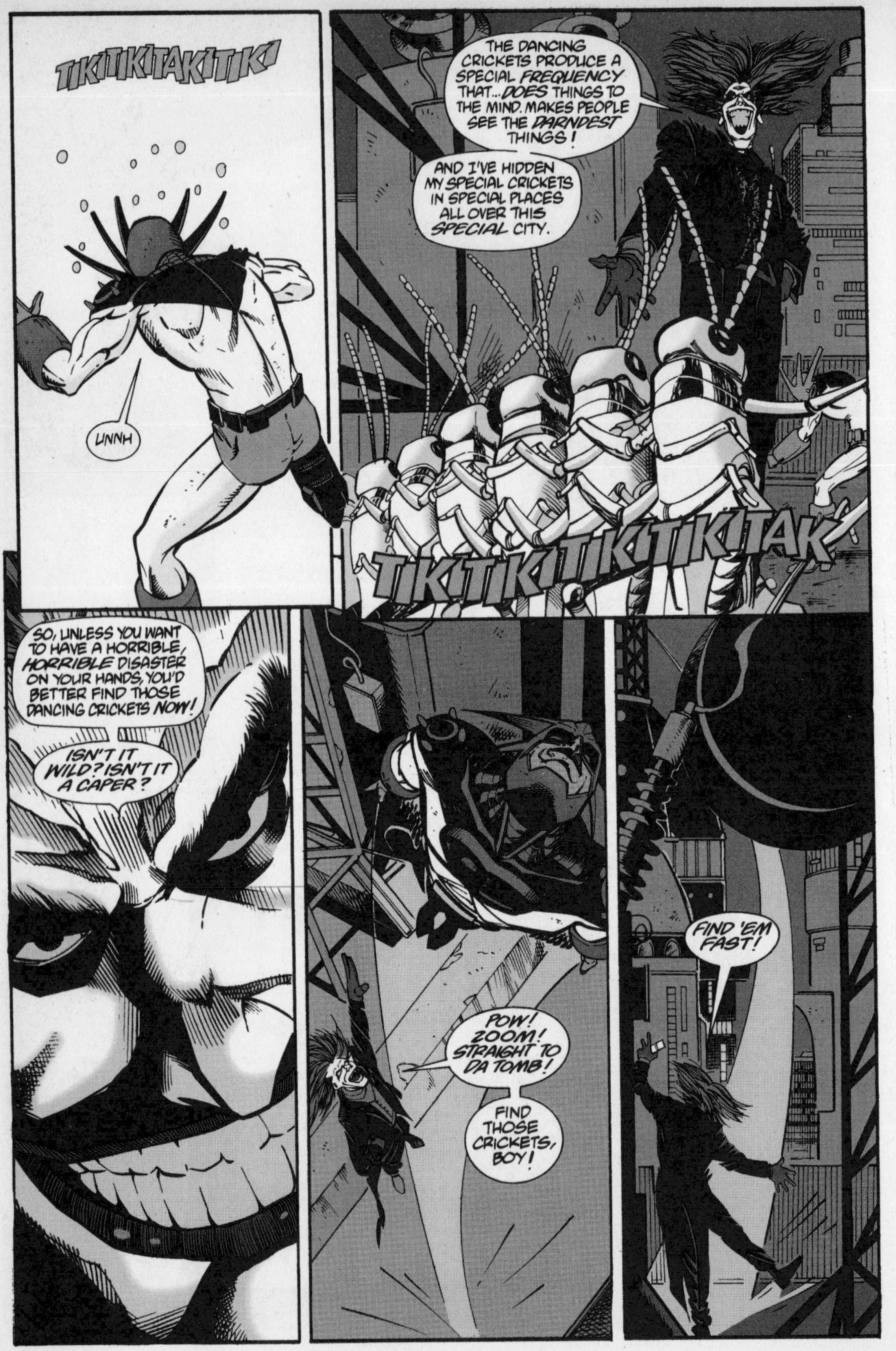
TIKITIKITAKITIKI
UNNH
THE DANCING CRICKETS PRODUCE A SPECIAL FREQUENCY THAT...DOES THINGS TO THE MIND. MAKES PEOPLE SEE THE DARNDEST THINGS!
AND I'VE HIDDEN MY SPECIAL CRICKETS IN SPECIAL PLACES ALL OVER THIS SPECIAL CITY.
TIKITIKITIKITIKITAK
SO, UNLESS YOU WANT TO HAVE A HORRIBLE, HORRIBLE DISASTER ON YOUR HANDS, YOU'D BETTER FIND THOSE DANCING CRICKETS NOW!
ISN'T IT WILD? ISN'T IT A CAPER?
POW! ZOOM! STRAIGHT TO DA TOMB!
FIND THOSE CRICKETS, BOY!
FIND 'EM FAST!

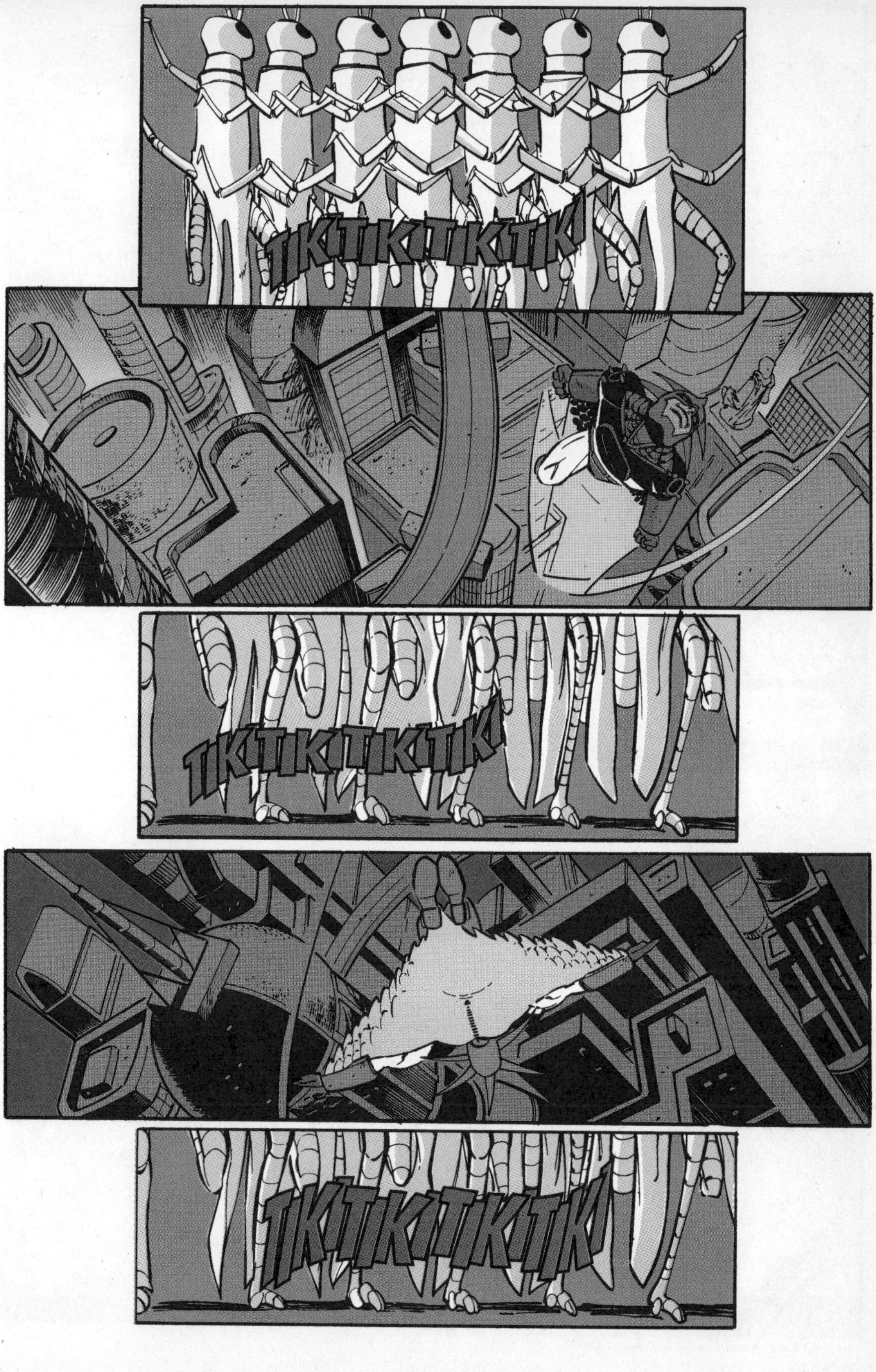
TIKITIKITIKITIKI
TIKITIKITIKITIKI
TIKITIKITIKITIKI

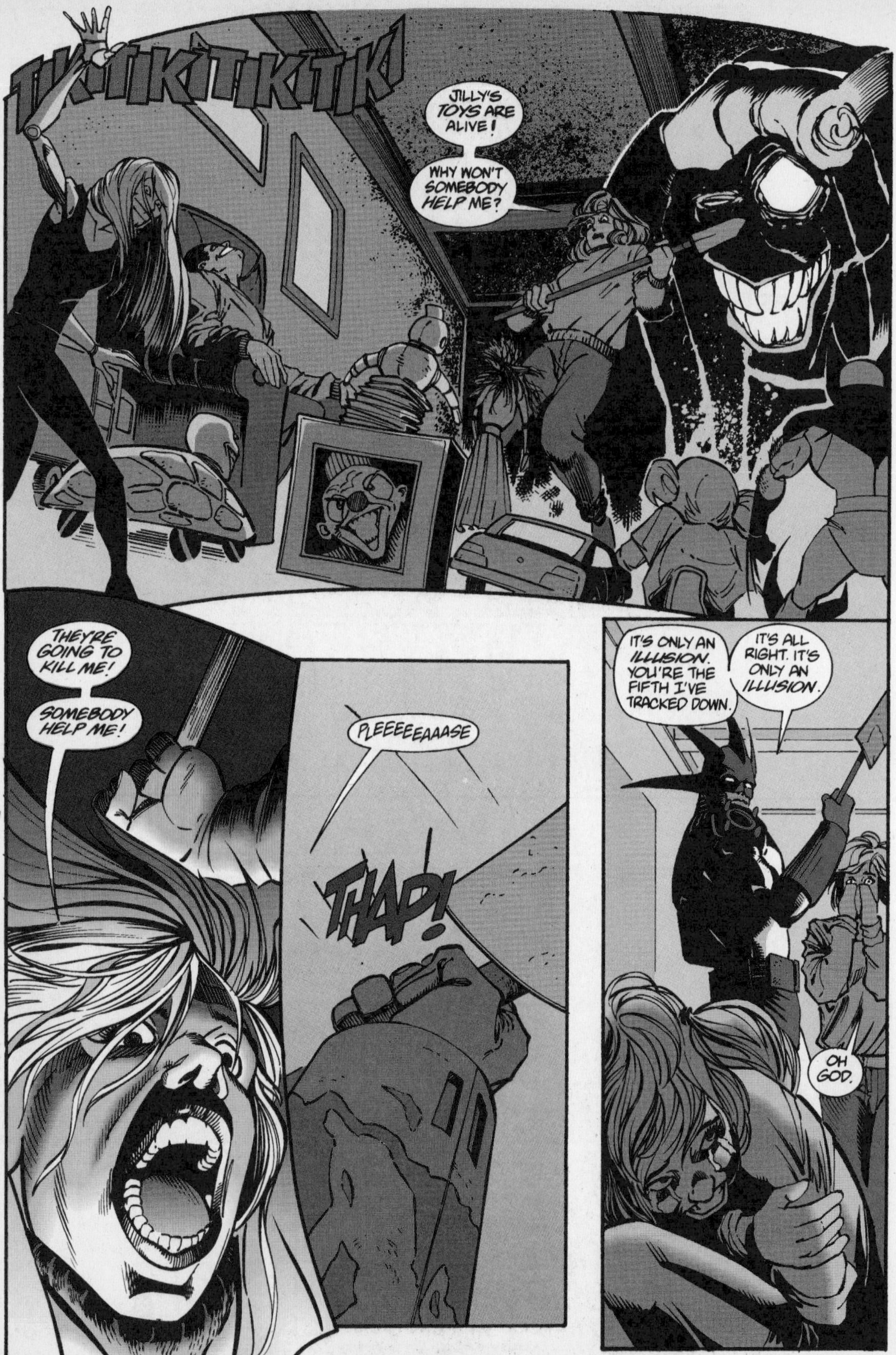
TIKITIKITIKITIKI
JILLY'S TOYS ARE ALIVE!
WHY WON'T SOMEBODY HELP ME?
THEY'RE GOING TO KILL ME!
SOMEBODY HELP ME!
PLEEEEEAAAASE
THAP!
IT'S ONLY AN ILLUSION. YOU'RE THE FIFTH I'VE TRACKED DOWN.
IT'S ALL RIGHT. IT'S ONLY AN ILLUSION.
OH GOD.

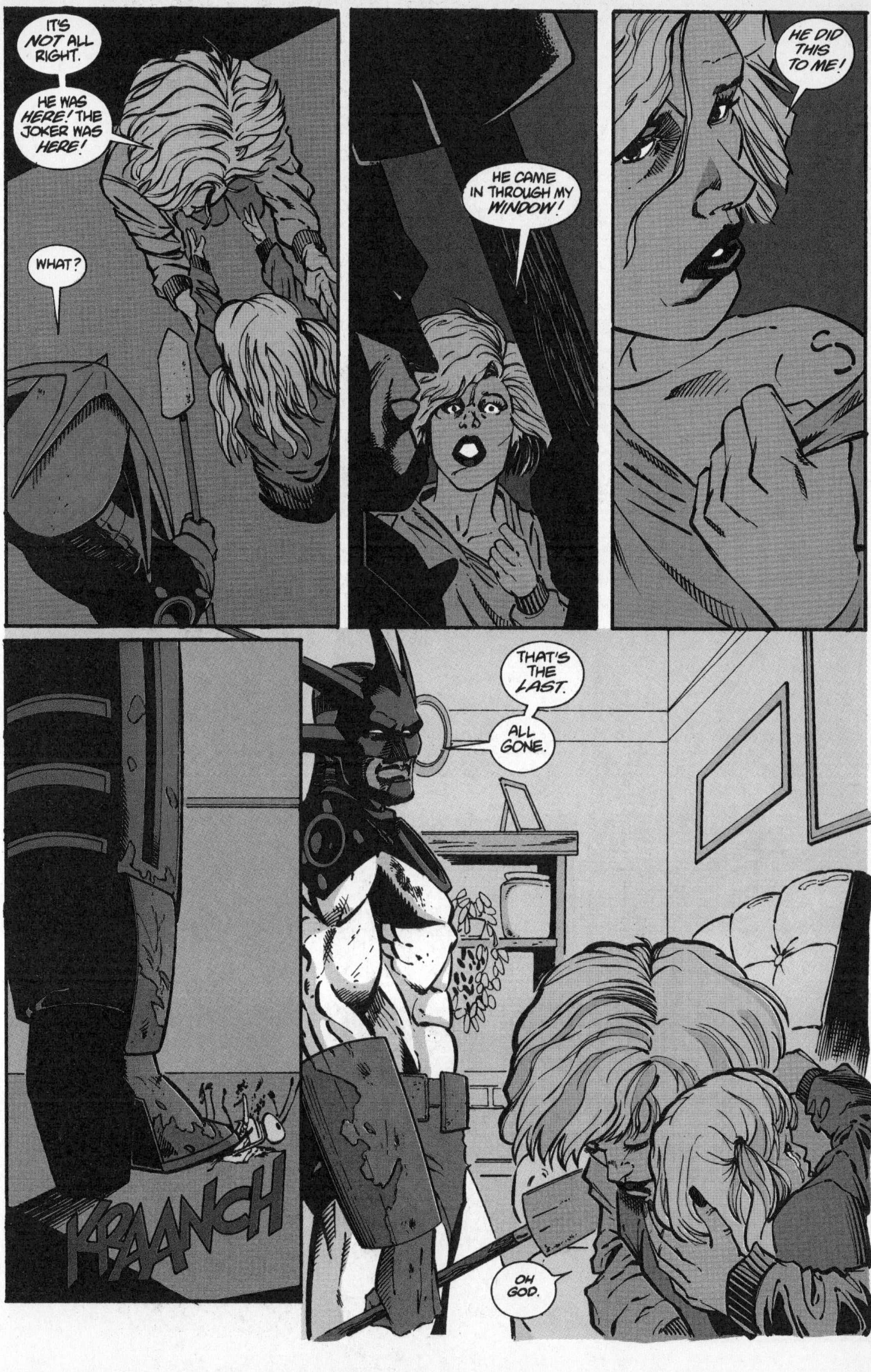
IT'S NOT ALL RIGHT.
HE WAS HERE! THE JOKER WAS HERE!
WHAT?
HE CAME IN THROUGH MY WINDOW!
HE DID THIS TO ME!
THAT'S THE LAST.
ALL GONE.
KRAANCH
OH GOD.

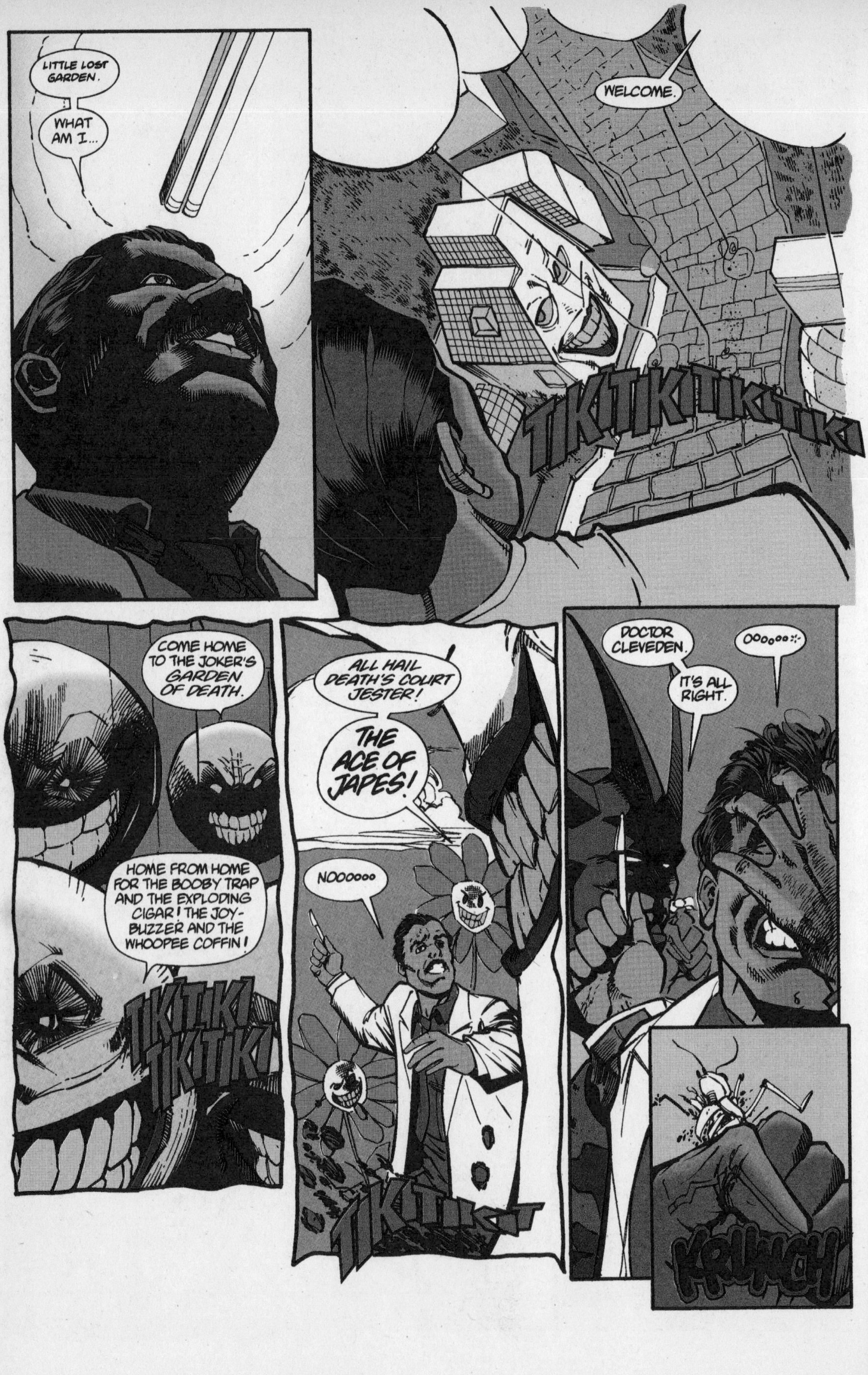

LITTLE LOST GARDEN.
WHAT AM I...
WELCOME.
TIKITIKITIKITIKITIKI
COME HOME TO THE JOKER'S GARDEN OF DEATH.
HOME FROM HOME FOR THE BOOBY TRAP AND THE EXPLODING CIGAR! THE JOY-BUZZER AND THE WHOOPEE COFFIN!
TIKITIKI TIKITIKI
ALL HAIL DEATH'S COURT JESTER!
THE ACE OF JAPES!
NOOOOOO
TIKITIKIT
DOCTOR CLEVEDEN.
IT'S ALL RIGHT.
OOOOOO
KRUNCH

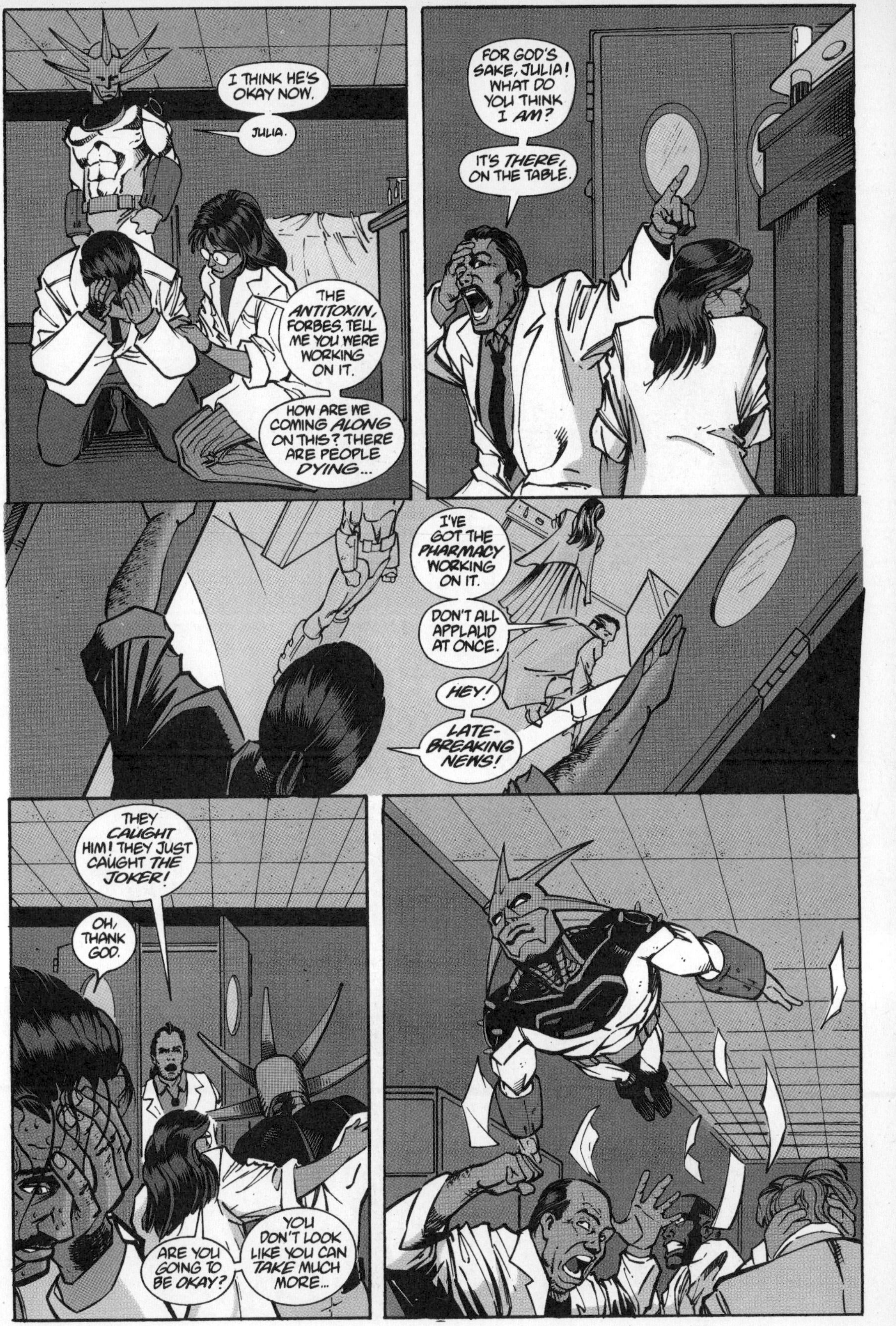
I THINK HE'S OKAY NOW.
JULIA.
THE ANTITOXIN, FORBES. TELL ME YOU WERE WORKING ON IT.
HOW ARE WE COMING ALONG ON THIS? THERE ARE PEOPLE DYING...
FOR GOD'S SAKE, JULIA! WHAT DO YOU THINK I AM?
IT'S THERE, ON THE TABLE.
I'VE GOT THE PHARMACY WORKING ON IT.
DON'T ALL APPLAUD AT ONCE.
HEY!
LATE-BREAKING NEWS!
THEY CAUGHT HIM! THEY JUST CAUGHT THE JOKER!
OH, THANK GOD.
ARE YOU GOING TO BE OKAY?
YOU DON'T LOOK LIKE YOU CAN TAKE MUCH MORE...

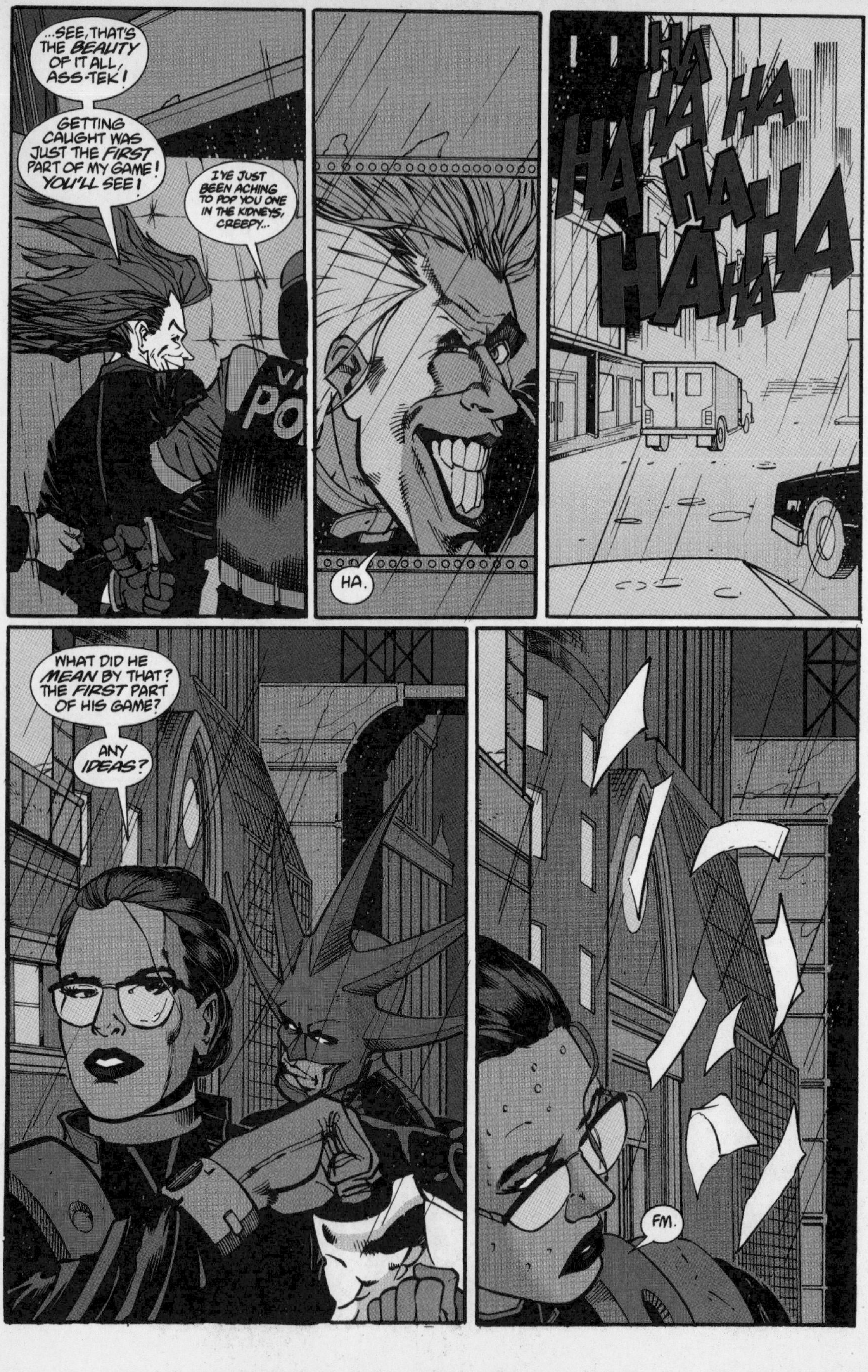
...SEE, THAT'S THE BEAUTY OF IT ALL, ASS-TEK!
GETTING CAUGHT WAS JUST THE FIRST PART OF MY GAME! YOU'LL SEE!
I'VE JUST BEEN ACHING TO POP YOU ONE IN THE KIDNEYS, CREEPY...
HA.
HA HA HA HA HA HA HA HA HA HA HA
WHAT DID HE MEAN BY THAT? THE FIRST PART OF HIS GAME?
ANY IDEAS?
FM.

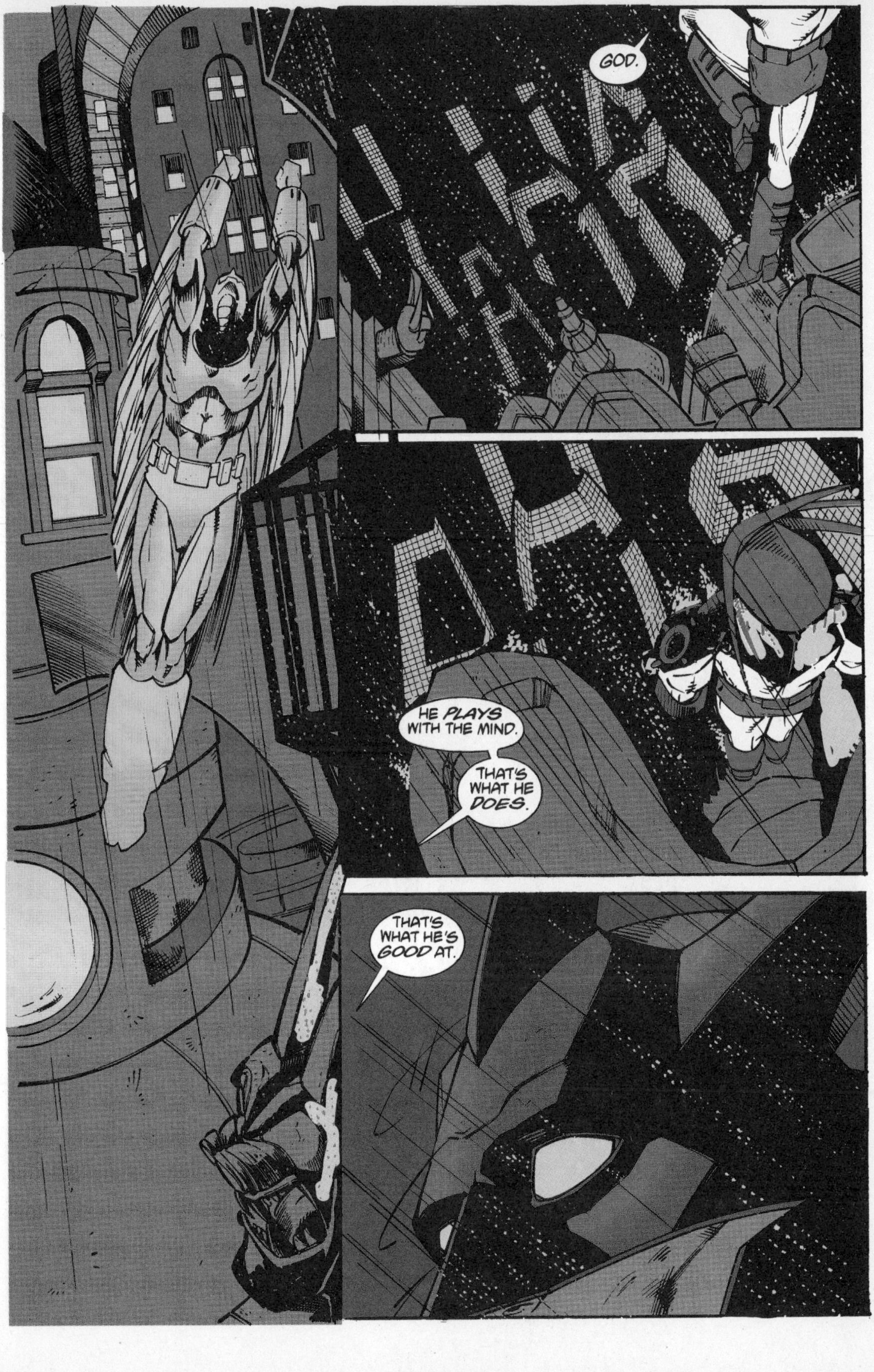
GOD.
HE PLAYS WITH THE MIND.
THAT'S WHAT HE DOES.
THAT'S WHAT HE'S GOOD AT.

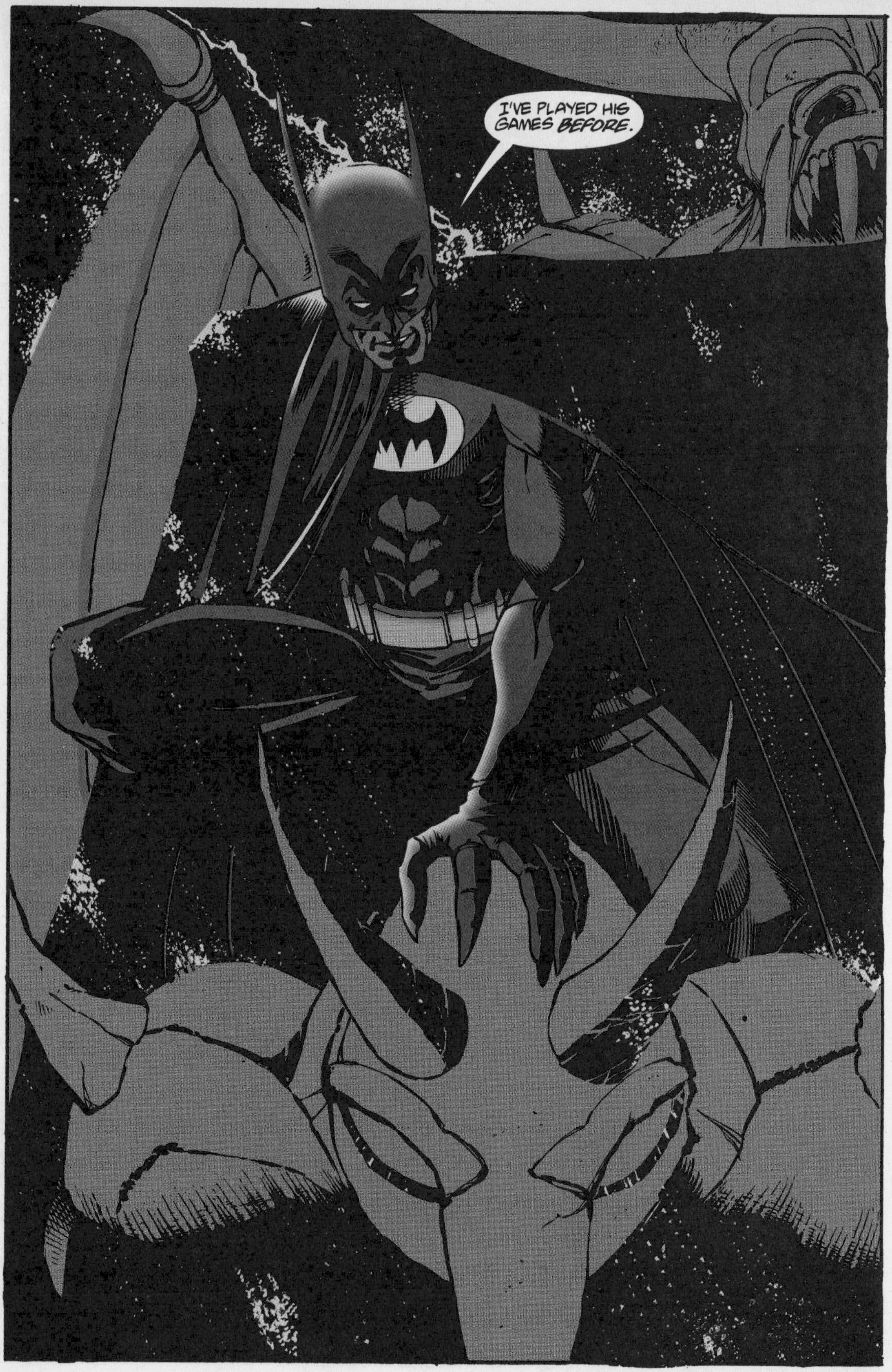
I'VE PLAYED HIS GAMES BEFORE.

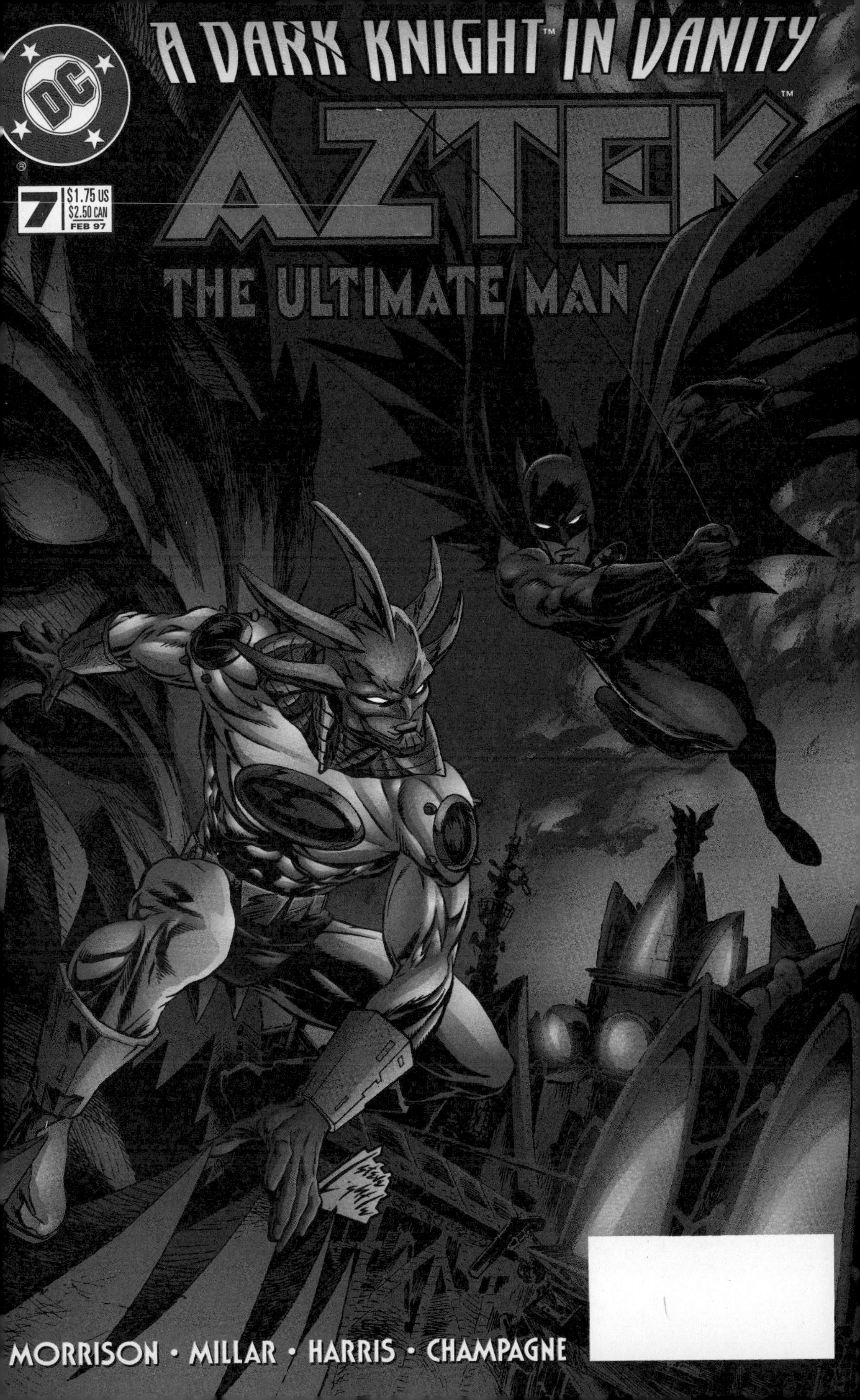
A DARK KNIGHT™ IN VANITY
AZTEK™
THE ULTIMATE MAN
7
$1.75 US
$2.50 CAN
FEB 97
MORRISON · MILLAR · HARRIS · CHAMPAGNE

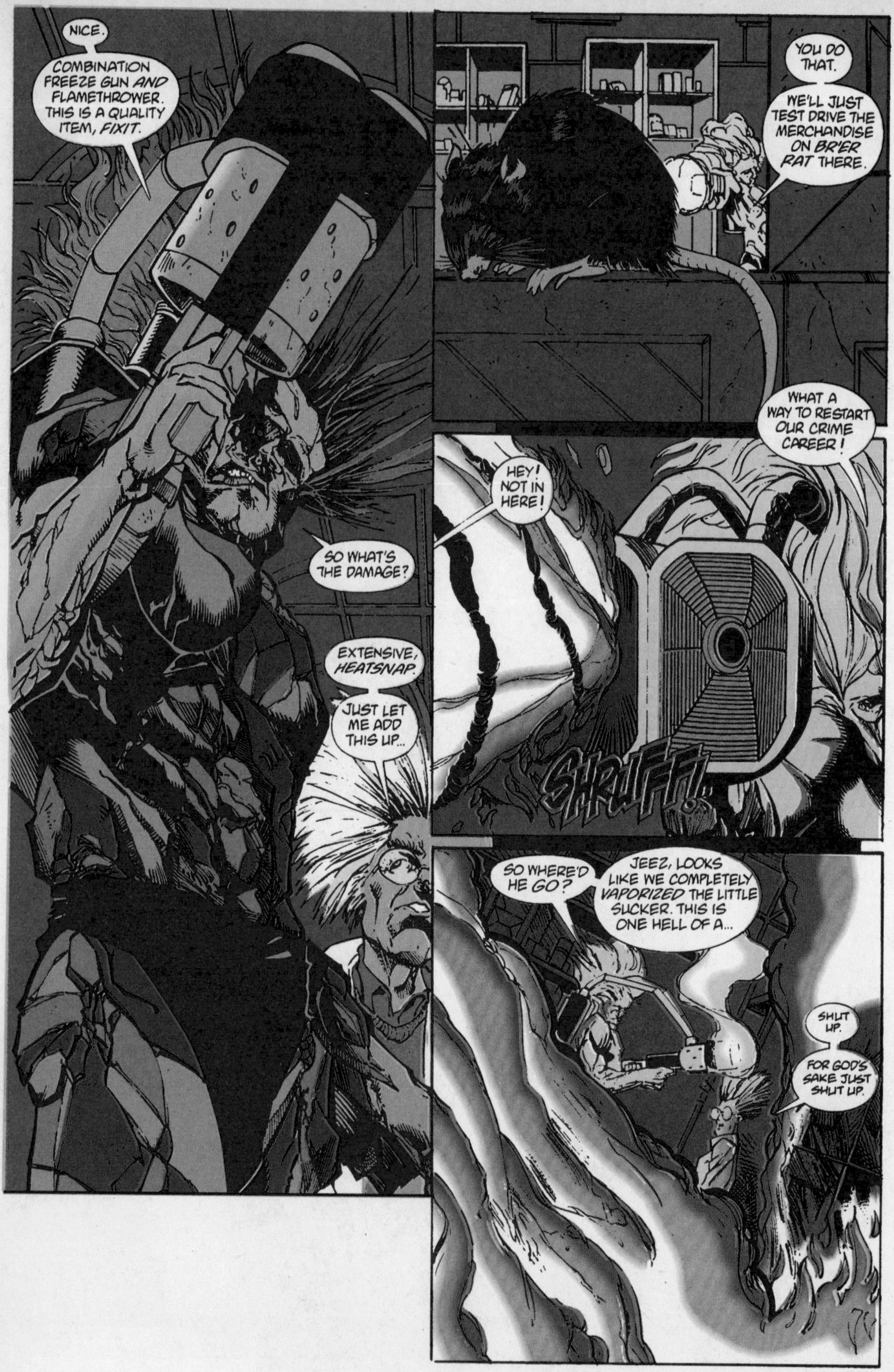
NICE.
COMBINATION FREEZE GUN AND FLAMETHROWER. THIS IS A QUALITY ITEM, FIXIT.
YOU DO THAT.
WE'LL JUST TEST DRIVE THE MERCHANDISE ON BR'ER RAT THERE.
WHAT A WAY TO RESTART OUR CRIME CAREER!
HEY! NOT IN HERE!
SHRUFF!
SO WHAT'S THE DAMAGE?
EXTENSIVE, HEATSNAP.
JUST LET ME ADD THIS UP...
SO WHERE'D HE GO?
JEEZ, LOOKS LIKE WE COMPLETELY VAPORIZED THE LITTLE SUCKER. THIS IS ONE HELL OF A...
SHUT UP.
FOR GOD'S SAKE JUST SHUT UP.

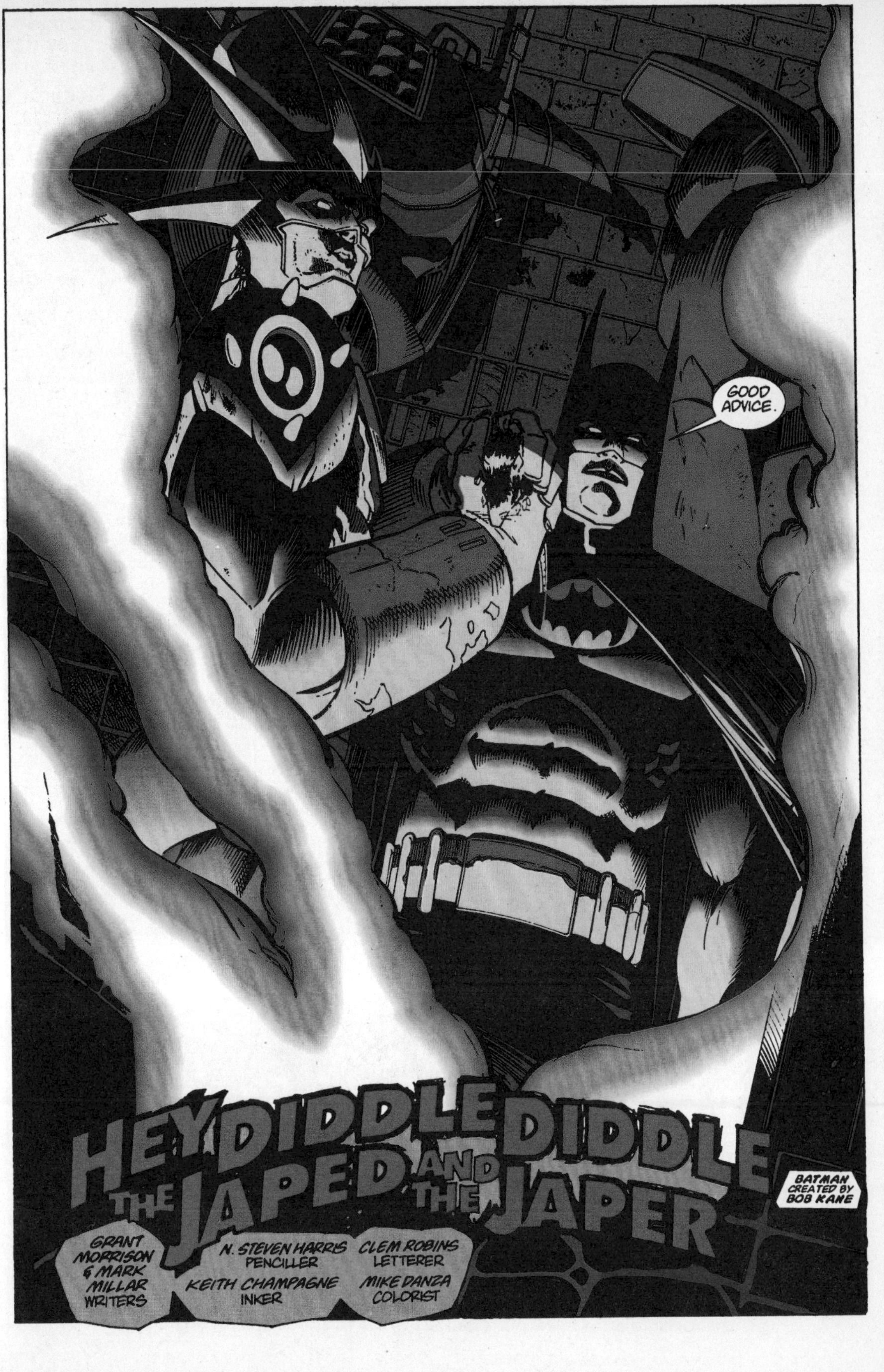
GOOD ADVICE.
HEY DIDDLE DIDDLE THE JAPED AND THE JAPER
BATMAN CREATED BY BOB KANE
GRANT MORRISON & MARK MILLAR WRITERS
N. STEVEN HARRIS PENCILLER
KEITH CHAMPAGNE INKER
CLEM ROBINS LETTERER
MIKE DANZA COLORIST

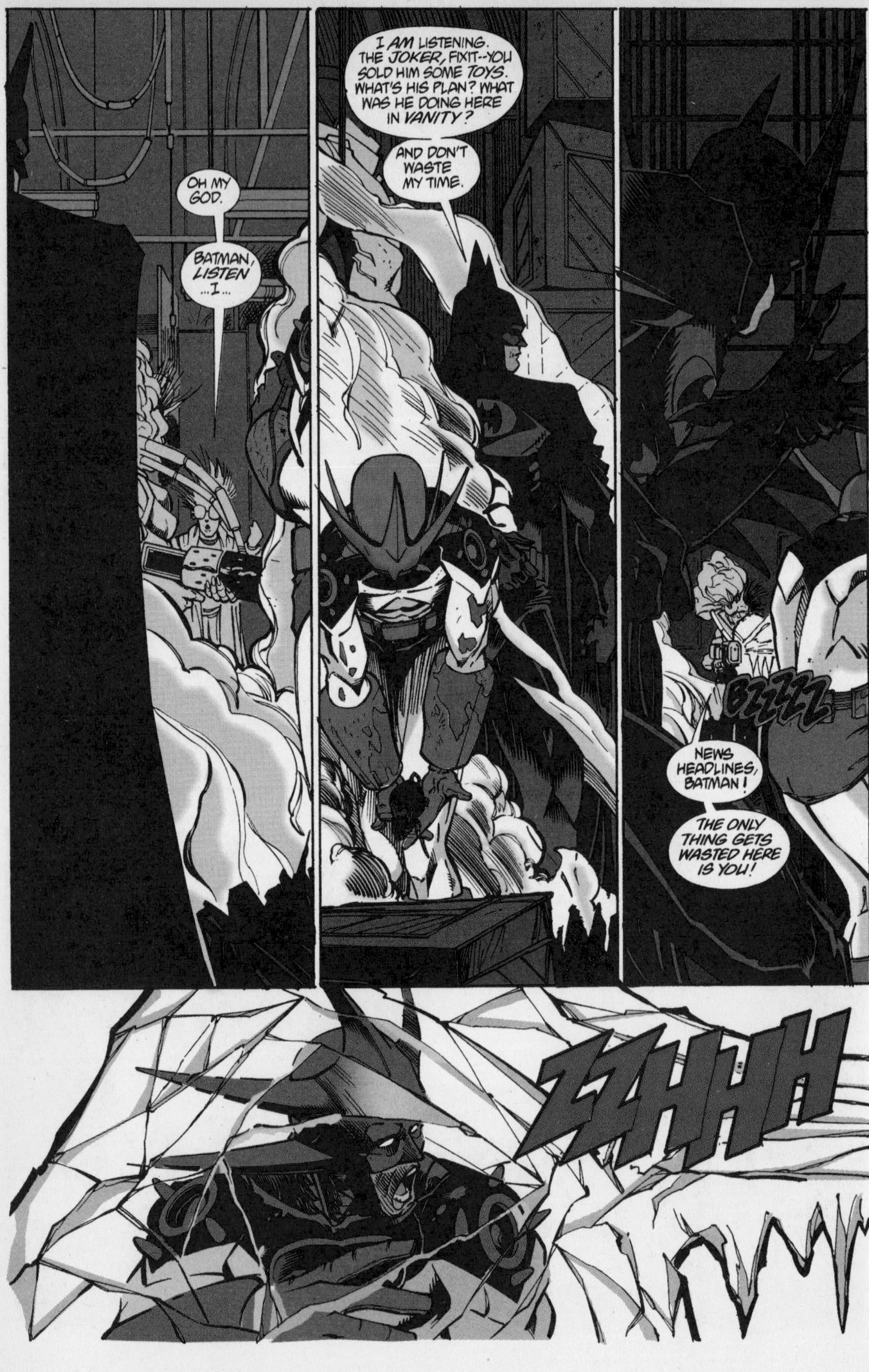
OH MY GOD.
BATMAN, LISTEN ...I...
I AM LISTENING. THE JOKER, FIXIT--YOU SOLD HIM SOME TOYS. WHAT'S HIS PLAN? WHAT WAS HE DOING HERE IN VANITY?
AND DON'T WASTE MY TIME.
BZZZZZ
NEWS HEADLINES, BATMAN!
THE ONLY THING GETS WASTED HERE IS YOU!
ZZHHH

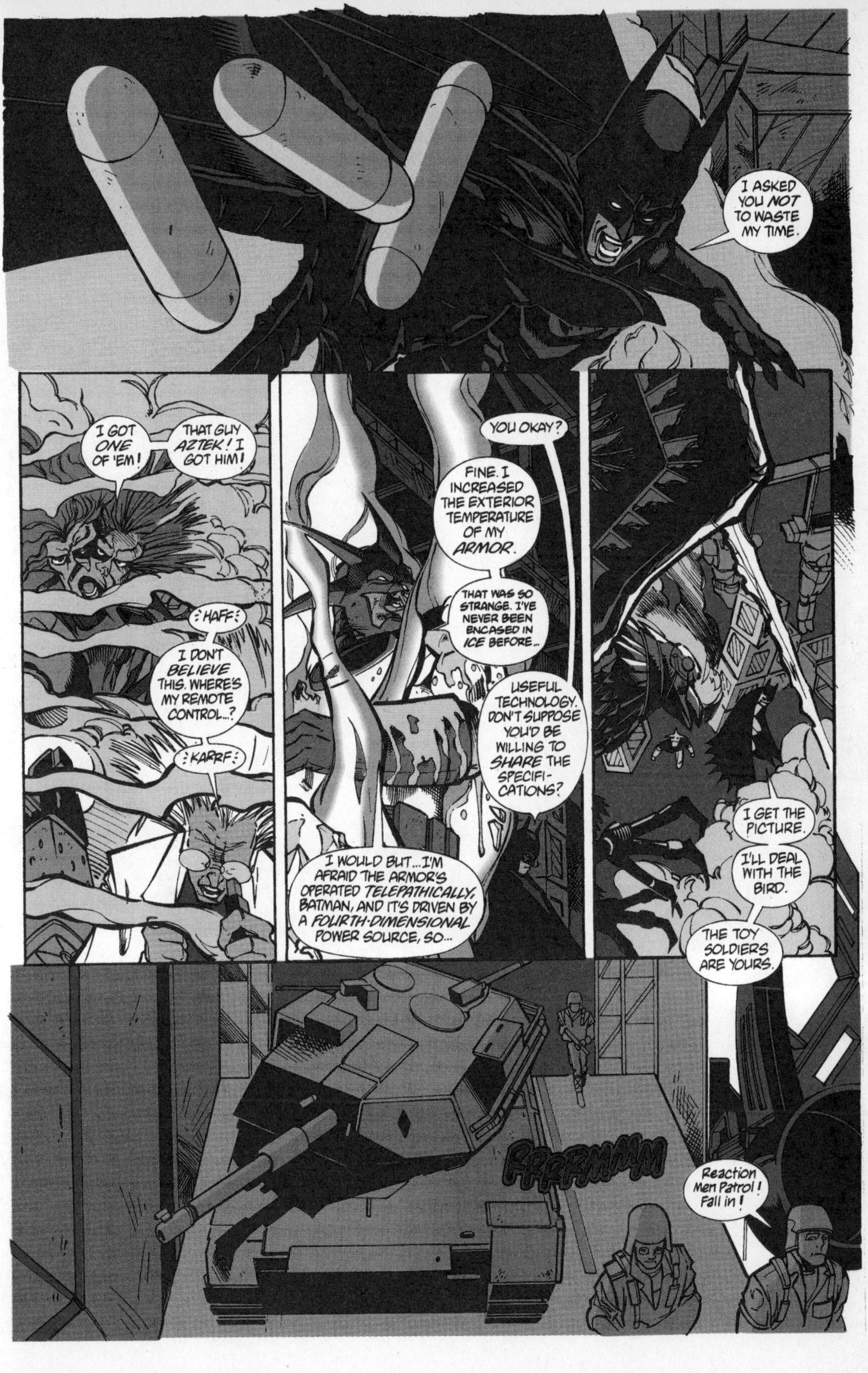

I ASKED YOU NOT TO WASTE MY TIME.
I GOT ONE OF 'EM!
THAT GUY AZTEK! I GOT HIM!
HAFF
I DON'T BELIEVE THIS. WHERE'S MY REMOTE CONTROL...?
KARRF
YOU OKAY?
FINE. I INCREASED THE EXTERIOR TEMPERATURE OF MY ARMOR.
THAT WAS SO STRANGE. I'VE NEVER BEEN ENCASED IN ICE BEFORE...
USEFUL TECHNOLOGY. DON'T SUPPOSE YOU'D BE WILLING TO SHARE THE SPECIFI-CATIONS?
I WOULD BUT...I'M AFRAID THE ARMOR'S OPERATED TELEPATHICALLY, BATMAN, AND IT'S DRIVEN BY A FOURTH-DIMENSIONAL POWER SOURCE, SO...
I GET THE PICTURE.
I'LL DEAL WITH THE BIRD.
THE TOY SOLDIERS ARE YOURS.
RRRRMMM
Reaction Men Patrol! Fall in!

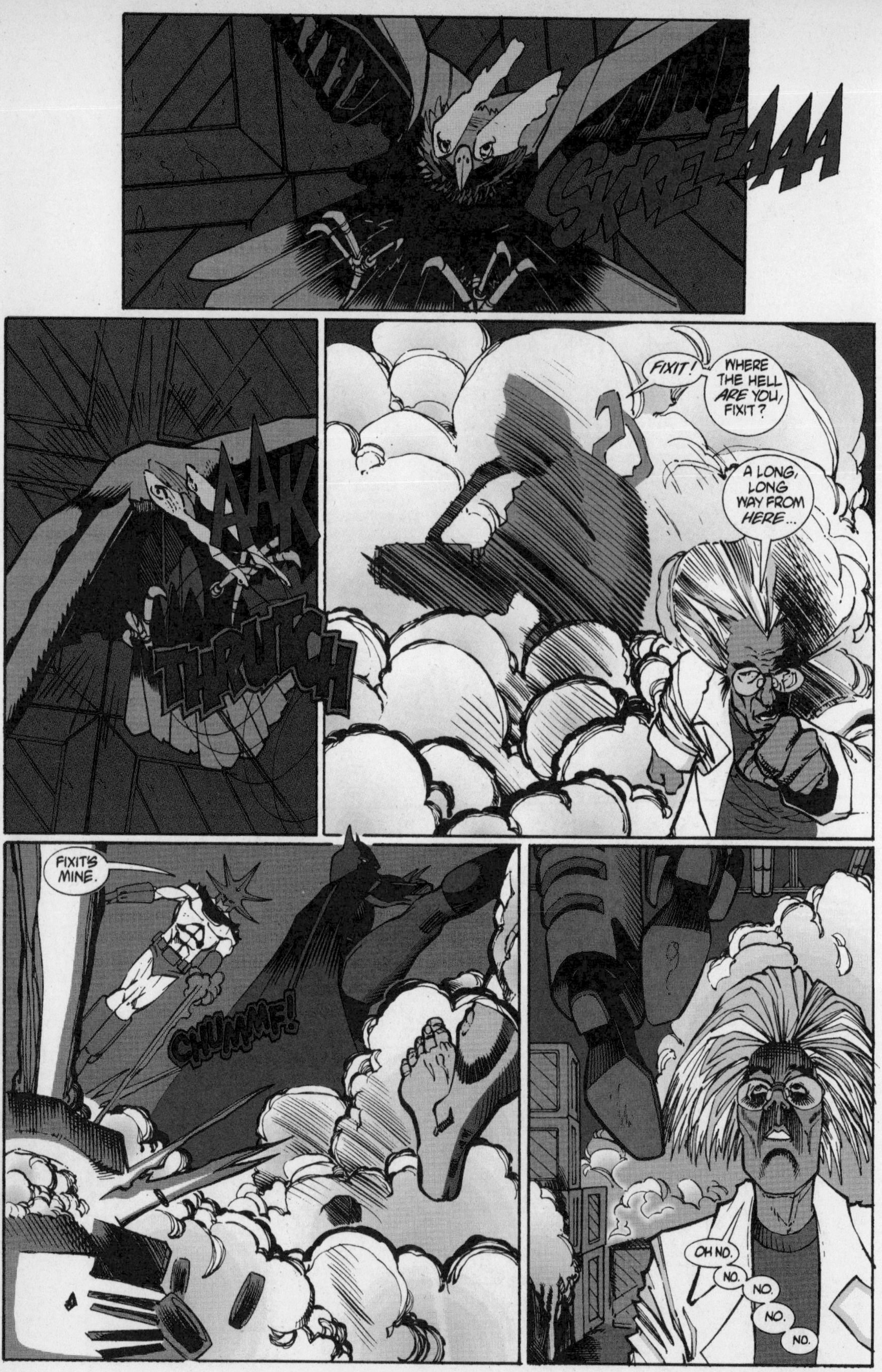

SKREEAAA
AAK
THRUTCH
FIXIT!
WHERE THE HELL ARE YOU, FIXIT?
A LONG, LONG WAY FROM HERE...
FIXIT'S MINE.
CHUMMF!
OH NO.
NO.
NO.
NO.
NO.

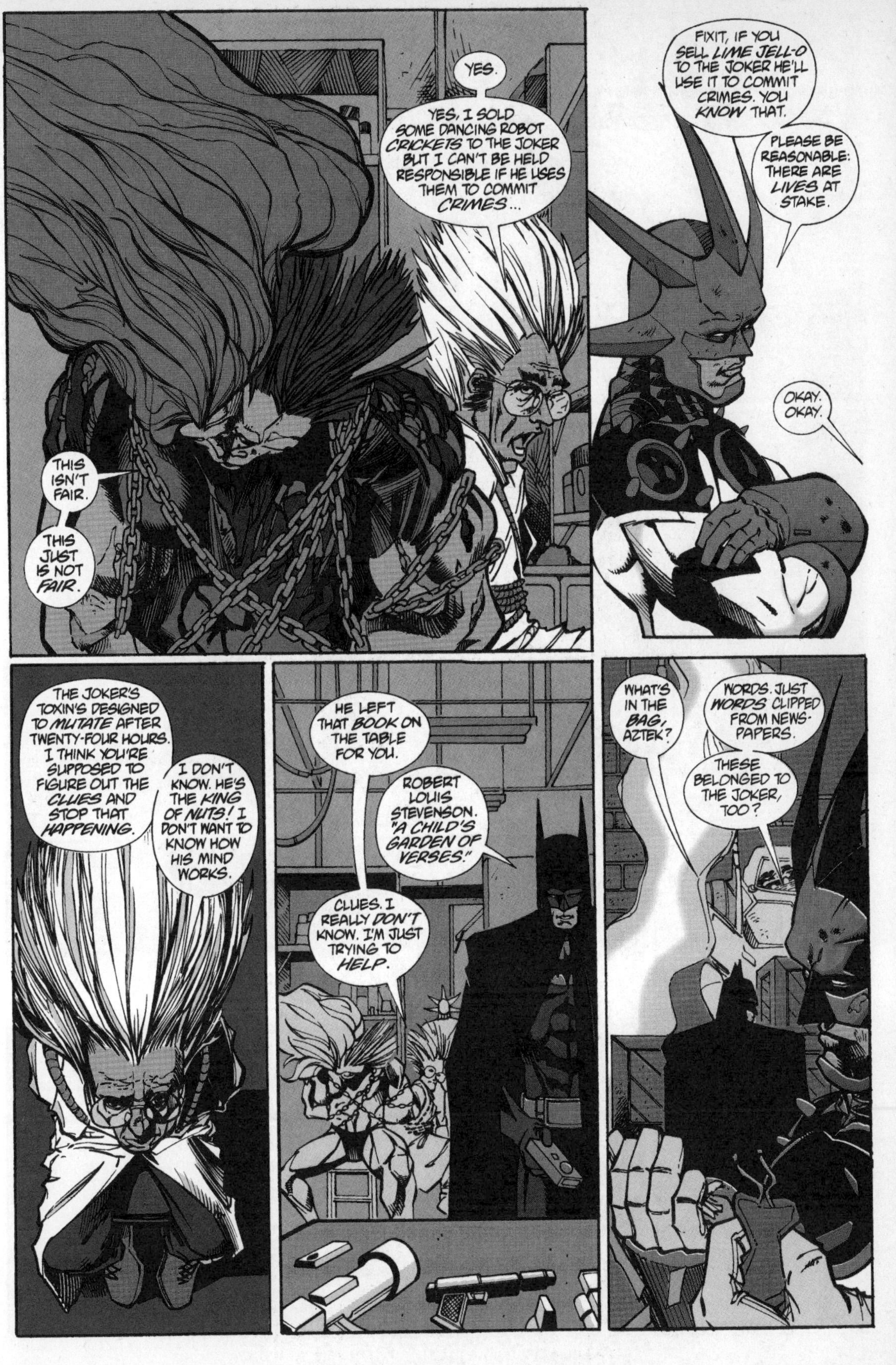
YES.
YES, I SOLD SOME DANCING ROBOT CRICKETS TO THE JOKER BUT I CAN'T BE HELD RESPONSIBLE IF HE USES THEM TO COMMIT CRIMES...
FIXIT, IF YOU SELL LIME JELL-O TO THE JOKER HE'LL USE IT TO COMMIT CRIMES. YOU KNOW THAT.
PLEASE BE REASONABLE: THERE ARE LIVES AT STAKE.
THIS ISN'T FAIR.
THIS JUST IS NOT FAIR.
OKAY. OKAY.
THE JOKER'S TOXIN'S DESIGNED TO MUTATE AFTER TWENTY-FOUR HOURS. I THINK YOU'RE SUPPOSED TO FIGURE OUT THE CLUES AND STOP THAT HAPPENING.
I DON'T KNOW. HE'S THE KING OF NUTS! I DON'T WANT TO KNOW HOW HIS MIND WORKS.
HE LEFT THAT BOOK ON THE TABLE FOR YOU.
ROBERT LOUIS STEVENSON. "A CHILD'S GARDEN OF VERSES."
CLUES. I REALLY DON'T KNOW. I'M JUST TRYING TO HELP.
WHAT'S IN THE BAG, AZTEK?
WORDS. JUST WORDS CLIPPED FROM NEWS-PAPERS.
THESE BELONGED TO THE JOKER, TOO?

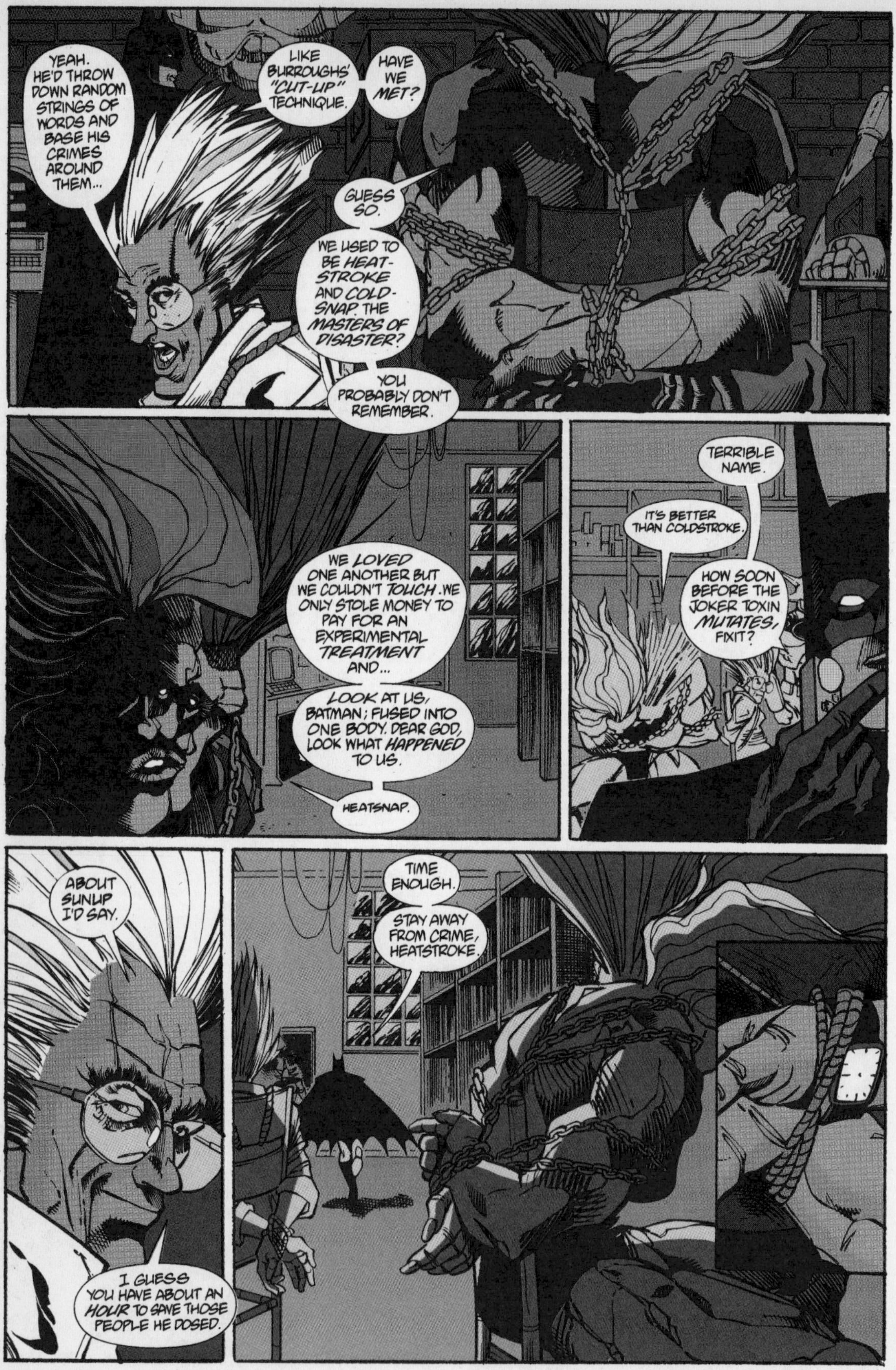
YEAH. HE'D THROW DOWN RANDOM STRINGS OF WORDS AND BASE HIS CRIMES AROUND THEM...
LIKE BURROUGHS' "CUT-UP" TECHNIQUE.
HAVE WE MET?
GUESS SO.
WE USED TO BE HEAT-STROKE AND COLD-SNAP. THE MASTERS OF DISASTER?
YOU PROBABLY DON'T REMEMBER.
WE LOVED ONE ANOTHER BUT WE COULDN'T TOUCH. WE ONLY STOLE MONEY TO PAY FOR AN EXPERIMENTAL TREATMENT AND...
LOOK AT US, BATMAN; FUSED INTO ONE BODY. DEAR GOD, LOOK WHAT HAPPENED TO US.
HEATSNAP.
TERRIBLE NAME.
IT'S BETTER THAN COLDSTROKE.
HOW SOON BEFORE THE JOKER TOXIN MUTATES, FIXIT?
ABOUT SUNUP I'D SAY.
I GUESS YOU HAVE ABOUT AN HOUR TO SAVE THOSE PEOPLE HE DOSED.
TIME ENOUGH.
STAY AWAY FROM CRIME, HEATSTROKE.

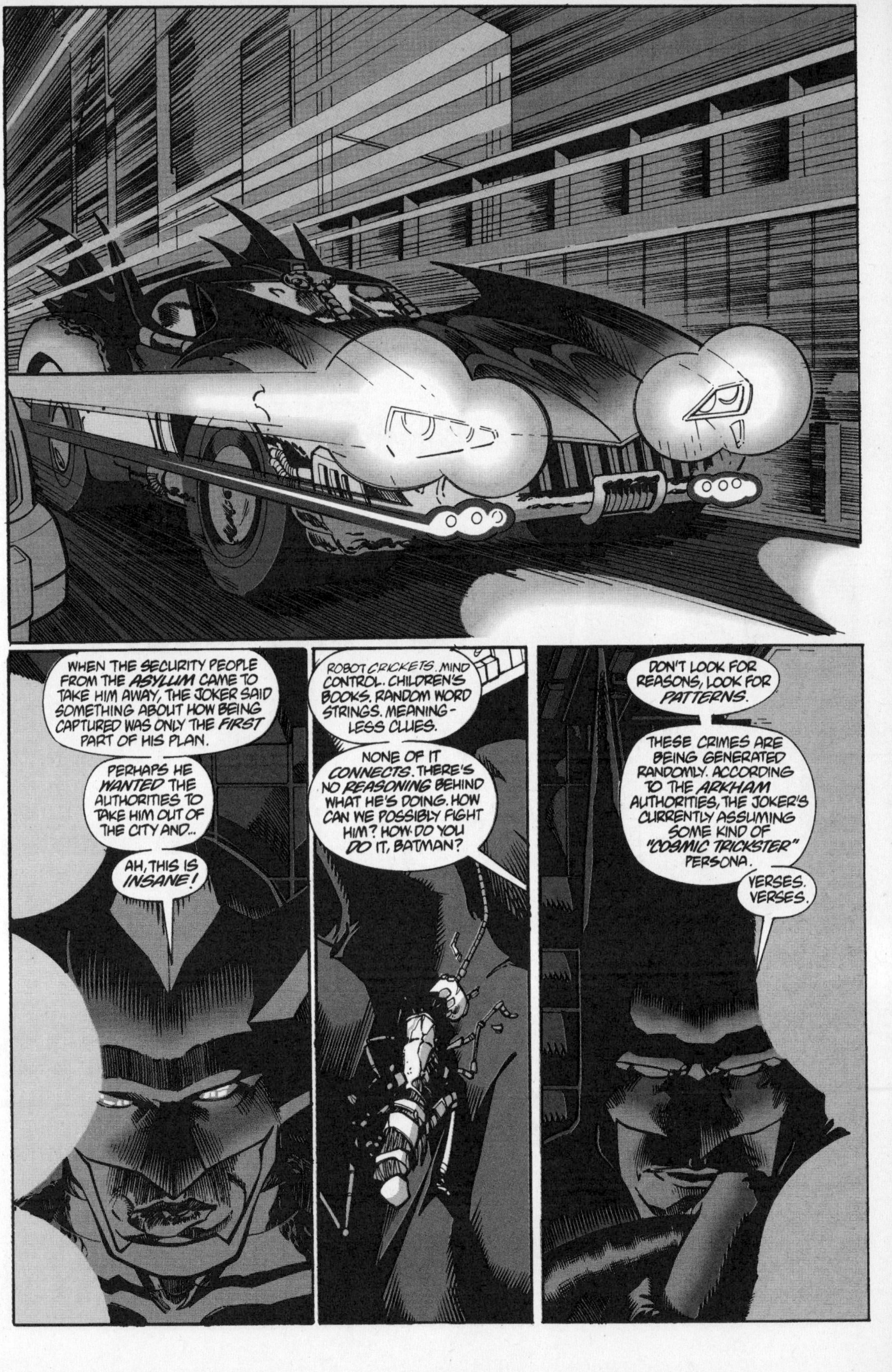
WHEN THE SECURITY PEOPLE FROM THE ASYLUM CAME TO TAKE HIM AWAY, THE JOKER SAID SOMETHING ABOUT HOW BEING CAPTURED WAS ONLY THE FIRST PART OF HIS PLAN.
PERHAPS HE WANTED THE AUTHORITIES TO TAKE HIM OUT OF THE CITY AND...
AH, THIS IS INSANE!
ROBOT CRICKETS. MIND CONTROL. CHILDREN'S BOOKS. RANDOM WORD STRINGS. MEANING-LESS CLUES.
NONE OF IT CONNECTS. THERE'S NO REASONING BEHIND WHAT HE'S DOING. HOW CAN WE POSSIBLY FIGHT HIM? HOW DO YOU DO IT, BATMAN?
DON'T LOOK FOR REASONS, LOOK FOR PATTERNS.
THESE CRIMES ARE BEING GENERATED RANDOMLY. ACCORDING TO THE ARKHAM AUTHORITIES, THE JOKER'S CURRENTLY ASSUMING SOME KIND OF "COSMIC TRICKSTER" PERSONA.
VERSES. VERSES.

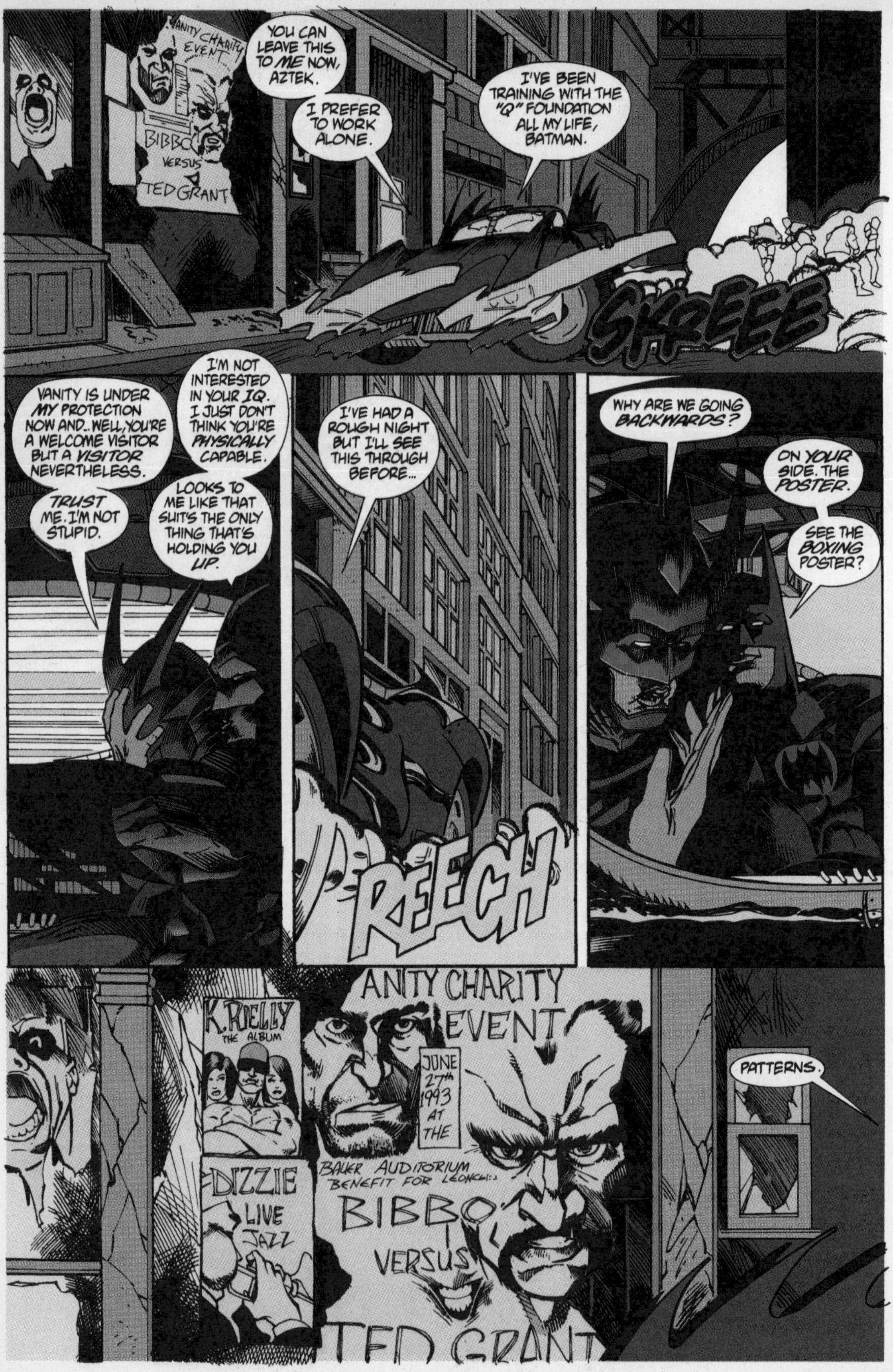
VANITY CHARITY EVENT
BIBBO VERSUS TED GRANT
YOU CAN LEAVE THIS TO ME NOW, AZTEK.
I PREFER TO WORK ALONE.
I'VE BEEN TRAINING WITH THE "Q" FOUNDATION ALL MY LIFE, BATMAN.
SKREEE
VANITY IS UNDER MY PROTECTION NOW AND... WELL, YOU'RE A WELCOME VISITOR BUT A VISITOR NEVERTHELESS.
I'M NOT INTERESTED IN YOUR IQ. I JUST DON'T THINK YOU'RE PHYSICALLY CAPABLE.
TRUST ME. I'M NOT STUPID.
LOOKS TO ME LIKE THAT SUIT'S THE ONLY THING THAT'S HOLDING YOU UP.
I'VE HAD A ROUGH NIGHT BUT I'LL SEE THIS THROUGH BEFORE...
REECH
WHY ARE WE GOING BACKWARDS?
ON YOUR SIDE. THE POSTER.
SEE THE BOXING POSTER?
ANITY CHARITY EVENT
K. RIELLY THE ALBUM
JUNE 27th 1993 AT THE
BAKER AUDITORIUM BENEFIT FOR LEONCII
BIBBO VERSUS
TED GRANT
DIZZIE LIVE JAZZ
PATTERNS.

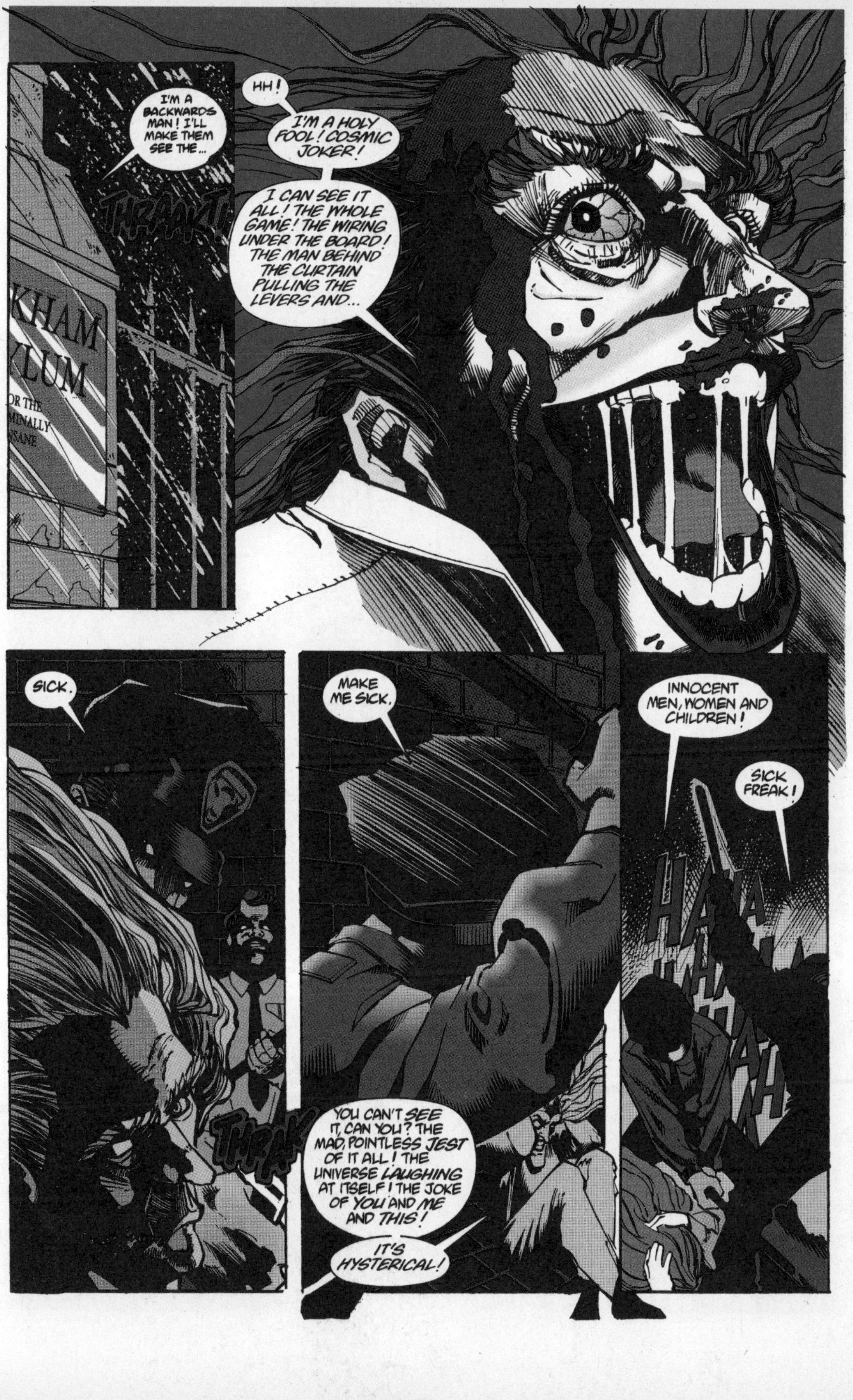
I'M A BACKWARDS MAN! I'LL MAKE THEM SEE THE...
THRAAK!
HH!
I'M A HOLY FOOL! COSMIC JOKER!
I CAN SEE IT ALL! THE WHOLE GAME! THE WIRING UNDER THE BOARD! THE MAN BEHIND THE CURTAIN PULLING THE LEVERS AND...
SICK.
MAKE ME SICK.
YOU CAN'T SEE IT, CAN YOU? THE MAD, POINTLESS JEST OF IT ALL! THE UNIVERSE LAUGHING AT ITSELF! THE JOKE OF YOU AND ME AND THIS!
IT'S HYSTERICAL!
INNOCENT MEN, WOMEN AND CHILDREN!
SICK FREAK!

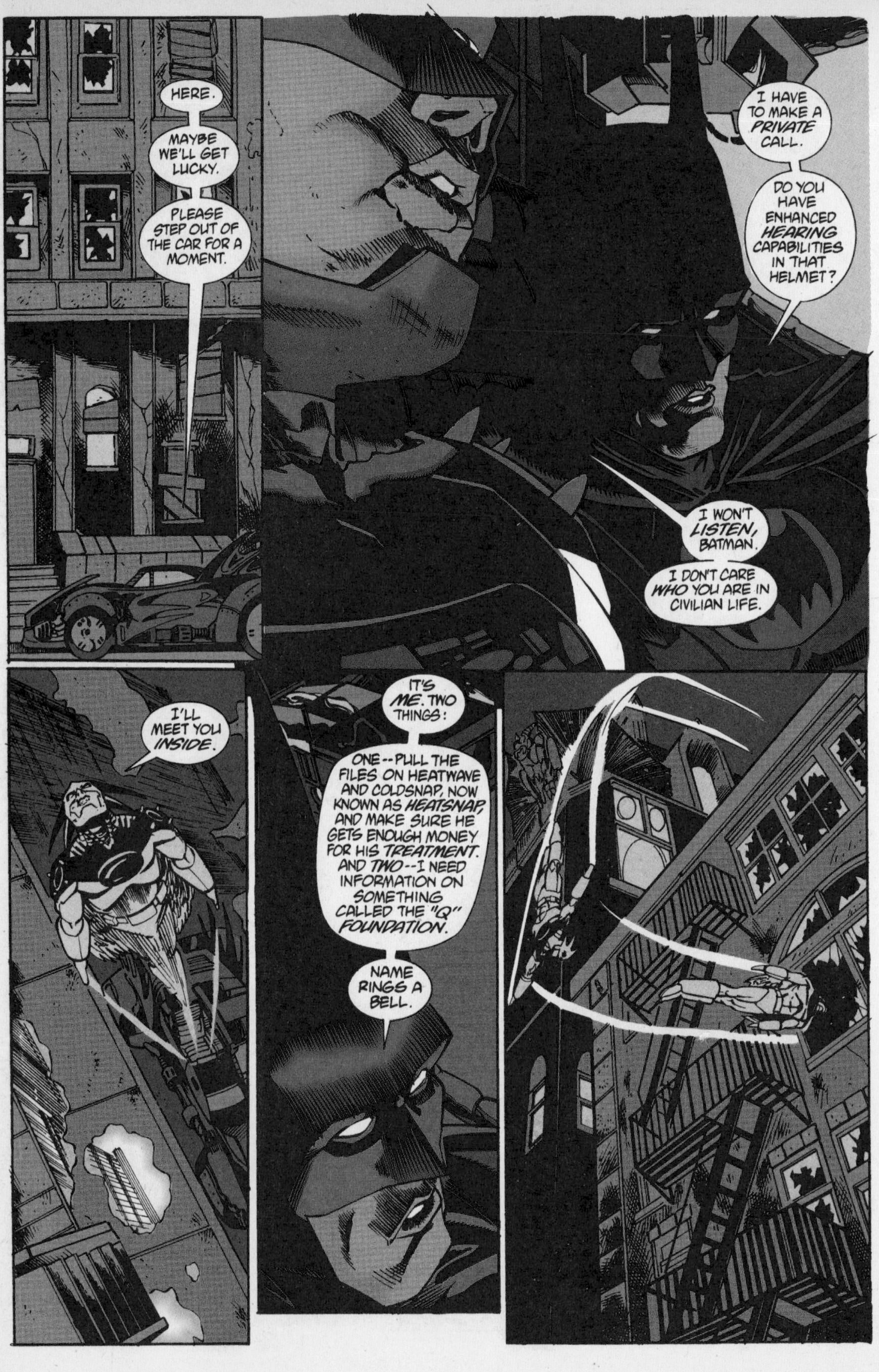
HERE.
MAYBE WE'LL GET LUCKY.
PLEASE STEP OUT OF THE CAR FOR A MOMENT.
I HAVE TO MAKE A PRIVATE CALL.
DO YOU HAVE ENHANCED HEARING CAPABILITIES IN THAT HELMET?
I WON'T LISTEN, BATMAN.
I DON'T CARE WHO YOU ARE IN CIVILIAN LIFE.
I'LL MEET YOU INSIDE.
IT'S ME. TWO THINGS:
ONE--PULL THE FILES ON HEATWAVE AND COLDSNAP, NOW KNOWN AS HEATSNAP, AND MAKE SURE HE GETS ENOUGH MONEY FOR HIS TREATMENT. AND TWO--I NEED INFORMATION ON SOMETHING CALLED THE "Q" FOUNDATION.
NAME RINGS A BELL.

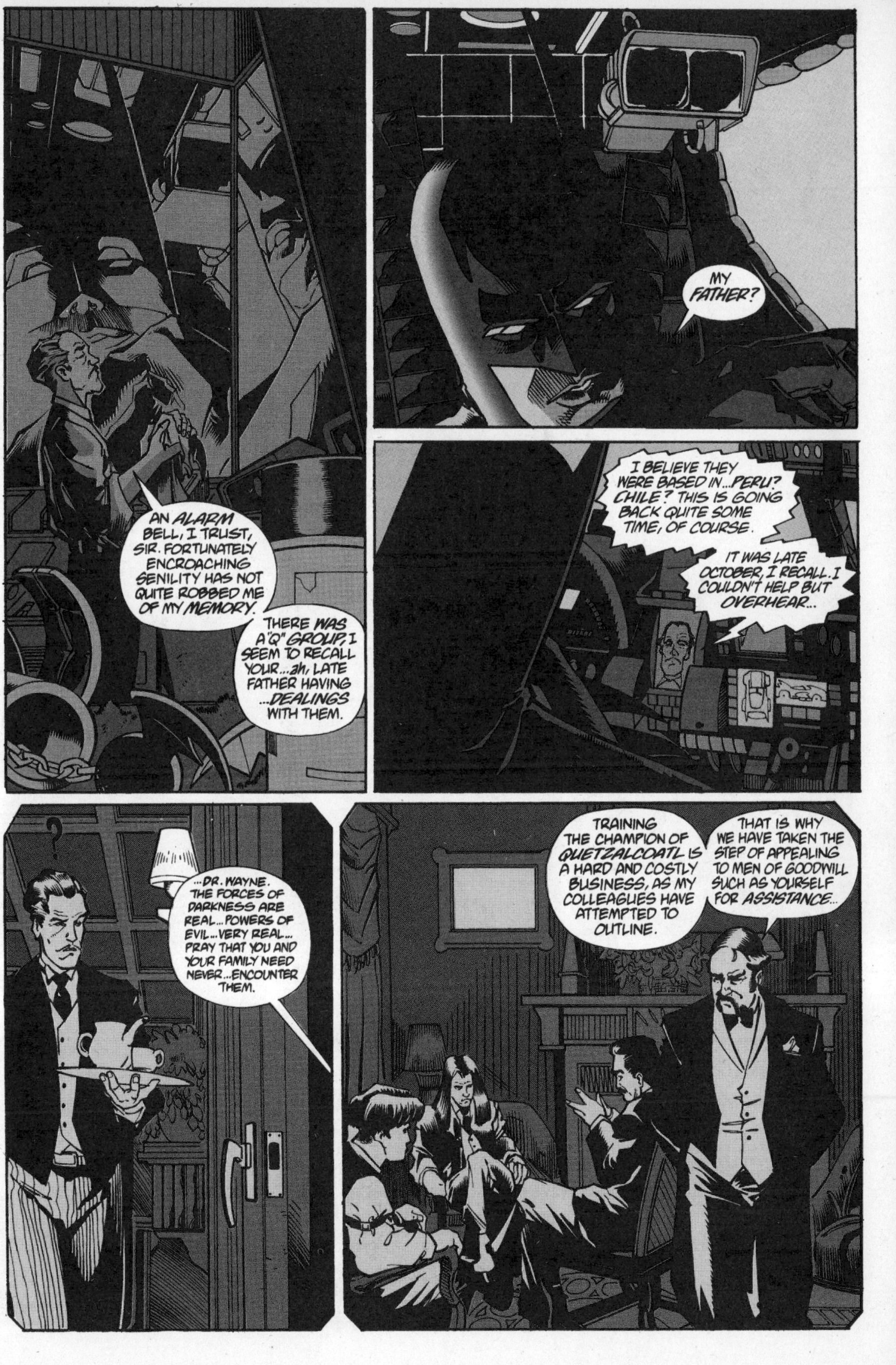
AN ALARM BELL, I TRUST, SIR. FORTUNATELY ENCROACHING SENILITY HAS NOT QUITE ROBBED ME OF MY MEMORY.
THERE WAS A "Q" GROUP, I SEEM TO RECALL YOUR...ah, LATE FATHER HAVING ...DEALINGS WITH THEM.
MY FATHER?
I BELIEVE THEY WERE BASED IN...PERU? CHILE? THIS IS GOING BACK QUITE SOME TIME, OF COURSE.
IT WAS LATE OCTOBER, I RECALL. I COULDN'T HELP BUT OVERHEAR...
?
...DR. WAYNE. THE FORCES OF DARKNESS ARE REAL...POWERS OF EVIL...VERY REAL... PRAY THAT YOU AND YOUR FAMILY NEED NEVER...ENCOUNTER THEM.
TRAINING THE CHAMPION OF QUETZALCOATL IS A HARD AND COSTLY BUSINESS, AS MY COLLEAGUES HAVE ATTEMPTED TO OUTLINE.
THAT IS WHY WE HAVE TAKEN THE STEP OF APPEALING TO MEN OF GOODWILL SUCH AS YOURSELF FOR ASSISTANCE...

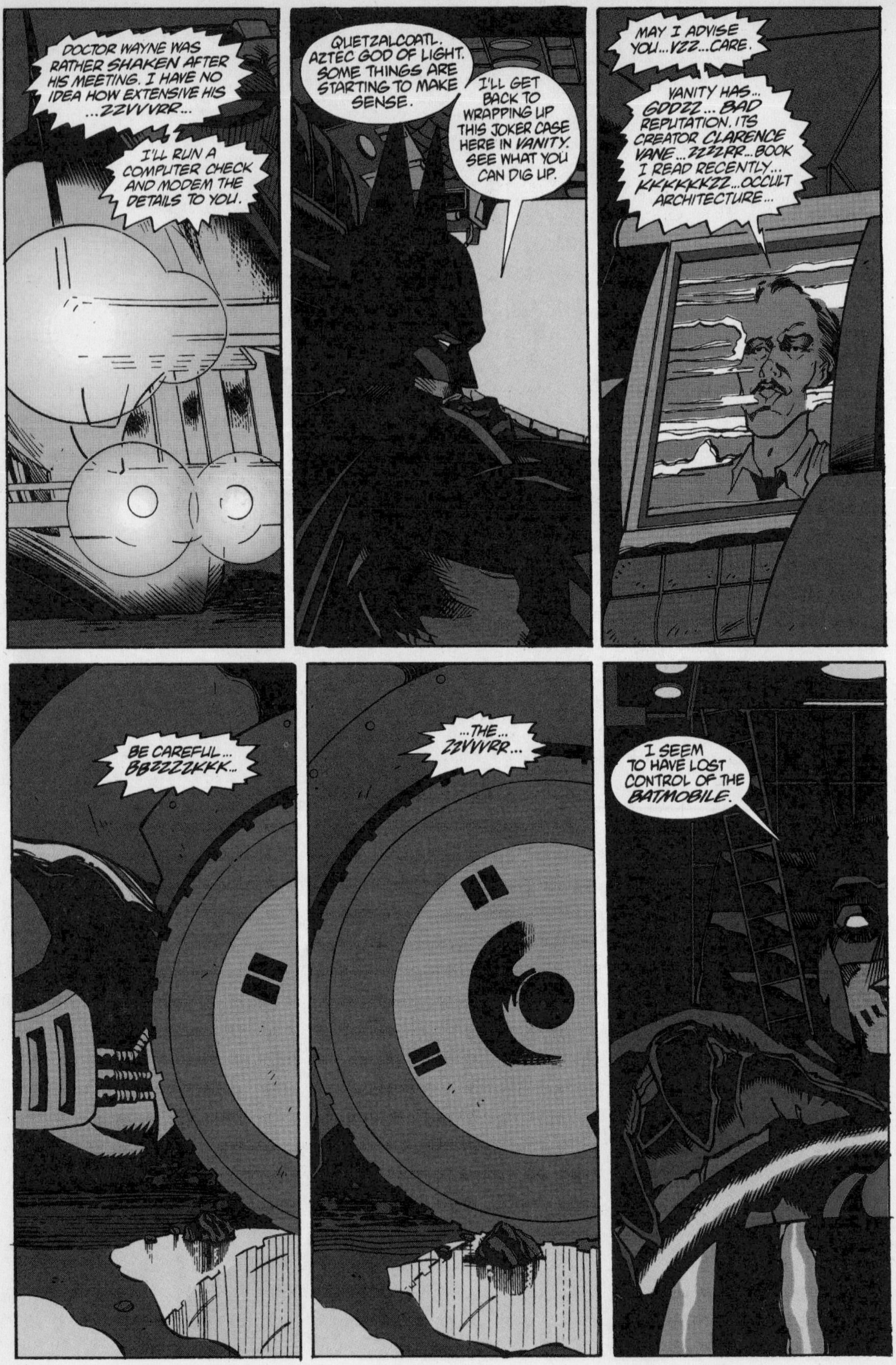
DOCTOR WAYNE WAS RATHER SHAKEN AFTER HIS MEETING. I HAVE NO IDEA HOW EXTENSIVE HIS ...ZZVVVRR...
I'LL RUN A COMPUTER CHECK AND MODEM THE DETAILS TO YOU.
QUETZALCOATL. AZTEC GOD OF LIGHT. SOME THINGS ARE STARTING TO MAKE SENSE.
I'LL GET BACK TO WRAPPING UP THIS JOKER CASE HERE IN VANITY. SEE WHAT YOU CAN DIG UP.
MAY I ADVISE YOU...VZZ...CARE.
VANITY HAS... GDDZZ... BAD REPUTATION. ITS CREATOR CLARENCE VANE...ZZZZRR...BOOK I READ RECENTLY... KKKKKKZZ...OCCULT ARCHITECTURE...
BE CAREFUL... BBZZZZKKK...
...THE... ZZVVVRR...
I SEEM TO HAVE LOST CONTROL OF THE BATMOBILE.

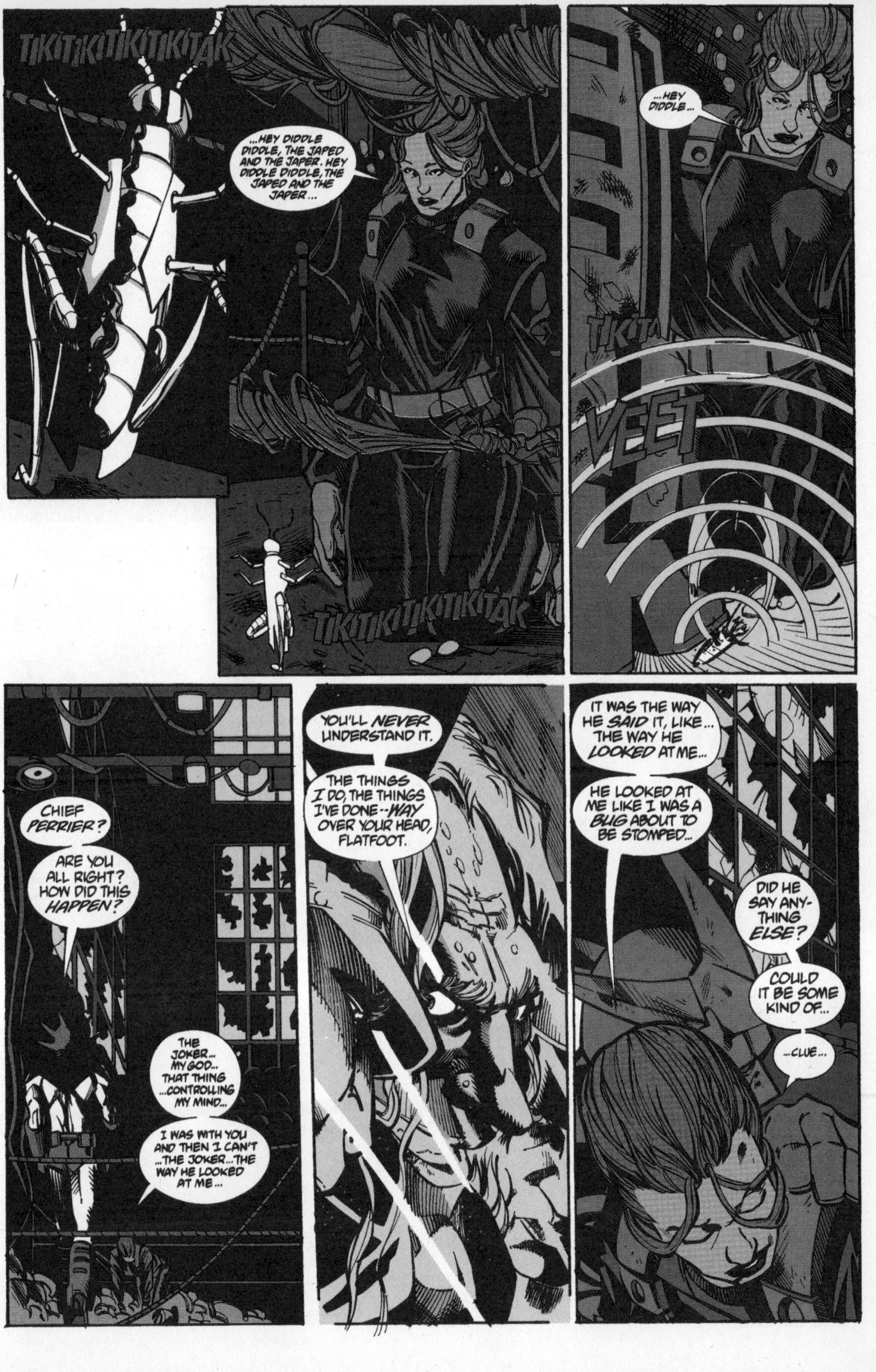
TIKITIKITIKITIKITAK
...HEY DIDDLE DIDDLE, THE JAPED AND THE JAPER. HEY DIDDLE DIDDLE, THE JAPED AND THE JAPER...
TIKITIKITIKITIKITAK
...HEY DIDDLE...
TIKITA
VEET
CHIEF PERRIER?
ARE YOU ALL RIGHT? HOW DID THIS HAPPEN?
THE JOKER... MY GOD... THAT THING ...CONTROLLING MY MIND...
I WAS WITH YOU AND THEN I CAN'T ...THE JOKER...THE WAY HE LOOKED AT ME...
YOU'LL NEVER UNDERSTAND IT.
THE THINGS I DO, THE THINGS I'VE DONE--WAY OVER YOUR HEAD, FLATFOOT.
IT WAS THE WAY HE SAID IT, LIKE... THE WAY HE LOOKED AT ME...
HE LOOKED AT ME LIKE I WAS A BUG ABOUT TO BE STOMPED...
DID HE SAY ANYTHING ELSE?
COULD IT BE SOME KIND OF...
...CLUE...

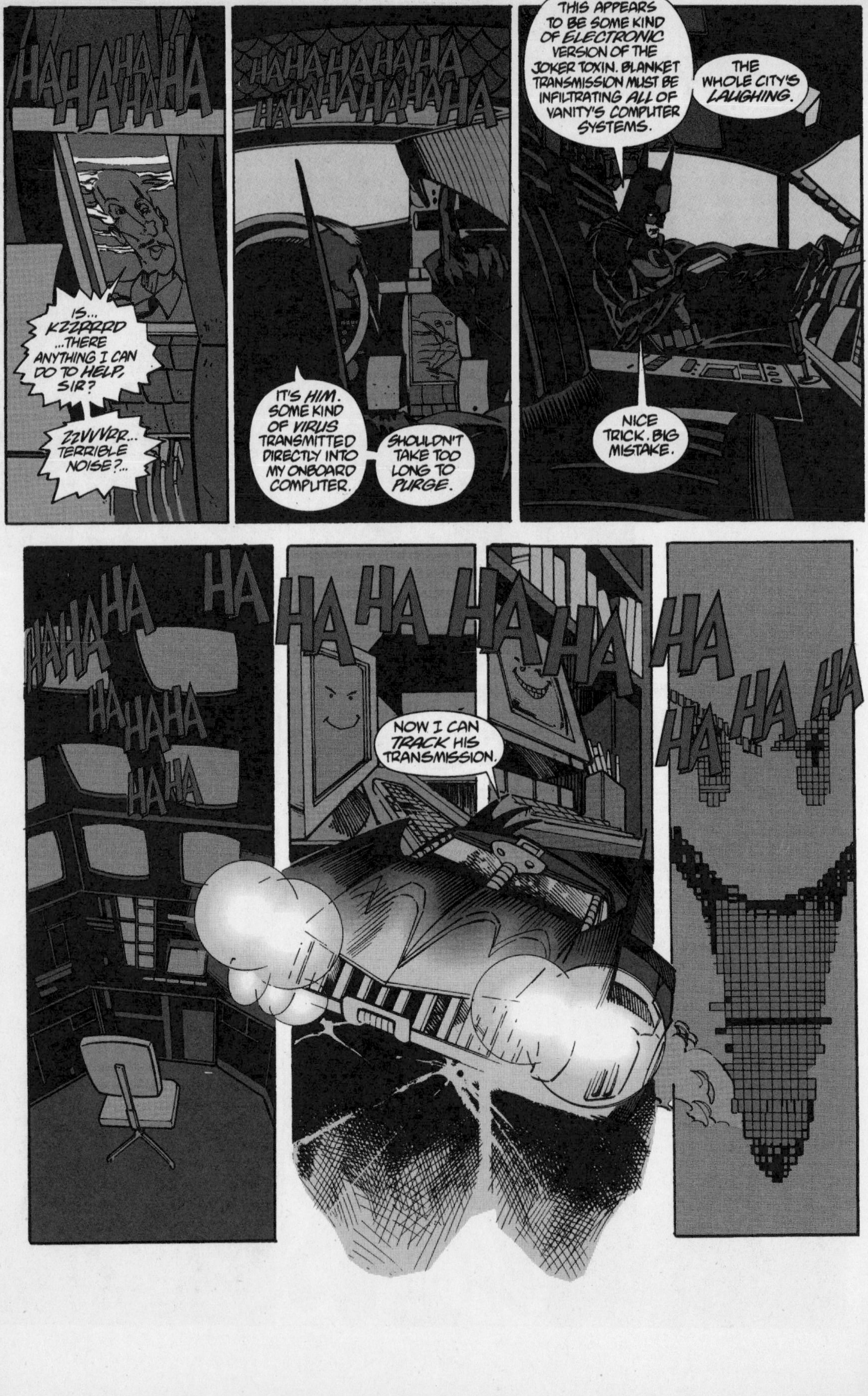
HAHAHAHA HAHAHAHA
IS... KZZRRRD ...THERE ANYTHING I CAN DO TO HELP, SIR?
ZZVVVRR... TERRIBLE NOISE?...
HAHAHAHAHAHA HAHAHAHAHAHAHA
IT'S HIM. SOME KIND OF VIRUS TRANSMITTED DIRECTLY INTO MY ONBOARD COMPUTER.
SHOULDN'T TAKE TOO LONG TO PURGE.
THIS APPEARS TO BE SOME KIND OF ELECTRONIC VERSION OF THE JOKER TOXIN. BLANKET TRANSMISSION MUST BE INFILTRATING ALL OF VANITY'S COMPUTER SYSTEMS.
THE WHOLE CITY'S LAUGHING.
NICE TRICK. BIG MISTAKE.
HAHAHA HAHAHA HAHA
HA HA HA HA HA HA HA HA HA HA HA HA
NOW I CAN TRACK HIS TRANSMISSION.

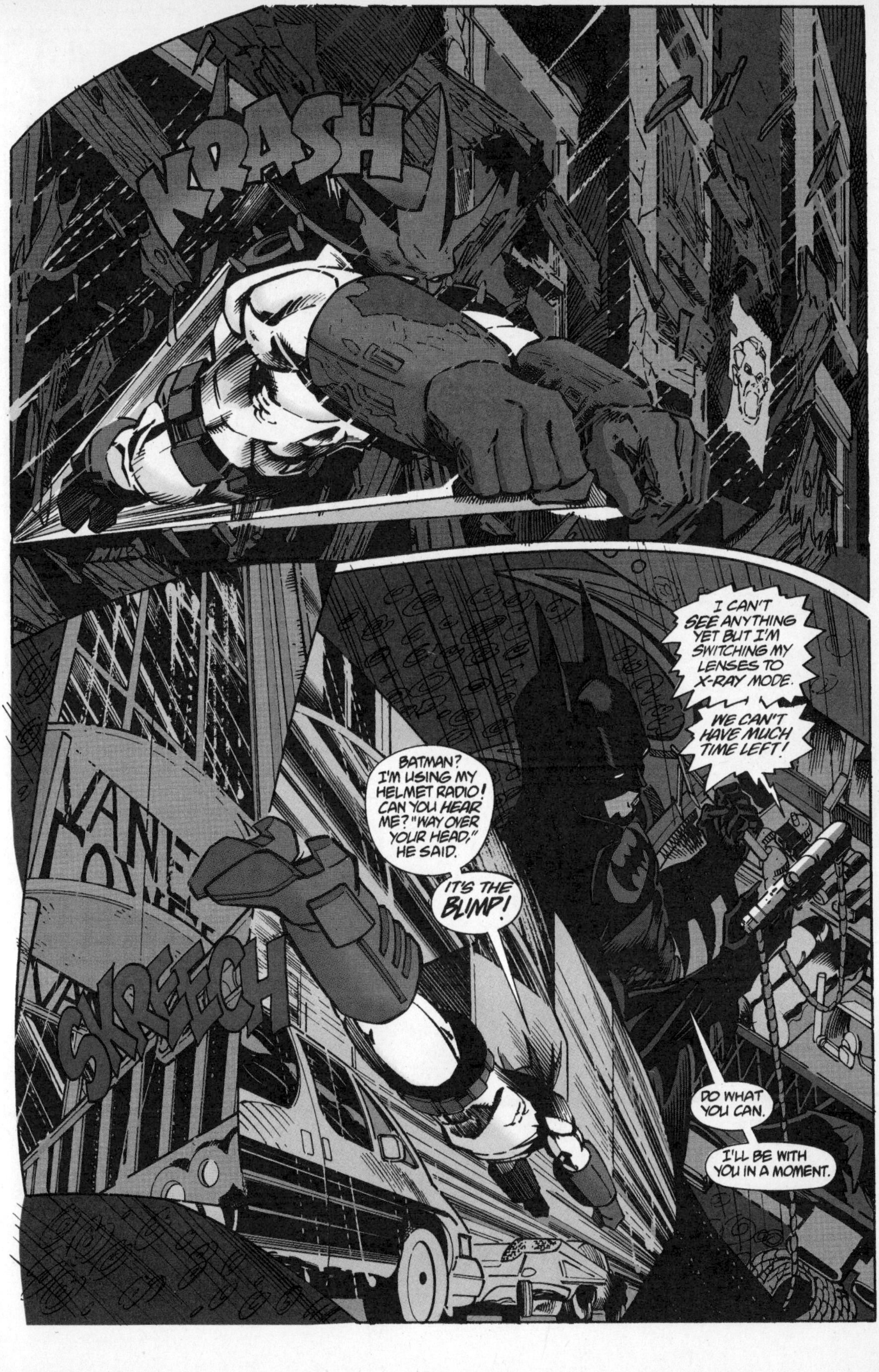
KRASH
I CAN'T SEE ANYTHING YET BUT I'M SWITCHING MY LENSES TO X-RAY MODE.
WE CAN'T HAVE MUCH TIME LEFT!
BATMAN? I'M USING MY HELMET RADIO! CAN YOU HEAR ME? "WAY OVER YOUR HEAD," HE SAID.
IT'S THE BLIMP!
SKREECH
DO WHAT YOU CAN.
I'LL BE WITH YOU IN A MOMENT.

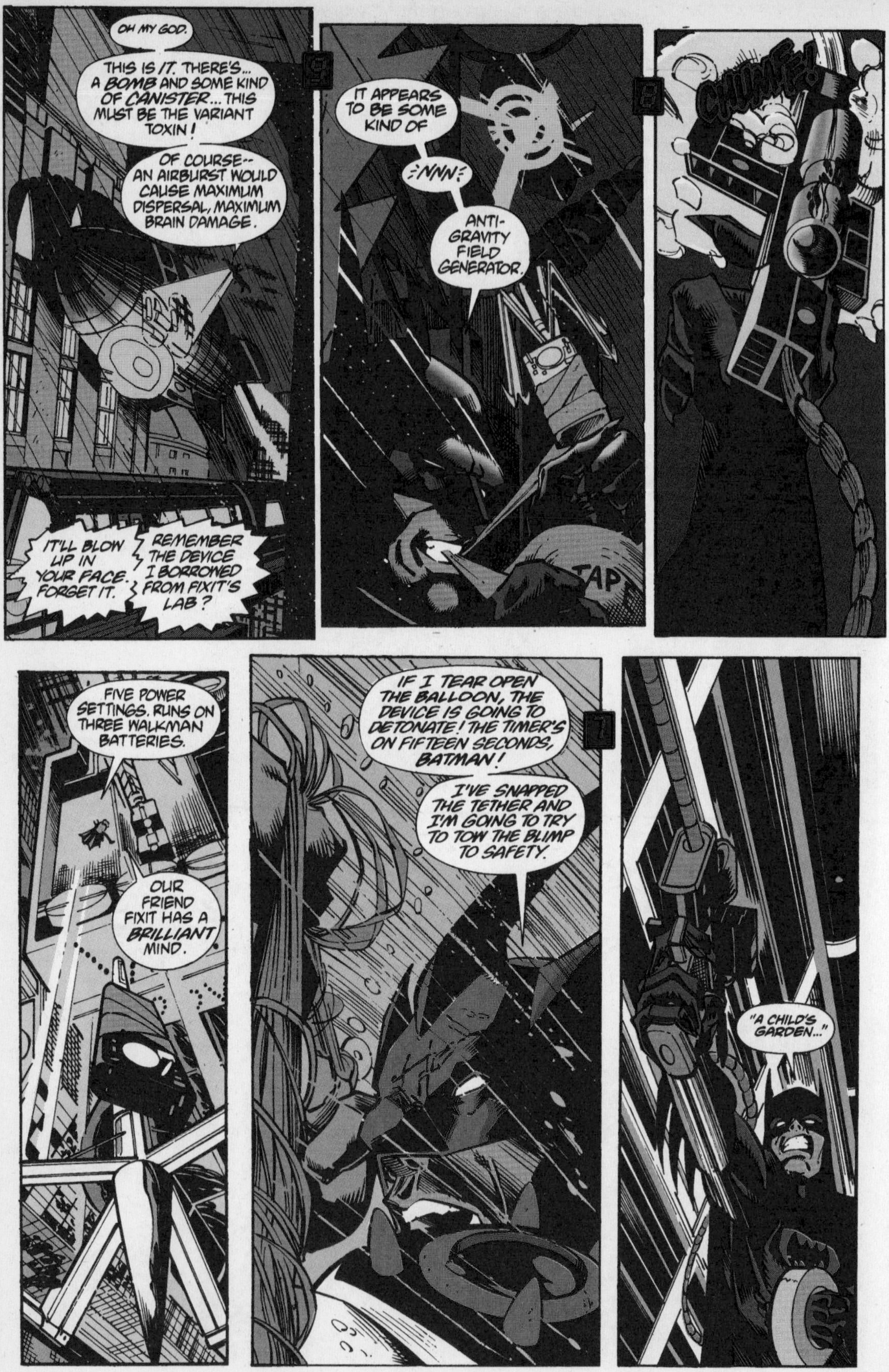

OH MY GOD.
THIS IS IT. THERE'S... A BOMB AND SOME KIND OF CANISTER... THIS MUST BE THE VARIANT TOXIN!
OF COURSE-- AN AIRBURST WOULD CAUSE MAXIMUM DISPERSAL, MAXIMUM BRAIN DAMAGE.
IT'LL BLOW UP IN YOUR FACE. FORGET IT.
REMEMBER THE DEVICE I BORROWED FROM FIXIT'S LAB?
9
IT APPEARS TO BE SOME KIND OF
NNN
ANTI-GRAVITY FIELD GENERATOR.
TAP
8
CHUNK!
FIVE POWER SETTINGS. RUNS ON THREE WALKMAN BATTERIES.
OUR FRIEND FIXIT HAS A BRILLIANT MIND.
IF I TEAR OPEN THE BALLOON, THE DEVICE IS GOING TO DETONATE! THE TIMER'S ON FIFTEEN SECONDS, BATMAN!
7
I'VE SNAPPED THE TETHER AND I'M GOING TO TRY TO TOW THE BLIMP TO SAFETY.
"A CHILD'S GARDEN..."

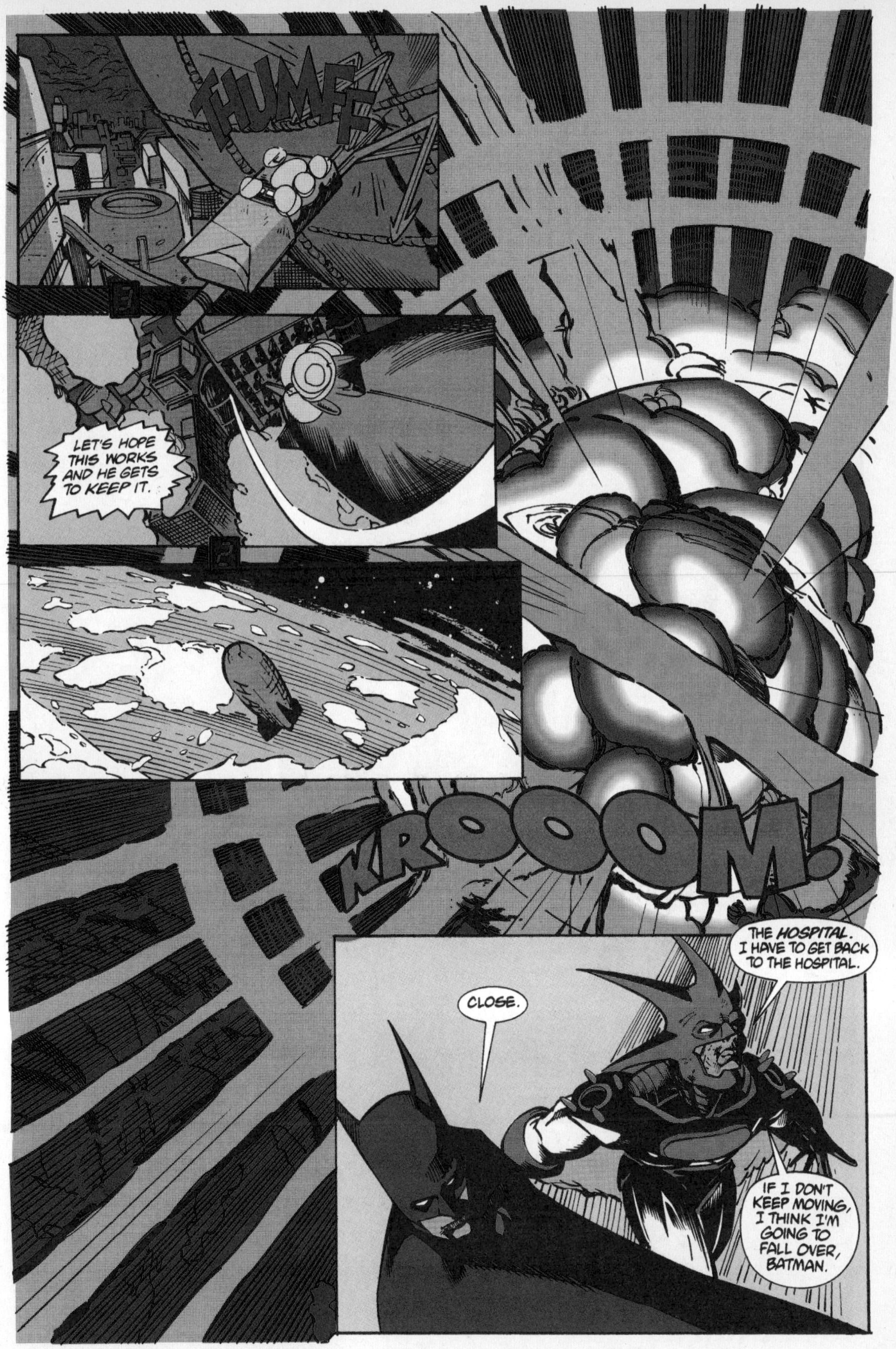
THUMF
LET'S HOPE THIS WORKS AND HE GETS TO KEEP IT.
KROOOOM!
THE HOSPITAL. I HAVE TO GET BACK TO THE HOSPITAL.
CLOSE.
IF I DON'T KEEP MOVING, I THINK I'M GOING TO FALL OVER, BATMAN.

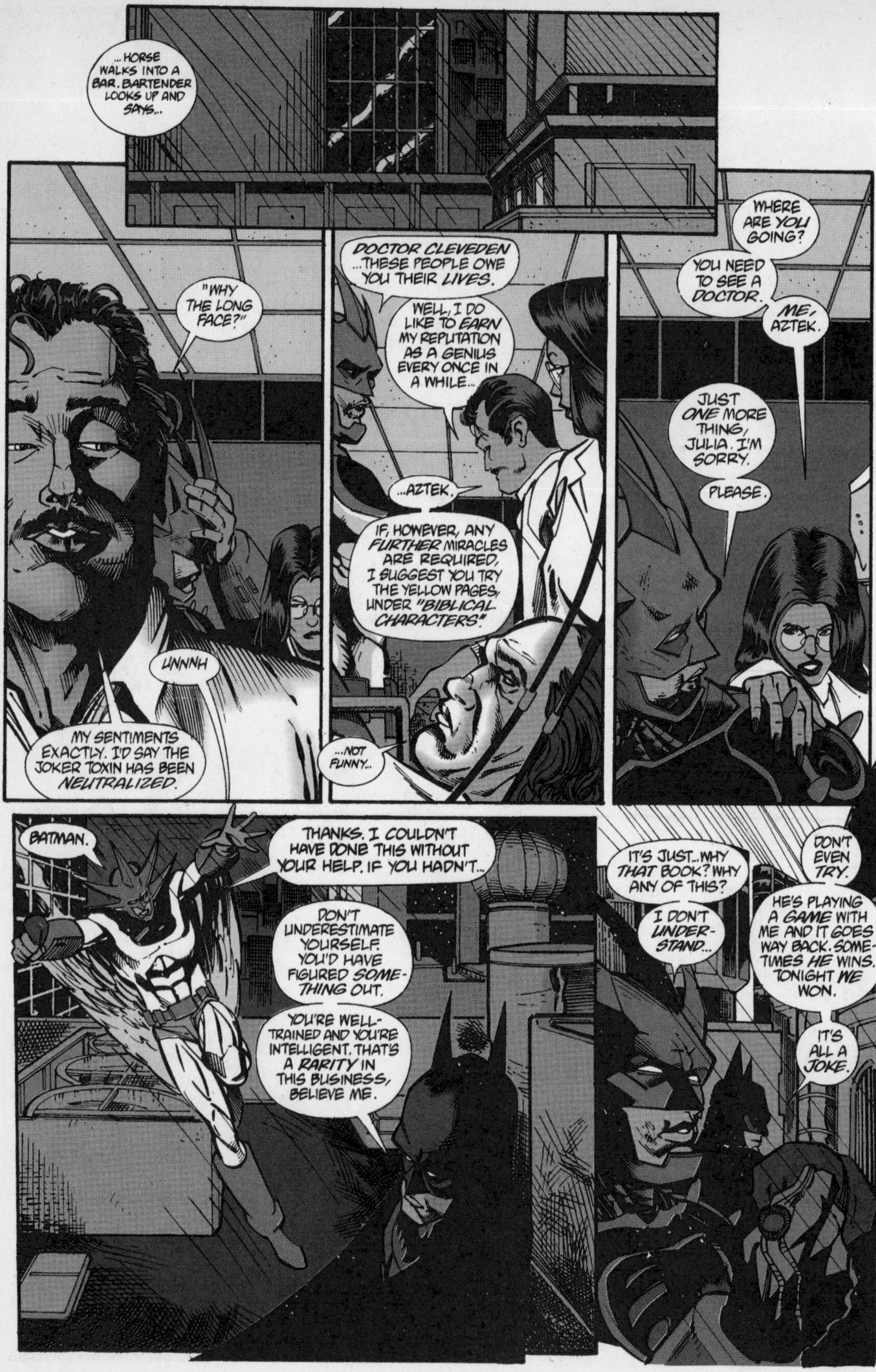
...HORSE WALKS INTO A BAR. BARTENDER LOOKS UP AND SAYS...
"WHY THE LONG FACE?"
UNNNH
MY SENTIMENTS EXACTLY. I'D SAY THE JOKER TOXIN HAS BEEN NEUTRALIZED.
DOCTOR CLEVEDEN ...THESE PEOPLE OWE YOU THEIR LIVES.
WELL, I DO LIKE TO EARN MY REPUTATION AS A GENIUS EVERY ONCE IN A WHILE...
...AZTEK.
IF, HOWEVER, ANY FURTHER MIRACLES ARE REQUIRED, I SUGGEST YOU TRY THE YELLOW PAGES, UNDER "BIBLICAL CHARACTERS."
...NOT FUNNY...
WHERE ARE YOU GOING?
YOU NEED TO SEE A DOCTOR.
ME, AZTEK.
JUST ONE MORE THING, JULIA. I'M SORRY.
PLEASE.
BATMAN.
THANKS. I COULDN'T HAVE DONE THIS WITHOUT YOUR HELP. IF YOU HADN'T...
DON'T UNDERESTIMATE YOURSELF. YOU'D HAVE FIGURED SOMETHING OUT.
YOU'RE WELL-TRAINED AND YOU'RE INTELLIGENT. THAT'S A RARITY IN THIS BUSINESS, BELIEVE ME.
IT'S JUST...WHY THAT BOOK? WHY ANY OF THIS?
I DON'T UNDERSTAND...
DON'T EVEN TRY.
HE'S PLAYING A GAME WITH ME AND IT GOES WAY BACK. SOMETIMES HE WINS. TONIGHT WE WON.
IT'S ALL A JOKE.

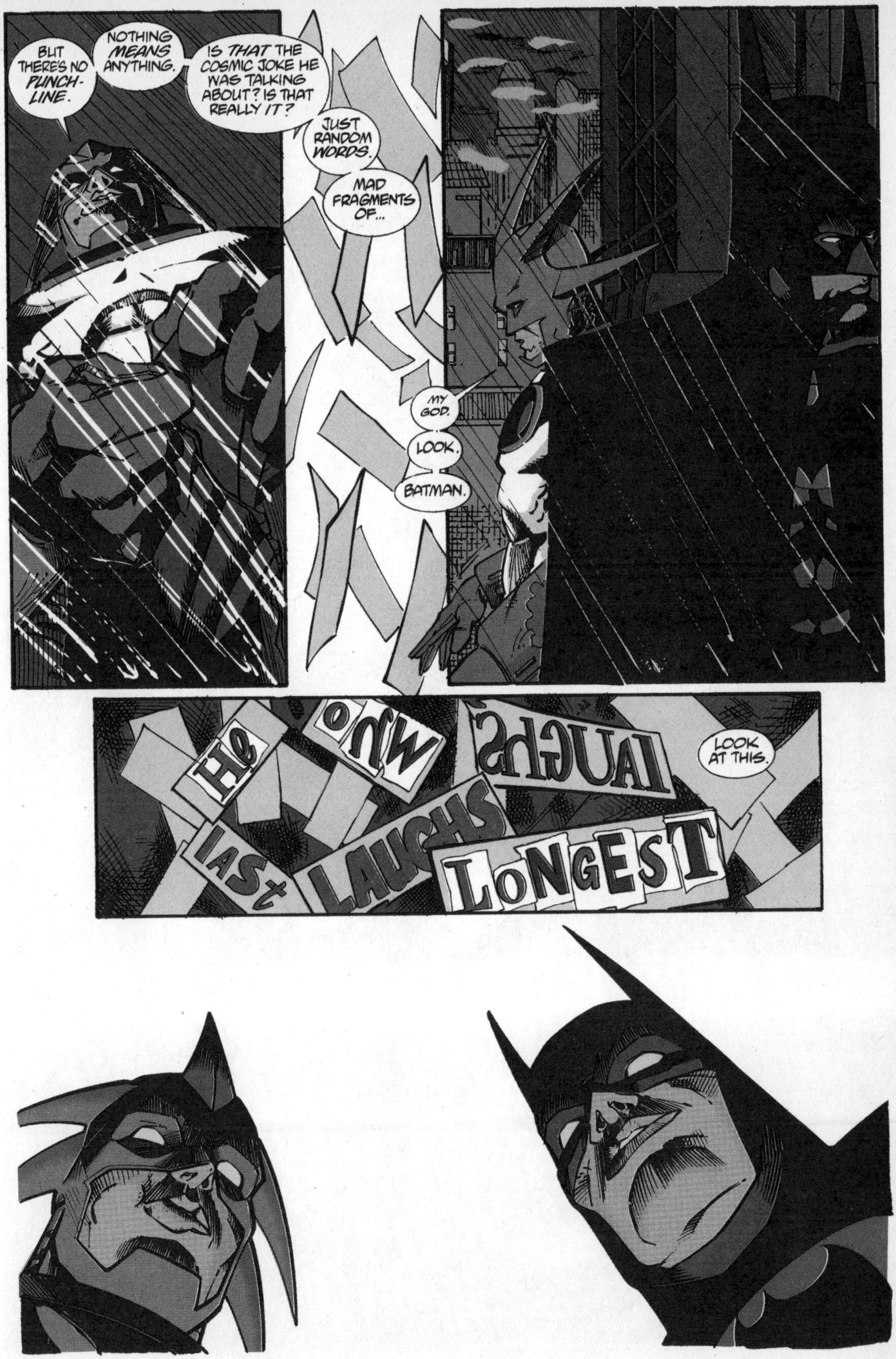
BUT THERE'S NO PUNCH-LINE.
NOTHING MEANS ANYTHING.
IS THAT THE COSMIC JOKE HE WAS TALKING ABOUT? IS THAT REALLY IT?
JUST RANDOM WORDS.
MAD FRAGMENTS OF...
MY GOD.
LOOK.
BATMAN.
He who LAUGHS
LOOK AT THIS.
lASt LAUGHS LONGEST

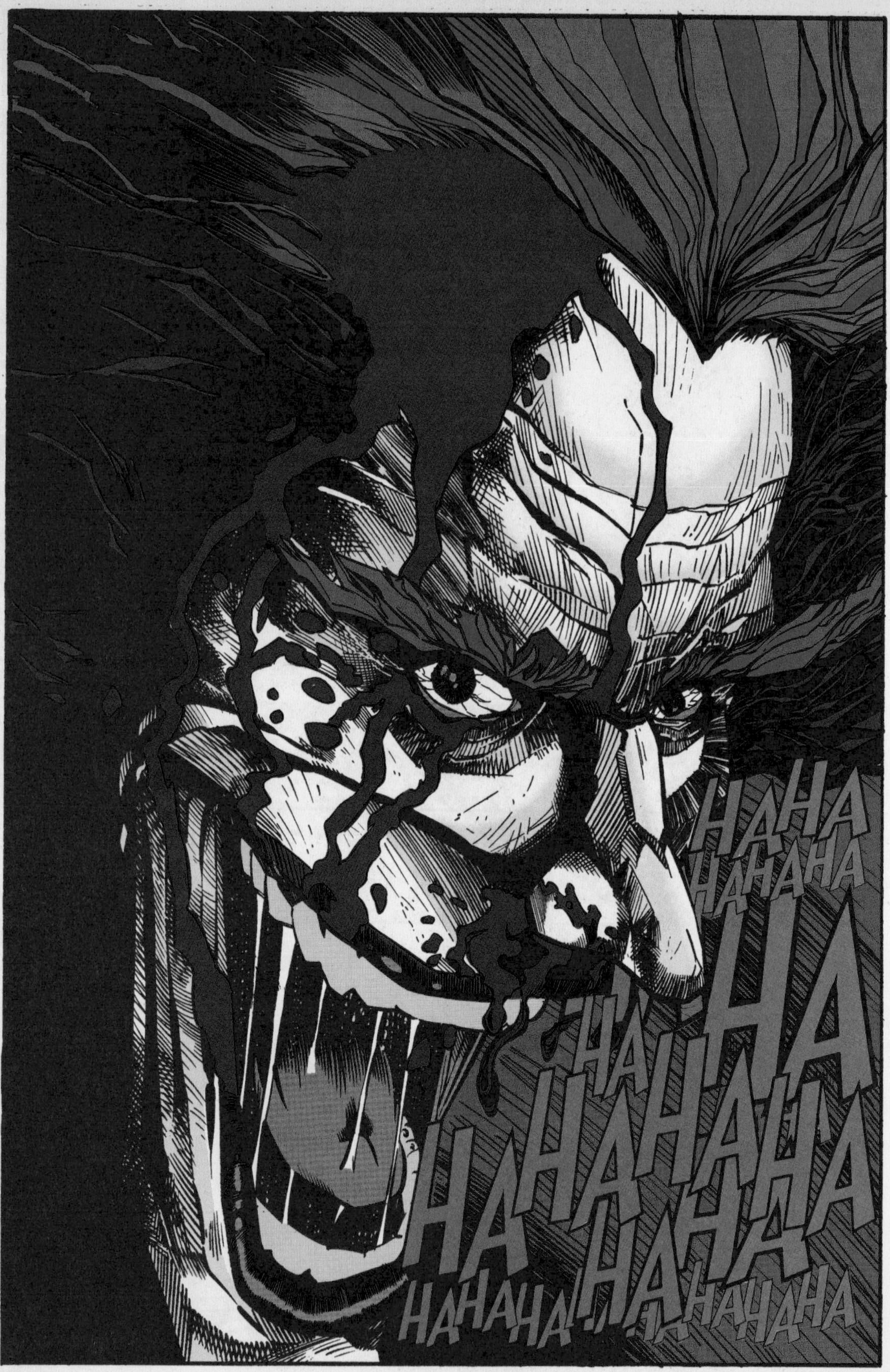
HAHA
HAHAHA
HA
HAHA
HAHAHA
HA
HAHAHAHA
HAHAHA
HAHAHAHA
HAHAHAHA

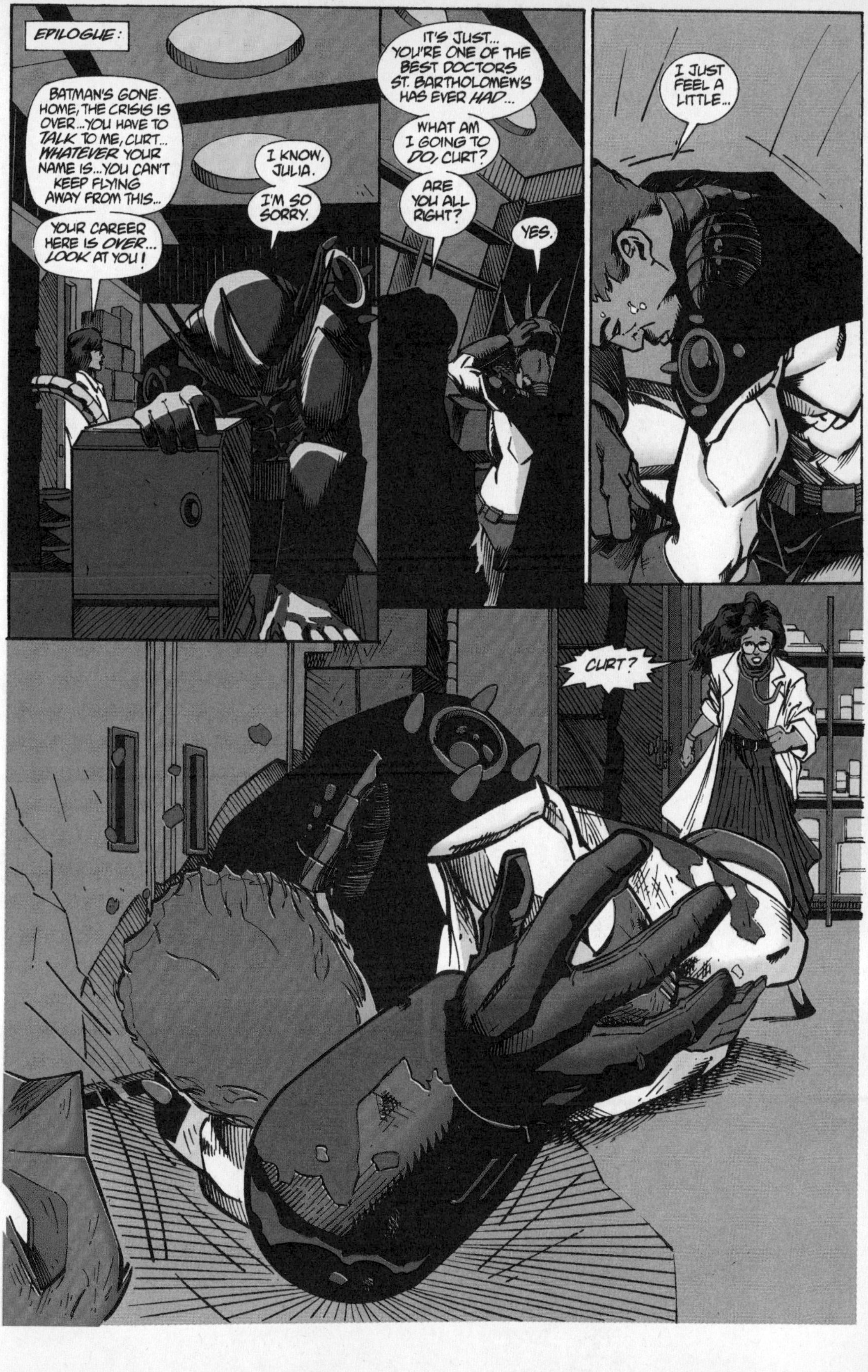
EPILOGUE:
BATMAN'S GONE HOME, THE CRISIS IS OVER...YOU HAVE TO TALK TO ME, CURT... WHATEVER YOUR NAME IS...YOU CAN'T KEEP FLYING AWAY FROM THIS...
YOUR CAREER HERE IS OVER... LOOK AT YOU!
I KNOW, JULIA.
I'M SO SORRY.
IT'S JUST... YOU'RE ONE OF THE BEST DOCTORS ST. BARTHOLOMEW'S HAS EVER HAD...
WHAT AM I GOING TO DO, CURT?
ARE YOU ALL RIGHT?
YES.
I JUST FEEL A LITTLE...
CURT?

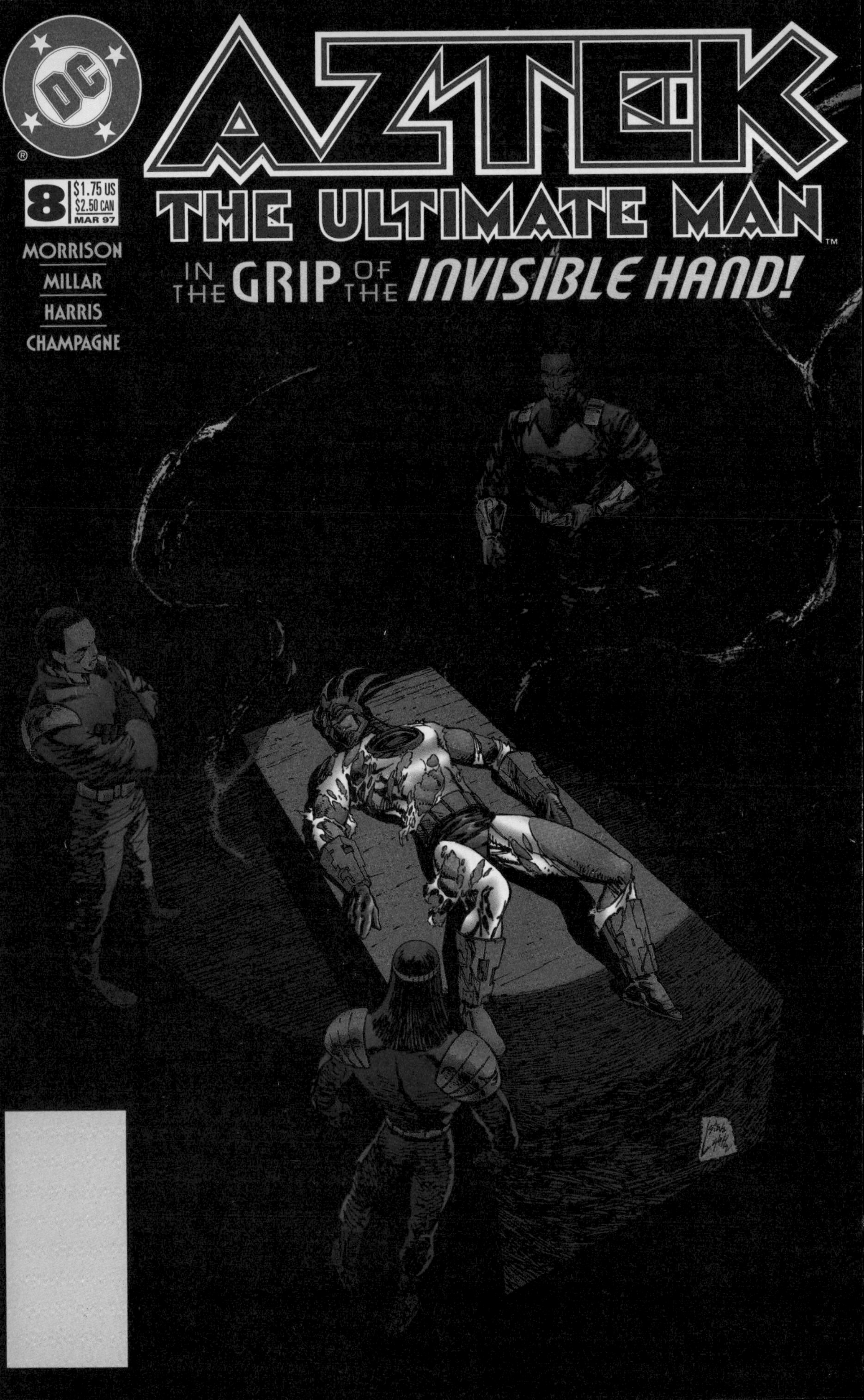

DC
AZTEK
THE ULTIMATE MAN
8
$1.75 US
$2.50 CAN
MAR 97
MORRISON
MILLAR
HARRIS
CHAMPAGNE
IN THE GRIP OF THE INVISIBLE HAND!

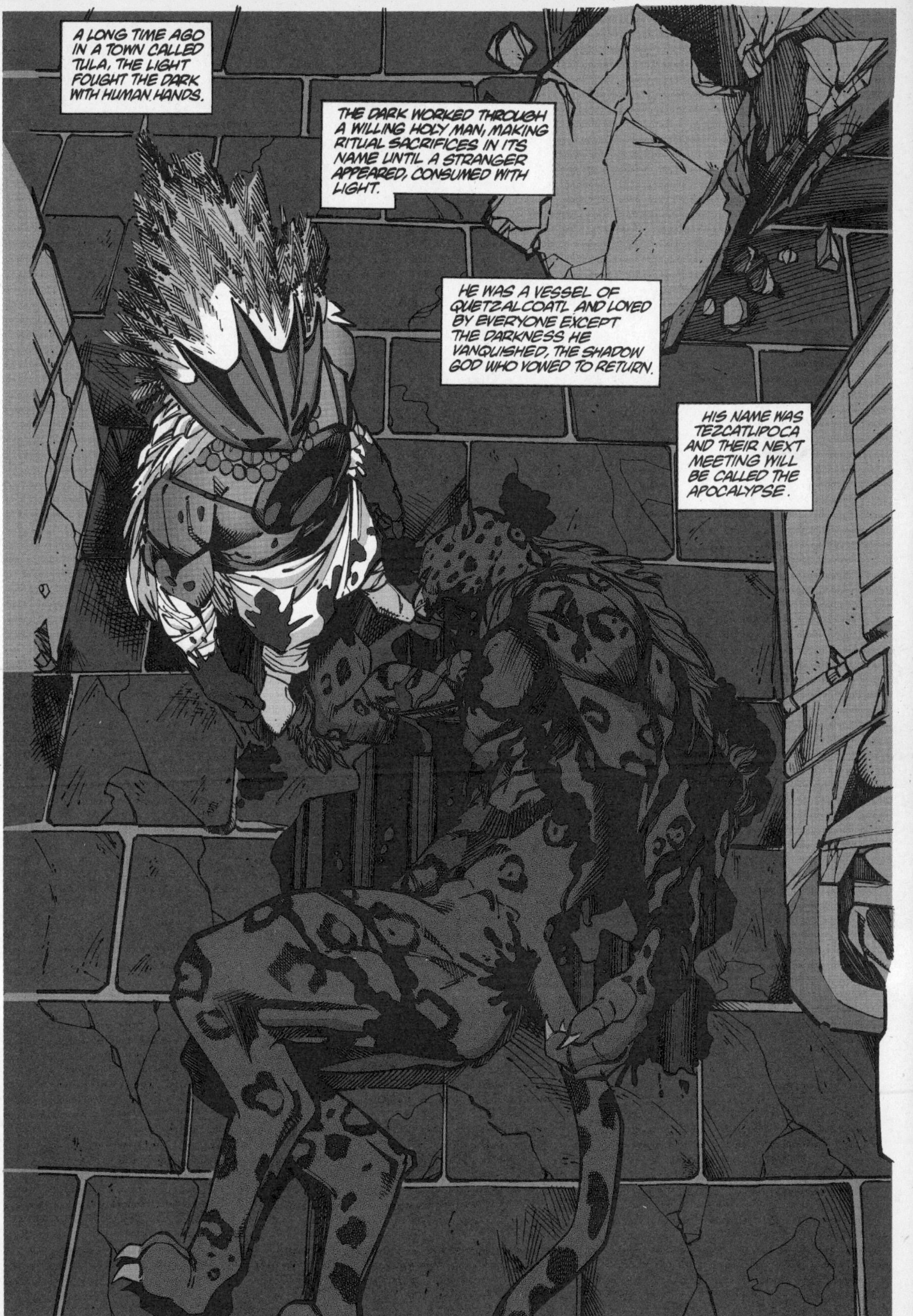

A LONG TIME AGO IN A TOWN CALLED TULA, THE LIGHT FOUGHT THE DARK WITH HUMAN HANDS.
THE DARK WORKED THROUGH A WILLING HOLY MAN, MAKING RITUAL SACRIFICES IN ITS NAME UNTIL A STRANGER APPEARED, CONSUMED WITH LIGHT.
HE WAS A VESSEL OF QUETZALCOATL AND LOVED BY EVERYONE EXCEPT THE DARKNESS HE VANQUISHED, THE SHADOW GOD WHO VOWED TO RETURN.
HIS NAME WAS TEZCATLIPOCA AND THEIR NEXT MEETING WILL BE CALLED THE APOCALYPSE.

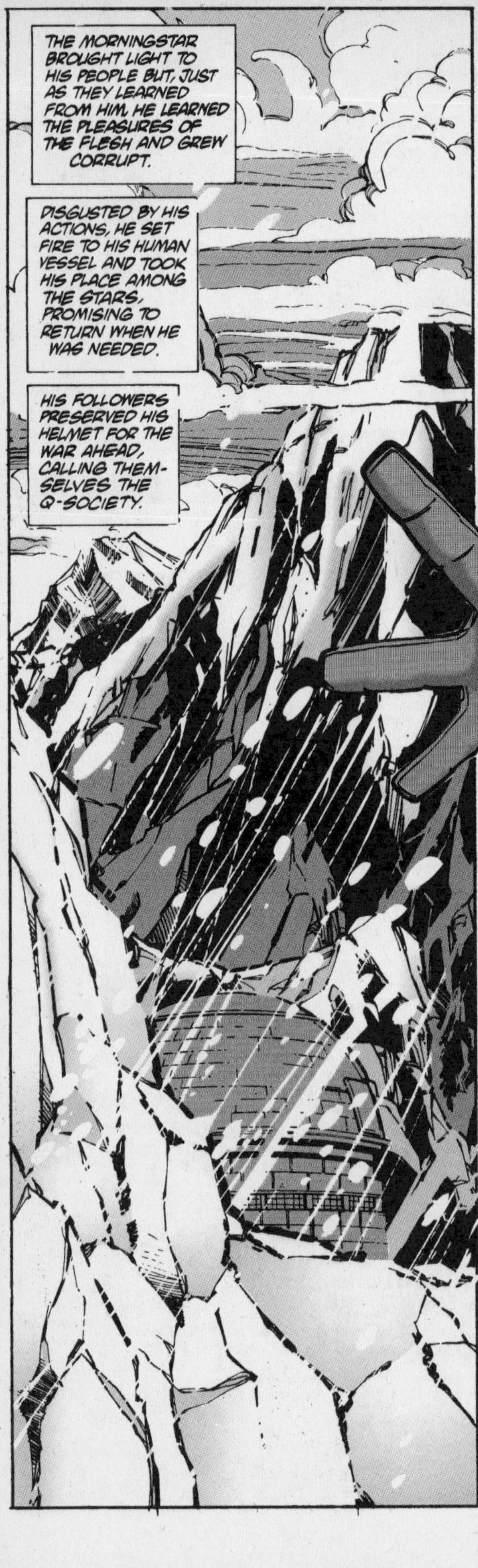
THE MORNINGSTAR BROUGHT LIGHT TO HIS PEOPLE BUT, JUST AS THEY LEARNED FROM HIM, HE LEARNED THE PLEASURES OF THE FLESH AND GREW CORRUPT.
DISGUSTED BY HIS ACTIONS, HE SET FIRE TO HIS HUMAN VESSEL AND TOOK HIS PLACE AMONG THE STARS, PROMISING TO RETURN WHEN HE WAS NEEDED.
HIS FOLLOWERS PRESERVED HIS HELMET FOR THE WAR AHEAD, CALLING THEMSELVES THE Q-SOCIETY.

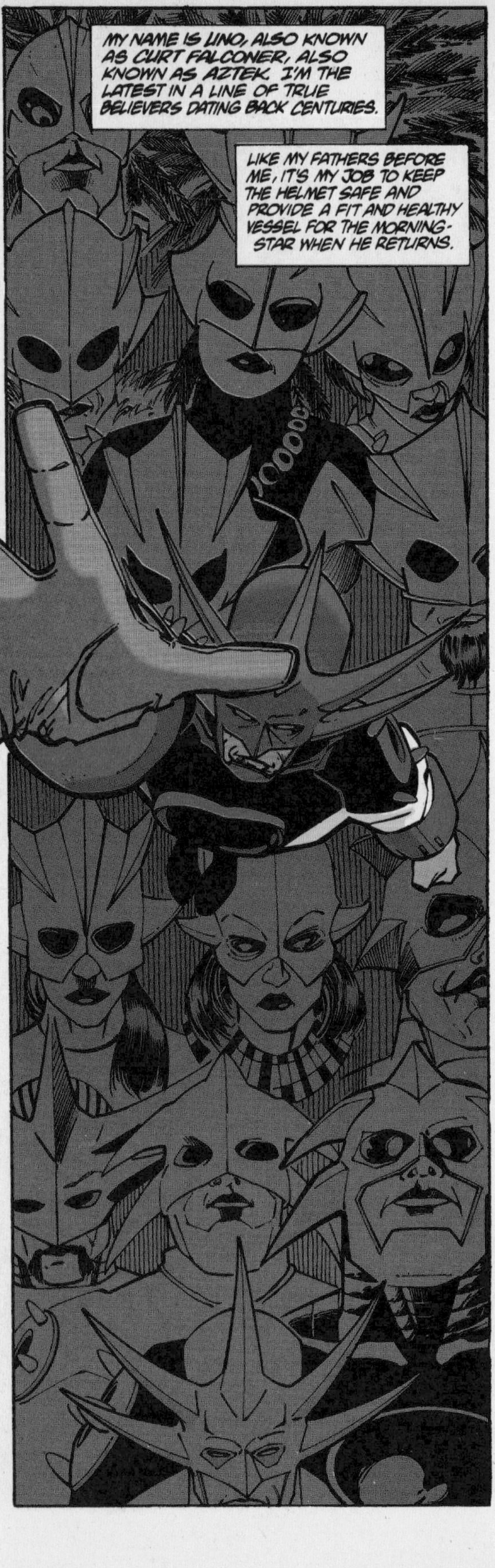
MY NAME IS UNO, ALSO KNOWN AS CURT FALCONER, ALSO KNOWN AS AZTEK. I'M THE LATEST IN A LINE OF TRUE BELIEVERS DATING BACK CENTURIES.
LIKE MY FATHERS BEFORE ME, IT'S MY JOB TO KEEP THE HELMET SAFE AND PROVIDE A FIT AND HEALTHY VESSEL FOR THE MORNING-STAR WHEN HE RETURNS.

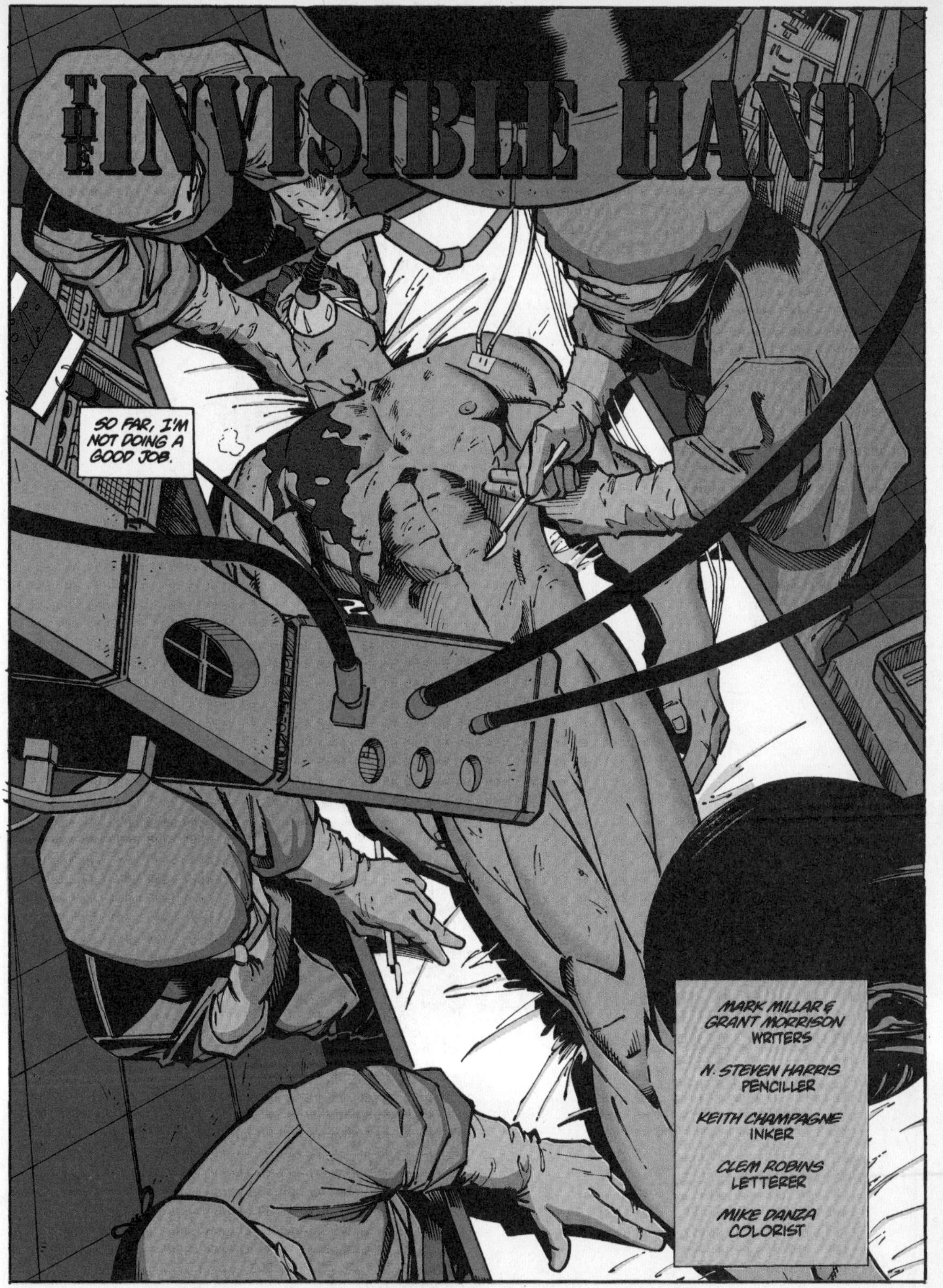
THE INVISIBLE HAND
SO FAR, I'M NOT DOING A GOOD JOB.
MARK MILLAR & GRANT MORRISON
WRITERS
N. STEVEN HARRIS
PENCILLER
KEITH CHAMPAGNE
INKER
CLEM ROBINS
LETTERER
MIKE DANZA
COLORIST

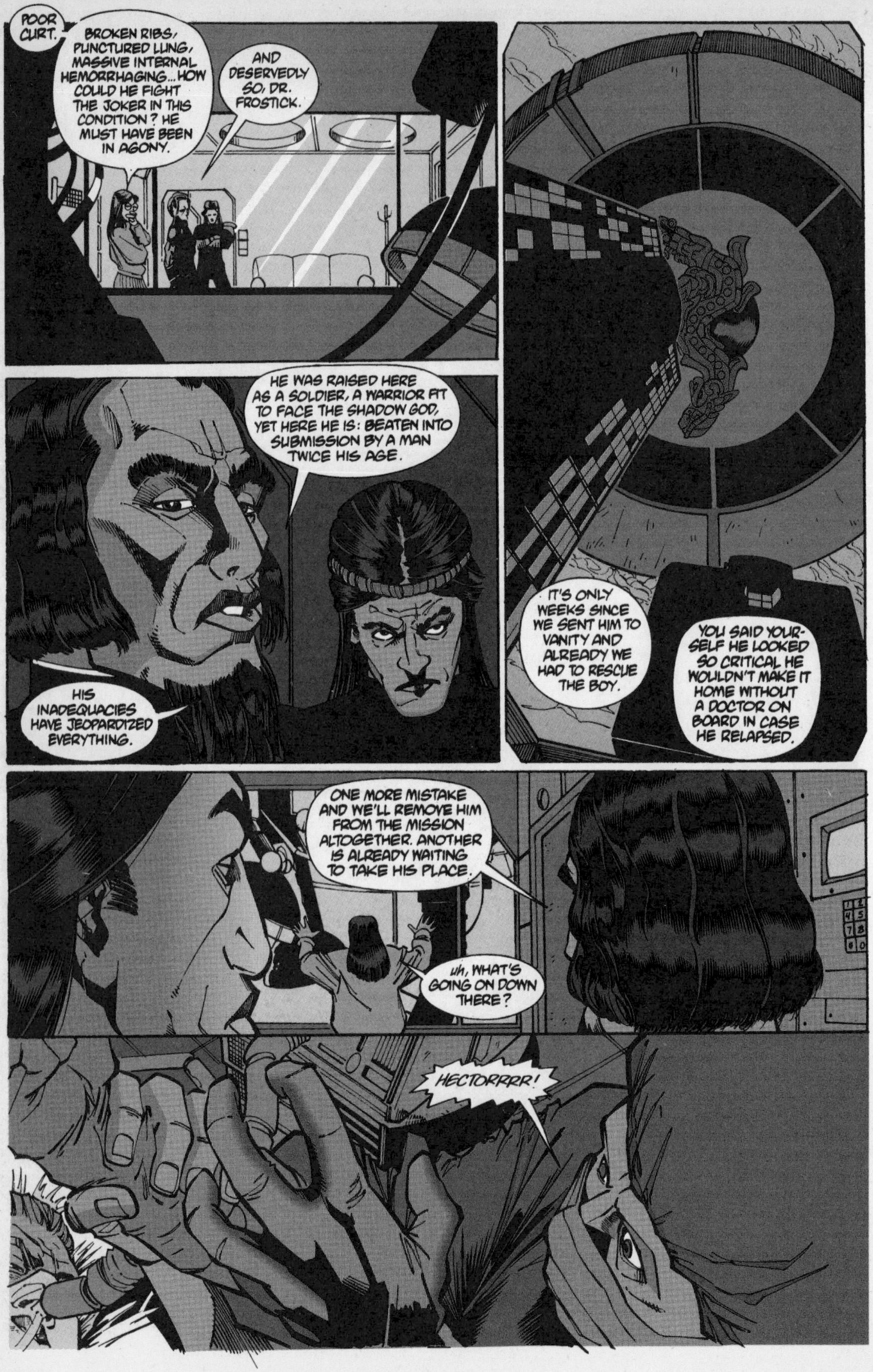
POOR CURT.
BROKEN RIBS, PUNCTURED LUNG, MASSIVE INTERNAL HEMORRHAGING... HOW COULD HE FIGHT THE JOKER IN THIS CONDITION? HE MUST HAVE BEEN IN AGONY.
AND DESERVEDLY SO, DR. FROSTICK.
HE WAS RAISED HERE AS A SOLDIER, A WARRIOR FIT TO FACE THE SHADOW GOD, YET HERE HE IS: BEATEN INTO SUBMISSION BY A MAN TWICE HIS AGE.
HIS INADEQUACIES HAVE JEOPARDIZED EVERYTHING.
IT'S ONLY WEEKS SINCE WE SENT HIM TO VANITY AND ALREADY WE HAD TO RESCUE THE BOY.
YOU SAID YOURSELF HE LOOKED SO CRITICAL HE WOULDN'T MAKE IT HOME WITHOUT A DOCTOR ON BOARD IN CASE HE RELAPSED.
ONE MORE MISTAKE AND WE'LL REMOVE HIM FROM THE MISSION ALTOGETHER. ANOTHER IS ALREADY WAITING TO TAKE HIS PLACE.
uh, WHAT'S GOING ON DOWN THERE?
HECTORRRR!

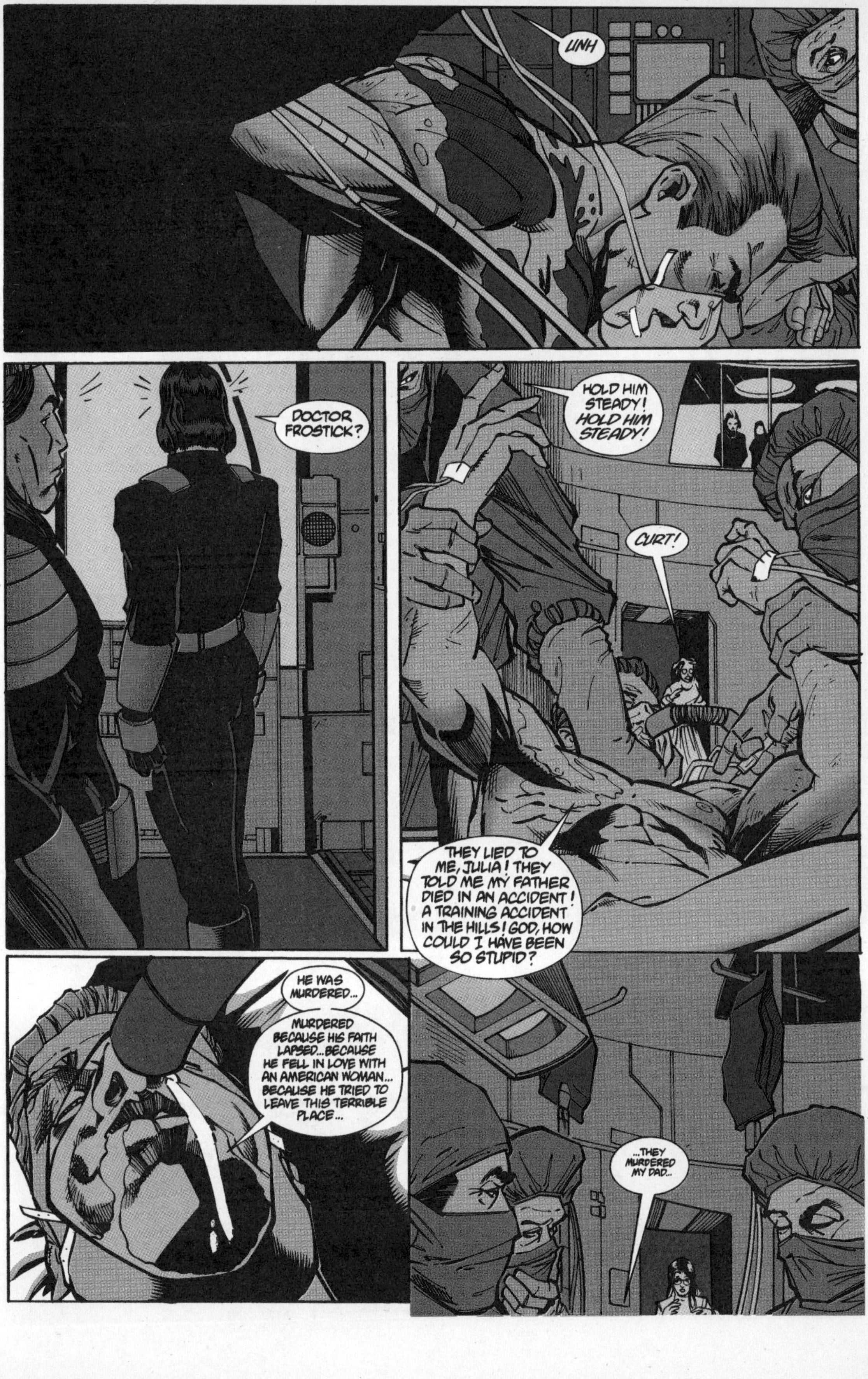
UNH
DOCTOR FROSTICK?
HOLD HIM STEADY! HOLD HIM STEADY!
CURT!
THEY LIED TO ME, JULIA! THEY TOLD ME MY FATHER DIED IN AN ACCIDENT! A TRAINING ACCIDENT IN THE HILLS! GOD, HOW COULD I HAVE BEEN SO STUPID?
HE WAS MURDERED...
MURDERED BECAUSE HIS FAITH LAPSED...BECAUSE HE FELL IN LOVE WITH AN AMERICAN WOMAN... BECAUSE HE TRIED TO LEAVE THIS TERRIBLE PLACE...
...THEY MURDERED MY DAD...

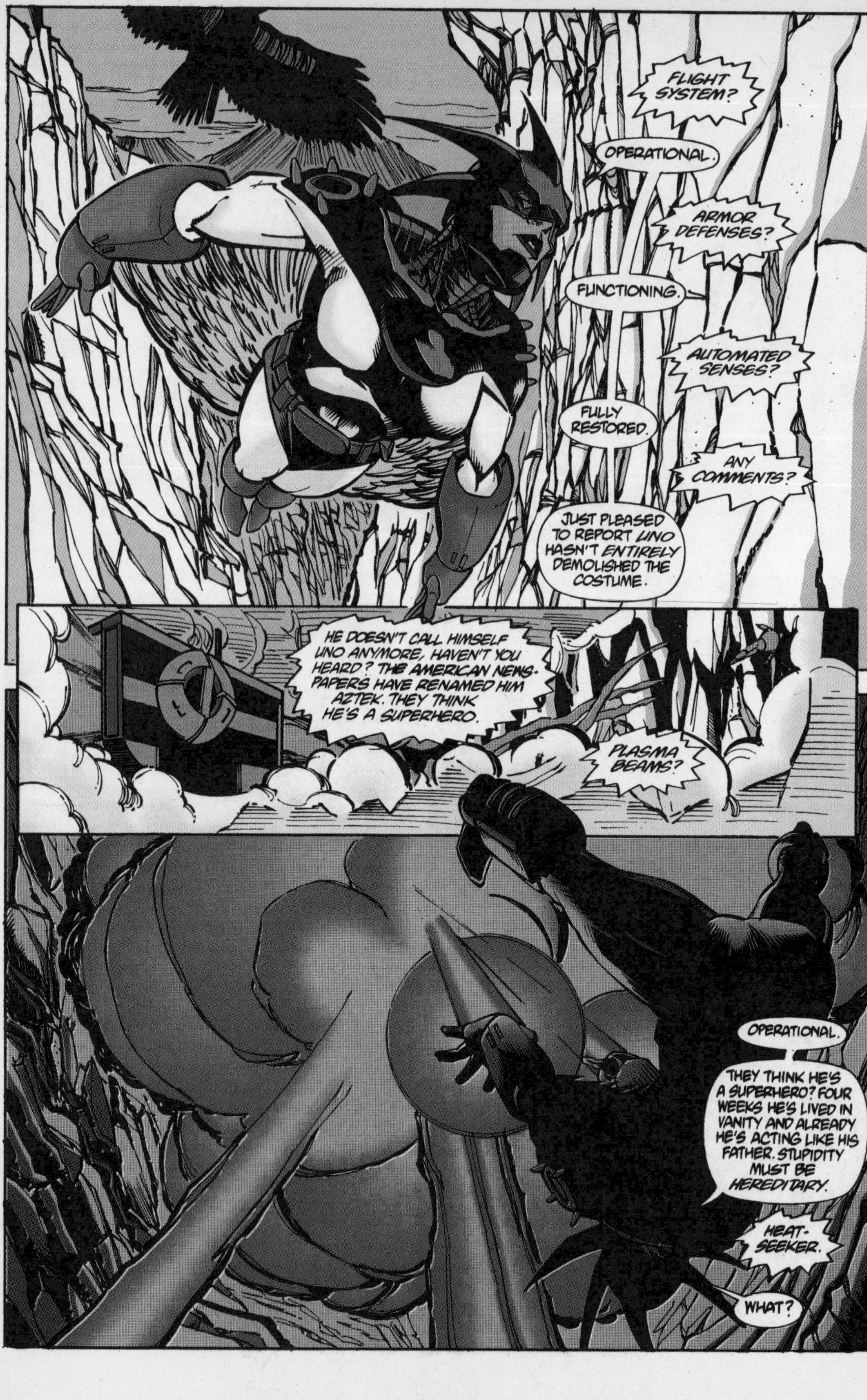
FLIGHT SYSTEM?
OPERATIONAL.
ARMOR DEFENSES?
FUNCTIONING.
AUTOMATED SENSES?
FULLY RESTORED.
ANY COMMENTS?
JUST PLEASED TO REPORT UNO HASN'T ENTIRELY DEMOLISHED THE COSTUME.
HE DOESN'T CALL HIMSELF UNO ANYMORE, HAVEN'T YOU HEARD? THE AMERICAN NEWS-PAPERS HAVE RENAMED HIM AZTEK. THEY THINK HE'S A SUPERHERO.
PLASMA BEAMS?
OPERATIONAL.
THEY THINK HE'S A SUPERHERO? FOUR WEEKS HE'S LIVED IN VANITY AND ALREADY HE'S ACTING LIKE HIS FATHER. STUPIDITY MUST BE HEREDITARY.
HEAT-SEEKER.
WHAT?

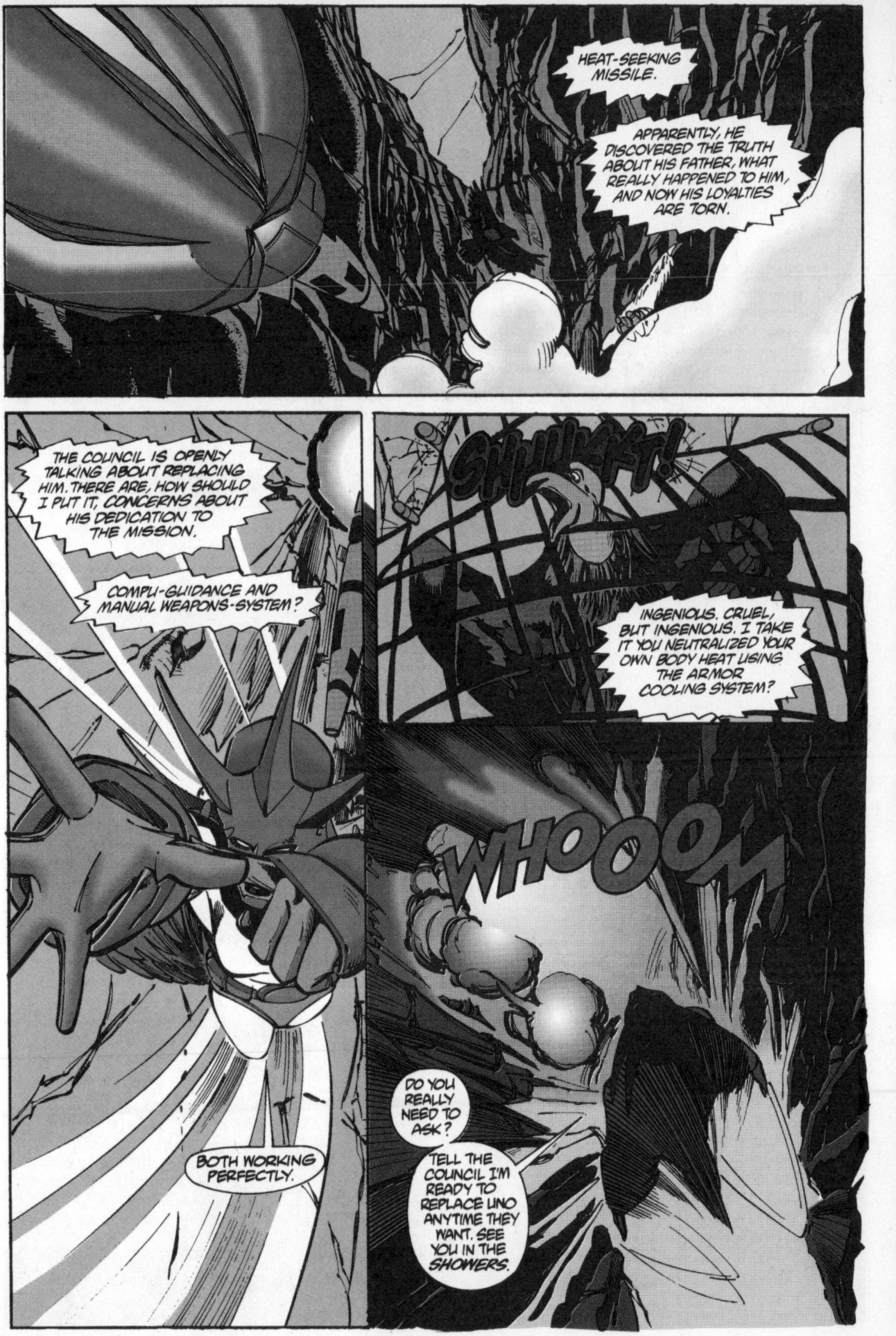
HEAT-SEEKING MISSILE.
APPARENTLY, HE DISCOVERED THE TRUTH ABOUT HIS FATHER, WHAT REALLY HAPPENED TO HIM, AND NOW HIS LOYALTIES ARE TORN.
THE COUNCIL IS OPENLY TALKING ABOUT REPLACING HIM. THERE ARE, HOW SHOULD I PUT IT, CONCERNS ABOUT HIS DEDICATION TO THE MISSION.
COMPU-GUIDANCE AND MANUAL WEAPONS-SYSTEM?
BOTH WORKING PERFECTLY.
SHHHKKT!
INGENIOUS. CRUEL, BUT INGENIOUS. I TAKE IT YOU NEUTRALIZED YOUR OWN BODY HEAT USING THE ARMOR COOLING SYSTEM?
WHOOOM
DO YOU REALLY NEED TO ASK?
TELL THE COUNCIL I'M READY TO REPLACE UNO ANYTIME THEY WANT. SEE YOU IN THE SHOWERS.

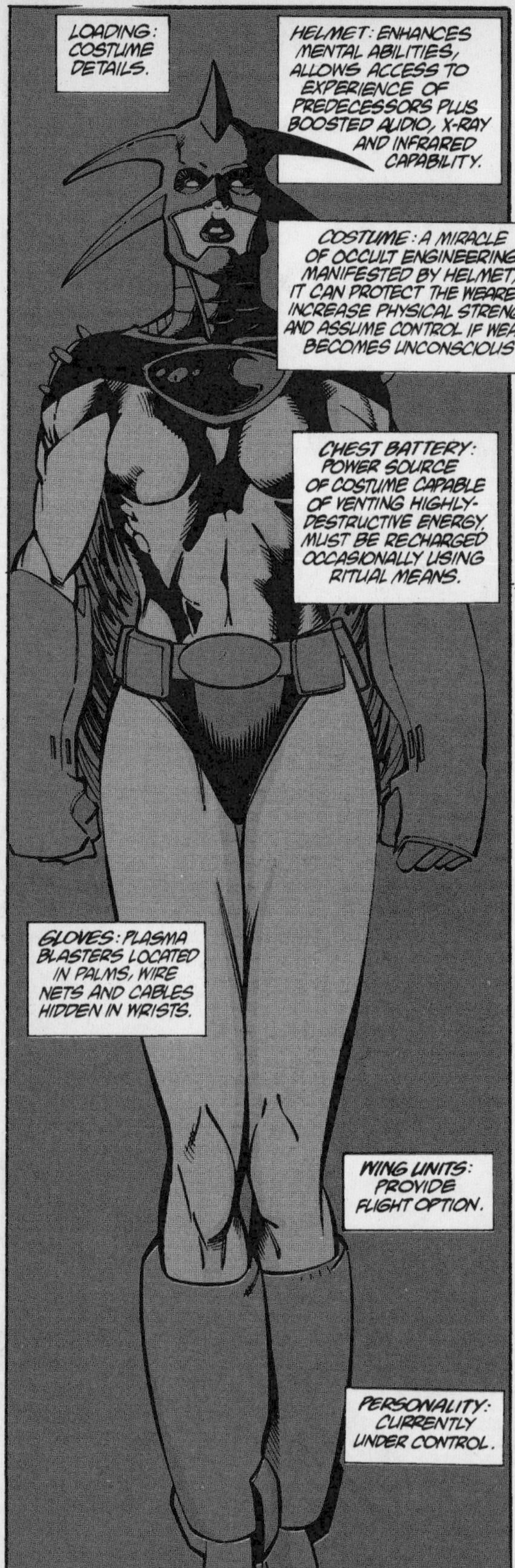
LOADING: COSTUME DETAILS.
HELMET: ENHANCES MENTAL ABILITIES, ALLOWS ACCESS TO EXPERIENCE OF PREDECESSORS PLUS BOOSTED AUDIO, X-RAY AND INFRARED CAPABILITY.
COSTUME: A MIRACLE OF OCCULT ENGINEERING MANIFESTED BY HELMET, IT CAN PROTECT THE WEARER, INCREASE PHYSICAL STRENGTH AND ASSUME CONTROL IF WEARER BECOMES UNCONSCIOUS.
CHEST BATTERY: POWER SOURCE OF COSTUME CAPABLE OF VENTING HIGHLY-DESTRUCTIVE ENERGY, MUST BE RECHARGED OCCASIONALLY USING RITUAL MEANS.
GLOVES: PLASMA BLASTERS LOCATED IN PALMS, WIRE NETS AND CABLES HIDDEN IN WRISTS.
WING UNITS: PROVIDE FLIGHT OPTION.
PERSONALITY: CURRENTLY UNDER CONTROL.
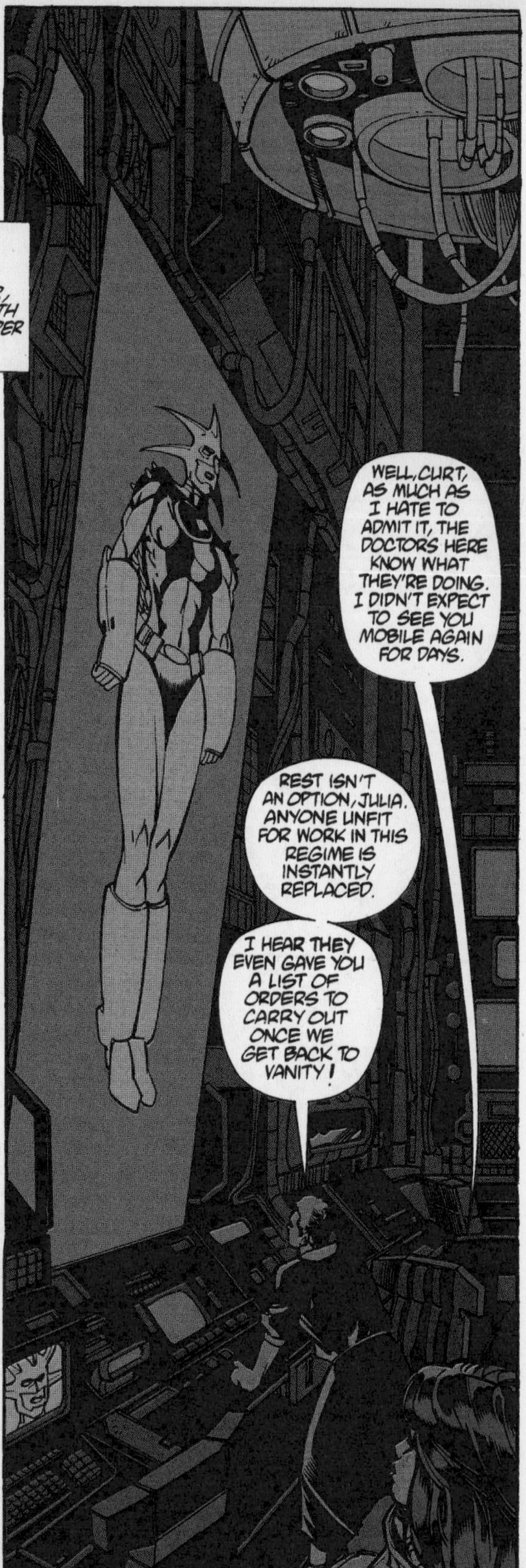
WELL, CURT, AS MUCH AS I HATE TO ADMIT IT, THE DOCTORS HERE KNOW WHAT THEY'RE DOING. I DIDN'T EXPECT TO SEE YOU MOBILE AGAIN FOR DAYS.
REST ISN'T AN OPTION, JULIA. ANYONE UNFIT FOR WORK IN THIS REGIME IS INSTANTLY REPLACED.
I HEAR THEY EVEN GAVE YOU A LIST OF ORDERS TO CARRY OUT ONCE WE GET BACK TO VANITY!

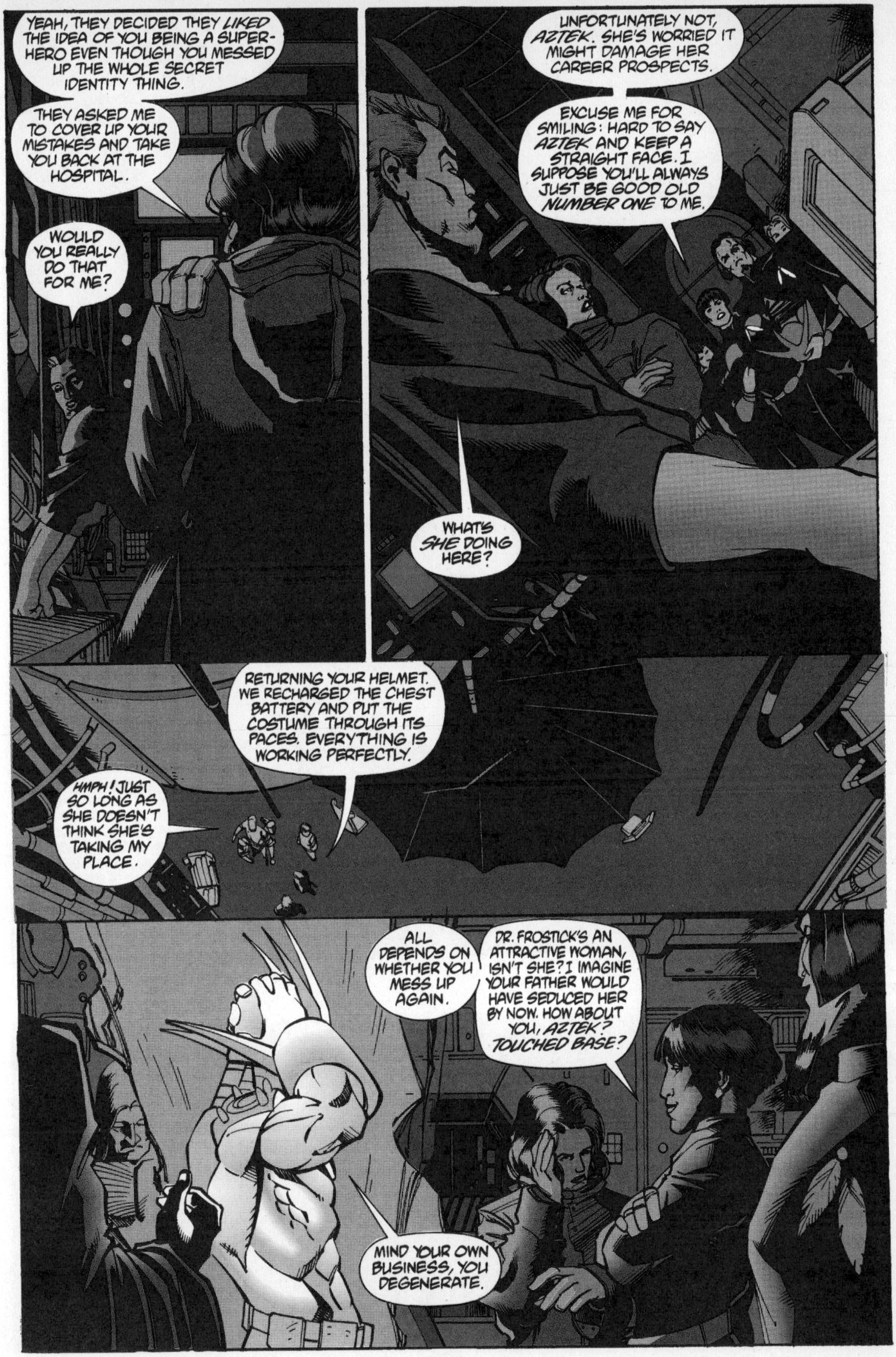
YEAH, THEY DECIDED THEY LIKED THE IDEA OF YOU BEING A SUPER-HERO EVEN THOUGH YOU MESSED UP THE WHOLE SECRET IDENTITY THING.
THEY ASKED ME TO COVER UP YOUR MISTAKES AND TAKE YOU BACK AT THE HOSPITAL.
WOULD YOU REALLY DO THAT FOR ME?
UNFORTUNATELY NOT, AZTEK. SHE'S WORRIED IT MIGHT DAMAGE HER CAREER PROSPECTS.
EXCUSE ME FOR SMILING: HARD TO SAY AZTEK AND KEEP A STRAIGHT FACE. I SUPPOSE YOU'LL ALWAYS JUST BE GOOD OLD NUMBER ONE TO ME.
WHAT'S SHE DOING HERE?
RETURNING YOUR HELMET. WE RECHARGED THE CHEST BATTERY AND PUT THE COSTUME THROUGH ITS PACES. EVERYTHING IS WORKING PERFECTLY.
HMPH! JUST SO LONG AS SHE DOESN'T THINK SHE'S TAKING MY PLACE.
ALL DEPENDS ON WHETHER YOU MESS UP AGAIN.
DR. FROSTICK'S AN ATTRACTIVE WOMAN, ISN'T SHE? I IMAGINE YOUR FATHER WOULD HAVE SEDUCED HER BY NOW. HOW ABOUT YOU, AZTEK? TOUCHED BASE?
MIND YOUR OWN BUSINESS, YOU DEGENERATE.

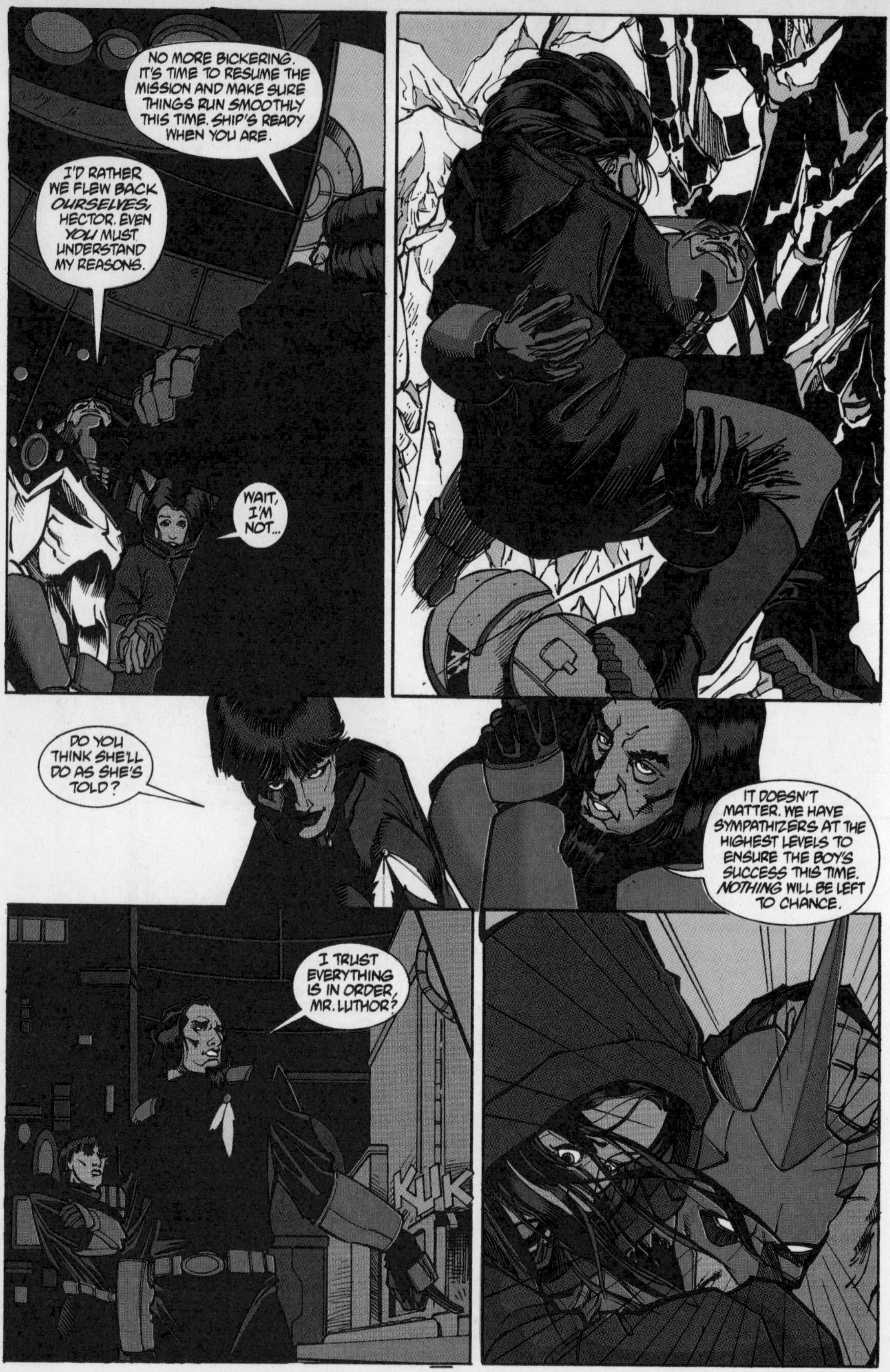
NO MORE BICKERING. IT'S TIME TO RESUME THE MISSION AND MAKE SURE THINGS RUN SMOOTHLY THIS TIME. SHIP'S READY WHEN YOU ARE.
I'D RATHER WE FLEW BACK *OURSELVES,* HECTOR. EVEN *YOU* MUST UNDERSTAND MY REASONS.
WAIT, I'M NOT...
DO YOU THINK SHE'LL DO AS SHE'S TOLD?
IT DOESN'T MATTER. WE HAVE SYMPATHIZERS AT THE HIGHEST LEVELS TO ENSURE THE BOY'S SUCCESS THIS TIME. *NOTHING* WILL BE LEFT TO CHANCE.
I TRUST EVERYTHING IS IN ORDER, MR. LUTHOR?
KLIK

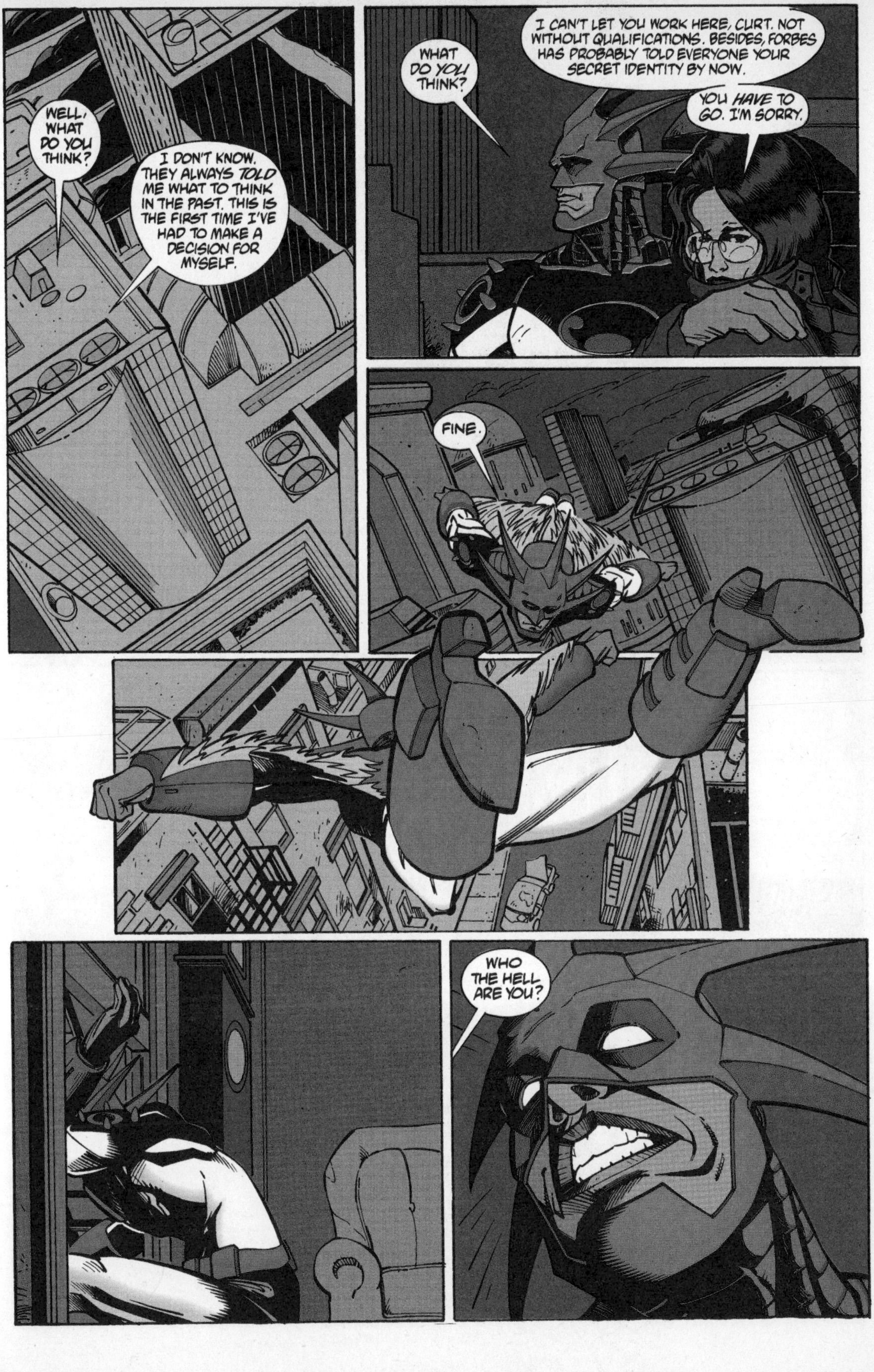

WELL, WHAT DO YOU THINK?
I DON'T KNOW. THEY ALWAYS TOLD ME WHAT TO THINK IN THE PAST. THIS IS THE FIRST TIME I'VE HAD TO MAKE A DECISION FOR MYSELF.
WHAT DO YOU THINK?
I CAN'T LET YOU WORK HERE, CURT. NOT WITHOUT QUALIFICATIONS. BESIDES, FORBES HAS PROBABLY TOLD EVERYONE YOUR SECRET IDENTITY BY NOW.
YOU HAVE TO GO. I'M SORRY.
FINE.
WHO THE HELL ARE YOU?

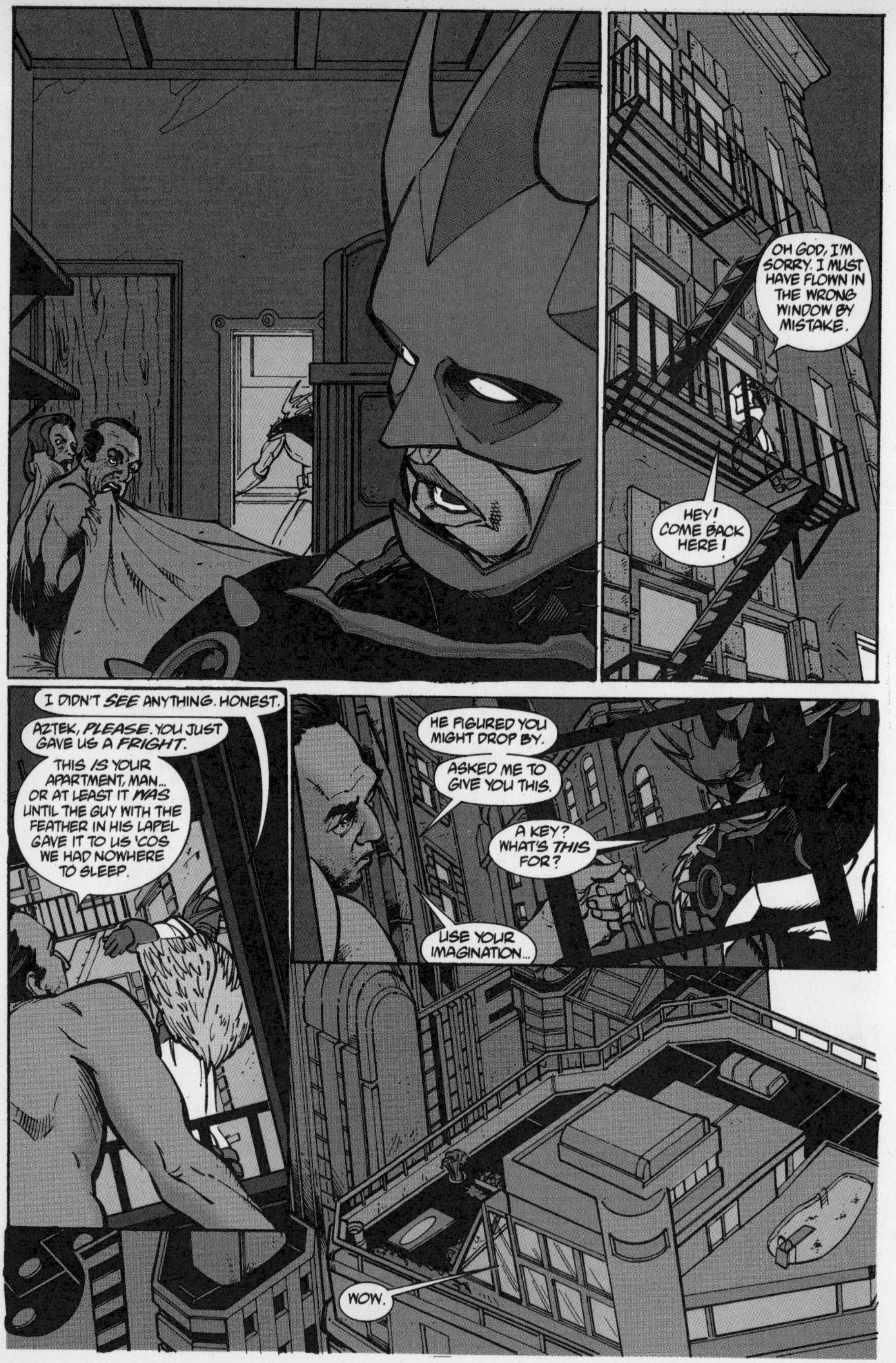
OH GOD, I'M SORRY. I MUST HAVE FLOWN IN THE WRONG WINDOW BY MISTAKE.
HEY! COME BACK HERE!
I DIDN'T SEE ANYTHING. HONEST.
AZTEK, PLEASE. YOU JUST GAVE US A FRIGHT.
THIS IS YOUR APARTMENT, MAN... OR AT LEAST IT WAS UNTIL THE GUY WITH THE FEATHER IN HIS LAPEL GAVE IT TO US 'COS WE HAD NOWHERE TO SLEEP.
HE FIGURED YOU MIGHT DROP BY.
ASKED ME TO GIVE YOU THIS.
A KEY? WHAT'S THIS FOR?
USE YOUR IMAGINATION...
WOW.

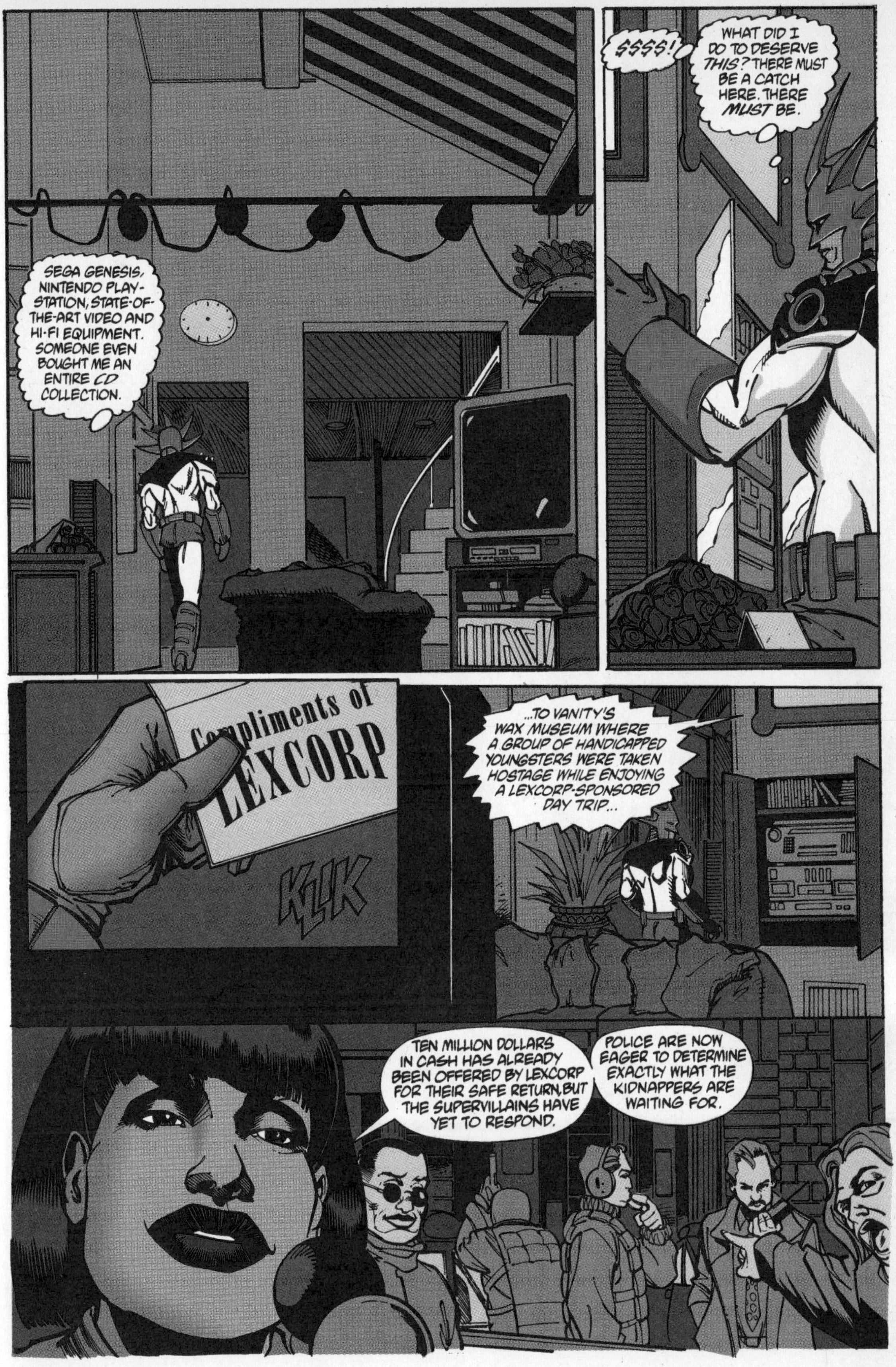
SEGA GENESIS, NINTENDO PLAY-STATION, STATE-OF-THE-ART VIDEO AND HI-FI EQUIPMENT. SOMEONE EVEN BOUGHT ME AN ENTIRE CD COLLECTION.
$$$$!
WHAT DID I DO TO DESERVE THIS? THERE MUST BE A CATCH HERE. THERE MUST BE.
Compliments of LEXCORP
KLIK
...TO VANITY'S WAX MUSEUM WHERE A GROUP OF HANDICAPPED YOUNGSTERS WERE TAKEN HOSTAGE WHILE ENJOYING A LEXCORP-SPONSORED DAY TRIP...
TEN MILLION DOLLARS IN CASH HAS ALREADY BEEN OFFERED BY LEXCORP FOR THEIR SAFE RETURN, BUT THE SUPERVILLAINS HAVE YET TO RESPOND.
POLICE ARE NOW EAGER TO DETERMINE EXACTLY WHAT THE KIDNAPPERS ARE WAITING FOR.

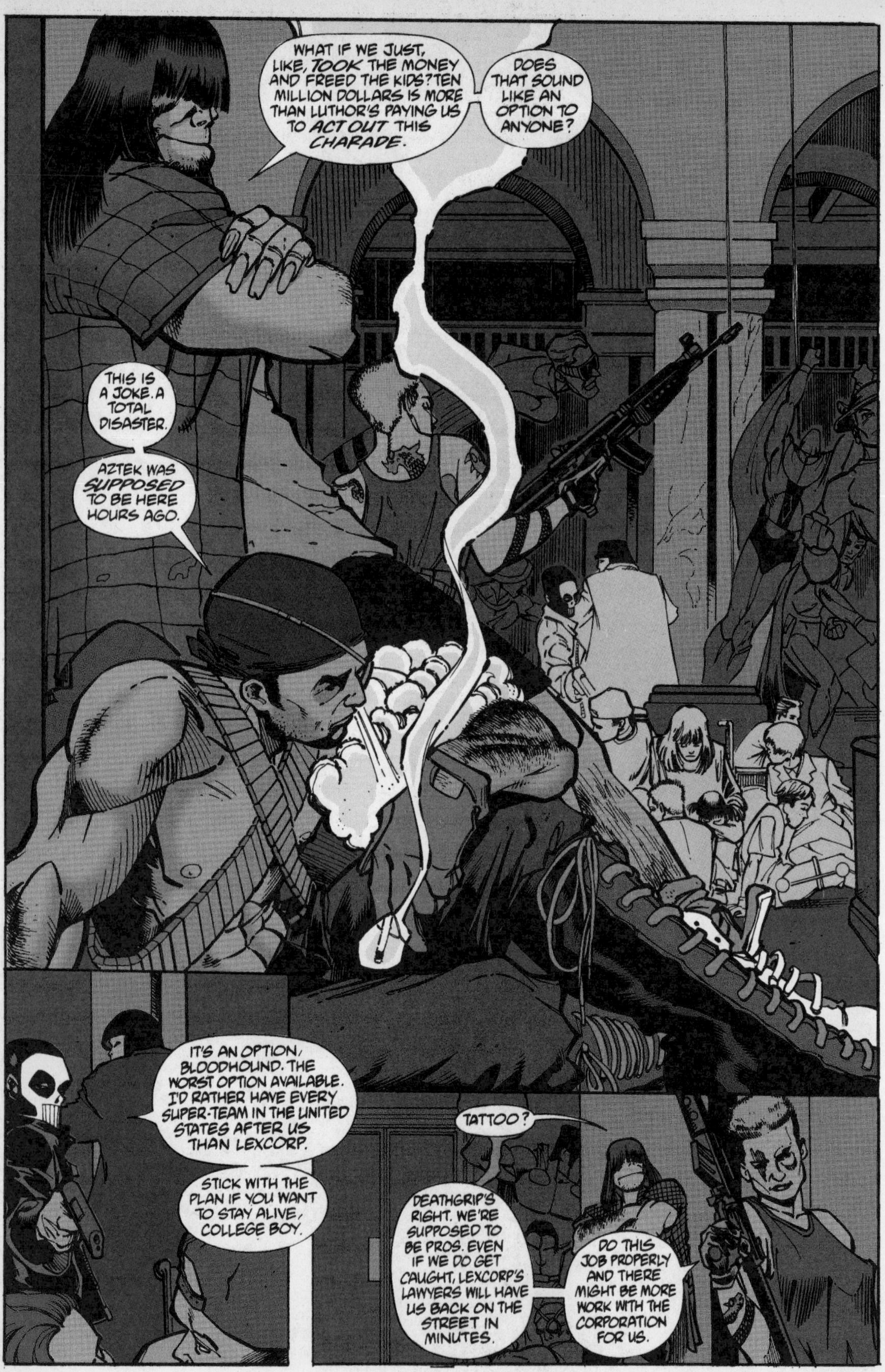
WHAT IF WE JUST, LIKE, TOOK THE MONEY AND FREED THE KIDS? TEN MILLION DOLLARS IS MORE THAN LUTHOR'S PAYING US TO ACT OUT THIS CHARADE.
DOES THAT SOUND LIKE AN OPTION TO ANYONE?
THIS IS A JOKE. A TOTAL DISASTER.
AZTEK WAS SUPPOSED TO BE HERE HOURS AGO.
IT'S AN OPTION, BLOODHOUND. THE WORST OPTION AVAILABLE. I'D RATHER HAVE EVERY SUPER-TEAM IN THE UNITED STATES AFTER US THAN LEXCORP.
STICK WITH THE PLAN IF YOU WANT TO STAY ALIVE, COLLEGE BOY.
TATTOO?
DEATHGRIP'S RIGHT. WE'RE SUPPOSED TO BE PROS. EVEN IF WE DO GET CAUGHT, LEXCORP'S LAWYERS WILL HAVE US BACK ON THE STREET IN MINUTES.
DO THIS JOB PROPERLY AND THERE MIGHT BE MORE WORK WITH THE CORPORATION FOR US.

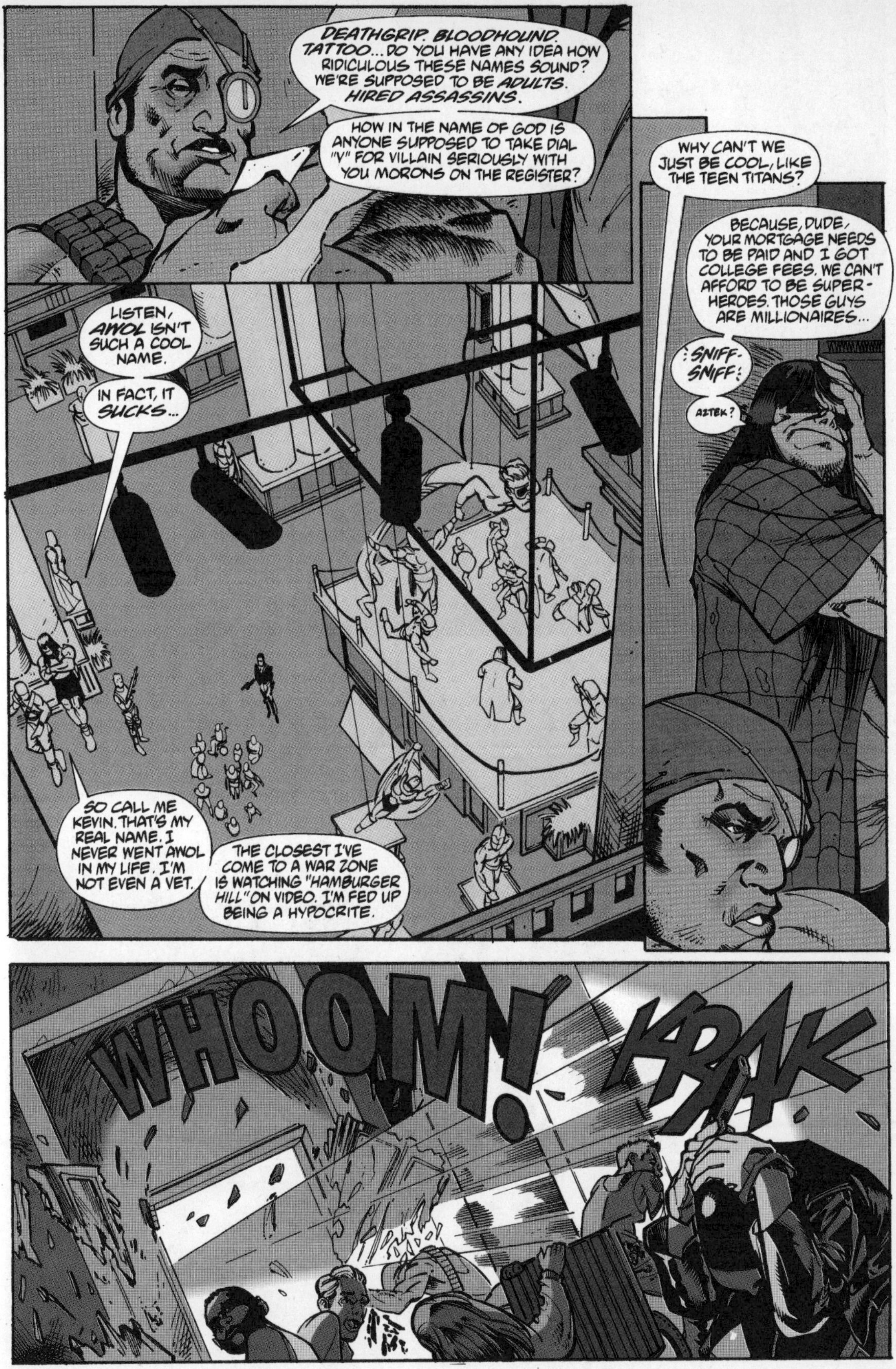
DEATHGRIP. BLOODHOUND. TATTOO... DO YOU HAVE ANY IDEA HOW RIDICULOUS THESE NAMES SOUND? WE'RE SUPPOSED TO BE ADULTS. HIRED ASSASSINS.
HOW IN THE NAME OF GOD IS ANYONE SUPPOSED TO TAKE DIAL "V" FOR VILLAIN SERIOUSLY WITH YOU MORONS ON THE REGISTER?
WHY CAN'T WE JUST BE COOL, LIKE THE TEEN TITANS?
BECAUSE, DUDE, YOUR MORTGAGE NEEDS TO BE PAID AND I GOT COLLEGE FEES. WE CAN'T AFFORD TO BE SUPER-HEROES. THOSE GUYS ARE MILLIONAIRES...
SNIFF-SNIFF
AZTEK?
LISTEN, AWOL ISN'T SUCH A COOL NAME.
IN FACT, IT SUCKS...
SO CALL ME KEVIN. THAT'S MY REAL NAME. I NEVER WENT AWOL IN MY LIFE. I'M NOT EVEN A VET.
THE CLOSEST I'VE COME TO A WAR ZONE IS WATCHING "HAMBURGER HILL" ON VIDEO. I'M FED UP BEING A HYPOCRITE.
WHOOM!
KRAK

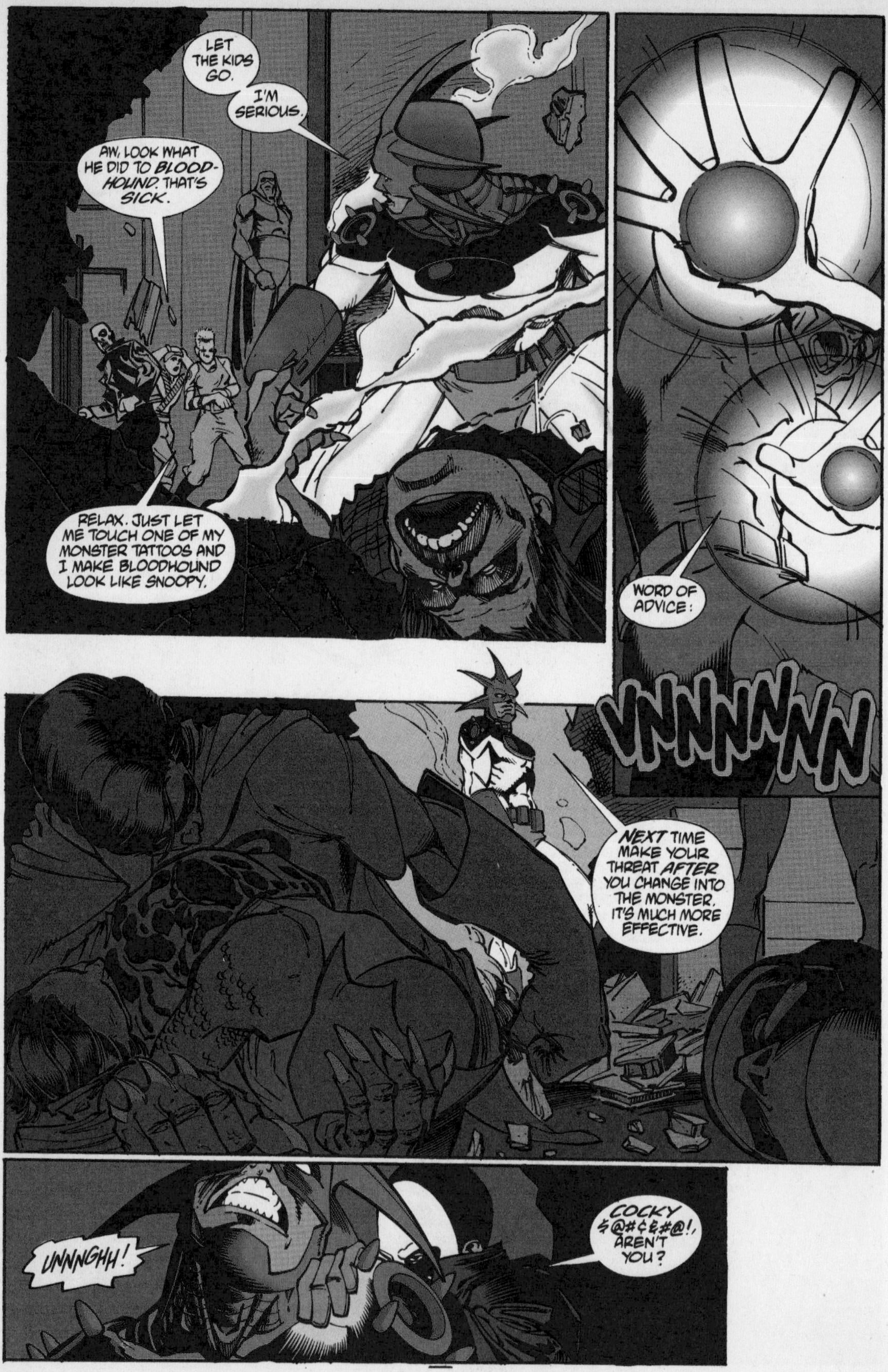

LET THE KIDS GO.
I'M SERIOUS.
AW, LOOK WHAT HE DID TO *BLOOD-HOUND*. THAT'S *SICK*.
RELAX. JUST LET ME TOUCH ONE OF MY MONSTER TATTOOS AND I MAKE BLOODHOUND LOOK LIKE SNOOPY.
WORD OF ADVICE:
VNNNNNNN
NEXT TIME MAKE YOUR THREAT *AFTER* YOU CHANGE INTO THE MONSTER. IT'S MUCH MORE EFFECTIVE.
UNNNGHH!
COCKY $@#¢&#@!, AREN'T YOU?

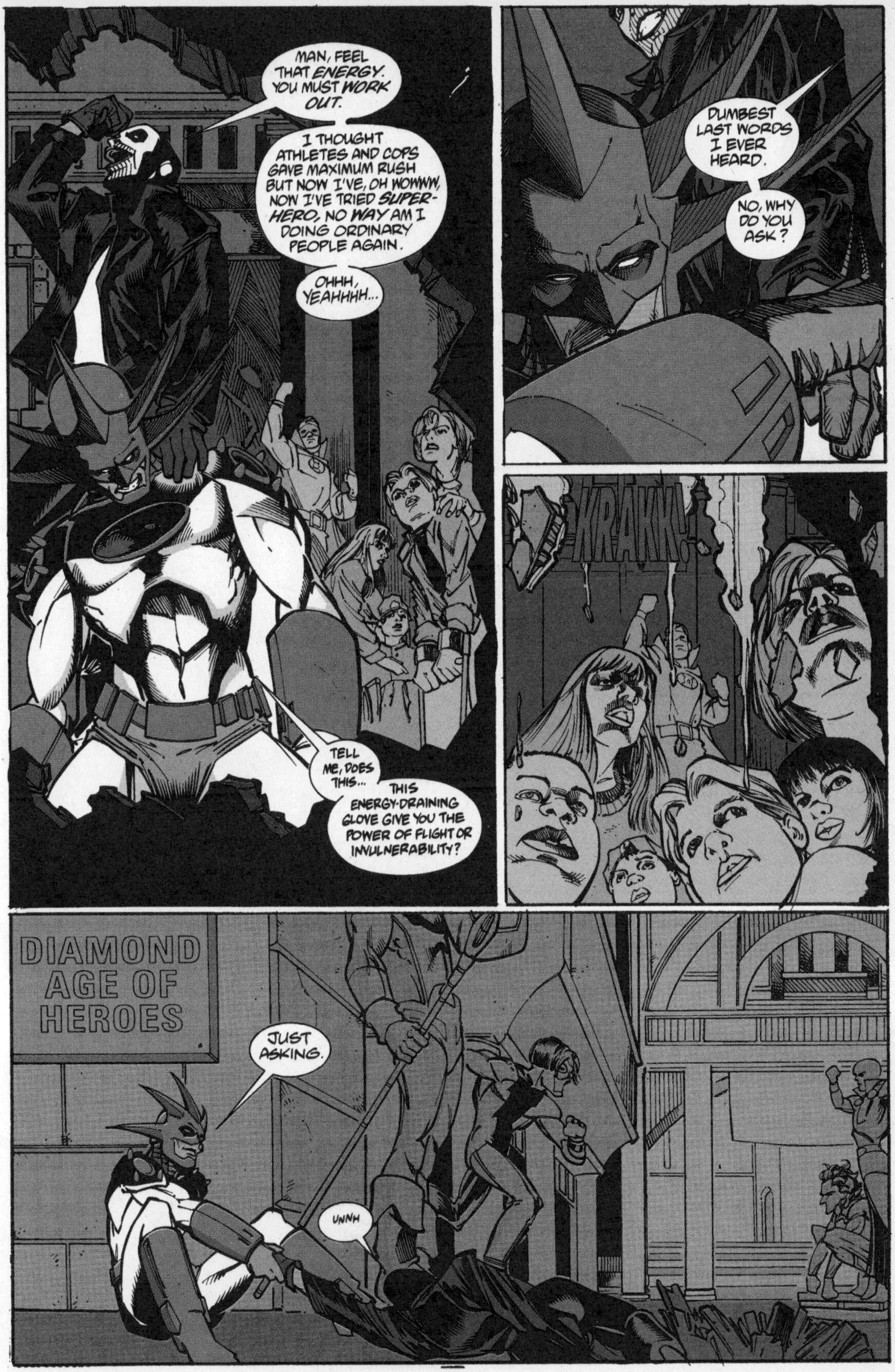
MAN, FEEL THAT ENERGY. YOU MUST WORK OUT.
I THOUGHT ATHLETES AND COPS GAVE MAXIMUM RUSH BUT NOW I'VE, OH WOWWW, NOW I'VE TRIED SUPER-HERO, NO WAY AM I DOING ORDINARY PEOPLE AGAIN.
OHHH, YEAHHHH...
TELL ME, DOES THIS...
THIS ENERGY-DRAINING GLOVE GIVE YOU THE POWER OF FLIGHT OR INVULNERABILITY?
DUMBEST LAST WORDS I EVER HEARD.
NO, WHY DO YOU ASK?
KRAKK!
DIAMOND AGE OF HEROES
JUST ASKING.
UNNH

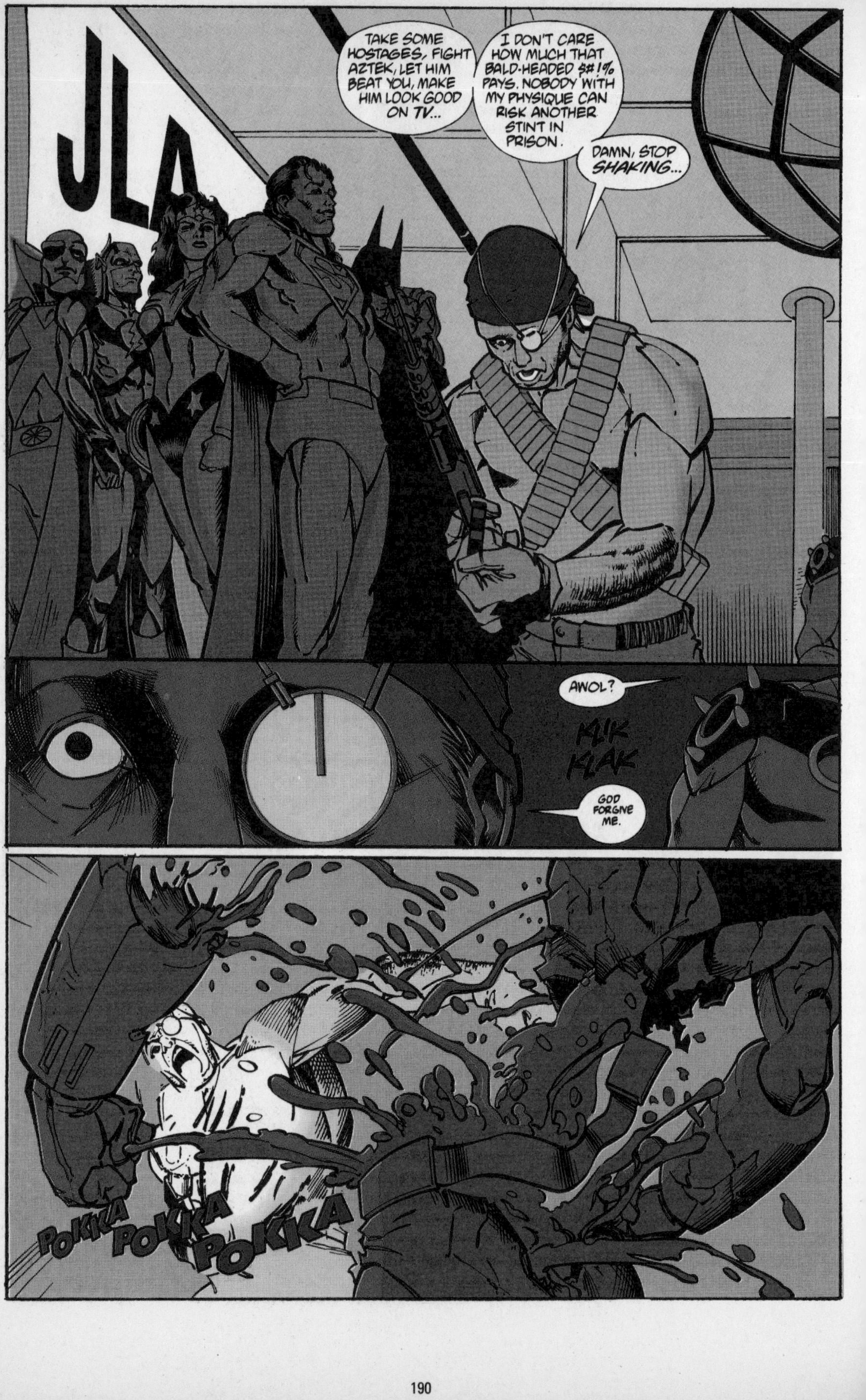
TAKE SOME HOSTAGES, FIGHT AZTEK, LET HIM BEAT YOU, MAKE HIM LOOK GOOD ON TV...
I DON'T CARE HOW MUCH THAT BALD-HEADED $#!% PAYS. NOBODY WITH MY PHYSIQUE CAN RISK ANOTHER STINT IN PRISON.
DAMN, STOP SHAKING...
JLA
AWOL?
KLIK KLAK
GOD FORGIVE ME.
POKKA POKKA POKKA

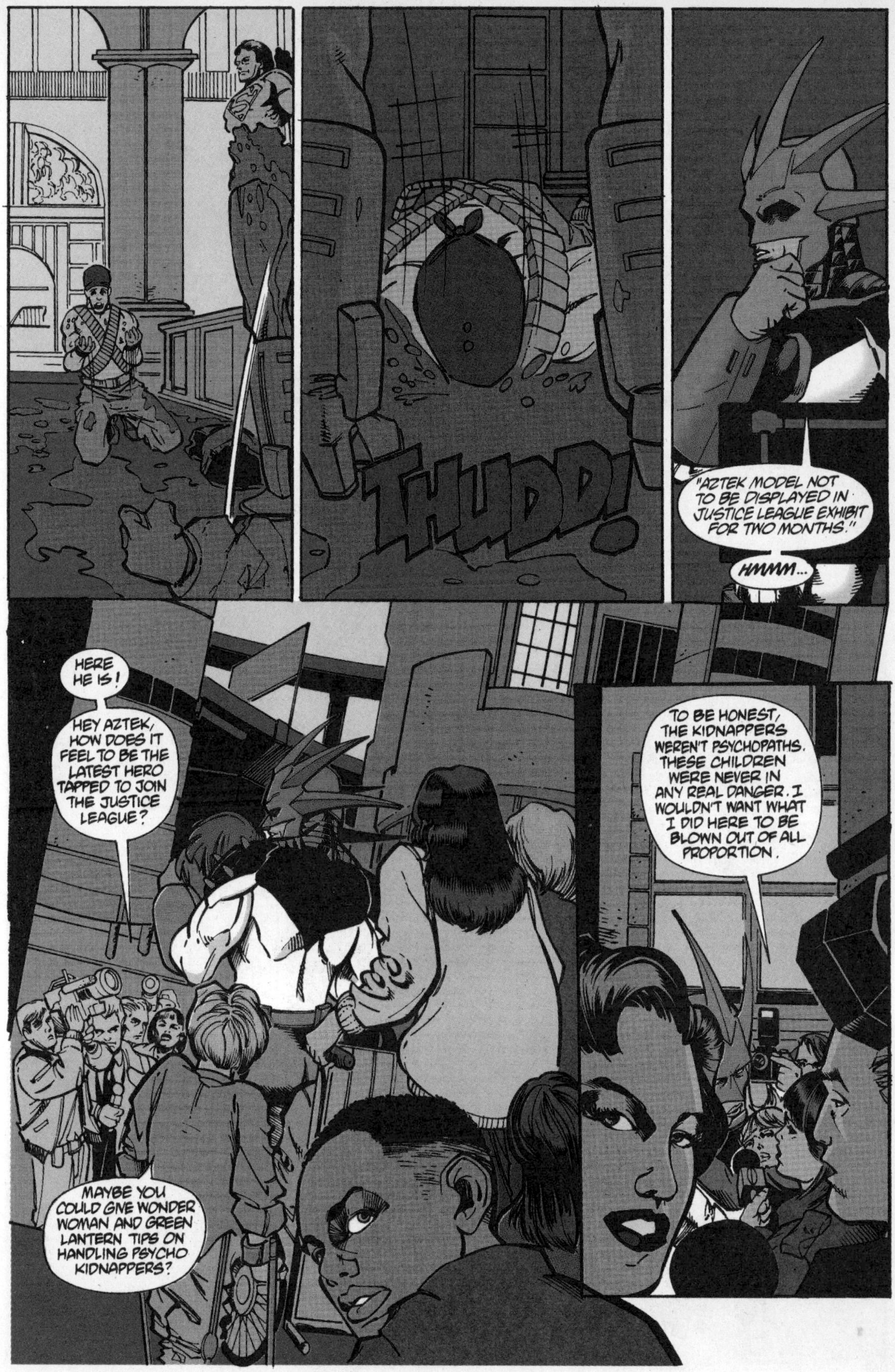
THUDD!
"AZTEK MODEL NOT TO BE DISPLAYED IN JUSTICE LEAGUE EXHIBIT FOR TWO MONTHS."
HMMM...
HERE HE IS!
HEY AZTEK, HOW DOES IT FEEL TO BE THE LATEST HERO TAPPED TO JOIN THE JUSTICE LEAGUE?
MAYBE YOU COULD GIVE WONDER WOMAN AND GREEN LANTERN TIPS ON HANDLING PSYCHO KIDNAPPERS?
TO BE HONEST, THE KIDNAPPERS WEREN'T PSYCHOPATHS. THESE CHILDREN WERE NEVER IN ANY REAL DANGER. I WOULDN'T WANT WHAT I DID HERE TO BE BLOWN OUT OF ALL PROPORTION.

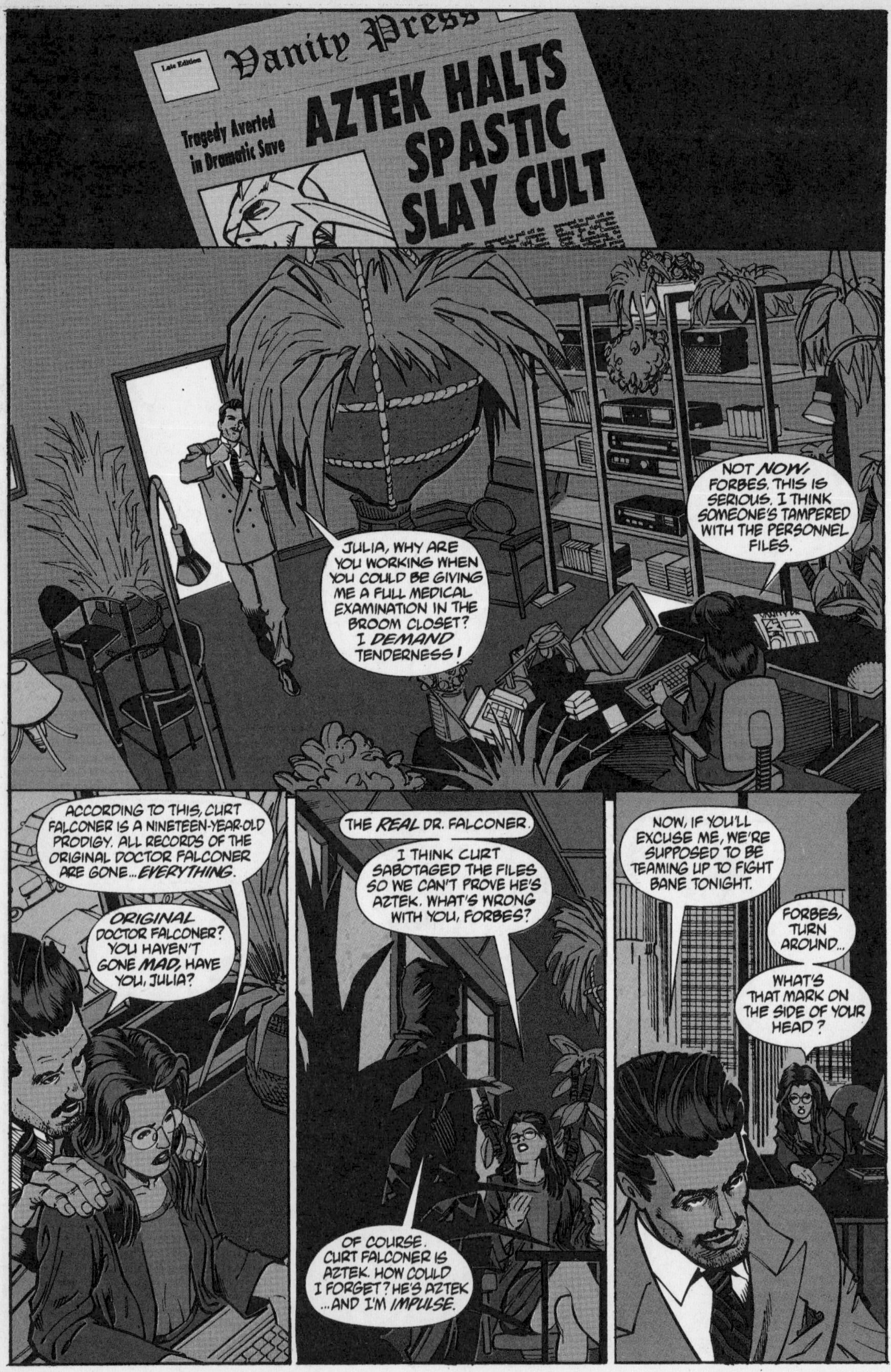
Vanity Press
Late Edition
AZTEK HALTS SPASTIC SLAY CULT
Tragedy Averted in Dramatic Save
JULIA, WHY ARE YOU WORKING WHEN YOU COULD BE GIVING ME A FULL MEDICAL EXAMINATION IN THE BROOM CLOSET? I DEMAND TENDERNESS!
NOT NOW, FORBES. THIS IS SERIOUS. I THINK SOMEONE'S TAMPERED WITH THE PERSONNEL FILES.
ACCORDING TO THIS, CURT FALCONER IS A NINETEEN-YEAR-OLD PRODIGY. ALL RECORDS OF THE ORIGINAL DOCTOR FALCONER ARE GONE... EVERYTHING.
ORIGINAL DOCTOR FALCONER? YOU HAVEN'T GONE MAD, HAVE YOU, JULIA?
THE REAL DR. FALCONER.
I THINK CURT SABOTAGED THE FILES SO WE CAN'T PROVE HE'S AZTEK. WHAT'S WRONG WITH YOU, FORBES?
OF COURSE. CURT FALCONER IS AZTEK. HOW COULD I FORGET? HE'S AZTEK ...AND I'M IMPULSE.
NOW, IF YOU'LL EXCUSE ME, WE'RE SUPPOSED TO BE TEAMING UP TO FIGHT BANE TONIGHT.
FORBES, TURN AROUND...
WHAT'S THAT MARK ON THE SIDE OF YOUR HEAD?

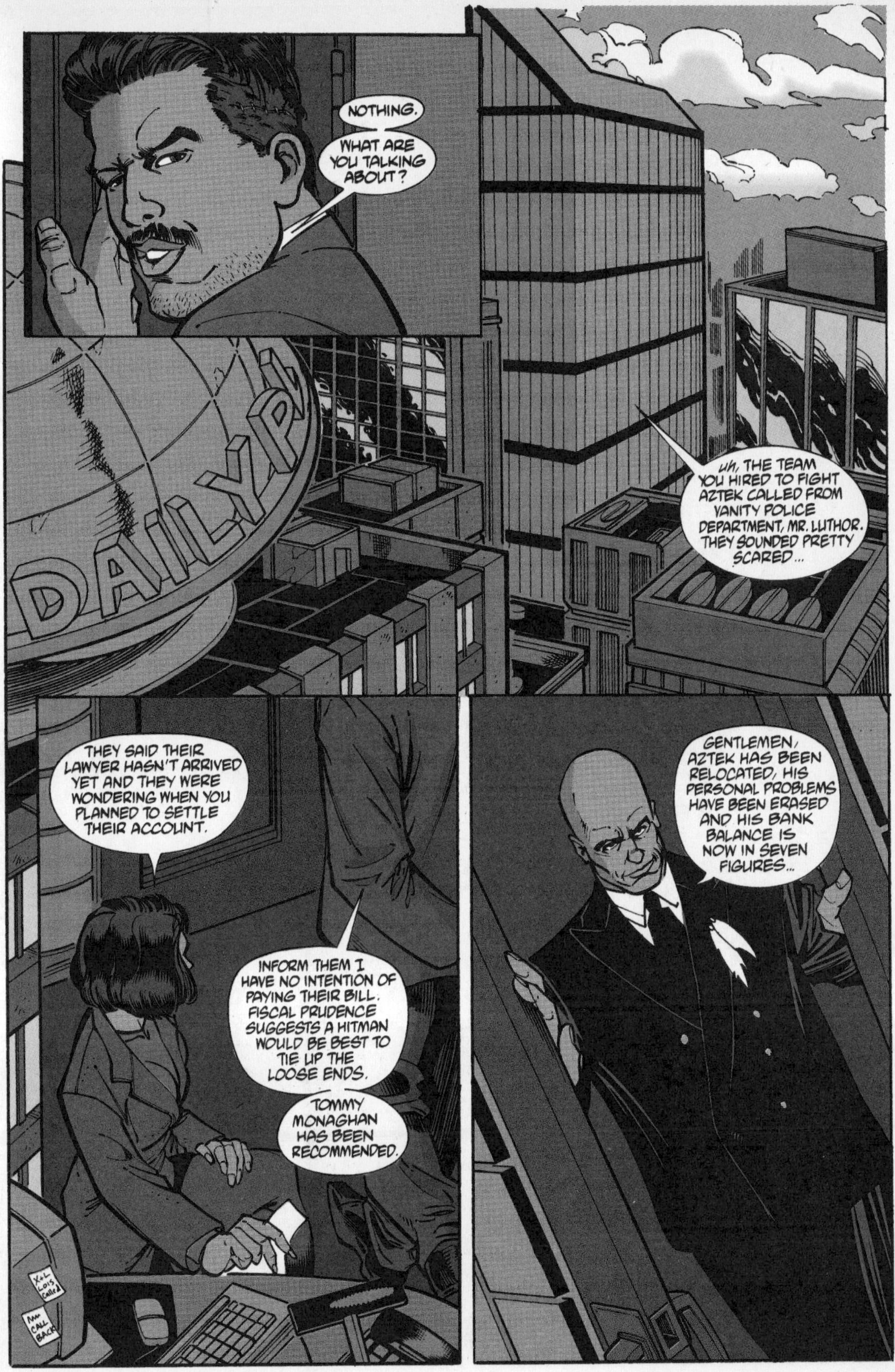
NOTHING.
WHAT ARE YOU TALKING ABOUT?
uh, THE TEAM YOU HIRED TO FIGHT AZTEK CALLED FROM VANITY POLICE DEPARTMENT, MR. LUTHOR. THEY SOUNDED PRETTY SCARED...
THEY SAID THEIR LAWYER HASN'T ARRIVED YET AND THEY WERE WONDERING WHEN YOU PLANNED TO SETTLE THEIR ACCOUNT.
INFORM THEM I HAVE NO INTENTION OF PAYING THEIR BILL. FISCAL PRUDENCE SUGGESTS A HITMAN WOULD BE BEST TO TIE UP THE LOOSE ENDS.
TOMMY MONAGHAN HAS BEEN RECOMMENDED.
GENTLEMEN, AZTEK HAS BEEN RELOCATED, HIS PERSONAL PROBLEMS HAVE BEEN ERASED AND HIS BANK BALANCE IS NOW IN SEVEN FIGURES...

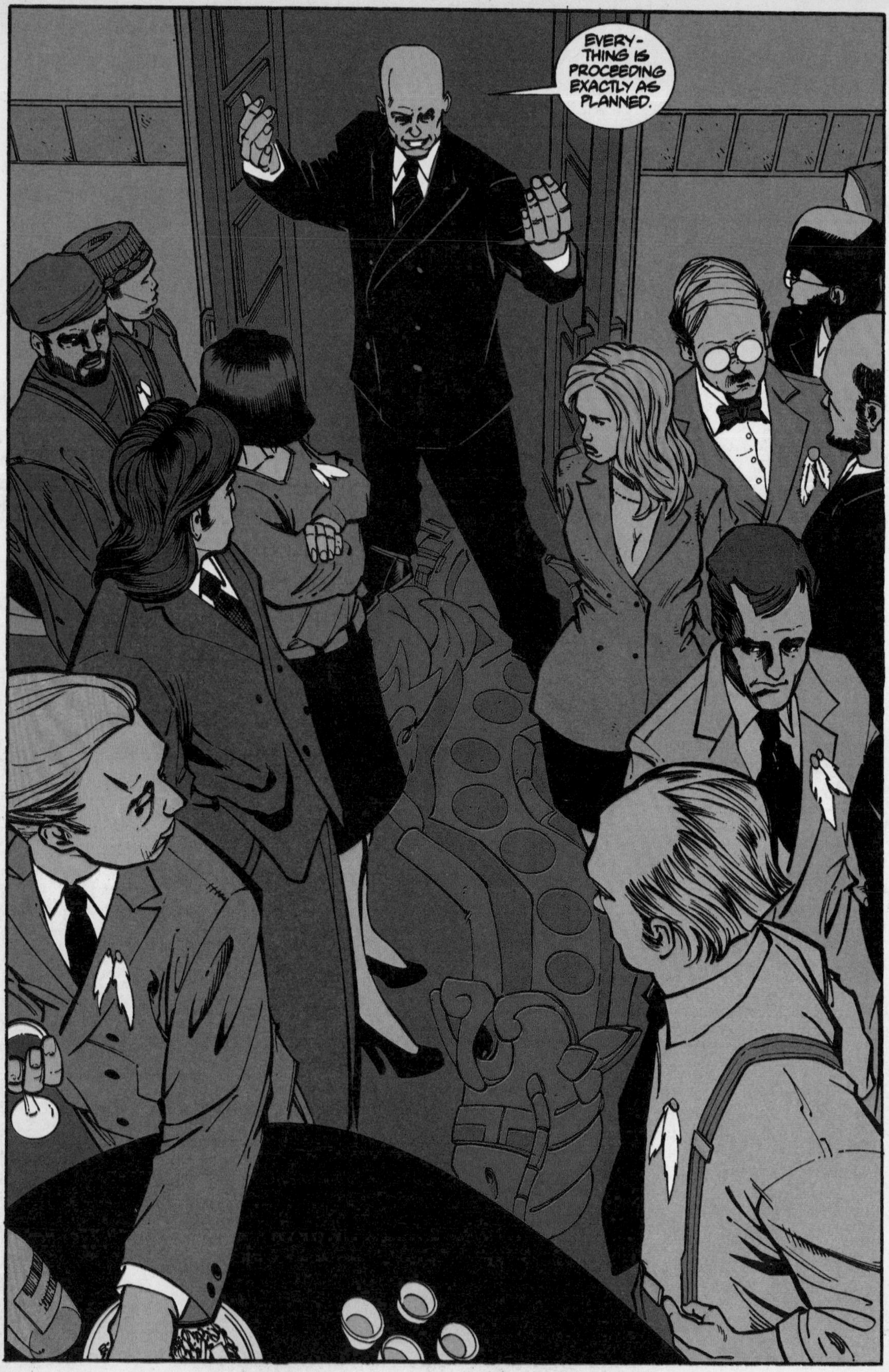
EVERY-THING IS PROCEEDING EXACTLY AS PLANNED.

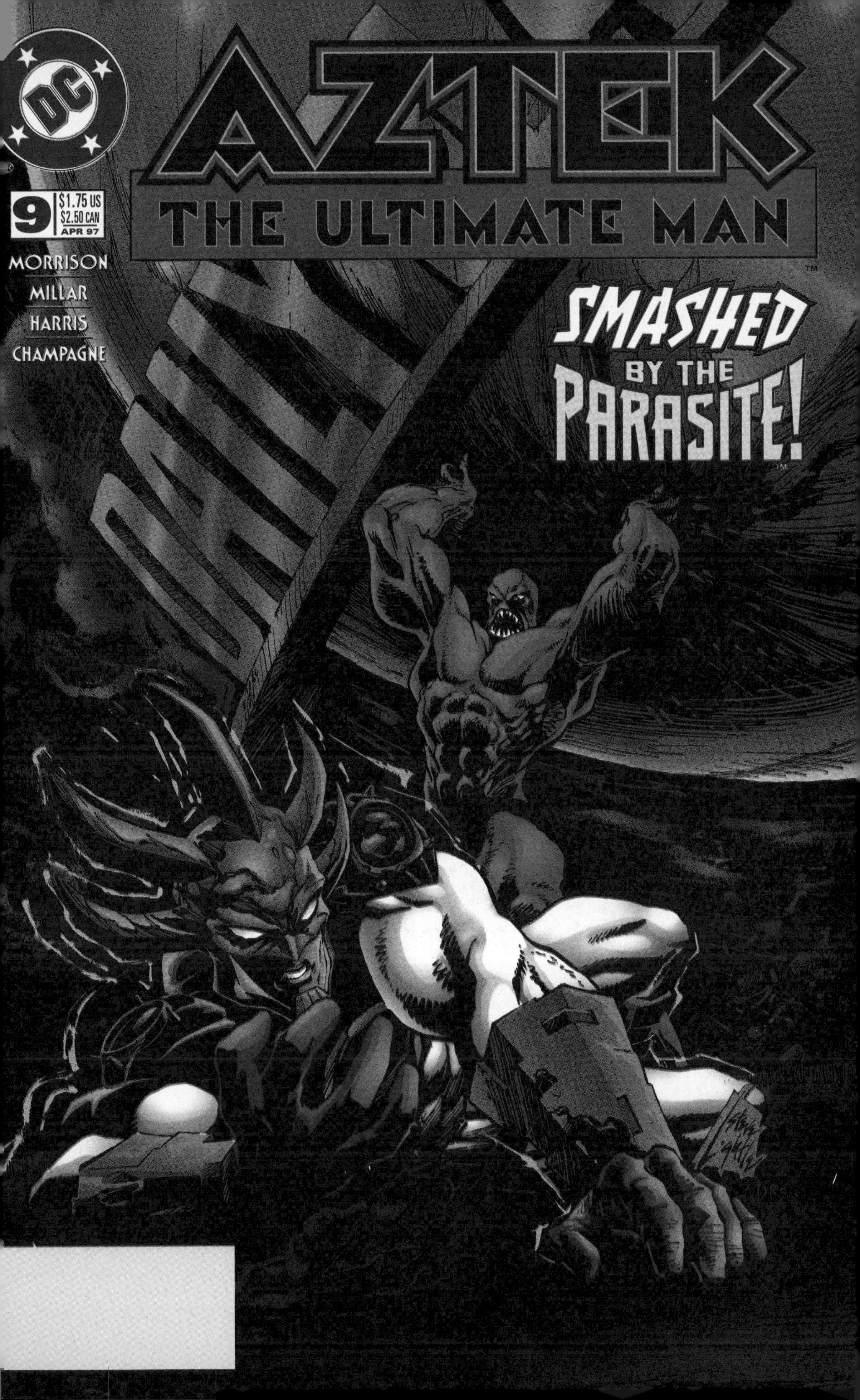
DC
AZTEK
THE ULTIMATE MAN
9
$1.75 US
$2.50 CAN
APR 97
MORRISON
MILLAR
HARRIS
CHAMPAGNE
SMASHED
BY THE
PARASITE!

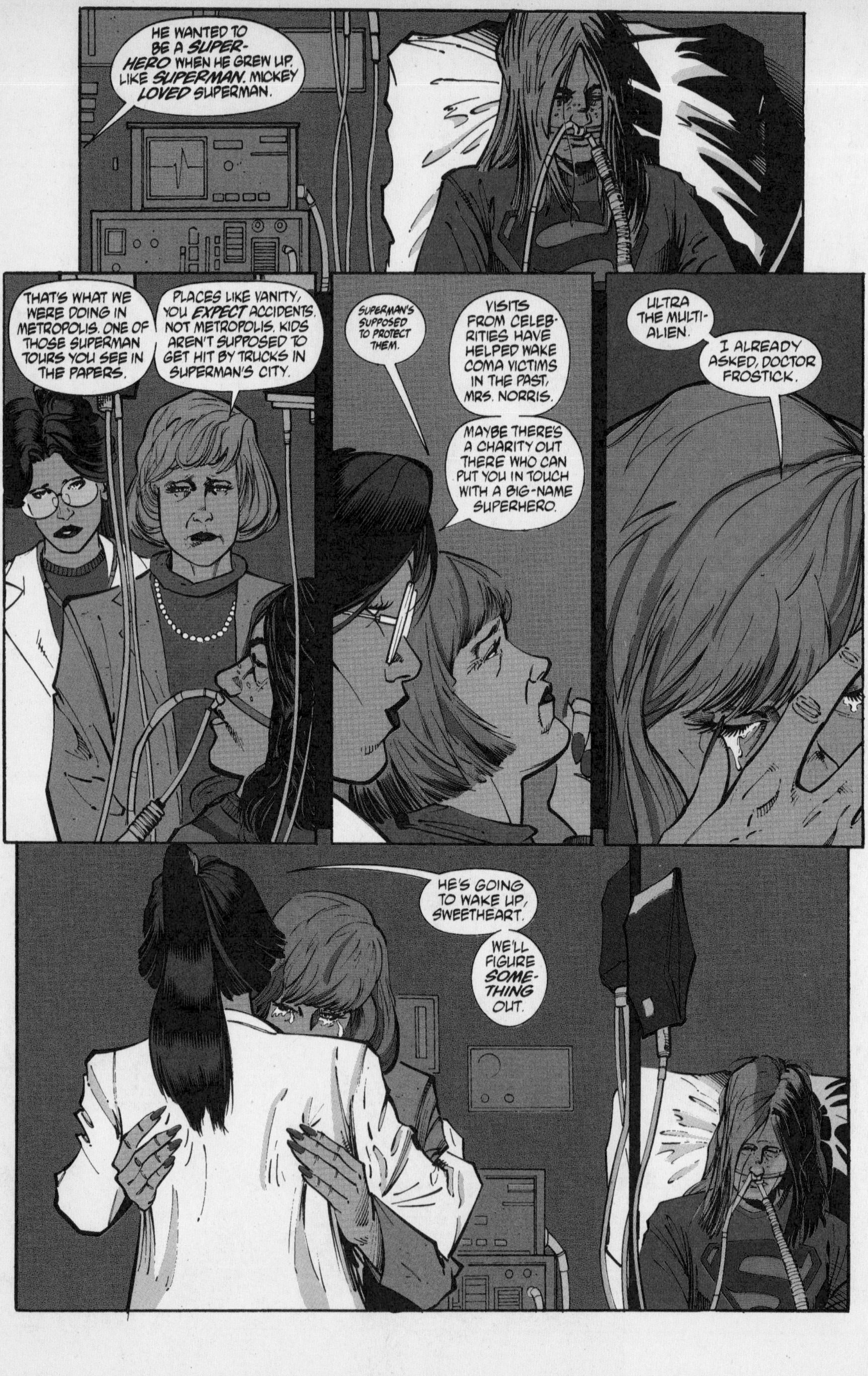

HE WANTED TO BE A SUPER-HERO WHEN HE GREW UP. LIKE SUPERMAN. MICKEY LOVED SUPERMAN.
THAT'S WHAT WE WERE DOING IN METROPOLIS. ONE OF THOSE SUPERMAN TOURS YOU SEE IN THE PAPERS.
PLACES LIKE VANITY, YOU EXPECT ACCIDENTS. NOT METROPOLIS. KIDS AREN'T SUPPOSED TO GET HIT BY TRUCKS IN SUPERMAN'S CITY.
SUPERMAN'S SUPPOSED TO PROTECT THEM.
VISITS FROM CELEB-RITIES HAVE HELPED WAKE COMA VICTIMS IN THE PAST, MRS. NORRIS.
MAYBE THERE'S A CHARITY OUT THERE WHO CAN PUT YOU IN TOUCH WITH A BIG-NAME SUPERHERO.
ULTRA THE MULTI-ALIEN.
I ALREADY ASKED, DOCTOR FROSTICK.
HE'S GOING TO WAKE UP, SWEETHEART.
WE'LL FIGURE SOMETHING OUT.

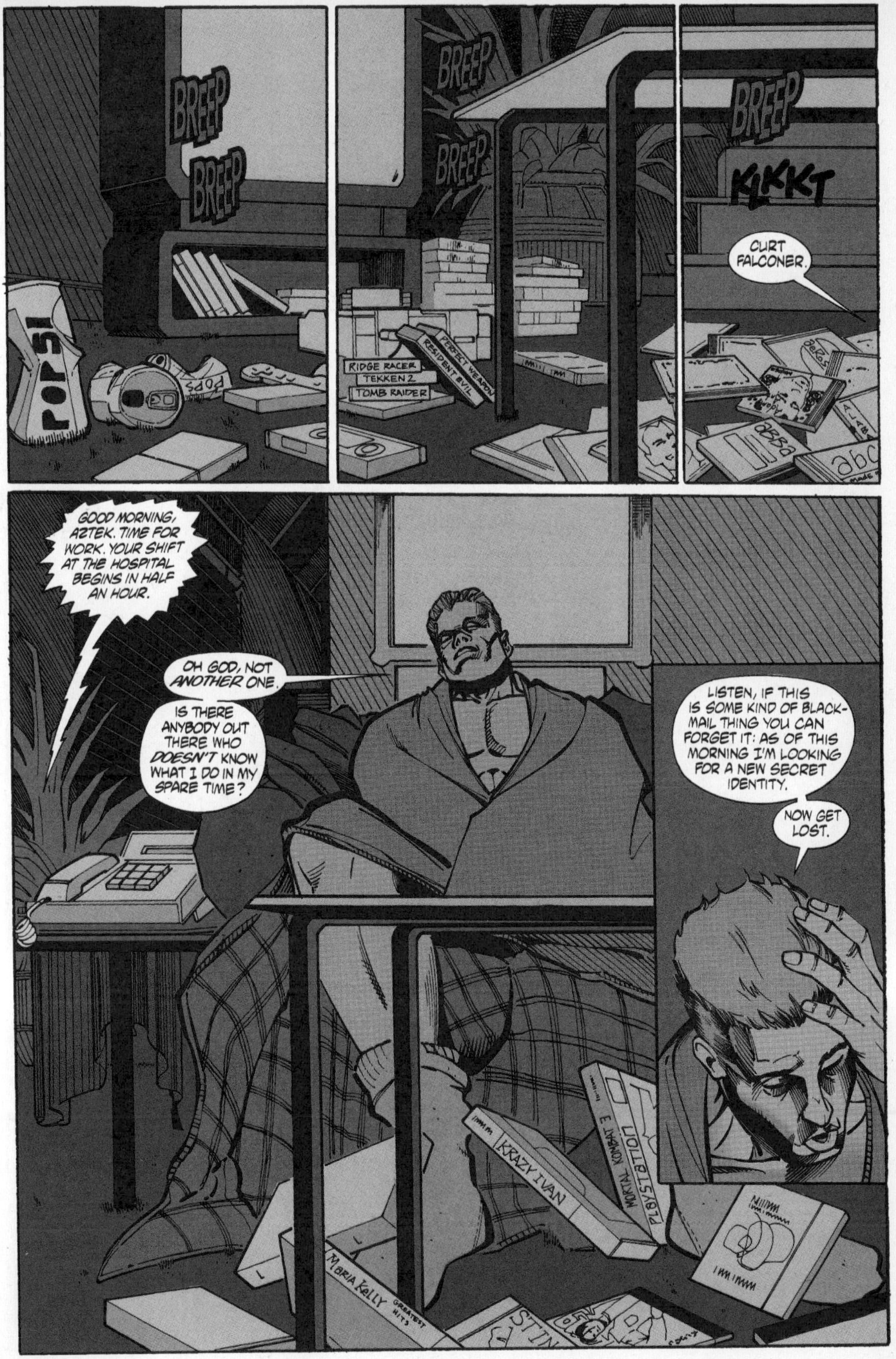
BREEP
BREEP
BREEP
BREEP
BREEP
KLKKT
CURT FALCONER.
PEPSI
RIDGE RACER
TEKKEN 2
TOMB RAIDER
RESIDENT EVIL
PERFECT WEAPON
GOOD MORNING, AZTEK. TIME FOR WORK. YOUR SHIFT AT THE HOSPITAL BEGINS IN HALF AN HOUR.
OH GOD, NOT *ANOTHER* ONE.
IS THERE ANYBODY OUT THERE WHO *DOESN'T* KNOW WHAT I DO IN MY SPARE TIME?
LISTEN, IF THIS IS SOME KIND OF BLACK-MAIL THING YOU CAN FORGET IT: AS OF THIS MORNING I'M LOOKING FOR A NEW SECRET IDENTITY.
NOW GET LOST.
KRAZY IVAN
MORTAL KOMBAT 3
PLAYSTATION
Maria Kelly GREATEST HITS

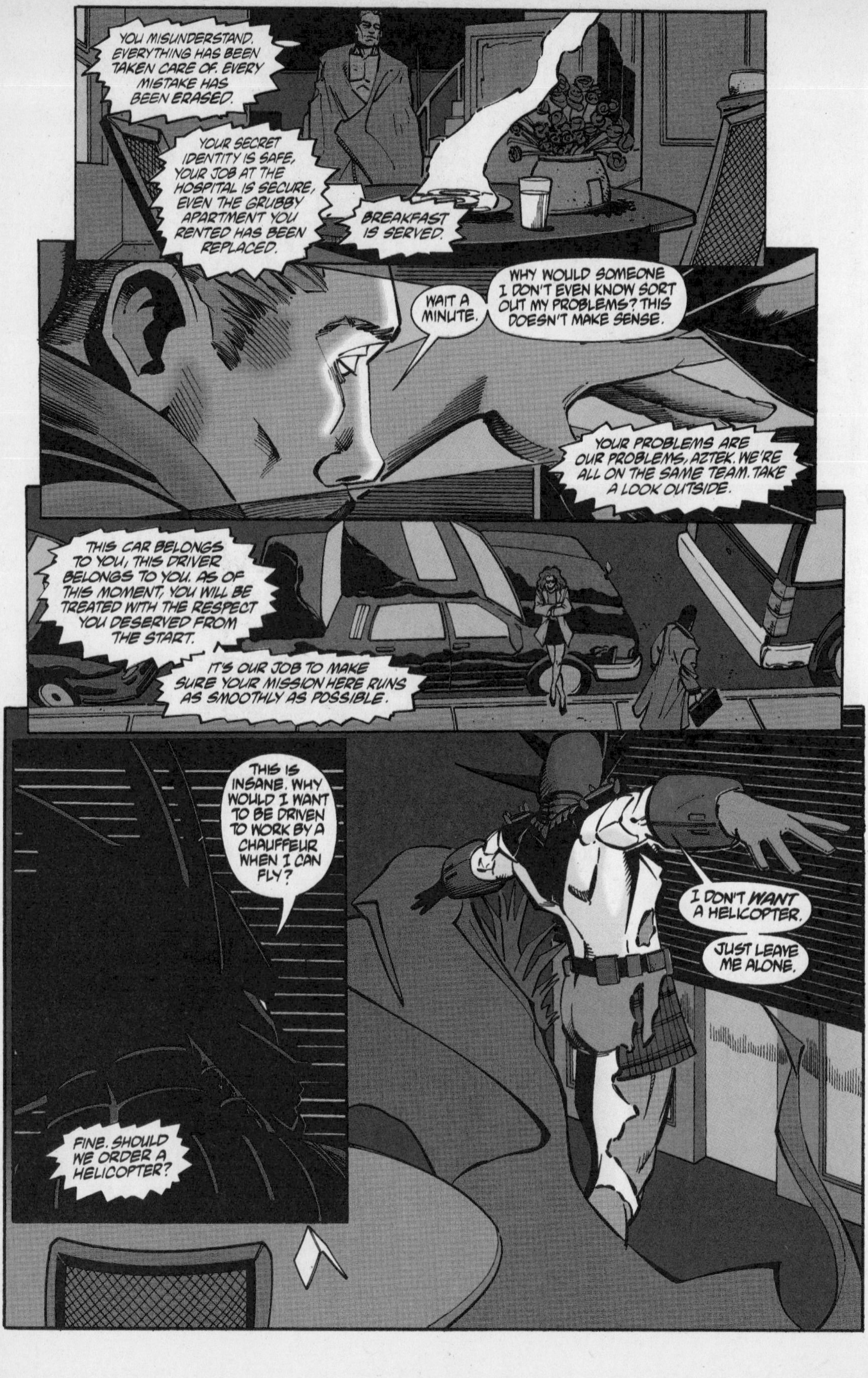
YOU MISUNDERSTAND. EVERYTHING HAS BEEN TAKEN CARE OF. EVERY MISTAKE HAS BEEN ERASED.
YOUR SECRET IDENTITY IS SAFE, YOUR JOB AT THE HOSPITAL IS SECURE, EVEN THE GRUBBY APARTMENT YOU RENTED HAS BEEN REPLACED.
BREAKFAST IS SERVED.
WAIT A MINUTE.
WHY WOULD SOMEONE I DON'T EVEN KNOW SORT OUT MY PROBLEMS? THIS DOESN'T MAKE SENSE.
YOUR PROBLEMS ARE OUR PROBLEMS, AZTEK. WE'RE ALL ON THE SAME TEAM. TAKE A LOOK OUTSIDE.
THIS CAR BELONGS TO YOU, THIS DRIVER BELONGS TO YOU. AS OF THIS MOMENT, YOU WILL BE TREATED WITH THE RESPECT YOU DESERVED FROM THE START.
IT'S OUR JOB TO MAKE SURE YOUR MISSION HERE RUNS AS SMOOTHLY AS POSSIBLE.
THIS IS INSANE. WHY WOULD I WANT TO BE DRIVEN TO WORK BY A CHAUFFEUR WHEN I CAN FLY?
FINE. SHOULD WE ORDER A HELICOPTER?
I DON'T WANT A HELICOPTER.
JUST LEAVE ME ALONE.

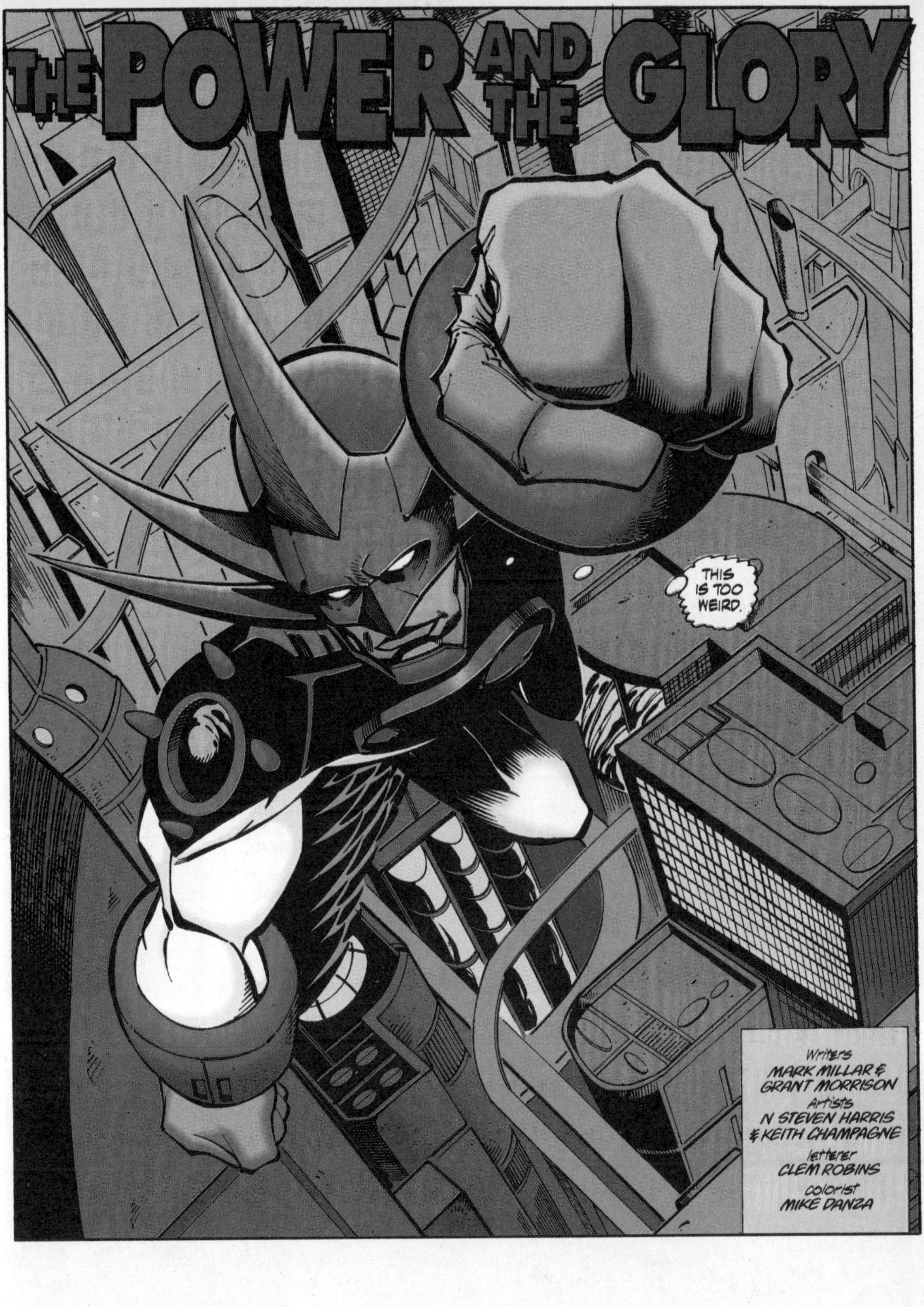
THE POWER AND THE GLORY
THIS IS TOO WEIRD.
Writers
MARK MILLAR & GRANT MORRISON
Artists
N STEVEN HARRIS & KEITH CHAMPAGNE
letterer
CLEM ROBINS
colorist
MIKE DANZA

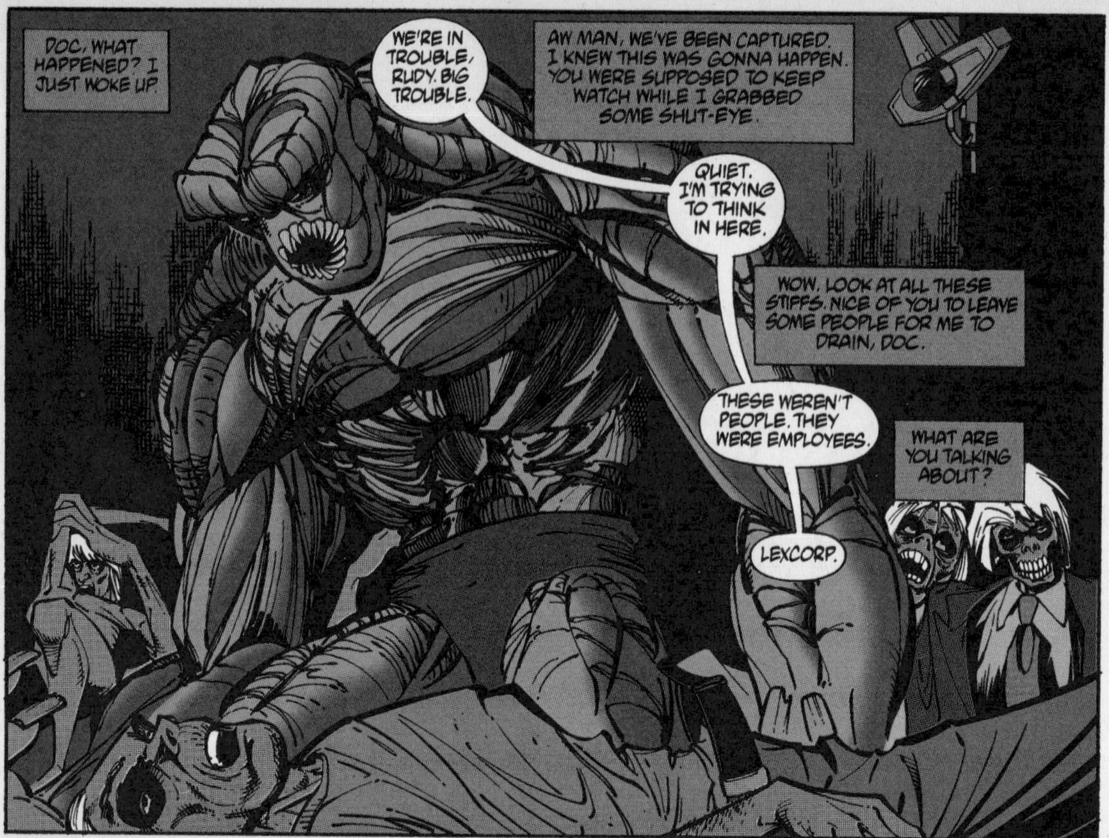
DOC, WHAT HAPPENED? I JUST WOKE UP.
WE'RE IN TROUBLE, RUDY. BIG TROUBLE.
AW MAN, WE'VE BEEN CAPTURED. I KNEW THIS WAS GONNA HAPPEN. YOU WERE SUPPOSED TO KEEP WATCH WHILE I GRABBED SOME SHUT-EYE.
QUIET. I'M TRYING TO THINK IN HERE.
WOW. LOOK AT ALL THESE STIFFS. NICE OF YOU TO LEAVE SOME PEOPLE FOR ME TO DRAIN, DOC.
THESE WEREN'T PEOPLE. THEY WERE EMPLOYEES.
WHAT ARE YOU TALKING ABOUT?
LEXCORP.

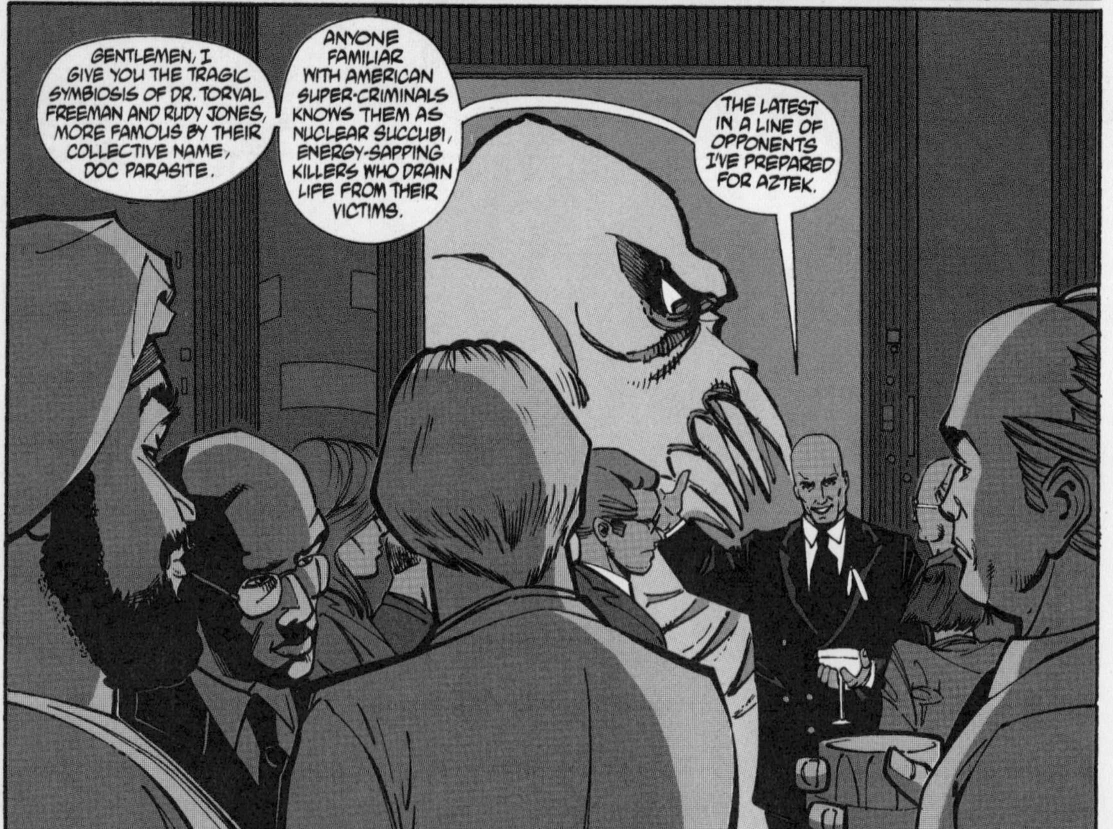
GENTLEMEN, I GIVE YOU THE TRAGIC SYMBIOSIS OF DR. TORVAL FREEMAN AND RUDY JONES, MORE FAMOUS BY THEIR COLLECTIVE NAME, DOC PARASITE.
ANYONE FAMILIAR WITH AMERICAN SUPER-CRIMINALS KNOWS THEM AS NUCLEAR SUCCUBI, ENERGY-SAPPING KILLERS WHO DRAIN LIFE FROM THEIR VICTIMS.
THE LATEST IN A LINE OF OPPONENTS I'VE PREPARED FOR AZTEK.

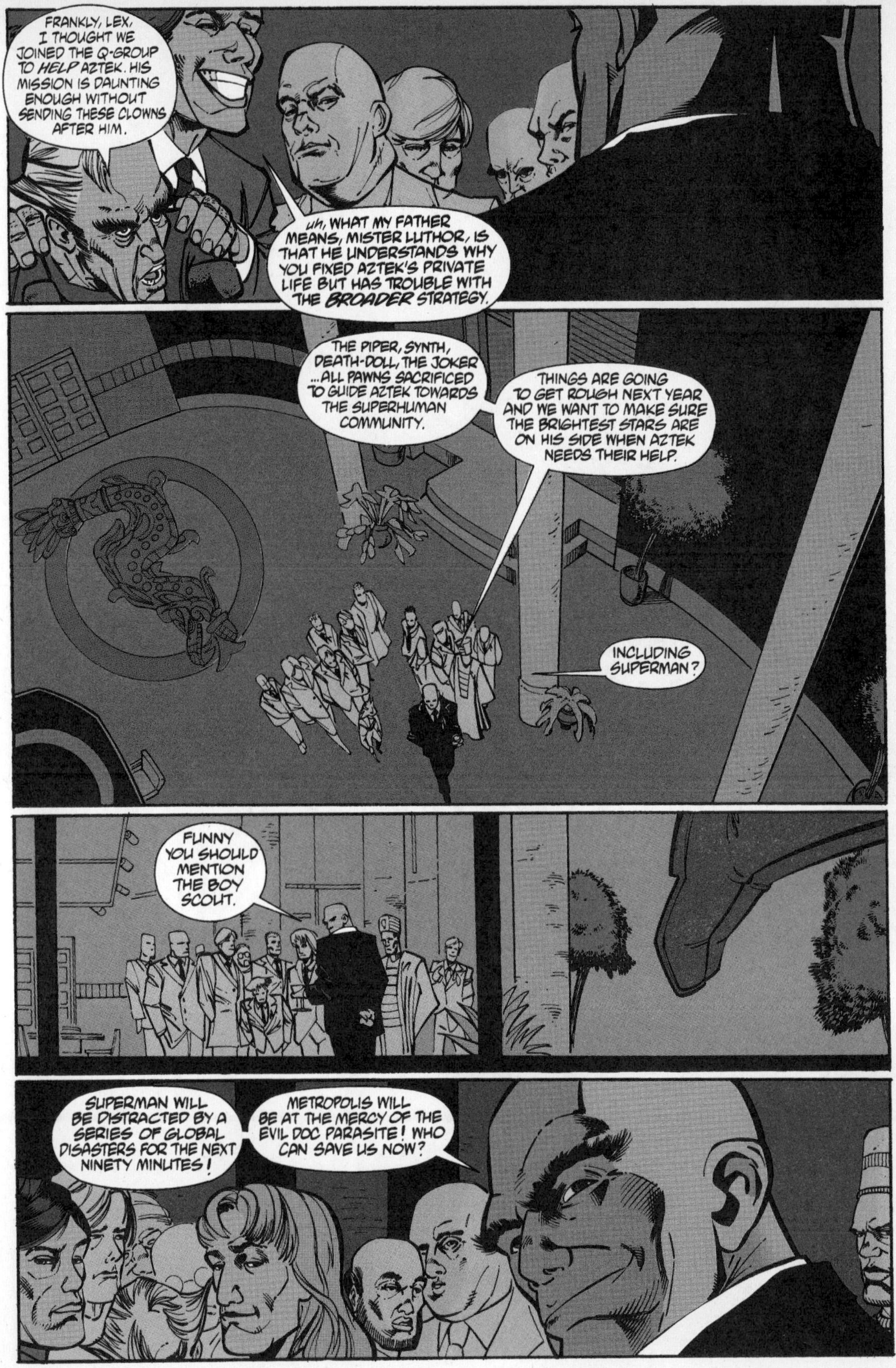
FRANKLY, LEX, I THOUGHT WE JOINED THE Q-GROUP TO HELP AZTEK. HIS MISSION IS DAUNTING ENOUGH WITHOUT SENDING THESE CLOWNS AFTER HIM.
uh, WHAT MY FATHER MEANS, MISTER LUTHOR, IS THAT HE UNDERSTANDS WHY YOU FIXED AZTEK'S PRIVATE LIFE BUT HAS TROUBLE WITH THE BROADER STRATEGY.
THE PIPER, SYNTH, DEATH-DOLL, THE JOKER ...ALL PAWNS SACRIFICED TO GUIDE AZTEK TOWARDS THE SUPERHUMAN COMMUNITY.
THINGS ARE GOING TO GET ROUGH NEXT YEAR AND WE WANT TO MAKE SURE THE BRIGHTEST STARS ARE ON HIS SIDE WHEN AZTEK NEEDS THEIR HELP.
INCLUDING SUPERMAN?
FUNNY YOU SHOULD MENTION THE BOY SCOUT.
SUPERMAN WILL BE DISTRACTED BY A SERIES OF GLOBAL DISASTERS FOR THE NEXT NINETY MINUTES!
METROPOLIS WILL BE AT THE MERCY OF THE EVIL DOC PARASITE! WHO CAN SAVE US NOW?

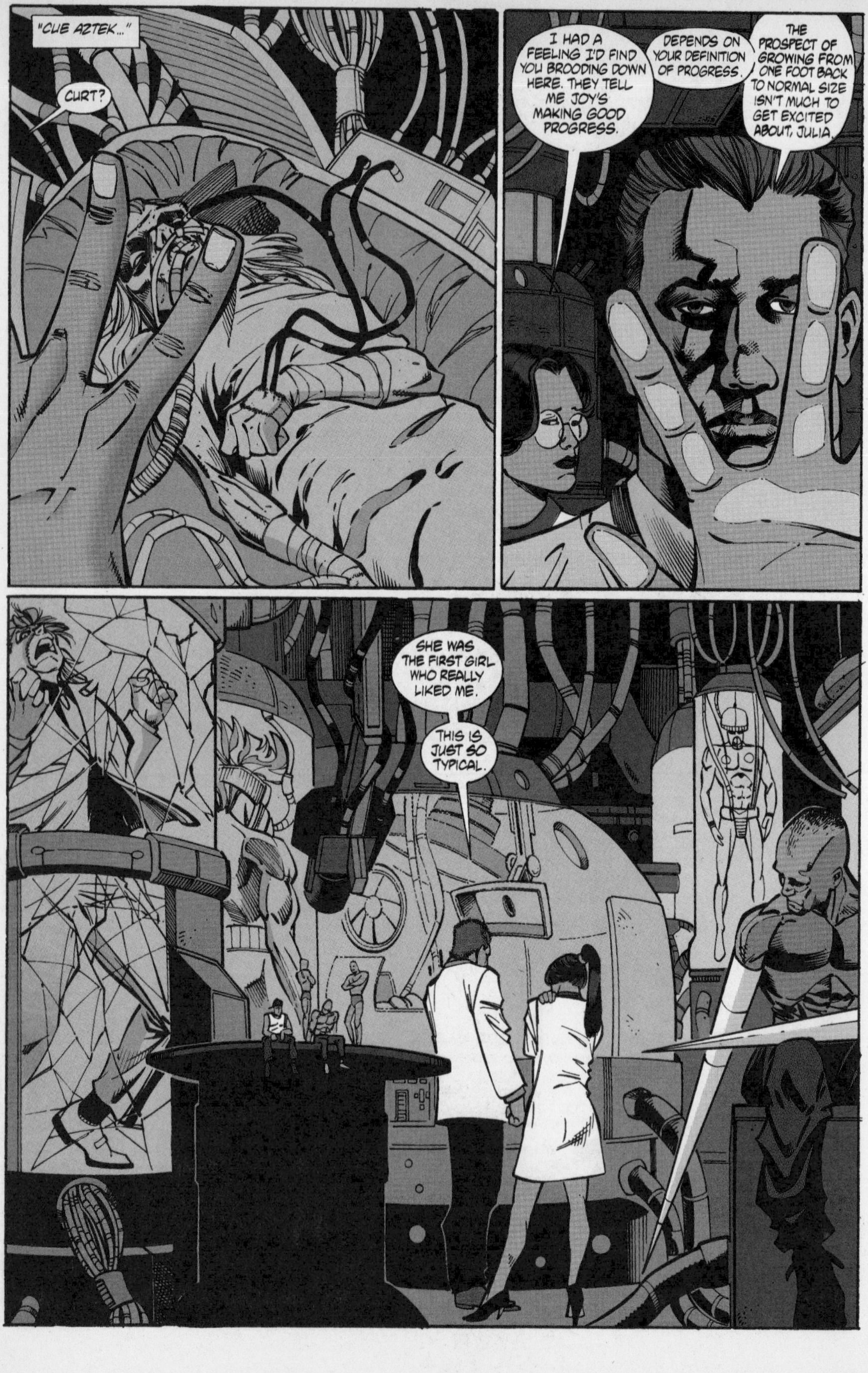
"CLIE AZTEK..."
CURT?
I HAD A FEELING I'D FIND YOU BROODING DOWN HERE. THEY TELL ME JOY'S MAKING GOOD PROGRESS.
DEPENDS ON YOUR DEFINITION OF PROGRESS.
THE PROSPECT OF GROWING FROM ONE FOOT BACK TO NORMAL SIZE ISN'T MUCH TO GET EXCITED ABOUT, JULIA.
SHE WAS THE FIRST GIRL WHO REALLY LIKED ME.
THIS IS JUST SO TYPICAL.

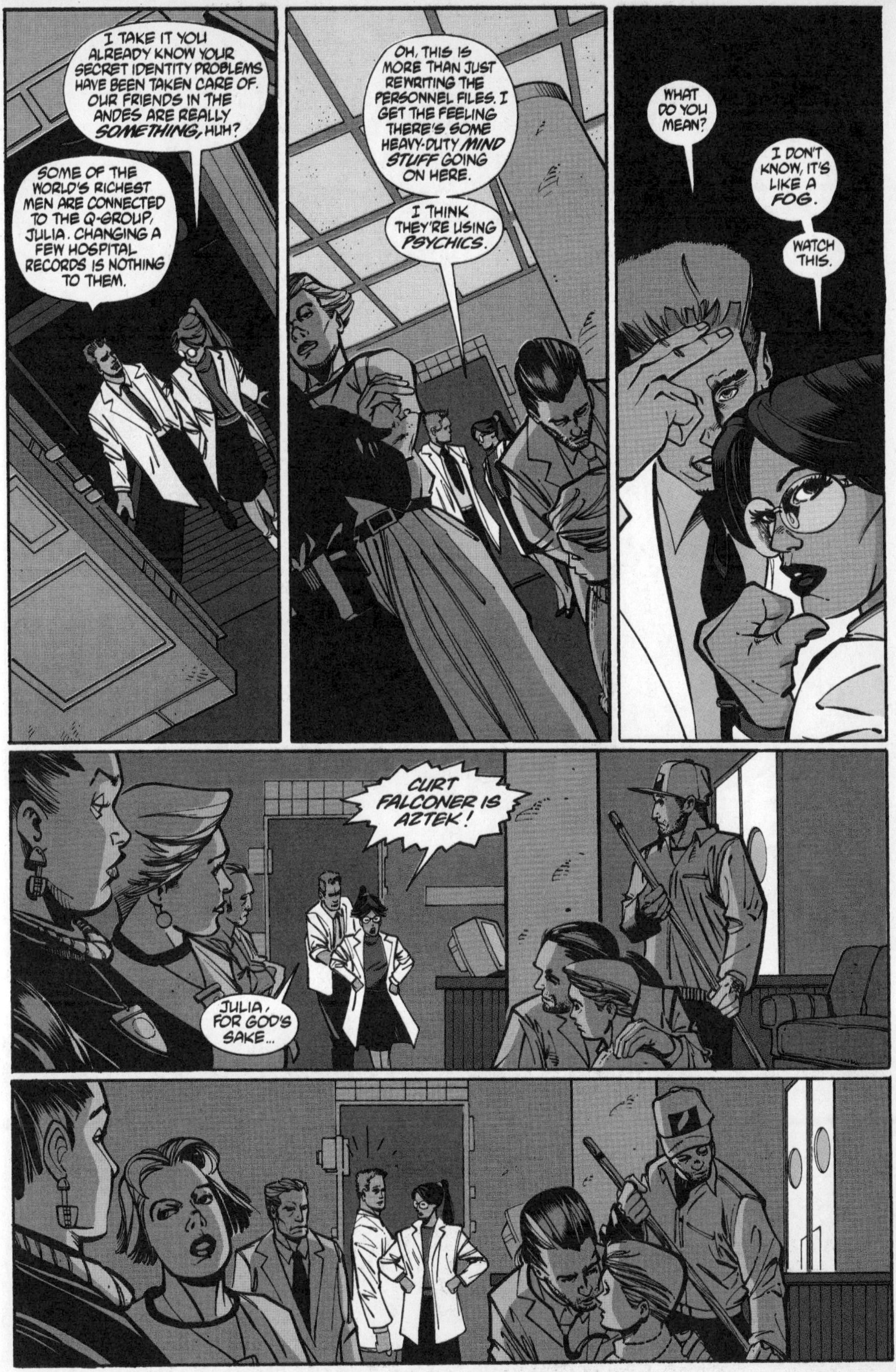
I TAKE IT YOU ALREADY KNOW YOUR SECRET IDENTITY PROBLEMS HAVE BEEN TAKEN CARE OF. OUR FRIENDS IN THE ANDES ARE REALLY SOMETHING, HUH?
SOME OF THE WORLD'S RICHEST MEN ARE CONNECTED TO THE Q-GROUP, JULIA. CHANGING A FEW HOSPITAL RECORDS IS NOTHING TO THEM.
OH, THIS IS MORE THAN JUST REWRITING THE PERSONNEL FILES. I GET THE FEELING THERE'S SOME HEAVY-DUTY MIND STUFF GOING ON HERE.
I THINK THEY'RE USING PSYCHICS.
WHAT DO YOU MEAN?
I DON'T KNOW, IT'S LIKE A FOG.
WATCH THIS.
CURT FALCONER IS AZTEK!
JULIA, FOR GOD'S SAKE...

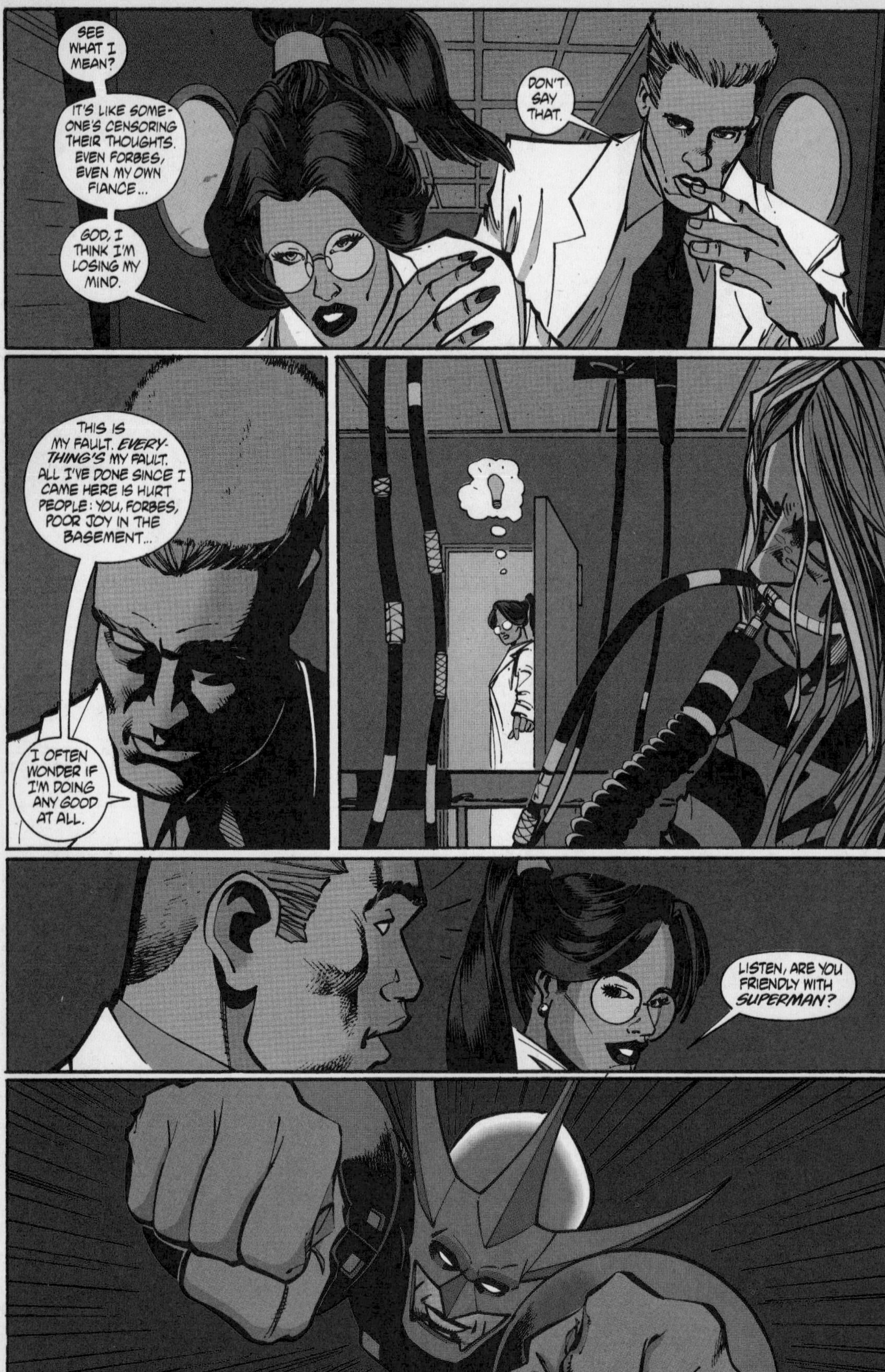
SEE WHAT I MEAN?
IT'S LIKE SOMEONE'S CENSORING THEIR THOUGHTS. EVEN FORBES, EVEN MY OWN FIANCE...
GOD, I THINK I'M LOSING MY MIND.
DON'T SAY THAT.
THIS IS MY FAULT. *EVERYTHING'S* MY FAULT. ALL I'VE DONE SINCE I CAME HERE IS HURT PEOPLE: YOU, FORBES, POOR JOY IN THE BASEMENT...
I OFTEN WONDER IF I'M DOING ANY GOOD AT ALL.
LISTEN, ARE YOU FRIENDLY WITH *SUPERMAN*?

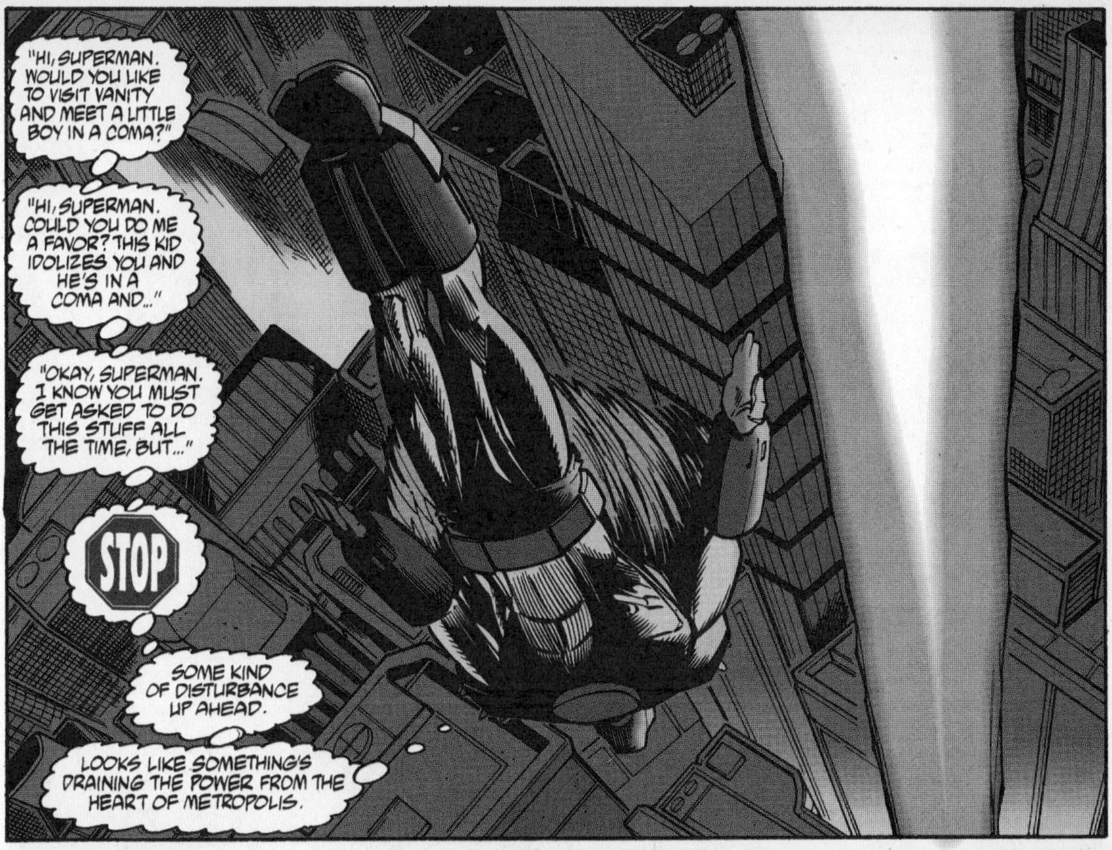
"HI, SUPERMAN. WOULD YOU LIKE TO VISIT VANITY AND MEET A LITTLE BOY IN A COMA?"
"HI, SUPERMAN. COULD YOU DO ME A FAVOR? THIS KID IDOLIZES YOU AND HE'S IN A COMA AND..."
"OKAY, SUPERMAN. I KNOW YOU MUST GET ASKED TO DO THIS STUFF ALL THE TIME, BUT..."
STOP
SOME KIND OF DISTURBANCE UP AHEAD.
LOOKS LIKE SOMETHING'S DRAINING THE POWER FROM THE HEART OF METROPOLIS.

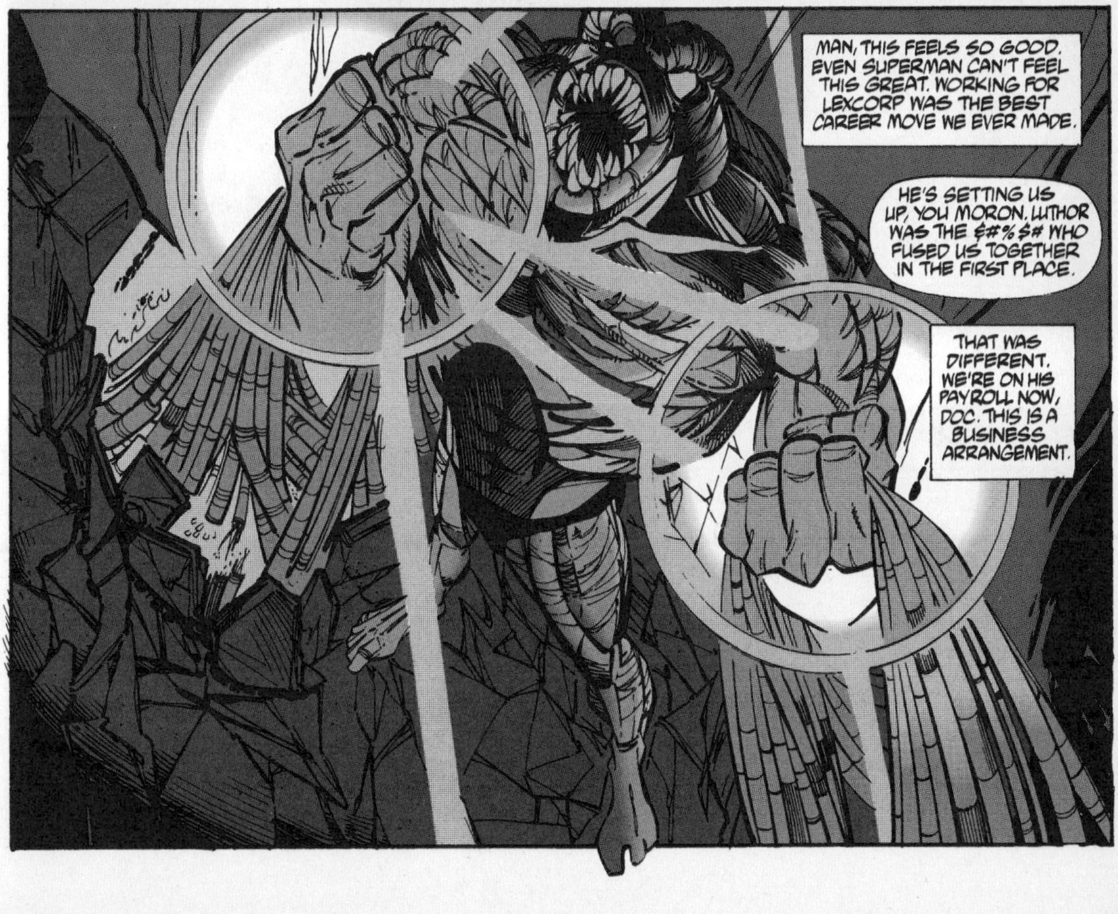
MAN, THIS FEELS SO GOOD. EVEN SUPERMAN CAN'T FEEL THIS GREAT. WORKING FOR LEXCORP WAS THE BEST CAREER MOVE WE EVER MADE.
HE'S SETTING US UP, YOU MORON. LUTHOR WAS THE $#%$# WHO FUSED US TOGETHER IN THE FIRST PLACE.
THAT WAS DIFFERENT. WE'RE ON HIS PAYROLL NOW, DOC. THIS IS A BUSINESS ARRANGEMENT.

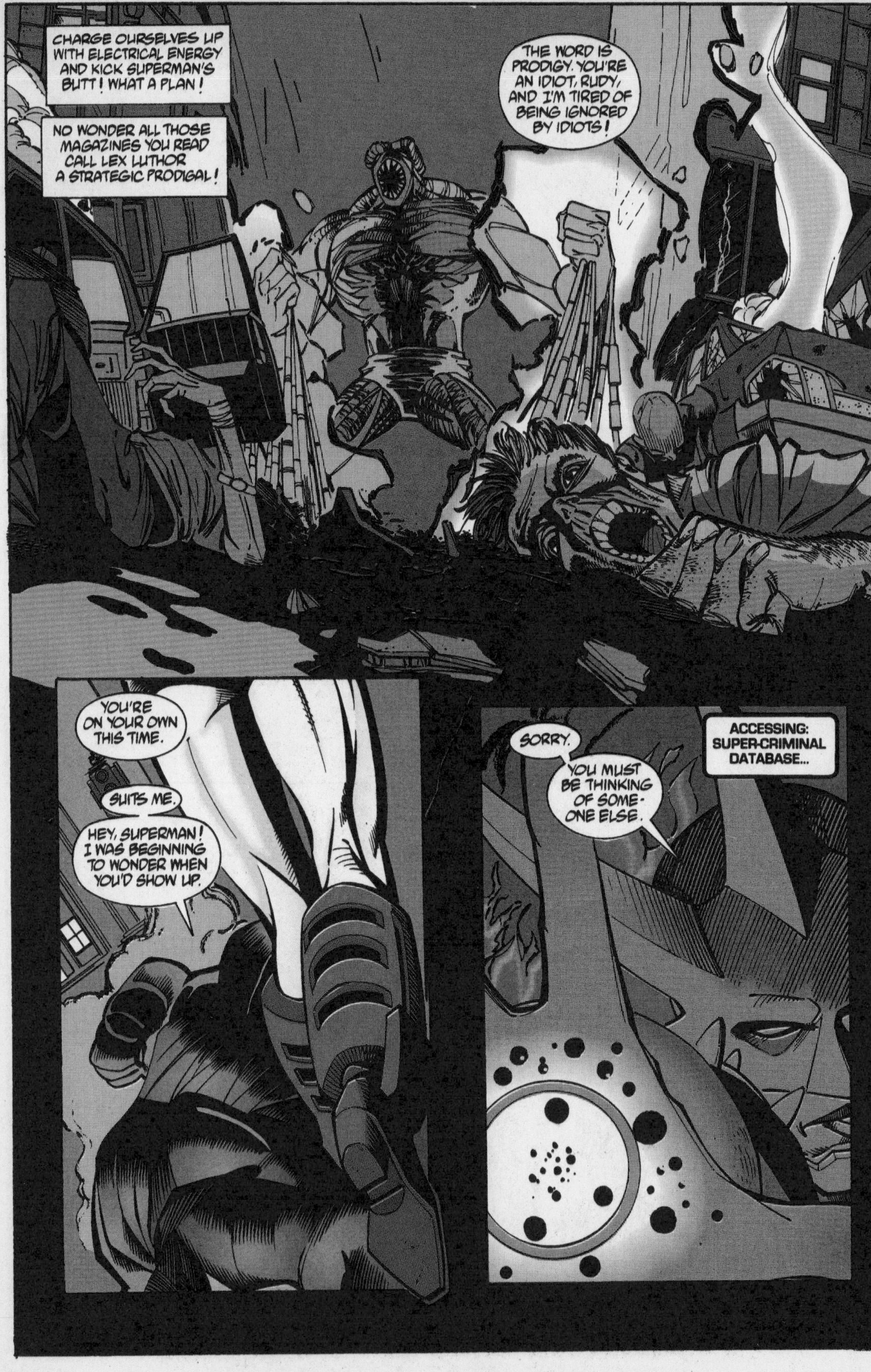
CHARGE OURSELVES UP WITH ELECTRICAL ENERGY AND KICK SUPERMAN'S BUTT! WHAT A PLAN!
NO WONDER ALL THOSE MAGAZINES YOU READ CALL LEX LUTHOR A STRATEGIC PRODIGAL!
THE WORD IS PRODIGY. YOU'RE AN IDIOT, RUDY, AND I'M TIRED OF BEING IGNORED BY IDIOTS!
YOU'RE ON YOUR OWN THIS TIME.
SUITS ME.
HEY, SUPERMAN! I WAS BEGINNING TO WONDER WHEN YOU'D SHOW UP.
SORRY.
YOU MUST BE THINKING OF SOME-ONE ELSE.
ACCESSING: SUPER-CRIMINAL DATABASE...

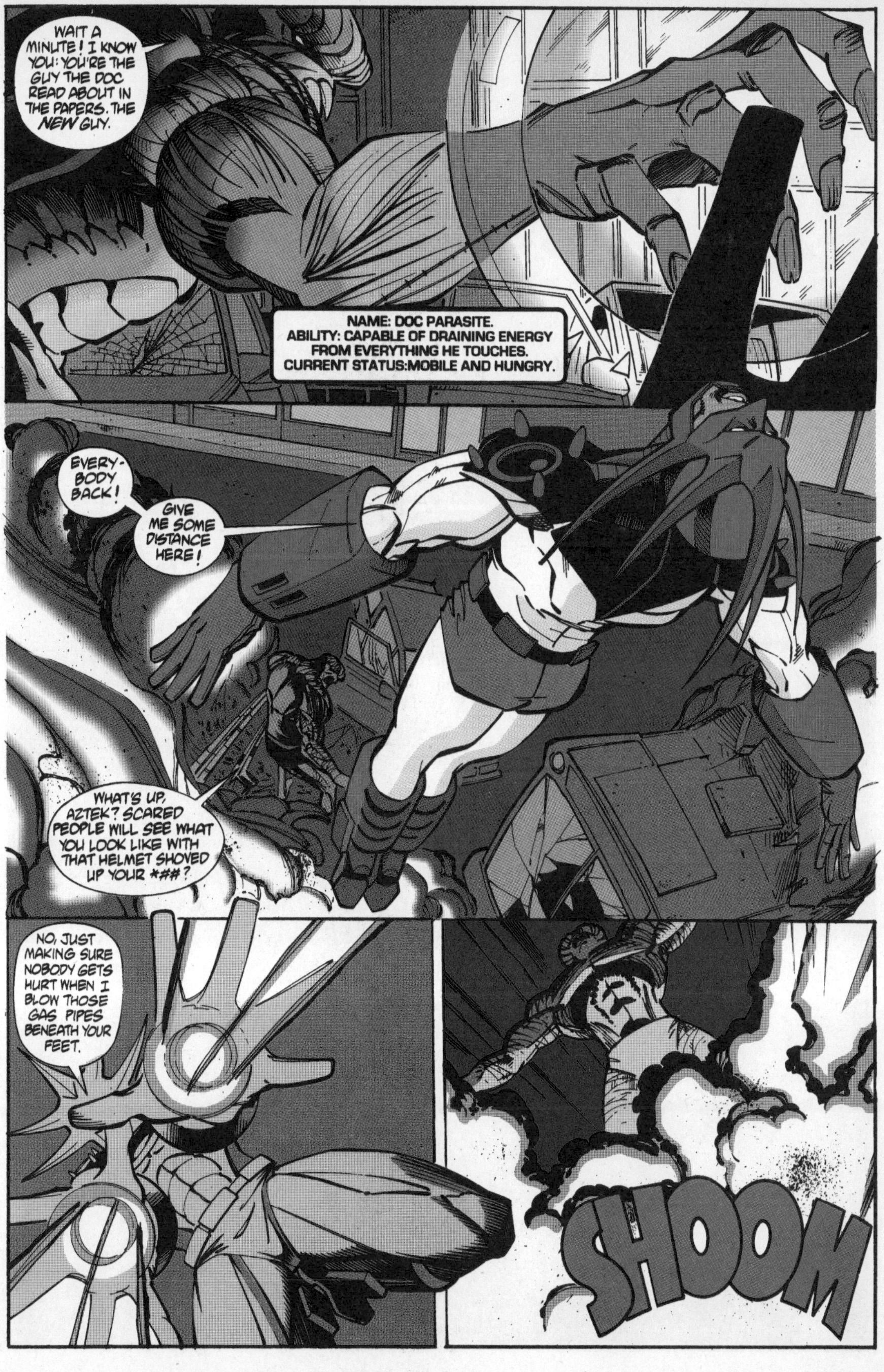
WAIT A MINUTE! I KNOW YOU: YOU'RE THE GUY THE DOC READ ABOUT IN THE PAPERS. THE *NEW* GUY.
NAME: DOC PARASITE.
ABILITY: CAPABLE OF DRAINING ENERGY FROM EVERYTHING HE TOUCHES.
CURRENT STATUS:MOBILE AND HUNGRY.
EVERY-BODY BACK!
GIVE ME SOME DISTANCE HERE!
WHAT'S UP, AZTEK? SCARED PEOPLE WILL SEE WHAT YOU LOOK LIKE WITH THAT HELMET SHOVED UP YOUR *##?
NO, JUST MAKING SURE NOBODY GETS HURT WHEN I BLOW THOSE GAS PIPES BENEATH YOUR FEET.
SHOOM

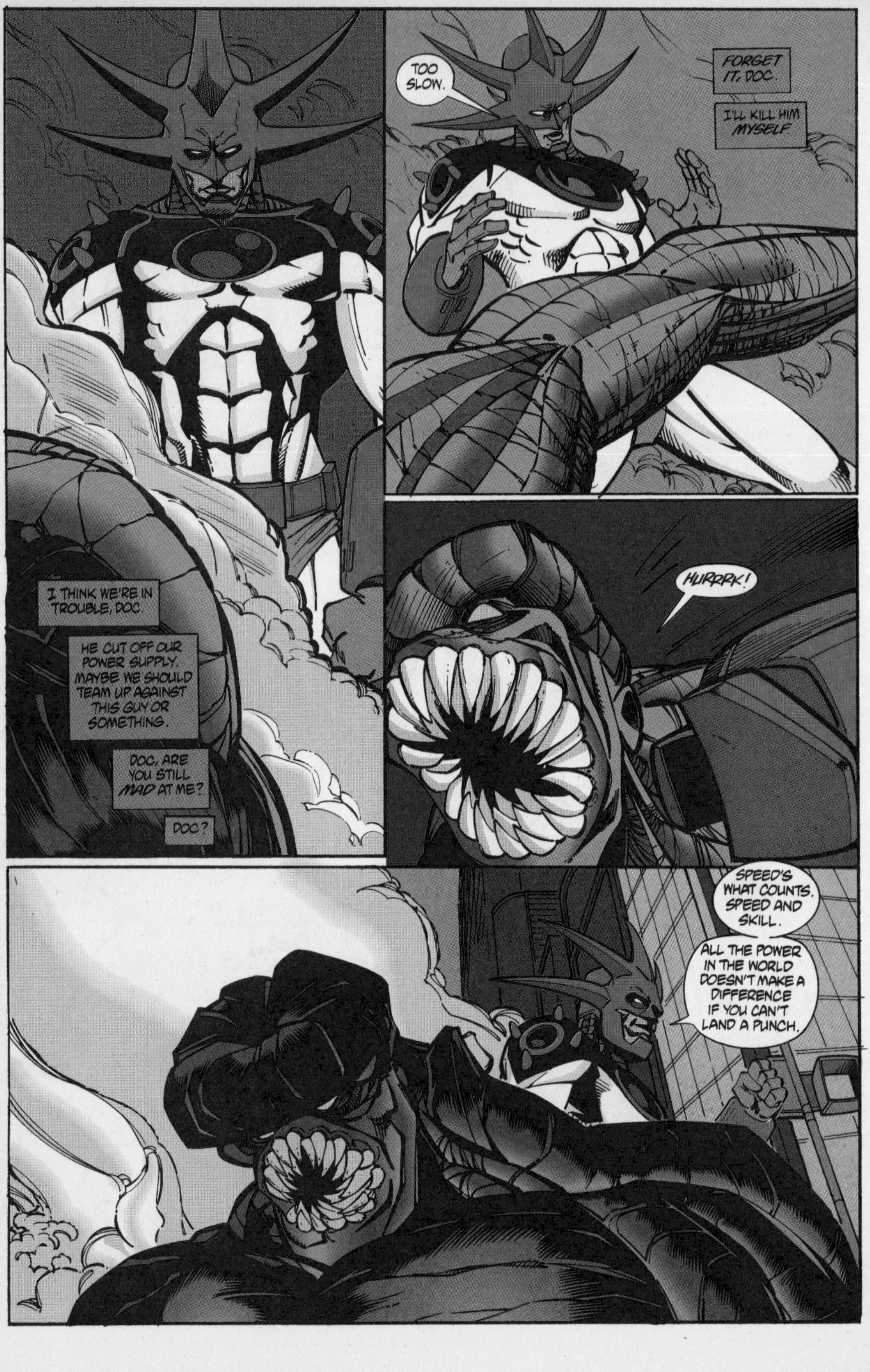

I THINK WE'RE IN TROUBLE, DOC.
HE CUT OFF OUR POWER SUPPLY. MAYBE WE SHOULD TEAM UP AGAINST THIS GUY OR SOMETHING.
DOC, ARE YOU STILL MAD AT ME?
DOC?
TOO SLOW.
FORGET IT, DOC.
I'LL KILL HIM MYSELF.
HURRRK!
SPEED'S WHAT COUNTS. SPEED AND SKILL.
ALL THE POWER IN THE WORLD DOESN'T MAKE A DIFFERENCE IF YOU CAN'T LAND A PUNCH.

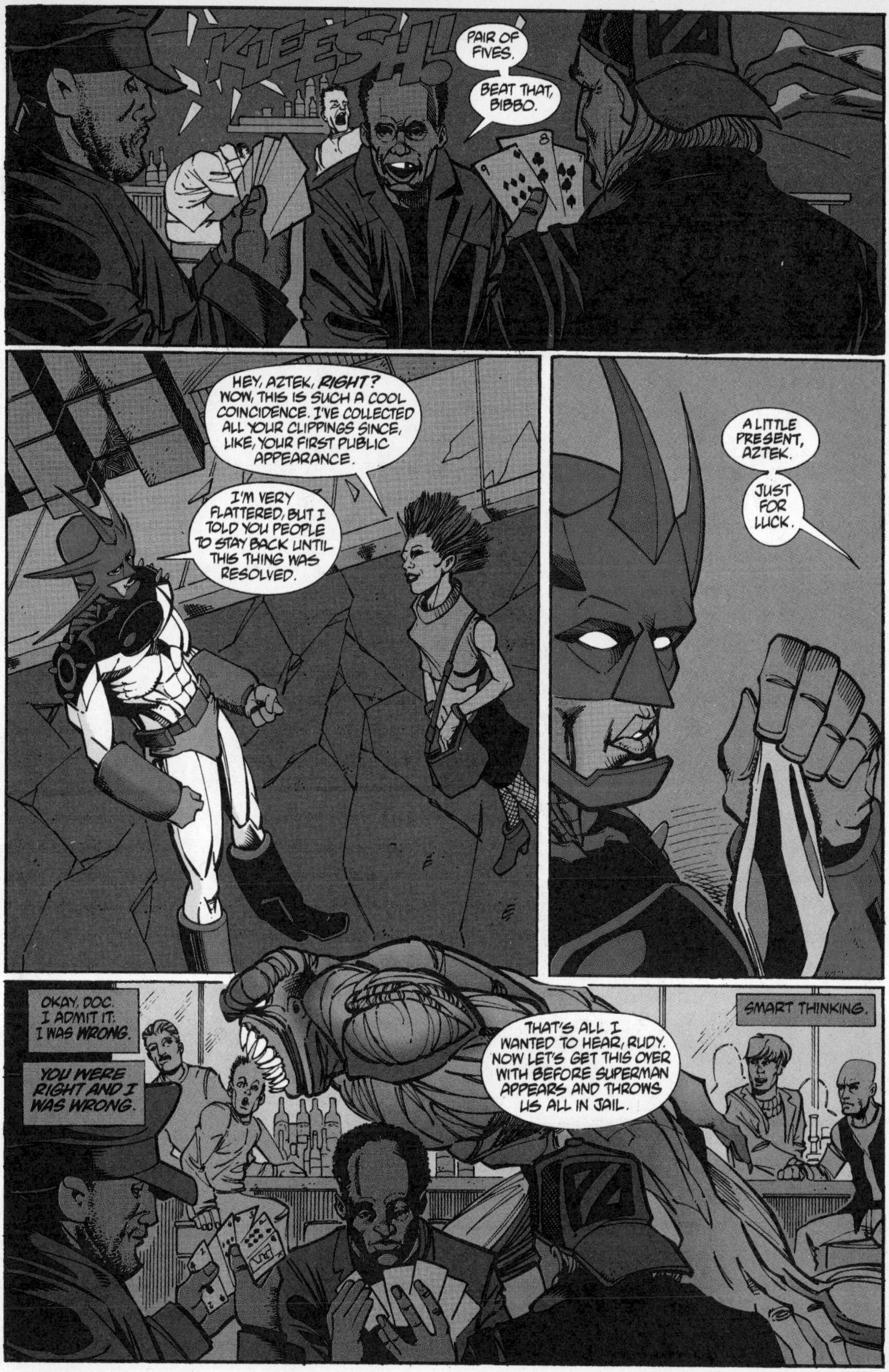
KLEESH!
PAIR OF FIVES.
BEAT THAT, BIBBO.
HEY, AZTEK, RIGHT? WOW, THIS IS SUCH A COOL COINCIDENCE. I'VE COLLECTED ALL YOUR CLIPPINGS SINCE, LIKE, YOUR FIRST PUBLIC APPEARANCE.
I'M VERY FLATTERED, BUT I TOLD YOU PEOPLE TO STAY BACK UNTIL THIS THING WAS RESOLVED.
A LITTLE PRESENT, AZTEK.
JUST FOR LUCK.
OKAY, DOC. I ADMIT IT: I WAS WRONG.
YOU WERE RIGHT AND I WAS WRONG.
THAT'S ALL I WANTED TO HEAR, RUDY. NOW LET'S GET THIS OVER WITH BEFORE SUPERMAN APPEARS AND THROWS US ALL IN JAIL.
SMART THINKING.

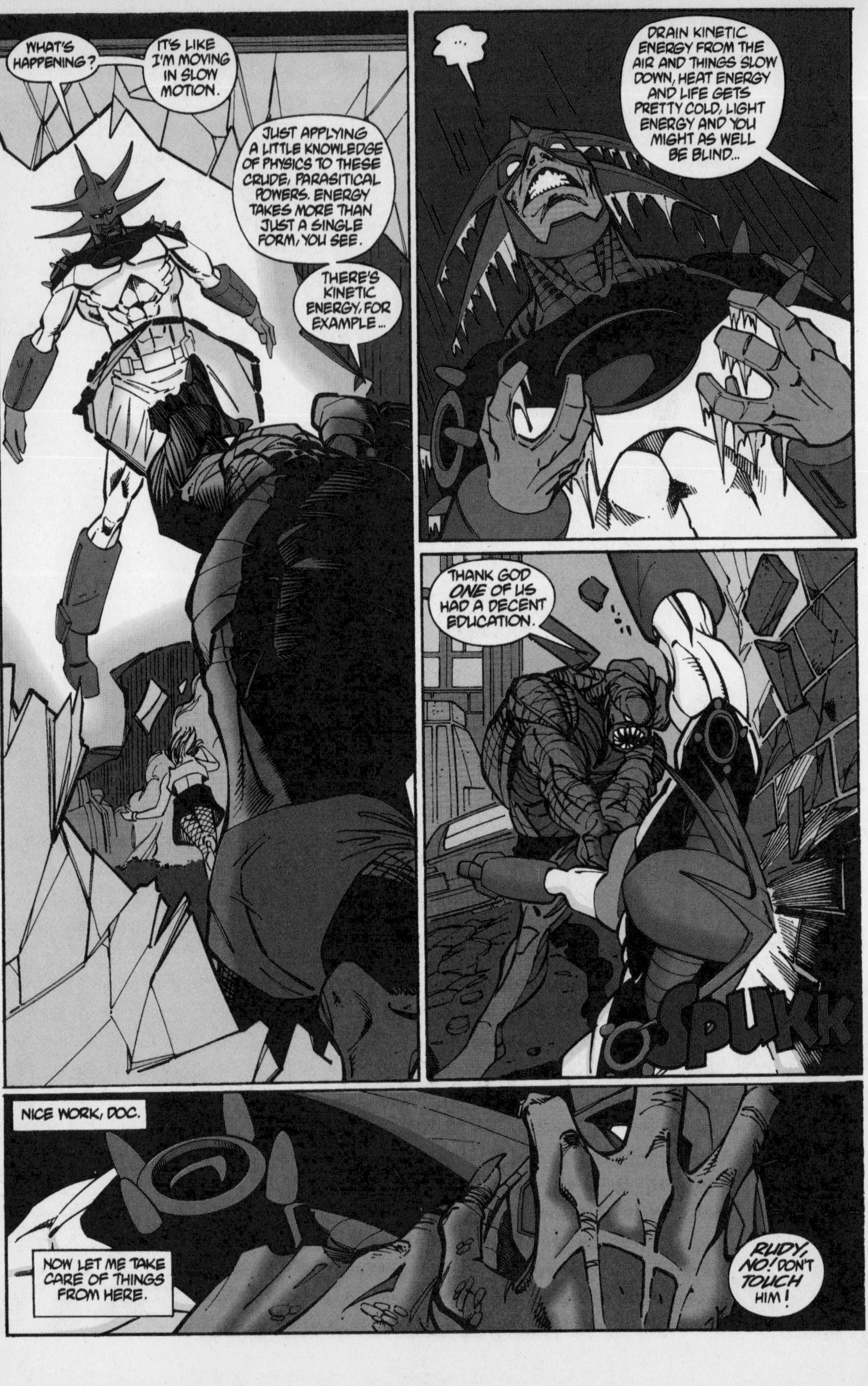
WHAT'S HAPPENING?
IT'S LIKE I'M MOVING IN SLOW MOTION.
JUST APPLYING A LITTLE KNOWLEDGE OF PHYSICS TO THESE CRUDE, PARASITICAL POWERS. ENERGY TAKES MORE THAN JUST A SINGLE FORM, YOU SEE.
THERE'S KINETIC ENERGY, FOR EXAMPLE...
...
DRAIN KINETIC ENERGY FROM THE AIR AND THINGS SLOW DOWN, HEAT ENERGY AND LIFE GETS PRETTY COLD, LIGHT ENERGY AND YOU MIGHT AS WELL BE BLIND...
THANK GOD ONE OF US HAD A DECENT EDUCATION.
SPUKK
NICE WORK, DOC.
NOW LET ME TAKE CARE OF THINGS FROM HERE.
RUDY, NO! DON'T TOUCH HIM!

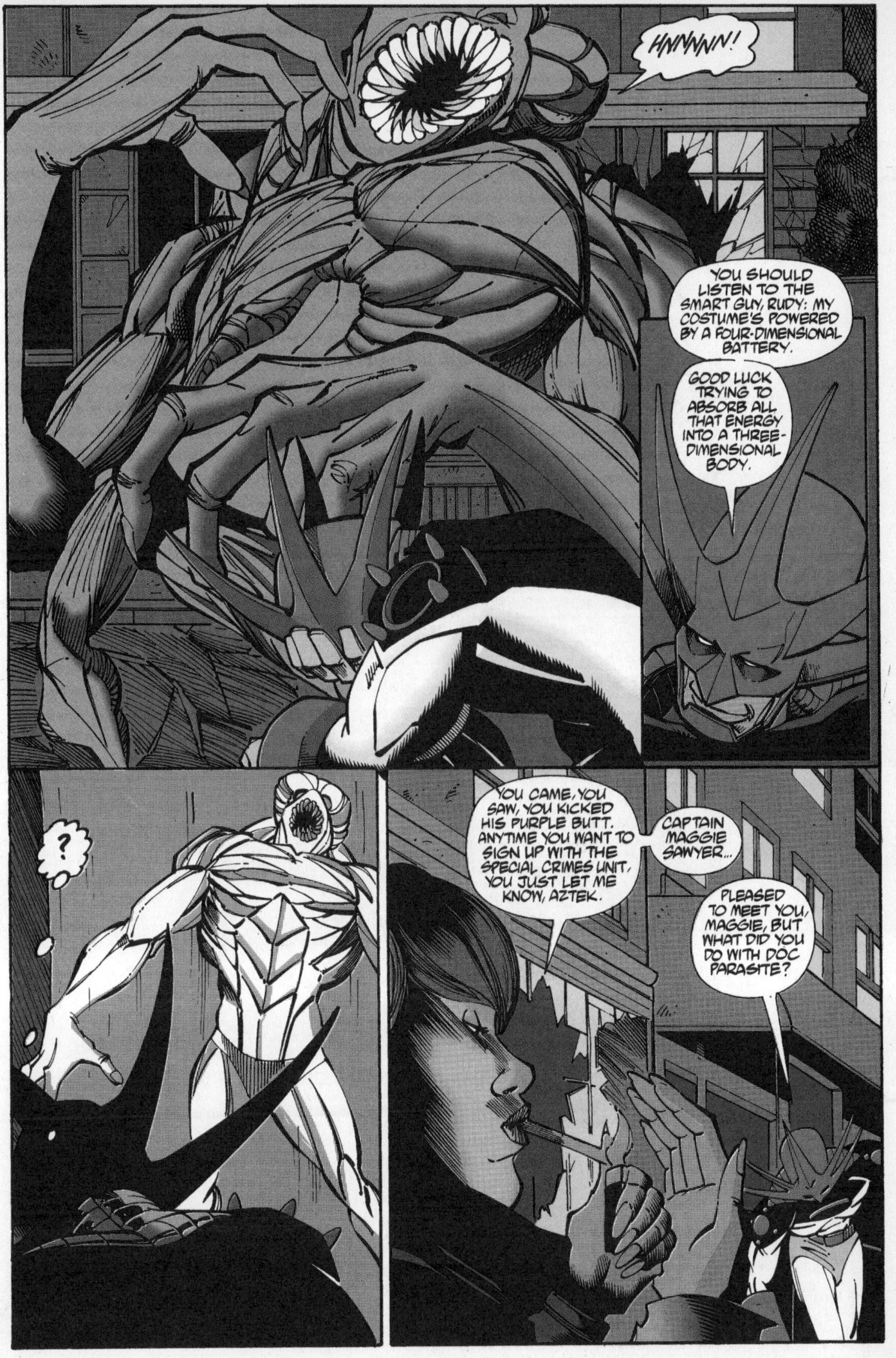
HNNNNN!
YOU SHOULD LISTEN TO THE SMART GUY, RUDY: MY COSTUME'S POWERED BY A FOUR-DIMENSIONAL BATTERY.
GOOD LUCK TRYING TO ABSORB ALL THAT ENERGY INTO A THREE-DIMENSIONAL BODY.
?
YOU CAME, YOU SAW, YOU KICKED HIS PURPLE BUTT. ANYTIME YOU WANT TO SIGN UP WITH THE SPECIAL CRIMES UNIT, YOU JUST LET ME KNOW, AZTEK.
CAPTAIN MAGGIE SAWYER...
PLEASED TO MEET YOU, MAGGIE, BUT WHAT DID YOU DO WITH DOC PARASITE?

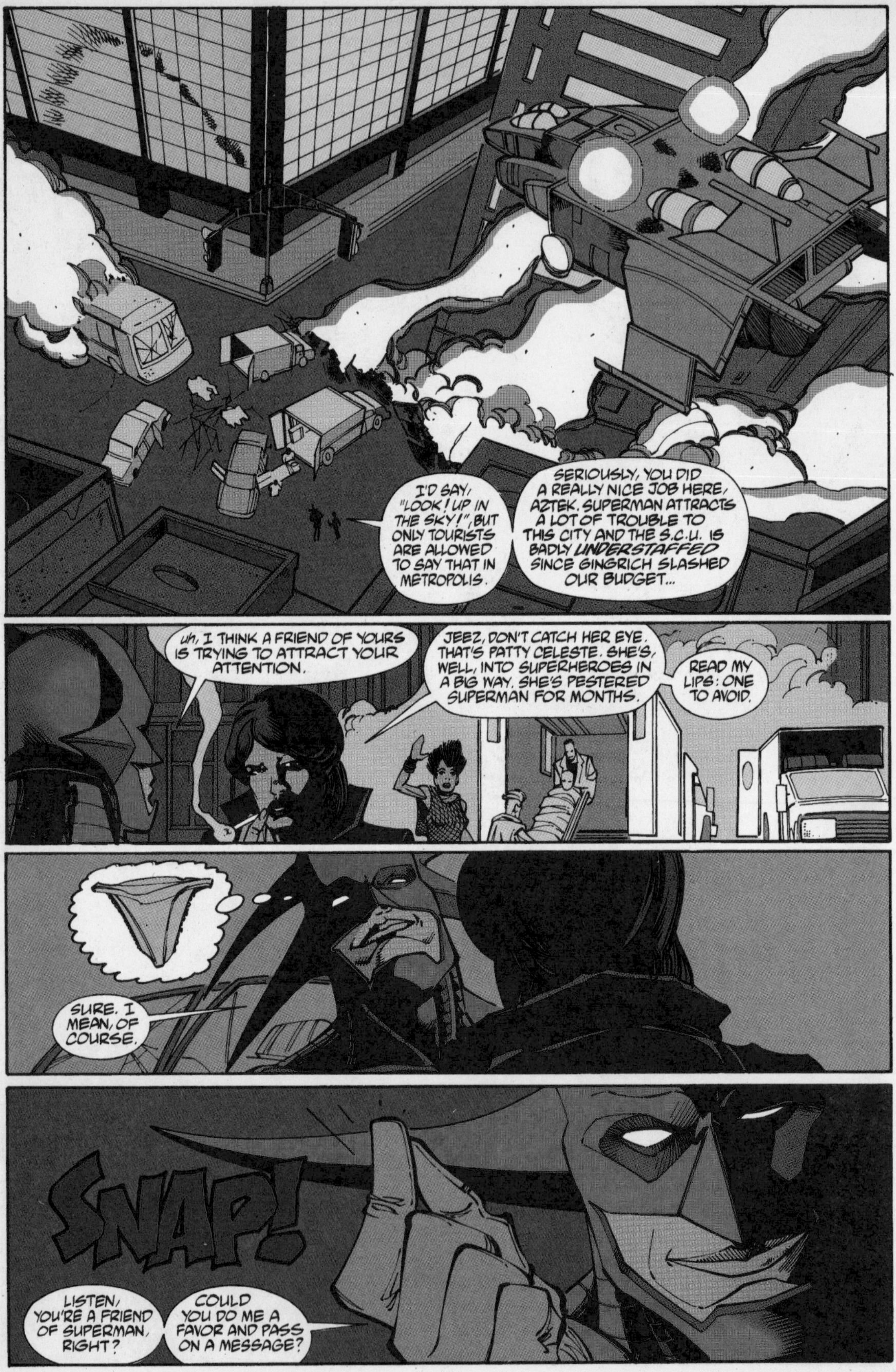
I'D SAY, "LOOK! UP IN THE SKY!", BUT ONLY TOURISTS ARE ALLOWED TO SAY THAT IN METROPOLIS.
SERIOUSLY, YOU DID A REALLY NICE JOB HERE, AZTEK. SUPERMAN ATTRACTS A LOT OF TROUBLE TO THIS CITY AND THE S.C.U. IS BADLY UNDERSTAFFED SINCE GINGRICH SLASHED OUR BUDGET...
uh, I THINK A FRIEND OF YOURS IS TRYING TO ATTRACT YOUR ATTENTION.
JEEZ, DON'T CATCH HER EYE. THAT'S PATTY CELESTE. SHE'S, WELL, INTO SUPERHEROES IN A BIG WAY. SHE'S PESTERED SUPERMAN FOR MONTHS.
READ MY LIPS: ONE TO AVOID.
SURE. I MEAN, OF COURSE.
SNAP!
LISTEN, YOU'RE A FRIEND OF SUPERMAN, RIGHT?
COULD YOU DO ME A FAVOR AND PASS ON A MESSAGE?

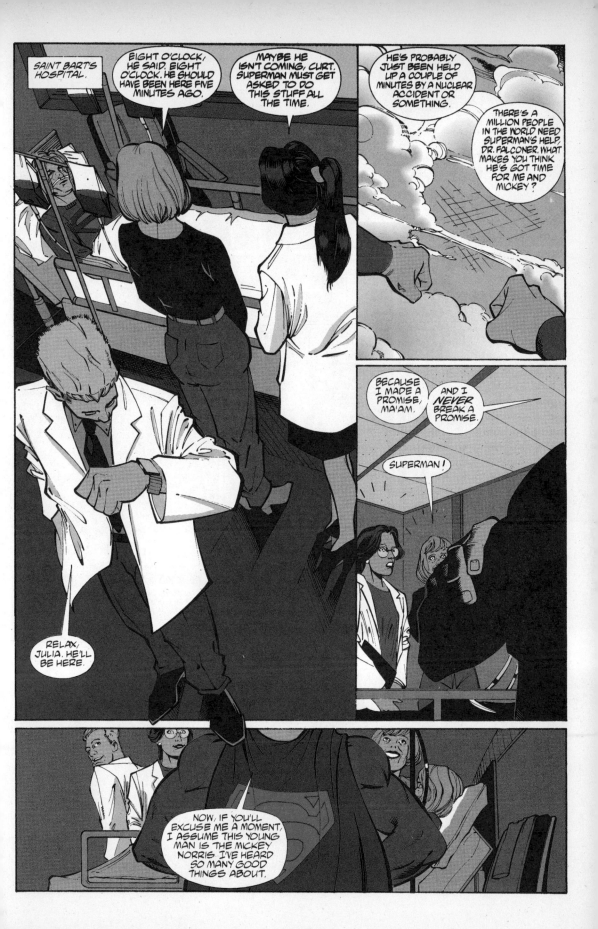

SAINT BART'S HOSPITAL.

EIGHT O'CLOCK, HE SAID. EIGHT O'CLOCK. HE SHOULD HAVE BEEN HERE FIVE MINUTES AGO.

MAYBE HE ISN'T COMING, CURT. SUPERMAN MUST GET ASKED TO DO THIS STUFF ALL THE TIME.

HE'S PROBABLY JUST BEEN HELD UP A COUPLE OF MINUTES BY A NUCLEAR ACCIDENT OR SOMETHING.

THERE'S A MILLION PEOPLE IN THE WORLD NEED SUPERMAN'S HELP, DR. FALCONER. WHAT MAKES YOU THINK HE'S GOT TIME FOR ME AND MICKEY?

BECAUSE I MADE A PROMISE, MA'AM.

AND I *NEVER* BREAK A PROMISE.

SUPERMAN!

RELAX, JULIA. HE'LL BE HERE.

NOW, IF YOU'LL EXCUSE ME A MOMENT, I ASSUME THIS YOUNG MAN IS THE MICKEY NORRIS I'VE HEARD SO MANY GOOD THINGS ABOUT.

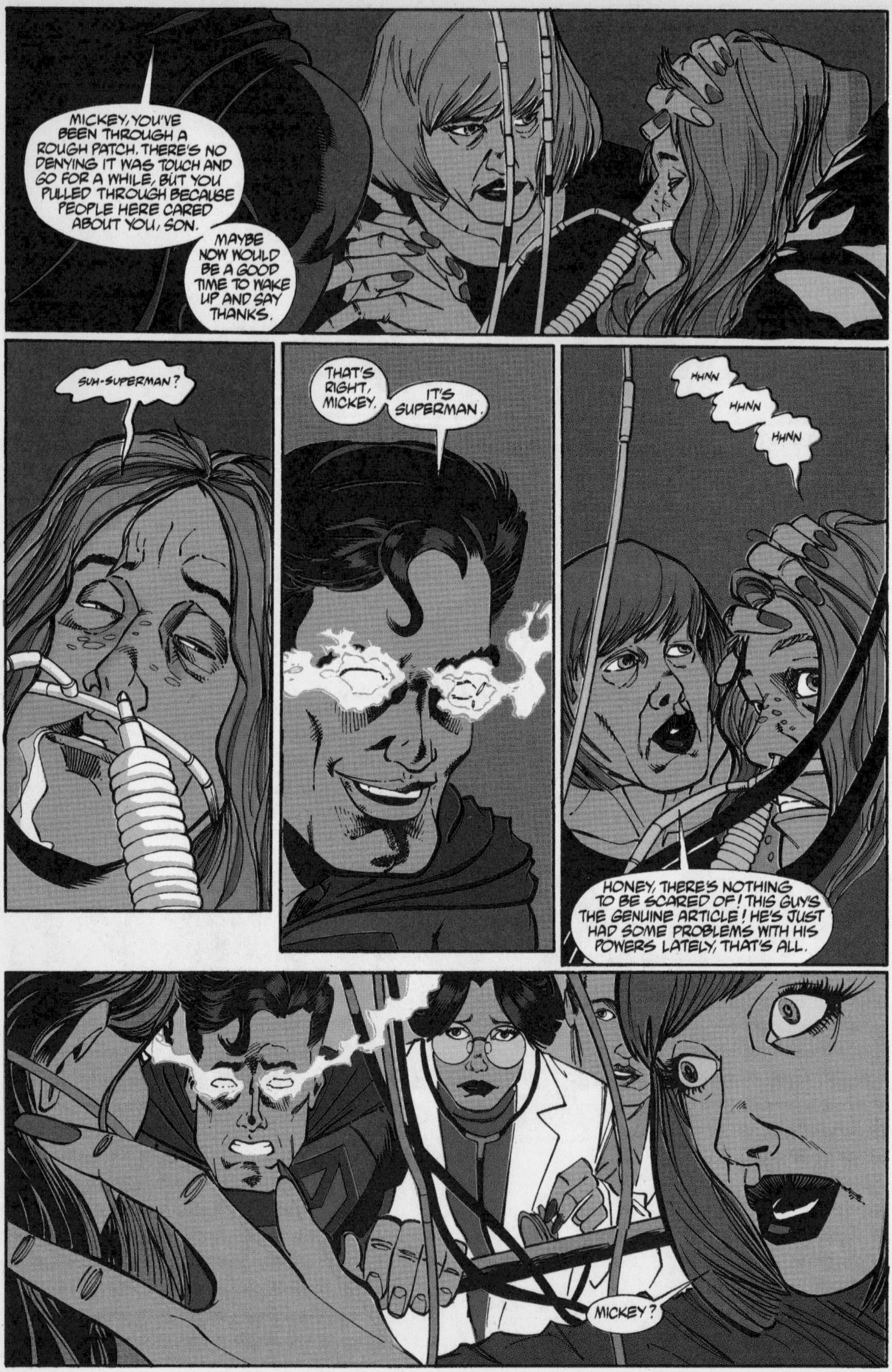
MICKEY, YOU'VE BEEN THROUGH A ROUGH PATCH. THERE'S NO DENYING IT WAS TOUCH AND GO FOR A WHILE, BUT YOU PULLED THROUGH BECAUSE PEOPLE HERE CARED ABOUT YOU, SON.
MAYBE NOW WOULD BE A GOOD TIME TO WAKE UP AND SAY THANKS.
SUH-SUPERMAN?
THAT'S RIGHT, MICKEY.
IT'S SUPERMAN.
HHNN
HHNN
HHNN
HONEY, THERE'S NOTHING TO BE SCARED OF! THIS GUY'S THE GENUINE ARTICLE! HE'S JUST HAD SOME PROBLEMS WITH HIS POWERS LATELY, THAT'S ALL.
MICKEY?

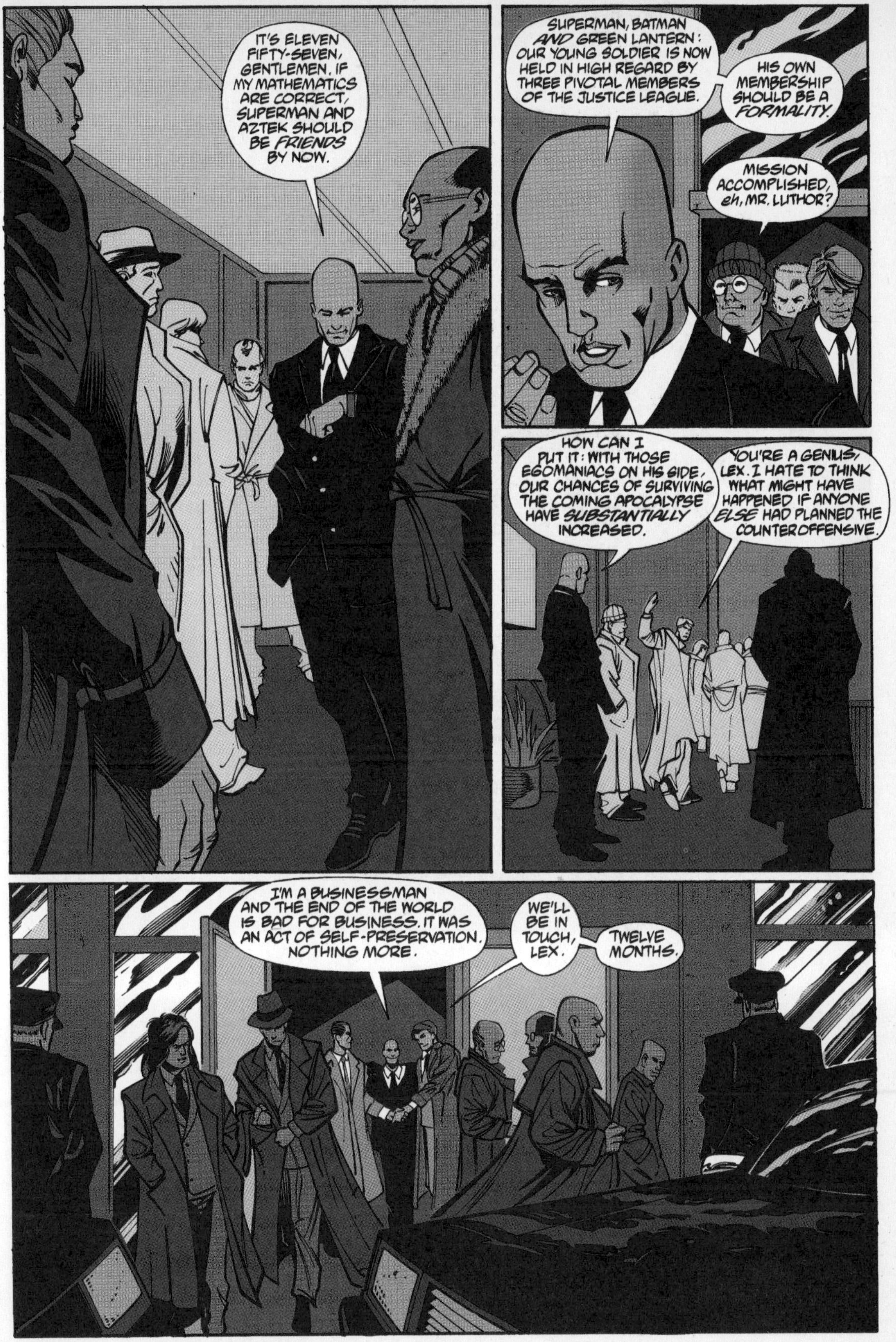
IT'S ELEVEN FIFTY-SEVEN, GENTLEMEN. IF MY MATHEMATICS ARE CORRECT, SUPERMAN AND AZTEK SHOULD BE FRIENDS BY NOW.
SUPERMAN, BATMAN AND GREEN LANTERN: OUR YOUNG SOLDIER IS NOW HELD IN HIGH REGARD BY THREE PIVOTAL MEMBERS OF THE JUSTICE LEAGUE.
HIS OWN MEMBERSHIP SHOULD BE A FORMALITY.
MISSION ACCOMPLISHED, eh, MR. LUTHOR?
HOW CAN I PUT IT: WITH THOSE EGOMANIACS ON HIS SIDE, OUR CHANCES OF SURVIVING THE COMING APOCALYPSE HAVE SUBSTANTIALLY INCREASED.
YOU'RE A GENIUS, LEX. I HATE TO THINK WHAT MIGHT HAVE HAPPENED IF ANYONE ELSE HAD PLANNED THE COUNTEROFFENSIVE.
I'M A BUSINESSMAN AND THE END OF THE WORLD IS BAD FOR BUSINESS. IT WAS AN ACT OF SELF-PRESERVATION. NOTHING MORE.
WE'LL BE IN TOUCH, LEX.
TWELVE MONTHS.

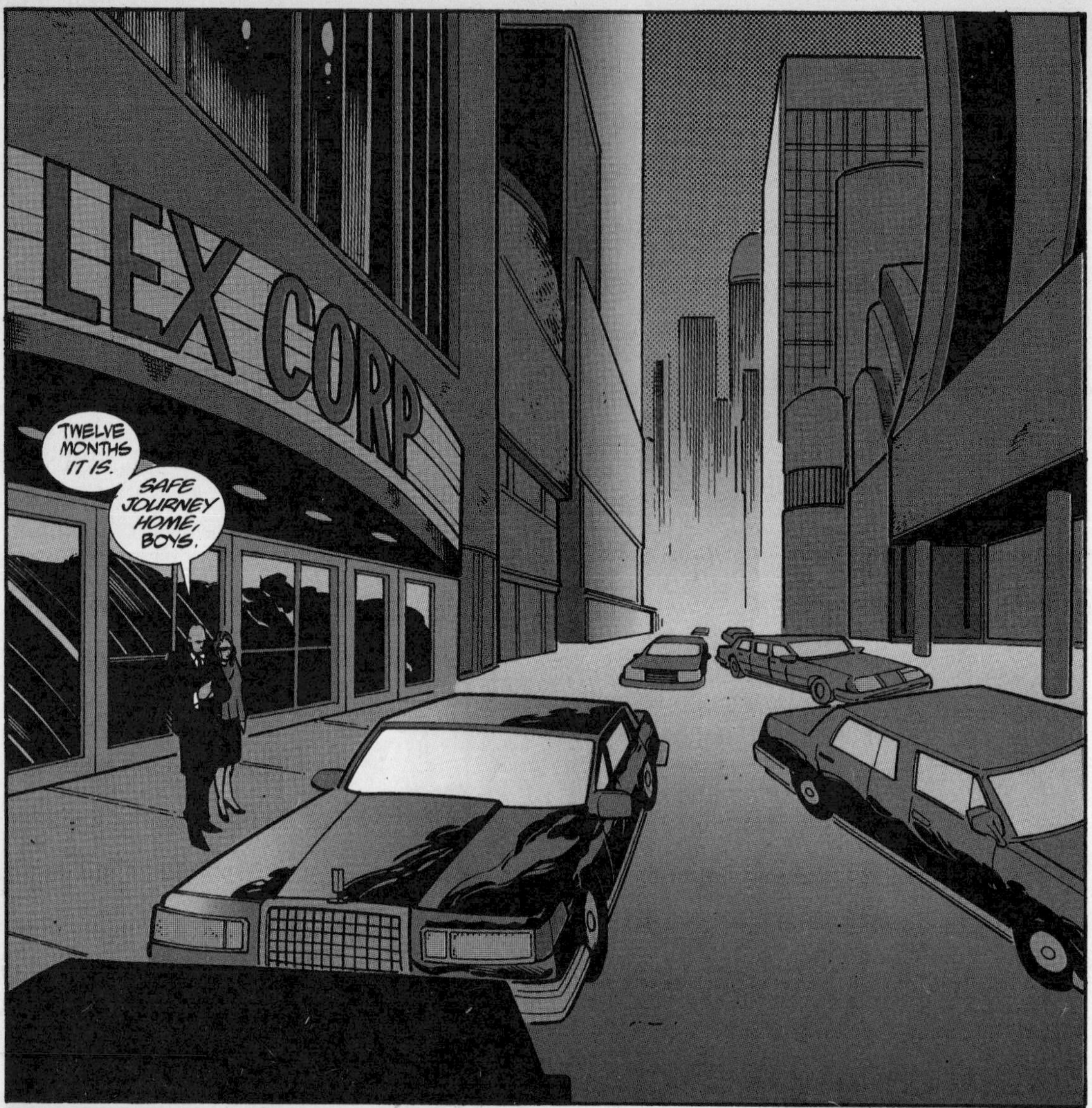
LEX CORP
TWELVE MONTHS IT IS.
SAFE JOURNEY HOME, BOYS.

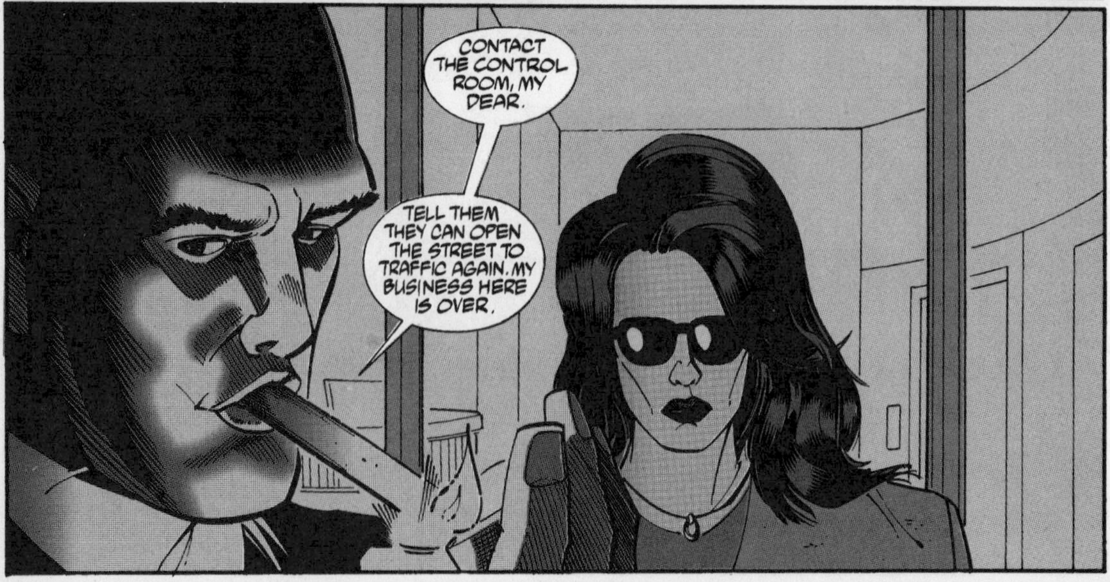
CONTACT THE CONTROL ROOM, MY DEAR.
TELL THEM THEY CAN OPEN THE STREET TO TRAFFIC AGAIN. MY BUSINESS HERE IS OVER.

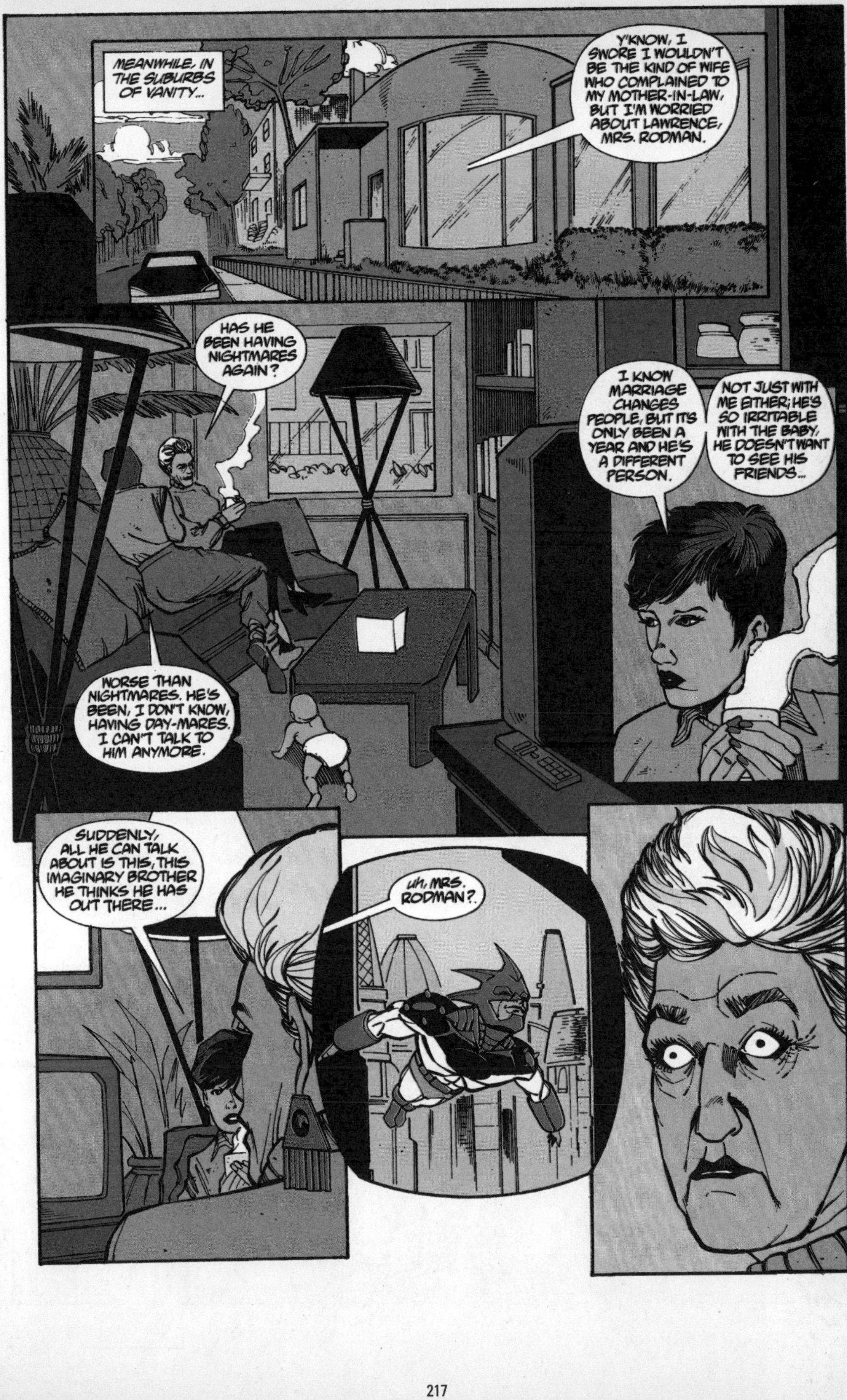
MEANWHILE, IN THE SUBURBS OF VANITY...
Y'KNOW, I SWORE I WOULDN'T BE THE KIND OF WIFE WHO COMPLAINED TO MY MOTHER-IN-LAW, BUT I'M WORRIED ABOUT LAWRENCE, MRS. RODMAN.
HAS HE BEEN HAVING NIGHTMARES AGAIN?
I KNOW MARRIAGE CHANGES PEOPLE, BUT IT'S ONLY BEEN A YEAR AND HE'S A DIFFERENT PERSON.
NOT JUST WITH ME EITHER; HE'S SO IRRITABLE WITH THE BABY, HE DOESN'T WANT TO SEE HIS FRIENDS...
WORSE THAN NIGHTMARES. HE'S BEEN, I DON'T KNOW, HAVING DAY-MARES. I CAN'T TALK TO HIM ANYMORE.
SUDDENLY, ALL HE CAN TALK ABOUT IS THIS, THIS IMAGINARY BROTHER HE THINKS HE HAS OUT THERE...
uh, MRS. RODMAN?.

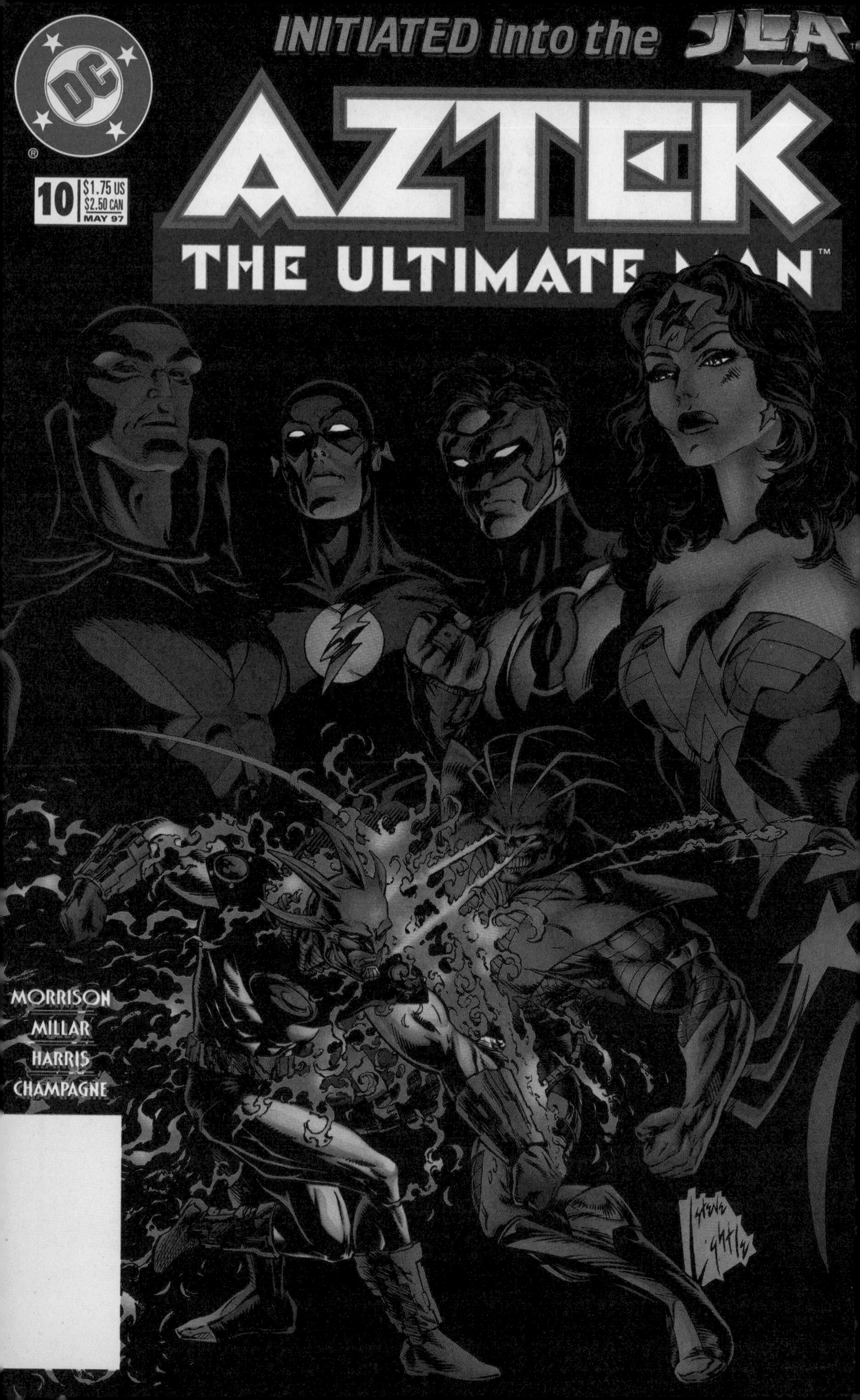
INITIATED into the JLA
DC
10
$1.75 US
$2.50 CAN
MAY 97
AZTEK
THE ULTIMATE
MORRISON
MILLAR
HARRIS
CHAMPAGNE

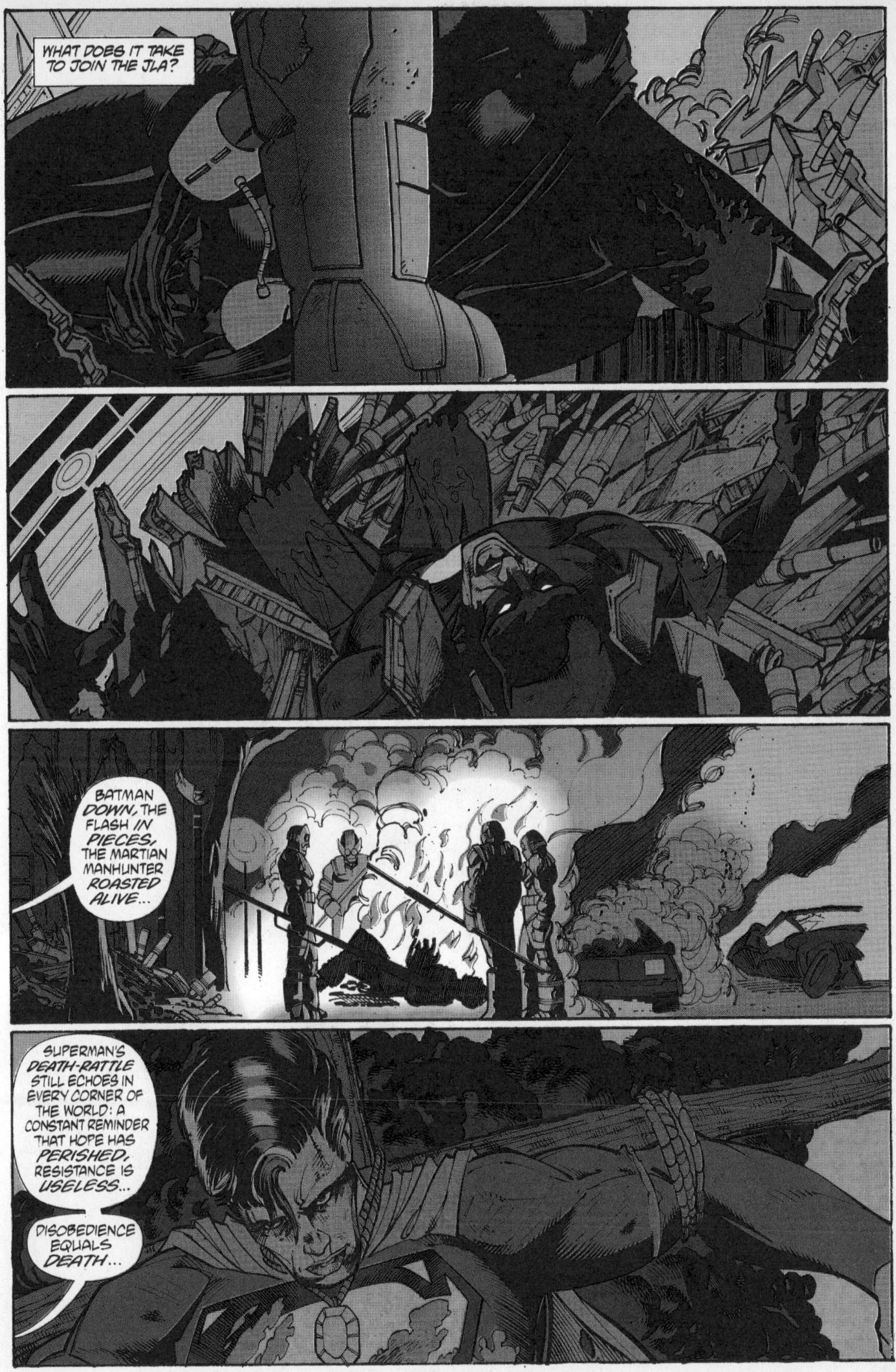
WHAT DOES IT TAKE TO JOIN THE JLA?
BATMAN DOWN, THE FLASH IN PIECES, THE MARTIAN MANHUNTER ROASTED ALIVE...
SUPERMAN'S DEATH-RATTLE STILL ECHOES IN EVERY CORNER OF THE WORLD: A CONSTANT REMINDER THAT HOPE HAS PERISHED, RESISTANCE IS USELESS...
DISOBEDIENCE EQUALS DEATH...

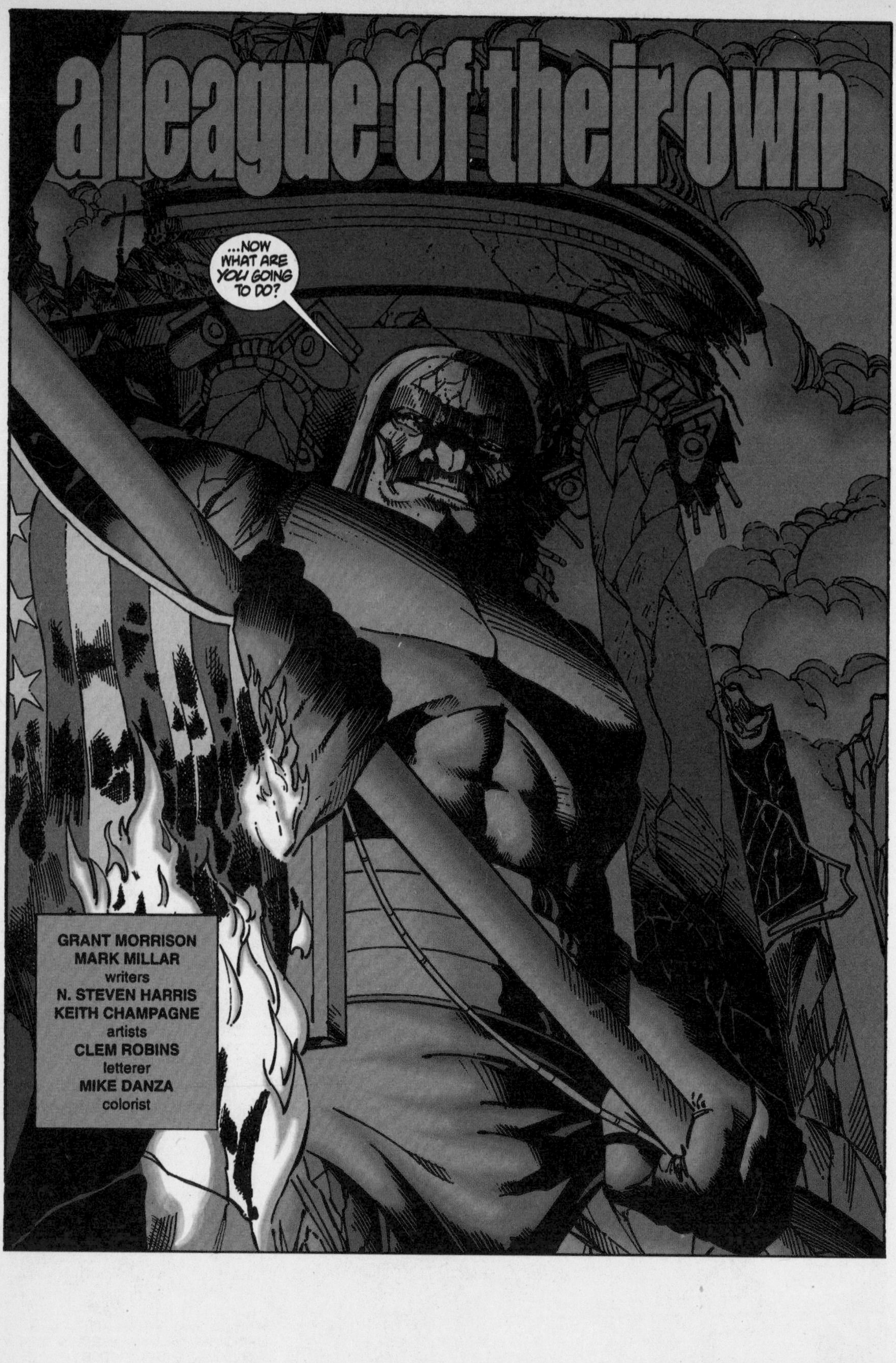
a league of their own
...NOW WHAT ARE YOU GOING TO DO?
GRANT MORRISON
MARK MILLAR
writers
N. STEVEN HARRIS
KEITH CHAMPAGNE
artists
CLEM ROBINS
letterer
MIKE DANZA
colorist

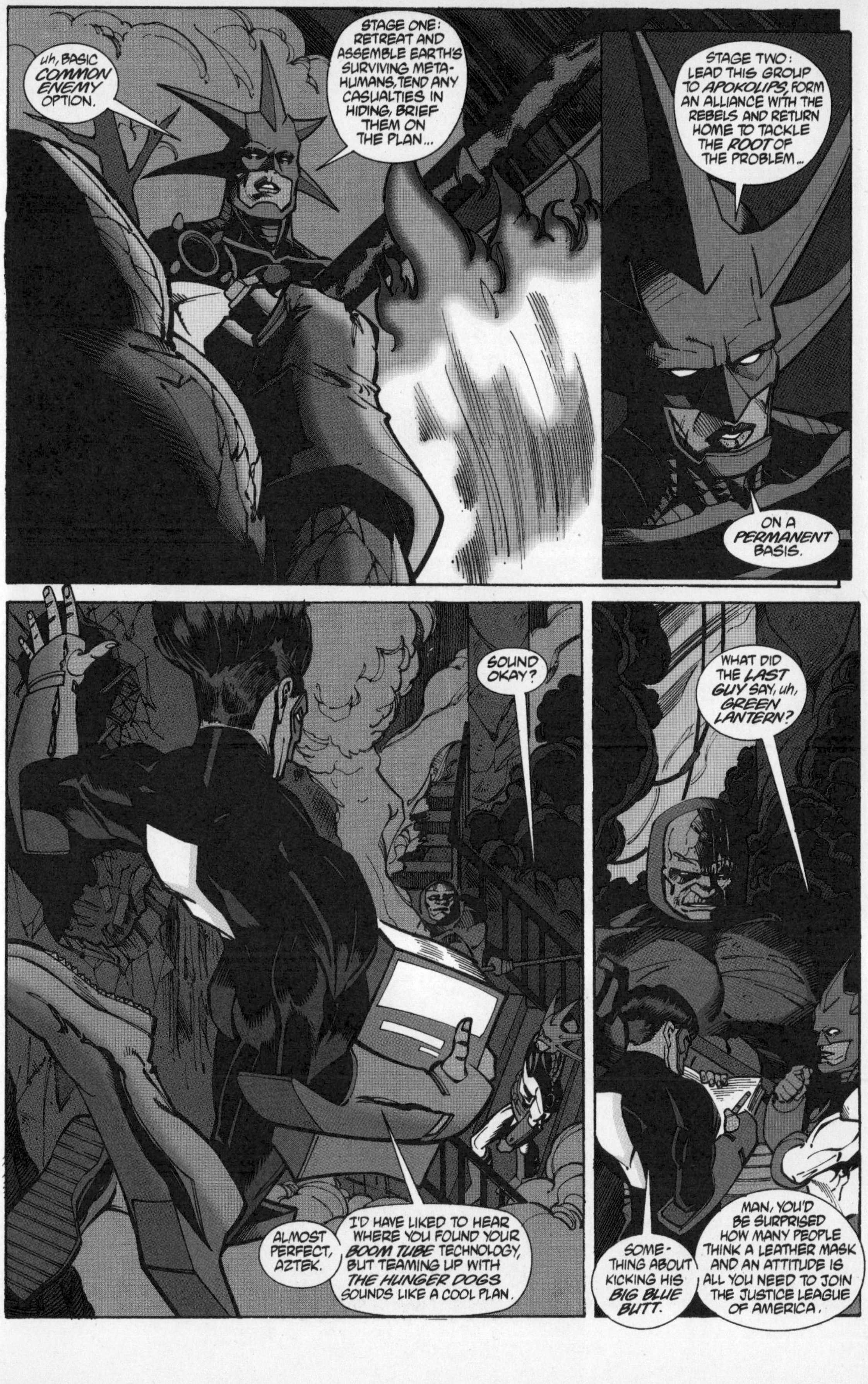
uh, BASIC COMMON ENEMY OPTION.
STAGE ONE: RETREAT AND ASSEMBLE EARTH'S SURVIVING META-HUMANS, TEND ANY CASUALTIES IN HIDING, BRIEF THEM ON THE PLAN...
STAGE TWO: LEAD THIS GROUP TO APOKOLIPS, FORM AN ALLIANCE WITH THE REBELS AND RETURN HOME TO TACKLE THE ROOT OF THE PROBLEM...
ON A PERMANENT BASIS.
SOUND OKAY?
ALMOST PERFECT, AZTEK.
I'D HAVE LIKED TO HEAR WHERE YOU FOUND YOUR BOOM TUBE TECHNOLOGY, BUT TEAMING UP WITH THE HUNGER DOGS SOUNDS LIKE A COOL PLAN.
WHAT DID THE LAST GUY SAY, uh, GREEN LANTERN?
SOME-THING ABOUT KICKING HIS BIG BLUE BUTT.
MAN, YOU'D BE SURPRISED HOW MANY PEOPLE THINK A LEATHER MASK AND AN ATTITUDE IS ALL YOU NEED TO JOIN THE JUSTICE LEAGUE OF AMERICA.

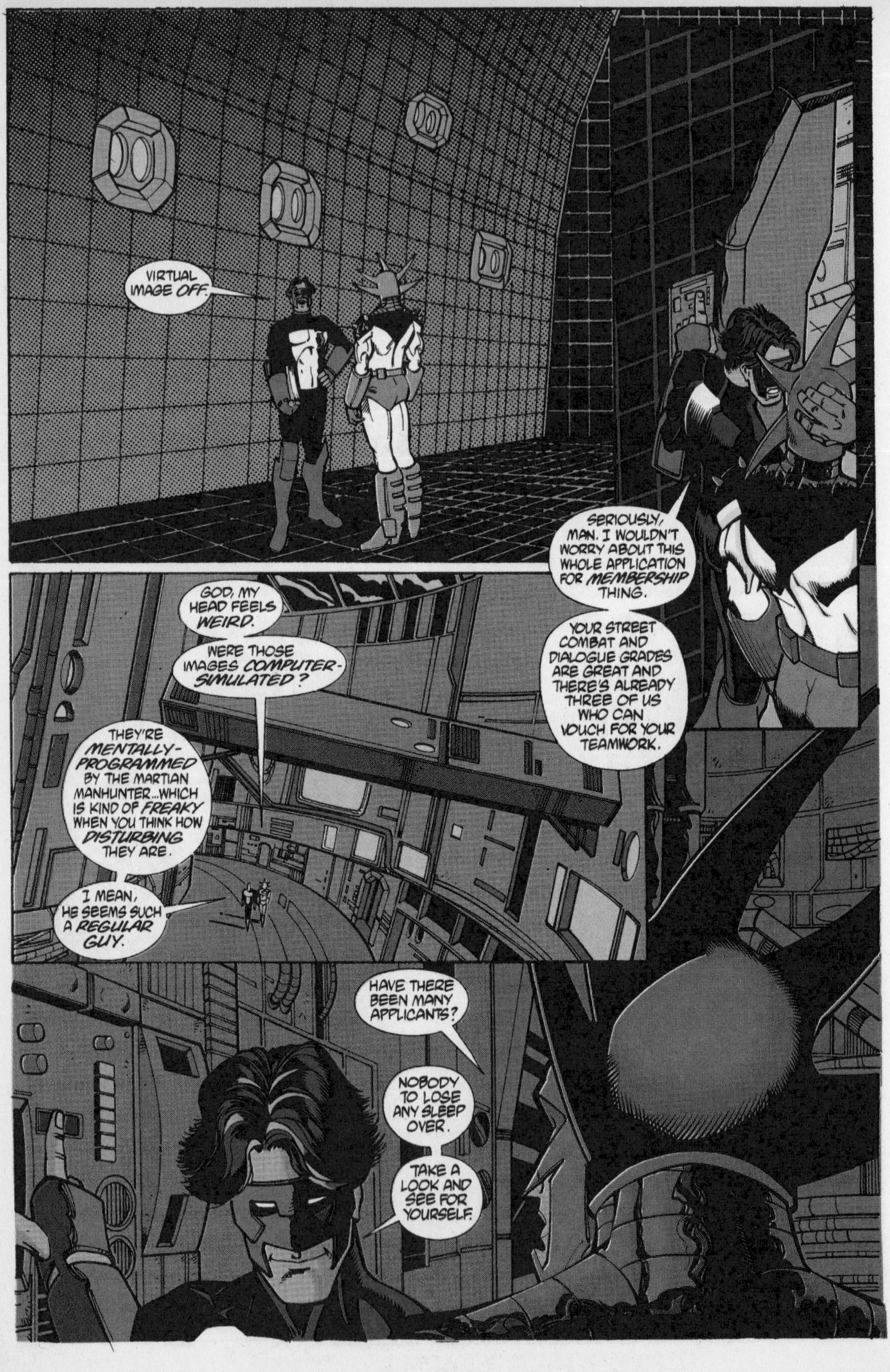
VIRTUAL IMAGE OFF.
SERIOUSLY, MAN. I WOULDN'T WORRY ABOUT THIS WHOLE APPLICATION FOR MEMBERSHIP THING.
YOUR STREET COMBAT AND DIALOGUE GRADES ARE GREAT AND THERE'S ALREADY THREE OF US WHO CAN VOUCH FOR YOUR TEAMWORK.
GOD, MY HEAD FEELS WEIRD.
WERE THOSE IMAGES COMPUTER-SIMULATED?
THEY'RE MENTALLY-PROGRAMMED BY THE MARTIAN MANHUNTER...WHICH IS KIND OF FREAKY WHEN YOU THINK HOW DISTURBING THEY ARE.
I MEAN, HE SEEMS SUCH A REGULAR GUY.
HAVE THERE BEEN MANY APPLICANTS?
NOBODY TO LOSE ANY SLEEP OVER.
TAKE A LOOK AND SEE FOR YOURSELF.

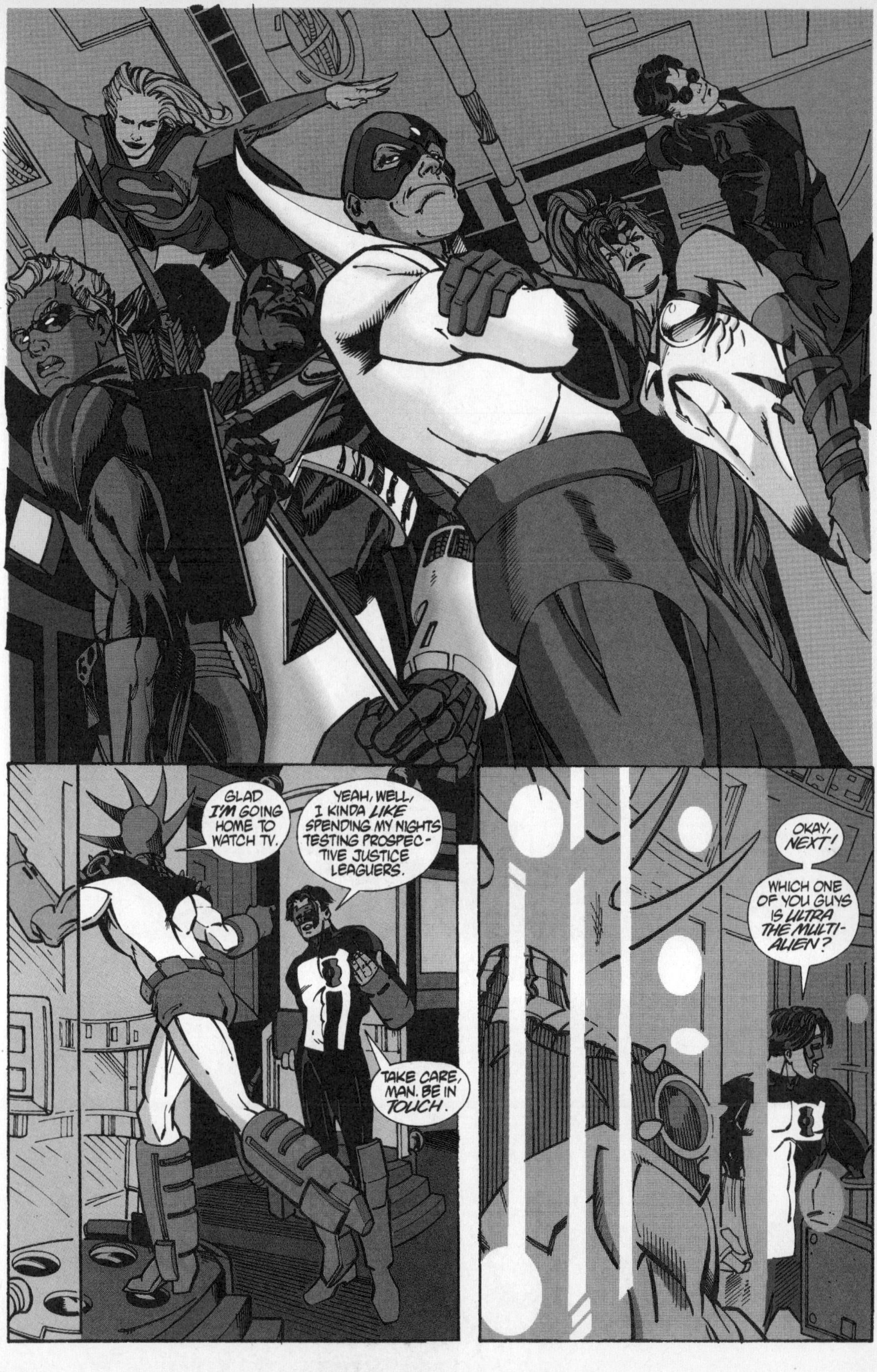
GLAD I'M GOING HOME TO WATCH TV.
YEAH, WELL, I KINDA LIKE SPENDING MY NIGHTS TESTING PROSPECTIVE JUSTICE LEAGUERS.
TAKE CARE, MAN. BE IN TOUCH.
OKAY, NEXT!
WHICH ONE OF YOU GUYS IS ULTRA THE MULTI-ALIEN?

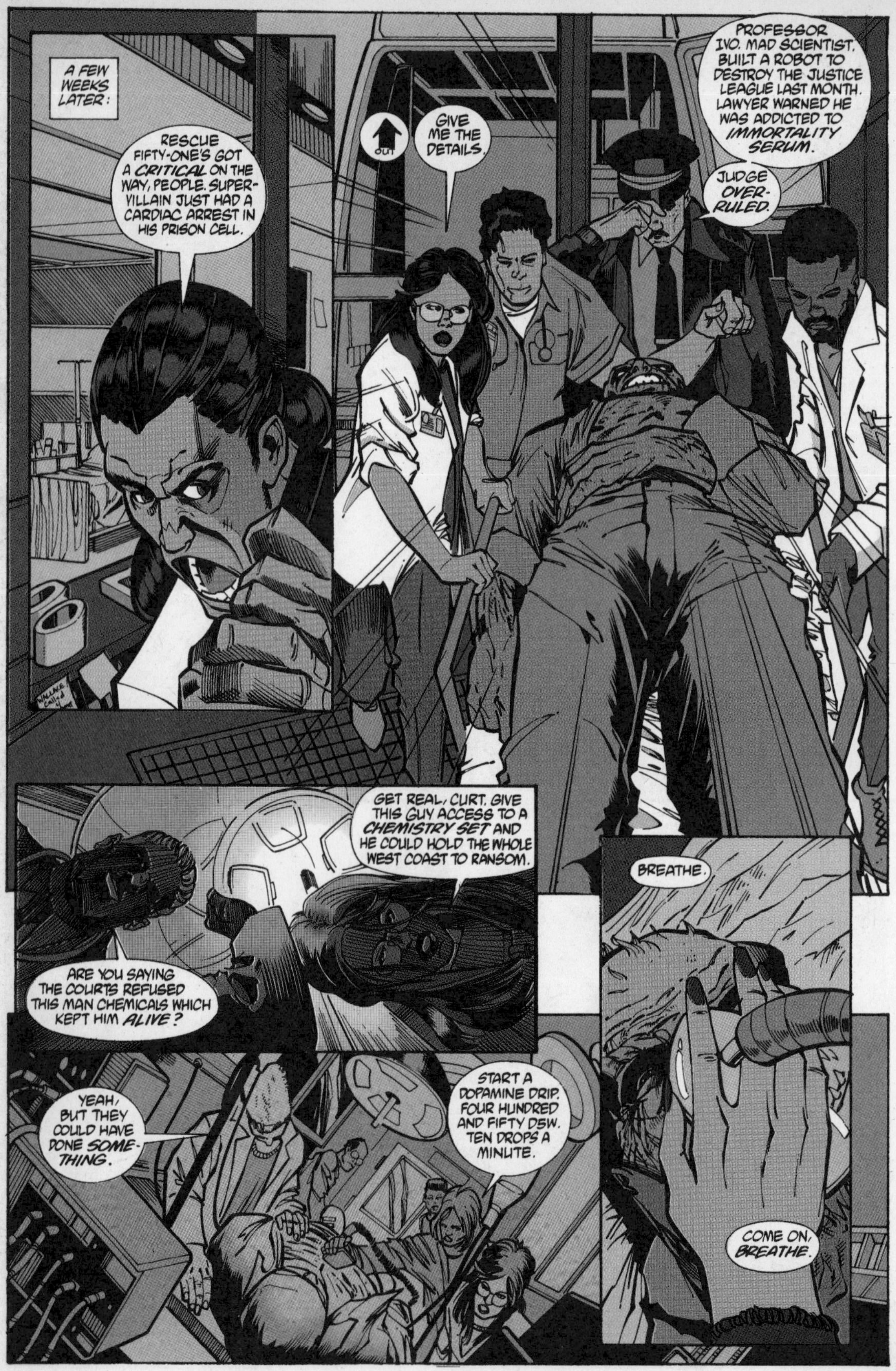
A FEW WEEKS LATER:
RESCUE FIFTY-ONE'S GOT A CRITICAL ON THE WAY, PEOPLE. SUPER-VILLAIN JUST HAD A CARDIAC ARREST IN HIS PRISON CELL.
OUT
GIVE ME THE DETAILS.
PROFESSOR IVO. MAD SCIENTIST. BUILT A ROBOT TO DESTROY THE JUSTICE LEAGUE LAST MONTH. LAWYER WARNED HE WAS ADDICTED TO IMMORTALITY SERUM.
JUDGE OVER-RULED.
GET REAL, CURT. GIVE THIS GUY ACCESS TO A CHEMISTRY SET AND HE COULD HOLD THE WHOLE WEST COAST TO RANSOM.
ARE YOU SAYING THE COURTS REFUSED THIS MAN CHEMICALS WHICH KEPT HIM ALIVE?
BREATHE.
YEAH, BUT THEY COULD HAVE DONE SOME-THING.
START A DOPAMINE DRIP. FOUR HUNDRED AND FIFTY D5W. TEN DROPS A MINUTE.
COME ON, BREATHE.

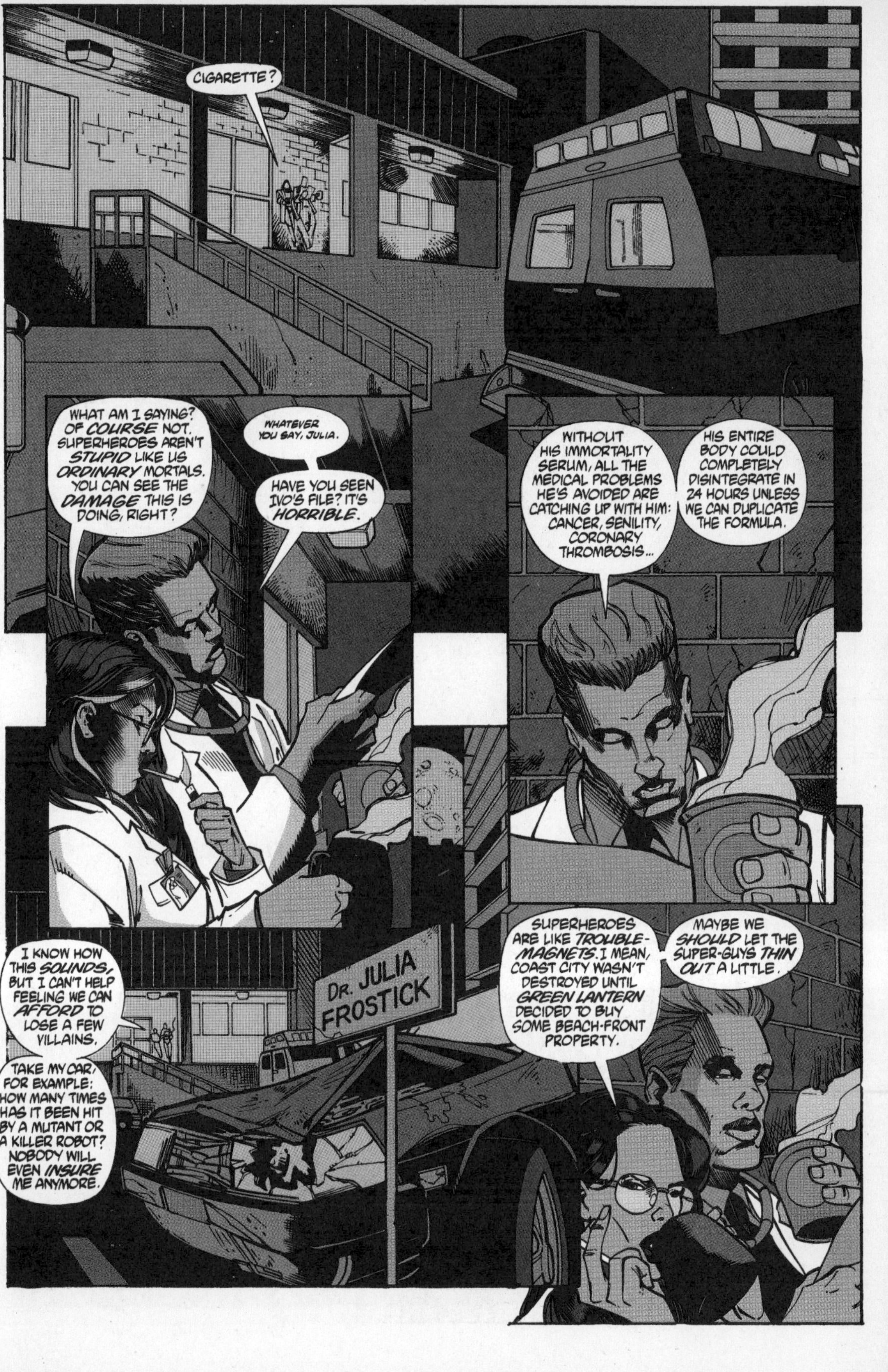
CIGARETTE?
WHAT AM I SAYING? OF COURSE NOT. SUPERHEROES AREN'T STUPID LIKE US ORDINARY MORTALS. YOU CAN SEE THE DAMAGE THIS IS DOING, RIGHT?
WHATEVER YOU SAY, JULIA.
HAVE YOU SEEN IVO'S FILE? IT'S HORRIBLE.
WITHOUT HIS IMMORTALITY SERUM, ALL THE MEDICAL PROBLEMS HE'S AVOIDED ARE CATCHING UP WITH HIM: CANCER, SENILITY, CORONARY THROMBOSIS...
HIS ENTIRE BODY COULD COMPLETELY DISINTEGRATE IN 24 HOURS UNLESS WE CAN DUPLICATE THE FORMULA.
I KNOW HOW THIS SOUNDS, BUT I CAN'T HELP FEELING WE CAN AFFORD TO LOSE A FEW VILLAINS.
TAKE MY CAR, FOR EXAMPLE: HOW MANY TIMES HAS IT BEEN HIT BY A MUTANT OR A KILLER ROBOT? NOBODY WILL EVEN INSURE ME ANYMORE.
Dr. JULIA FROSTICK
SUPERHEROES ARE LIKE TROUBLE-MAGNETS. I MEAN, COAST CITY WASN'T DESTROYED UNTIL GREEN LANTERN DECIDED TO BUY SOME BEACH-FRONT PROPERTY.
MAYBE WE SHOULD LET THE SUPER-GUYS THIN OUT A LITTLE.

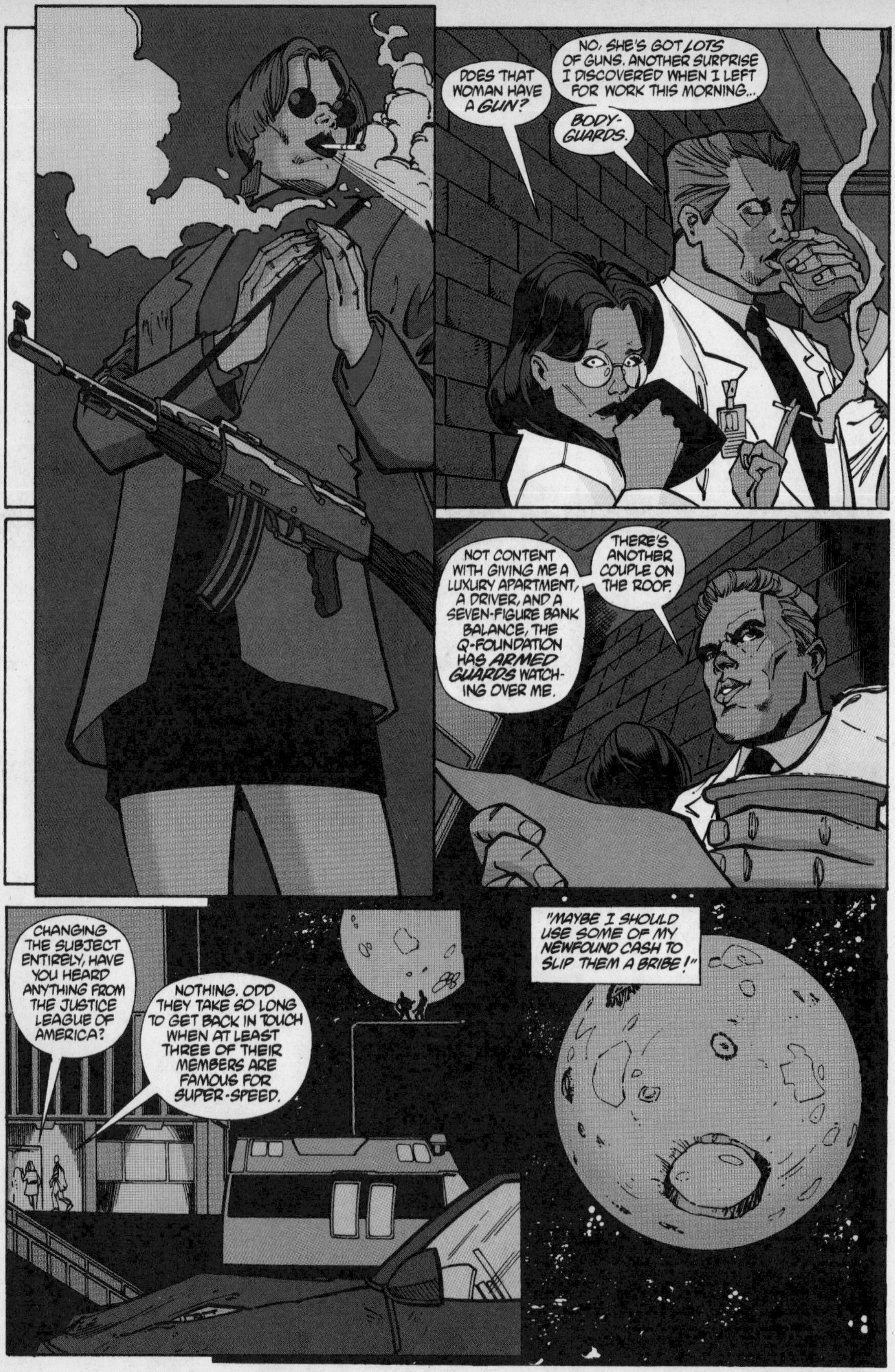
DOES THAT WOMAN HAVE A GUN?
NO, SHE'S GOT LOTS OF GUNS. ANOTHER SURPRISE I DISCOVERED WHEN I LEFT FOR WORK THIS MORNING...
BODY-GUARDS.
NOT CONTENT WITH GIVING ME A LUXURY APARTMENT, A DRIVER, AND A SEVEN-FIGURE BANK BALANCE, THE Q-FOUNDATION HAS ARMED GUARDS WATCHING OVER ME.
THERE'S ANOTHER COUPLE ON THE ROOF.
CHANGING THE SUBJECT ENTIRELY, HAVE YOU HEARD ANYTHING FROM THE JUSTICE LEAGUE OF AMERICA?
NOTHING. ODD THEY TAKE SO LONG TO GET BACK IN TOUCH WHEN AT LEAST THREE OF THEIR MEMBERS ARE FAMOUS FOR SUPER-SPEED.
"MAYBE I SHOULD USE SOME OF MY NEWFOUND CASH TO SLIP THEM A BRIBE!"

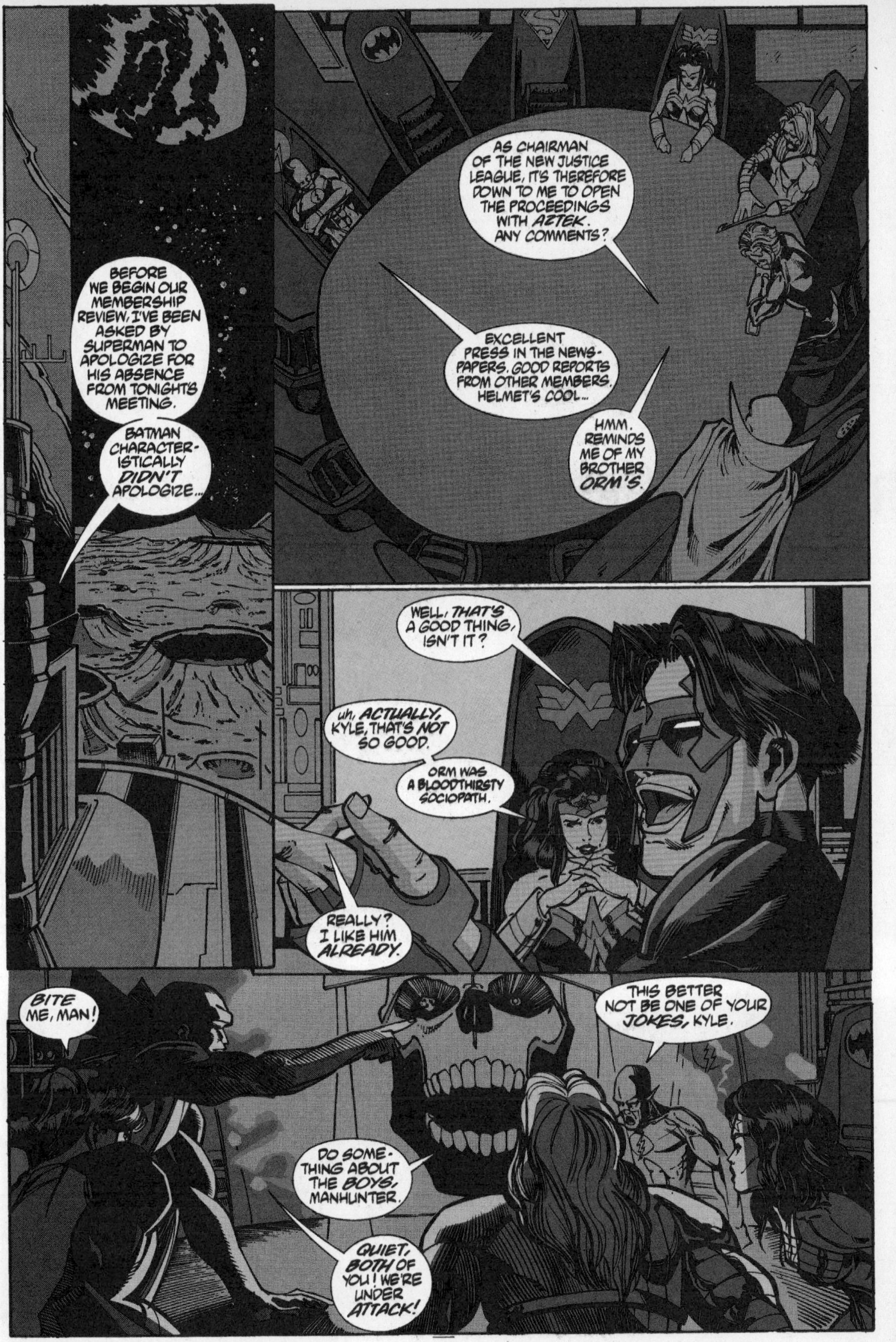
BEFORE WE BEGIN OUR MEMBERSHIP REVIEW, I'VE BEEN ASKED BY SUPERMAN TO APOLOGIZE FOR HIS ABSENCE FROM TONIGHT'S MEETING.
BATMAN CHARACTER-ISTICALLY DIDN'T APOLOGIZE...
AS CHAIRMAN OF THE NEW JUSTICE LEAGUE, IT'S THEREFORE DOWN TO ME TO OPEN THE PROCEEDINGS WITH AZTEK. ANY COMMENTS?
EXCELLENT PRESS IN THE NEWS-PAPERS. GOOD REPORTS FROM OTHER MEMBERS. HELMET'S COOL...
HMM. REMINDS ME OF MY BROTHER ORM'S.
WELL, THAT'S A GOOD THING, ISN'T IT?
uh, ACTUALLY, KYLE, THAT'S NOT SO GOOD.
ORM WAS A BLOODTHIRSTY SOCIOPATH.
REALLY? I LIKE HIM ALREADY.
BITE ME, MAN!
THIS BETTER NOT BE ONE OF YOUR JOKES, KYLE.
DO SOME-THING ABOUT THE BOYS, MANHUNTER.
QUIET, BOTH OF YOU! WE'RE UNDER ATTACK!

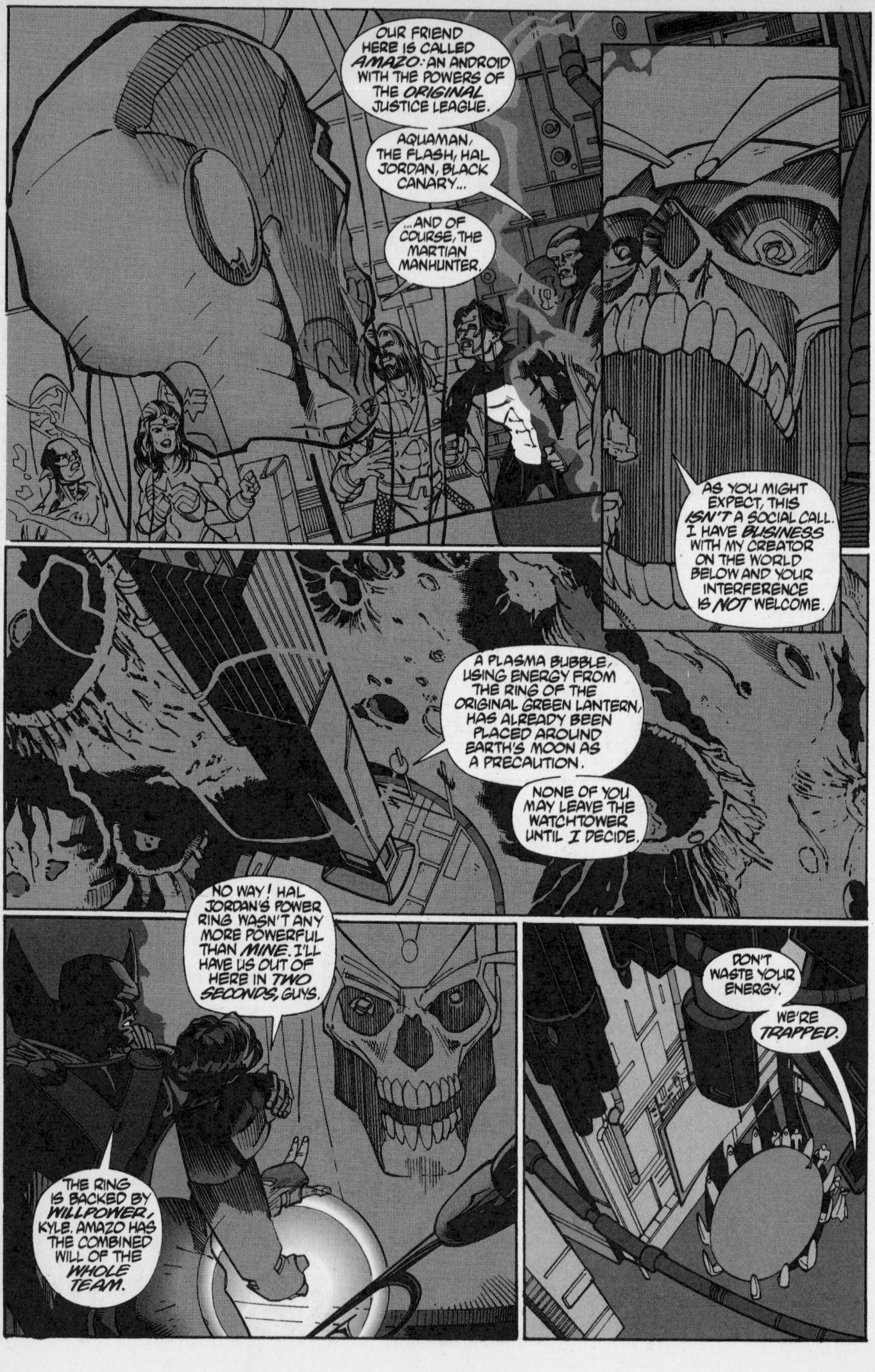
OUR FRIEND HERE IS CALLED AMAZO: AN ANDROID WITH THE POWERS OF THE ORIGINAL JUSTICE LEAGUE.
AQUAMAN, THE FLASH, HAL JORDAN, BLACK CANARY...
...AND OF COURSE, THE MARTIAN MANHUNTER.
AS YOU MIGHT EXPECT, THIS ISN'T A SOCIAL CALL. I HAVE BUSINESS WITH MY CREATOR ON THE WORLD BELOW AND YOUR INTERFERENCE IS NOT WELCOME.
A PLASMA BUBBLE, USING ENERGY FROM THE RING OF THE ORIGINAL GREEN LANTERN, HAS ALREADY BEEN PLACED AROUND EARTH'S MOON AS A PRECAUTION.
NONE OF YOU MAY LEAVE THE WATCHTOWER UNTIL I DECIDE.
NO WAY! HAL JORDAN'S POWER RING WASN'T ANY MORE POWERFUL THAN MINE. I'LL HAVE US OUT OF HERE IN TWO SECONDS, GUYS.
THE RING IS BACKED BY WILLPOWER, KYLE. AMAZO HAS THE COMBINED WILL OF THE WHOLE TEAM.
DON'T WASTE YOUR ENERGY.
WE'RE TRAPPED.

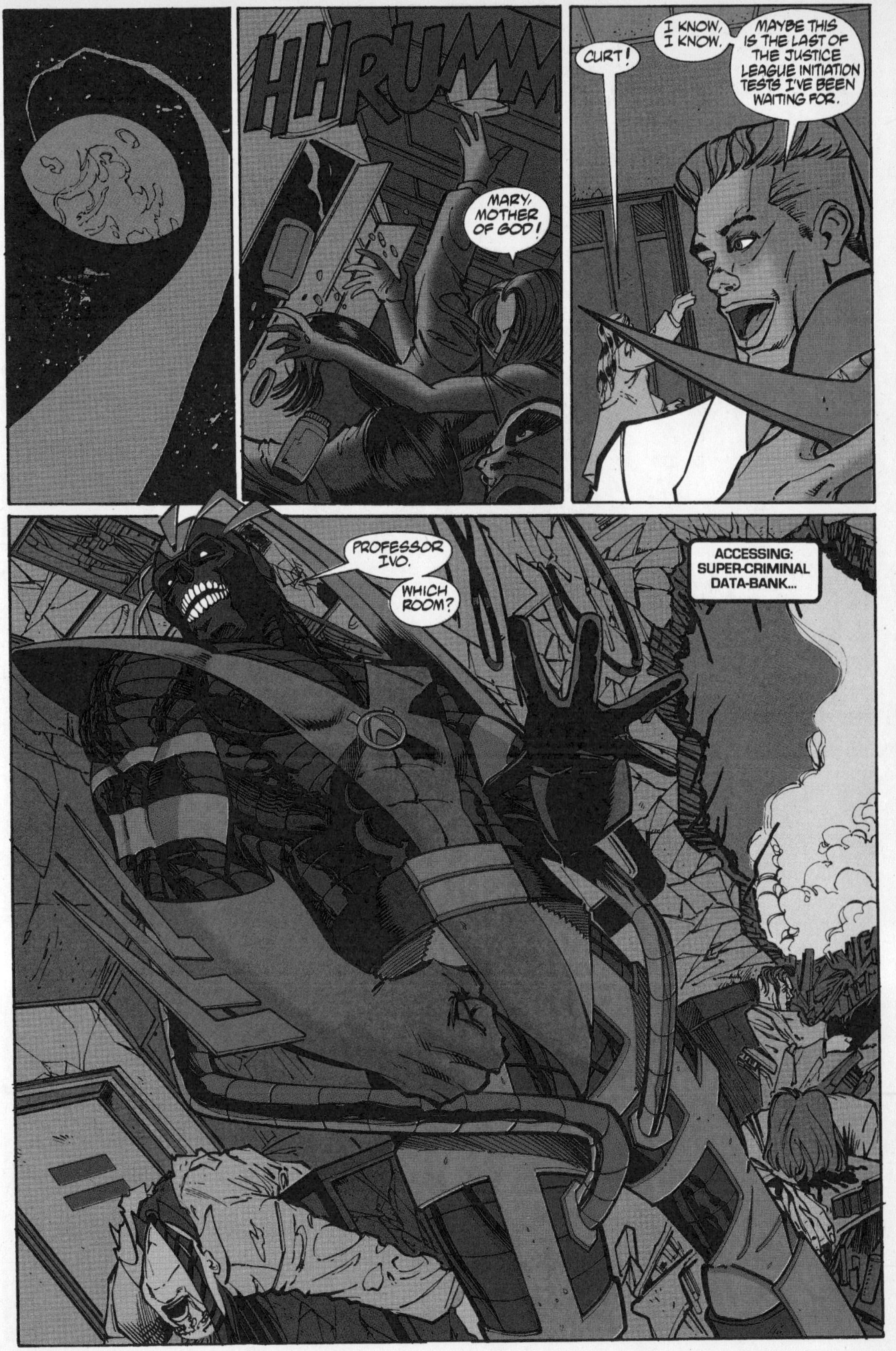
HHRUMM
MARY, MOTHER OF GOD!
CURT!
I KNOW, I KNOW.
MAYBE THIS IS THE LAST OF THE JUSTICE LEAGUE INITIATION TESTS I'VE BEEN WAITING FOR.
PROFESSOR IVO.
WHICH ROOM?
ACCESSING: SUPER-CRIMINAL DATA-BANK...

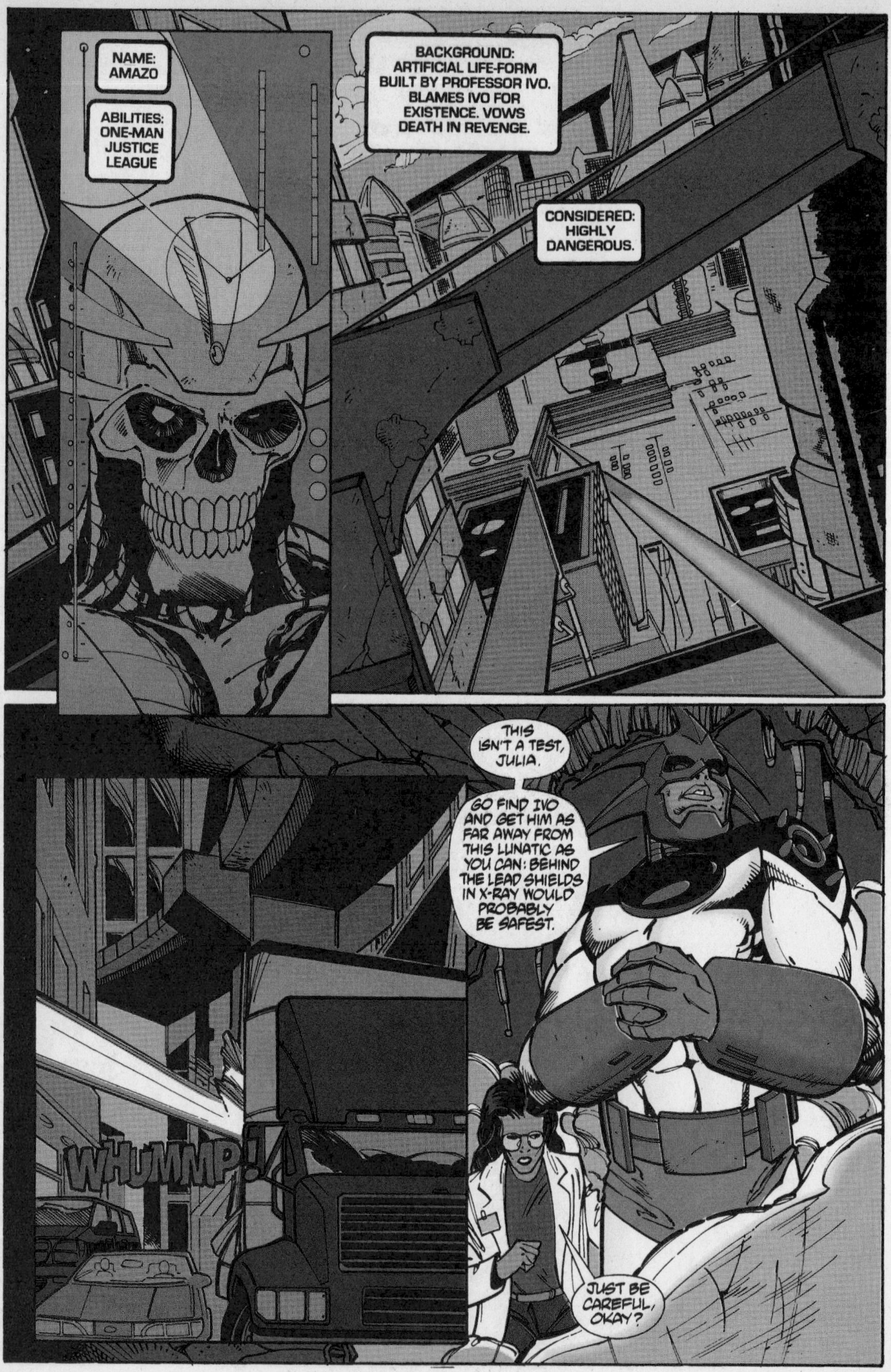
NAME: AMAZO
ABILITIES: ONE-MAN JUSTICE LEAGUE
BACKGROUND: ARTIFICIAL LIFE-FORM BUILT BY PROFESSOR IVO. BLAMES IVO FOR EXISTENCE. VOWS DEATH IN REVENGE.
CONSIDERED: HIGHLY DANGEROUS.
THIS ISN'T A TEST, JULIA.
GO FIND IVO AND GET HIM AS FAR AWAY FROM THIS LUNATIC AS YOU CAN: BEHIND THE LEAD SHIELDS IN X-RAY WOULD PROBABLY BE SAFEST.
WHUMMP!
JUST BE CAREFUL, OKAY?

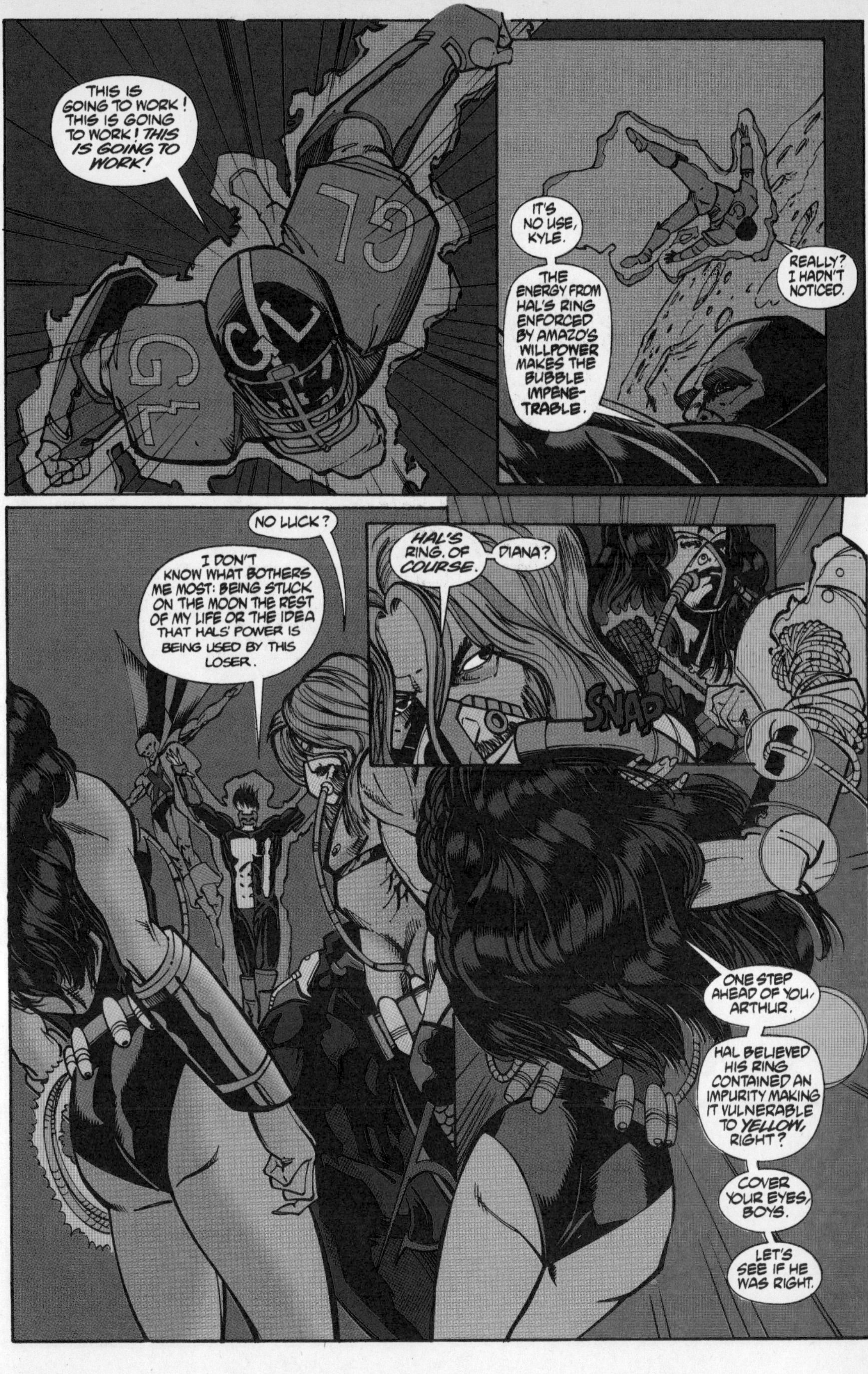

THIS IS GOING TO WORK! THIS IS GOING TO WORK! *THIS IS GOING TO WORK!*
IT'S NO USE, KYLE.
THE ENERGY FROM HAL'S RING ENFORCED BY AMAZO'S WILLPOWER MAKES THE BUBBLE IMPENE-TRABLE.
REALLY? I HADN'T NOTICED.
NO LUCK?
I DON'T KNOW WHAT BOTHERS ME MOST: BEING STUCK ON THE MOON THE REST OF MY LIFE OR THE IDEA THAT HALS' POWER IS BEING USED BY THIS LOSER.
HAL'S RING. OF *COURSE*.
DIANA?
SNAP
ONE STEP AHEAD OF YOU, ARTHUR.
HAL BELIEVED HIS RING CONTAINED AN IMPURITY MAKING IT VULNERABLE TO *YELLOW*, RIGHT?
COVER YOUR EYES, BOYS.
LET'S SEE IF HE WAS RIGHT.

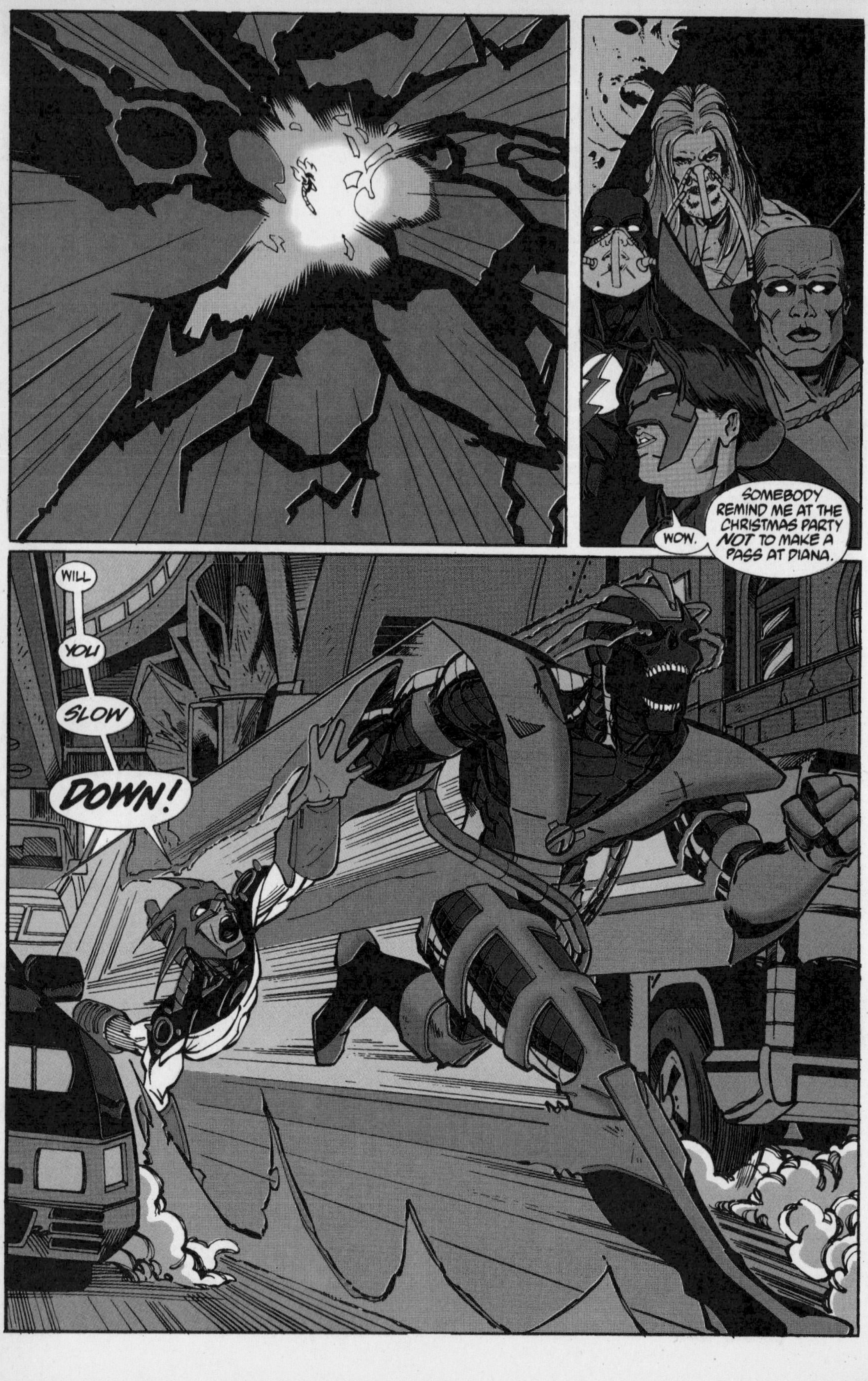
WOW.
SOMEBODY REMIND ME AT THE CHRISTMAS PARTY NOT TO MAKE A PASS AT DIANA.
WILL
YOU
SLOW
DOWN!

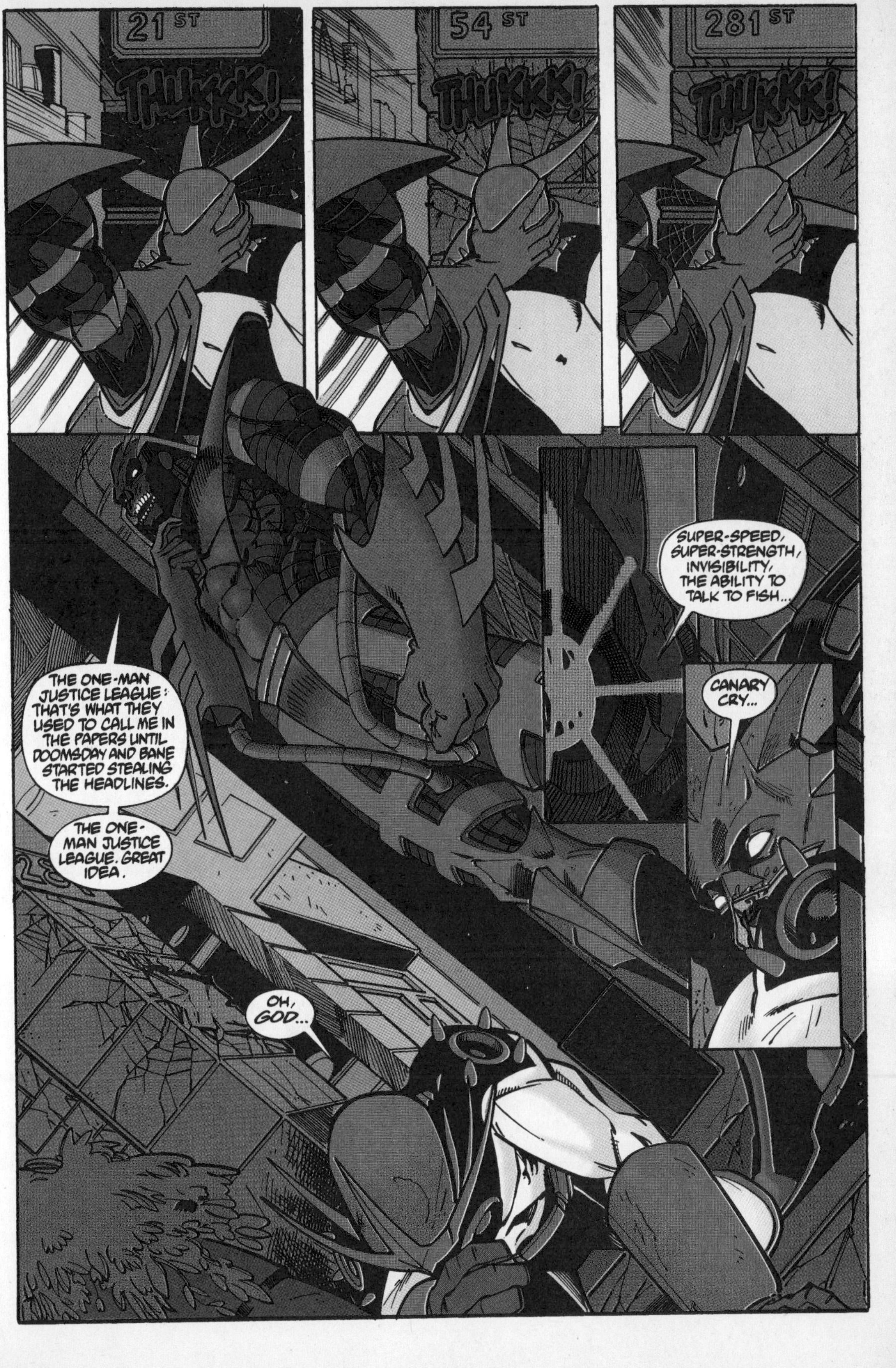
21 ST
THUKKK!
54 ST
THUKKK!
281 ST
THUKKK!
SUPER-SPEED, SUPER-STRENGTH, INVISIBILITY, THE ABILITY TO TALK TO FISH...
CANARY CRY...
THE ONE-MAN JUSTICE LEAGUE: THAT'S WHAT THEY USED TO CALL ME IN THE PAPERS UNTIL DOOMSDAY AND BANE STARTED STEALING THE HEADLINES.
THE ONE-MAN JUSTICE LEAGUE. GREAT IDEA.
OH, GOD...

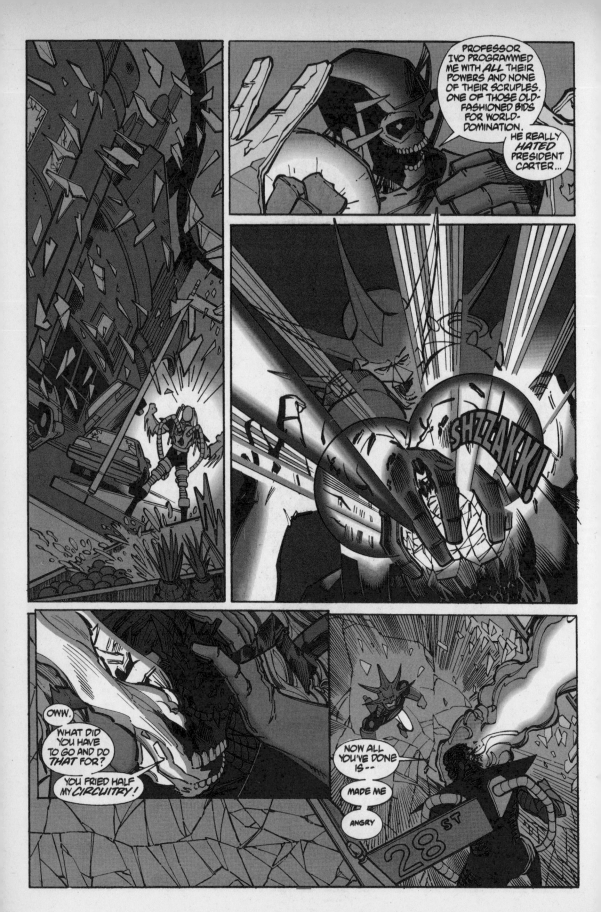

PROFESSOR IVO PROGRAMMED ME WITH *ALL* THEIR POWERS AND NONE OF THEIR SCRUPLES. ONE OF THOSE OLD-FASHIONED BIDS FOR WORLD-DOMINATION.

HE REALLY *HATED* PRESIDENT CARTER...

SHZZAK-K!

OWW. WHAT DID YOU HAVE TO GO AND DO *THAT* FOR?

YOU FRIED HALF MY *CIRCUITRY*!

NOW ALL YOU'VE DONE IS--

MADE ME

ANGRY

28 ST

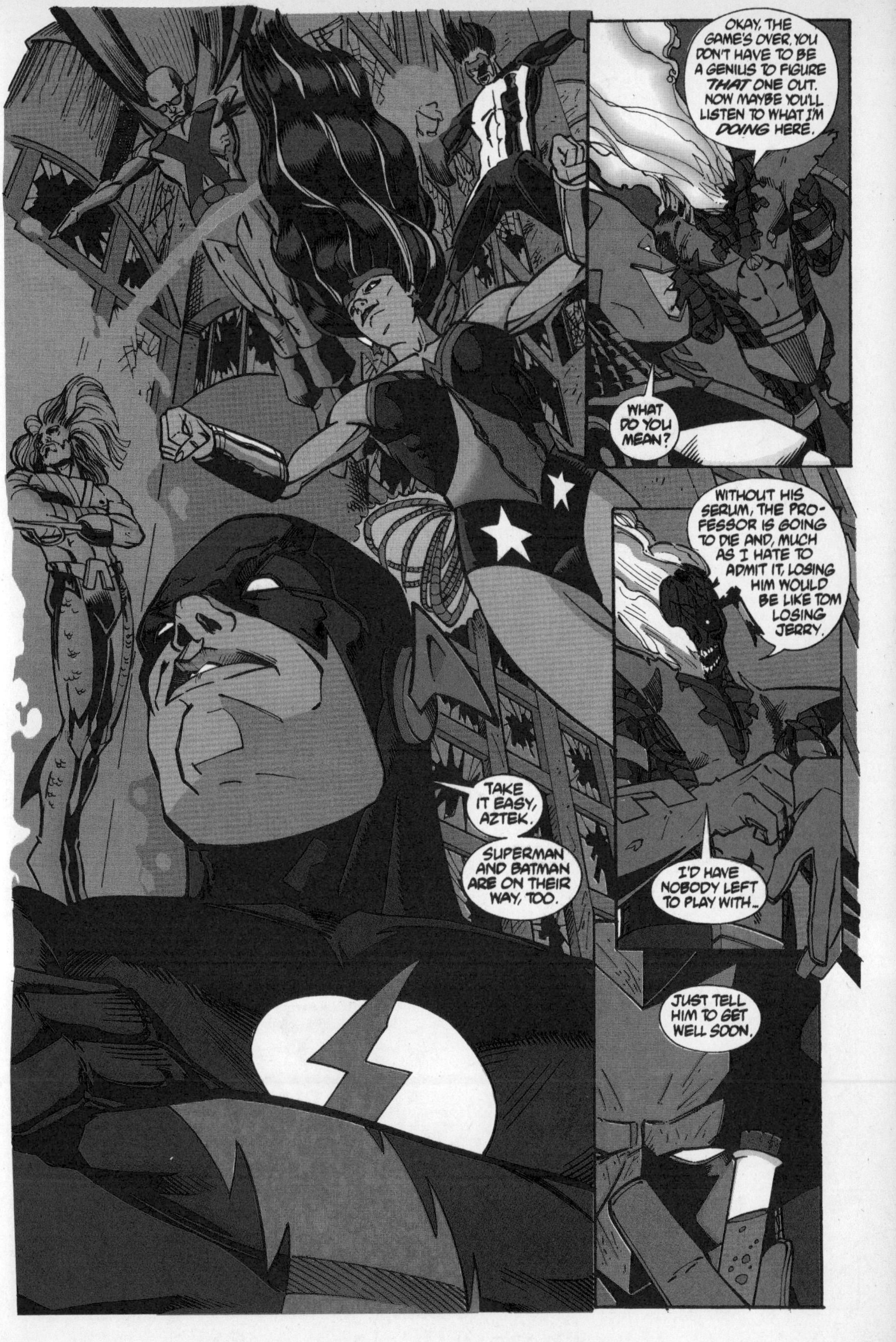
OKAY, THE GAME'S OVER. YOU DON'T HAVE TO BE A GENIUS TO FIGURE *THAT* ONE OUT. NOW MAYBE YOU'LL LISTEN TO WHAT I'M *DOING* HERE.
WHAT DO YOU MEAN?
WITHOUT HIS SERUM, THE PROFESSOR IS GOING TO DIE AND, MUCH AS I HATE TO ADMIT IT, LOSING HIM WOULD BE LIKE TOM LOSING JERRY.
TAKE IT EASY, AZTEK.
SUPERMAN AND BATMAN ARE ON THEIR WAY, TOO.
I'D HAVE NOBODY LEFT TO PLAY WITH...
JUST TELL HIM TO GET WELL SOON.

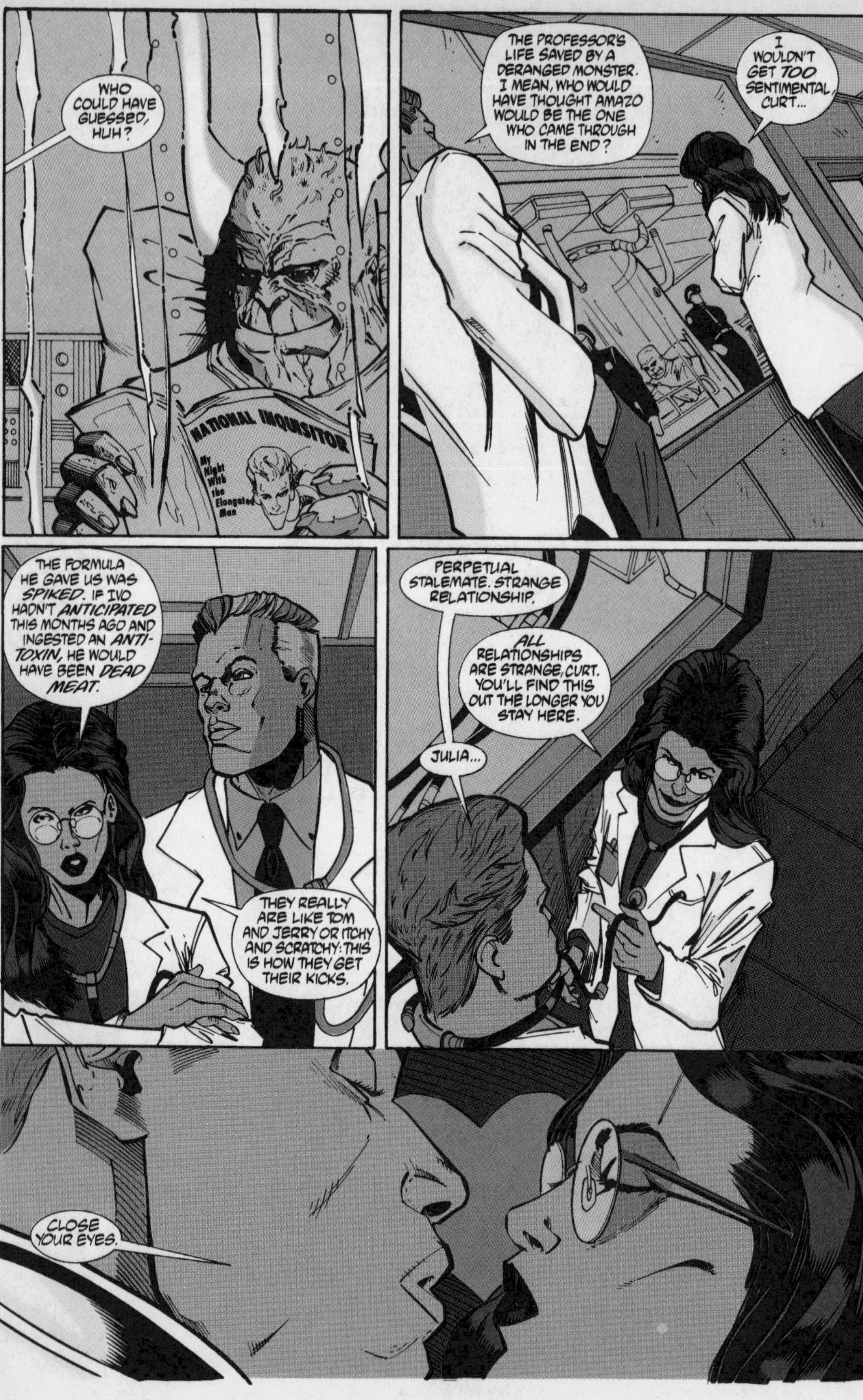
WHO COULD HAVE GUESSED, HUH?
NATIONAL INQUISITOR
My Night With the Elongated Man
THE PROFESSOR'S LIFE SAVED BY A DERANGED MONSTER. I MEAN, WHO WOULD HAVE THOUGHT AMAZO WOULD BE THE ONE WHO CAME THROUGH IN THE END?
I WOULDN'T GET *TOO* SENTIMENTAL, CURT...
THE FORMULA HE GAVE US WAS *SPIKED*. IF IVO HADN'T *ANTICIPATED* THIS MONTHS AGO AND INGESTED AN *ANTI-TOXIN*, HE WOULD HAVE BEEN *DEAD MEAT*.
THEY REALLY ARE LIKE TOM AND JERRY OR ITCHY AND SCRATCHY: THIS IS HOW THEY GET THEIR KICKS.
PERPETUAL STALEMATE. STRANGE RELATIONSHIP.
ALL RELATIONSHIPS ARE STRANGE, CURT. YOU'LL FIND THIS OUT THE LONGER YOU STAY HERE.
JULIA...
CLOSE YOUR EYES.

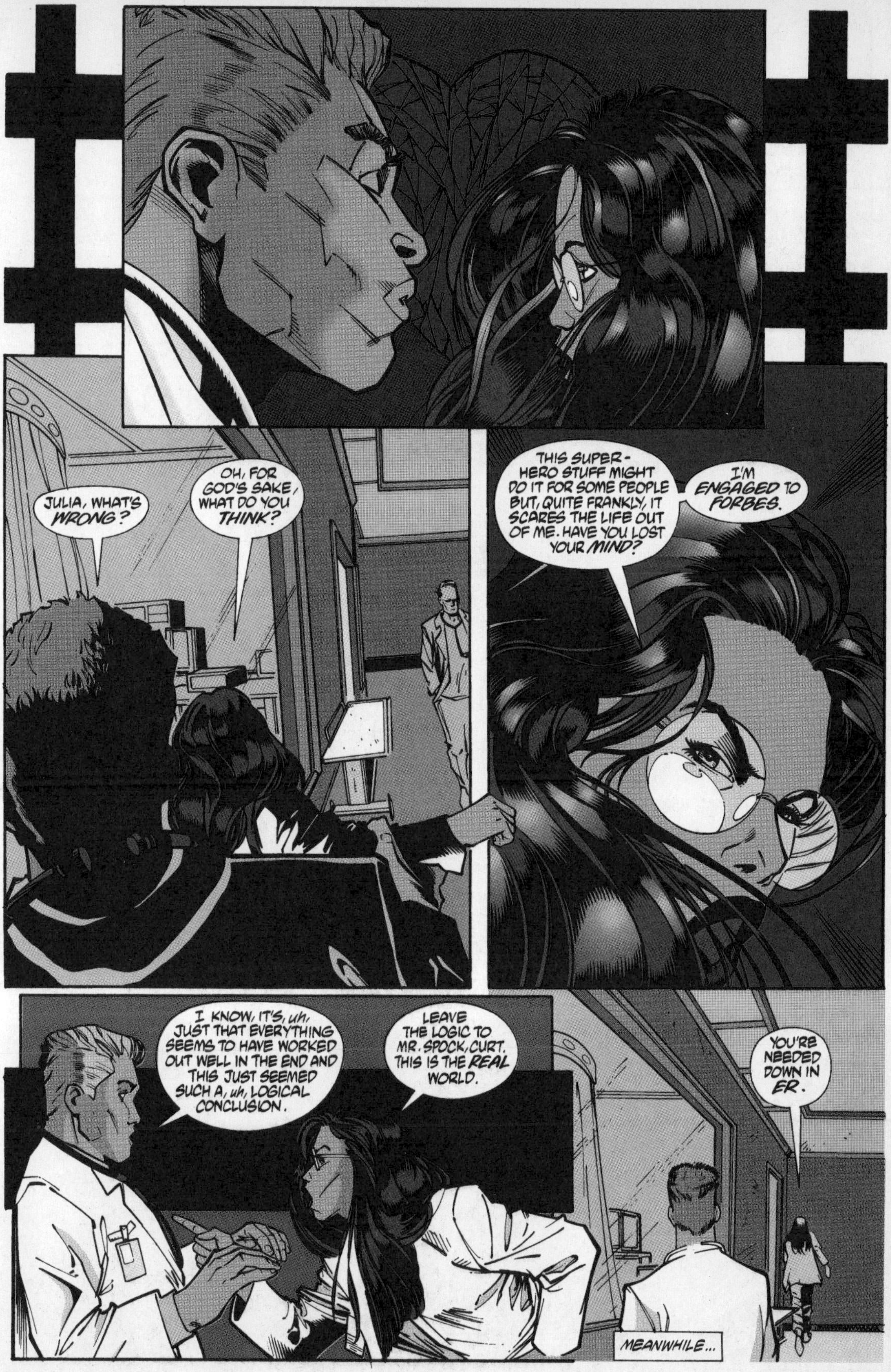

JULIA, WHAT'S WRONG?
OH, FOR GOD'S SAKE, WHAT DO YOU THINK?
THIS SUPER-HERO STUFF MIGHT DO IT FOR SOME PEOPLE BUT, QUITE FRANKLY, IT SCARES THE LIFE OUT OF ME. HAVE YOU LOST YOUR MIND?
I'M ENGAGED TO FORBES.
I KNOW, IT'S, uh, JUST THAT EVERYTHING SEEMS TO HAVE WORKED OUT WELL IN THE END AND THIS JUST SEEMED SUCH A, uh, LOGICAL CONCLUSION.
LEAVE THE LOGIC TO MR. SPOCK, CURT. THIS IS THE REAL WORLD.
YOU'RE NEEDED DOWN IN ER.
MEANWHILE...

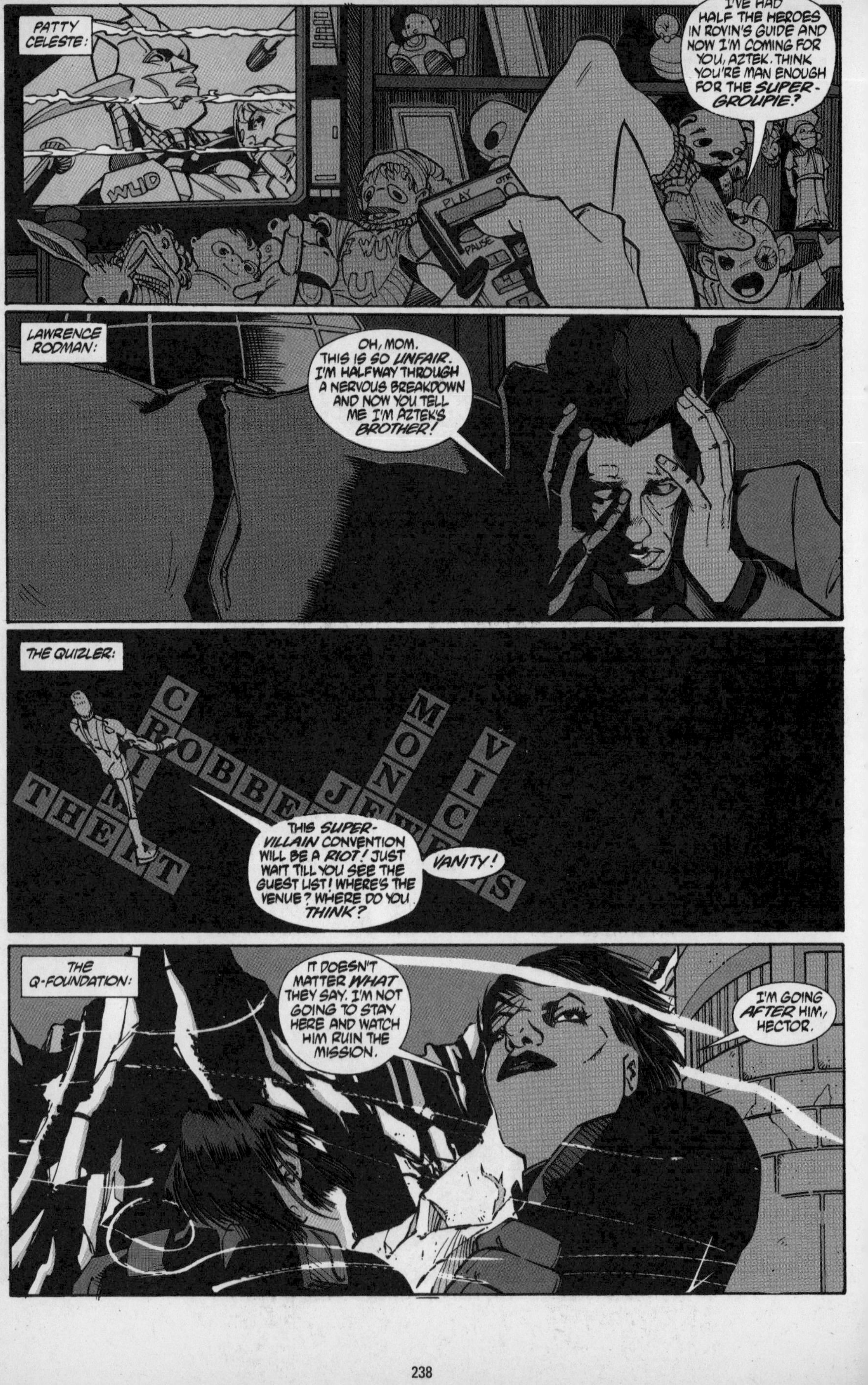

PATTY CELESTE:
I'VE HAD HALF THE HEROES IN ROVIN'S GUIDE AND NOW I'M COMING FOR YOU, AZTEK. THINK YOU'RE MAN ENOUGH FOR THE SUPER-GROUPIE?
LAWRENCE RODMAN:
OH, MOM. THIS IS SO UNFAIR. I'M HALFWAY THROUGH A NERVOUS BREAKDOWN AND NOW YOU TELL ME I'M AZTEK'S BROTHER!
THE QUIZLER:
THIS SUPER-VILLAIN CONVENTION WILL BE A RIOT! JUST WAIT TILL YOU SEE THE GUEST LIST! WHERE'S THE VENUE? WHERE DO YOU THINK?
VANITY!
THE Q-FOUNDATION:
IT DOESN'T MATTER WHAT THEY SAY. I'M NOT GOING TO STAY HERE AND WATCH HIM RUIN THE MISSION.
I'M GOING AFTER HIM, HECTOR.

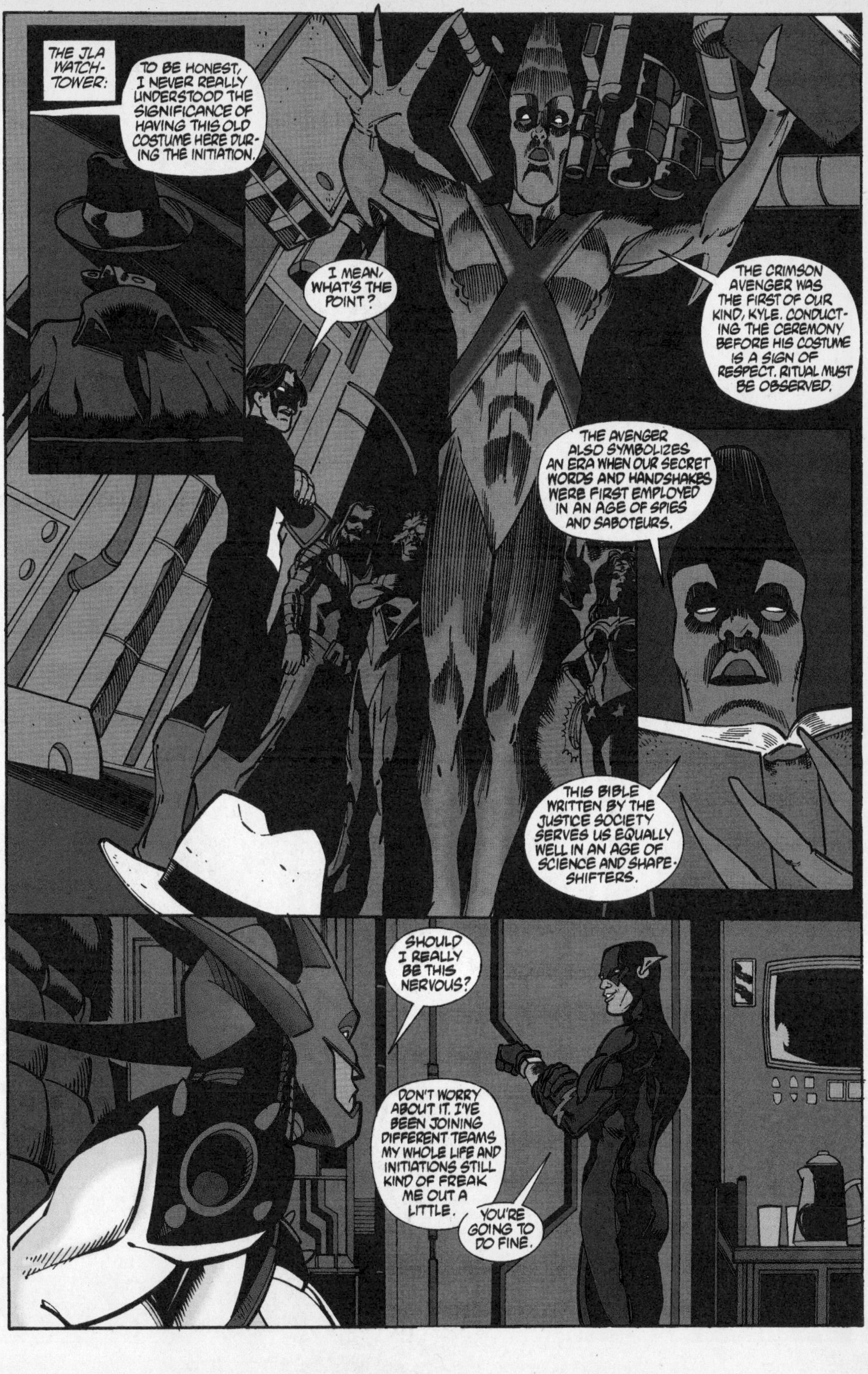
THE JLA WATCH-TOWER:
TO BE HONEST, I NEVER REALLY UNDERSTOOD THE SIGNIFICANCE OF HAVING THIS OLD COSTUME HERE DURING THE INITIATION.
I MEAN, WHAT'S THE POINT?
THE CRIMSON AVENGER WAS THE FIRST OF OUR KIND, KYLE. CONDUCTING THE CEREMONY BEFORE HIS COSTUME IS A SIGN OF RESPECT. RITUAL MUST BE OBSERVED.
THE AVENGER ALSO SYMBOLIZES AN ERA WHEN OUR SECRET WORDS AND HANDSHAKES WERE FIRST EMPLOYED IN AN AGE OF SPIES AND SABOTEURS.
THIS BIBLE WRITTEN BY THE JUSTICE SOCIETY SERVES US EQUALLY WELL IN AN AGE OF SCIENCE AND SHAPE-SHIFTERS.
SHOULD I REALLY BE THIS NERVOUS?
DON'T WORRY ABOUT IT. I'VE BEEN JOINING DIFFERENT TEAMS MY WHOLE LIFE AND INITIATIONS STILL KIND OF FREAK ME OUT A LITTLE.
YOU'RE GOING TO DO FINE.

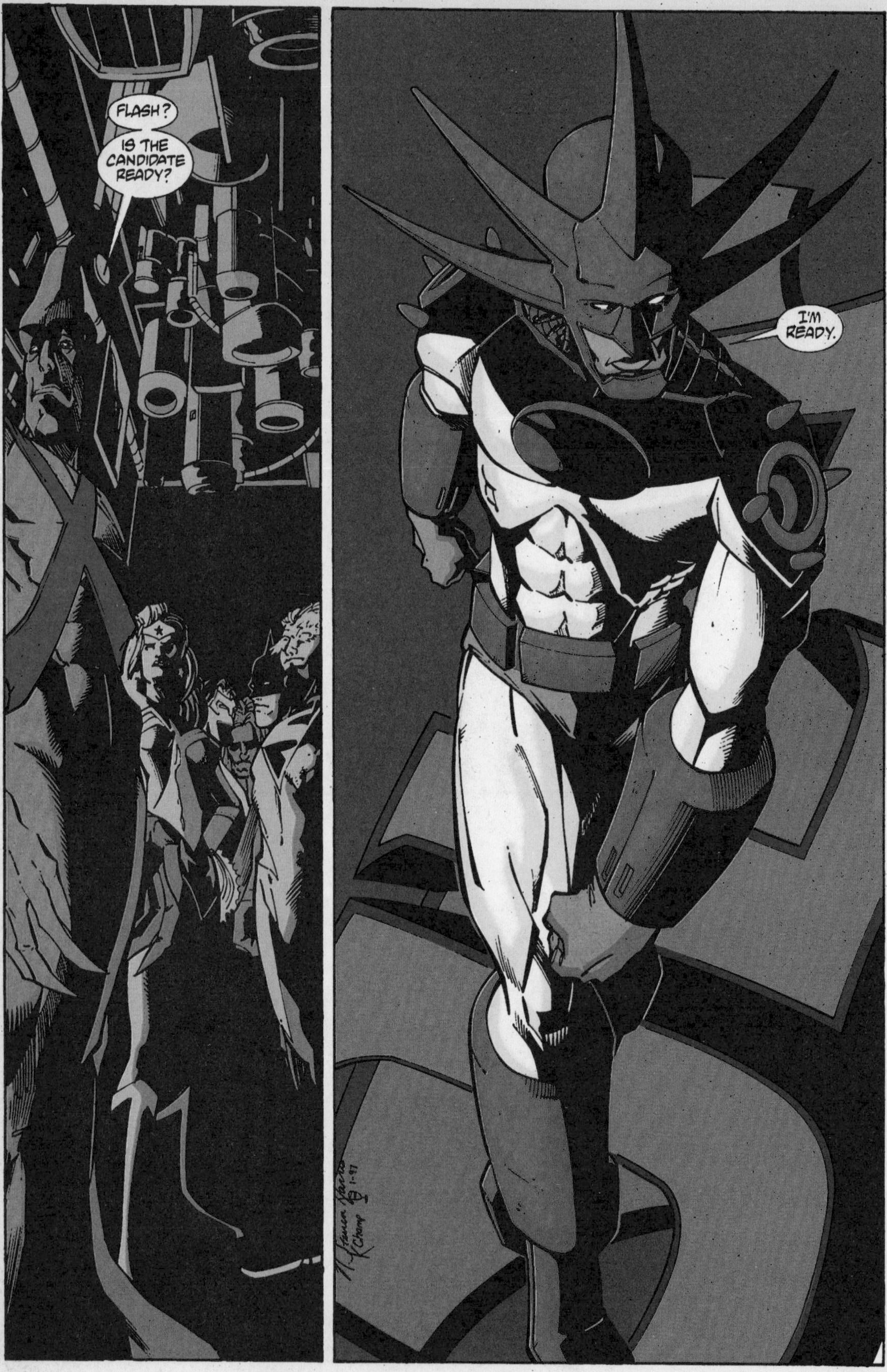
FLASH?
IS THE CANDIDATE READY?
I'M READY.